BALL & BELL ON

ENVIRONMENTAL LAW

THE LAW AND POLICY RELATING TO THE PROTECTION OF THE ENVIRONMENT

BALL & BELL ON

ENVIRONMENTAL LAW

THE LAW AND POLICY RELATING TO THE PROTECTION OF THE ENVIRONMENT

Fifth Edition

Stuart Bell LLB Hons, Barrister
and
Donald McGillivray LLB Hons, MA

OXFORD
UNIVERSITY PRESS

OXFORD
UNIVERSITY PRESS

Great Clarendon Street, Oxford OX2 6DP

Oxford University Press is a department of the University of Oxford.
It furthers the University's objective of excellence in research, scholarship,
and education by publishing worldwide in

Oxford New York

Auckland Bangkok Buenos Aires Cape Town Chennai
Dar es Salaam Delhi Hong Kong Istanbul Karachi Kolkata
Kuala Lumpur Madrid Melbourne Mexico City Mumbai Nairobi
São Paulo Shanghai Taipei Tokyo Toronto

Oxford is a registered trade mark of Oxford University Press
in the UK and in certain other countries

Published in the United States
by Oxford University Press Inc., New York

A Blackstone Press Book

© S Ball and S Bell 1991
First published 1991
Second edition 1994
Third edition 1995
© S Bell 1997
Fourth edition 1997
© S Bell and D McGillivray 2000
Fifth edition 2000

British Library Cataloguing in Publications Data

A record for this book is available from the British Library

Library of Congress Cataloguing in Publications Data

Data applied for

ISBN 1-85431-887-X

5 7 9 10 8 6 4

Typset by Style Photosetting Limited, Mayfield, East Sussex
Printed in Great Britain
on acid-free paper by
Ashford Colour Press Ltd, Gosport, Hampshire

Contents

Environmental — Law — Some themes of the book — The shape of the book — The history of environmental law — The modern age of environmental law — The future of environmental policy — The future of environmental law — The costs of compliance — The costs of non-compliance — Policy and environmental law

Values and environmental law — The interaction between values and law — What's different about environmental values — Law and balancing environmental values — Law and risk — Perspectives on environmental issues — Environmental principles — Sustainable development — Sustainable development as a legal instrument — Sustainable development as a policy instrument — Achieving sustainable development in practice — The precautionary principle — The precautionary principle as a legal instrument — The precautionary principle as a policy instrument — Applying the precautionary principle in practice — Human rights and environmental values

3 Sources of environmental law   58

The development of sources of environmental laws — Features of environmental legislation — Environmental laws as practice — Categories of environmental legislation — Case law — Administrative appeals — European
Community (EC) law — International law — Judicial review — Remedies —
Procedure — Standing — Delay — Is delay the 'new standing'? — Judicial
review and other avenues of challenge — The usefulness of judicial review —
The Ombudsman — Other complaints mechanisms

4 International law and environmental protection   84

Why is international law important for environmental protection? — International law and the UK — International law and the EC — Nation states and
global commons — A tragedy of the commons? — Sources of international
law: 'hard law' — Sources of international law: 'soft law' — International law
and policy development — The Stockholm Conference — The Brundtland
Report — The Rio Conference — Post-Rio — Institutional organisations and
other actors — Dispute settlement and dispute settlement bodies — The
Gabcíkovo-Nagymaros case — International environmental treaty post-Rio
— International trade and the environment — Future directions in international environmental law and policy

5 The European Community and the environment   113

The nature of the EC — The institutions of the EC — Other bodies — The
European Environment Agency — Voting procedures — Sources of EC law
— Validity of EC legislation — The rationale for EC environmental law and
policy — The EC's environmental policy — The constitutional basis of the
EC's environmental policy — Which Article? — The scope of EC environmental law — The range of environmental directives — Towards uniformity
or flexibility? — Free trade and environmental protection — Compliance by
Member States — Non-compliance: enforcement by the Commission —
Non-compliance: individual remedies — Non-compliance: the Commission's
proposals — Future directions in EC environmental law and policy — EC
environmental law and Britain

6 The administration of environmental law and policy   152

Scotland, Northern Ireland, Wales and the regions — Central government —
Parliamentary select committees — Royal Commission on Environmental
Pollution (RCEP) — Other advisory bodies — Department of the Environment, Transport and the Regions (DETR) — Regulatory agencies — Regulatory agencies: Scotland — Regulatory agencies: Northern Ireland — The
Environment Agency — The Environment Agency: an overview — Sewerage
undertakers — Countryside bodies — Local authorities — Decision-making
in local authorities

protection mechanism — Human rights law — Private law, public regulation and 'the public interest' — The way ahead? Civil liability in statutes and EC proposals

The main features of town and country planning — Town and country planning as a tool of environmental policy — Town and country planning and some themes of this book — The planning legislation — What is town and country planning? — The centrality of planning policy and the Secretary of State — A change of direction? — Local planning authorities — Wales, Scotland, Northern Ireland — Forward planning: development plans — Changes to the nature of development planning — Challenges to development plans — Development plans: critique and future — Non-statutory plans and guidance — Development control: the meaning of 'development' — Exemption from the need to apply for planning permission — 'Development' activities for which planning permission is granted by statute — Special cases — Is planning permission required? — Applying for planning permission — Determining the planning application — Summary of rights of third parties — The local planning authority's discretion — Environmental considerations as material considerations — Planning conditions — Conditions and policy — Planning conditions and environmental protection — Planning obligations — Planning obligations: the case law — Planning obligations: policy and practice — 'Environmental planning gain' — Planning appeals — Procedure on appeals — Challenging the decision of the Secretary of State — Enforcement under planning law — Injunctions under local government law — Immunity from enforcement under planning law — Appeals against notices — Enforcement discretion — Powers where there is no breach of planning law — Planning, the environment and risk — Planning and hazardous substances

What is environmental impact assessment? — The Environmental Impact Assessment Directive — Amendments to Directive 85/337 — The EIA Directive and direct effect — Is the project subject to EIA? — 'Salami-slicing' of projects — EIA and permitted development — What is a 'project'? And what is a 'consent'? — Pre-application procedures for establishing the need for EIA — Pre-application directions from the Secretary of State — Challenges to the decisions of local planning authorities or the Secretary of State — Other procedures for determining the need for EIA — The environmental statement — Determination of the planning application — Transboundary effects — EIA: an overall assessment — Towards strategic environmental assessment?

17 Waste management   460

18 Contaminated land   523

19 Water pollution and water quality   552

of State — Appeals — How are consents set? — Water quality objectives — Groundwater pollution — Water pollution offences — Sampling and enforcement powers — Enforcement policy — Access to information — Preventative and remedial powers — Overlapping controls — Water pollution and private law controls

Trade effluent discharges — Applying for a trade effluent consent — How are consents set? — Trade effluent charges — Public participation — 'Red List' substances — Enforcement — Discharges from sewage works — Domestic sewage discharges

The history and development of controls — Types of legal protection — The nature conservation agencies — The protection of individual animals and plants — Habitat protection — Sites of special scientific interest — Duties on owners and occupiers — Specific nature conservation duties — Nature conservation orders — National nature reserves (NNRs) — Local nature reserves (LNRs) — Marine nature reserves (MNRs) — Limestone pavements — Management agreements — Planning permission — Loss and damage to SSSIs — SSSIs: proposals for reform — EC conservation law — EC Wild Birds Directive 79/409 — EC Habitats Directive 92/43 — The 1994 Regulations — European marine sites — European sites and other regulatory systems — Summary of protection under EC conservation law — International conservation law

Regulatory mechanisms — The international and EC dimension — Town and country planning — Extra protections under planning law — The Countryside Agency — Landscape protection and management agreements — Agriculture and landscape — Trees, woodland and hedgerows — Trees and planning permission — Tree preservation orders (TPOs) — Conservation areas — Compensation — Proposals for change — Afforestation — Felling licences — Consultation on felling and afforestation — Community forests and the National Forest — Consumer information and certification schemes — Hedgerows

Preface

The first edition of this book, which was published in 1991, contained 15 chapters and ran to some 381 pages. Nine years later, this fifth edition has 22 chapters and nearly 700 pages. Given that one of the aims of the first edition was to provide a concise, accessible introduction to environmental law this seemingly exponential growth needs some explanation.

First of all, additional material reflects the fact that the nature of environmental law is becoming increasingly complex. For example, the regulation of contaminated land has recently acquired a detailed and complicated set of rules which deserve to be considered in depth.

Secondly, existing environmental laws are acquiring more and more 'baggage'. This includes new environmental quality standards, guidance documents, framework strategies and case law. All of these need to be incorporated into pre-existing texts if there is to be some understanding of the context in which environmental laws work.

Thirdly, many of the ideas which were in their infancy in the late 1980s when the first edition was being written have begun to mature in legal and policy terms. Although such things as the aim of sustainable development and the precautionary principle were prevalent at that time they had little effect upon the way in which environmental laws were implemented and had received scant recognition in official policy documents.

Fourthly, the plethora of good general texts dealing with environmental law requires us to try to continue to offer something distinctive, which we attempt to do by maintaining a central commitment to looking at both environmental law and policy, and at the environmental rule-making process in all its stages from the crystallisation of values to enforcement.

Finally, and perhaps most importantly, this book is a labour of love (it would have to be given the tortuous time it takes to produce). It has always reflected the interests and concerns of the authors and the additions to the text mirror new enthusiasms or issues which we feel should be explored further.

After this lengthy plea in mitigation, a word of explanation about the new areas covered in this edition. There are a number of completely new chapters. Chapter 2 covers new ground (for this book) by looking at the issue of the way in which environmental values interact with law, including some consideration of the precautionary principle and the aim of sustainable development. Chapter 4 signals a belated acceptance that international environmental law should be covered in some detail. Chapters 15 and 16 cover statutory nuisance and noise respectively. Although these areas were covered in previous editions, they have now been given more coverage and prominence as individual topics in their own right. Finally, Chapter 18 covers the regulation of contaminated land. Once again, this topic had previously been dealt with alongside waste management but with the implementation of legislation dealing with the area (and the bonus of making the waste management chapter more manageable), it seemed to make sense to isolate the material in a new stand-alone chapter. Other chapters have been extensively rewritten as they were becoming a little dated in terms of structure and coverage. These include Chapters 3, 6, 8, 9, 10, 13, 14 and 22 (the last mentioned being our limited concession to consolidation).

This book is primarily aimed at the student market, but the coverage of material is probably too wide to form the basis of most under-graduate courses. Therefore, we do not expect it will be read progressively from cover to cover. Rather, it can be dipped into as appropriate, even within some chapters. Part I of the book is, however, structured in what we hope is a useful progression of topics for those coming to the subject for the first time. In the subject specific material in Part II, we have endeavoured to summarise the 'meatier' material by giving brief overviews as part of the introduction to many of the chapters. The purpose of these overviews is to enable a first time student to find their bearings and to try and place the detail within some contextual framework.

It has become something of a tradition in the Preface to this book to take a snapshot of 'where are we now' in terms of current environmental law and policy. Some general issues which could be more significant in the short term are considered below.

(a)   The impact of devolution

Although in previous editions we have struggled to provide a very basic coverage of environmental law and policy on a UK basis, the impact of devolution should mean that discernible differences between law and policy in England, Scotland, Wales and Northern Ireland gather more significance over the first decade of the 21st century. Broad similarities will always remain as a result of a need to meet European and international obligations as a United Kingdom. There is, however, a good chance that the phrase 'a "British" approach to environmental regulation', which is used in various parts of this book, may be replaced in future editions by an 'English' approach which may be contrasted against a 'Scottish', 'Welsh', or 'Northern Irish' approach. Indeed, in relation to some areas, notably nature conservation, these differences are already apparent. Given that we are at a relatively early stage of the devolution process, we hope that any readers or colleagues in the devolved countries will forgive us if we are too Anglocentric or inadvertently and incorrectly conflate the law across the UK.

There is a liberal use of 'Britain' and 'British' in the text. This is often clumsy shorthand for the UK and is not meant to exclude Northern Ireland.

This phraseology does, however, reflect the fact that up until the very recent past, substantive Northern Irish environmental law did not mirror the position in other countries in the United Kingdom. Once again, we hope that Northern Irish readers will forgive us for this form of abbreviation (with the excuse that the Bibliography contains references to more specialised texts).

(b)   European issues

At a European level we are faced with a number of significant developments over the next few years. On a mundane policy level we should see the publication of the Sixth Action programme which will hopefully have a more practical and perceptible impact than the Fifth Action Programme. At the Member State level there is the challenge of enlargement. This brings with it the search for a more 'flexible' European Community which is capable of expanding eastwards to include new Member States which combine extreme industrial legacies and large areas of high conservation importance. At the institutional level we have an interesting role reversal with a number of Ministers with 'Green' sympathies sitting in the Council of Ministers but a more conservative flavour to the Parliament, traditionally seen as the most radically environmental EC institution.

(c)   Environmental risk

Issues involving environmental risk and the public perception of that risk continue to feature prominently in the media, the political arena and legal processes. At the time of writing, recent issues to the fore have included the risks associated with: the deliberate (or otherwise) planting of genetically modified seeds; the use of mobile phones and their masts; the lapse in safety standards when dealing with radioactive material at BNFL; and the emission of dioxins from, amongst other things, waste incinerators. Although there is nothing new about such 'scares', the increasing complexity of the issues and the intensity of feeling on all sides of the debate underlines the need for deliberative processes which can resolve the apparently irresolvable. In particular we need to examine the ways in which law can give effect to collectively held values on the environment and differentiate them from genuinely held individual preferences, a theme we consider in more detail in Chapter 2.

(d)   New Labour and environmental modernisation

On the wider political front, we have yet to see New Labour adopt environmental concerns with any real fervour. The creation of the DETR, the 'super-ministry' linking environment, transport and regional affairs, has yet to really bear fruit when it comes to integrating environmental protection with other key policy areas, and within government, the environment remains in need of a higher profile (although the current Environment Minister, Michael Meacher, can sometimes appear to be a 'lone voice crying in the wilderness' in support of environmental protection in tussles with other government departments — particularly noticeable in relation to the debate on genetically modified crops). In an attempt to push 'the environment' up the political agenda by making it more politically acceptable and homogenous with other New Labour policies, we may see increasing reference to environmental or ecological modernisation. This idea emphasises the extent to which environmental problems can be solved by technological advances which can contribute to, rather than hinder, economic growth. In this sense environmental modernisation is essentially an optimistic and hopeful approach which has the advantage of not only fitting well with the 'modernist' agenda being pursued by New Labour but also a weak version of the sustainable development principle.

(e) Implementation and enforcement

There is an increasing recognition that more work needs to be done to assess the adequacy of the implementation and enforcement of environmental laws. On the international front, this lack of an effective remedy for any breaches or failure to implement has long been a cause for concern. This will be heightened with the implementation of the Kyoto Protocol on the reduction of emissions which contribute to climate change. At the time of writing, the overall picture does not look particularly rosy and there are legitimate fears that even with the 'flexible mechanisms' of implementation, the overall reduction targets will not be met (a view which has been echoed in the Royal Commission on Environmental Pollution's 22nd Report, *Energy — The Changing Climate*, Cm 4749, 2000).

On a European level, the acceptance that there needs to be more done to police the implementation and enforcement of EC environmental law will be found in the forthcoming Sixth Action Programme. In addition, the Commissioner, Margot Wallström, has expressed her determination not to allow Member States to disregard EC environmental laws. Although there has been a lot of activity in giving 'reasoned opinions' to Member States, there is little evidence yet that it is anything more than 'business as usual'.

On a domestic level, implementation and enforcement will be important both substantively (in relation to the new system of integrated pollution prevention and control, the Landfill Directive, the contaminated land regime and the much anticipated reform of nature conservation law) and institutionally (at the time of writing, the Environment Agency has been criticised by the Parliamentary Select Committee for being too 'soft' on polluters and lacking focus in relation to environmental quality). At the sharp end of enforcement we have recently seen the Court of Appeal ignoring the Sentencing Advisory Panel's advice on the sentencing for environmental offences. It would be easy to criticise the Court which refused to take a strict line against environmental offenders. Perhaps it would be more worthwhile, however, to reflect upon whether we should be looking for uniform sentencing guidelines for offences which varied from the dumping of special waste to failing to register under the packaging waste legislation. Or, put differently, how should the courts formulate general rules on sentencing when they are dealing with complex matters relating to the risk of perhaps unquantifiable environmental harm rather than actual damage?

(f) The development of environmental jurisprudence

More generally, the courts are gradually developing small pockets of environmental jurisprudence through case law. In particular we have seen significant numbers of cases in relation to the need for environmental impact assessment and statutory nuisances. If there is one underlying characteristic in all of these cases, however, it is the lack of consistent principles which emerge. This can leave a student trying to grapple with many seemingly contradictory decisions (e.g. in relation to whether the EIA Directive has 'direct effect', whether an abatement notice has to specify the works required to abate a statutory nuisance, or even procedural matters such as whether an applicant has standing or there has been prejudicial delay). These seeming contradictions merely underline the essential discretionary nature of much environmental law. In some instances, however, a measure of consistency is now being achieved (e.g. in relation to environmental assessment).

Although it is nearly four years since his death, Simon Ball remains a strong influence on a text that, true to his passions, still attempts both to introduce environmental law to students whilst, at the same time, offers a critique of a bigger picture and some pointers to the kinds of principles and policy directions that might emerge to develop the subject. We continue to dedicate the book to him but, of course, remain wholly responsible for any errors. We have endeavoured to state the law as at 1 May 2000, although some later additions have sneaked in at proof stage. The authors would welcome comments on this edition of the book, and of course suggestions for future issues, to *sbell@dial.pipex.com* and *d.mcgillivray@bbk.ac.uk*.

A new edition of this book normally appears approximately every two years. The fact that it is nearly a year late reflects the extra work which has been put into it, and the additional pressures experienced by all who work in the academy. This in turn has meant that we have had an incredible amount of support and additional assistance which has been given to us by our colleagues.

Donald is indebted to numerous friends and colleagues at Kent and at London over the years, some of whom kindly read through drafts of chapters. In addition, thanks to Liz Cable and her team in the Kent Law School office for much appreciated help, and to Sarah Carter and Jane Venis for superb library support. Finally, a more general thank you to everyone at Kent Law School who were, without exception, the very definition of collegiality, but particularly to Bill Howarth, first amongst equals in that regard.

Stuart would like to thank his friends and colleagues in the Centre for Legal Research at Nottingham and all of the National Environment Team at Eversheds for their support and (sometimes!) helpful comments. In particular he would like to thank Philippa, Nicholas, Oliver, Andrew and Thomas for allowing him to take an occasional break from the chaos of family life to the calm of the writer's study.

Both of us are grateful to all those, too numerous to mention, who continue to give so freely of their time to answer our numerous questions and queries, and to our students, who do so wittingly and unwittingly.

Stuart Bell
Donald McGillivray

Abbreviations

AONB	area of outstanding natural beauty
APC	air pollution control
AQMA	air quality management area
AQS	air quality standards
BAT	best available techniques
BATNEEC	best available techniques not entailing excessive cost
BPM	best practicable means
BREF	BAT reference document
BS	British Standard
BTU	British Thermal Unit
CFC	chlorofluorocarbon
CIA	Chemical Industry Association
CITES	Convention on the International Trade in Endangered Species
COMAH	Control of Major-Accident Hazards
COPA 1974	Control of Pollution Act 1974
CPR	Civil Procedure Rules
CPRE	Council for the Protection of Rural England
CRI	chemical releases inventory
DETR	Department of the Environment, Transport and the Regions
DoE	Department of the Environment
DTI	Department of Trade and Industry
EA	Environment Agency
EC	European Community
ECHR	European Convention on Human Rights
ECJ	European Court of Justice
EEZ	exclusive economic zone
EIA	environmental impact assessment
EMAS	eco-management and audit scheme (EC)
EMS	environmental management system
EPA 1990	Environmental Protection Act 1990
ES	environmental statement
ESA	environmentally sensitive area
FAO	Food and Agriculture Organisation (UN)
GATT	General Agreement on Tariffs and Trade
GBR	general binding rule

GDP	gross domestic product
GDPO	General Development Procedure Order
GMO	genetically modified organism
GPDO	General Permitted Development Order
GLA	Greater London Authority
GQA	general quality assessment
HMIP	Her Majesty's Inspectorate of Pollution
HSA	hazardous substances authority
HSE	Health and Safety Executive
ICJ	International Court of Justice
IPC	integrated pollution control
IPPC	integrated pollution prevention and control
ISO	International Standards Organisation
IUCN	International Union for the Conservation of Nature
JNCC	Joint Nature Conservancy Council
LAAPC	local authority air pollution control
LTCS	Landfill Tax Credit Scheme
MAFF	Ministry of Agriculture, Fisheries and Food
MNR	marine nature reserve
NCC	Nature Conservancy Council
NGO	non-governmental organisation
NNR	national nature reserve
NRA	National Rivers Authority
NVZ	nitrate vulnerable zone
OECD	Organisation for Economic Cooperation and Development
OSPAR	Convention for the Protection of the Marine Environment of the North East Atlantic
PPCA 1999	Pollution Prevention and Control Act 1999
PPG	Planning Policy Guidance
PRN	packaging waste recovery note
RCEP	Royal Commission on Environmental Pollution
RDA	Regional Development Agency
RPB	Regional Planning Bodies
RPG	Regional Planning Guidance Note
RSPB	Royal Society for the Protection of Birds
SAC	special area of conservation
SEA	strategic environmental assessment
SEA 1986	Single European Act 1986
SEPA	Scottish Environment Protection Agency
SPA	special protection area
SLF	substitute liquid fuels
SPL	significant pollution linkage
SSSI	site of special scientific interest
TPO	tree preservation order
UDP	unitary development plan
UNEP	United Nations Environment Programme
VOC	volatile organic compounds

WDA	waste disposal authority
WMP	Waste Management Paper
WRA	waste regulation authority
WTO	World Trade Organisation

Table of Cases

Table of Statutes

Table of Statutory Instruments

European secondary legislation

PART I   GENERAL PRINCIPLES OF ENVIRONMENTAL LAW

ONE

What is environmental law?

In the 1980s and 90s some commentators predicted that the issue of 'the environment' would be transitory. Although the interest in subject specific environmental concerns can ebb and flow, it is clear that the general topic is one of the big issues, perhaps the biggest contemporary issue we face.

It is a big issue in political terms, since protection of the environment is high on most people's priorities in the 21st century. As a result political parties and governments are falling over each other in their eagerness to appear green, even if as yet their actions rarely match their rhetoric. It is big in terms of the size of the problems faced and the solutions required; global warming, the destruction of the ozone layer, acid rain, deforestation and toxic waste are all global issues which require an appropriately global response. It is big in terms of the range of problems and issues — air pollution, water pollution, noise pollution, waste management, radioactivity, pesticides, countryside protection, conservation of wildlife — the list is virtually endless. In the words of the White Paper on the Environment, *This Common Inheritance* (Cm 1200, 1990) the issues range 'from the street corner to the stratosphere'. Finally, it is big in terms of the knowledge and skills required to understand a particular issue. Law is only one element in what is a major cross-disciplinary topic. Lawyers need some understanding of the scientific, political and economic processes involved in environmental degradation. Equally, all those whose activities and interests relate to the environment need to acquire an understanding of the structure and content of environmental law, since it has a large and increasing role to play in environmental protection. The book is entitled 'Environmental Law' and an explanation of these two words will clarify some preliminary points about its content.

Environmental

This is a difficult word to define. Its normal meaning relates to 'surroundings', but obviously that is a concept that is relative to whatever object it is which is surrounded. Used in that sense environmental law could include virtually anything; indeed, as Einstein once remarked, 'The environment is everything that isn't me'. However, 'the environment' has now taken on a rather more specific meaning, though still a very vague and general one, and may be treated as covering the physical surroundings that are common to all of us, including air, space, waters, land, plants and wildlife.

A definition of this nature is used in the Environmental Protection Act 1990 (EPA 1990), s. 1, which defines the environment as consisting of 'all, or any, of the following media, namely, the air, water and land'. Rather than offering a hostage to fortune by attempting to lay down some impossibly precise definition, we propose to adopt this one for the general description of the book's content. A more precise description can be given simply by stating what is and what is not covered by the book. We intend to concentrate on those laws and practices which relate primarily to the protection of the whole or part of the general surroundings, as opposed to those where the true objective is the protection of public health, or individual people such as workers or consumers.

Obviously, it is not possible to consign some areas of law with certainty to one category or another and, as a result, the exact dividing line between what is and what is not included is rather artificial. But a line has to be drawn somewhere. Accordingly, we cover the law and practice on the protection of air, water and land against pollution, laws relating to development and the conservation of biodiversity and landscape features, together with those ancillary issues which help to explain these areas, such as public participation, access to information, remedies and procedures.

Such things as consumer protection laws, product liability laws, health and safety legislation and animal protection laws are not covered, although they can often be relevant to solving environmental problems. There are also a number of areas of what is undeniably environmental law which are omitted on grounds of space. The growing package of legislation on the protection of the cultural heritage is omitted. Little will be said about radioactivity, where the law is very complex indeed and where there is a large overlap between the environmental and human protection parts of the law. The provisions in the EPA 1990 on the introduction of genetically modified organisms into the environment and on litter are also omitted.

Law

This book is not intended to be merely a description of the various rules and regulations, although obviously that is a part of any useful book on the law. Such a description would give little clue to what happens in practice. Whether, and how, the law is enforced is just as important as what the law is. Indeed, given the discretionary nature of many of the powers and duties imposed on environmental decision-makers, it is unreal to draw a hard and fast distinction between what the law is and how it is used. This book will therefore seek to emphasise policy as much as law, and practice as much as principle.

Law in practice is also affected by the values and culture of those who make the rules; set the standards by which those rules operate; implement and enforce the rules and standards; and those whose activities are controlled, by those rules and standards. In environmental law and policy this extends to us all and the impact of these values can be stretched further to include non-human interests and the interests of future generations. The word 'values' covers the things which are important to us and the priority we give to them. There is therefore a direct connection between that which we consider to be a priority and the laws and policies which are introduced to 'control', promote or otherwise regulate the area concerned. We therefore cover the role that values play in environmental law and policy and the various perspectives on environmental issues or decisions.

The terms 'rules' and 'law' are often used interchangeably in many parts of the book. That is because environmental 'law' arguably comes from different sources, many of which would not necessarily fall within the definition of statutes or regulations. Thus there are guidance notes, circulars, official policy documents, codes of practice, even politicians' speeches which can have a marked effect upon the way in which the law operates in practice. For example, the Environment Agency or the Department of the Environment, Transport and the Regions may publish some guidance on the interpretation of a vague statutory phrase, such as the meaning of 'waste'. Although there may be arguments over whether the guidance is 'correct', it can only be overturned by a legal challenge. Unless a challenge is made, this interpretation may become the new rule for practical purposes. In other situations, the statutory scheme may require either policy or technical guidance to flesh out the general definitions. Thus decisions on whether to grant planning permission for out of town retail development are closely controlled by a series of rules (known collectively as the sequential test) dressed up as policy in Planning Policy Guidance Notes. In the area of pollution control, there are many technical guidance notes which set process or other standards which act as rules which guide decision-makers (or more properly, structure their discretion) in granting authorisations, consents or permissions. Understanding the role of these rules and in particular the legal effect which is created when such rules exist is crucial to any understanding of the way in which environmental law works in practice.

There are some other general limitations on the subject matter of the book in addition to the ones mentioned above. It is not about all those laws which 'relate to' the environment, since that too could cover virtually anything. Instead we intend to concentrate on those laws and practices which have as their object or effect the *protection* of the environment. Those things which merely have an indirect impact on the state of the environment, such as general tax levels, grants and incentives, are thus excluded from full coverage, although their relevance is referred to in passing and they may frequently be of crucial importance to the policy-maker.

As the understanding of the global nature of environmental impacts grows, there is an increasing recognition that principles and rules need to be agreed in the international arena if there is to be a concerted effort to address common issues. Thus the role played by international agreements and principles in influencing and moulding our domestic law is covered in outline. We do not, however, attempt to deal with truly international problems in any detail, leaving such coverage to specialised works which are referred to in the bibliography.

The crucial relevance of European Community (EC) law must be emphasised. We adopt the attitude that EC law *is* domestic law in the sense that it cannot be ignored even though it does not always give rise to enforceable obligations and remedies. Therefore EC controls, both current and proposed, will be integrated into each part of the book where relevant. In addition, there is a separate chapter on the basic constitutional rules of the EC and on the history, philosophy and current direction of its environmental policy. It is hard to overestimate the central importance of EC law and policy to British environmental law. This importance is often masked by the fact that in the environmental field, EC law tends to require some form of transposition and implementation in this country before it is formally recognised. Once implemented, the EC derivation of the rule is then frequently forgotten because the domestic law is cited as the applicable law.

Some themes of the book

This description of the scope of the book highlights a number of important themes. One is that there is a great deal of interaction between rules which have as their main objective the protection of the environment and those which aim to protect people. Just as in nature conservation it has become accepted in the last 30 years that there is no use in protecting individual animals or species unless you also protect their habitats, in all matters we now accept that protection of human beings involves protection of their environment. The converse is also true in that many rules originally aimed at protection of people end up protecting the environment. For example, standards in relation to radioactivity are often set with the protection of humans in mind, but have an important impact on environmental levels of radiation. Similarly, the presence or absence of laws on cruelty to animals has a significant impact on nature conservation even though that is not their primary motive.

A related theme is that the rules are simply the tools of the trade of law-makers, environmental protection agencies and environmentalists. A rule which has as its objective one goal is frequently of enormous use in an entirely different way. For example, the law of nuisance owes its existence and shape to the objective of protecting property rights, but it still has an important, though often unpredictable, part to play in regulating environmental standards in the interests of the community. This is one of the major themes of this book: that there is often more than one way of tackling a problem and that the environmental lawyer must be seen as a problem-solver who chooses the most appropriate tool for the particular problem encountered. Often this will involve using a combination of different tools. As an example, many rules of property law may be used to further environmental ends: the Royal Society for the Protection of Birds follows a policy of buying land for nature reserve purposes on the principle that the exercise of ownership rights will often provide a better method of protection than many statutory designations or protections. This is not to say that the whole of property law must be somehow annexed as a part of environmental law, but that environmental lawyers should make use of any piece of law which has a relevance to the problem in hand.

A further issue relates to the nature of law. It is often stated that law is not constructive; that it does not build houses or plant trees. We regard this as an inaccurate notion. There is no doubt that many laws do lay down straightforward negative rules restricting specified forms of behaviour. But many laws lay down rights as well as wrongs. Much of environmental law consists of setting out a framework for behaviour — who should make decisions, how they should make them, what procedures must be followed. Such law is clearly not just negative.

In *Countryside Conflicts* (Lowe et al., 1986), the authors state that, 'planning control is no more than an essentially negative power; a device for stopping objectionable proposals'. This pessimistic view, which is undoubtedly widespread (especially amongst non-lawyers), seems to miss the point that planning law, like much of environmental law, is also about positive concepts, as expressed in the word 'planning' and illustrated by the production of development plans as an integral part of the process. In relation to pollution control, a similar point can be made by noting that the regulatory agencies spend a far greater proportion of their time providing positive advice on how to reach the standards they set than on enforcing those standards through legal threats and remedies.

This distinction between negative and positive tools links to a division in the subject matter of environmental law. It is common to equate environmental protection with pollution control. However, whilst pollution control undoubtedly represents a major part of environmental law, there are many other issues, such as the retention of biological diversity and the preservation of landscape, which also make up the subject. These issues often require slightly different legal mechanisms. Indeed the evidence of a growing maturity of environmental law can be seen in the use of a more extensive range of these positive tools. The producer responsibility legislation which sets out targets for the recycling and recovery of waste packaging (with the implicit incentive to reduce the amount of waste packaging produced) is a good example of the use of positive legal rules to bring about environmental improvement.

Finally, and perhaps most importantly, the law provides remedies. To many people, whether they are environmentalists or industrialists or lawyers giving advice, this is the most central aspect of law, since they want to know what they can do about a situation. One of the interesting developments of recent years has been the search for adequate remedies for environmental problems. Legal tools have been accepted as legitimate devices for helping to solve environmental problems. Law plays an often underrated but enormously important role, alongside scientific, technological, social and economic solutions, in helping to combat environmental degradation. In this role, many novel legal concepts have been developed.

The shape of the book

A major aim of this book is to illustrate the proposition that there has developed such a thing as environmental law. Most lawyers are brought up on the idea that there are a number of core, or basic, subjects which are essentially about techniques and in which a set of central organising principles can be distilled from the law. Criminal law, constitutional law, public law, contract law, torts, equity and property law would be good examples. The traditional view would then be that, alongside those basic subjects, there are as many areas of law as there are areas of life, in each of which the techniques of the basic subjects are used; for example, the law relating to family relationships, the law relating to housing. But over a period of time, there is no doubt that these topic-related areas build up their own principles and reasoning processes. A good example of this process would be the development of the principles of family law over the last 30 years.

We would argue that environmental law has its own conceptual apparatus, in the sense that there is a set of principles and concepts which can be said to exist across the range of subjects covered. Although there is a valid debate about the extent to which these principles have gained universal acceptance as principles with meaningful legal effect, the process of establishing environmental law as an identifiable discipline has begun. Clearly these principles provide a theoretical context in which to view the detail of environmental law and thus it is important to provide near the beginning of the book some explanation of what we think principles such as the 'precautionary principle' or the 'polluter pays' mean. It also explains the division of the book into two parts, one on the general themes of environmental law and the other on the law relating to specific environmental issues. As suggested above, an environmental lawyer needs to understand the law in practice as well as the detailed rules in order to possess the tools required to carry out the task of solving particular problems properly.

Part I of the book looks at those general issues which cut across all issues of environmental protection, but which are in practice an essential part of any understanding of the law. The discussion in this part should also provide a form of vocabulary to help with an understanding of the context of the specific laws and practices which are dealt with in Part II.

Part I thus covers perspectives on the environment and how the law overlaps with environmental issues, the nature of the regulatory systems adopted for environmental protection, the sources of the law, the institutions and agencies involved in environmental protection, the process of setting environmental standards and the different types of standards that may be adopted, the role of the EC and international law, secrecy and freedom of access to information, the role of the common law and the important question of how environmental laws are actually enforced.

In *Part II* the specific laws relating to particular environmental issues are treated on a chapter by chapter basis. However, there is a significant problem of organisation here. Should the law be divided up according to the medium in which the environmental threat manifests itself (e.g. air, water, land etc.)? Should it be divided according to the identity of the polluter (e.g. cars, factories, power stations etc.)? Should it be divided according to the nature of the pollutant (e.g. radiation, lead, pesticides, CFCs etc.)? Or should it even be divided according to the nature of the target which is being protected (e.g. people, animals, ecosystems, the atmosphere)?

There is no single answer. The laws are not designed on any one of these four axes, but on all four at once. The best that can be done is to select groupings of laws that more or less hang together in a way that makes sense to someone faced with a problem. It must then be remembered that in reality all these things interrelate, so that a problem on the disposal of waste to land cannot be considered without some consideration of the law on incineration, or discharges to water, or recycling. Integrated pollution control and the adoption of the related concept of best practicable environmental option in the EPA 1990 are explicit recognitions of this interrelation.

Certain issues also play a role which it is impossible to explain in terms of any one of the four axes set out above. The law on town and country planning is an example. It clearly has a central role in protecting against threats to amenity and is in other ways an important part of the law on environmental protection. For example, hazardous or undesirable developments can be prevented or controlled by the imposition of conditions making the need for planning permission an essential part of most systems of pollution control. But it also has a role in organising economic development which is outside environmental law in its strict sense.

As a result the chapter divisions in Part II may be seen as artificial in a number of ways. We try to cover the protection of the major environmental media — air, land and water — from pollution, whilst considering the various means of disposing of and managing waste — sewage disposal, incineration, landfill, discharge to rivers, discharge to the sea, reuse and recycling.

One of the characteristics of the law and policy of environmental protection is that it evolves, constantly reflecting the various values and priorities which we place upon different aspects of environmental issues. This means that in recent years as environmental issues have gained in importance, we have seen a period of unprecedented rapid change (see below). We have therefore tried to give special prominence to those areas where there have been recent changes and to refer to potential future developments wherever possible. In a subject area such as this where activities have to be planned reasonably far in advance, it is always helpful to know what is likely to happen in the future as well as what is the law at the time. In this sense environmental law is forward-looking law. In some areas this can create problems where there is an overlap between the existing rules and those which are to be phased in (the control of industrial processes under the existing system of integrated pollution control and the new pollution prevention and control legislation covered in Chapter 13 is a good example). In such cases, we have tried to emphasise those features of the new system which are clearly distinguishable from the existing framework.

Finally, it must be stressed that environmental law is often thought to be a complex and opaque area of study. Without wishing to oversimplify the subtle nuances of environmental rules and policy, we believe that it should be possible to give an outline of the substantive provisions of a subject area which should give the reader a general idea of the scope of the particular area of control. We have attempted to provide such summaries.

The history of environmental law

An understanding of the current state of environmental law requires some understanding of its history. Not surprisingly for such a densely populated country, environmental controls have a long history, going back to medieval statutes on small-scale pollution and the development of private law principles to deal with threats to communal assets such as water. Of course, until recently, few would have thought of these laws as part of something called 'environmental law', since their main focus was on the protection of private and common property.

Britain's position as the cradle of the Industrial Revolution led to the very early development of public controls specifically related to environmental protection. The most significant provisions were developed in response to public health problems in the mid-nineteenth century, culminating in the landmark Public Health Act 1875.

Britain can boast what is normally considered the world's first national public pollution control agency, the Alkali Inspectorate, which was established by the Alkali Act 1863 to control atmospheric emissions primarily from the caustic soda industry. Water pollution controls followed in the Rivers Pollution Prevention Act 1876, although these proved to be virtually unenforceable in practice. Britain also introduced some of the earliest provisions on town planning. The first legislation to cover this subject was the Housing, Town Planning etc. Act 1909, which again derived from public health pressures and which vested controls in local authorities, at this stage on a non-obligatory basis. Obligatory town and country planning controls were introduced on a nationwide scale in 1947 — again early in world terms.

In addition to these public controls, the law of nuisance was developed (especially in the nineteenth century) as a means of providing private redress for environmental harm, although on a very selective basis. Britain also had some of the earliest voluntary bodies concerned with environmental protection.

National, centralised control of problems (such as through the Alkali Inspectorate) was very much the exception in this period of development, and most public health and environmental protection was carried out at a local level by a vast array of local boards and, at a later stage, local authorities. Some uniformity was effected by the Public Health Act 1875, which produced model by-laws for such things as the design and layout of housing, but most of the early provisions reflect a tendency (which is still apparent) to regulate only the most dangerous or sensitive matters at a central level.

In these formative years, law-making tended to be ad hoc in the extreme. This is self-evident with case law, which by its very nature must react to the facts of cases brought. But legislative changes were also reactive, with Parliament tending to legislate for problems on an individual basis, in isolation from other areas and without any thought for wider development or consolidation of the law. For example, one effect of the early Alkali Acts and the controls over atmospheric emissions is reputed to have been an immediate worsening of water quality as industries chose liquid discharge as a replacement method for the disposal of their wastes. The same reactive tendency can be seen more recently. An example is the enactment of the Deposit of Poisonous Wastes Act 1972, which passed through Parliament in only a few days in response to a much-publicised discovery of the fly-tipping of poisonous waste near a school playground.

As a result, environmental law has traditionally been split amongst a number of statutes, many of them covering much other material with little to do with environmental protection. Grandiose titles have often concealed the fact that an Act only covers part of the law on a particular area. For example, the Wildlife and Countryside Act 1981 did not really have much to offer for the protection of the wider countryside outside sites protected for nature conservation and landscape purposes, and even the Control of Pollution Act 1974, which was the first of the modern breed of large statutes concerned exclusively with pollution control, had very little to say about air pollution.

One reason for this fragmentation was often lack of Parliamentary time provided by the government of the day, fuelled by the perceived lack of importance of environmental issues. This is undoubtedly changing rapidly as the political importance of environmental protection has grown immensely in recent years. But many environmental measures in the past have resulted from single issue campaigns, or from private members' bills. For example, one of the reasons why the protection of birds has always been at a greater level than the protection of animals and plants is the passage of the Protection of Birds Act 1954 as a Private Member's Bill sponsored by the Royal Society for the Protection of Birds. A further example to show that this still happens is the Control of Pollution (Amendment) Act 1989, a Private Member's Bill to require the registration of carriers of controlled waste, passed in response to fly-tipping in London.

One effect of this long, and unplanned, history is that modern Britain has inherited a far less coherent system of pollution control than many other countries. The same historical factors also explain the relatively large number of agencies dealing with environmental matters, although changes in institutional responsibility have significantly improved matters in this respect.

A further effect is the survival of anachronisms. The name 'Alkali Inspectorate' lasted until the 1980s (when it became part of Her Majesty's Inspectorate of Pollution) and, although there have been changes in the EPA 1990, we still have laws on statutory nuisances (which have also been adopted as a loose model for the regulation of historically contaminated land) which retain the essential shape they were given in the Public Health Act 1875. Anachronisms may also be seen in the limitations on access to environmental information and public participation in environmental decision-making (see Chapter 8) and in the historical widespread immunity of the Crown in relation to environmental regulation (although this is being removed gradually).

Of course, as well as a long history of pollution control, Britain has a long history of pollution. This has left a legacy of problems that require urgent action, such as abandoned waste tips, derelict land, discharges of toxic wastes and untreated sewage into estuaries and the sea, and a host of other matters. There are other problems, stemming from the fact that many matters were not perceived as problems in the past, or that lower standards were accepted then. For example, perpetual planning permissions for peat extraction or minerals extraction were commonly granted in the 1940s and 1950s. Many of these are in areas now accepted as sensitive and worthy of protection, but it is only recently that there have been progressive legislative amendments which enable such permissions to be revoked or modified to take account of modern environmental concerns.

Britain's ageing industrial base also creates difficulties when new, improved controls and standards are introduced. Fairness requires that existing producers are given some time to adapt to new standards, yet there is at the same time a problem of unfairness if controls are introduced so as to produce an inequality between new and existing producers.

The modern age of environmental law

Environmental law has changed rapidly over a period of 15 years with the pace of change accelerating since the beginning of the 1990s. Further change can be expected in the future to reflect the vastly increased prominence of environmental issues. Although it is not possible to specify a precise date or event, the modern age of environmental law can tentatively be said to have begun some time in the early 1970s.

There has been an obvious shift in the emphasis of the law since then to reflect newer environmental concerns. Many problems were simply not perceived as such in the 1960s, or were subordinated to other more pressing matters, such as the raising of living standards or the provision of full employment. The emphasis at that stage was on health and safety matters, a point well illustrated by the placing of the Alkali and Clean Air Inspectorate within the Health and Safety Executive when it was established in 1974. Land use was also emphasised; indeed, it could be argued that the very fact that Britain had (and still has) what is probably the world's most advanced system of land use planning led to the concentration of controls at that stage rather than to encouraging the development of adequate continuing pollution controls.

By comparison, the focus of modern legislation is on the control of pollution, and growing concern is being expressed about global and transfrontier problems, the control of hazardous substances and processes, the minimisation and management of waste, the conservation of natural resources and protection of ecosystems. In short, current concerns tend to reflect the need to control the almost inevitable by-products of the modern, technological, post-industrial information age.

In terms of legislation, the law is becoming more concentrated in a smaller number of Acts. The Environmental Protection Act 1990 contains the main bulk of provisions on air pollution from stationary sources, waste management and disposal, the integrated control of the most potentially polluting processes, litter, the environmental impact of genetically modified organisms, noise and statutory control of environmental nuisances. The provisions controlling industrial processes are to be replaced by the permitting system which is to be found in the Pollution Prevention and Control Act 1999. The Water Resources Act 1991 contains the law on water pollution and water resources, whilst the Water Industry Act 1991 (which has been amended in certain areas such as the power to charge for water supply by the Water Industry Act 1999) covers matters relating to water supply and sewerage. The

Wildlife and Countryside Act 1981 includes much of the relevant law on nature conservation in Parts I and II. The Environment Act 1995 introduced new legal provisions in relation to liability for contaminated land. It also created the Environment Agency, which took over functions related to integrated pollution control, waste regulation, water pollution and water resources, and radioactive substances, although without any major changes in the substance of the law. The Town and Country Planning Act 1990 includes in consolidated form most of the relevant statutory law on town and country planning and tree protection. There is also the Planning and Compensation Act 1991, which made some significant amendments to the 1990 Acts.

None of these Acts is a full code in relation to the relevant subject matter. There are numerous individual issues which are dealt with by separate pieces of legislation, such as on radioactivity, or on pesticides. There are other issues where the controls are still spread amongst a large number of Acts, such as in relation to landscape protection. It is also necessary to point out that much of the detailed law in any area is actually provided in statutory instruments and a wide range of other documents made under the relevant Acts. The process of producing a coherent body of environmental law, begun in the Control of Pollution Act 1974 (which put most of the law on water pollution and waste disposal in one place, but which is now virtually fully replaced by later legislation in England and Wales), has certainly moved forward some distance.

One of the important features of this process is that the development and direction of the statutory controls is more planned than before. The main Acts referred to above are all government-sponsored Acts, illustrating an increasing tendency to plan and interlink legislation properly, although there is still a habit of including unrelated matters in legislation just in case no other opportunity arises in a packed Parliamentary timetable. For example, the EPA 1990 includes miscellaneous provisions on the control of dogs, the dismantling of the Nature Conservancy Council and the prohibition of straw and stubble burning. The publication of the wide-ranging White Paper on the environment, *This Common Inheritance* (Cm 1200, 1990), underlined this commitment to a planned development of environmental policy. The latest incarnation of this planned development is the White Paper on Sustainable Development, *A Better Quality of Life* (Cm 4345, 1999) which demonstrates a shift away from the declaration of wide-ranging environmental policies (such as those under *This Common Inheritance*) to the setting of indicators on such complicated issues as 'quality of life' and the equal distribution of the consequences of pollution.

There is also an increasing institutional coherence. The National Rivers Authority was established in 1989 as a national body regulating water pollution and a number of other activities affecting water quality. Her Majesty's Inspectorate of Pollution was established in 1987 to bring together a number of sectoral Inspectorates and was given integrated powers over the most hazardous industrial processes in the EPA 1990, an Act which also created greater coherence in relation to the control of air pollution by local authorities and the management of waste and waste disposal. Once again it is clear that controls over stationary sources of pollution are more coherent than those over mobile or non-point sources. In 1996, the creation of the Environment Agency brought the main pollution control functions (integrated pollution control, waste management and the regulation of water pollution) under one administrative body for the first time.

A different aspect of developments in relation to institutional responsibilities has been the policy of splitting production from regulation. This may be termed the need to differentiate the poachers from the gamekeepers. In more recent years this was achieved by the creation of the National Rivers Authority. Prior to that the regulation of water pollution was the responsibility of the regional water authorities, who were also responsible for causing pollution from sewage works which they operated. Another example is the enforced separation of waste regulation functions from waste disposal functions in the EPA 1990 (see Chapter 17), a process that was taken further in the Environment Act 1995.

A final change, which may be seen from the examples referred to, is that environmental protection is becoming increasingly centralised, although this must be seen against the perspective that, as stated above, the system inherited from earlier years was particularly decentralised. There are many reasons for this — the increasing complexity of environmental risks which create technological and scientific demands on regulators, many years of central government antipathy towards local government, the growth in emphasis on uniform and integrated planning of solutions to problems, the increase in institutional coherence and the impact of EC membership. This issue of centralisation is considered further in Chapter 7.

A most important factor in all of these changes has been the influence of the European Community (EC). The EC has a well-developed environmental policy and has passed numerous pieces of environmental law. At a general level, membership of the EC has led to the consideration and adoption of new methods of control and to the need to confront environmental issues in an organised way at central government level. More specifically, EC legislation and pressure has led to many actual and proposed changes in the law (often after British resistance), for example, on sulphur dioxide emissions, the dumping of sewage sludge in the sea and reductions in emissions from vehicles. Other changes have been more indirect; for example, the Wildlife and Countryside Act 1981 was necessary to comply with EC Directive 79/409 on Wild Birds, and the opportunity was taken to modify other areas of the law at the same time. Without the EC obligation there must be some doubt whether any legislation would have been brought forward at that time — and even greater doubt as to whether it would have been persevered with in the light of the widespread opposition to the Government's original proposals, which were significantly altered as the Bill passed through Parliament.

The future of environmental policy

In the light of EC membership and the pressure now brought to bear by the whole international community on environmental issues, it is difficult to disentangle British policies from global and regional ones. It is also difficult to predict the future accurately in this area because environmental policy continues to be a highly political area. For example, the obligations entered into under the treaty on climate change provide targets without necessarily identifying the specific legal (or otherwise) instruments; the range of options put forward (including a tax on the use of energy) provide a large number of separate, highly charged political issues. Nevertheless, a number of key directions for future policy present themselves:

(a)   The emphasis is shifting away from the more traditional reactive methods of solving environmental problems towards the prevention of harm. This is illustrated by the progressive adoption of laws that set standards for products or the processes by which they are made, rather than for discharges or emissions. The adoption of the Integrated Pollution Prevention and Control Directive which is characterised by holistic preventive, process-based controls, is an important step in this direction.

(b)   The importance of the market in controlling environmental problems will continue to be stressed. Originally, this stemmed from the philosophical basis of the Conservative Government whilst it was in power. Subsequently, it has been related to the preference for market mechanisms (often referred to as 'economic instruments'), which may help to prevent pollution occurring by sending signals to consumers about the true environmental costs of their activities. Examples can be seen in the proliferation of schemes for charging for environmentally harmful activities; in the increasingly frequent reference to the 'polluter pays' principle; and in direct measures such as the introduction of the landfill tax. The current Government has made it clear that over the next few years there will be more reforms of the taxation system to increase incentives which will reduce environmental damage. The 1999 budget heralded a tax on the use of energy under the Climate Change Levy. In addition, the EC is looking at a variety of economic instruments including full cost recovery pricing for water (i.e. charging for the full environmental costs for the use of water, see further p. 570).

(c)   At EC level, we are currently between Action Programmes. The Fifth Action Programme for the period 1993 to 2000, entitled *Towards Sustainability*, began the process of integrating environmental considerations into a limited number of other policy sectors and this process will continue under the EC's revised Treaty principles which were agreed at Amsterdam in 1997. Under the forthcoming Sixth Action Programme we can expect greater efforts to enforce existing EC environmental law across all Member States and a continuation of the theme of 'shared responsibility' meaning that responsibility for environmental problems is shared between government, producers and consumers. By suggesting that producers and consumers should be empowered to make decisions that have an impact on environmental performance, it heralds the development of a wider range of legal and policy responses to environmental problems.

(d)   A further matter that links all of the above together is the provision of information about the environment. It is obvious that increased interest in environmental issues has led to a political need for greater access to information. But there is a further reason why freedom of information is a central issue. This is that market mechanisms do not work, and concepts such as shared responsibility mean nothing, unless there is access to accurate information. On a policy level, purposefully linking access to environmental information with other aspects of environmental policy can be seen in the links between access to information and shared responsibility, and with public participation and access to justice (as evidenced by the recent Århus Convention on these issues).

(e)   An important issue is the internationalisation of many problems. A number of high-profile issues, such as global warming, depletion of the ozone layer and the global conservation of biological diversity, have galvanised interest in environmental issues, and there is no doubt that the future agenda will increasingly be set on the international stage. The clearest expression of this process was the United Nations Conference on Environment and Development (UNCED), held in Rio de Janeiro in June 1992. Although this was rightly criticised for failing to produce anything of enormous immediate significance, it did produce agreement on a number of things. These included a framework convention on climate change, a convention on biological diversity, a declaration on the sustainable development of forests, and Agenda 21, which is effectively a very wide-ranging environmental action plan for the twenty-first century. The implications of these commitments continue to feed through into domestic policies, so Rio is probably most accurately seen as the beginning of a process rather than the end of one, a view which is supported by the fact that a further 'Rio + 10' conference will be held in 2002 to reflect on progress.

(f)   A central strand of policy at Rio was the emphasis on the conservation of natural resources. The key concept was that of 'sustainable development', an idea that was originally developed by the World Commission on Environment and Development (the Brundtland Commission) in its report, *Our Common Future*, in 1987. *Our Common Future* defined sustainable development in general terms as 'development that meets the needs of the present without compromising the ability of future generations to meet their own needs', thus suggesting that global resources (including environmental resources) should be measured, with the objective of ensuring that they are not depleted over time. Clearly, this idea requires some further development itself, in particular in relation to how one goes about measuring intangible global assets and whether it is permissible to substitute one type of asset for another. One thing that is clear is that sustainable development still represents a commitment to growth.

In national policy this commitment has been reflected in the policy initiatives which have been published in the sustainable development strategy. In *This Common Inheritance*, the then Conservative Government stressed the view that continued growth was a necessary (although not a sufficient) condition for maintaining the quality of life, and this view was reiterated in the follow-up document, *Sustainable Development: The UK Strategy* (Cm 2426, 1994). The Labour administration has adopted a similar line in its own sustainable development policy, *A Better Quality of Life: A Strategy for Sustainable Development for the United Kingdom* (Cm 4345, 1999). Thus, the idea of sustainable development which has been embraced within national policy should therefore be distinguished from the concept of sustainability, which merely reflects the state of something being sustainable in the long term.

(g) At a national level, the Labour Government has been in power long enough to discern that any shift in environmental policy has been subtle (to put it at its highest). Certain policy areas, such as the use of economic instruments, are attractive across party political boundaries (although there can be significant differences over detail rather than principle). Others, such as an emphasis on resource management and efficiency (e.g. waste reduction targets), are more the result of external pressures (such as the EC) and the increasing sophistication of environmental instruments rather than any internal policy shift. There has, however, been some identifiable shift in policy in more general areas such as the integration of environmental policies within other areas of government. This can be seen with the introduction of the 'Greening Government' initiative (see p. 155) which included the Cabinet committee on the environment and the establishment of 'Green Ministers' with individual environmental responsibility.

(h) Arguably the most noticeable shift in policy has been the introduction of a more strategic approach to many environmental issues. In a response to the traditional reactive mode of policy and rule making, we appear to be entering the phase of the 'national strategy'. This is partly because of the need to flesh out the policy framework in the sustainable development strategy; partly to indicate the manner of achieving certain goals or targets which have been set down either nationally or internationally; and partly because of the history of inadequate policy making in many areas of environmental policy. Thus we have (or in some cases will have) strategies on sustainable development, waste management, air quality, chemicals, climate change, soil protection, sustainable distribution and sustainable construction. Whilst these can provide a helpful framework for future action and specific targets which can be aimed at, there is a danger that the overuse of such strategies can be used to present mere 'aspirations' which can be manipulated or dropped if progress in meeting the targets is slow.

(i) One of the key concepts in future policy making will be flexibility in the selection of the instruments which are used to meet policy aims. For example, consultation papers on the Climate Change programme have considered a range of instruments including voluntary agreements to reduce energy consumption, a direct tax on the use of energy, emissions trading schemes, growth in renewable energy and emission controls under the implementation of the Integrated Pollution Prevention and Control Directive. In addition the Kyoto Protocol (which contains the latest agreed programme for reduction in emissions which contribute to climate change) has other innovative mechanisms for achieving compliance with cuts in emissions of greenhouse gases including: 'emissions trading' whereby an industrialised country can buy or sell emission 'credits' to or from other countries; or the use of the so-called 'clean development mechanism' whereby industrialised countries can earn cuts in their own targets by investing in greenhouse gas reduction projects in developing countries. These 'flexible mechanisms' are not without criticism but they reflect an increasing concern that policies should be as adaptable as possible in order to meet the specified goals and targets. Thus the blending of different types of instruments means that if one mechanism is less effective, another mechanism may reduce the gap between aspiration and the achievement of the policy objective.

(j)   Perhaps most significantly, the full implications of sustainability will need to be addressed and difficult choices made. These are most obvious in relation to steps which are being taken to tackle consumption of resources (such as the production of waste and the use of energy or water). Other areas which continue to pose problems include transport policy and house building. The nature of the controversy reflects the fact that the most important message of sustainability (and environmental policy) appears to be getting across. This is that these policy issues are not only the concern of a remote group of individuals or companies with the label of 'polluters' and everything will be all right if their activities can be regulated efficiently, but that environmental protection is a matter for everyone and involves everyone making informed decisions about their own lifestyles. In a connected point it has become fashionable to talk of environmental policy assisting with the identification and delineation of 'rights' such as the right to a clean environment. When the full implications of sustainability are considered, there should be an equal emphasis placed upon the corresponding duties which such environmental rights can impose upon us all as individuals. Thus when we assert the language of 'rights' (e.g. I have a right to breathe clean air), the difficult dilemma posed is that the duty to prevent the pollution of the atmosphere is often a corollary of that assertion (e.g. I have a duty to ensure that I do not contribute to the pollution of the air). Once again, environmental law and policy can clarify the scope of such duties and inform the debate about the nature of the duties as they apply to each individual and our community.

The future of environmental law

An introductory chapter may seem a strange place to consider the future of the law, since any such discussion must inevitably involve an understanding of the present position. However, it is useful to sketch out some general ideas about the direction in which environmental law might be going at this stage so as to set the rest of the book in context.

The starting point is to repeat the proposition that environmental law has not been developed as a self-contained discipline, but has simply borrowed concepts from other areas of law. One result is undoubtedly a degree of incoherence, but another is that the objective of the protection of the environment is not always best served by the legal mechanisms available, because these other areas were not developed with the particular problems of environmental protection in mind. For example, the private law concentrates on the protection of private interests and has difficulties when it comes to protecting common or public interests in the unowned environment. No damages are payable for harm to the environment as such, and only those with personal or property rights may bring an action (thus excluding animals, trees, rivers etc). No value is placed on the environment itself and environmental protection is simply an incidental by-product of the protection of other interests. As Lord Scarman pointed out in 1974 in *English Law — The New Dimension*:

> For 'environment' a traditional lawyer reads 'property': English law reduces environmental problems to questions of property . . .. The judicial development of the law, vigorous and imaginative though it has been, has been found wanting.

Public law does recognise the public interest, but difficulties arise out of a lack of acceptance of the idea that the environment has some independent status or value, as distinct from rights conferred on individuals and communities. Even the criminal law struggles with environmental 'crimes', since it has often been pointed out in the courts that many of the offences created are not criminal in the 'true' sense (see the acceptance by the House of Lords in *Alphacell Ltd* v *Woodward* [1972] AC 824 that water pollution offences are in the category of 'acts which in the public interest are prohibited under a penalty'). Finally, the structure of the judicial system (with its emphasis on adversarial and backward-looking two-party litigation and with its procedural rules which are not user-friendly to those wishing to bring environmental cases and which fail to give the public interest a separate voice) is not particularly well-suited to consideration of environmental disputes, because typically they have multiple causes; give rise to complex scientific arguments; involve a complex interplay between public, private and criminal law; and require the balancing of difficult political or policy questions.

With these current defects in mind, the following thoughts can be put forward about the future development of environmental law.

(a)   In terms of civil law, there may well be the development of some sort of redress for purely environmental harm. For example, the EC proposals on civil liability cover damages for impairment of the environment or at least damage to conservation areas protected under EC law (see p. 287).

(b)   At a wider level, the work of environmental philosophers may be adopted so as to establish a legal concept which accords the environment some status in its own right (one hesitates to use the unclear phrase 'environmental rights', which might be better used to describe procedural rights possessed by individuals, such as rights to information, rights to be consulted, rights to have reasons provided for a decision and rights to make a complaint). This could be achieved by the recognition that, in line with the discussion about sustainability above, the planet is effectively held in trust for future generations. It could thus lead to the development of some sort of public trust doctrine. However, the development of such a concept is fraught with problems, since there is an all too obvious potential conflict between the precautionary and restrictive measures that are often required for sensible action on the environment and the traditional legal emphases on personal freedom and protection of property. This conflict can only really be resolved by the development of some sort of 'environmental constitution' that sits alongside other constitutional protections.

(c)   With regard to the criminal law, one reason that is often given for the failure to enforce against environmental laws is that a criminal remedy is inappropriate. Consideration may, therefore, be given to the 'decriminalisation' of whole areas of environmental law, so that a distinction could be drawn between, on the one hand, infringements that are properly characterised as administrative in nature and, on the other, truly criminal breaches, such as blatant cases of environmental vandalism. One advantage of this may be to encourage stiffer penalties for those in the second category. In turn this is linked with the idea of improving the effectiveness of sentencing for environmental crimes. Although there have been attempts to introduce consistent sentencing principles which would encourage judges to impose higher fines, particularly in relation to wealthy defendants, these will only magnify the problems associated with conflating true environmental crime with routine administrative breaches. Neither is acceptable but sentencing for the former should be based upon the need to sanction and deter whilst in the case of the latter it should be aimed at ensuring any environmental harm is rectified and prevented in future.

(d)   There is, perhaps, a growing realisation that the different areas of law — public law, private law, criminal law — merely provide, in the environmental context, a set of different tools to achieve a specified objective, in this case the protection of the environment. For example, in relation to contaminated land it is clear that someone has to 'pay' for the contamination, either by cleaning it up, or by living with the consequences. There are essentially four possible options: the polluter could be made liable; the current owner or occupier could be liable; the state could pay (i.e. through some public clean-up mechanism) — this really means that the public pays through some form of taxation; or, finally, the loss could lie where it falls, meaning that the environment and the local community effectively 'pay'. For a policy-maker the issue is how to come up with a solution that is effective, efficient and fair, whilst the tools that are available include, but are not limited to, legal mechanisms. The interesting thing about the solution provided in the Environment Act 1995 is that it combines the various tools in quite a sophisticated fashion and produces a situation where the public interest is protected by a combination of mechanisms that borrow from public, private and criminal law (see Chapter 18).

(e)   The above example raises the question of whether the development of the law is a matter for the courts or for Parliament. In *Cambridge Water Co. v Eastern Counties Leather plc* [1994] 2 AC 264, Lord Goff stated in respect of environmental protection:

. . . given that so much well-informed and carefully structured legislation is now being put in place for this purpose, there is less need for the courts to develop a common law principle to achieve the same end, and indeed it may well be undesirable that they should do so.

This can be interpreted as a reflection of the fact that Parliament is able to create a coherent and structured system, rather than one developed on an ad hoc, case-by-case basis; but it also reflects the point that Parliament has a greater democratic legitimacy than the courts when it comes to allocating responsibility for environmental harm. In the same passage Lord Goff also stated:

As a general rule, it is more appropriate for strict liability in respect of operations of high risk to be imposed by Parliament, than by the courts.

This raises a different point about the *nature* of the liability that should be imposed. At present there is a clear division between those, such as the Government and most industrial organisations, who see the imposition of strict liability as unfair and punitive and therefore wish to retain a fault-based system as far as possible, and those, including the EC Commission, who see strict liability as the most efficient and effective method of allocating responsibility for environmental harm. This issue is likely to remain a controversial one for many years.

(f)   Notwithstanding the above points about the shortcomings of the courts system, there is a healthy debate as to whether there should be a separate court or tribunal dealing with environmental cases. Some tentative steps towards this goal have already been made with the amalgamation of administrative appeals within the Planning Inspectorate. The proponents of such a court argue that many of the procedural hurdles which are inherent in the current system could be by-passed with the creation of a new institutional framework for resolving environmental disputes. Although there is a strong connection between the inadequacies of the current system and certain procedural flaws (e.g. the rules on standing, delay, representative actions, funding and expert evidence), it must be borne in mind that there are many occasions where the substantive defects of the law would remain.

(g)   What does current experience tell us about the way in which the approach of British Courts may develop in future? Whilst acknowledging the dangers of generalisation, it is possible to detect different approaches to different types of cases. In the civil or common law cases, the courts appear to be keen to restrict the extension of liability for environmental harm unless there are clearly identifiable parameters within which future decisions can be made. In *Cambridge Water Co.* v *Eastern Counties Leather plc* [1994] 2 AC 264 and *Hunter* v *Canary Wharf Ltd* [1997] 2 WLR 684, the House of Lords refused to extend common law principles to accommodate the concept of environmental damage or damage to those who did not have any property interests respectively.

(h)   Administrative challenges to environmental decisions have also been dealt with in a very narrow fashion by the courts. There have been a series of challenges to administrative decisions ranging from the acceptance of derogation from standards set under the Drinking Water Directive to failure to designate a special protection area under the Wild Birds Directive. Whilst the courts have not rejected every challenge, it is uncommon for environmental decisions to be overturned. Although this often reflects the essentially discretionary nature of the decision-making process in many environmental matters, it also suggests that, in the main, the courts have been very cautious when it comes to developing new ideas on environmental protection.

(i) A final example of the judicial reluctance to develop the law on environmental protection can be found in relation to cases which have an aspect of European law to them. Time and time again the courts have appeared to be unwilling to develop the principles of European environmental law or to refer the most complicated matters to the European Court of Justice under the Article 234 (ex 177) procedure. In *R* v *Secretary of State for Trade and Industry, ex parte Duddridge* [1995] Env LR 151, the Divisional Court (subsequently upheld in the Court of Appeal [1996] Env LR 325) refused in very clear terms even to consider the application of the precautionary principle set out in Article 130R(2) (now 174(2)) of the EC Treaty as part of English law. There are other decisions where it is interesting to contrast the ECJ's view with the conclusions of the domestic courts (see, for example, case C-72/95 *Aanemersbedrijf P.K. Kraaijeveld BV* v *Gedeputeerde Staten van Zuid-Holland* [1996] ECR I-5403 on the direct effect of the Environmental Assessment Directive and the UK cases (p. 351) or the decisions in the *Lappel Bank* case, p. 642). It is quite clear from these cases that, on the whole, the courts in the UK struggle with the application of European environmental law.

(j) In relation to criminal cases, however, the courts have increasingly adopted a purposive approach to construing statutes. For example, in the case of water pollution offences, the interpretation that successive courts have been willing to place on the word 'cause' has been very wide (see p. 589). This can also be seen in relation to waste management offences (e.g. *Shanks and McEwan (Teesside) Ltd* v *Environment Agency* [1997] Env LR 305). This purposive approach appears to stem from the judicial desire to provide law that is effective in terms of environmental protection. One of the exceptions to this purposive approach is in the case of nature conservation matters. In *Southern Water Authority* v *Nature Conservancy Council* [1992] 1 WLR 775, the House of Lords adopted a very literal interpretation of the Wildlife and Countryside Act 1981 in finding against the NCC (see p. 631).

(k) There is another area where the courts have proved active. In more recent years, there has been an increased willingness to develop judicial review mechanisms to provide for openness in decision-making and accountability to the public for decisions made in its name. For example, the courts are now accepting a wider role for environmental and other public interest groups in litigation. Although this liberalisation of some of the principles of judicial review has seen a rise in the number of challenges to environmental decisions, there is still more than a degree of uncertainty involved in bringing such an action. Partly this is because even on relatively settled questions as to who has standing to bring an action, there is still a residual judicial discretion to reject an application for lack of a sufficient interest (see e.g. *R* v *N. Somerset DC, ex parte Garnett* [1998] Env LR 91 and p. 77). In addition, even where standing is indisputable, other procedural hurdles such as a prejudicial delay in making the application for review or the availability of an alternative remedy are used to prevent a challenge (see p. 77).

(l) Despite the negative points that have emerged in the previous discussion, there will certainly be a continuing increase in environmental litigation. The increased formality of many areas of environmental policy increases the possibility of a successful public law challenge; practising lawyers are increasingly aware of the possibilities thrown up by legal action; environmental interest groups have learnt the usefulness of the legal process in making political points as well as in winning cases; and EC law throws up a whole new area of litigation arising out of the doctrines of claims about EC rights.

(m) Finally, whatever happens in relation to these major issues, there will continue to be some fine-tuning of the mechanisms that already exist. One of the defects of the law has been its piecemeal development, and it is clear that measures that have proved successful in one area are likely to be adopted in others.

The costs of compliance

Whatever the exact direction that the law takes, one thing is clear about the future; the cost of compliance with the law is going to rise sharply, both for polluters and for society in general. This is mainly because regulatory standards are getting stricter and are being enforced more rigorously. But there are other factors, such as a heightened perception of the true environmental cost of many activities (which is further increased when explicit links are drawn with the introduction of environmental taxes) and the greatly increased pressure that is being brought to bear by the public, environmental groups and green consumers and investors.

The cost of sewage disposal illustrates the point. Disposal to the sewers has traditionally been thought of as a fairly cheap and efficient way of disposing of wastes. But the introduction of integrated pollution control meant that increased controls have been applied to discharges of prescribed substances to the sewers. The costs of sewage treatment are also increasing because of changes relating to the disposal of their own wastes by sewage works. For example, the standards set for discharges to controlled waters are being tightened as the Environment Agency reviews existing consents, in the light of the need to meet the requirements of EC Directive 91/271 on Urban Waste Water Treatment. The cost of disposal of sewage sludge is rising fast. Not only has the cheap option of dumping sewage sludge in the sea been phased out, after strong international pressure, but the cost of disposal on land has risen significantly. Incineration is another possibility for disposal of sludge, but that too is coming under increasingly tight regulation. The privatised nature of the sewerage undertakers emphasises the need to take these factors into account. At the moment these sewerage undertakers are reviewing existing trade effluent consents for discharges to the sewers, and it is clear that conditions restricting the discharge of certain substances are being imposed and that charges for discharges to sewers are rising.

The costs of non-compliance

Apart from the direct cost to business of complying with stricter regulatory controls, the potential liabilities for non-compliance are also increasing. These liabilities fall into five general categories:

(a) *Criminal liabilities.* The number of criminal offences for non-compliance with environmental legislation is immense, and the regulatory agencies have shown an increased willingness to resort to prosecution. Private prosecution is also a possibility. Fines will be the usual penalty, though in a number of cases sentences of imprisonment have been imposed (there is normally a potential personal liability for directors and senior managers). Maximum fine levels have risen as have actual levels of fines imposed.

(b) *Administrative sanctions.* In most regulatory systems there is a range of options available to the regulator, including variation, suspension or revocation of a licence. Since these steps may lead to the closure of a plant, they are obviously of great importance.

(c) *Clean-up costs.* In most environmental legislation there is a power to clean up after a pollution incident and recover the cost from the polluter or (in some cases) the occupier. These costs often exceed the levels of fine which can be imposed.

(d) *Civil liability.* There is growing interest in the 'toxic torts', although many of the actions have in fact been around for a long time. Many environmental actions rest upon strict liability. Although liability may often be difficult to establish, the size of claims may be very high indeed.

(e) *Adverse publicity.* In practice the publicity attracted as a result of infringements of the law may be as costly as any direct costs, as evidenced by corporate hostility to the Environment Agency's 'Name and Shame' policy for major polluters.

In the light of all these risks, not to mention the increased costs of waste disposal and of complying with stricter standards, some of the most significant recent developments in the environmental field relate to management issues. For example, there is an international standard for environmental management systems (ISO 14001). Although this scheme is voluntary in the sense that there is no compulsion to join, there are pressures from within industry (e.g. the supply chain) and outside (e.g. from the public, insurers, and financial institutions) which mean that, in practice, environmental management systems need to be adopted.

Policy and environmental law

A final introductory thought, but a most important one, is that environmental law is a political discipline. It is political in the narrow sense that major differences can be discerned between political parties as to the correct policy to apply. These differences do not normally relate to the ends to be achieved, but to the methods to be adopted in doing so, and the costs to be incurred.

A clear example is the controversy provoked by the passage of the Wildlife and Countryside Act 1981 over whether voluntary or compulsory controls should be adopted in relation to the protection of important natural sites (see Chapter 21). A further example relates to the whole history of town and country planning in the 1980s, when the very dramatic changes to planning policy led to disagreement and dispute. These are clear examples of the application of 'Thatcherism' to the environment, as a Government with a deep suspicion of planning and regulation sought to grapple with a system based on coherent planning for the future. However, there are others which relate to such things as privatisation and deregulation. The Deregulation and Contracting Out Act 1994 showed that little has really changed since the 1980s and also emphasised the point that the whole context of environmental law can change when a different administration is elected.

Environmental law is also political in the wide sense that it involves the making of policy decisions about the best way to achieve certain objectives. This is emphasised in this book by looking at law as being about techniques or tools for solving problems. It is not just lawyers and environmentalists who have a choice of tools they may use to achieve a particular objective. Legislators and policy-makers also have a range of tools available to them. The law is one tool alongside such things as fiscal policy, education, research, and voluntary solutions. There are different types of legal mechanism that may be used, such as the setting of environmental quality objectives, or of strict limits on emissions, or controls attached to processes or products. These various possibilities are discussed in detail in Chapter 7, but it ought to be recognised that, in order to combat complex problems of pollution and environmental harm, a combination of methods is often required.

It is impossible to say that Britain always adopts one method rather than another, but it is clear that the tendency has been to adopt flexible mechanisms of control, where what is permitted is judged by reference to its effect on the receiving environment. As a result, the British approach to pollution control tends to be fairly pragmatic, and involves a great deal of discretion. This discretion is normally exercised by specialist regulatory agencies, although local authorities also have very significant environmental protection functions. An important point is that this discretion is exercised on grounds that are not restricted to environmental factors. There is a traditionally close connection in British environmental regulation between social, political and economic factors and decisions on environmental protection.

This emphasis on taking into account a wide range of factors before making a decision links to a fundamental point about the way that 'pollution' and 'environmental harm' are defined. Once again, it is difficult to formulate precise definitions, but a general guide would be to say that they cover situations where there is an excess of something over what is desirable. There is no doubt that they are relative concepts; one person's waste is another's raw material. This relativity also applies to other forms of environmental harm. For example, a rock concert for some is a noise nuisance for others and what would be thought as intrusive development in one locality will blend in in another. As a result, Nicholas Ridley's famous comment that 'Housing is not a form of environmental pollution' can be seen as inaccurate in some cases.

The level of pollution is also relative. For example, because of the self-cleansing properties of the environment, it may well be said to be less polluting to discharge into a large fast-flowing river than into a small sluggish one, and higher levels of pollution from industrial sources may be tolerated in one area than in another because of the corresponding advantages of the economic prosperity that the industries bring. It is nonsensical to talk of getting rid of pollution. It only makes sense to consider how to reduce it and the levels which are acceptable.

Everything depends on what is considered acceptable. This involves economic, political, social and cultural criteria as well as scientific and environmental ones. It is therefore important to understand that, in implementing environmental protection policies, regulatory agencies are effectively carrying out a political balancing process. As Hawkins puts it in *Environment and Enforcement* (OUP, 1984), 'The power to define and enforce consents is ultimately a power to put people out of business, to deter the introduction of new business or to drive away a going concern'.

TWO

Environmental values and environmental law

Having identified, in Chapter 1, that the answer to the question, 'what is environmental law?' is complex and to a certain extent subjective, this chapter deals with equally complex questions such as, 'why do we have environmental laws?', 'what approaches can be taken when making environmental decisions?' and 'how do regulators make rules and decisions against the background of these different approaches?'. These questions reflect some of the problems facing anyone who studies environmental law. Although we may understand that pollution control or planning legislation sets down a framework for making decisions which can assist in environmental protection, there is no necessary connection between this and the decisions on what pollutants to ban, at what level to set an acceptable legal emission standard or what to decide in relation to an individual application for planning permission or pollution control authorisation.

In the light of this it should be clear that simplistic approaches which characterise environmental law as being about 'protecting the environment' fail to deal with the primary issue of the weight to be given to environmental protection as against important matters such as economic development and other concerns in the modern world. Nor do they assist in understanding the more difficult question of the part that law plays in giving significance to all of these factors. In other words, law provides both substantive and procedural mechanisms to give effect to all of these different considerations (e.g. economic, social, scientific and environmental). For example, the fact that ideas such as the precautionary principle and the goal of sustainable development have been incorporated into substantive environmental laws (see the examples below) adds to the legitimacy and authority of what some would argue are political ideas. In time, it could be argued that the increasing usage of such ideas within environmental rules indicates an acceptance of their legal effect (i.e. they may become a legal norm).

In this chapter, therefore, we consider the interaction between values and environmental law; this involves some reflection on differing attitudes to the environment. We then examine some of the ways in which these values are translated into political principles such as the goal of sustainable development or the precautionary principle and the question of whether these principles are capable of being rules or law in the sense that they create legally enforceable rights and duties. Finally we consider the role of human rights and environmental protection.

Values and environmental law

It is an inescapable fact that environmental law and environmental lawyers do not operate within a value-free vacuum. In Chapter 1 we outlined the way in which environmental law is law for the real world, where political, social, scientific and economic factors influence the way that law works in practice. Thus, when environmental rules are placed into a practical context there is a need to be aware that law is not some stand-alone monolith which can be interpreted in isolation from external issues, in particular values.

What do we mean by values? In its 21st Report, *Setting Environmental Standards* (Cm 4053, 1998), the Royal Commission on Environmental Pollution suggested that values were 'beliefs, either individual or social, about what is important in life and thus about the ends or objectives which should govern and shape public policies'. The Royal Commission went further and identified certain factors which may influence individuals' attitudes to the environment. These included such things as the environment as a vital resource for humans; the richness of biodiversity; and the cultural, historical or social significance of the environment (e.g. an industrial landscape may be an important part of the local environment, or such natural features as the 'seven oaks' of the eponymous Kent town).

Taking the broad definition adopted by the RCEP, we can characterise 'environmental values' as 'what people believe to be important about the environment and thus what should be the priorities for environmental policy and ultimately environmental law'. At the outset, however, it is important to distinguish between, on the one hand, 'opinions and attitudes' and on the other, the wider, deeper sort of values which are held by groups and sections of society as a whole. Individual 'values' can be sincerely held opinions that fluctuate or are mutually inconsistent; at their worst they are little more than consumer-type preferences for a favourite brand of chocolate bar or washing powder. Representative values held by groups and sections of society should be the product of debate, participation and where possible the attainment of consensus and therefore much more likely to be consistent and underpin rational rule- and decision-making.

The definition of values stated above, which is adopted for the purposes of this chapter, distinguishes 'environmental values' from a different categorisation of environmental ethics. The latter is not covered in detail. Partly this is because the subject has been covered more than adequately elsewhere (in particular see Alder and Wilkinson, *Environmental Law and Ethics* (Macmillan Press, 1999)). More importantly, perhaps, the aim of this chapter is to place values as part of a matrix, which includes strongly held moral and ethical positions and environmental principles such as sustainable development and the precautionary principle. It also includes formal law and other rules and the values contained in these, which can be environmental values (e.g. the need to take into account the interests of future generations) or legal values (e.g. legal certainty and respect for the 'rule of law'). There is, therefore, no deep analysis of underlying ethical issues nor is there much detailed discussion of so-called normative ethics, that is the question of what is right and wrong or what the law should be (as opposed to what it is).

That is not to say that these normative questions are irrelevant or that these aspects of environmental ethics are unimportant. There is, however, no necessary connection between normative environmental ethics and the way people behave in practice (just as most murderers probably believe murder is wrong). There are many people who subscribe to the idea that environmental protection is important and that certain things are 'right' or 'wrong' but that view makes no impact on the way in which they live their lives. Alternatively, there are others who follow what we might term 'green' lifestyles (e.g. do not own a car and recycle their waste) but do not adopt this stance from an environmentalist perspective. Also, the domestic courts appear not to be interested in the concept of normative environmental ethics. This is true of both administrative and public law but also in relation to judge-made law such as the common law tort of nuisance. Although many of the participants in the environmental disputes which end up in the courts are concerned with the fundamental issues of what is 'right' and 'wrong', the judiciary tend to refocus attention on legalistic interpretation of rules; deference to Parliament's capacity and authority to decide complicated questions of what is in the public interest; and the exercise of lawful administrative powers. We consider below whether this is likely to change when the courts have to consider human rights legislation.

The interaction between values and law

Environmental values affect the way in which law is made and the way it operates on a practical level. Although there is no direct connection between the two, there are many ways in which values play a part in the operation of an environmental regulatory system.

(a) Triggering the formulation of new policy and law

The rules which make up environmental law are a consequence of the establishment of political aims and goals and the setting of scientific standards which form a framework for the law. The ignition of the policy 'fuse', however, can be brought about by shifts in environmental values, in the sense that new priorities are identified and action called for. This book has many examples where the policy shifts were brought about by a public outcry over a particular incident or situation (these include the Clean Air Acts in the 1950s and the Deposit of Poisonous Waste Act 1972).

These shifts in values have tended to be narrowly focused and resulted in piecemeal, reactive legislation. For this reason, they should be distinguished from more fundamental changes in the way in which we view the environment. The general public is now much more aware of the need for environmental protection at an individual, local, regional, national and international level. This means that although issues-based values continue to be important (e.g. the controversy over GMOs or the disposal of the *Brent Spar* oil platform in the North Sea), there are shifts in the general way of looking at environmental issues, in particular, the future impacts of current pollution levels and the pursuit of the goal of sustainable development.

(b)   Influencing the interpretation and enforcement of environmental laws

The day-to-day interpretation of environmental law shifts slowly to reflect changing public values. If we take a relatively straightforward pollution control provision which is designed to protect water from pollution (now contained in the Water Resources Act 1991, s. 85(1)), we can compare and contrast judicial attitudes underlying the interpretation of similar provisions over a period of 20 years in which environmental values have shifted. First we have the comment of Viscount Dilhorne in *Alphacell Ltd* v *Woodward* [1972] 2 All ER 475:

> This Act is, in my opinion, one of those Acts . . . which . . . deals with acts which are not criminal in any real sense, but are acts which in the public interest are prohibited under a penalty.

The suggestion here is that, by their nature, pollution control offences were commonly seen to be part of the group of regulatory offences which could be termed 'technical' where no moral blame attaches. In comparison in *National Rivers Authority* v *Alfred McAlpine Homes East Ltd* [1994] 4 All ER 286, Moreland J categorised the breach of the analogous provision clearly as 'criminal' and placed much more emphasis on the importance of environmental protection in stating:

> The object of the relevant words of s. 85(1) and the crime created thereby is the keeping of streams free from pollution for the benefit of mankind generally and the world's flora and fauna. Most significantly deleterious acts of pollution will arise out of industrial, agricultural or commercial activities. The damage occasioned may take years to repair and often at a cost running into thousands or millions of pounds. The act or omission by which the polluting matter enters a stream may result from negligence or may not. It does not matter.

It is possible to read too much into two quotes taken in isolation but these cases tend to illustrate a much wider picture of the way in which the courts reflect changing public attitudes to the environment. In addition to pollution, we also see wider purposive approaches now being taken to waste management offences and nature conservation provisions (see p. 494 and p. 651 respectively).

(c) Influencing individual decision-making

As we discuss in Chapter 7, the 'British approach' to environmental law is heavily dominated by discretionary decision-making based upon political factors. It is possible to identify the impact that shifting values have upon the way in which new policies are given weight in the context of individual decision-making. As we shall see, the principle of sustainable development and the precautionary principle are particularly difficult to transform into legal rules. In the context of policy formulation and individual decision-making, however, the principles can be fleshed out and applied in a practical manner with practical consequences. For example, the policy of developing 'brownfield' sites and the consequent effect on planning applications for such developments reflects an understanding and acceptance of the need to use resources effectively and sustainably (see further p. 333). We can also see the effect of the public perception of environmental risks and associated values in the sequence of planning cases which suggest that even where such perceptions of risk are 'unsubstantiated' they may still be taken into account when making development decisions (see further p. 342).

(d) Influencing the regulated

Changing public values can affect those who are regulated. For example, regulated companies may change their behaviour in response to shifting consumer values even where their activities are officially sanctioned and supported at the highest level (as *Brent Spar* nicely illustrated when consumer pressure overrode governmental support for a particular disposal route).

One of the more recent innovations in environmental regulation is the increasing reliance upon self-regulatory or voluntary instruments such as the acceptance of corporate environmental reporting or the introduction of accredited systems of environmental management (see further p. 208). There are various explanations for the growth of the 'privatisation' of environmental regulation but at least part of the reason is that there has been a commercial recognition of the importance of environmental values as weighed against the accumulation of profit. It could be argued that certain unrelated factors such as the cost of environmental compliance (with a consequent need for cost reduction and risk minimisation) and the maintenance of a competitive industrial advantage have been particularly influential. The impact of changing public perceptions of environmental values has, however, also been significant, leading to, amongst other things, the promotion of 'green advertising' (see further p. 231).

(e) Assisting with the legitimacy of environmental laws

Just as values provide a trigger for new environmental laws, they also ensure that laws are considered to be legitimate by those who are regulated and the general public. For example, one of the reasons for the many delays in the introduction of the contaminated land regime under Part IIA of the Environmental Protection Act 1990 was the perceived unfairness of a system of law which introduced retrospective strict liability. Where environmental legislation does not reflect contemporary values it becomes difficult to police as the regulated feel justified in ignoring 'unfair' requirements.

What's different about environmental values?

Should environmental values be viewed in a different way from other areas of life in which values play a part (e.g. social values, cultural values, family values and even corporate values)? There is a clear link between what is considered to be important for society generally and for the environment in particular. In Chapter 1, the description of the history of environmental law demonstrated that the first pollution control legislation was introduced primarily to protect public health. Even the first 'nature conservation' legislation was concerned with the protection of flora and fauna as a commodity (see p. 618). In recent years, however, there has been an emerging consensus that environmental issues and the values informing the debate about those issues are distinguishable in two main areas. First, that the environment is worthy of protection in its own right and not necessarily as an adjunct to the protection of human health or property rights. Secondly, environmental issues must be considered in the context of the potential effect upon future generations in addition to the present one. These factors have a tremendous impact upon the way in which environmental issues are addressed. For example, the protection of a habitat may be warranted because it provides a home for a species of animal which humans like to hunt or to eat, because the habitat is seen by many as particularly beautiful, because it is worthy of scientific study, because it contributes to the maintenance of biodiversity or simply because it is 'wrong' to interfere with nature.

We need therefore to consider various aspects of these two issues which are distinctive in relation to environmental values. First, there should be an awareness that current and past actions may have long-term and wide effects which cannot be fully understood contemporaneously. Secondly, the use of finite natural resources is not only relevant in terms of humans and this generation. Finally, there are international aspects to environmental values that cross national, social and cultural boundaries (e.g. in relation to species and habitat protection) and include the way in which natural resources are traded in global markets and the environmental impacts of transportation. Thus, there are environmental values that can only be held in relation to global issues which can raise problems given the lack of authority over individual nation states and groups within those states. For example, truly international issues such as climate change give rise to the creation of values that could be characterised as international environmental values in the sense that they underpin international action.

Law and balancing environmental values

There is a general consensus that environmental protection is an important matter, indeed one of the justifications for introducing a system of comprehensive environmental regulation was that it was and is in the public interest to protect the environment. Thus, everyone from the judiciary to regulators to industrial interests stresses that environmental protection should be at the heart of our activities (or to put it another way it is very rare to hear the contrary view, i.e. that it is desirable to destroy the environment). This general consensus, however, masks fundamental differences in the choices which different people might make and the emphasis they might place upon the importance of the environment as weighed against other factors.

Environmental law is controversial and thus interesting because it deals with questions of changing values and therefore priorities. The key question is 'how does the law interact with the process of change?'. If there is a spectrum of views on the importance of environmental protection, it might range from one end where environmental interests were paramount and all other considerations overridden, to the other end where environmental interests were inconsequential and did not play a part in any aspect of life. Of course simplistic views such as these tend to caricature the problems involved in regulating for environmental protection. For example, should the law make owners clean up contaminated land notwithstanding the fact that they were not responsible for the original pollution? What if the owners were a company and they had to make workers redundant to balance the books? What if they were to be made bankrupt? Should the law protect the habitat of a rare species? What if the destruction of the habitat was going to be of direct benefit to people living in a village on the basis that localised pollution from traffic congestion was to be transferred onto a new bypass? These are very specific questions, but there are other more general concerns such as how we should use resources today so that they can be used by future generations (we discuss 'resource' issues more in relation to 'strong' and 'weak' forms of sustainability below).

Each of these issues magnifies the problem of establishing a legal framework of rules which can assist in the balancing of competing interests. They also raise the question of whether the law should have anything to do with these issues at all. Some might argue that law is unsuited to dealing with political balancing acts where competing interests need to be 'traded off' with one another. We would argue that law, in the many forms of 'rules' which are discussed in Chapter 3, promotes the consistency, transparency and accountability of decision-making and controls the discretion of the decision-maker (although there are other things that law could do, e.g. increase the legitimacy of some of the environmental principles which are discussed below).

Law and risk

In addition to these uncertain priorities, decisions are further complicated by elements of risk to the environment and human health. One of the characteristics of many of the hottest debates about environmental issues has been the role of risk and the perception of that risk. If we think of the BSE crisis, the *Brent Spar* fiasco, or most recently the controversy over the potential hazards to the environment and human health posed by genetically modified crops and foods, we can see that the disagreement and doubts over the long-term implications of associated risks have only helped to obscure the decision-making process. The problem of risk is not, however, confined to individual issues, but permeates the whole of environmental regulation whether it be by way of analysing the costs and benefits of taking action against pollution as the Environment Agency is required by law to do (see p. 168), in assessing whether it is appropriate to clean up a contaminated site, or in determining the appropriate strategy to reduce the threat of climate change. It is hard enough to decide upon individual priorities or policy goals where the issues are clear without the additional complexity of factoring in short- or long-term risks which are the subject of scientific and non-scientific debate.

There are different ways of approaching the question of defining and assessing environmental risks (which are similar to the general perspectives on environmental issues discussed below). These approaches influence the way in which decisions are made about regulating environmental risks (e.g. banning a pollutant) or making an individual decision where risks are involved (e.g. to grant permission for an incinerator). Thus the decision- or rule-maker may be influenced differently depending upon whether risk is measured economically, i.e. through balancing costs and benefits; scientifically, i.e. based around a statistical basis of probabilities based upon past experiences or by assessing the incidence of hazards across large numbers of people; or psychologically, i.e. based around people's perception of the risk with, for example, voluntary risks such as those associated with smoking seen as more acceptable than imposed risks such as risks associated with the granting of planning permission for a landfill site in the locality.

Environmental risks can be addressed in a number of ways from increasing the accuracy and independence of 'expert' analysis (e.g. with the creation of a 'Risk Commission'), to improving public participation in rule-making and decision-making. Ultimately, however, the problem of how to deal with environmental risks is concerned with underlying issues such as priorities for regulatory action, the trade-off between environmental protection (including human health) as against other goals and the acceptance of priorities for action by the general public.

Perspectives on environmental issues

We have seen how values underpin many aspects of environmental law but values on their own can only progress matters so far. In the case of many of the difficulties that environmental law and policy seek to resolve, the under-lying values may not be controversial. Collective or public values like the need to protect human health, the need to use our resources wisely or the need to provide food, warmth and accommodation would not raise much debate. Problems arise, however, when competing values need to be prioritised.

When it comes to rule-making, for example, there may be benefits from banning a pollutant which has a causal link with disease or is degrading our environment. But what if the ban means the closure of factories in a number of depressed areas which puts people out of work, lowers the quality of life for many others, and has an overall detrimental effect on the national economy? What if scientists could 'prove' that the effects of the pollutant would only be revealed over a 250-year period or that it would only result in one death per 100,000 residents per year?

These practical problems highlight a number of theoretical issues. How do we compare costs and benefits which appear to be so different? What weight should we give to environmental interests over other considerations? How do we assess what we should forfeit today in order to do justice to future generations? What sort of information should assist in the decision as to whether or not regulatory intervention is required? Of course these issues are magnified when they are put into the context of individual decision-making such as planning applications. In these circumstances the subjectivity of the participants in the decision-making process makes the choices much starker (although there is often some confusion between individual attitudes and collective values perhaps best illustrated by the so-called 'NIMBY' — not in my backyard — argument).

These issues are complex without any obvious solution. In seeking some way out of the problem of making environmental rules and decisions we have to examine some of the different approaches which may be taken. In doing so, there is no suggestion that these perspectives are strictly drawn or exclusive. Indeed, people may adopt different perspectives in relation to different issues. There is, however, some value in trying to disassemble some of the justifications for making (or not making) rules or decisions. These perspectives provide some way of trying to balance competing values and explain how and why opposing arguments are put forward to support individual positions. By 'perspective', we imply an overview of values rather than a particular view on a particular issue. In general, when rules or decisions are made, they are often influenced by many different perspectives; the significance lies in the weight which is attached to each perspective or perhaps the perspective which can best justify the end result which the maker of the decision or rule desires. These differing perspectives can usefully be illustrated by thinking about how decisions would be reached about a local habitat threatened with development.

(a) Environmental perspectives

An environmentalist perspective can be characterised as placing greatest weight (and at its extreme to the exclusion of other balancing factors) on the need to protect the environment and, where there is no conflict with such protection, human health. Thus, an 'environmentalist' would presume that environmental protection was paramount and outweighed considerations such as cost, or scientific arguments that any associated risks were small (although in the context of the examples quoted above where environmental protection is to be balanced against 'quality of life' issues and societal inequalities, this crude representation of views masks more sophisticated arguments).

There is a spectrum of views which might fall within the category of what we have termed 'environmentalist' perspectives. The spectrum can be linked to basic viewpoints associated with environmental ethics. The critical distinction between these viewpoints is the extent to which they give the environment moral worth in its own right (what we might term 'ecocentric') as opposed to placing it within the sphere of human interests (i.e. the environment has a value only within the context of its relationship to humans — what we might term 'anthropocentric').

For example, the ecological perspective would view the destruction of the habitat in purely ecological terms. The ecocentrist would view the benefits of the provision of the new development as an irrelevant factor, indeed the status of the habitat (whether it was protected or 'special' in any way) would also be irrelevant. The guiding principle would be that humans did not have any right to interfere with nature. The anthropocentrist perspective might, however, involve different considerations. For example, although the habitat would be considered to be of great importance, there would be some justifications for its destruction where the overall contribution to human welfare was substantial (i.e. building a much needed hospital) or where the environmental importance of the site was limited (i.e. it was of little ecological significance).

(b) Economic perspectives

The economic perspective of environmental issues and values is concerned with making rational decisions on the basis of an analysis of the costs and benefits of individual options. In this sense some argue that it allows more representative forms of decision-making as there can be an acknowledgement of intensity of people's preferences (e.g. to what extent they value a habitat, not simply whether a development of that habitat should be allowed to go ahead). Accordingly, it would be concerned with only taking action where it is economically efficient, such that the benefits which accrued from the action outweighed the costs of doing so. Thus an economist aims to identify underlying measures of value including attaching worth to such intangibles as a human life and the environment. On a theoretical level, this sort of valuation is, however, fraught with difficulties. For the purposes of this discussion, however, economic techniques are simply one way of determining whether or not a particular decision will generate the maximum benefit to the most people (and therefore be a basis for decision- or rule-making).

Valuation of intangibles such as the environment can be based upon the preferences which people have (i.e. by examining people's behaviour and analysing the choices that they make). For example, the reduction in house prices of properties surrounding a polluted area or the increase in prices where the environment is desirable may form the basis of such a valuation (termed 'hedonistic pricing'). Even in the case of a human life, it is possible to determine, on an objective level at least (sometimes referred to as a 'statistical life'), what someone might be willing to pay to avoid the risk of death. For example someone might be willing to pay £1,000 to avoid a 1 in 10,000 chance of death. From the economic perspective this would make a statistical life worth £10,000,000.

It is not possible to value everything on the basis of explicit preferences particularly in the case of things which are unrelated to human life or property (which typically includes the unowned environment). For example in the case of a remote wilderness, it is unlikely that there are any objective measures of what people would be willing to pay to preserve it. In these circumstances, economists use 'contingent values' by carrying out a survey of people, asking them the amount of money they would be willing to pay to conserve some environmental feature (or *be* paid to compensate them for its loss).

In the case of the habitat threatened with development, the economist would undertake a valuation of the development (after deducting construction costs). This represents what a buyer would be willing to pay for the development. There is an assumption that this valuation reflects, in the absence of any value which could be attached to the habitat, what the development is 'worth'. If we assume that the habitat has no direct connection to local people (i.e. it cannot be valued by its use alone), an economist would undertake a survey to determine what an accurate contingent valuation might be. If that survey showed that local residents would be willing to pay (or be paid) more than the value of the development, the development should be refused. Of course much depends upon how widely the survey sample is drawn.

(c) Social and cultural perspectives

Taking social and cultural perspectives into account in decision-making has been relatively late in coming, but is gaining currency. In contrast to economic perspectives, this approach questions whether it makes sense, e.g. to ask people how much they are willing to pay for environmental assets. Instead, it argues that values are not static, in the sense of being beliefs that we argue *from*, but rather are things that we reason *towards*. We would therefore need to construct ways of decision-making that involve some form of collective deliberation about what things we value and why, rather than asking for individual preferences in surveys.

A socially and culturally informed perspective would also question attitudes to natural scientific assessments of risk. This might be for failing to take local attitudes or 'lay' knowledge seriously enough; for example, by having too much confidence that 'laboratory' assumptions apply to the real world in which regulation takes place. It might also be for the wider reason that, inevitably, risk is constructed culturally. That is, our attitudes to risk (and therefore also to precaution) are related, at an individual level, to how risk-seeking or risk-averse we are, and to broader issues about how much trust we place in regulators and in 'official' knowledge. They are also affected by wider public perceptions, formed by numerous factors, about how fragile the environment is.

From this perspective, therefore, cost-benefit and other economic approaches to habitat conservation will be rejected for wrongly equating natural resources with consumer goods; or as one writer has neatly put it, equating 'corncrakes' and 'cornflakes' (see the chapter by Clark in a useful set of essays, Guerrier et al (eds), *Values and the Environment* (Wiley, 1995)). Instead, more discursive valuation techniques will be preferred. There are already some signs of this: the Environment Agency now requires the use of deliberative valuation techniques, involving small groups discussing which criteria they think are important, to be used when Local Environment Agency Plans are drawn up.

A social or cultural approach would also hesitate before accepting any quantitative valuation of harm to a species or habitat. It would almost certainly find problematic the idea of 'translocating' habitat elsewhere, since the value of the habitat is not only its contribution to national or global biodiversity but also includes its meaning and importance for (usually local) people. A good illustration of how law may fail to take cultural importance seriously enough is provided by the Hedgerows Regulations 1997 which arguably take too narrow an approach to the local cultural importance of these landscape features (see p. 678).

(d)   Scientific perspectives
Broadly, a scientific perspective (by which we mean here a natural science approach) embodies what we might call a 'technocratic' approach to environmental regulation. That is, it both suggests that a range of environmental issues and disputes can be resolved 'scientifically', and provides a means for reaching 'objective', conclusive opinions about such matters. Arguably, much UK pollution control law has, at least ostensibly, been framed along such lines, in particular standards relating to public health such as drinking water standards. The approach has also been seen in something of an elitist 'we know best' attitude by regulators towards things like granting environmental licences. To operate successfully, such a 'top down' approach requires a considerable degree of public trust in science and in scientists acting for regulatory bodies and governments. (Recent events such as the BSE crisis have led to something of a crisis of confidence here, and levels of public trust in scientific evidence, especially evidence produced by government, is low compared with the trust placed in research seen as being more 'independent', e.g. by respected environmental pressure groups.) Faith in official science has also been one of the reasons behind the traditionally secretive nature of decision-making, since a technocratic approach has little reason for public involvement other than, perhaps, to rubber-stamp decisions already taken (on the other hand it must be recognised that those who are sceptical of the role of science in decision-making still tend to rely upon scientific evidence to *reveal* environmental problems).

A scientific or technocratic approach to conservation is exemplified in the approach to the designation of sites of special scientific interest under the Wildlife and Countryside Act 1981, and to the early stages of designating protected conservation areas under EC law, where only scientific criteria can be taken into account (see generally Chapter 21). It can also be seen in the fact that, at least in England and Wales (the position is different in Scotland), there are no mechanisms to appeal the designation (or non-designation) of sites, and no public participation. By contrast, the planning system that decides whether development will be permitted is more open to participation, and is less technocratic in the sense that decisions are taken at both local and national level by elected politicians. In contrast to other perspectives, therefore, a scientific or technocratic approach would only form part of the overall assessment of whether economic development could outweigh the nature conservation interests.

Environmental principles

As a response to some of the problems of approaching environmental rules or decisions from any one particular perspective, attempts have been made to formulate general concepts and principles which can accommodate at least some of the features of these various perspectives. The difficulty in doing this is that there has to be flexibility in the manner in which the principle can be interpreted. This flexibility can create problems of certainty and precision. By their very nature such principles need to be applied across sweeping expanses of environmental law and policy and also beyond the environmental field.

The most common substantive principles associated with environmental law and policy are those relating to sustainable development, the precautionary principle, the preventative principle, the polluter pays principle and the principle that environmental damage should be rectified at source. Other general underpinning approaches, particularly of a procedural nature, also have an impact (see e.g. the process of environmental assessment covered in Chapter 12). We focus here on sustainable development and the precautionary principle as these are the most developed as matters of law and policy within international, European and domestic law. Others are referred to in passing elsewhere, for example the polluter pays principle is discussed on p. 207.

Sustainable development

The concept of sustainable development is central to the recent and future development of environmental law and policy. The idea of 'sustainability' (indicating the state of something being sustainable in the long term) has always been considered as part of the system of land-use planning within the UK in the sense that the long-term implications of resource depletion and other environmental factors have always been material considerations when determining planning applications. The precise principle of 'sustainable development' which has gained credibility within international law is, however, both relatively new and uncertain although its all-pervasive characteristics can be found explicitly in many environmental policy documents in relation to different topic areas. The fullest discussion of the subject can be found in the recent White Paper, *A Better Quality of Life: A Strategy for Sustainable Development for the United Kingdom* (Cm 4345, 1999).

What is meant by the phrase 'sustainable development'? Although the idea can be traced back at least to 1972 and the United Nations Stockholm Conference on the Human Environment, the common definition which is used most often comes from the Brundtland Commission's 1987 Report, *Our Common Future*, in which it was suggested that the phrase covered: 'Development that meets the needs of the present without compromising the ability of future generations to meet their own needs'. This definition is, however, vague, and requires further elaboration.

First, the primary objective of the principle is to meet current and future *human* needs and aspirations (there is a further issue in relation to what is meant by 'needs and aspirations'). Thus the emphasis is anthropocentric although under the Brundtland Commission's definition, the environment is considered to be an integral part of human well-being. Secondly, there is an underlying objective of fairness in the manner of development which applies as between different sectors of the current generation (e.g. 'poor' and 'rich' nations and classes of society) and future generations (i.e. inter-generational equity). Thus, future generations have the same rights to develop as we do and preventing such development would be unfair. Finally, there is an inherent assumption that we can identify the impact of current activity in terms of resource depletion and the ability of the environment to absorb pollution. Any doubts over the nature of the risks involved will inevitably cloud the decisions which need to be made to achieve the goal of sustainable development.

Sustainable development as a legal instrument

The goal of sustainable development has been translated into some form of legal obligation in a number of international, European and domestic sources of law, although the nature of the legal effects of the obligation is the subject of some debate. The transposition of the goal of sustainable development into legal forms, perhaps a legal principle, is becoming increasingly common and is set to continue. The implementation of the principle is perhaps more problematic.

(a)   International law
In international law, sustainable development as a *legal* concept has tended to be found mostly in 'soft law' documents, i.e. documents that are not directly binding and which have more of a policy feel to them. The most important document here is 'Agenda 21', signed at the 1992 Rio 'Earth Summit', which is essentially a lengthy blueprint for realising sustainable development. This pays particular attention to action at the local level, and picks up many of the recommendations in the Brundtland Report about greater public involvement in decision-making through, e.g. access to environmental information. As we discuss more fully in Chapter 4, there are signs that at least some of the judges of the International Court of Justice are beginning to recognise the procedural dimension to issues of sustainable development, and recognise sustainable development as a *principle* rather than just a *concept*. However, beyond agreement on basic procedural requirements, of the kind referred to in the Rio Declaration (information, public participation etc.), there is little sign yet of anything resembling an international legal consensus on what sustainable development might mean substantively.

(b)   European law
Perhaps most significantly the principle has been made a fundamental *justification* for the existence of the EC with the incorporation of sustainable development into Article 2 of the EC Treaty which states that the Community

'shall have as [one of its tasks] . . . to promote throughout the Community harmonious, balanced and sustainable development of economic activities'. This justification applies across all policy areas and legislation and is not necessarily restricted to environmental considerations, and is backed up by a further provision explicitly requiring integration of environmental protection requirements into other policy areas 'in particular with a view to promoting sustainable development' (Article 6 EC).

The relative newness of these constitutional amendments (made under the 1997 Treaty of Amsterdam) means that there has been little opportunity for the ECJ to interpret or flesh out the concept, although it is possible to identify judgments which implicitly incorporate some of the more important aspects of sustainable development, including the relative significance of environmental considerations over other issues (e.g. in relation to the drawing up of the boundaries of certain nature conservation sites where economic considerations have been judged to be irrelevant, see *R* v *Secretary of State for the Environment, ex parte RSPB* [1997] QB 206 and further p. 642 below).

(c) UK law

The transformation and integration of the principle of sustainable development into formal rules within the UK reflects the European experience in the sense that it is relatively recent and is taking place within an overarching administrative and institutional framework rather than through changes to substantive environmental laws. Although 'sustainable' was introduced in the Natural Heritage (Scotland) Act 1991 as something which Scottish Natural Heritage must have 'regard to the desirability of securing' (s. 1(1)), the initial step of incorporating sustainable *development* in UK law was taken with the introduction of the Environment Agency's principal aim under s. 4 of the Environment Act 1995. This requires the Agency, in discharging its functions so to protect or enhance the environment, taken as a whole, as to make the contribution towards attaining the objective of achieving sustainable development (see further p. 165).

The pace of this administrative and institutional integration is increasing. The 1999 White Paper on Sustainable Development contained a government commitment to consider incorporating the sustainable development principle as a legal goal for any newly created public body. Indeed, there are a number of examples of the implementation of this commitment with the Welsh Assembly (under s. 121 of the Government of Wales Act 1998), Regional Development Agencies (RDAs) (under s. 4(e) of the Regional Development Agencies Act 1998) and the Greater London Authority (GLA) (under s. 30(4) of the Greater London Authority Act 1999) all being subject to some form of requirement to take into account the goal of sustainable development. The impact of these changes will take some time to be realised but with the duty to promote environmental well-being applying to all local government bodies if and when the Local Government Bill is passed in its current form (see clause 2), it will be interesting to see whether there is any consistency of application.

These legal instruments are of interest because they demonstrate a formal commitment to the sustainable development principle but there are a number of factors affecting the practical implementation of the legal duty. First, and perhaps most significantly, there is no specific definition of the phrase 'sustainable development'. Even if the Brundtland Commission definition were to be adopted as a suitable definition by default, there would still be a number of ambiguities which would make precise legal interpretation impossible. Secondly, the wording of the relevant sections is too wide to create a legally enforceable duty, even if a suitably consistent definition of the principle could be agreed. Thirdly, the content and objectives of the duty are, in some of the cases (e.g. RDAs and the Environment Agency) controlled centrally by way of a requirement to 'have regard to' guidance set by central government. Finally, the different Acts have slightly different impacts on the activities of the statutory bodies concerned. For example, the Welsh Assembly is under a duty to produce a scheme to 'promote' sustainable development, whereas the RDAs have as one of their statutory purposes the contribution to 'the achievement of sustainable development' and the GLA has to 'have regard to the effect of exercising its powers' on the achievement of sustainable development. Clearly, the duty imposed on the Welsh Assembly to make a scheme creates a legal obligation whereas the other provisions are much more flexible without any obvious legal effect. Whether there is any practical distinction in terms of the consequences for environmental law or decision-making is perhaps more difficult to anticipate.

All of these factors suggest that the principle of sustainable development is too loose a concept to be developed by the courts (fitting in nicely with the discretionary, policy based approach of other aspects of environmental decision-making). This is not to say that the principle will have no practical impact, as the aims and objectives of administrative bodies play an integral part in influencing the setting of policies and the making of individual decisions.

Sustainable development as a policy instrument

The most coherent attempts to flesh out the bare bones of the Brundtland Commission's definition of sustainable development can be found in policy documents, although even here there is a great deal of 'woolliness' as befits the breadth of the matters covered under the principle. Most of the significant policy work is aimed at providing meaningful goals and objectives against which the pursuit of sustainable development can be benchmarked. As we have already touched on the main policy text on sustainable development at international level, Agenda 21, we restrict discussion here to European and national level.

(a) European policy
At a European level, the current policy framework on sustainable development can be found in the Fifth Environmental Action Programme: *Towards Sustainability*, which sets out a series of long-term objectives in relation to major issues of concern. These objectives, are, however, general and not intended to be legally binding (see Case C–142/95P *Associazone Agricoltori*

della Provincia di Rovigo and Others v *Commission* [1996] ECR I-6669). There is a strong suggestion that the forthcoming Sixth Environmental Action Programme will set out clearer objectives through the use of measurable indicators, but it is unlikely that they will carry any greater legal force.

(b) Domestic policy — the White Paper, *A Better Quality of Life: A Strategy for Sustainable Development for the United Kingdom*
As in the case of legal instruments, domestic policy is following the same path as European measures (although unusually perhaps the use of specific measures of sustainable development is slightly more advanced). The 1999 White Paper sets out four main objectives, i.e. social progress which recognises the needs of everyone; the effective protection of the environment; the prudent use of natural resources; and the maintenance of high and stable levels of economic growth. These objectives provide some indication that economic, social and environmental factors have equal weight.

These objectives are fleshed out with the introduction of seven 'priorities for action' (e.g. reducing social exclusion; promoting energy efficiency and waste reduction; and improving the quality of life in cities and large towns). Finally, the White Paper offers 15 'headline indicators' (there are a further 150 indicators) which are to be used for assessing progress towards sustainable development: total economic output (GDP); expected years of healthy life; unfit accommodation; levels of crime; traffic levels; wild bird populations; and waste arisings. The stated policy aim is to 'move in the right direction over time, or where a satisfactory level has been reached, to prevent a reversal'. The White Paper does not set any specific targets, although in relation to some areas, such as waste arisings or greenhouse gas emissions, binding targets have been set in other legislation (see further p. 472 and p. 416 respectively). The lack of measurable targets in some areas (e.g. traffic reduction) means that in these areas, there is only a broad commitment to enhance the current state of affairs which does not necessarily coincide with the principle of sustainable development (in the sense that a shift from a terrible situation to a bad one might still be detrimental, by merely prolonging the reaching of a crisis point).

(c) Domestic policy — other initiatives
Although the White Paper sets out general domestic policy, it is only part of a broad incorporation of the sustainable development principle within all areas of administration. At a national level, the Sustainable Development Commission is responsible for monitoring progress on sustainable development and for building consensus on action to accelerate its achievement. In addition the 'Greening Government' initiative is intended to monitor the achievement of sustainable development across all government activities (see further p. 155). At a regional and local level, the regional sustainable development frameworks are to be prepared for eight English regions, whilst Local Agenda 21 strategies (see p. 175) are to be prepared by all local authorities; both the frameworks and the strategies should set policies which are closely linked to the 'headline indicators' set out in the White Paper.

Finally, other areas of domestic policy will be linked to business sectors (sustainability strategies are being considered for the chemicals, vehicles, retail and printing sectors amongst others) and consumers (see p. 231).

Achieving sustainable development in practice

Anyone reading the above discussion of the burgeoning legal and policy instruments might consider that there has been a great deal of progress towards a practical, workable definition of sustainable development. This would, however, mask some of the fundamental problems underlying the principle. In particular, the feasibility of sustainable development is dependent on the manner in which some of these problems are addressed.

(a)   'Weak' v 'Strong' versions of sustainable development

Although not without criticism, a distinction is often made between 'strong' and 'weak' versions of sustainable development. The distinction is really about matters of emphasis as much as it relates to matters of principle. Thus, a 'strong' approach to sustainability emphasises the extent to which natural assets are irreplaceable in the sense that their loss cannot be adequately replaced by compensatory benefits. In contrast, 'weak' sustainability would accept that natural assets may be consumed or sacrificed if the overall benefit is positive, that is if the total stock of resources passed on to future generations is not diminished. 'Resources' here, however, would include non-environmental resources such as human knowledge and creativity; this would mean that there should not be too much concern about losing any individual environmental resource so long as there is sufficient ingenuity (or sufficient investment to ensure that there will be sufficient ingenuity) to come up with something equivalent or better.

On one view, strong sustainability is said to be morally abhorrent since it privileges environmental 'assets' above all others, suggesting that we should devote whatever it takes to save a species even if this means that individual humans starve. Further, weak sustainability is seen as no different from the kinds of trade-offs that have been made for centuries in the interests of raising human standards of living, and in this sense is simply 'business as usual'. Many environmental economists and philosophers agree that, presented in these terms, weak sustainability is something of an empty concept. However, others stress, for example, that environmental and human resources are not completely interchangeable: no matter how skilful we become, we will still need a base of natural resources to live off. A difficulty is therefore knowing *which* resources future generations will need and value or rather maintaining a sufficient *diversity* of resources.

(b)   The definition of 'needs'

The 'needs' of future generations are central to the Brundtland definition of sustainable development. But beyond those things which form the very minimum necessary for survival — food, clean air and water, shelter, a tolerable climate — there is considerable debate about what we really 'need', even amongst present generations. Even thinking about some of these basic needs shows some of the problems involved. For example, humans are not dependent on any single food source in the way that giant pandas require bamboo shoots, nor do we need to make our homes out of any particular raw material. We cannot therefore say that the sources of even our most common foodstuffs must be conserved, even for present generations (although we might make an argument that a sufficient *diversity* of seeds, genetic material etc. should be conserved to guard against the impacts of climate change and other unknowns). The problem is also compounded when we engage in judging what the needs of those perhaps several generations hence will be, since apart from the basics necessary for survival the things that have been valued over the centuries have of course changed. Even where things have been treasured as 'necessary' in the past and present, this is no guarantee that future generations will 'need' or even value them. While conceivably we might find agreement across the generations in relation to what humans need, it is difficult to say objectively that anything particular must be conserved or preserved to satisfy such needs.

Ultimately, there is some connection between one's view of sustainability, in strong or weak terms, and the question of needs, since those with more optimistic views of human ingenuity to 'fix' environmentally-related problems will be more sanguine about exploiting resources today in the confidence that future generations will be able to satisfy their needs through a lesser abundance of natural resources. There is also the thorny question of the 'right to develop' (central to the Rio Declaration), and thus the liberty of present generations to destroy the natural environment in the interests of development.

(c) The role of technology

Central to weak and strong sustainability, and to the question of needs, is the role of technology. There are various strands to this, including how much faith to place in technological progress as against the conservation of natural resources, and whether we can say that developing countries 'need' technology from the developed world to give practical effect to their right to develop. Central to the two Conventions signed at Rio, on Climate Change and on Biodiversity, is the idea that there should be a transfer of technology to developing countries; either 'clean technology' to reduce greenhouse gas emissions, or pharmaceutical-type technology to allow for the commercial exploitation, and thus, it is argued, sustainable use, of biological diversity.

This approach marks something of a shift from earlier 'waves' of environmentalism which have generally been sceptical of technical 'fixes' to what have been seen as deeper-seated problems with the structuring of societies and economies. However, the Brundtland Report stressed that it did not consider capitalism as necessarily destructive of the environment and therefore advocated solutions from within the existing economic framework. In a climate where support for alternative models of organisation is practically non-existent, it is perhaps inevitable that there is growing backing for fine-tuning the current model, and reliance on more effective technology and its more efficient use are central to what has been coined 'ecological modernisation'. Put more straightforwardly, this is the idea that environmental resources can be more efficiently managed to produce the same or higher levels of goods and services, leading to so-called 'win-win' results where both the economy and the environment benefit. (Since social issues are generally included within sustainable development, however, we really need to find virtuous circles leading to 'win-win-win' solutions.) This has obvious relevance to issues such as waste management or climate change, and in some senses is obviously furthered by making polluters pay for the 'external' costs imposed on society caused by their activities (such as air pollution which does not infringe on private rights). But a 'more from less' approach could also mean more efficient use of space and therefore less pressure on land of conservation interest. A growing body of what we might call the 'literature of hope' therefore argues that there is a path to sustainability which does not involve adopting a strong environmentalist perspective (as defined above).

(d)   The assessment of fairness and inter-generational equity

Finally, there are considerable difficulties in deciding what is 'fair' to future generations. As discussed above, the background to this question will include factors like faith in human creativity and what 'needs' are, which in practice tend to be highly subjective. There is also the problem that there will never be a consensus on values, even if values did not shift over time.

One influential attempt to guide decisions about future generations is given by Brown Weiss (the argument is summarised in 'Intergenerational Equity: A Legal Framework for Global Environmental Change', in Brown Weiss (ed.) *Environmental Change and International Law* (United Nations University, 1991)). She argues for three principles to underpin inter-generational equity: 'conservation of options' (e.g. conserving biodiversity contributes to the robustness of ecosystems); 'conservation of quality' (i.e. handing on environmental quality, at local and global level, without worsening its state); and 'conservation of access' (equitable rights of access to what past generations have handed on, while keeping open equitable access for future generations). A virtue of this approach is that it tries not to second-guess what future generations will want or value, e.g. conserving options does not require any particular species to be saved from extinction. But difficulties remain. For example, how is environmental quality to be measured? How are the trade-offs between the principles to be handled, e.g. if improving conservation of access within the present generation means that someone's environmental quality is necessarily reduced? And why should one generation not decide to sacrifice a measure of environmental quality in the interests of future generations? As issues like climate change testify, there are no easy answers to deciding who, within the current generation, should have to bear burdens for past greenhouse gas emissions, or whether these burdens (or at least changes) should be sufficient to allow developing countries to continue increasing their emissions to further their chosen development path (on climate change see further p. 416).

The precautionary principle

The second major environmental principle which assists in the process of environmental rule- and decision-making is the precautionary principle. Although there are a number of different interpretations of the principle, it generally describes an approach to the protection of the environment or human health based around precaution even where there is no clear evidence of harm or risk of harm from an activity or substance. For example, the precautionary principle suggests that we should ban a pollutant suspected of causing serious harm even in circumstances where there is no conclusive scientific proof of a clear link between the substance and the harm. In other words, although scientific evidence is never final in the sense that it is only conclusive to the extent that it is based on premises which have not yet been overturned, there comes a point where we have to rely upon 'instinct' and take action regardless.

The precautionary principle is often associated with areas of high public controversy and concern where there are unknown (or in some cases arguably unknowable) risks to the environment or human health. Obvious examples which have been mentioned elsewhere in this book include the BSE crisis, the planting of genetically modified crops or the link between diseases such as cancer and overhead power lines. The precautionary principle is often used in the debates about such issues to support the notion that scientific analysis of risks should form the core of environmental rules and decisions notwithstanding the fact that such analysis may be uncertain. Alternatively, the principle could be used to support an argument that there are limits to the extent that science can inform the debate and that ultimately, rules and decisions have to be made having regard to other considerations such as the public perception of the risk and the potential for harm.

As an illustration, it is interesting to compare and contrast the Nature Conservancy Council's view of the precautionary principle as being 'not so much a practical guide to decision-making as a moral injunction *not* to ignore possible environmental impacts which cannot be proven', with the RCEP's view (in *Setting Environmental Standards*) that the principle is a 'rational response to uncertainties in the scientific evidence relevant to environmental issues and uncertainties about the consequences of action or inaction'.

These mutually inconsistent views underline the fact that the principle is necessarily subject to interpretations of concepts such as the significance of risks, and the acceptability of scientific evidence as 'proof'. Ultimately, the use of the precautionary principle is subject to the same limitations restricting the resolution of any debate about environmental values. In other words the precautionary principle provides a framework for any discussion about how to 'trade-off' the risk of environmental harm as against other considerations, but it does not necessarily provide any 'right' answer. In this sense, the principle is merely another ingredient which goes into the melting pot of environmental rule- and decision-making along with other relevant considerations such as the public perception of risk, the benefit of the proposed activity, the notion of the 'public interest' and protection of individual rights.

The precautionary principle as a legal instrument

The development of the precautionary principle as a legal instrument mirrors the development of the principle of sustainable development in a number of ways. The formal origin of the principle can be traced back to Germany in the 1970s with the *vorsorgeprinzip*. This principle, of taking protection against specific environmental hazards by avoiding or reducing environmental risks before specific harms are experienced, was rapidly integrated into a variety of international conventions from the late 1980s onwards (e.g. the Ministerial Declarations of 1987 and 1990 which followed the 2nd and 3rd North Sea Conferences both expressly incorporated the principle).

(a) International law
A number of important international conventions have incorporated the principle including the Conventions on Climate Change, the Protection of the Ozone Layer, and on Biological Diversity (and its associated Protocol on Biosafety which is concerned with the handling and use of genetically modified organisms). However, each convention tends to contain a slightly different formulation of the principle, which makes it difficult to identify an interpretation with which all states can be said to agree implicitly as a matter of binding international law. Nevertheless, a measure of international consensus on the principle was reached in the Rio Declaration, Principle 15 of which provides:

> Where there are threats of serious or irreversible damage, lack of full scientific certainty shall not be used as a reason for postponing cost-effective measures to prevent environmental degradation.

Like sustainable development, precaution has found only limited judicial support so far in international law, this despite many commentators arguing that it has reached the status of a principle of customary international law (see more generally p. 102). In a case challenging the right of France to carry out nuclear tests in the South Pacific (*New Zealand v France* [1995] ICJ Rep, 288), Judge Weeramantry's opinion suggests that the precautionary principle — which he says is 'gaining increasing support as part of the international law of the environment' — should be used where there is insufficient material before the Court to justify action, even if this means acting ahead of 'full scientific evidence'.

This opinion, however, was a dissent, and it is worth comparing a more recent example where the precautionary principle has featured in international trade disputes. The US and Canada brought a dispute settlement case before the World Trade Organisation against the EC, which in 1989 had banned the import of beef fed with growth hormones on the grounds that it was not safe for human health to eat such meat (see *EC Measures Concerning Meat and Meat Products (Hormones)*, WT/DS26/AB/R and WT/DS48/AB/R, 16 January 1998). The EC argued that its import ban was justified in the light of the precautionary principle, which it presented as a binding rule of international customary law. The USA and Canada denied that the principle already had such a status. (Canada did admit that it was an emerging principle.) The WTO found that the EC import ban violated WTO law, although the EC has continued to impose its ban and has been forced by the WTO to compensate Canada and the US for lost trade.

(b) European law
The requirement to take account of the precautionary principle in European law and policy is now enshrined in Article 174(2) of the EC Treaty.

In comparison with the principle of sustainable development, however, the precautionary principle is explicitly or implicitly incorporated into a number of different substantive European laws. For example, the Environmental Assessment Directive (85/337/EEC, as amended) makes express reference to the need to assess the environmental impact of development projects within the context of the precautionary principle. Another example would be the Nitrates Directive (91/676/EEC) which creates a system of nitrate vulnerable zones in which farming activities are restricted notwithstanding that pollution and the risk of environmental harm may have come from a different source. Thus, even where there is no evidence of pollution from individual farms, activities are restricted on those farms based upon the need to take precaution in areas which are vulnerable to nitrate pollution. The institutional antipathy towards the directive and its precautionary basis is, however, evidenced by the fact that the European Commission alleged that 13 out of 15 Member States (including the UK) had breached the terms of the directive within the first six years of its life (see COM(97)473, *The Implementation of the Nitrates Directive*). A further example is provided by the establishment of various environmental quality standards implicitly adopting the precautionary approach where substances are liable or likely to cause harm (e.g. in relation to the Titanium Dioxide Waste Directive 78/109/EEC and the Pesticides Directive 91/414/EEC). As the dates of these directives show, precautionary measures were being taken before precaution found its way into the Treaty of Rome. The classic example of this is Directive 90/220/EEC, perhaps the most explicitly precautionary EC measure, which restricts the deliberate release of genetically modified organisms despite the complete lack of evidence then about possible harmful impacts.

Furthermore, the ECJ has upheld the validity of the precautionary principle in the case of the protection of human health in relation to the banning of exports of beef from the UK in order to reduce the risk of BSE infection even where there were significant economic considerations which could have been taken into account (see Case C-180/96R *United Kingdom* v *Commission* [1996] ECR I-3903).

(c) UK law
The precautionary principle has not been incorporated directly into domestic legislation (i.e. there is no overarching duty or aspiration as in the case of the principle of sustainable development). Indeed, in *R* v *Secretary of State for Trade and Industry, ex parte Duddridge* [1995] Env LR 151, the High Court

determined that the principle had no legal effect over and above the need to take into account the potential for environmental risk as a material consideration in any decision-making procedure. In addition, the court considered that the precautionary principle in European law did not create any direct obligation within Member States, nor should it be applied as a matter of 'common sense'. On the contrary, Art. 130R(2), the predecessor of the current Art. 174(2), merely formed the basis upon which future policy should be based. More recently, the ECJ has hinted that, in extreme cases, it may be prepared to find that EC legislation has not taken the precautionary principle into account, but this would probably require complete oversight or wilful disregard (see Case C-341/95 *Bettani* v *Safety Hi-Tech Srl* [1998] ECR I-4355; see also p. 128). The failure to incorporate the precautionary principle explicitly does not mean that it is irrelevant. Just as there are elements of European legislation which incorporate the principle, those domestic rules which implement the requirements of that legislation also transpose the principle into substantive domestic legislation.

In addition there are other rules which are not directly linked to European legislation which involve aspects of the precautionary principle. For example, the Water Resources Act 1991, s. 92 gives the Secretary of State power to make regulations in order to take precautions against water pollution (a power which has been exercised in relation to precautions to be taken in the storage of oil and silage, see further p. 600). Other examples include the powers to serve works notices to prevent water pollution under s. 161 of the Water Resources Act 1991 (see p. 599) and the concept of the 'best available techniques' process standard adopted under IPPC to prevent unacceptable environmental impacts (see p. 396).

The precautionary principle as a policy instrument

The first international recognition of the precautionary principle was in the World Charter for Nature, adopted by the UN General Assembly in 1982. There has, however, been little movement on the development of the principle as a policy instrument compared with sustainable development. Partly this is because there are underlying disagreements about the way in which the principle applies across an institutional and administrative frame-work (as opposed to the context of individual decision-making). Moreover, there are fundamental questions about the role of science and the question of risk assessment and how this should be applied within the context of the 'trade-offs' that need to be made. These uncertainties have led to a certain amount of confusion about the application of the precautionary principle.

(a) European policy
A distinction should be made, here, between EC policy and policy adopted for other European issues such as the pollution of the North Sea. Under the latter, there have been various Declarations that have been based upon the precautionary principle. For example, the Esjberg Declaration to the 4th North Sea Conference in 1995 agreed that the precautionary principle be adopted as the 'guiding principle' for achieving a clean North Sea, with reference

to reducing discharges, emissions and hazardous substances with a goal of zero emission within 25 years (a similar approach has been taken in relation to the reductions of radioactive substances under the 1992 'OSPAR' Convention).

By contrast, EC policy on the precautionary principle has been relatively undeveloped. The first attempt at a detailed explanation of the policy came early in 2000 with the publication of a communication from the European Commission (COM(2000)1) which sets out the Commission's guidelines to using the precautionary principle. The Commission sets out the risk-based context of the precautionary principle, emphasising the relationship between the principle and the management of risks which might impinge upon the environment, human, animal or plant health. The communication also makes it clear that the precautionary principle is not to be invoked defensively (i.e. as a 'disguised form of protectionism') reflecting the fact that the principle has been invoked as a justification of what might more appropriately be called a 'trade ban' (e.g. in relation to the French and German ban on British beef, although this might be contrasted with the EC's own use of precaution in relation to beef hormones, discussed above).

In particular, the policy makes it clear that identifying an 'acceptable' level of risk is an essentially political decision, which must take into account such things as proportionality (i.e. the steps taken must be in proportion to the risks involved), an analysis of the costs and benefits associated with the measure (involving non-economic considerations such as public acceptability of other options and their effectiveness), and consistency (in relation to the measures taken in similar areas). Up until the publication of this document, there were few policies in relation to the precautionary principle and those which existed were aimed more at regulating food safety (see e.g. *The General Principles of Food Law* (COM(97)176)).

(b) UK policy
One of the first detailed references to the precautionary principle can be found in the 1990 White Paper, *This Common Inheritance*. This put forward a 'weak' form of the precautionary principle on the basis that there would be action against 'significant risks' even in cases of scientific uncertainty if the 'balance of costs and benefits' justified it. (This approach was confirmed in the government's guidance to the Environment Agency under s. 4 of the Environment Act 1995.) Although this was a firm policy commitment to the *idea* of the precautionary principle, the practical significance of this statement was little more than an acceptance of the growing international and European recognition of the principle (a view seemingly endorsed by Smith J in the *Duddridge* decision discussed above). Developments since 1997 suggest that current government policy increasingly favours a strong commitment to a 'weak' form of the precautionary principle. This is illustrated by the decision not to make a final decision on the acceptability of genetically modified crops before the results of trial plantings are known.

Of more practical significance was the publication, in 1995, of the Department of the Environment's *A Guide to Risk Assessment and Risk Management for Environmental Protection* which contained guidance on risk assessment and

the use of the precautionary principle for public bodies involved in environmental decision-making. The guide suggested that the principle was likely to
be appropriate in a number of cases, namely: where environmental hazards
had long 'environmental lifetimes'; where there were accumulative or irreversible consequences; where the consequences had a widespread distribution; and where there was 'considerable uncertainty' about the link between
the hazard and the consequence.

The adoption of policies incorporating the precautionary principle can be
seen in relation to other bodies. For example, the RCEP has recommended
a precautionary policy in relation to the disposal of sewage sludge on land in
order to restrict the transfer of pathogens into the food chain (see RCEP, 19th
Report: *Sustainable Use of Soil*, Cm 3165, 1996). The Environment Agency
has a similar approach in relation to the protection of drinking water supplies
and other groundwater (see *Policy and Practice for the Protection of Groundwater*, discussed below at p. 605).

Perhaps the most significant consequence of the adoption of policy in
relation to the precautionary principle is the impact on individual decision-
making. There have been a number of decisions based around the need to
take precaution, particularly in relation to drinking water supplies (e.g. the
dismissal of a planning application for a landfill site in Hampshire, see ENDS
Report 280, p. 15). The quantity and quality of the policies on risk
assessment and the precautionary principle should increase dramatically as a
result of the risk assessment basis for taking action against contaminated land
under Part IIA of the Environmental Protection Act 1990 (see p. 533). In
general terms, however, there is relatively scant mention of precaution in
things like planning policy guidance notes compared with the now ritual
mention of sustainable development, although draft planning policy to
control development in the flood plain takes an overtly precautionary approach. Otherwise, at best we find modestly precautionary policies such as
giving 'draft' sites for protection under EC habitat conservation law the same
level of protection as fully designated areas (although it is somewhat difficult
to say that the level of protection actually given to such sites is precautionary;
see generally p. 644). And whether precaution is wholly compatible with
moves to speed up things like planning decisions might be questioned.

Applying the precautionary principle in practice

The practical application of the precautionary principle is afflicted with
similar issues as those besetting sustainable development. First there is the
problem of 'weak' and 'strong' versions of the principle. In the case of the
former the requirement to take precaution is modified by balancing the costs
and benefits of taking action (mirroring current EC and UK approaches to
the principle). At its extreme, the 'strong' version of the principle would
prohibit any action resulting in significant or irreversible environmental harm,
regardless of the cost of doing so. Both versions of the principle raise
theoretical concerns. For example, under the weak version, there are difficulties in assessing the costs and benefits of uncertain risks that may need to be

extrapolated over a long period of time. On the other hand, a 'strong' interpretation of the principle could result in a prohibition on beneficial activities simply on the basis that the understanding of the risks was uncertain. Science cannot provide 100% certainty on any risk, with the result that all activities would be proscribed.

Secondly, in government policy, much reliance is placed on the use of 'sound science'. As we have just noted, this can never be 'certain' or 'exact' science, but it does suggest a privileging of natural science over other forms of knowledge or constructions of belief, and therefore a certain rationality and unresponsiveness to shifts in public opinion. It should be noted that the 1999 White Paper suggests a slight change of emphasis here from the language previously used in *This Common Inheritance* (which spoke starkly of 'fact not fantasy'):

> When taking decisions, it is important to anticipate early on where scientific advice or research is needed, and to identify sources of information of high calibre. Where possible, evidence should be reviewed from a wide-ranging set of viewpoints.

This emphasises that it is the wider scientific process that is important, as much as the end result. However, it also continues the approach to decision-making which assumes that assessing risks and then agreeing responses to risk (either legally or politically) are completely separate. Many now question whether this can ever be the case. As Jasanoff observes:

> Studies of scientific advising leave in tatters the notion that it is possible, in practice, to restrict the advisory process to technical issues or that the subjective values of scientists are irrelevant to decision-making. The negotiated and constructed model of scientific knowledge, which closely captures the realities of regulatory science, rules out the possibility of drawing sharp boundaries between facts and values or claims and context. (*The Fifth Branch: Science Advisers as Policymakers* (Harvard UP, 1990), p. 231)

Thirdly, precaution does not determine what kinds of standards should be used. Inserting precaution into the EC Treaty, e.g. has not resolved the tension between environmental quality standards and process controls (see further p. 184), even if resolving this were desirable. Indeed, as we have seen, for countries like Germany precaution implied the use of the best pollution abatement techniques (i.e. process controls), while the UK response was to emphasise 'sound science' and costs and benefits, on which the traditional 'British' preference for quality standards was based.

Finally, and perhaps most importantly, the precautionary principle does not fit easily into the institutional and administrative framework which so happily accommodates the principle of sustainable development. It is not so much an aspiration which cuts across departmental boundaries and which can be the subject of 'indicators' and fleshed out policy documents. Rather, many see it as a response to the public mistrust of scientific 'objectivity' and a recognition that there will be circumstances where there is a policy gap between what a decision-maker 'knows' about a risk (or can be told by science) and what the public are concerned about. Thus the precautionary principle fills that gap and provides the decision-maker with a flexible principle which assists with the balance or trade-off between different options involving environmental risks which may be little more than a further justification for decisions which would have been reached anyway. At its worst, by suggesting a clear divide between the certain and uncertain, the precautionary principle may, paradoxically, give strength to the idea of certainty in some situations.

Human rights and environmental values

It may seem surprising to conclude a chapter on *environmental* values and *environmental* law with discussion of something that might not appear directly concerned with either. But, as we have said, environmental regulation does not take place in a vacuum, but within its own 'matrix' of values, practices and moral standpoints relating to our interaction with the natural environment. Beyond this, however, environmental law also exists in a wider context of generally held values that underpin modern liberal-democratic societies. These include things like respect for individual rights and for private property, for procedural fairness in decision-making and respect for the 'rule of law', which generally fall under the rubric of human rights law. We outline some of the more important provisions of human rights law and its case law elsewhere (see especially pp. 110–111 and 282–3), and generally touch on relevant human rights issues throughout this book. The purpose of this section is therefore to consider the impact that the increasing attention given to human rights will have, and how the various perspectives described above are furthered or constrained when human rights enter the equation.

The idea that individuals *should* enjoy various general rights and freedoms has a long heritage, but only relatively recently have these values been laid down in binding legal texts. In a European context, the most important is the 1950 European Convention on Human Rights and Fundamental Freedoms. This was a response both to the aftermath of the Second World War and to the onset of the Cold War, and sought to embed a number of civil rights and freedoms in law. The Convention provides for various degrees of protection for the interests it covers; for example, while freedom from torture is protected absolutely, with most other interests the state has a 'margin of appreciation' to decide whether a stated exception should apply (e.g. the right to privacy and the protection of home life can be outweighed by economic interests, so long as these are 'necessary in a democratic society'). Under the Human Rights Act 1998, which comes into force in October 2000, UK courts and public bodies will be bound to act in accordance with the Convention. There is one exception to this, which is that the Convention right to an individual remedy is not transposed. Instead, what is envisaged are 'collective' remedies, in the sense that legislation can be declared incompatible with the Convention and fast-tracked through Parliament for reform (there will be some scope for individual remedies in practice). The ECJ has already accepted that the European Convention on Human Rights provides one of the general principles of law it must uphold.

(a) The European Convention on Human Rights and the environment

In broad terms, European human rights law operates at three levels in relation to the environment. At a general level, it clearly gives great symbolic weight to the idea that human rights are deserving of protection, and that they are actually protected (there is considerable debate on this latter point). Alongside trade freedom, human rights are one of the major 'narratives' of our times. For the vast majority of people, human rights will tend to outweigh environmental rights or interests.

Secondly, as we discuss elsewhere (see p. 110), the European Court of Human Rights has interpreted some civil and political rights to protect against environmental harms. For example, the Court has, in fairly extreme cases, creatively interpreted the right to respect for home life (in Article 8) to provide a remedy against extreme pollution (although it is also notable that those who have suffered more serious injury, unconnected with property, have been less successful; see e.g. *LCB* v *UK* (1999) 27 EHRR 212).

Thirdly, human rights law may have a more indirect impact in the environmental sphere. For example, the Convention provides for various qualified freedoms such as the freedom of expression (Article 10) and the right to assemble peacefully (Article 11). To the extent that changes to environmental law or policy are argued for through public protest rather than lobbying, depending on various factors human rights law may justify such protest or, conversely, it may be restricted by the use of one of the exceptions which the Convention allows governments to rely on.

(b) 'Pros' and 'cons' of environmental rights

Because the European Convention on Human Rights mostly protects civil and political freedoms, it is rather light on protections for other interests. In particular, the Convention, and human rights law generally, has yet to protect or further genuinely collective rights such as rights relating to environmental quality or resources. One reason for this is the extent to which broad questions of public interest, and often a complex balancing of various factors, are involved. Alternatively, as with European law, a rights-based approach to environmental law has been shunned in the EC Treaty in favour of integrating environmental protection into other policy sectors and reference to 'protecting the quality of the environment' (Articles 6 and 174(1) EC). Although the European Court of Justice sometimes speaks the language of 'rights', what is really at stake is compliance by the Member States with specific, existing, legal obligations (see p. 138).

The 1992 Rio Declaration consciously avoids reference to environmental rights, although it does speak of national 'rights' to exploit the environment, and the right to develop. Elsewhere in international law, however, we can see a gradual coming together of various 'strands' including sustainable development and human rights, indicating the extent to which rights *within* generations, or *intra-generational rights*, are seen as indivisible from the pursuit of sustainability. For example, Art. 4 of the IUCN's Draft International Covenant on Environment and Development from 1995 provides that: 'Peace, development, environmental protection and respect for human rights and fundamental freedoms are interdependent'.

On the other hand, it is notable that most modern constitutions make some reference to environmental rights, usually by enshrining a very general right to a 'clean' or 'decent' environment. Although often this gives little hard legal edge to the right, attempts to flesh out a human 'right to environment' have been made. This is the approach taken in parts of the 'Ksentini' Report, a report by the UN Special Rapporteur on Human Rights and the Environment from 1994 (see further p. 110). This report identifies various substantive rights and freedoms, such as freedom from pollution and environmental degradation, and the right to the highest attainable standard of health free from environmental harm, qualified by exceptions similar to those found in the European Convention on Human Rights. From what has been said above, however, it should be apparent that whether these are anything more than policy aspirations or symbolic gestures is questionable. While they may guide decision-makers in a general sense, it is difficult to see courts requiring potentially vast sums of money to be spent on environmental improvement works to uphold such rights, not least because this might involve protecting the 'first right to get to court' at the expense of other, perhaps more worthy, improvement schemes. (For an example of the courts shying away from requiring massive public spending see *Baxter* v *Camden (No. 2)* [2000] Env LR 112, discussed at p. 258, and also *ex parte Duddridge*, referred to above).

On the other hand, human rights law does offer some advantages from an environmental perspective. First, as against 'environmental rights', it uses concepts familiar to judges — individuals against the state — and deals with issues with which judges are generally not completely unfamiliar (such as balancing individual rights not to be libelled and collective interests in free speech). This may lead to judicial activism in favour of individually-based environmental actions such as tort claims (although it may also protect individuals as against collective interests like those of environmental regulators). Secondly, and perhaps more importantly, it opens up the possibility of arguing cases on their merits, usually where there is a margin of appreciation, rather than applicants being confined to showing that a decision-maker has acted perversely or that some procedural rule has not been followed correctly. For example, a number of residents living in the path of night flights at Heathrow have brought a claim under Article 8 of the Convention because of night noise disturbance; the European Court of Human Rights is currently deciding whether the UK Government can justify the noise when the negative impacts are weighed against the economic benefits derived from the flights.

(c)   From human rights to 'animal' and 'environmental' rights

Many now argue for extending rights to the non-human world, e.g. according great apes 'rights' based on certain similarities to humans, or even protecting the 'rights' of natural habitats. Even if we accept that non-humans can have rights, there is a fierce dispute about whether this is progressive, or whether such an approach, at least when taken to extremes, in fact lowers the status of humans and human rights in a reactionary way or is, in any case, too individualistic for a holistic environmental 'ethic'. For more detailed discussion of animal and environmental rights see Alder and Wilkinson, *Environmental Law and Ethics* (Macmillan Press, 1999).

(d) Procedural rights

Because of the difficulties in relation to complex resources questions, most efforts to elevate environmental interests within a 'rights' tradition have so far concentrated more on procedural rather than substantive rights. Despite its background, these are not terribly well provided for in the European Convention on Human Rights, which provides guarantees only in relation to fair trials (see *R* v *Hertfordshire CC, ex parte Green Environmental Industries*, discussed at p. 518) and free elections, and a right to receive and impart information (under Article 10) which has been construed quite narrowly (see *Guerra* v *Italy*, discussed at p. 222).

As we have seen, some have argued that concepts like sustainable development are best approached by trying to lay down general procedural principles. These might facilitate greater public involvement, and the expression of environmental concerns, in decision-making, and be used to check the exercise of power so that environmental concerns are not marginalised. The approach of the important 1998 Århus Convention on Access to Information, Public Participation in Decision-Making and Access to Justice in Environmental Matters can be seen in this light. In effect, this Convention provides a procedural complement to the more substantively-oriented but less environmentally-relevant European Convention on Human Rights. The Århus Convention should be seen alongside other existing measures at European level, such as the Directive on Environmental Impact Assessment (85/337/EEC, as amended), which go some way towards fleshing out the concept of sustainable development.

As discussed elsewhere, some of the bolder judges have also begun fleshing out some of the procedural principles — such as impact assessment — which are increasingly seen as 'operationalising' sustainable development (see p. 102). Such 'proceduralisation', of course, is an important way of giving voice to those individuals or groups who want to speak for 'the' or 'their' environment. Increasingly it is being seen in decision-making contexts more generally, such as the use of consensus conferences where a small group of the public deliberates, privately and then by public questioning of 'witnesses', about policy matters, often of technical complexity such as how to manage nuclear waste. Procedural mechanisms also have the considerable virtue of being flexible in the light of substantive values changing over time, given their emphasis on processes rather than outcomes. They can be the 'rules of a game' whose participants, and their objectives, are always changing.

THREE
Sources of environmental law

If environmental laws are the tools of the environmental lawyer's trade, where can they be found? If we accept the notion that environmental law includes not only specific sets of rules laid down in statutes but also any mechanism which seeks to control or influence activities which cause environmental harm, we could find that all of the potential sources of environmental law are impossible to capture meaningfully in a book of this sort. As the nature of environmental issues becomes more complex and their diversity increases, so the sources of environmental law expand and the traditional boundaries and divisions of legal mechanisms blur. As described below, we find such concepts as environmental agreements; imposed self-regulation where industry groups or other organisations regulate the activities of their own members; taxes and incentives; and information-based strategies such as requiring companies to report on environmental performance within their annual reports.

When people talk of environmental law they commonly mean that branch of public law (i.e. laws which control the relationship between citizens and the state) which contains statutes which cover pollution control and wider environmental issues (e.g. the Environmental Protection Act 1990 or the Wildlife and Countryside Act 1981). This can be contrasted with private law mechanisms (covered in Chapter 10) which control the relationships between private individuals (e.g. contractual relationships). It is becoming increasingly clear that there are sources of environmental law which derive their status as law from both of these branches and the combination of public and private law can lead to innovation in the control over environmental problems. This chapter considers some of these sources of law and their characteristics. To some extent there is a degree of overlap between this chapter and others in this book. Therefore, a few of these sources are only covered in outline here but are dealt with in detail elsewhere (e.g. European law, international law and private law). Finally, we consider the role of the courts in supervising the way in which environmental laws are implemented and enforced, through the mechanism of judicial review.

The development of sources of environmental laws

When we look at the development of environmental law as a separate system of law we can identify three distinct phases of growth in the sources of law (it should be stressed, however, that there are and will continue to be substantial overlaps in different sources of environmental law). The first phase of development was dominated by the growth of private law ideas such as the protection of property rights. This appears to have reached what we might call a peak when the excesses of the industrial revolution started to cause significant impacts on public health and amenity in the mid to late nineteenth century. During this phase, the concepts of nuisance and other mechanisms for environmental protection were developed outside the statutory framework.

The second phase began in the late stages of the nineteenth century but only really gained momentum in the early 1970s (characterised by the formation of the Department of the Environment) when the limitations of the private law mechanisms meant that there was increasing recognition that the state had to take a more active role in the control of pollution and protection of the environment. There are a number of possible explanations for this shift stretching from the theoretical (e.g. the private law failed either to reflect the external costs of pollution or to protect the interests of future generations by conserving resources) to the pragmatic and political (e.g. impending membership of the European Community or the growth in environmental regulation in other developed countries which required some form of governmental response). Whatever the reason, this phase of environmental law has been characterised by the passing of environmental 'laws' or statutory frameworks in relation to aspects of environmental protection. Typically, the environmental statutes have been based upon a model which has become known as 'command and control' whereby centralised environmental standards are set and policed by a combination of government and regulatory agencies. This growth in the number of environmental laws over the last thirty years reflects the readiness with which the UK government has adopted this type of environmental regulation. In this chapter we concentrate principally on these public laws as they continue to represent the majority of the 'tools of the trade' for the environmental lawyer.

There is, however, evidence that the traditional sources of environmental law are being supplemented by more innovative mechanisms (these are considered in greater detail in Chapter 7). These include:

(a) Instruments which are hybrids of the public and private law (e.g. environmental agreements made under statutory powers by public bodies with private individuals or groups. These would include such things as planning obligations under s. 106, Town and Country Planning Act 1990 or management agreements in nature conservation).

(b) Instruments which impose self-regulatory requirements. An example of this would be the existence of compliance schemes under the producer responsibility legislation for the recovery and recycling of packaging waste. The regulations exempt all companies who would otherwise have had to comply with the producer responsibility obligations if they are members of a compliance scheme which is registered for the purposes of the regulations. The compliance scheme takes on collective responsibility for meeting its members' obligations under the legislation (see further Chapter 17). Thus the regulation of the activities is delegated to a small number of self-regulated organisations.

(c)   Instruments based upon increasing public information about polluting activities. These include not only rights of access to information on specific emissions and activities regulated under licences which are held on public registers, but also more sophisticated information such as inventories of general and aggregated pollution levels, product labelling and possible requirements to include environmental information in companies' annual reports (see Chapter 8).

(d)   Economic instruments which can cover a range of measures from the direct taxation of polluting substances through to fees and charges for licences which reflect the level of environmental risk or harm which an authorised activity causes.

(e)   It is arguable that even threats made by senior politicians could constitute a source of environmental 'law' if they cause changes in behaviour which bring about long-term environmental improvement. An example of this occurred when the Secretary of State for the Environment 'requested' that the water companies should offer leakage detection and repair service for private water supplies; this was agreed to with a consequent reduction in consumption of water (see Editorial, 'Regulation by Request' [1997] 9 Water Law 117).

This use of a broader range of instruments reflects a third phase in the growth of sources of environmental law: traditional public law 'command and control' legislation is combined with different regulatory approaches to secure the most effective forms of control over environmental pollution. This blend of instruments has been termed 'smart regulation' (see Gunningham and Grabosky, *Smart Regulation: Designing Environmental Policy*, Clarendon Press, 1998). Whilst it is clear that these regulatory innovations are an important form of control, for the purposes of this chapter we focus primarily on environmental legislation which is the principal source of environmental law in the UK.

Features of environmental legislation

Environmental legislation covers a wide range of areas which means that the substance of the legislation is often very different. There are, however, some characteristics which could be said to be common to all.

(a)   Complex tiers of rules
Much of the detail of environmental statutes is left to be worked out in various forms of delegated legislation. There is no typical type of delegated legislation within UK environmental law and detailed laws come under

names such as regulations, rules, orders and schemes. This is particularly true of some of the main pieces of legislation in environmental law — the Environmental Protection Act 1990, the Water Resources Act 1991, the Environment Act 1995, the Town and Country Planning Act 1990 and the Pollution Prevention and Control Act 1999. In each case, the statute only provides a limited description of what the law is. For example, in the Town and Country Planning Act 1990, the central definition of what requires planning permission owes just as much to statutory instruments — the General Permitted Development Order and the Use Classes Order — as to the general definition laid down in s. 55 of the Act (see p. 310).

As this detailed type of delegated legislation is often technical and complex, there is a further layer of rules which form what we might term 'tertiary' or 'quasi' legislation. There is no set pattern to this type of rule but it is made up of different forms of guidance, circulars and other technical advice. As environmental regulation becomes more multifaceted, this type of rule-making is becoming more popular as it provides a simple, flexible and efficient way of expanding upon basic statutory concepts.

The upshot of all of these different types of legislation and other rules is that it is often difficult to find out about the law on a particular issue in anything other than a very general manner. For example although Chapter 13 covers controls over industrial processes, if one wanted to find out about the rules which governed an application for pollution prevention and control permit, the basic information about application procedures would have to be supplemented with technical guidance on specific industrial sectors and general guidance on such things as monitoring requirements. The complexity and interaction of these many tiers of rules can obscure the effects of the law in that the informal rules and guidance can have greater practical significance than the primary or secondary legislation.

(b)   Commencement
Legislation often requires implementation by statutory instrument before it comes into force. The Control of Pollution Act was enacted in 1974, yet Part II relating to water pollution was not brought into force until 1986, and then only in a piecemeal and gradual manner. Some parts of the Act were never brought into force (e.g. s. 46(1)–(3) on the powers of water authorities to vary consents after an act of pollution). Apart from the suspicion that such delays are used for political purposes, this gradualist approach obscures what the law is and brings it into disrepute by creating uncertainty for the public, regulatory bodies and industry alike.

The EPA 1990 included a provision for most of it to be brought into force by commencement order. This led to the provisions on waste management licensing not being brought into force until May 1994. It seems contrary to the rule of law that the decision on whether, and how far, to implement enacted legislation should be left entirely to the discretion of the Secretary of State. However, that is the position and the same approach was adopted for the Environment Act 1995, virtually all of which required a commencement order before it came into force.

(c) Definitions

Definitions are often left unclear in the legislation. Normally this is to preserve flexibility in the application of the law. For example, until the enactment of the EPA 1990, the central concept in the law on air pollution was that of 'best practicable means' (BPM). This phrase was never statutorily defined. Instead, it was explained in relation to different processes in BPM Notes published by Her Majesty's Inspectorate of Pollution (HMIP) and its predecessors. Even these were not comprehensive, since an important feature of BPM was that it allowed flexibility to cater for local and individual circumstances. Interestingly, the BPM Notes were often drawn up in consultation with interested parties, including representatives of the industry concerned.

A similar process can be seen in the Town and Country Planning Act 1990, where fundamental concepts such as development and material change of use have deliberately been left as open as possible in the legislation. In this case, they have been further defined by the courts in numerous cases, but the original flexibility has been retained by the courts' insistence that the application of the law to the facts of any individual case is a matter for the relevant decision-maker (the so-called 'fact and degree' test). If anything, this approach is becoming more common. In the Environment Act 1995, Part II, a new system providing for remediation of contaminated land was established, yet the fundamental question of whether land is 'contaminated' owes as much to guidance issued by the Secretary of State which local authorities must follow, as it does to the partial definition set out in the Act. What should be determined as a matter of law is thus relegated to a matter of administrative discretion. An even more remarkable example is provided by the Deregulation and Contracting Out Act 1994, which included a general power for any Minister to amend or repeal existing legislation by means of a statutory instrument if it appeared that the measure imposed a burden on any trade, business or profession, and that the amendment or repeal would reduce that burden. These examples illustrate a clear shift in power away from Parliament and the courts to the executive government.

(d) Purposive and listing approaches

One of the consequences of having to balance such wide definitions against the technical nature of much of environmental law is that there are two typical approaches to drafting legislative concepts. First, and probably the most common, is the approach outlined above where the rule maker balances flexibility and certainty by creating complex tiers of rules. Characteristically, this will involve having a broad definition within primary legislation followed by lists of a more technical nature in secondary regulations. Examples of this can be found in the formation of exemptions from the legislative system in many areas of environmental legislation (e.g. from the need for planning permission or waste management licences). The primary statute empowers the rule maker to create classes of exempt activities and these are set down in detailed secondary legislation. The main alternative to this approach is to set down a purposive definition which stands alone without any need for further clarification. The purpose of the definition is self-explanatory. An example of this can be found in s. 85, Water Resources Act 1991, which makes it an offence to cause the entry of 'polluting' matter into controlled waters. The key phrase 'polluting' is not defined in the Act.

Finally, certain environmental laws combine both of these approaches. For example, the exemptions from the need for an IPC authorisation are listed in regulations (see further p. 407), however, there is a further, more general purposive exemption where prescribed processes would give rise to emissions which are 'trivial' in terms of their environmental impact. Another more controversial example can be found in the definition of waste (see further p. 487) where the relationship between a purposive definition ('substances or objects which have been discarded') and descriptions of wastes, waste recovery and disposal operations have been examined by the courts.

Interestingly in this context, European law sets out the specific purposes of legislation in recitals which form part of directives. Since more and more European law is being transposed into domestic law by means of straight translation (also referred to as 'copy out', see further p. 149), and the doctrine of indirect effects (that national laws should be interpreted so as to comply with EC law, see further p. 140), this means that courts are interpreting national environmental laws in accordance with the underlying purposes.

(e) Discretions

Wide discretions are frequently given in the legislation. This is a particularly clear feature of British environmental law (see p. 194). There are many examples, ranging from the discretion given to the Secretary of State on the form of delegated legislation, through discretion as to whether an area should be designated for special protection, discretion on the setting of standards (e.g. in the permitted level of a pollutant discharged or emitted), to discretion over the enforcement of the law. In all areas of environmental law it is hard to get away from discretionary decision-making.

However, two important trends must be pointed out at this stage — the increased structuring of the discretions and the increased role of central government. In the past, it has been normal for environmental legislation to grant public agencies and bodies a large amount of discretion, often in the form of a subjective power which is then regulated by the courts. More recently, the agencies have themselves structured the exercise of their discretion through such things as internal agency guidelines and strategies, and have thus made the whole system more formalised (an example is the adoption by the Environment Agency (EA) of a formal policy on prosecution and other enforcement action). This gives the courts a greater potential role in environmental decisions. However, the effect is arguably limited by the other trend which, as pointed out above, is that ever greater powers are being given to central government to dictate the sorts of considerations that must be taken into account in any exercise of a discretion. This process is seen very clearly in the Environment Act 1995. As a specific example, s. 39 imposes a requirement that the EA take into account the likely costs and benefits before making decisions; but, more generally, the whole way in which the EA operates is effectively decided by guidance and directions issued by central government.

These features of environmental legislation help to explain some of the essential characteristics of the 'British approach' to environmental protection, such as flexibility and pragmatism (see p. 191). The width of the discretions given also militates against uniformity in either the definition or the application of the law.

Environmental laws in practice

As much of the above discussion illustrates, the reading of environmental statutes may provide us with a source of environmental law but it does not necessarily represent how such laws work in the real world. One of the key characteristics of environmental law is that it is (or rather should be) law in action rather than law for lawyers. It involves the solving of practical problems, so everything which is likely to have an impact on the solution of a problem should be understood including tertiary rules such as guidance and evidence of practice. For example, the use of political threats to bring about improvements in water leakage rates referred to above would not normally be cited as a typical source of law. However, it clearly resulted in some action being taken, perhaps more efficiently and in a shorter period than would have been the case had specific legislation been introduced.

The sources of environmental law are also forward-looking in the sense that they often provide frameworks for future action (e.g. the structured implementation of the integrated pollution prevention and control (IPPC) legislation, see p. 386). Thus, it is often desirable to know what the law is going to be as well as what it is. Finally, it may also be argued that the sources of law should include the actual practice of agencies with responsibilities in the environmental field; an argument which is at its strongest when dealing with enforcement. This makes it desirable that as much as possible about the practice and policy actually relied upon by decision-makers is published officially, an aim which is still not yet met in practice.

Categories of environmental legislation

Although the boundaries between different types of legislation and rules are often blurred in practice, the source of domestic environmental legislation can be broken down into three main categories.

(a) Primary legislation

Acts of Parliament (also known as statutes or enactments) provide the basic framework for most domestic environmental law. They display most of the characteristics which are discussed above (i.e. delayed commencement, wide definitions and discretion, and essentially a framework). Although they are subject to full Parliamentary scrutiny, these general characteristics mean that there is often little controversy concerning the substantive provisions of environmental statutes as they do not contain anything of sufficient certainty to give rise to party political disputes (although there are notable exceptions to this; the primary example being the Wildlife and Countryside Act 1981).

Another notable feature of environmental statutes is that legislation on single environmental issues is often promoted in the form of Private Members' Bills, reflecting the individual interests of MPs and the effective lobbying of non-governmental organisations (NGOs). Examples of Private Members' Bills on environmental issues which have reached the statute book in recent years include the Pesticides Act 1998 and the Waste Minimisation Act 1998.

There is little direct public participation (e.g. by way of public consultation) in the creation of environmental statutes. The main justification for this is that Parliament has representative accountability through the electorate and is therefore presumed to pass laws on behalf of everyone. In addition, both Houses of Parliament scrutinise new legislation in standing committees and debates. In reality, this scrutiny is often no more than passing consideration because of pressure on Parliamentary time and commonly the numerical strength of the incumbent government.

Although there has been a consolidation of the administration of environmental protection over recent years, environmental legislation still extends over a relatively large area. The main Acts include:

(a) The Environmental Protection Act 1990 which covers the controls over emissions from industrial processes, waste management, statutory nuisances, litter, and genetically modified organisms.

(b) The Water Resources Act 1991 which covers controls over water pollution, water quality regulation, water resource issues (e.g. controls over abstraction and flood defence) and miscellaneous water related matters including fisheries and navigation.

(c) The Water Industry Act 1991 and the Water Industry Act 1999 which cover the control of the supply of water and the provision of sewerage services by the water and sewerage undertakers.

(d) The Environment Act 1995 which sets out the duties and powers of the Environment Agency, duties and powers in respect of the clean up of historically contaminated land, the framework for national strategies on waste and air quality and general producer responsibility obligations for waste.

(e) The Pollution Prevention and Control Act 1999 which sets out the basic framework for the implementation of the Integrated Pollution Prevention and Control Directive.

(f) The Town and Country Planning Act 1990 which controls land use planning and sets out procedures for strategic development planning.

(g) The Wildlife and Countryside Act 1981 which provides for a scheme for the management and protection of habitats and species.

There is another more general statute which could be said to be a primary source of environmental law. The European Communities Act 1972, s. 2(2) gives powers for the passing of secondary legislation which is necessary to comply with EC law (see further below). One of the main disadvantages of this power is that it only permits bare implementation measures (i.e. secondary legislation must accord exactly with the European obligations, no more and no less). This power has been supplemented with a wider power to

transpose and modify environmental obligations under EC law under the
Pollution Prevention and Control Act 1999, sch. 1, para. 20.

(b) Secondary legislation

The second main source of environmental law stems from the first. Beneath
the tier of primary legislation there is a range of detailed secondary legislation
which is used to flesh out much of the detail of environmental law. Regulations
are commonly made by the appropriate Secretary of State under the delegated
authority of Parliament. Typically, they are known as regulations or statutory
instruments although in relation to environmental laws, there are other types
of secondary legislation (e.g. the Use Classes Order). This tier of legislation is
entirely dependent upon the powers which have been granted within the
primary statute. In environmental law, there has been some controversy about
the breadth of some of the powers which have been granted by primary
statutes. There appears to have been an desire to broaden the scope of the
power to make secondary legislation in order to give more and more flexibility
to the rule makers. The Pollution Prevention and Control Bill featured a
particularly wide power allowing the Secretary of State to pass regulations in
respect of a series of statutory purposes relating to environmental pollution.
This would have given a virtually unlimited scope to control any activity which
gave rise to pollution without any Parliamentary scrutiny. This power was
subsequently amended after objections were lodged in the House of Lords.

This controversy illustrates some of the concerns about using secondary
legislation for many of the elements of environmental laws. Unlike primary
legislation, there is little Parliamentary scrutiny of detailed secondary legislation. Many environmental regulations are passed under what is known as the
negative resolution procedure which, in practice, consists of laying the
statutory instrument before both Houses of Parliament for a specified period
before it comes into force. Some more controversial aspects of secondary
legislation are subject to the alternative affirmative procedure which ensures
that there are debates in both Houses before the legislation is passed.

One of the main reasons for the lack of Parliamentary scrutiny is that
environmental secondary legislation tends to be highly technical and the lack
of any sufficient expertise would make Parliamentary scrutiny less than
effective. Secondly, environmental secondary legislation is commonly sent out
for public consultation which enables a broad range of technical views to be
taken into account prior to finalising the details. In these circumstances, the
lower levels of Parliamentary scrutiny can be justified as there is a broader
public scrutiny which is involved in the law-making process.

It is impossible to provide any comprehensive list of environmental secondary legislation but there are certain categories which can be identified.

(i) Procedural

Certain aspects of environmental regulation are too detailed and complex to
be placed in primary legislation. Procedures for applications for licences and
for appealing against refusals or enforcement action can often be found in
secondary legislation. In addition, provisions on other procedural matters

such as registers of information on emissions are left to delegated powers. For examples see the Environmental Protection (Applications, Appeals and Registers) Regulations 1991 (as amended) (SI 1991/507) and the Statutory Nuisance (Appeals) Regulations 1995 (SI 1995/2644).

(ii)   Detailed categories
Primary legislation may set down general definitions which can be more properly defined in technical secondary legislation. Thus categories of processes prescribed for control under IPC (see Environmental Protection (Prescribed Processes and Substances) Regulations 1991, SI 1991/472), exemptions from the need for planning permission (e.g. see the Town and Country Planning Use Classes Order 1987, SI 1987/764) or categories of special waste (see the Special Waste Regulations 1996, SI 1996/972) are all to be found in secondary legislation.

(iii)   Standards
It is common for the many different types of standards which play an important role in environmental regulation (see further p. 183) to be set out in secondary legislation. Examples include the Air Quality (England) Regulations 2000 (SI 2000/928) and the Surface Waters (Dangerous Substances) (Classification) Regulations 1992 (SI 1992/337).

(iv)   Transposing European obligations
Certain European obligations have been transposed directly into secondary legislation. The justification for using secondary legislation is that there should be little political controversy over the transposition of measures which have been agreed at a European level. Thus these regulations are direct translations of the corresponding European measures and examples include the Environmental Information Regulations 1992 (SI 1992/3240) (transposing the Access to Environmental Information Directive (90/313)), the Conservation (Natural Habitats etc.) Regulations 1994 (SI 1994/2716) (transposing the Habitats Directive (92/43)), and the Waste Management Licensing Regulations 1994 (SI 1994/1056) (transposing the Framework Directive on Waste (91/271)).

(c)   Tertiary legislation, guidance and other 'rules'
Although secondary legislation provides the bulk of the technical details of environmental law, it is still not particularly user-friendly nor does it set out a comprehensive set of definitions. There is an increasing reliance on other rules and guidance to explain the practical workings of environmental laws and to provide a structure for some of the statutory discretion which is referred to above. There are so many different types of this source of law that it is impossible to identify any meaningful classification other than looking at the purpose behind the guidance or rule. These rules can have a number of purposes.

(i)   As an aid to the interpretation of statutory provisions
As the main statutory provisions in primary and secondary legislation can be complex and technical, there is often a need to flesh out definitions and

provide an interpretation of such provisions in non-legalistic language. An example is the definition of waste which is defined in the primary statute in a few lines, fleshed out in different ways in the Waste Management Licensing Regulations 1994 (SI 1994/1056) but is explained in simpler terms in the Department of the Environment Circular 11/94. Another example is the series of Air Quality Notes which are issued by the Department of the Environment, Transport and the Regions (DETR) to local authorities as an aid to interpreting certain of the statutory provisions on air pollution control under Part I of the Environmental Protection Act 1990. The Environment Agency has also issued a number of documents which purport to interpret and flesh out statutory definitions. For example there is a series of notes which provide detailed interpretations of issues associated with the producer responsibility legislation dealing with packaging waste.

(ii)   As a more flexible form of informal guidance or rule
There are some areas which do not lend themselves to the traditional sources of environmental law. These include matters which cannot easily be reduced to simple rules as there is a need for a little more flexibility and less legal rigidity in the use of language. An example is the code of practice on the duty of care (see p. 512) which provides detailed guidance on the type of conduct which might be considered to be reasonable when handling materials throughout the waste management chain. Another example is the statutory guidance in the contaminated land regime (see p. 532). Both of these examples set out principles and rules in a prose style which enables a wider range of issues to be discussed and balanced than would be the case if they were set out in formal legislation. In addition, broad strategic documents are more easily framed in informal documents than in formal legislation as they set out general policies, strategies and programmes which are to be used in meeting statutory or non-statutory environmental quality targets. Examples include the national strategies on waste and air quality, the action plan for phasing out polychlorinated biphenyls (PCBs) or the programme for reducing sulphur dioxide and oxides of nitrogen.

(iii)   As statements of regulatory agency policy and practice
Regulatory agencies will often publish policy documents which set out their aims and policies on particular areas. The EA has policy and practice documents in a number of areas including the protection of groundwater and of floodplains. These documents are used in liaison with other agencies (primarily the planning authorities) in carrying out overlapping functions and in exercising decision-making powers such as determining planning applications.

(iv)   As a way of structuring discretion and promoting consistency and transparency in decision-making
Where environmental agencies implement and enforce wide discretionary statutory powers there is often guidance which aims to direct them in the exercise of those powers. Documents such as the Environment Agency's Enforcement and Prosecution Policy (see p. 253) set out objective principles

which guide individual officers as to when and how enforcement action should be taken when environmental laws are breached. This should ensure that there is a degree of consistency and uniformity in enforcement practices across the country and thereby increases the transparency and fairness of the otherwise unstructured use of enforcement powers.

(v)   As rules and guidance on procedure or other technical matters
Although secondary legislation often sets out the formal legislative requirements for procedural or other technical matters, it does not deal with many of the practical issues which can arise on a day-to-day basis. Thus there is a need to provide information and practical guidance in non-legalistic language. Examples of this can be found in general guidance notes issued by the DETR to local authorities in relation to procedural and other matters under air pollution control legislation and process guidance notes which are issued by the Secretary of State and the Environment Agency in relation to BATNEEC process standards under Part I of the EPA 1990.

These types of tertiary rules and guidance have become a common method of supplementing formal primary and secondary legislation as a source of environmental law. In areas of policy rather than law, the use of circulars and other guidance documents is relatively well established. Whilst there is a very significant degree of overlap between law and policy (see p. 24), the range of tertiary rules in modern environmental law goes much further than mere policy documents providing assistance with decision-making. The use of technical guidance and documents which interpret general statutory concepts is one of the ways in which environmental laws operate in the real world. The use of such documents is not, however, without its own set of difficulties. The level of formality of such rules differs. Some, such as the code of practice on the duty of care or the statutory guidance on contaminated land, have their origins in primary or secondary legislation (and which could be referred to as sub-delegated legislation). Others appear somewhat spontaneously and do not have any formal basis.

The key problem with the use of tertiary rules is, however, that there is a great deal of uncertainty and confusion about the extent to which such rules have legal effect. For example, if an interpretive guidance document sets out a detailed interpretation of a general statutory definition (such as the government's interpretation of the definition of waste in Circular 11/94 or the EA's view on the definition of packaging), does that interpretation have any legal force? Theoretically, at least, such interpretations or rules do not have any determinative status as law (indeed, it is common for such guidance documents to make it clear that the individual interpretation is no substitute for a court's view). This theory unfortunately ignores the fact that in practice the interpretation often supplants the general definition in the minds of the regulator and the regulated. Moreover, if the interpretation is ever challenged in court, there is a great temptation for a judge to 'adopt' the official interpretation over any other.

Generally speaking, tertiary rules will have a persuasive status, either as a material consideration (e.g. in the case of planning circulars) which cannot be ignored but is not prescriptive, or as a presumptive starting point for a decision-maker or regulatory agency (e.g. in the case of process guidance notes in relation to IPC where the process standard set out is presumed to represent BATNEEC but other circumstances could give rise to alternatives).

Case law

In addition to legislative sources of environmental law, case law, that is the decisions made by judges in the courts, forms a growing source of law. On a very general level, substantive environmental cases come before the courts in three main ways. First, where there is a dispute about a statutory definition in primary or secondary legislation, a court can be asked to interpret the statutory phrase. This can be in the context of criminal proceedings (e.g. in relation to the definition of 'causing' in the Water Resources Act 1991, see *Empress Car Co. (Abertillery) Ltd* v *National Rivers Authority* [1998] Env LR 396) or in the Chancery Division by way of seeking the court's declaration (e.g. in relation to the definition of 'waste', see *Mayer Parry Recycling* v *Environment Agency* [1999] Env LR 489). In these cases, the court's interpretation of the definition becomes the law (in this context it is also important to note the role and influence of the European Court of Justice; see further p. 116). Secondly, there are common law disputes which have an environmental flavour. These include actions in nuisance, negligence and trespass (see Chapter 10). In these cases, the courts are developing principles which have a long history in order to address modern environmental disputes (e.g. nuisances arising out of the pollution of groundwater, see *Cambridge Water Co.* v *Eastern Counties Leather* [1994] Env LR 105; personal injury arising from emissions of asbestos dust, see *Hancock and Margereson* v *JW Roberts Ltd* [1996] Env LR 304; and breach of statutory duty giving rise to stigma damages for radioactive contamination, see *Blue Circle Industries* v *Ministry of Defence* [1997] Env LR 22 and p. 286). Finally, as most of the sources of environmental law are statutory, cases arise where the powers granted to government and regulatory agencies are used unlawfully or statutory procedures ignored and the courts are asked to judicially review the exercise of the power.

These broad categories of cases are, of course, simplistic in the sense that environmental disputes arise in all sorts of ways which are impossible to categorise but nevertheless they illustrate that in certain areas environmental law is organic and develops to reflect the views and values of the judiciary and arguably the general public. In Chapter 1 we considered the different approaches which judges take to different categories of various environmental cases (see p. 21). In summary, the courts appear to be willing to adopt a wide purposive approach to interpreting statutory provisions which create environmental criminal offences but take a less interventionist approach to the judicial review of environmental powers and duties or the private law.

Administrative appeals

In addition to judicial decisions, there is a range of quasi-judicial decisions which can provide a source of law in its widest sense (in the same way that tertiary rules form a source of law). In a subject which is heavily dominated by policy, it is clear that the Secretary of State (which we use loosely to cover the relevant decision-makers in Scotland, Wales and Northern Ireland), in his role as ultimate arbiter on questions of policy in the system of administrative appeals, can set precedents in terms of the manner in which central rules or guidance are to be interpreted both generally and on a case-by-case basis. Although such administrative decisions are not binding upon other decision-makers (i.e. not in the way that judicial pronouncements bind lower courts), they can effectively dictate the decision-making processes of the regulatory agencies to whom such powers have been devolved. An example of this can be found in the way in which decisions in planning appeals were used to reinforce deregulatory planning policies in the 1980s.

The system of environmental appeals addresses questions of law (e.g. whether or not something is 'development' within the meaning of the Town and Country Planning Act 1990), fact (e.g. whether a planning use was commenced more than 10 years ago), policy (e.g. whether a particular development should be situated outside a town centre in contravention of central government guidance), scientific and technical issues (e.g. whether a particular process option represents BATNEEC) or any combination of these. In this way, such appeals are concerned with the substantive (as opposed to procedural) 'rights and wrongs' of environmental decision-making with all of the consequential impact that this has on public participation; provision of adequate and objective evidence; and clarity and transparency of the decision itself.

In many ways, the 'battleground' of environmental decision-making lies within the context of the administrative appeals system. Although the courts have supervisory powers under the judicial review process this is not concerned with the substantive decision but the manner in which the decision was made. One of the main problems with this approach is that there can be a tendency for administrative appeals to be viewed by the public as being more concerned with going through the correct procedures than with debating and adjudicating on the substantive issues at hand, as the appeal process is primarily concerned with applying central policy within an individual set of facts rather than debating whether that policy is in itself acceptable (e.g., whether an incinerator is acceptable at a particular location, rather than whether we should be using waste minimisation techniques to ensure that there is no need for further incinerators).

European Community (EC) law

It would not be proper to conclude a discussion of the sources of the law without a reference to EC law, which is of enormous importance in the environmental field. Membership of the EC has clearly involved a distinct loss of sovereignty for Member States, and in this country this is given constitutional force by the European Communities Act 1972. Section 2(1) provides that EC legislation is recognised as law in Britain, although by no means all EC environmental legislation is directly effective in the sense that it can be relied upon by individuals before it is implemented by domestic measures.

In addition to the concept of EC law as British law, there are rules and principles which can be applied to the institutions of the EC (i.e. EC law as it affects internal bodies). Thus such things as the precautionary principle and the need to integrate environmental considerations into all areas of EC policy apply to the Commission when it is formulating legislative proposals and the European Parliament and Council of Ministers when they are debating and making European environmental laws.

EC law is explained in greater detail in Chapter 5, but an important point to establish here is that, as with the position in domestic law, EC environmental law consists of far more than legal rules. It is as necessary to understand the policies, principles and future direction of EC law as it is to understand its current legal content.

International law

International law governs relations between states. Unlike EC law, it has no direct effect on domestic law or on individuals. However, it will often have an indirect effect, for example by publicising a particular issue, by laying down generally accepted standards, or by imposing political pressure on states to change their laws or practices. Thus the North Sea Conferences have had an important impact on British domestic policies in relation to the dumping of sewage sludge in the North Sea, which has now ceased. Many pieces of legislation include powers for the government to introduce changes into domestic law in order to comply with international obligations. For example, the EPA 1990, s. 156 enables the Secretary of State to make regulations to modify other parts of the Act in order to comply with EC or international obligations.

For the most part, international environmental law consists of Conventions agreed by signatory states, such as the Ramsar Convention on Wetlands of International Importance (see p. 653), or the Vienna Convention for the Protection of the Ozone Layer. These may provide general guidance on activities or they may lay down precise standards and requirements (for example, the Montreal Protocol to the Vienna Convention does this). The important point is that such law is not ultimately binding, except in a political sense, because of the lack of sanctions available for non-compliance. However, it is often implemented by domestic or EC legislation, a process which has happened to the Montreal Protocol. It is anticipated, by analogy with the development of international law in other spheres, that it will develop some generally agreed principles to cover such things as trans-boundary pollution, that will apply even without the need for a treaty.

International law is covered in Chapter 4. It is however worth pointing out that the role of the EC in negotiating international agreements and the globalisation of environmental issues means that international law will continue to grow in significance as an influencing factor in domestic law.

Judicial review

Environmental enforcement authorities are public bodies exercising public powers. Mostly, these powers are exercised under statute and consequential delegated legislation. However, in exercising these powers, it may be that such bodies do not follow statutory procedures, that they arrive at decisions unfairly, or that they attempt to make decisions which they have no power to make. The High Court oversees the exercise of these powers by administrative bodies by means of judicial review. The main ground for judicial review is that an administrative body has made a decision which was outside the statutory powers given to it (i.e. *ultra vires*). This may happen in one of three ways.

(a) No power to make the decision itself

If the Environment Agency decided to issue a trade effluent discharge consent for a discharge made to a sewer, a matter which is controlled by the water and sewerage undertaker, then the decision would be subject to judicial review because it could not be made within the statutory powers under the Water Resources Act 1991.

(b) The improper exercise of discretion

This principle was first expounded by Lord Greene MR in the case of *Associated Provincial Picture Houses Limited* v *Wednesbury Corporation* [1948] 1 KB 223:

> . . . a person entrusted with a discretion must, so to speak, direct himself properly in law. He must call his own attention to the matters which he is bound to consider. He must exclude from his consideration matters which are irrelevant to what he has to consider. If he does not obey those rules, he may truly be said, and often is said, to be acting 'unreasonably'. Similarly there may be something so absurd that no sensible person could ever dream that it lay within the powers of the authority. Warrington LJ in *Short* v *Poole Corporation* gave the example of the red-haired teacher, dismissed because she had red hair. That is unreasonable in one sense. In another it is taking into account extraneous matters. It is so unreasonable that it might almost be described as being done in bad faith; and, in fact, all these things run into one another.

Therefore, the improper exercise of discretion can be crudely subdivided into a number of different categories: taking into account irrelevant considerations; failing to take into account relevant considerations; and acting so irrationally that the decision could only have been made in bad faith. Examples include taking into account the political party that an applicant supported when deciding an application for a waste disposal licence and failing to consider the special attention to be paid to the provisions of the development plan when considering a planning application.

(c) Procedural unfairness

Although, in theory, the review of decisions made with procedural impropriety falls within the unreasonableness ground above, it is distinct enough to form its own head of review. There are two elements making up procedural fairness. These are that every person has a right to a fair hearing and that there should be no bias (or perception of bias) in a decision-making process. The right to a fair hearing includes the right to meet any case put against an applicant and the right to present cogent and coherent evidence in support of a case. The prohibition against bias covers such situations as local authority planning committee members participating in decisions to grant planning applications on land which they own. In such circumstances it is impossible for the decision-maker to reach a fair decision.

When a decision is made in any of the above circumstances, an aggrieved person has the right to apply to the High Court for judicial review. Such a right should not be confused with any statutory right of appeal, which may give rise to a reconsideration of the merits of a case, rather than consideration of questions of law. Indeed, theoretically, a court exercising its power of judicial review is not entitled to substitute its own decision for that of the administrative body. This general right to challenge administrative decisions is supplemented in certain cases by specific statutory rights to challenge decisions. For example, s. 288 of the Town and Country Planning Act 1990 makes provisions for High Court challenges to decisions of the Secretary of State on points of law. Although there are procedural distinctions between the two types of challenge (in particular there are often much stricter time limits), the substantive issues remain broadly the same. It is important to note, however, that the statutory challenge is often an exclusive power which prevents any further challenge under general judicial review proceedings.

Remedies

The High Court has several remedies available to it to overturn a decision made unlawfully.

(a) Certiorari

An order of certiorari is used to quash an administrative decision made unlawfully. Thus, where a noise abatement order has not been made correctly because of procedural defects, the order itself would be declared null and void.

(b) Prohibition

Where there is a threat that a statutory power will be unlawfully exercised then a prohibition forbids a statutory body from exercising its power in the threatened way.

(c) Mandamus

An order for mandamus forces a statutory body to carry out its statutory duty. For example, where the Environment Agency is under a statutory duty to supervise sites governed by a waste management licence under the EPA 1990, such an order would force them to carry out this supervision properly. This is perhaps the remedy which is most obviously concerned with the control of environmental bodies. Many authorities are under a duty to carry out activities which have a consequential effect on environmental protection. A failure to carry out these duties may be due to the 'unreasonableness' of the body making the decision. Thus, the rights of people aggrieved by such a lack of activity are considerably enhanced.

(d) Declaration
When a declaration is sought the court seeks to give a statement as to the legal relations between the parties, but that is all it does and the declaration cannot be enforced. A declaration seeks no more than to state the legal position and does not seek to change the respective legal positions of the parties. Thus, a declaration is suitable for a situation where there are uncertainties over whether or not a certain set of facts falls within a category of law.

(e) Injunctions
Although an injunction is available as a remedy under the judicial review procedure, it is the least used remedy, primarily because there are procedural hurdles, such as the requirement to pay money into court as a financial guarantee.

Procedure

Although civil procedure has undergone a major change with the introduction of the Civil Procedure Rules 1998 (CPR), the general framework for judicial review procedure remains largely unaffected. The main principles of judicial review, such as the need to have standing, the need to commence proceedings without delay and the need to have an arguable case, remain (and are explained further below). The terminology has changed with applicants applying for permission to seek judicial review by way of claim form (as opposed to leave by way of notice of motion in pre-CPR days). In addition the making of an 'ex parte' application has been replaced by making an application without serving notice or evidence on any other party. Interestingly, the Latin terms for remedies in judicial review, namely certiorari and mandamus, have been maintained notwithstanding the general abandonment of Latin within the CPR. The other change of significance is that the overriding objective of the CPR (i.e. to enable the court to deal with cases justly) applies to judicial review proceedings. This overriding objective includes ensuring that all parties are on an equal footing and could mean that individual parties (e.g. objectors or litigants in person) are assisted by the court in obtaining disclosure of documents, or in other ways where the court considers that the public body which is the subject of the challenge is making matters difficult for the applicant.

The procedure for judicial review is contained within the Rules of the Supreme Court, Order 53 (now to be found in CPR, sch. 1). An application has to be made within three months from the date when the grounds of the application first arose, unless the court considers that there is good reason for extending the period (Ord. 53, r. 4). This time limit does not apply where there is any other statutory provision which has the effect of limiting the time within which an application for judicial review may be made (Ord. 53, r. 4(3)). In addition, the court may refuse to hear an application if there has been undue delay in bringing it, even if it is brought within the three months period (see, for example, *R v Swale Borough Council, ex parte Royal Society for the Protection of Birds* [1991] 1 PLR 6 and the discussion of delay, below)).

However, in order to bring a claim for judicial review, the applicant must show a 'sufficient interest' in the decision or power to which the application relates (Supreme Court Act 1981, s. 31(3)). There has been some suggestion that this interest has to be greater where the application is for the remedies of prohibition or certiorari, but it is generally accepted that the only test is to show a sufficient interest. The phrase 'sufficient interest' is of tremendous importance in matters of environmental protection. As will be shown in Chapter 10, the protection of private law rights is contained within the common law and thus anyone seeking to protect their own private interest in land may resort to the common law rather than going through the even more expensive procedure of judicial review. But it is clear that somebody with a private interest in land affected by an administrative decision would have 'sufficient interest' or standing. It is more difficult to show that a person has the necessary standing by virtue of an interest in the environment as a whole, as it is not generally accepted that there are 'environmental rights' available to the public at large.

Standing

The basis of the law on standing is contained in *Inland Revenue Commissioners v National Federation of Self Employed and Small Businesses Ltd* [1982] AC 617, where Lord Wilberforce said that the decision as to who had a 'sufficient interest' under the Supreme Court Act 1981, s. 31 had to be considered with the known merits of a case:

> It will be necessary to consider the powers or the duties of those against whom the relief is asked, the position of the applicant in relation to those powers or duties, and to the breach of those duties said to have been committed. In other words, the question of sufficient interest cannot, in such cases, be considered in the abstract, or as an isolated point: it must be taken together with the legal and factual context.

In the planning system many actions have been brought by local interest groups where sufficient interest can be demonstrated by objecting to proposals or giving evidence at a local inquiry and an analogy can be drawn in relation to groups bringing challenges in connection with local environmental issues (e.g. waste management licences, statutory nuisances, or local air pollution). The position of general environmental interest groups (e.g. Friends of the Earth or Greenpeace) is more problematic as there is no necessary geographic connection with the matter being challenged.

In *R v Inspectorate of Pollution, ex parte Greenpeace Ltd (No. 2)* [1994] 4 All ER 329, Greenpeace challenged the decision to allow the thermal oxide reprocessing plant at Sellafield (THORP) to commence operations. Pointing to Greenpeace's genuine interest in the issues raised and to its expertise and resources, Otton J decided that the group had sufficient interest, although he did note that it also had many members in the region who might be affected. In *R v Secretary of State for Foreign and Commonwealth Affairs, ex parte World Development Movement Ltd* [1995] 1 WLR 386 (the *Pergau Dam* case), the court, if anything, went even further in allowing a pure public interest claim to proceed, since there were clearly no local residents involved. In particular, it was emphasised that if the applicants were not granted standing then a clear illegality would not be subject to challenge.

Although general environmental interest groups have become increasingly accepted as having standing in judicial review actions, there is still a degree of uncertainty and there have been cases where the courts have required a special interest in the subject matter of the challenge (e.g. see *R v N. Somerset District Council, ex parte Garnett* [1998] Env LR 91). In *R v Somerset County Council, ex parte Dixon* [1998] Env LR 111, however, the decision in *Pergau Dam* was reaffirmed and the law on standing continued to be liberalised. In that case, the answer to the question of who had sufficient interest in the subject matter of the challenge was wide enough to include anyone who was not a busybody or a troublemaker. Public law challenges were concerned with the abuse of power, not the protection of private rights and therefore the classes of those who sought to draw attention to those abuses must include anyone who had a genuine interest in the subject matter of the challenge irrespective of any private law interest. There is a degree of contradiction in the case of *Garnett* and *Dixon*. The two cases were strikingly similar in their facts with very different results. Whilst these differences emphasise the discretionary nature of judicial review proceedings, they also illustrate that there is little precedent value in previous decisions.

This liberalisation of the law on standing reflects the recommendations of the Law Commission. In *Administrative Law: Judicial Review and Statutory Appeals* (Law Com. No. 226, 1994) it recommended that standing should be found where the application is in the 'public interest', unincorporated associations should be enabled to make applications in their own name, and costs should be awarded from central funds where there is a public interest challenge.

It should be noted that there is one exception to all of this. The Attorney-General, as guardian of the public interest, always has standing. An applicant without 'sufficient interest' could therefore ask the Attorney-General to bring an action on their behalf. This is called a 'relator' action. The shadow applicant pays the costs but manages to side-step the rules on standing. However, the Attorney-General has an unchallengeable discretion whether to bring an action in this manner.

Delay

The second procedural hurdle for any application for judicial review is that the application must be made 'promptly'. Under Order 53, r. 4(1) and the

Supreme Court Act 1981, s. 31(6), a court must refuse an application for permission or grant any relief where there has been a lack of promptness, unless there are good reasons for extending the time or it is unlikely that the persons affected by the grant of the relief would suffer hardship or prejudice.

There are three aspects to the issue of delay. The first relates to the time limit which is laid down for particular applications to be made. For example, challenges to planning decisions made by the Secretary of State must be brought within six weeks from the Secretary of State's decision (s. 288, Town and Country Planning Act 1990), whereas Order 53 applications must be brought within three months of the decision which is being challenged. Although these time limits are important, there is a degree of flexibility in the sense that applications which have not been made 'promptly' but fall within the time period can be dismissed (see *R v Swale BC, ex parte RSPB* [1991] 1 PLR 6 where an application for leave was made ten weeks after the decision but was dismissed for lack of 'promptness') and applications made outside the period can be permitted where there are good reasons to do so.

The second aspect of delay is the issue of when the time for challenge starts to run. Clearly, the decision-making process can have a number of stages from informal resolution to conditional and full permission. In addition, it may become clear, early on in the decision-making process, that an error of law has been made (e.g. taking into account an irrelevant consideration). Order 53, r. 4(2) makes it clear that time starts to run from the date on which grounds for the application first rose which is not necessarily the same as the date on which any final decision is made. If an application is made too early, there is a risk that it will be premature, too late and it will not have been made promptly. A good example of this dilemma can be found in *R v Secretary of State for Trade and Industry, ex parte Greenpeace Limited* [1998] Env LR 413, where Greenpeace sought to challenge the grant of licences to explore for North-Sea oil, on the ground that the decision-making process was contrary to the requirements of the Habitats Directive (some of the areas subject to the licences were the habitat of a protected species under the Directive). Greenpeace sought to challenge the decision to grant licences which was made in April 1997. The court dismissed the application on the basis that any application should have been made much earlier (i.e. before November 1995) when it was probable that licences would be granted in breach of the Directive.

In relation to planning cases, the *ex parte Dixon* and *ex parte Garnett* decisions referred to above illustrate that there can be differences of judicial opinion on the trigger date for the commencement of time for an application. In both cases, the question was whether time started to run at the date of the resolution to grant planning permission or actual formal grant of planning permission. As with the question of standing, Popplewell J (in *Garnett*) and Sedley J (in *Dixon*) came to mutually antagonistic conclusions. Popplewell J held that although planning permission had not been formally granted, there was an inevitability that it would be granted once a s.106 agreement had been completed. Sedley J on the other hand considered that it would have been premature to challenge the permission before the formal grant of planning permission. It is difficult to reconcile these two decisions other than to say that the issue of promptness is ultimately a question of discretion to be applied on the facts of each application and according to the nature of the specific grounds of challenge.

The third and arguably most important aspect of delay is the question of extending the time for bringing an application beyond the need for 'promptness'. Generally, the courts have taken a strict line over the question of delay in environmental cases. The speed or otherwise of an application would appear to depend largely upon whether an affected third party would have suffered prejudice. This might include such things as spending large sums of money after being granted permission or a licence to do something (see e.g. *R* v *Secretary of State for Trade and Industry, ex parte Greenpeace Limited* [1998] Env LR 413 and *Mass Energy Limited* v *Birmingham CC* [1994] Env LR 298), or doing other things in reliance on the grant of permission (e.g. commencing development). The extent of this prejudice can be minimised by the applicant putting the affected third party on notice of potential proceedings.

Generally, the issue of delay is considered within the context of the facts of the application and is essentially a question of discretion for the court. As is evidenced by the *Dixon* and *Garnett* decisions, judicial attitudes to delay can differ. At one end of the spectrum there is a strict view that time is of the essence and any delay in commencing the application (even if it is justified, e.g. trying to find specialist representation or raising funds to support a group action) could be fatal to the application. At the other end there is the view that the question of delay is to be viewed generally within the context of fairness and reasonableness.

Is delay the 'new standing'?

Is delay becoming 'the new standing' in the sense that it is a procedural mechanism upon which judges can rely when they want to reject an application? As the rules on standing have been liberalised, the courts have tended to view delay in a strict fashion. One example of this sort of approach can be see in *R* v *North West Leicestershire DC, ex parte Moses* (unreported, 12 April 2000). At first instance, the application for judicial review of a decision to grant planning permission for an extension to the runway at East Midlands airport was rejected on the ground that the named applicant had moved 8 miles away from the airport since making the application and therefore no longer had standing to bring the action. On appeal the Court of Appeal did not bother to consider the question of standing (primarily because it would have been possible to substitute another local applicant), preferring instead to concentrate on the question of delay in bringing the proceedings and the prejudice it would cause.

The attraction of delay over standing as a ground for rejecting applications could have many explanations, but the most obvious would be that, unlike standing which has acquired a degree of structured principles and where there is an obvious trend towards extending the classes of those who would have a 'sufficient interest', delay still allows the courts a wide discretion to determine applications in accordance with general principles such as fairness, good administration and prejudice. The width of this discretion can, however, be used to override any unfairness, where it is in the public interest to do so (e.g. where there have been clear and serious breaches of European legislation). In *R v Secretary of State for Trade and Industry, ex parte Greenpeace (No. 2)* [2000] Env LR 221, in which Greenpeace brought a second challenge to the grant of oil exploration licences, Maurice Kay J. considered that the application for judicial review had not been made 'promptly' (thus mirroring the first challenge discussed above). He went on, however, to find that the implementation of the Habitats Directive had been incomplete within UK law (in particular in relation to offshore habitats) and that the failure to implement the Directive was more important than any prejudice which would have been caused by the delay in making the application.

When all of these principles are aggregated we can identify a matrix of considerations which can be taken into account in determining the issue of delay. First, there is the actual amount of time which has expired since the decision. Secondly, there is the financial or other administrative implications of quashing the decision. Finally, there is the nature of the illegality which is the subject of the challenge. These factors interact in different ways which are dependent upon the facts of each case. For example, the prejudice which is caused by a long delay in making a challenge might be outweighed by the serious nature of the breach — such as the failure to transpose a Directive in *Greenpeace (No. 2)*.

Judicial review and other avenues of challenge

Although judicial review remains as one way of challenging a decision which has been made unlawfully, there are, in some cases, alternative remedies for aggrieved parties by way of a statutory right to administrative appeal. For example, where the EA serves a revocation notice under Part I of the EPA 1990 (covering IPC authorisations) which could be said to be irrational or oppressive, the recipient of the notice could arguably challenge the decision to serve the notice in one of three ways. First, they could appeal to the Secretary of State under powers found in s. 15, EPA 1990 and relevant regulations, secondly they could apply for permission to seek judicial review or thirdly, they could fail to comply with the revocation notice and in any subsequent prosecution for that failure, challenge the validity of the notice.

When considering the appropriate avenue of challenge, the courts have established two tests. First, would the statutory appeal process afford an adequate alternative remedy? If so, any application for permission to seek a judicial review would be refused. The adequacy of the statutory right of appeal as an alternative remedy is dependent upon a number of variables, including comparative speed, expense and finality of the alternative procedure; the need and scope for fact finding; the desirability of an authoritative ruling on any point of law arising; and the apparent strength of the applicant's challenge (see *R v Falmouth & Truro Port Health Authority, ex parte South West Water Limited* [2000] NPC 36 and see also *R v Environment Agency, ex parte*

Petrus Oils Ltd [1999] Env LR 732, where the court found that there was an adequate alternative remedy available to challenge the service of a revocation notice under Part I of the EPA 1990).

In the third situation, where a collateral challenge is brought (i.e. as an incidental challenge to the main proceedings) the courts have dismissed such challenges as being an abuse of process where the decision which is being challenged was made many years before and the period for statutory challenge had passed (see *R* v *Ettrick Trout Company Limited* [1994] Env LR 165).

The usefulness of judicial review

How useful is judicial review as a mechanism for controlling the activities and decision-making of environmental bodies? There are the various procedural hurdles which must be overcome before an application for permission to bring a judicial review action will be granted, such as having standing, bringing any application 'promptly' and ensuring that there are no alternative adequate remedies available. The main problem here is not with the hurdles themselves but that the determination of whether an applicant succeeds in 'jumping the hurdles' is largely discretionary and rests with the particular judge hearing the case. Although the basic principles of standing and delay are laid down, the manner in which these principles are applied within the factual context of an individual application can vary depending upon the way in which a judge views the purposes of the procedural hurdles. As we have seen in the *Dixon* and *Garnett* cases, two different judges can approach similar issues in entirely different ways. This discretion naturally leads to a degree of uncertainty as to whether an applicant might succeed, which in turn reduces the likelihood that an action will be taken.

In addition to these procedural hurdles, there is the difficult question of funding the cost of a judicial review action. As most environmental actions tend to be brought on a representative basis (either from local groups or interested parties), there is little direct financial interest in the outcome of an application (although there is a notable exception in the planning arena where commercial developers feature largely). The costs of going to litigation can be high particularly when considering that legal aid is seldom available in judicial review cases (see *R* v *Legal Aid Area No. 8 (Northern), ex parte Sendall* [1993] Env LR 167, although there are notable exceptions including cases where children have been selected as applicants in particular cases, see e.g. *R* v *Secretary of State for Trade and Industry, ex parte Duddridge* [1995] Env LR 151).

An extra pressure upon applicants is the fact that costs in judicial review proceedings normally follow the event, meaning that where an applicant loses (either at the full hearing or at the stage of seeking permission) they are normally obliged to pay the costs of the other side (again there are notable exceptions to this rule, in particular see *R* v *Secretary of State for the Environment, ex parte Greenpeace Limited* [1994] Env LR 401 where there was no award of costs against the applicant as the application was considered to be brought 'in the public interest').

Although the procedural issues and the costs of taking action represent significant factors in deciding whether to pursue a judicial review action, there are other substantive restrictions on the usefulness of judicial review. First, when an application for judicial review is heard, there is no consideration of the merits of a case. Thus, when a decision is quashed or a duty is enforced, it does not necessarily mean that the final decision of the administrative body will be to the liking of the person seeking judicial review. A good example of this is in the case of the judicial review of planning decisions. If an inspector, on appeal, makes a decision which is contrary to the Inquiries Procedure Rules (for instance by not taking into account written representations from objectors), the resulting decision may be challenged. The inspector's decision in those circumstances could be overturned by the High Court, but the final decision would be referred back to a fresh inspector, who could very well arrive at the same decision as the first inspector, even though taking into account the representations made.

Furthermore, where individuals with 'sufficient interest' apply for judicial review of a decision they have to be able to show that they have suffered prejudice. Therefore, although the court is not entitled to make a judgment on the merits of the individual case, it may be that the substance of the point raised by the interested party shows an unlawful act, but, on the facts of the individual case, the applicant did not suffer any prejudice from the decision itself. Thus, where an interested party was not entitled to put its views across at a planning inquiry, there may well be a breach of the right to a fair hearing. However, where it could be shown that other people had put over a similar case, a judicial review remedy may be refused.

The Ombudsman

There may be instances where, although there is no abuse of the statutory power which would render a decision reviewable, there is some maladministration which could give rise to a public complaint. In such cases a complaint can be made to the Ombudsman in control of those activities. In the case of central government activities (e.g. the DETR) the investigating Ombudsman is the Parliamentary Commissioner for Administration, whereas in the case of complaints against a local authority (e.g. in relation to planning, waste collection or air pollution matters), the matter is dealt with by the Commissioner for Local Administration. The governing factor in such complaints is whether or not the authority concerned has acted within appropriate standards of administrative conduct, rather than whether or not it has acted lawfully.

Complaints to the Ombudsman normally go through either a local councillor or an MP (depending upon the level of authority concerned), although they need not do so in all cases. The nature of the Ombudsman remedy is both singular and advisory. Therefore, an aggrieved party who has other rights of action, whether under the common law or by means of judicial review, must pursue that particular avenue, as long as it is realistic to do so. Secondly, an Ombudsman has no statutory power to impose an award of damages, or to alter the legal position (e.g. by quashing a decision). Normally, the Ombudsman will make a recommendation for compensation which, although having no statutory backing, is accepted by the statutory body concerned in over 95% of cases. The role of the Ombudsman should not be underestimated. The incidence of complaints to the Ombudsman has risen in recent years because it is a quick, cheap, and often effective mechanism for channelling complaints about public authorities. It is a mechanism which the public are happy to utilise because of its informal nature and simple procedure. It is perhaps worthwhile to point out that the stages of a complaint are relatively straightforward and provide an adequate opportunity for the proper presentation of grievances. It is also important that the Ombudsman has significant investigatory powers: these will have an impact on the practices of the public bodies over which jurisdiction is exercised.

Other complaints mechanisms

In the case of the privatised utilities, the regulators (e.g. Ofwat) act as a controlling influence through various means such as the amendment of undertakers' licences and more informal mechanisms (such as threats of action in the case of continuous underperformance). The effectiveness of the Ombudsman in dealing with maladministration in central and local government and the alternative avenues of redress in relation to the utilities can be contrasted with the gaping accountability hole in relation to other important bodies with environmental responsibilities such as the Environment Agency, English Nature and the Regional Development Agencies. In cases of public bodies such as these, incompetence, unfairness or otherwise unsatisfactory performance can only be dealt with by way of internal complaints procedures.

FOUR
International law and environmental protection

There are some unique features about international law which make it, and thus international environmental law, rather different from the other areas of law at which this book looks. Perhaps the most important of these is the absence of a single international body with the power to make and enforce law effectively. The absence of such a body, and of coercive powers to compel states, companies and individuals to act in ways they would not otherwise choose to, has often resulted in international 'law' being regarded as something rather closer to international policy. This view is receding, although the essential feature of international law as something that states may agree to or not both pervades the subject and poses a challenge for the effective regulation of environmental affairs at the international level. Nevertheless, this essential feature of international law arguably means that the gap between law and policy is not so great here as in national or EC law.

Another key feature of international law worth noting here is that it does not have a direct impact on domestic law or on individuals. Treaties need to be given effect to through national legislation, and are concerned with the action of states, not individuals within states. In this sense, international law differs greatly from national law and, to the extent that it confers individual rights, EC law.

This chapter describes the development of international environmental law, which has expanded significantly in scope and quantity since the late 1960s. The focus is on international treaties relating to environmental protection. However, 'customary' international law, i.e. that part of international law which applies even without a treaty, on the assumption that states have implicitly agreed to it, is also of some importance. If generally agreed principles of international law are to emerge, this is likely to be through customary law.

In general, this chapter is restricted to discussing public rather than private international law, that is, the law between states rather than the conflict of legal systems. The latter is, of course, relevant in environmental law, for example questions concerning the appropriate forum in which to hear pollution-related claims against transnational corporations. Such cases raise the issue of whether different standards can be employed by such companies working in developing countries (which covers similar ground to wider questions about international environmental law and sustainable development), but are not directly addressed here.

Why is international law important for environmental protection?

In summary, international law is important for environmental protection, and for the issues covered in the rest of this book, in the following central ways:

(a)   Transboundary and global problems require international (or at the very least, bilateral) solutions, and international legal regulation of some kind will be either necessary or desirable.

(b)   International agreements may generate standards which are adopted in national law, or by regional groupings like the European Community.

(c)   The international arena is of some importance for the development of principles of environmental law, such as sustainable development or the precautionary principle (see further Chapter 2). Indeed, such principles often develop precisely because of their often non-binding origins.

(d)   Because of its nature, recent developments in international law have focused on how an attention to procedures, and on positive inducements to comply rather than negative 'command and control' style enforcement mechanisms, can be used to secure compliance. Although borne of necessity, there is again much for national and EC law to learn from this experience.

(e)   Perhaps negatively, the development of environmental law at all levels may be subject to restrictions originating in international law, for example import restrictions which are deemed to be incompatible with the rules regulating international trade.

International law and the UK

The relationship between international law and the UK has two dimensions. First, the extent to which international law affects rights and duties and policy-making at national level. Secondly, the contribution of the UK to developments in international environmental law and policy.

In the UK, international agreements only become part of national law once they are given effect to by Parliament, usually through legislation. Moreover, both the making of treaties (*Blackburn* v *Attorney-General* [1971] 1 WLR 1037) and their implementation (*ex parte Molyneaux* [1986] 1 WLR 331) are seen by the courts as a matter solely for government: 'Treaties . . . are not self-executing. Quite simply, a treaty is not part of English law unless and until it has been incorporated into the law by legislation' (*Maclaine Watson* v *Department of Trade and Industry* [1989] 3 All ER 523 per Lord Oliver at 545). This is the case even where the treaty has been ratified, because in the UK ratification is a matter for central government, not Parliament. Following devolution, the power to ratify treaties remains with the UK government, being a matter of foreign affairs. All of this means that international agreements, in general, have what might be called 'high-level' rather than 'low-level' effect: they create obligations that bind the UK in its international relations, rather than obligations of the kind on which individuals can rely. In the UK, international agreements cannot be used as the basis for an action by groups or individuals against the state or a public body (in the way that EC directives may be), nor are they in themselves a source of rights and duties in legal actions between individuals.

Courts will, however, prefer interpretations of statutes which conform with international treaties to which the UK is a party to those which do not, although this does not necessarily mean that in all cases of discretion, there is a presumption in favour of the convention (*R* v *Secretary of State for the Home Department, ex parte Brind* [1991] 1 AC 696). But where national legislation is introduced to give effect to a treaty or treaty obligation, then the treaty *can* be used as an aide to interpreting the national law and it is presumed that Parliament did not intend to legislate contrary to the UK's international commitments. In some cases, the relationship between the treaty and implementing legislation will be spelt out more precisely. For example, the Human Rights Act 1998, which 'incorporates' the European Convention on Human Rights, makes it clear that the English courts must take account of previous decisions of the European Court of Human Rights when interpreting the Act. This is important because of the limited steps that the European Court of Human Rights has already taken to interpret the Convention in a creative way to give incidental protection to the environment. Rights under the Convention may also challenge some of the traditional common law rules on environmental protection. This is seen in the recent decision of the European Court of Human Rights in *Osman* v *UK* (1999) 5 BHRC 293, which challenges the approach of the UK courts to limiting the liability of public bodies in negligence (see *Barret* v *London Borough of Enfield* [1999] 3 WLR 79; on negligence, see Chapter 10). This approach might be used to argue that there is no effective remedy for some householders in private law in relation to amenity losses in private nuisance.

Developments in international law are often reflected in policy developments at national level. *Sustainable Development: The UK Strategy* (Cm 2426, 1994) was a response to Agenda 21, the soft law document agreed at the 1992 UN Conference on Environment and Development (the 'Rio Earth Summit'), and national policy in many areas reflects commitments made at Rio. These agreements, however, tend to contain general principles which give a considerable degree of latitude to governments in their implementation. The UK government has arguably used this latitude to translate soft international law into soft policy commitments, for example in relation to improving access to environmental justice. Where policy does have a sharper edge, as with town and country planning policy, there is some evidence of emerging policies based on sustainability thinking, although so far these have been limited to discrete areas like minerals planning or out of town shopping centres. General guidance on the aims of the planning system, although now containing some central government policies on planning and sustainability, does not yet reflect a wholesale shift of attitude in this area.

As far as the role of the UK in developing international law is concerned, the record has tended to be patchy at best (see Churchill, 'International Environmental Law and the UK' in Churchill, Warren and Gibson (eds) *Law, Policy and the Environment* (Blackwell, 1991)) and it is difficult to identify key environmental treaties where the UK has taken a lead in the negotiations. However, very often it is now the EC as a bloc which negotiates, which makes it difficult to assess the particular stance taken by the UK, although its role often appears to be negative, attempting to weaken the wording of commitments. Where the UK has shown most leadership has tended to be in relation to treaties like the 1946 Whaling Convention, an area where the UK no longer has any economic interests. In recent years, however, the attitude of the UK towards the making of international environmental agreements appears to have softened somewhat, although there is often a certain dragging of heels when it comes to the details, such as with radioactive discharges at sea.

International law and the EC

In some cases, treaties may be open to signature by 'regional economic integration organisations', a term covering the EC, which has signed all the most recent multilateral environmental agreements. The basic procedure is that the Commission does the negotiating, but the Council signs any treaty: a unanimous vote in the Council may be needed if the treaty deals with issues which require unanimity within the EC (such as town and country planning).

This should not hide the often hotly contested division of competence between the EC and the Member States as regards external matters. International trade and marine fisheries conservation are areas of exclusive Community competence, which means that it is the Community which negotiates any agreements in these areas (such as the GATT/WTO Agreement). Beyond these fields there is a considerable amount of scope for disagreement about the proper balance of competence in the environmental field. At a time when there are pulls both towards globalisation and devolution, we might any way question what 'exclusive competence', either for the EC or for the Member States, actually means.

Where both the EC and the Member States are parties to a treaty, there needs to be some way of coordinating their obligations. A unique example of how this is done is under the 1997 Kyoto Climate Change Protocol. Both the UK and the EC are parties to this, which requires specified reductions of emissions. Under art. 4 of the Protocol, the Member States can 'bubble' their reductions, so that the EC decides which states take heavier and lighter loads depending on things like their state of economic development.

Although EC environmental law is said to flow from developments in international law, specifically the Stockholm Conference (see p. 95), the unique nature of the EC has in some respects made it a testing ground for international environmental cooperation. For example, the balancing of trade and environmental concerns in the EC is often held up as a model for integration. Also, the insertion of environmental policy principles in the EC Treaty (now contained in Art. 174(2)) means that their legal status can be explored within the EC, but also contributes to the development of similar principles in international environmental law. In this way there is a clear synergy between EC and international law and policy.

Nation states and global commons

Because international law is the law of nation states, different considerations apply depending on whether we are concerned with activities:

    (a)   taking place within a state and affecting only the environment of that state (such as most contamination of land);

    (b)   having an impact as between states, neighbouring or otherwise (e.g. transboundary air pollution, or pollution of an international river by an upstream state); or

    (c)   which affect the 'global commons' (that is, all natural resources beyond the territory of any individual state).

The global commons includes things like the atmosphere and the ozone layer. It also includes the oceans and deep seabed beyond the 200 nautical mile limit of states' 'exclusive economic zones' (although this does not apply to a state's continental shelf if it goes beyond this limit) and space.

Antarctica, often mentioned in the context of the global commons, is a special case. Some states consider it to be *terra nullius* (land belonging to no one, but capable of appropriation), and a number of territorial claims to it have been made. Others, like the US and the former Soviet Union, have reserved the right to make such claims, while for other states (perhaps unsurprisingly, those without interests there) the continent is the common heritage of humankind. The Antarctic treaty regime displays elements of a global commons system, e.g. putting the various territorial claims into abeyance, an international management regime and benefits sharing. But it very clearly privileges the position of those states first involved in the area, and clearly does not regard the continent as part of the 'common heritage of humankind'. This concept developed, from the 1960s onwards, alongside demands for a new international economic order, and focused on the equitable sharing of benefits arising from the use of resources such as the Moon, the Antarctic and the deep seabed. Perhaps inevitably, such calls have largely gone unheard, and equity considerations are, regrettably, confined largely to such matters as the 'fair' sharing of the costs of clean technology.

The global commons should not be confused with resources that might be said to form a global 'common heritage'. The vast majority of known species, for example, live within or between national borders, which helps explain why the 1992 Biodiversity Convention refers only to the conservation of biodiversity (by definition, a global resource) as a matter of 'common concern' and makes explicit reference to principles of national sovereignty over natural resources.

Finally, the idea of nations owing obligations to all members of the international community (obligations said to be owed *'erga omnes'*) is especially relevant to international environmental law. In the first *Nuclear Tests* cases (*Australia* v *France* ICJ Rep (1974) 253; *New Zealand* v *France* ICJ Rep (1974), 457), Australia and New Zealand tried to stop French atmospheric nuclear testing in the South Pacific. An unsuccessful attempt was made in the International Court of Justice to argue that they could bring the claim because France owed a general obligation to all states to be free from nuclear tests generally or that France was in violation of the freedom of the high seas. Nevertheless, there were judges in the minority prepared to accept that the right to bring an action of behalf of the international community (an *'actio popularis'*) might exist, and who linked the right to bring such an action with the substantive nature of such *'erga omnes'* obligations.

Although a matter of considerable dispute, there are those who would argue for the right of a state to bring such an action in relation not just to the global commons, but also to matters of common concern. But as the example of international trade law shows (see p. 105), the difficulty is for states to avoid unilaterally imposing national standards beyond their borders, and to try to identify appropriate rules of international law that might apply. In treaty law, however, there are now examples of any state being able to enforce a treaty obligation without having to show it has suffered material damage from the alleged failure. The non-compliance and dispute-settlement mechanisms under the 1987 Montreal Protocol on Ozone Depletion, discussed below, are an example.

A tragedy of the commons?

A frequent justification for environmental regulation is to prevent damage to areas that are beyond effective individual control (the idea of environmental 'externalities' is discussed in more depth on p. 202). This is a particular problem in international law, especially for the 'global commons'. Of course, there are some examples from international relations where it is always in all countries interests to cooperate: e.g. it makes no sense for one state to 'go it alone' when it comes to running international postal services. However, in environmental regulation there may be one-off situations where individual states have an incentive not to cooperate, even though mutual cooperation would ultimately benefit the state concerned (the so-called 'prisoner's dilemma'). This can be seen, for example, in the difficulties in reaching effective agreement about climate change, or over-fishing.

A variant of this argument is Hardin's infamous 'Tragedy of the Commons' thesis ((1968) 162 *Science* 1243). Hardin's main argument is that common or open access resources will always be prone to over-exploitation. His preferred solution is to 'privatise' common resources wherever possible. Failing this, 'mutual coercion, mutually agreed upon' is required. The former solution can be seen in, for example, the 1982 Law of the Sea Convention which extended the exclusive economic zone (EEZ) to 200 nautical miles, effectively 'privatising' as much as 90% of the known living resources of the seas.

As the failure to stem the decline in world fisheries demonstrates, however, such moves may not be enough in themselves to counter unsustainable resource use and, at a national level, the thesis is subject to various theoretical and empirical criticisms, principally that individuals and groups do not always (or necessarily) act in possessively individualistic ways. Whether states always act as rational individual actors at the international level is also subject to debate, but various factors appear to influence the extent to which states come together to reach international agreements (discussed in more detail at p. 103). Hardin's thesis does, however, point to a role for law and legal institutions in providing the necessary framework for states to have confidence that all parties are honouring the agreements into which they enter.

The global commons is only one area requiring international environmental regulation. Resources shared between states may also be subject to 'commons'-type problems, as evidenced by the use of the North Sea as little more than an international dumping ground for its riparian states, not least the UK. Shared resources, however, also include things like migratory species, some of which were subject to very early international 'conservation' law (for example, the 1902 Convention for the Protection of Birds Useful to Agriculture) and which now receive a measure of protection for less directly economic reasons (1979 Bonn Convention on the Conservation of Migratory Species of Wild Animals). Finally, activities in one state may impact negatively on another state, for example through transboundary pollution (see the *Trail Smelter* case, discussed at p. 95 below. (For a fuller discussion see Stone, *The Gnat is Older than Man*, Princeton UP, 1993, chs 2-4.)

What is becoming discernible, however, is the way that the linkages between globalisation and continued economic development, and the natural environment on which that development depends, are becoming better understood. Notably, the emergence of global (as opposed to international or transboundary) issues requiring regulation is perhaps the most important development of recent years. These include global issues such as those which affect everyone and which require common solutions (global warming, ozone layer protection etc.). But they also include the range of concerns about the linkage between the global economy and environmental degradation that lie at the heart of theories of sustainable development (see p. 39). These include both the 'environmental shadow' cast by developed economies on less developed regions, and the relationship between poverty and environmental damage.

Sources of international law: 'hard law'

The sources of international law are generally divided into 'hard' and 'soft' law'. 'Hard law', which takes the various forms listed below (and is recognised by Art. 38 of the ICJ Statute), is binding in the sense that any legal rule or principle binds a state only in its relations with *other states*. It is not necessarily of any relevance in deciding legal disputes between individuals and the state, such as a judicial review action, or as between individuals such as in nuisance law. By way of example, the 1992 Convention for the

Protection of the Marine Environment of the North East Atlantic (the 'OSPAR' Convention) requires states to take 'all possible steps to prevent and eliminate pollution' and, in doing so, to apply the polluter pays principle. These provisions matter, if at all, only as between the parties to the Convention. They do not create general obligations of the kind that individuals can rely on. Nor can they be used as the basis for an action against the state or a public body, in the way that EC directives can sometimes be.

The same can be said of any rules of customary international environmental law. If it were decided that the UK was bound by the precautionary principle as customary law, this would not directly assist an individual in bringing a legal argument based on precaution, although it might add weight generally to precautionary arguments.

(a) Treaties (or 'conventions' or 'agreements')

These are in many ways the pre-eminent form of international law. The basic rules are laid down in the Vienna Convention on the Law of Treaties 1969. The fundamental principle is that states may only be bound with their consent, which is only fully given once the convention has been ratified. The various terms, 'treaties', 'conventions' and 'agreements' all mean the same thing. A 'Protocol' also has the same legal force, although it is a sub-agreement to a treaty, generally used to flesh out or amend the treaty (e.g. the 1997 Kyoto Protocol contains the carbon emissions reductions that states committed themselves to agreeing to in the 1992 Framework Convention on Climate Change).

Treaties generally come into force a specified number of days after a certain number of states have ratified, although the 1992 Climate Change Convention and 1997 Kyoto Protocol, to give two environmental examples, specify a formula designed to ensure that a core of carbon-emitting developed world states must have ratified. There are several factors which determine how quickly a treaty comes into force, most importantly the strictness and clarity of the obligations under it. Thus, the 1992 Convention on Biological Diversity entered into force within 18 months, in part because of the generality of its provisions. On the other hand, the 1982 United Nations Law of the Sea Convention took 12 years to come into force, largely because details about mining the resources of the deep sea bed were not satisfactorily agreed until the end of this period.

Ratification usually requires the approval of the legislature. This can delay treaties from coming into force, or from binding key states: the lobbying of the genetic and pharmaceutical industries has meant that the US has yet to ratify the Convention on Biological Diversity. But it does mean that treaties will only bind a state once the body responsible for enacting legislation to make the treaty work gives its approval. This is an important consideration in practice where (as in the US) the executive and legislature may be controlled by different groupings. But it may also be relevant where a convention is agreed by a government which then loses power in an election.

Of course, the success of a treaty will usually depend on whether key states are parties and have ratified: the success of the 1979 Moon Treaty in safeguarding environmental resources is unlikely given that the USA is not a party. There are some treaties, however, which may extend in practice to non-parties (see discussion of CITES below at p. 105).

(b) Custom

Customary international law is created by implicit rather than explicit agreement, and needs both the practice of states and their conviction that what is done is done not because of usage but because of some felt legal obligation. There are problems in ascertaining exactly what a state does, and problems of identifying customs in the wider global community. However, custom does offer the potential for flexibility by its uncertainty, and scope for creative argument to develop principles of customary international environmental law.

In this sense, flexibility here offers possibilities for the development of principles in a way that vagueness elsewhere cannot, e.g. in more developed areas of law and policy.

Many commentators, for example, assert that a number of the central principles of environmental law (including the precautionary and preventive principles and the polluter pays principle) are now established international customary law, at least for those states that are a party to a sufficient number of the many texts that now make reference to them. On the other hand, the precise scope and content of, for example, the precautionary principles laid down in various treaties and 'soft law' documents is rarely ever duplicated, which leads to the problem of identifying what it is *exactly* that states can be said to have implicitly agreed to.

(c) Generally recognised principles of law

These are of limited scope, and used where no treaty provision or custom can be utilised. They are mostly used to identify basic principles of procedure on which to decide particular issues, e.g. evidence that is admissible. They should not be confused with the 'principles' of international environmental law which are contained either in treaties or which may be distilled from treaties, or principles inferable from customary international law (see below).

(d) Judicial decisions and the work of international jurists

Judicial decisions include not just decisions of the International Court of Justice (ICJ) but also those of regional bodies (e.g. the European Court of Justice) and national courts. Previous decisions of the ICJ are binding only between the parties, and only as to the case under consideration (Article 59, ICJ Statute), hence their subsidiary nature. They do not create precedents, although in practice they function in a not too dissimilar way. The dearth of previous case law may help explain why academic writing is often referred to in international law, although this also reflects a closer relationship between legal academics and the ICJ. The work of jurists is often used to support dissenting opinions where relatively new ground is being covered. A good example of this is the *Nuclear Tests II* case (*New Zealand* v *France* [1995] ICJ Rep 288) where academic opinion about the requirements of the sustainable development principle was referred to in the dissenting opinion of Judge Weeramantry.

Sources of international law: 'soft law'

'Soft law' is not binding in form, is often neither clear nor specific in content, and is not readily enforceable in character. Examples include:

(a) Declarations

Two key documents in international environmental law are the 1992 Rio Declaration on Environment and Development and its Stockholm predecessor of 1972 (see p. 95). Such declarations perform a number of functions: they consolidate and restate what are already rules of customary international law (e.g. national sovereignty over natural resources); they contribute towards moving principles forward to the status of custom; and they reflect the agreed aspirations of the international community. The four Declarations of the North Sea Conferences, which fall into this category, have had a marked impact on EC and UK policy on, for example, the dumping of industrial waste and sewage sludge at sea.

(b) Principles

In addition to hard, binding obligations (however vaguely expressed), treaties may also contain what are essentially principles. Examples include Article 3 of the 1992 Framework Convention on Climate Change, which sets out a list of principles intended to guide the parties in implementing the treaty. These include principles relating to duties owed to future generations, and to the 'common but differentiated responsibilities and respective capabilities' of the parties (see further p. 104). The elaboration of specific principles in the treaty itself, as opposed to the preamble, is increasingly common.

(c) Recommendations

Towards the 'softer' end of the spectrum, recommendations may embody the germs of principles or even treaties. Good examples are the many Recommendations of the OECD which relate directly to the development of environmental policy, e.g. on the Polluter Pays Principle (1974) and on the Use of Economic Instruments in Environmental Policy (1991) (for a more complete list see Sands, *Principles of International Environmental Law*, Manchester UP, 1995, pp. 87-8).

(d) Standards

International standards can be a useful way to encourage environmentally beneficial changes in behaviour. In practice, drinking water quality standards in the EC have been much influenced by World Health Organisation standards, while the 1995 FAO Code of Conduct on Responsible Fishing, for example, contains non-binding provisions intended to prevent the by-catch of non-target species such as marine mammals. There are also some international standards, however, which may be accorded the status of binding law.

The EC Regulation on Environmental Management and Auditing Systems, for example, allows for participation through compliance with specified national, European and international standards, such as ISO14001 (see p. 210). Perhaps most importantly, some non-legislative international standards provide the benchmark against which international trade restrictions may be justified, for example the *Codex Alimentarius* in relation to certain food standards under the WTO agreements.

The key feature of soft law, seen most clearly in relation to principles, is that it contains general norms rather than specific rules: it provides a guide to how disputes might be resolved rather than hard-and-fast rules applying to specific situations. Whether the principle extends beyond the treaty, for example by suggesting a wider commitment to it sufficient to establish a principle of customary international law, will depend on the exact wording and context. An example is Article 3 of the 1992 Biodiversity Convention, which provides that Principle 21 of the Stockholm Declaration (see p. 96) concerning certain limitations to national sovereignty over natural resources is the sole principle of the treaty. However, the UK government attached a Declaration stating that it understood that it 'sets out a guiding principle to be taken into account in the implementation of the Convention', a clear attempt to limit the principle to the treaty itself, and then in a non-binding fashion.

The adoption of soft law over binding, treaty law has several potential advantages: domestic treaty ratification processes can be avoided; it provides an autonomous form of law-making for international organisations; it is more easily amended or replaced than treaties; it provides immediate evidence of consensus; and it is easier to reach agreement on its content *because* of its non-binding character. Soft law instruments may codify existing law; interpret/amplify treaties and other existing legal rules; act as a step in the process of concluding binding agreements; and serve as evidence of the obligations states feel they are under. They are an important part of the repetition and interplay with multilateral treaties and state practice. Too soft, however, and they may be virtually meaningless. Arguably the 1992 Non-Binding Authoritative Statement of Principles on Forests (see p. 97) serves only to highlight the absence of any measure of consensus in this area at the time.

International law and policy development

The development of international environmental law can be traced back at least to the nineteenth century and the adoption of a number of bilateral treaties concerning fishing stocks. Thereafter, other bilateral and regional treaties were adopted, but tended to cover things like species conservation. Although some bilateral treaties sought to regulate transboundary pollution, on the whole developments in treaty law were, as Sands notes, 'ad hoc, sporadic and limited in scope' (*Principles of International Environmental Law*, 1995, p. 26). Enforcement issues, in particular, received scant attention, and many conventions were little more than 'sleeping treaties', existing only on paper because of the absence of any effective institutional and enforcement arrangements (see further p. 103). There was little development of customary international environmental law.

The approach of international law generally to environmental problems is well illustrated by two international arbitrations. In the *Behring Fur Seals Arbitration* (1898) 1 Moore's Int. Arbitration Awards 755, the dispute was between the US and Great Britain over alleged over-exploitation of fur seals in areas beyond the (then) three nautical mile limit of US territorial waters. The panel found that the US had no right of 'protection or property' in the seals, despite the importance of their conservation for local US citizens and their migration between the high seas and US territory. The argument that the US was acting 'for the benefit of mankind', i.e. an '*erga omnes*' or perhaps even 'common heritage' argument, was also rejected. However, the outcome of the dispute was a series of provisions, binding on the two parties, to regulate seal fishing in the area, displaying many of the features of modern conservation treaties: closed seasons, limited means of killing or taking etc. But the decision did not bind the other states sealing in the area, who continued unrestricted until a treaty binding all relevant states was agreed in 1911.

The second decision of note was in the *Trail Smelter* arbitration between the US and Canada (3 *RIAA* 1907 (1941)) over sulphur emissions from a factory in Canada which damaged crops, trees and pastures in the US State of Washington. The issue was not the right to exploit natural resources on Canadian territory, but rather whether the manner of doing so was limited because of neighbouring states' interests. The tribunal held that:

> No state has the right to use or permit the use of its territory in such a manner as to cause injury by fumes in or to the territory of another of the properties or persons therein, when the case is of serious consequence and the injury is established by clear and convincing evidence.

From these beginnings an extensive body of international treaty law has emerged, together with the more tentative emergence of new norms of customary international environmental law. Three key landmarks, however, deserve special mention.

The Stockholm Conference

The United Nations Conference on the Human Environment (Stockholm, 1972) was the first occasion at which the international community of states united to discuss international environmental issues more generally and more coherently. Although no treaty was signed, the conference adopted an Action Plan of 109 Recommendations and a Declaration of 26 Principles. It also adopted a resolution on institutional and financial arrangements that led, amongst other things, to the establishment of the United Nations Environment Programme (UNEP).

For some, the Stockholm Declaration is the foundation of modern international environmental law. Its principles, however, are largely aspirational rather than mandatory — 'should' rather than 'shall' — and few impose clear duties on states. Nevertheless, the Declaration does include principles relating to the following:

(a) the sovereign right [of States] to exploit their own resources pursuant to their own environmental policies, and the responsibility to ensure that activities within their jurisdiction or control do not cause damage to the environment of other States or of areas beyond the limits of national jurisdiction (Principle 21);

(b) a duty on states to cooperate in the further development of international law regarding liability and compensation for environmental damage caused by activities within national jurisdiction to areas beyond their jurisdiction (Principle 22);

(c) a requirement (though not a duty) for international co-operation to 'effectively control, prevent, reduce and eliminate adverse environmental effects resulting from activities conducted in all spheres, in such a way that due account is taken of the sovereignty and interests of all States' (Principle 24).

Perhaps more importantly, the Stockholm Conference marked the beginning of a rapid increase in the number of international environmental agreements concluded. It has been said that the development of EC environmental law is the Conference's most tangible outcome.

The Brundtland Report

Although a strictly non-legal text, the report of the World Commission on Environment and Development (*Our Common Future*, 1987: the 'Brundtland Report') was pivotal in changing the direction of international environmental law. Its central concern was the increasing globalisation of various crises (environmental, developmental, energy, etc.), and the connections between them. As it memorably summarised this: 'They are all one'. The report is a landmark in respect of modern thinking about environmental problems, and gives prominence to the language of sustainable development, defined as 'development that meets the needs of the present without compromising the ability of future generations to meet their own needs' (see further Chapter 2). However, the report provided little solid guidance on the exact components of what such a duty to future generations might entail.

What was perhaps most important was the attention it gave to the linkages between economic and environmental considerations. Amongst other things it advocated greater use of international financing of environmentally-beneficial projects, and arrangements under which the debts of developing countries might be traded for commitments to conserve their biodiversity. It is not at all clear, however, that the developing world should continue to bear the burden of debts often incurred by former regimes, and although there are some examples of so-called 'debt-for-nature swaps', their use has not been extensive.

The Rio Conference

The UN Conference on Environment and Development (Rio, 1992) provided a platform for putting flesh on the bones of sustainable development in international law and to address the concern, noted in the Brundtland report, of the 'sectoral' and 'piecemeal' nature of international environmental law. Although the legal texts to emerge from Rio mark an important stage in the development of international environmental law, it can be argued that they fall some way short of providing the radical change in direction some had envisaged. The legal texts to emerge were:

(a) the Rio Declaration (see below);
(b) the Convention on Biological Diversity (see p. 654);
(c) the Framework Convention on Climate Change (see p. 416);
(d) Agenda 21 (an 800 page global action plan on development and the environment); and
(e) (in the absence of agreement on a Global Forest Convention) a 'non-legally binding authoritative statement' of principles in this area.

In terms of the general development of customary international environmental law, however, the Rio Declaration is central. Agreed to by all 176 states attending, it is a key soft law document, and an important text as regards the consolidation of a number of principles of customary international environmental law, including the precautionary approach (Principle 15, and see further Chapter 2), the polluter pays principle (Principle 16) and risk communication (Principles 18 and 19), as well as the development of customary principles concerning, for example, environmental impact assessment (Principle 17) and the fostering of public awareness and participation in environmental decision-making (Principle 10).

Although the preamble states that it is reaffirming and building upon the Stockholm Declaration, important principles are conspicuously modified (Principle 21, Stockholm) or even weakened. Thus Principle 1 of Stockholm, which refers to the 'fundamental right to . . . an environment of a quality that permits a life of dignity and well-being' becomes, in Principle 1 of Rio: 'Human beings are at the centre of concerns for sustainable development. They are entitled to a healthy and productive life in harmony with nature'. Interestingly, the Brundtland Commission had mandated an expert group, from North and South, to elaborate a set of general principles which could be submitted to the UN General Assembly with a view to their forming the basis of a universal declaration (see Munro and Lammers (ed.) *Environmental Protection and Sustainable Development: Legal Principles and Recommendations*, Graham and Trotman, 1987). Ultimately, the Commission failed to give its endorsement to this work, which might have underpinned a more ecological 'Earth Charter' akin to the Universal Declaration of Human Rights, as advocated by some states.

The effect of the Rio Declaration, therefore, is something of a mixed bag as regards the development of international environmental law and legal principles. Specifically, the double-edged quality of the explicit incorporation of developmental concerns (see Principles 2 and 3) might be seen either as an important accommodation of developing world interests or as allowing generally for 'business as usual'. Similarly, the lack of development of common heritage concepts might be viewed differently according to whether the focus is the global commons or biodiversity, and depending on whether one adopts a 'northern' or 'southern' perspective. The failure, in 1997, of the follow-up 'Rio + 5' meeting in New York to advance the debate further is perhaps evidence of the many tensions that remain unresolved.

Post-Rio

Developments up to and beyond Rio suggest a maturing of international environmental law, although numerous problems remain. As regards treaty law, many issues continue to be dealt with sectorally, e.g. ozone depletion and biodiversity conservation. Elsewhere, specific processes or products are coming under international regulation, e.g. the trade in hazardous waste under the 1989 Basle Convention, or the recent agreement of a 1998 Protocol on Persistent Organic Pollutants to the 1979 Convention on Long Range Transboundary Air Pollution. A range of different types of agreements are now found, from bilateral, sub-regional and regional agreements to global conventions, and there has been no let-up in the number of agreements reached.

Sadly, sudden shocks rather than creeping crises — Chernobyl or the 'Ozone Hole' discovery, rather than global warming forecasts and concerns about biodiversity — tend to help secure agreement. This illustrates the continuing nature of international law as, in general, reactive rather than proactive.

As with developments in the EC, there has been a perceptible shift in recent years from promulgating new agreements to putting effort into making existing agreements more effective and achieving higher levels of compliance. These issues, and other future developments, are discussed in more depth below.

Institutional organisations and other actors

A feature of international environmental law is the wide range of bodies involved either in the development of treaties or their enforcement. This is because, unlike international trade law, for example, there is no main or 'umbrella' convention governing the area like the General Agreement on Tariffs and Trade (GATT) regulates international trade. Nor is there a body similar to the World Trade Organisation (WTO) when it comes to compliance (international trade and the environment is discussed more fully below).

The key player in international law remains the individual state. Treaties are often advocated by individual states keen to see regulation in an area of particular importance to them, or conversely opposed by states, usually for economic reasons, and of course there can be no international law without the agreement of states.

A slightly less reactive and piecemeal approach to treaty-making ought to be a responsibility of the United Nations Environment Programme (UNEP), which was established following the Stockholm Conference (see p. 95). Based in Nairobi, UNEP is now the only UN body charged exclusively with international environmental matters, and has played an important role in the development of international environmental law, not least through its promotion of numerous regional seas treaties, the 1985 Vienna 'Ozone' Convention and the 1992 Biodiversity Convention. But in general terms UNEP has been a weak institution, somewhat under-funded and of relatively low visibility.

Although not a specialist environmental body, the International Law Commission (ILC) plays an important role in the drafting of treaties and the development of customary international law and general principles, although its work is not specific to the environmental area.

An institution that deserves special mention is the International Union for the Conservation of Nature (IUCN), established in 1948, which has a unique mix of governmental and non-governmental members and a quasi-institutional status. The IUCN was an influential force behind the Convention on the International Trade in Endangered Species (CITES) treaty, and the driving force behind the influential 1982 World Charter for Nature, both of which have played an important role in bringing nature conservation to international legal attention.

Increasingly, non-governmental organisations (NGOs) representing environmental and other interests are also involved in the negotiating of international agreements. Usually this is at the fringes, although in an interesting development NGOs were formally involved in the negotiation of the 1998 Århus Convention (on this convention see p. 111). Even if they are not involved in negotiations, it is unquestionable that environmental NGOs have played an important role in shaping the general political climate that has spawned increased activity in this area in the last 30 years.

Like negotiation, enforcement is usually handled on a treaty-by-treaty basis, and treaties tend to establish their own 'executive' organisations like the CITES Secretariat or the OSPAR Commission. Some soft law documents also do this: the UN Commission on Sustainable Development is charged with implementing Agenda 21 (see p. 97). This proliferation of organisations (and of treaties) may frustrate attempts to establish policy coherence in this area, as well as making policy and legal integration more difficult.

Environmental NGOs also have an increasingly important role in relation to compliance. Formerly, this tended to be limited to their 'observer status' at the meetings of parties to conventions such as CITES and the 1946 Whaling Convention, with some scope for bringing implementation problems to wider attention. In some cases, their role now extends more directly to enforcement matters. For example, TRAFFIC (an arm of the World Wildlife Fund which monitors wildlife trade) has a formal role in policing the international trade in certain elephant species under the CITES convention. In the *Shrimp/Turtle* case (see p. 107), it was notable that environmental NGOs were allowed to make unsolicited representations to the WTO.

A final point is that the role of bodies with primarily economic remits should not be overlooked. This is seen below in relation to the role of the

WTO, and its Committee on Trade and the Environment which is mandated to 'identify the relationship between trade measures and environmental measures in order to promote sustainable development' and make appropriate recommendations, but other bodies are also important. The lending policy of the World Bank, for example, is crucial in relation to a wide range of development projects, and the OECD has played a very significant role, e.g. in promoting the use of economic instruments and in advancing the polluter pays principle (the latter being largely promoted in the interests of trade harmonisation rather than environmental protection). The integration of environmental objectives into economic and other policy areas is likely to increase the number of bodies which pursue (or ought to pursue) environmental issues, especially if, institutionally, international environmental law remains as fragmented as it is.

Dispute settlement and dispute settlement bodies

There are a number of reasons why resolving disputes before the International Court of Justice (ICJ) is particularly problematic:

(a)   Only states may be parties in cases, although the Court can also be asked to deliver Advisory Opinions by specialist UN agencies (as it was by the UN General Assembly in relation to the *Legality of the Threat or Use of Nuclear Weapons* 35 ILM 809 and 1343 (1996) where environmental arguments were raised).

(b)   Taking a case to the ICJ, even though this can only happen if both states have accepted its jurisdiction, is often viewed as politically unfriendly. Where possible, international diplomacy is usually preferred.

(c)   Seeking a diplomatic solution, such as mediation or negotiation, is less risky, since the likelihood of accepting a politically unacceptable decision is much reduced.

(d)   Very few disputes are exclusively, or even primarily, legal disputes. To make them so requires the ignoring of dimensions which are irrelevant legally, but crucial politically or otherwise. For the more powerful states, the temptation is not to submit to rules which mean that their advantages are left at the door of the Court and not exploited politically.

All of this means that non-legal routes are generally preferred, but where international disputes need to be resolved formally, they will tend to be settled by arbitration. It is also worth noting here that, increasingly, consultation provisions are built into treaties where other states may be affected by actual or risky activities beyond their boundaries (see generally para. 39.10 of Agenda 21), i.e. a preventive approach to dispute resolution.

Very little resort is made to the ICJ, a UN body consisting of fifteen judges elected by the General Assembly and the Security Council to represent the 'main forms of civilisation and the principal legal systems of the world', and less than one third of UN members have accepted its compulsory jurisdiction (although the UK has). The ICJ's case load has not been substantial, amounting to roughly three decisions per year. Although an Environmental Chamber of the ICJ was established in 1993, it has yet to hear any cases, and the full ICJ has only ever heard one environmental 'case' (the *Gabcikovo-Nagymaros* case, discussed below). Because the mechanisms available in international law have been under-utilised in the environmental sphere, the extent to which they are appropriate for resolving international environmental disputes remains, perhaps at best, unclear.

A telling example of the limits of the ICJ's jurisdiction is the *Fisheries Jurisdiction Case (Spain v Canada)* 4 December 1998, unreported. This was brought after Canada had used force to stop a Spanish trawler fishing in an area important for Canadian fisheries interests, but which lay beyond the 200 mile limit of its exclusive economic zone. In 1994, Canada amended its coastal fisheries law to allow it to board such vessels if they were violating the law, which ostensibly aimed to prevent over-fishing. However, aware of the possible inconsistencies of this national law with the international law of the sea, two days before its coastal fisheries law was amended Canada effectively refused to let the ICJ hear cases involving Canadian fisheries conservation matters like the one at stake. This was sufficient for the ICJ to decide that it had no right to hear the complaint, even though Canada's actions were at best of dubious legality otherwise.

A final point is to note the role of specialist bodies such as the World Trade Organisation (see p. 106), the International Tribunal for the Law of the Sea, and older bodies like the European Court of Human Rights (see p. 54). This range of tribunals raises concerns about their ability to decide cases with an environmental dimension, and the equally important question of which body is most appropriate to decide any particular dispute (Sands, 'International Environmental Litigation: What Future?' (1998) RECIEL 1). This has important implications for the development of a coherent international environmental law. Even so, disputes arise when national, rather than individual, interests are at stake, and there are few opportunities for individuals to raise actions in international fora (although the right to take cases to the European Court of Human Rights is a notable exception).

The Gabcíkovo-Nagymaros case

In 1977, Hungary and Czechoslovakia agreed, by treaty, to dam a section of the River Danube to facilitate the development of their economies. This meant that, over a significant stretch of the river, most of the Danube would be diverted into an immense artificial waterway. The treaty contained some very rudimentary provisions to protect the environment. Following concerns about the environmental impact of the project, Hungary abandoned construction work in 1989. In 1991 the Czechoslovak government proceeded to a provisional solution involving construction work entirely on Slovak territory, and in 1992 the Danube was diverted, leading to considerable environmental damage. Hungary then terminated the treaty. The two countries eventually agreed to take their dispute to the ICJ (see *Case concerning the Gabcikovo-Nagymaros Project (Hungary/Slovakia)* 37 ILM (1998) 162).

What is most important is the way in which the dispute was dealt with. The central question was whether the situation was sufficiently serious to justify Hungary's actions. As a matter of the rules on treaties, the Court accepted that concerns about its natural environment could justify this, but then found that the environmental damage was not sufficiently serious or immediate. The ICJ also found that the Czechoslovak action in 1991 was disproportionate, violating the principle that shared watercourses should be utilised 'equitably'. But nor, finally, could Hungary lawfully terminate as it had done, since the 1977 Treaty provided, in theory, a means to adjust the obligations of the parties to new conditions.

The Court therefore emphasised the extent to which relations between the two countries continued to be governed primarily through terms agreed to between the parties rather than norms imposed by the Court. In this sense the decision was a considerable disappointment for those who had hoped for a bolder decision offering guidance, in particular, on how sustainable development principles might be given effect to in international law. The decision was more important for what it did *not* say than for what it did.

What the case does do, however, is illustrate:

(a)   the way in which, as a matter of law, the situation was restricted to a dispute between the two parties (even though the area affected was Europe's last inland delta, and arguably of much wider importance);

(b)   how the dispute was restricted to the issues the parties agreed to put before the court; and

(c)   how the ICJ made every effort to resolve the case by interpreting the 1977 Treaty, rather than seeing it as an opportunity to develop wider principles which might govern environmental disputes.

On this last point, the separate opinion of Vice-President Weeramantry is notable. He argued that sustainable development is not merely a *concept* but a recognised *principle* of customary international law, albeit one which suggests procedural rather than substantive obligations. For him the principle includes a duty of 'continuous' environmental impact assessment, i.e. one which requires continual assessment of environmental impact in the light of modern knowledge, although he does not spell out how this might be given effect to in practice. His separate opinion indicates what some might regard as a welcome, if so far minority, move towards the development of genuine international environmental law principles, and recalls his remarks in *New Zealand* v *France* (the *Nuclear Tests II* case) [1995] ICJ Rep 288:

I regret that the Court has not yet availed itself of the opportunity to enquire more fully into . . . making a contribution to some of the seminal principles of the evolving corpus of international environmental law. The Court has too long been silent on these issues and, in the words of ancient wisdom, one may well ask 'If not now, when?'.

International environmental treaty law post-Rio: towards more effective agreements?

As noted above, international law cannot be 'enforced' in the same way as domestic law or even EC law. The limited role for the courts in resolving international environmental disputes is also clear. This has meant a focus on other means of securing compliance with international agreements, especially positive inducements rather than negative sanctions. It is also important to bear in mind that few states ever have individual incentives to initiate action for non-compliance. On the other hand, states are often reluctant to delegate enforcement matters to bodies like treaty secretariats. The following conclusions may be drawn as to what makes for a more 'successful' treaty.

(a) Who is a party?
Attention should be paid to which states will be party to any treaty or any agreements made under treaties. A good, and perhaps unique, example is the 1979 Bonn Convention on Migratory Species, which provides for AGREE-MENTS (sic) open to accession by all states across whose borders species migrate regardless of whether they are parties to the convention (see, e.g. the 1995 AGREEMENT on the Conservation of African-Eurasian Migratory Waterbirds). These 'sub-treaties' allow states to benefit from positive conservation measures without signing up to the negative restrictions imposed in relation to species which the convention lists as endangered.

(b) Implementation and monitoring
Increasing attention is now paid to implementation and monitoring provisions, both at an institutional level and in relation to procedures. For example the establishment of an active treaty secretariat, regular meetings of the parties, and sometimes provision for NGO involvement are now common. NGOs have built up considerable adeptness in gathering information about non-compliance with treaties, and passing this on either to secretariats or to other sympathetic states.

More generally, success is likely to correlate with the extent to which information about compliance and non-compliance is collected and disseminated to the actors concerned; this task may be given to a specialist body such as the Subsidiary Body for Implementation established under the Framework Convention on Climate Change. Adverse reports about implementation may in themselves be sufficient to edge a party into compliance. Although information is usually gathered by the parties, there are examples of the possibility of on-site monitoring responsibilities. The 1971 Ramsar Wetlands Convention, e.g. allows for monitoring at the request of the host state authorities, which may prevent allegations of 'free-riding'. The functions of the Commission established under the 1992 'OSPAR' Convention on the North Sea include requiring the assessment of compliance, and where appropriate enable it to call for necessary compliance measures. Nevertheless, there is still a general problem of ensuring adequate monitoring, even where there are treaty arrangements under which developed countries pay for monitoring in developing countries.

(c)   Positive assistance

Effectively designed institutions will also be better able to administer the financial aspects of treaties (financing, technology-transfer etc.) that are increasingly a central aspect of environmental treaties. These began with the London amendments (1990) to the Montreal Protocol to the 1985 Vienna Ozone Treaty, establishing the Global Environment Facility (GEF), which is also used for the 1992 Framework Convention on Climate Change (FCCC) and for the 1992 Biodiversity Convention. Financial aid has been given for the agreed incremental costs of compliance with control measures (1990 London Amendments) and the agreed full costs of compliance with reporting and full incremental costs to secure compliance (FCCC). Multilateral development banks such as the World Bank now acknowledge the need to incorporate environmental considerations into their lending policy. In this context the increasing attention to taking the 'common but differentiated responsibilities' of parties seriously should be noted. An example of this is the 1992 FCCC, under which no new commitments are to be imposed on developing countries. Some would see the 'flexibile implementation' provisions of the 1997 Kyoto Protocol (such as the Clean Development Mechanism, which allows industrialised parties which invest in emissions reduction projects in developing country parties to use accruing reductions to offset a part of their emissions reduction commitments; see further p. 416) as also falling within this general principle. Technical assistance and education provisions are also found in some treaties.

(d)   Cross-checking non-compliance

One possible approach is to design agreements that reduce the practical possibilities for non-compliance. For example, the requirements in the 1973 International Convention for the Prevention of Pollution from Ships (the 'MARPOL' treaty) to install pollution-prevention equipment would have to be violated by several parties (builders, classifiers, insurers) for the rules to be evaded. Similarly, by requiring both import and export permits for species deemed most endangered, the CITES treaty reduces the scope for individual parties to evade their obligations.

(e)   Involving non-state actors

In light of the considerable difficulties of inter-state actions, increasing attention is being paid to the possibility of enforcement-type measures by non-state actors (governmental and non-governmental organisations and individual legal persons). As far as individual and group rights are concerned, however, even the limited mechanisms provided for in EC law (see p. 138) have yet to be replicated in international environmental treaty law more generally, although there are signs that non-state bodies will enjoy greater access to international environmental justice in the future.

(f)   Comparing treaties for effectiveness: a brief case study

Comparison of the Ozone, CITES and Biological Diversity treaties illustrates some general points about reaching effective international environmental agreements. The relative success of the Ozone treaty regime is usually said to be because of the very small number of parties (those states producing ozone-depleting chemicals) from which to get agreement; a scientific consensus over the issue; the fact that no one state could be sure that they might lose if they did not cooperate (as some states might think is the case in relation to global warming); and the relatively low costs involved in addressing the problem (including the non-availability of alternatives). The initial use in 1985 of a framework convention, fleshed out by later protocols, also helped facilitate compliance (as it has with the 1992 Framework Convention on Climate Change, which has allowed the parties to move from 'soft' standards to more binding targets for emissions reductions under the 1997 Kyoto Protocol).

CITES is also widely regarded as one of the more successful treaties. Despite a large membership, the Convention pays close attention to procedural issues, establishing a funded and effective secretariat, and requiring (and in practice, helping) states to establish national management and scientific authorities. And the import-permitting requirement applies even to parties outside the Convention which must comply with this provision on export, providing less incentive for non-participation. By contrast, the 1992 Biological Diversity Convention is something of a disappointment. The vagueness of the language used in many of its central provisions, often qualified with phrases such as 'as far as possible and as appropriate', testifies to the considerable difficulties in trying to reconcile North-South tensions between environmental and development goals. Moreover, the Convention is essentially based on the route to biodiversity conservation being through realising the commercial value of biodiversity (e.g. for pharmaceuticals), which may be optimistic.

It seems likely that, for the short term, the emphasis will be on the implementation of existing treaties and improving compliance, especially with framework conventions like those on climate change and biodiversity, rather than on the negotiation of new treaties. In this context the developing of procedural rights under international law is an important development (see p. 111).

International trade and the environment

A potent mechanism for making international agreements effective is the prospect of trade restrictions being imposed against non-compliant states, and some treaties (as discussed below) make provision for such restrictions. However, trade controls are often used by one state against another when the import of goods is banned or restricted, often on ostensibly environmental grounds.

National measures may hinder free international trade in one of two main ways; either by imposing restrictions on the manner in which commodities are produced (process and production methods) or by regulating the quality of the commodities themselves (product standards). Process controls may be concerned with the polluting impact on a neighbouring state, or the way in which a national or global resource is exploited. Thus, restrictions may be enacted to protect the environment of the importing state, the exporting state or the global commons. Regulating the extent to which measures enacted for environmental protection reasons may unlawfully hinder international trade is therefore of central importance to environmental law and to sustainable development.

The regulation of international trade rests primarily with bodies connected to the World Trade Organisation (WTO). It is arguable that these bodies (e.g. General Agreement on Tariffs and Trade (GATT) panels and the Appellate Body of the WTO) are effectively becoming international courts of sustainable development, since they are taking the lead in deciding, under the GATT, where the balance between global free trade and environmental protection lies. This has raised understandable concerns amongst environmentalists and others, and is in contrast to the position in the EC, for example, where the European Court of Justice decides both trade and environment cases, and cases combining both issues. This section focuses on two leading cases, decided before and after the GATT 1994 and the WTO agreement which governs this area, the preamble to which now qualifies emphasis on the 'full use of the resources of the world' with their:

> optimal use . . . in accordance with the objective of sustainable development, seeking both to protect and preserve the environment and to enhance the means for doing so in a manner consistent with the respective needs and concerns at different levels of economic development.

(a)   'Tuna/Dolphin'

The *Tuna/Dolphin* dispute (1992) 30 ILM 1598 centred around import restrictions imposed by the US because of concerns about the incidental effect on dolphin populations of Mexican (and other) tuna-fishing methods. The panel upheld the complaint of Mexico that this violated the GATT's 'national treatment' provision (Article III) which requires that all 'like products' receive similar treatment in international trade law, regardless of how they are produced: imported and domestic tuna had to be compared as *products*.

The issue was then whether the US action amounted to a 'quantitative restriction' under Article XI of GATT 1994, i.e. an obstacle in practice to a level playing field for international trade. This had to be determined in light of various exceptions in Article XX. This provides that so long as measures do not unjustly or arbitrarily discriminate between countries where the same conditions apply, or act as a disguised restriction on international trade, contracting parties to the GATT may adopt measures including those:

> (a)   necessary to protect human, animal, or plant life or health (Art. XX(b)); or which
>
> (b)   [relate] to the conservation of exhaustible natural resources if such measures are made effective in conjunction with restrictions on domestic production or consumption (Art. XX(g)).

The panel held that these exceptions only applied to activities within the national jurisdiction of the country adopting the measure. By impacting on activities in international waters, the US action was unlawful. The objective of the GATT — reducing trade restrictions and barriers — would be 'eviscerated' if the US could dictate conservation measures to Mexico as a condition of Mexican access to US markets. Even if the US could take action beyond its borders, it had not shown that doing so would be necessary. There were other means by which the US might pursue its conservation objectives, e.g. through financial incentives or through negotiating international agreements. (In 1992 the US, Mexico and eight other nations, responsible for 99% of the tuna catch in the disputed area, signed an international accord to phase out, by 1994, the use of 'dolphin-unfriendly' nets.) In a further, related dispute issue, brought by the EU against the US (*Tuna/Dolphin II* (1994) 33 ILM 839), a GATT panel again found that US action, adopted following the initial dispute, fell foul of the GATT. But it did hold that there could be circumstances where a country could employ trade restrictions to influence environmental policies beyond its jurisdiction where this was necessary to protect a global resource pursuant to an international environmental agreement and where there was a direct causal connection between the measure and the environmental objective pursued.

The *Tuna/Dolphin* disputes raised important questions about the interplay between trade freedom and environmental protection. For example, should it be unlawful unilaterally to block the import of products because they have been produced through relatively high energy use, contributing to global warming? How does the distinction between product and process restrictions allow for the polluter pays principle to be given effect to? Linking these is the issue of what counts as an 'externality' in international law; should this require proof of actual harm to the importing state, or are global or commons concerns sufficient?

(b) 'Shrimp/Turtle'
Disputes since 1994, illustrated here by the recent view of the WTO Appellate Body in the *Shrimp/Turtle* dispute (*US — Import Prohibition of Certain Shrimp and Shrimp Products* (1999) 38 ILM 121) suggest few radical departures from the basic stance illustrated above. At issue here was the GATT 1994 compatibility of US national measures which required any state exporting shrimp to the US to demonstrate that its harvesting methods did not endanger sea turtles, or were at least regulated and no less damaging to sea turtle conservation than standards actually achieved in the US. *Shrimp/Turtle* confirms that a two stage test, first elaborated in *US Standards for Reformulated and Conventional Gasoline* (1996) 35 ILM 603, will be used in relation to Article XX of GATT 1994: first, provisional justification if the measure correctly comes within one of the exceptions; secondly, further appraisal of these measures under the introductory clauses of Article XX.

On the first point, the US measures were acceptable under Article XX(g). The view of a previous panel that 'exhaustible natural resources' were not to be limited to non-renewalable resources such as minerals but extended to any finite resource and therefore covered living resources, was reaffirmed. But it appears that the turtle species in question were 'exhaustible' because of their recognised endangered status, not because action was required to prevent endangering them. (In *US — Gasoline*, clean air was held to be an exhaustible natural resource.) Nevertheless, the remaining requirements to come within Article XX(g) were fulfilled: the measure 'related to conservation' in light of an assessment of its primary aim, having regard both to its purpose and effect (see *US — Gasoline*) and was sufficiently 'even-handed' as between imported and domestic shrimp. Because it satisfied Article XX(g), the Appellate Body did not need to consider also whether it was 'necessary' under Article XX(b).

In this sense, the US measures were substantively acceptable. However, the US failed to show that the measures were not an 'arbitrary or unjustified discrimination between countries where the same conditions prevail'. As to unjustified discrimination, four points were central. First, in practice the US rules forced importing states to adopt US policy without any flexibility of approach. In short, the US only looked to see whether importing states required the fitting of 'turtle excluder devices' (TEDs), as required in the US, rather than authorising comparable measures. (Using its own inspectors to certify was hardly helpful, and raises the question of whether something closer to 'mutual recognition' would have been preferable.) Secondly, the US also banned the import of shrimp caught by boats using TEDs if they did so in the waters of otherwise non-compliant states. Thirdly, the US had failed to engage the importing states in serious negotiations for an international treaty on sea turtle conservation before imposing trade sanctions. This was in violation of several important statements emphasising multilateralism, including Principle 12 of the Rio Declaration. Finally, the US had provided different levels of support through technology transfer to different countries, affecting the ability of all states to comply on equal terms. The measures were also 'arbitrary' because of their informality, lack of transparency and absence of procedural protections, e.g. the absence of appeal or review rights.

A final point on *Shrimp/Turtle* is the tension evident between the interests of nation states and a 'common heritage' approach. 'Go it alone' approaches are strongly rejected, the Appellate Body encouraging the negotiation of multilateral agreements in the interests of opening up international decision-making to those affected. This is consistent with what the WTO calls its preference for a 'rules-based' approach to free trade; see below. Yet it also deals rather unconvincingly with the question of jurisdictional limits to nation states' legitimate interests, doing little more than stating, rather than positively arguing towards, the connection in law between the turtle populations involved and the US.

(c) Future developments

For the future, however, it is not yet clear where the balance will be struck between the GATT and multilateral environmental agreements. Some, for example, would like to see the GATT amended to insert a defence that action was taken pursuant to treaties like CITES, the Basle Convention on Hazardous Wastes or the Montreal Ozone Protocol, all of which provide for enforcement through trade restrictions, although it is unlikely that two parties to such an agreement will raise a dispute over GATT-incompatibility. Nor is it clear how the increasing use of packaging and labelling requirements (which throw up their own problems; see Ward (1997) 6 RECIEL 139) will be viewed. And future disputes about what are 'like' products can be expected: for example, is a tax based on the recycled content of bottles a product or process-based measure? Indeed, although the details of GATT law are important, as Vogel points out the debate 'reflects a more profound clash of culture and world views between the trade community and environment-alists' (*Trading Up: Consumer and Environmental Regulation in a Global Economy*, Harvard Univ. Press, 1995, p. 134).

This clash is based in part upon competing views of whether security through free trade, or environmental security, is the more fragile. But it is also based on disagreement over the extent to which unilateral action contributes either to the progressive ratcheting up of international standards or to a deregulatory 'race to the bottom', raising difficult questions concerning sustainable development. It should be noted that in *Tuna/Dolphin*, however, the greatest reduction in dolphin deaths occurred before the import ban, by which time there was no evidence that the dolphin populations affected were endangered. Trade restrictions may serve only to depress the commercial value of natural resources in other states, driving up the number of units (of tropical hardwood trees, of endangered species) that must be sold to maintain revenues, and driving down the incentives of national governments to invest in measures (e.g. anti-poaching measures or habitat conservation) to conserve the resource.

Finally, it is worth noting the views of those who argue for the creation of a World Environment Organisation as the institutional and legal counterpart to the WTO (see also the pessimistic advocacy of such a body by Esty, *Greening the GATT*, Institute for International Economics 1994, pp. 77–83 and 98). However, in the words of one proponent of this view, a former Director-General of the WTO, the WTO system has now, post *Shrimp/Turtle*, 'demonstrated how — through consensus — we can build a rules-based international trading system where all countries, large and small, developing and developed, can find a place'. If this is true, it does somewhat beg questions about the role of any future 'WEO', about the remit of the WTO's Committee on Trade and Environment and about the effective integration of trade and environmental objectives in global management. This suggestion also seems far removed from a global ombudsman or guardian, charged with responsibility for common resources and able to bring actions against nation states for harm to the international environment. For the immediate future, however, states are likely to prefer the speed and certainty provided by the WTO over dispute resolution under multilateral environmental agreements, which typically lack these features (see Cameron, 'Dispute Settlement and Conflicting Trade and Environment Regimes', in *Trade and the Environment: Bridging the Gap*, Earthscan, 1998). This has important implications for the development of customary principles of international law, which may become biased towards free trade concerns.

Future directions in international environmental law and policy

In addition to greater attention to matters of compliance, it is arguable that
a mix of approaches will colour the future of international environmental law.
These are likely to give increasing weight to protecting individual 'environmental' rights. But in some cases an approach emphasising duties towards the
environment may develop (this really means an approach emphasising the
rights of states or international organisations to take actions against individuals for environmental harm). In both cases, increased attention is likely to
be paid to individuals and to organisations, rather than the traditional
'state-centric' approach of international law.

(a)   Rights-based approaches
There have been some attempts to advance an environmental human right,
most notably in a report by a UN Sub-Commission on Prevention of
Discrimination and Protection of Minorities on the relationship between
human rights and the environment (Ksentini, *Human Rights and the Environment*, UN Doc. E/CN.4/Sub.2/1994/9, 6 July 1994). Finding that over sixty
national constitutions contained some form of environmental rights protection, the report concluded that there had been 'a shift from environmental
law to the right to a healthy and decent environment', comprising substantive
rights to life, health and development. This, it claimed, was rather more than
a 'greening' of international human rights law, and the report proposed the
adoption of Principles of Human Rights and the Environment which would
be enforceable by human rights organisations. Following Rio, however, the
willingness of the international community to sign up to a rights-based
approach may be questioned and the Principles are making no progress in the
UN system.
    While we have already discussed human rights law in the context of
environmental values (see p. 54), it is worth recalling that the European
Convention on Human Rights is an international treaty of considerable
importance. Although it does not contain explicit mention of the environment, experience of the Convention does suggest a number of possible ways
of framing environmental disputes as human rights violations. Some of these
may be substantive in character, e.g. the right to life (Article 2), which may
be violated where, e.g. national authorities fail to advise those affected of
certain risks of nuclear contamination (*LCB* v *UK* (1998) 4 BHRC 447, but
see *Osman* v *UK* (1999) 5 BHRC 293); or the right to privacy and home life
(Article 8), which may be violated in cases of severe environmental pollution
such as in *López Ostra* v *Spain* (1995) 20 EHRR 277 but which may also give
rise to procedural safeguards such as in *Guerra* v *Italy* (1998) 26 EHRR 357,
a successful claim following a failure to be informed of chemical pollution
risks.
    Procedural rights are also protected under the Convention, e.g. through the
right to a fair hearing (Article 6(1)), which might be breached where a person
affected by the grant of an environmental licence is unable to challenge this
judicially (*Zander* v *Sweden* (1993) 18 EHRR 175). However, a 'victim' test

is used and there may be problems of standing; nor is there a 'right to nature' with all that entails for protection of the unowned environment (*X and Y* v *Federal Republic of Germany* (1976) 5 Eur Com HR Dec & Rep). Proximity problems can also be seen in *Balmer-Schafroth* v *Switzerland* ((1997) 25 EHRR 598), where the court rejected a claim based on the absence of the right of residents to review or appeal the grant of a power station authorisation. The applicants had failed to show that the operation of the power station exposed them to a danger that was not only serious but specific and imminent. The connection between the decision by the government and the right invoked by the applicants was too tenuous and remote to qualify as a 'civil right'.

It is clear, therefore, that under the ECHR, environmental protection is at best incidental to protecting human rights, rather than human rights protection securing environmental and conservation objectives. Of course, the latter would involve balancing social and environmental interests, and an individual right to sustainable development is bound to be problematic. A less extreme option may be to reinterpret existing rights — such as the right to life — creatively. This is the approach taken in the Ksentini Report, and has been taken most notably by the Indian courts (for an excellent summary see Anderson, 'Environmental Protection in India', in Boyle and Anderson (eds) *Human Rights Approaches to Environmental Protection*, Claredon, 1996).

(b) Procedural rights

A definite shift towards establishing and protecting procedural rights in international environmental law is certainly emerging. This can be seen in, for example, Principle 10 of the Rio Declaration. This notes that environmental problems are best handled with the participation of all concerned citizens, at the relevant level. Specifically, at national level individuals should have access to publicly-held environmental information and the opportunity to participate in decision-making processes, while states should foster public awareness and participation by making information widely available, and provide effective access to judicial and administrative proceedings. More specific elaboration of procedural rights is contained in the 1998 UN/ECE Århus Convention on Access to Information, Public Participation in Decision-making and Access to Justice in Environmental Matters. References there to 'the public concerned' includes references to non-governmental organisations promoting environmental protection, which are deemed to have a sufficient interest in environmental decision-making. However, the secrecy surrounding the initial negotiation of the Multilateral Agreement on Investment, considered by many the harbinger of a 'race to the bottom' in transnational environmental standards, suggests there is a long way to go.

(c) Rights of future generations

The Århus Convention does not make any reference to the rights of future generations. These have been upheld, both substantively and in the right for a group of children to take legal action on their behalf to oppose various logging permits, in the Philippines case of *Minors Oposa* v *Secretary of the Department of the Environment and Natural Resources* (1994) 33 ILM 173, a national case. An interesting example of future generational considerations was the rejection, in negotiating the 1997 Kyoto Climate Change Protocol, of 'temporal flexibility', which would have allowed states to 'borrow' carbon credits from future generations at a penalty rate. As noted above, there are signs that the ICJ would prefer to avoid defining 'sustainability', but has so far made little contribution to the development of procedural principles.

(d) Duty-centred approaches

A range of duty-centred approaches now exists. In national law, many constitutions include provisions requiring either individuals or the state (or both) to protect the environment. The Spanish Constitution, for example, provides that: 'Everyone has the right to enjoy an environment suitable for the development of the person as well as the duty to preserve it' (1978, Article 45), while some texts also require states or citizens to 'improve' the environment (e.g. Turkish Constitution 1982, Article 56). More specifically, there have been moves in the Council of Europe to establish a Convention for the Protection of the Environment Through Criminal Law (see the 1996 Draft). And perhaps the starkest example of legislating for individual responsibility is contained in the 1998 Rome Statute of the International Criminal Court, Article 8 of which provides for an international war crime against the environment.

FIVE

The European Community and the environment

Notwithstanding its economic basis, the EC is a major and increasing source of British environmental protection law. It also has a central and profound influence on the direction of environmental policy, both at a Community level and within each Member State. As a result, every subject covered by this book is affected, either directly or indirectly, by the activities of the EC.

There are four main ways in which the EC plays a role in shaping British environmental law and policy:

(a)   Some pieces of EC legislation lay down rules and standards that are directly enforceable in Member States without any need for further implementation. In these cases EC law is British law.

(b)   Other pieces of EC legislation are addressed to Member States and require changes in British law or administrative practice. This is normally the situation in relation to environmental legislation, because of the predominant use of directives, which are not necessarily directly effective within Member States (see p. 121). British law is therefore not the same as EC law until the EC law has been implemented. In such cases the precise role of the EC in initiating the change is often forgotten, since the domestic legislation resulting from the EC requirements will constitute the law which is applied in practice. An important point to note is that EC law and British law often differ in such circumstances, because EC law frequently consists of aims and goals and procedural frameworks rather than precise legal rules, and allows for some discretion in the Member States as to how and when to implement it.

(c)   The third role is somewhat wider and rests upon the constitutional position that the UK now occupies as a Member State of the EC. The EC not only passes environmental laws, it has an environmental policy. This policy and the general economic and environmental principles which underpin it exert an important influence on British policy-making and on British attitudes towards environmental law and its enforcement. The direction in which environmental protection will go therefore depends as much on wider

European attitudes as it does on ingrained British ideas, although of course British ideas will in turn help to mould the general EC view and to affect the attitudes of the other Member States.

(d)   Finally, the economic policies of the EC have a profound effect on the direction of both EC and domestic environmental law. Environmental protection cannot be isolated from economic policy and the substantial completion of the single internal market by the end of 1992 had significant spin-off effects on the environment. Indeed, many 'green' commentators would argue that the economic policies of the EC, based as they are on economic growth and on economies of scale in industrial and agricultural production, are themselves antithetical to the achievement of the aims of a clean environment and conservation of natural resources.

The specific pieces of EC law and policy that have an influence on British law are integrated into the relevant chapters of the rest of the book. This chapter concentrates on more general matters, such as the place of environmental policy within the EC, the history and principles of that policy, the institutions of the EC and their law-making and enforcement powers, and the way in which the policies and laws are implemented in Britain. However, it must be stressed that all the nuances of EC law cannot be covered in one chapter; accordingly, this chapter will concentrate on those issues which are of relevance to environmental protection and does not seek to provide an exhaustive account of general EC law principles.

The nature of the EC

The EC is more than just a free trade agreement between 15 fairly similar Western European states. It has institutions and law-making powers of its own, making it a form of supranational state in which the Member States have limited their sovereign rights, albeit within limited fields (although for political reasons the extent of this is often denied).

The activities over which the EC has powers are set out in the Treaties which establish the EC, which are effectively the EC's constitution. In the past there have been three Treaties and three linked Communities, the European Economic Community (EEC), the European Coal and Steel Community (ECSC) and the European Atomic Energy Community (Euratom). It has been the EEC, established by the Treaty of Rome 1957, which has been the central Community and to which environmental policy relates. The Treaty of Rome was amended by the Single European Act 1986, which first introduced references to the environment. All the Treaties were further amended by the 1992 'Maastricht' Treaty on European Union, which came into force on 1 November 1993 and altered the name of the EEC Treaty to the EC Treaty. In this book all references to Treaty Articles are to the EC Treaty, as amended. Only aspects relating to the EC, which (together with foreign and defence matters, and justice and home affairs) forms one of three 'pillars' of the European Union (EU) are considered here, so references are to the EC rather than the EU. Most recently, less significant amendments to the EC Treaty were agreed at the Amsterdam Summit in 1997, and changes made under the Treaty of Amsterdam came into force on 1 May 1999. These include a renumbering of the EC Treaty. References below are generally to the new articles, with the old article numbers in brackets (although when we look at them in an historical context, we do so the other way round).

The institutions of the EC

The four main EC institutions are the Commission, the Council, the Parliament, and the European Court of Justice. Each has powers and duties specified in the Treaty and an obligation to further the aims of the EC. There is also an advisory Economic and Social Committee and a Court of Auditors.

(a)   The Commission

The Commission is the executive of the EC. It consists of 20 independent members appointed by the Member States (two each from the five larger states — Germany, France, the UK, Italy and Spain — and one each from the others), serviced by officials. It has responsibility for implementing EC policies and initiates and draws up proposals for legislation for the Council to approve. It also has a major responsibility for policing and enforcing EC law, in which role it has extensive investigatory powers.

It is the Commission which draws up the environment action programmes and drafts proposed EC legislation. By means of information agreements with the Member States, the Commission is informed of proposals for domestic legislation and these often give rise to a Commission proposal for a common policy across the EC. However, the ambivalent nature of the Commission must be appreciated. On the one hand it is often the driving force behind new environmental policies: on the other it is responsible for enforcing the economic aims of the EC (see its position in the *Danish Bottles* case — p. 135).

Internally the Commission is divided into a number of Directorates-General. The Environment Directorate-General deals with environmental matters. As a result of the formal adoption of the principle that environmental policies should form a component of the EC's other policies, the Environment Directorate-General has had its hand strengthened slightly in relation to its dealings with other Directorates–General, such as those with responsibility for transport and energy policy, which have traditionally tended to have greater influence.

(b)   The Council

The Council is a political body made up of one representative of each Member State. The identity of this representative alters according to the nature of the business. Thus, transport ministers normally agree transport measures, environment ministers normally agree environmental measures and so on. As a body it has a duty to ensure the attainment of the Treaty objectives, but clearly national interests play a central role in the Council's decisions.

As a result the Council's voting procedures are crucial. There are some differences in the procedures to be adopted for different matters. Some pieces of legislation have to be passed unanimously by the Council, acting on a proposal from the Commission, and after consultation with Parliament and the Economic and Social Committee. Others can be passed by a qualified majority of the Council, a system of weighted voting in which Member States can be outvoted (see p. 118).

(c)   The European Parliament

The powers of the European Parliament, which began life as an unelected consultative Assembly, have grown considerably in recent years. Although the Parliament still has no formal right to initiate proposals for new legislation (it can only request that the Commission consider new legislation in an area), it now has a much greater role in the making of new legislation (see below). The Parliament has also been a significant mouthpiece of concern over environmental issues. For example, despite its inability formally to initiate legislation, it set in motion a ban on the imports of sealskin products, and for many years has had a vigorous Committee on the Environment, Public Health and Consumer Protection subjecting proposals to quite searching scrutiny. Since the last elections in 1999, however, its political complexion has changed somewhat, as the balance of power in the Parliament has swung towards the more conservative end of the spectrum. This may see it become something of a less radical voice on environmental issues, at least in the short term.

(d)   The European Court of Justice

The European Court of Justice consists of judges appointed by common agreement of the Member States. It is assisted by Advocates-General, one of whom makes reasoned submissions to the Court in each case. It has supreme authority on matters of EC law. This means that it has ultimate power to interpret the meaning of the Treaties and of any legislation made by the other institutions. The Court can thus, if asked, review the legitimacy of the actions of the other institutions, provide answers on matters of EC law to Member States' courts and declare whether Member States are implementing EC law properly.

Article 234 (ex 177) plays a major role here. Under Article 234, any court or tribunal in a member state can refer any matter of EC law to the European Court of Justice for its interpretation of the law. This procedure aims to ensure uniformity between Member States in their application of the law. It also provides a method of obtaining an authoritative ruling. Since the Court is the ultimate arbiter of any law having an EC input, Article 234 references should be made where there is any doubt as to the meaning of EC law, or the compatibility of domestic law with it. However, one drawback is that national courts effectively have a discretion whether to make a reference or not.

In carrying out its functions the European Court of Justice has been exceptionally activist and creative. It has developed several novel principles, including the doctrines of the supremacy of EC law and of direct effects, and has been responsible for extending the scope of the powers of all the institutions (including itself). It has done this by adopting a purposive approach to interpretation in which it looks as much at the spirit as at the letter of the law. On matters of EC law, therefore, the Court's view is central to any discussion of the law. For example, in *Vessoso* (Cases C-206 & 207/88 [1990] ECR I-1461), it ruled that the definition of waste in the Framework Directive on Waste 75/442 included waste which was to be recycled, since it was waste as far as the disposer was concerned irrespective of the intentions of the recipient and its judgments on the Wild Birds Directive (79/409) have given forceful expression to safeguarding ecological interests.

The Court gives one agreed judgment. These are often very brief and formal and for the full reasoning the opinion of the Advocate-General must be read, although sometimes the Court and the Advocate-General do not agree. The European Court of Justice should not be confused with the European Court of Human Rights, which exists to police the European Convention on Human Rights (see p. 54).

Other bodies

Other bodies of note include the Court of Auditors, an EC institution, which oversees Community expenditure. The Court of Auditors has been a particlarly critical voice, e.g. in relation to the way in which Community regional funding has been spent on environmentally-damaging projects generally (Special Report No. 3/92), or in specific sectors like subsidising water pollution (Special Report No. 3/98). Mention should also be made of the Committee of the Regions and the Economic and Social Council, which play important advisory roles.

The European Environment Agency

Although not formally an EC 'institution', the European Environment Agency, provided for in Regulation 1210/90 and established in October 1993, plays an important role. Based in Copenhagen, the Agency has the role of gathering information and data on the state of the environment in the EC. A report on the state of the environment must be published every three years and the two reports published in 1995 and 1998 provide a valuable account of pressures on the European environment (see further p. 223). In recognition of the international nature of environmental pollution, the Agency is open to non-EC members.

The Agency has not been given any enforcement or policing powers in relation to environmental legislation. Despite determined efforts by the European Parliament to see this happen, it must be unlikely that such a role will emerge, at least in the short-term because of the enormity and complexity of the task, and the political unpopularity it would probably generate. What is more likely to happen is that bodies like IMPEL (an Implementation Network set up by the Commission, consisting of representatives from the Member States) will try to develop best practice and benchmarking standards for monitoring implementation, i.e. that the EC will try to raise the profile of non-compliance rather than create an EC body to police environmental legislation on the ground.

Voting procedures

The making of EC environmental legislation involves either unanimity or, more usually, qualified majority voting, subject to some form of involvement of the Parliament.

(a) The role of the Council and the Parliament
The involvement of the Parliament has always been required, although to begin with this involved no more than mere consultation. A rather complex procedure, the 'co-operation procedure', was introduced by the Single European Act in 1987, and gave some additional legislative power to the Parliament. This procedure did not prove particularly satisfactory, however, and is no longer used to pass legislation of any great environmental relevance. At Maastricht, a new procedure — the 'co-decision procedure' — was introduced. Following the Amsterdam Treaty, legislation adopted under both Articles 95 (ex 100a) and 175 (ex 130S), the main bases in the EC Treaty for environmental legislation (see further p. 126 below) is now adopted by this procedure, which is contained in Article 251 (ex 189b).

The co-decision procedure, which was streamlined under the Amsterdam Treaty, gives a strengthened role in the legislative process to the Parliament, although this is still quite negative in character. For example, the Parliament still has no right to initiate new proposals. One feature of this procedure is the resolution of disputes, on matters of detail, by a Conciliation Committee made up of representatives of the Parliament and Council. This conciliation procedure has been invoked on a number of occasions in the environmental area, e.g. in relation to the first 'Auto-Oil' Directive 98/69/EC and the draft Framework Water Directive (see p. 570). One important consequence of the greater involvement of the Parliament is that decision-making is rather more open that it used to be, which goes some way towards tackling problems of secrecy and lack of democratic accountability inherent in EC legislative procedures (see p. 223).

(b) Unanimity or majority voting?
The other key development in this area has been the extension of qualified majority voting, the system whereby the number of votes in the Council are weighted roughly according to population (thus, the UK has 10 votes in the Council out of 87). This has restricted the number of areas where unanimity amongst all the Member States is needed, and therefore the scope for one unsupportive Member State to veto a proposal.

For example, the objections of the Danish government (which wanted stricter standards than those proposed) to Directive 88/76 on Emissions from Large Cars resulted in it being outvoted in the Council and the UK government was outvoted on the EC list of hazardous wastes adopted pursuant to Directive 91/689 on Hazardous Waste. However, another reason is that the system encourages the Member States to reach a compromise position within the Council. The combined effect may enable some proposed directives to avoid the fate of, for example, Directives 88/609 on Emissions from Large Combustion Plants (which deals with the causes of acid rain) and 85/337 on Environmental Impact Assessment, both of which were delayed for many years by the opposition of one or two Member States. However, this does not mean that directives will always be agreed swiftly, even with qualified majority voting, because there are also complex political consider-ations to take into account, although less-developed Member States may now be bought off by concessions based on Article 175(5) (ex 130S(5)). The increasing involvement of the European Parliament is also relevant to whether a compromise position can be reached.

Prior to the Single European Act 1986, unanimity was required for all environmental legislation, whether agreed under Article 100 or Article 235 (now Articles 94 and 308). This was changed by the Act, so that, in order to move more quickly to the single internal market, a qualified majority would suffice for directives agreed under Article 100A (now 95). Unanimity was still required under Article 130S (now 175), although a little-used exception was introduced in the second subparagraph to cover situations where a unani-mous Council had agreed in advance that a qualified majority would apply.

This was changed again by the Maastricht Treaty, which amended Article 130S (now 175) so that most environmental legislation agreed under it is subject to qualified majority voting. The only types of environmental legisla-tion where unanimity is still required are those primarily of a fiscal nature (for example, the proposed carbon energy tax), measures relating to town and country planning or land use (unless they are concerned with waste manage-ment), measures concerning the management of water resources, and measures affecting national policies on energy supply (for example, a proposal restricting the use of coal on environmental grounds).

Sources of EC law

EC law is contained in the Treaties, legislation passed by the institutions, international treaties to which the EC is a party, and the judgments and principles of the European Court of Justice.

To understand the relevance of these sources, an explanation of the concepts of the supremacy of EC law and direct effect is required. The doctrine of the supremacy of EC law is that, where there is a conflict between EC law and national law, EC law prevails, even if the national law is later in time; national courts should thus apply EC law rather than national law which does not comply with EC law. This is, however, intimately linked with the idea of direct effect. A law has direct effect if it gives rise to rights and obligations which can be enforced by individuals and companies before national courts. If an EC law is directly effective in this sense, the doctrine of supremacy means that the non-conforming national law can simply be ignored.

Not all EC law is directly effective in this sense. For any provision to be directly effective it must be sufficiently clear and precise to form a cause of action. It must also be unconditional and must not require further definition at the discretion of the member state. There are also limitations on direct effect related to the source of the EC law. Treaty Articles and regulations are capable of having direct effect, as long as they fulfil the above tests. For directives, the Treaty suggested that they would not be capable of having direct effect. However, the European Court of Justice has indulged in some significant judicial creativity and has decided that directives may have direct effect if the action is against the state or an emanation of the state, but not if against another private body (see further p. 121).

Even if not directly effective, EC law may have some effect in domestic courts through sympathetic interpretation. The European Court of Justice held in Case 14/83 *Von Colson* v *Land Nordrhein-Westfalen* [1984] ECR 1891 that domestic legislation must be interpreted so as to comply with EC law if the domestic law was passed to implement it. Since then, the European Court of Justice has decided in Case C-106/89 *Marleasing SA* v *La Comercial Internacional de Alimentación SA* [1990] ECR I-4135 that national courts should interpret national legal provisions in accordance with EC law, irrespective of whether they pre-date or post-date it. However, it appears that national courts may decline to adopt this approach in circumstances where to do so would breach the legitimate expectations of parties to the action.

(a) Treaty provisions

The provisions of the EC Treaties lay down the powers of the EC institutions and the procedures for decision-making as well as laying down certain substantive legal requirements. They are of enormous importance in actions before the ECJ relating to the legality of EC actions. In addition, some Treaty provisions are directly effective (e.g. Article 141 on equal pay), but this is not the case for the Articles concerned with the environment because of their policy orientation.

(b) Regulations

Regulations are legislative acts of general application. They are normally directly effective, as long as they are sufficiently precise. However, there are few regulations in the environmental sphere, except those relating to the process of giving effect to international treaties, agricultural policy and administrative matters, such as the European Environment Agency and the eco-auditing and eco-labelling schemes.

(c) Directives

Directives are addressed to Member States and are binding as to the result to be achieved. They are well-suited to environmental measures, since they leave the choice of how to implement them to the Member States, which will each have different methods for setting environmental laws. Most EC environmental legislation is in the form of directives. In this book we refer to directives by their common names (e.g. the 'Habitats Directive') rather than the often lengthy titles they are given formally ('Council Directive 92/43/EEC of 21 May 1992 on the conservation of natural habitats and of wild fauna and flora'). The full titles of key directives are given in the Index.

Normally implementation is required within a specified time period (often two years). This will be done by the Member State changing its domestic law and it will be in breach if it has not *fully and correctly* implemented the directive within the time limit. In Britain, once the Directive is transposed the domestic rule will constitute the relevant law, unless there has been partial or incomplete transposition.

A distinction must be drawn here between formal and actual compliance. Changing the law to comply with EC law constitutes formal compliance. However, this is no guarantee that the law is complied with in practice since, for example, a regulatory agency may exercise its discretion not to enforce the law. Increasingly the Commission is looking for evidence of both formal and actual compliance, although its lack of resources for monitoring developments in all the Member States hampers this. The creation of the European Environment Agency should help here.

A directive cannot be relied upon in the courts of a member state unless it is directly effective. Originally it was assumed that directives could not be directly effective, since discretion was given to the Member States on the method of their implementation. But the European Court of Justice has held that directives which are sufficiently precise as to the ends to be achieved are directly effective once the time limit has expired. However, even then, directives have direct effect *only* against a member state or an emanation of the state (this is known as vertical direct effect), not against another private body or person (horizontal direct effect). The reason for this distinction is that the state itself cannot plead a failure to implement the directive properly as a defence — a form of the estoppel principle (see the European Court of Justice decision in Case 152/84 *Marshall* v *Southampton and South West Hampshire Area Health Authority (Teaching)* [1986] QB 401). The continuing existence of the distinction was re-asserted in Case C-91/92 *Faccini Dori* v *Recreb Srl* [1994] ECR I-3325.

An 'emanation of the state' has been defined widely by the European Court of Justice in Case C-188/89 *Foster* v *British Gas plc* [1991] 1 QB 405, where it was stated that:

a body, whatever its legal form, which has been made responsible pursuant to a measure adopted by the state, for providing a public service under the control of the state, and has for that purpose special powers beyond those which resulted from the normal rules applicable in relations between individuals, is included among the bodies against which the provisions of a directive capable of having direct effect might be relied upon.

One limitation is that it is up to the national courts to apply this test. However, in *Griffin* v *South West Water Services Ltd* [1995] IRLR 15, it was decided, in the context of employment law, that a privatised water company is an emanation of the state. The judge made it clear that it is the functions that the body carries out, rather than its precise legal ownership and structure, which determine the point. It is thus likely that all the privatised utilities will be treated as emanations of the state, at least as far as their 'public' functions are concerned.

The effect of these cases is that some environmental directives will be directly effective in some circumstances. If that is the case, an incompatible domestic law can be ignored and the directive applied instead by the national court. A number of environmental directives have now been held to be directly effective in British courts (see p. 150). Other remedies for failure to implement a directive are also discussed below.

(d) Decisions, recommendations and opinions

Decisions are binding on the individual or group to whom they are addressed, and may also be directly effective. They are again rare in environmental law, being limited mainly to matters of monitoring and information gathering, but precautionary steps in relation to CFCs were taken in the 1980s by means of decisions. The institutions may also issue recommendations and opinions. These are not binding and only have a persuasive effect.

(e) Court decisions

The decisions of the European Court of Justice give rise to law and this has been a particularly fertile area. The Court has borrowed and developed general principles of law from the jurisprudence of the Member States, such as the principles of natural justice, proportionality, certainty, equality and the protection of legitimate expectations. The concept of proportionality is a particularly important one in environmental law and was applied in the *Danish Bottles* case (Case 302/86 *Commission* v *Denmark* [1988] ECR 4607 (see p. 135)).

Validity of EC legislation

The validity of regulations, directives and decisions can be challenged within two months under Article 230 (ex 173). This Article sets out grounds which are slightly wider than the English *ultra vires* rules. As a judicial review action it also requires the applicant to have standing. Member States, the Commission, the Council and Parliament have it, whilst an individual has to show direct and individual concern. Such a requirement virtually restricts individuals to challenging decisions addressed to them specifically, rather than relating to the environment generally (see Case C-321/95P *Greenpeace* v *Commission* [1998] ECR I-1651).

The rationale for EC environmental law and policy: the common market

The fundamental basis of the EC has always been economic. The primary aims were originally set out in Articles 2 and 3 of the Treaty of Rome, which established the EEC in 1957. These are the creation of a 'common market' (i.e. a fully integrated single internal market within the boundaries of the Member States) in 'goods, persons, services and capital', together with the progressive harmonisation of the economic policies of the Member States. In order to achieve these primary aims, internal barriers to trade and competition need to be dismantled, so that there are no internal frontiers to hamper the free movement of goods, persons, services and capital, and no discrimination between people or firms on the grounds of nationality. This policy of free competition may be referred to as the provision of a level playing-field for producers across the EC. Common tariff barriers against the outside world are also to be erected and common policies developed in relation to certain key sectors of the economy, such as agriculture, transport, coal and steel, and energy.

This fundamental economic basis remains. In 1985, the Member States agreed to push for the completion of a fully integrated internal market by the end of 1992, and this requirement was incorporated into the Treaty as Article 8A by the Single European Act 1986. There is little doubt that this led to fresh impetus towards economic integration, although there is equally little doubt that full economic integration has yet to appear in some sectors (e.g. fiscal policy).

It is clear that there is a fundamental conflict between some of these aims and the protection of the environment. This problem has been tackled by the creation of an environmental policy.

The EC's environmental policy

There was no mention of the environment in the original Treaty of Rome. To some extent this was because the primary aims of the EEC were, as explained above, economic, but it was mainly because the potential environmental impact of the expansionist, growth-related economic policies adopted at the time was not perceived. By the early 1970s, however, the need for some form of policy on the protection of the environment was accepted. There were two reasons for this. One was the acceptance of the interrelationship between economic growth and environmental degradation. The other was that the environment was then emerging as a significant political issue. Environmental protection thus fits into the activities of the EC in two overlapping ways: first as an adjunct to economic policy, and secondly as a positive end in itself.

In October 1972, declaring that 'economic expansion is not an end in itself', the heads of state of the Member States accordingly requested the Commission to draw up an EC environmental policy. It responded by formulating the first Action Programme on the Environment. (This has been followed by four further Action Programmes in 1977, 1982, 1987 and 1992.) This was the effective beginning of what is now a very wide-ranging environmental strategy. (Even so, it was not actually the beginning of EC involvement in environmental matters — as long ago as 1967, Directive 67/548 provided specifically for the classification, packaging and labelling of dangerous substances.) Well over 200 items of environmental legislation have now been agreed as part of this policy, ranging across the whole spectrum of matters covered by this book.

The constitutional basis of the EC's environmental policy

The constitutional basis for an environmental policy must be considered in two distinct phases: before and after the Single European Act 1986. The history of the development of the EC's environmental policy will be considered first, because it is a good illustration of the way that the institutions have in practice widened the scope of what the EC deals with by a generous reading of the Treaty.

(a) Before the Single European Act 1986

Before 1986 the legal justification for the policy was not entirely clear. In practice, two Articles of the Treaty, Articles 100 and 235 (the former relating to the harmonisation of national laws in order to further the establishment of the common market, the latter relating to the EC's general and residual powers), were used as justification. The majority of directives, especially those relating to pollution control and common standards, tended to be justified on the basis of Article 100 (now 94), whilst those where the content was almost purely environmental, such as Directive 79/409 on Wild Birds, were justified on the basis of Article 235 (now 308). It was quite common for both Articles to be cited, just in case of a challenge.

In cases that did come to the European Court of Justice, the environmental policy was supported, which is not surprising since it had been formulated with the agreement of all the Member States. In Case 91/79 *Commission* v *Italy* [1980] ECR 1099, the Court held quite clearly that environmental matters could fall within Article 100. It stated:

Provisions which are made necessary by considerations relating to the environment and health may be a burden on the undertakings to which they apply, and if there is no harmonisation of national provisions on the matter, competition may be appreciably distorted.

Then, in Case 240/83 *Procureur de la République* v *Association de Défense des Brûleurs d'Huiles Usagées* [1985] ECR 531, on the legitimacy of Directive 75/439 on Waste Oils, the European Court of Justice stated that environmental protection was 'one of the Community's essential objectives', and as such it justified some restrictions on the operation of the common market. In a sense this amounted to a rewriting of the Treaty by the European Court of Justice as a matter of political reality.

(b) Single European Act 1986

In 1986, the Single European Act (SEA 1986) went some way towards reflecting the reality of the situation by amending the Treaty to add a whole new title relating to the protection of the environment. By adding new Articles 130R, 130S and 130T (now 174, 175 and 176), the SEA 1986 introduced explicit law-making powers in relation to environmental matters making reliance on ex-Article 235 redundant. In addition, it effectively amended Article 100 by adding a new Article 100A (now 95), which has been of great importance for the development of environmental policy, even though it is primarily aimed at speeding up the completion of the single internal market. To some extent these changes regularised the existing *de facto* position, but they also established some clearer constitutional rules than there had been in the past on the extent of the law-making powers and on how decisions were to be made. For some, however, the insertion of an environmental title was more about structuring and perhaps even *restricting* the competence of the Community, through procedural provisions such as requiring available scientific and technical data to be taken account of, than about regularising and strengthening the role of the Community in the field of the environment by giving it an explicit legal base. Regardless, they failed to check the rapid growth in environmental legislation following the SEA.

(c) Treaty on European Union ('Maastricht Treaty') 1992

The Maastricht Treaty continued the process of integrating environmental matters into the heart of the EC's activities by making further amendments to the Articles mentioned above. It also recognised for the first time that the development of 'a policy in the sphere of the environment' is one of the EC's main activities (see Article 3), and replaced Article 2, which sets out the objectives of the EC, with a new version that included the tasks of promoting throughout the Community 'a harmonious and balanced development of economic activities' and 'sustainable and non-inflationary growth respecting the environment'. Article 2 thus acknowledges that there is a balance to be struck between economic and environmental factors. Of course, there remains a very live political debate about how far this widening of the aims of the EC has moved it away from a strictly economic union towards political union. Environmental policy is perhaps a good indicator of this process, since the more that explicit environmental objectives are adopted, the more it looks as if the EC is moving towards full political union.

(d) Treaty of Amsterdam 1997

Further amendments to the Treaty were agreed at Amsterdam in June 1997 and came into force in May 1999. Although not generally as significant as those made at Maastricht, they continue the development of European environmental policy. Although sustainable development is not defined, a new main goal of 'promoting a harmonious and balanced and sustainable development of economic activities', together with 'a high level of protection and improvement of the quality of the environment' is now found in Article 2, and therefore applies to all policies and all institutions, not just to Commission initiatives. These goals are reinforced by a new Article 6 which provides that 'environmental protection requirements must be integrated into the definition and implementation of Community policies and activities . . . in particular with a view to promoting sustainable development'. Although a version of this objective previously appeared in the environmental title, its elevation to the start of the Treaty is of considerable symbolic, legal and policy importance. It is leading, for example, to publication by the Commission of a number of policy documents exploring the integration of the environment into Community policy generally (e.g. COM(98)333)) or in specific sectors like energy (COM(98)571) or agriculture (COM(2000)20).

Which Article?

The difference in the voting procedure in the Council has been one reason why, following the Single European Act, the Article that was used in adopting a directive was often of considerable importance. Another reason related to the involvement of the European Parliament. In attempting to speed up completion of the internal market, the SEA introduced qualified majority voting for measures adopted under Article 100A but made no change to measures adopted under the new environmental provisions in the Treaty, so legislation adopted under Article 130S still required unanimity. This encouraged the Commission to introduce proposals under Article 100A, to speed their process into legislation. However, the different voting procedures meant that the Parliament had a greater legislative role in 'internal market' legislation than in proposals introduced under the environmental title.

Tensions came to a head when the Commission challenged the adoption of Directive 89/428 on the Titanium Dioxide Industry on the grounds that the wrong Article (and thus the wrong voting procedures) had been used (see Case C-300/89 *Commission* v *Council* [1991] ECR I-2867). The Commission, in proposing the directive, had argued that it could be adopted under Article 100A (now 95), because it related to the harmonisation of rules relating to an industrial process. The Council, however, unanimously agreed that it should be adopted under Article 130S (now 175), since the content of the directive related to environmental protection. The Court of Justice decided that the Commission's argument was essentially correct. It stated that where environmental measures also contributed to the establishment of the internal market they fell within Article 95, thus suggesting that most environmental directives could be based on Article 95. It also suggested that, where there was a choice between alternative Articles, Article 95 should be chosen because it allowed greater input from Parliament through the co-operation procedure, a conclusion difficult to square with its view that only 'objective factors . . . amenable to judicial review' counted. This decision opened the way at the time for the wider use of qualified majority voting on environmental matters.

However, in a later case, (Case C-155/91 *Commission* v *Council* [1993] ECR I-939, which concerned the correct legal basis of Directive 91/156 amending the framework Directive on Waste 75/442), the Court of Justice altered its view and adopted instead a test based on the centre of gravity of the Directive. In this case it decided that the principal objective of the Directive, which was the protection of the environment, was the crucial factor, and not any ancillary effect on the functioning of the internal market. Directive 91/156 could thus be distinguished from Directive 89/428. It is notable that this decision followed the conclusion of the Maastricht negotiations which sanctioned the general use of qualified majority voting under Article 175 (ex 130S) (see also Case C-187/93 *Parliament* v *Council* [1994] ECR I-2857).

These cases suggest that most environmental directives should now be based on Article 175, although it remains possible to adopt harmonisation directives having some environmental elements under Article 95. Because the decision-making procedures are now virtually identical for internal market harmonisation and environmental directives, however, these 'legal base' battles are less important when measures having both trade and environmental dimensions to them are proposed (and also because the ability of states to set higher standards is now broadly similar under both Articles).

Instead, we may be more likely to see disputes where measures in other fields have an environmental component to them, something which should be ever more frequent now that the Treaty requires the integration of environmental protection requirements when legislative proposals are made in *all* other areas. For example, in Cases C-164 and 165/97 *Parliament v Council* [1999] ECR I-1139, the Parliament challenged the validity of regulations protecting forests from air pollution and from fire. The regulations had been adopted by the Council under Article 43 of the Treaty (now 37) which relates to agriculture, under which the Parliament only needs to be consulted, the very weakest form of Parliament involvement in decision-making. The Parliament was successful in having the regulations annulled on the grounds that the measures were primarily environmental in nature; they were primarily intended to protect forest ecosystems and forests were not agricultural products as the Council, rather weakly, argued. While this was a fairly straightforward decision to reach, more difficult cases will doubtless emerge.

The scope of EC environmental law

(a)   Harmonising legislation

Article 94 (ex 100) enables directives to be made that seek to harmonise laws and administrative practices of Member States which directly affect the establishment or functioning of the common market. The normal methods of achieving this are to lay down uniform, common standards or to outlaw specified discriminatory practices.

The relationship with the environment here is that a unified internal market depends upon trade and competition not being distorted by Member States applying different rules and standards. The EC has therefore tried to harmonise laws in all the Member States so that a producer in one country does not have an unfair advantage over one in another. Initially used to harmonise product standards, this soon extended to *process* standards. A law permitting producers in one country to pollute more than an equivalent producer in another country is seen as anti-competitive, since it amounts to a form of disguised subsidy. In this sense environmental policy is little more than incidental to the central economic policy.

By inserting Article 100A (now 95), the Single European Act introduced qualified majority voting for many proposals of this nature. However, as a safeguard, it also required as an objective that, if action is taken under Article 95 concerning health, safety, environmental or consumer protection, a high level of protection should be taken for those standards. In addition, Member States may derogate from the common standards in certain limited ways (Article 95(4) — see p. 132).

(b)   'Environmental' legislation: objectives and policy

Articles 174 to 176 (ex 130R–T), on the other hand, provide a specific justification for environmental protection laws, even where there is no direct link to the economic aims of the EC. Article 175 provides the mechanics by setting out the voting procedures in the Council (see below). In contrast with

Articles 94 and 95, either directives or regulations are possible, although few environmental regulations have been made. A further contrast is that, whilst Articles 94 and 95 generally require uniform baseline standards (subject to the environmental guarantee), under these Articles that is not always required, since the motivating force behind them is the improvement of environmental standards rather than the creation of the common market. Accordingly, Article 176 specifically provides for the possibility that stricter measures than those agreed under Article 175 may be employed by Member States, as long as they are compatible with the rest of the Treaty (for fuller discussion of the need for uniformity, see p. 132).

Article 174(1) includes as *objectives* of the EC's environmental activities the preservation, protection and improvement of the quality of the environment, the protection of human health, and the prudent and rational utilisation of resources. Article 174(2) uniquely sets out the central *principles* of EC environmental policy, which should be taken into account when framing policy and legislation:

(a)   preventative action should be preferred to remedial measures;
(b)   environmental damage should be rectified at source;
(c)   the 'polluter pays' principle; and
(d)   policy should be based on the precautionary principle.

A high level of environmental protection must also be aimed at, while the principle that environmental policies should form a component of the EC's other policies is now a general principle of the EC Treaty (Art. 6 EC).

The principles are essentially policy principles, the purpose of which is to guide the form and content of EC environmental legislation. As noted, they must be taken into account; at best, this means that if legislation has been adopted which completely fails to have regard to a principle, it might be annulled. For example, the ECJ has held that it would only review the compatibility of the Ozone Regulation 3093/94 with the precautionary principle if there had been a 'manifest error of appraisal' (Case C-341/95 *Bettani* v *Safety Hi-Tech Srl* [1998] ECR I-4435).

A difficulty, however, is that the meaning of the principles is far from settled. For example, the degree of risk needed to invoke the precautionary principle is contested (see p. 52), but would probably be something other than the worst case scenario as the Commission argued in a case concerning nuclear testing (Case T-219/95R *Danielsson* v *Commission* [1996] ECR II-3051). Similarly, the polluter pays principle is vague, both as to who the polluter is and what 'pollution' means (see further p. 207). It is not clear whether the approach of the ECJ in the *Safety Hi-Tech* case is to avoid difficulties by deciding that only if the principle has not been considered will legislation be reviewable, or whether it also allows arguments based on fundamental misconceptions of the principles.

It is important to note that the principles are not directly enforceable obligations. That is, they cannot be relied on in the abstract by an individual claiming that a polluter has not 'paid' for some aspect of pollution (e.g. by a claimant in a private nuisance case arguing that a polluter should pay for damage to property even where this was unforeseeable) or that all regulatory action should be precautionary (see *R v Secretary of State for Trade and Industry, ex parte Duddridge* [1995] Env LR 151, discussed further on p. 49).

Under Article 174(3) (ex 130R(3)), the EC institutions are required to *take account of* available scientific and technical data, environmental conditions in the various regions of the EC, and the balanced development of those regions when preparing any proposals. In addition, some form of cost-benefit analysis should be performed before environmental measures are agreed — another example of the close interrelationship between environmental and economic matters.

The international dimension is covered by Article 174(4). Many pollution, conservation and environmental matters, such as acid rain, the protection of migratory species, or pollution of the North Sea, are international in scope. A supranational body such as the EC is well-placed to tackle them by having a common internal environmental policy with agreed standards. It may also act by putting forward a common platform in dealings with the rest of the world. Article 174(4) specifically permits the negotiation and conclusion of international agreements, a power which justifies the EC's independent involvement in international treaties and dealings with Eastern Europe. Promoting international co-operation is also an objective of the EC (Article 174(1)).

Article 175(5) (ex 130S(5)) provides that if a measure agreed under Article 175 involves disproportionate costs for a particular member state, the Council may allow for temporary derogations and/or for financial support to meet those costs out of the special Cohesion Fund. This provision was inserted at Maastricht to buy off complaints from a number of the less-developed Member States that the burden of EC environmental policy fell unfairly on them since it hindered their industrial and economic development. They perceive this to be unfair because the other Member States have arguably reached their current level of development only by taking advantage of the absence in the past of the standards now imposed by modern environmental laws.

(c)   The scope of EC environmental law
The scope of the future content of EC environmental policy can also be seen from the five environmental Action Programmes. The first two Action Programmes were reactive in nature and concentrated on pollution control and on remedial measures. This fitted in with the economic justification of environmental policy under Article 100 (now 94), but was also designed to tackle the most obvious and pressing problems first. The third and fourth Action Programmes emphasised preventive measures at the same time as continuing the work on pollution control. For example, a number of directives were agreed on product standards and on the design of industrial plant and processes. They also stressed the need to integrate environmental protection into other EC policies. Whilst there are not too many clear examples where this has happened as yet (the designation of environmentally

sensitive areas for agricultural grant purposes is one of the few direct examples), the importance of this principle for the shape of future policy should not be underestimated. However, perhaps the most significant feature of the third and fourth Action Programmes was that attention was increasingly paid to structural, or 'horizontal', measures that laid down procedures or ancillary administrative matters. For example, legislation was passed on the assessment of the environmental impact of major projects (Directive 85/337), eco-labelling (Regulation 880/92), freedom of access to environmental information held by public bodies (Directive 90/313), and eco-management and audit (Regulation 1836/93).

There is no doubt that the amendments made by the Single European Act aided this shift in emphasis by encouraging more wide-ranging measures. For example, because of Danish objections to the use of Article 235 (now 308), it was accepted after the passage of the Wild Birds Directive 79/409 that no further legislation would be passed on wildlife unless it related to trade. Such a limitation is now clearly removed, as the passage of the Habitats Directive 92/43 illustrated. As a further example, Directive 90/313 on Freedom of Access to Information on the Environment was made under Article 175 and there is little doubt that it would have been difficult to justify such a measure under Articles 94 or 95.

The fifth Action Programme, entitled *Towards Sustainability*, was agreed at the end of 1992 and covers the period 1993 to 2000. It reflects in part the agreements adopted at the Rio 'Earth Summit' earlier that year and, as its title suggests, stresses the sustainable management of natural resources and provides a more wide-ranging environmental policy than before. It further switches the emphasis away from grouping environmental controls by reference to environmental media, such as air, water or land, to looking horizontally at all the environmental implications of various sectors of the economy. In particular, as part of the principle of integrating environmental policies within the EC's other policies, it concentrates on the following sectors: industry, transport, agriculture, energy and tourism.

A central concept in the scheme of the fifth Action Programme is that of 'shared responsibility'. This is the idea that responsibility for solving environmental problems is shared between government, industry and consumers. The idea reflects not just concerns about subsidiarity and proportionality but also equity considerations. The programme heralded a movement away from using legislation and regulation to solve problems towards a greater use of financial and other market mechanisms. It also suggested a more inventive use of legal instruments, including civil liability and voluntary mechanisms, the provision of more information on the state of the environment, a greater role for NGOs, and scrutiny of the financial sector's contribution towards sustainable development.

The range of environmental directives

It is not possible in the space available to list all EC directives that relate to the environment. What follows is a selective list intended to illustrate the major areas of EC involvement. Greater detail on individual directives is given in the relevant chapters of Part II of this book and in Haigh, *Manual of Environmental Policy: the EC and Britain* (Longman, looseleaf), which explains each directive, and its implementation, in turn. Where the number of a directive is given below, it normally refers to the original piece of legislation, which may subsequently have been amended. In some cases, such as in relation to the use and production of CFCs or emissions from vehicles, no number is given simply because the amount of legislation is very great.

EC directives have been made in relation to the following:

(a)   setting quality standards for water (e.g. Surface Waters for Drinking 75/440; Drinking Water 80/778; Bathing Waters 76/160; Water Standards for Freshwater Fish 78/659; Shellfish Waters 79/923; Nitrates 91/676);

(b)   setting emission standards for discharges to water (e.g. Dangerous Substances in Water 76/464; Groundwater 80/68);

(c)   setting quality standards for air (e.g. Smoke and Sulphur Dioxide 80/779; Nitrogen Dioxide 85/203; Lead in Air 82/884 and now Directive 96/62);

(d)   setting emission standards for emissions to the atmosphere (e.g. various Directives on Emissions from Vehicles such as 70/220, 88/76, 89/548 and 91/441; Emissions from Industrial Plants 84/360; Emissions from Large Combustion Plants 88/609; New and Existing Municipal Waste Incinerators 89/369 and 89/429; Hazardous Waste Incinerators 94/67);

(e)   setting noise standards (e.g. Noise in the Workplace 86/188; various Directives on Noise from Vehicles; Noise from Construction Plant 84/532);

(f)   controlling emissions of dangerous pollutants (e.g. Dangerous Substances in Water 76/464; Toxic Waste 78/319 as amended by 91/689; Mercury 84/156; Lindane 84/491; Cadmium 83/513; Disposal of PCBs 76/403 and various Directives on CFCs, Lead and Pesticides);

(g)   controlling the disposal, management and reduction of waste (e.g. Framework Directive on Waste 75/442 as amended by 91/156; Toxic Waste 78/319 as amended by 91/689; Sewage Sludge 86/278; Urban Waste Water Treatment 91/271; Landfill 99/31); Packaging and Packaging Waste 94/62);

(h)   controlling the storage and use of hazardous materials (e.g. Major Accident Hazards 82/501 and 96/82 (the 'Seveso' I and II Directives); Asbestos 87/217);

(i)   controlling dangerous activities (e.g. Transfrontier Shipment of Toxic Waste Regulation 259/93);

(j)   setting product standards (e.g. Lead in Petrol 88/195; the various Directives on Noise and Emissions from Vehicles; Classification, Packaging and Labelling of Dangerous Substances 79/831);

(k)   setting standards for the operation of certain industries (e.g. Emissions from Industrial Plants 84/360; Titanium Dioxide Industry 78/176 and 89/428; Emissions from Large Combustion Plants 88/609; Integrated Pollution Prevention and Control 96/61);

(l)   procedures for the planning of development (e.g. Environmental Impact Assessment 85/337);

(m)   protection of wildlife (e.g. Wild Birds 79/409; Habitats 92/43; Trade in Endangered Species Regulation 338/97);

(n)   protection of the countryside (e.g. the Rural Development Regulation 1257/99);
(o)   the use and release of genetically modified organisms (e.g. Directives 90/219 and 90/220);

There are also important directives and regulations on an ever-widening range of ancillary matters. Regulation 1210/90 establishes the European Environment Agency (see p. 223). Directive 90/313 on Freedom of Access to Information on the Environment is another essential part of the process of providing accurate information, which is so important if responsibility for environmental improvement is to be shared between regulators, industry and the public. Regulation 880/92 on Eco-Labelling and Regulation 1836/93 on Eco-Management and Audit further emphasise the role that voluntary initiatives by business will play in future policy. Lastly, there is the Financial Instrument for the Environment (LIFE), originally contained within Regulation 1973/92, which provides financial support for environmental matters, especially on the promotion of sustainable development and nature conservation.

Towards uniformity or flexibility?

As explained above, there is now a considerable body of EC environmental law, some of which has its origins in economic integration and some which has been adopted as more explicitly 'environmental' measures (under ex Art. 235 or now Art. 175). In one sense, all of this legislation aims at harmonising practice across the Community, although the desirability of setting uniform standards is somewhat greater when it comes to measures passed to complete the internal market (i.e. under Art. 95), especially product standards. Nevertheless, all of this legislation is essentially *minimum harmonisation* legislation — it sets baseline standards which should not be breached. With both types of legislation, however, there is some room for Member States to set stricter standards at national level. Two issues therefore arise. The first is the extent to which any Member State may go beyond environmental standards set at Community level (where there is a difference depending on whether the EC measure relates primarily to the internal market or to the environment). The second is the more general issue as to whether directives tend towards uniform standards or impose different standards on different Member States (i.e. how much flexibility there is *in the directive itself*).

For 'internal market' legislation, under Article 95(4), national provisions may be stricter than the directive if the national provision is justified by the need to protect the environment or the working environment, and the Commission verifies this. This exception was intended to cover the situation where a directive was agreed under Article 95 despite the opposition of a member state (and for this reason is called the 'environmental guarantee'). It was central to the political balance agreed in the Single European Act because it provided a palliative to qualified majority voting. Article 95(4) has been invoked successfully by the German government in relation to what effectively amounts to a ban on the use of pentachlorophenol in Germany, although not before the original decision by the Commission to accept the ban was annulled by the European Court of Justice (see Case C-41/93 *France* v *Commission* [1994] ECR I-1829). The Court did not address the scope of the then Article 100A(4) directly, but it did state that the exception should be interpreted restrictively because it derogates from the single internal market and therefore suggests that it applied only where a Member State has an *existing* piece of legislation that is more stringent than the directive at the time the directive is adopted. This is now given effect to by the Amsterdam Treaty, which provides for such national provisions to be *maintained* rather than *applied* (Article 95(4)). Under Article 95(5), however, further national provisions may be *introduced* in the light of new scientific evidence.

Although this seems exhaustive, some measures adopted under Article 100A (now 95) allow for more flexibility. The Packaging Waste Directive (94/62), for example, requires Member States to establish national systems to provide for the collection and recovery of packaging. It then provides for recovery and recycling targets, though Member States may set higher targets if they wish. In addition, three Member States (Portugal, Greece and Ireland) were allowed to meet lower targets. It is clear that these differences were agreed as a political expedient, but it is hard to see how this fits in with the normal requirements of uniformity under Article 95 (see London and Llamas, 'EC Packaging Directive' (1995) 145 NLJ 221).

By contrast, Article 175(5) (ex 130S(5)) allows disproportionate costs to be alleviated by temporary derogations and/or financial support from the Cohesion Fund. It is worth noting that there is a move away from resorting to reliance on derogations (which must generally be granted by the Commission) towards setting out different targets in directives (see, e.g. the different national targets effectively provided for in the Landfill Directive 99/31, and further below). The latter may be preferable politically, since the Member States can exercise more influence on the Council than on the Commission.

More generally, however, stricter measures are allowable under Article 176, subject to unlawful trade distortions (see below). But what does Article 174, and the Treaty generally, require when it comes to agreeing the content of directives?

The starting point is the general principle of subsidiarity, first introduced specifically to the environmental title by the SEA 1986 and now contained in Article 5 (ex 3b). This states that:

> In areas which do not fall within its exclusive competence, the Community shall take action, in accordance with the principle of subsidiarity, only if and in so far as the objectives of the proposed action cannot be sufficiently achieved by the Member States and can therefore, by reason of the scale or effects of the proposed action, be better achieved by the Community. Any action by the Community shall not go beyond what is necessary to achieve the objectives of this Treaty.

In part this is a competency clause, but it also relates to the amount of discretion given to Member States in EC environmental legislation. Following the Maastricht negotiations, the concept was much discussed. The

Edinburgh Summit in December 1992, for example, resolved that the Community should only legislate to the extent necessary, that framework directives should be preferred (see below), and voluntary codes used where appropriate. In the event, the hit list of directives that were candidates for amendment or repeal did not include any environmental measures. However, the threat posed by subsidiarity was shown by the UK Government's action in bringing forward a list of directives it wished to see amended and a further list of proposals it wished to see discontinued. The first category included the various directives on air quality standards, drinking water, bathing waters and hazardous waste, whilst the second included the proposed directives on landfill, packaging waste and ecological quality of water, as well as proposals for strategic environmental assessment. This pressure has largely been resisted although not without some drift towards more flexible legislation.

Alongside subsidiarity must be considered Article 175 (ex 130R). This provides, for example, that Community policy should be based on the principle that environmental damage should, as a priority, be rectified at source. But it also provides that, in preparing its environmental policy, the Community must take account of environmental conditions in, and balanced development of, the various regions of the Community. Arguably, the former points to a preference for emission standards, while the latter suggests a preference for target standards.

In general terms, the EC appears to be resolving this contradiction by a subtle mixture of approaches which may require 'best available techniques' and similar types of standards to be used for things like industrial emissions, but then tempers this by requiring these standards to be set having regard to regional differences. A good example of this is the Integrated Pollution Prevention and Control Directive (96/61) under which emissions must be controlled with regard to firms' 'geographic location and local environmental conditions'. Thus, while all regulated firms have to use the best available techniques to minimise pollution, regional differences will play a part in determining what is 'best' for any installation.

A slightly different example of taking regional differences into account is the 'bubbling' of the EC's greenhouse gas emission reduction targets. Thus, the Community's target of reducing its emissions by 8 per cent by 2008–2012 (compared to 1990 levels) is imposed unequally on Member States, so that some states must reduce emissions (e.g. the UK must make a 12.5 per cent cut) while others can increase their emissions (e.g. Greece is allowed a 25 per cent increase). This is a good illustration of the idea of 'common but differentiated responsibilities' in EC law (see further p. 104).

Free trade and environmental protection

The tensions between uniformity and flexibility, or between harmonisation and national interests, are also seen in the extent to which environmental considerations may override the free movement of goods within the EC. Thus Article 30 (ex 36) permits national laws effectively to restrict imports under Article 28 (ex 30) if there is a genuine need to protect, amongst other things, human, plant or animal health or national treasures. 'Animal health' has recently been defined to include wider biodiversity conservation concerns (Case C-67/97 *Bluhme* [1998] ECR I-8033), an important extension from its narrower agricultural origins.

The very important decision of the European Court of Justice in the *Danish Bottles* case (Case 302/86 *Commission v Denmark* [1988] ECR 4607) amplifies this point into a more general rule. The Court concluded that the protection of the environment is one of the EC's so-called 'mandatory requirements'. As such it can justify an interference with the operation of the common market, as long as the method adopted is proportionate to the aim which is being protected. However, it will not justify derogation from a full harmonisation directive agreed under Article 95.

The case arose from a Commission challenge to Danish laws which required beer and soft drink containers to be returnable, arguing they were a form of disguised discrimination against foreign manufacturers and hence an impediment to free trade under Article 28. The European Court of Justice held in clear terms that it was permissible to use environmental protection as an excuse for such discrimination. It went on to hold that such a derogation from the free market must be proportionate to the end to be achieved. Since a returnability requirement was clearly more environment-friendly than a recycling one, this requirement was acceptable. But a further licensing requirement, whereby only a limited number of container shapes was permitted, was disproportionate and thus illegal in EC law.

This decision has an obvious impact on the ability of Member States to pass environmental legislation that is stricter than in other Member States and which thus interferes with the common market. But it also has an impact on the attitude of the Commission, since in order to re-establish the single internal market, it will seek to lay down common standards by proposing EC legislation. There is an incentive to move towards common standards based on the stricter environmental protection legislation of the non-conforming state, using Article 95(3) as a justification.

Some extension of the *Danish Bottles* principle can be seen in the *Wallonian Waste* case (Case C-2/90 *Commission v Belgium* [1992] ECR I-4431). This case concerned what was effectively a ban on waste imports imposed by the Walloon Regional Executive. The European Court of Justice decided that waste constituted goods for the purposes of the Treaty and thus there was a clear infringement of the provisions on free movement of goods. However, it went on to decide that the ban was justified on environmental grounds. In so doing, it held that wastes are goods of a special character. Accordingly, the general principle set out in Article 174(2), that pollution should be rectified at source, was called into play to suggest that wastes should be disposed of as close to their place of origin as possible. This enabled the Court to avoid the otherwise inevitable conclusion that the ban was discriminatory and is an important example of how these general principles can be used so as to have an impact on the development of the law. A further interesting feature of the case was the rather bizarre (but logical) result that the ban was legal as far as it applied to ordinary wastes, but not as far as hazardous wastes were concerned, because Directive 84/631 laid down an exhaustive system for the transfrontier shipment of hazardous waste. Therefore, the ban on hazardous waste was illegal because it contravened the provisions of the Directive.

Some attempt to formalise these decisions was made by the Maastricht Treaty, which added a new paragraph to Article 174(2). This allows directives seeking to harmonise EC laws to include a safeguard clause permitting a Member State to take *provisional* measures for environmental reasons. This does not appear to alter anything decided by *Danish Bottles,* but the Article does add a further requirement that such measures are subject to inspection by the Commission.

Compliance by Member States with EC law

Under Article 10 EC, Member States are required to 'take all appropriate measures, whether general or particular, to ensure fulfilment of the obligations arising out of this Treaty or resulting from action taken by institutions of the Community'. A further requirement is to 'abstain from any measure which could jeopardise the attainment of the objectives of the Treaty'. Abiding by EC law therefore entails a positive and a negative obligation: implementation of relevant directives, and not doing anything contrary to EC law. Since environmental law consists mainly of directives, compliance will be discussed in terms of them.

In order to comply with a directive, a member state must implement it fully and within the time limit. Any incompatible law must be repealed. It is irrelevant whether other states have also failed to comply.

It thus appears that there are a number of ways in which there may be non-compliance with a directive:

(a) failure to implement at all within the time allowed (the case law is clear that there is no real excuse for this, since the member state will have agreed the time limit in the first place);

(b) failure to implement all the requirements of the directive;

(c) implementation by adopting an incorrect interpretation of the directive, the European Court of Justice being the ultimate arbiter of this point;

(d) attempting to implement by mere changes in administrative practice; Case 102/79 *Commission* v *Belgium* [1980] ECR 1473 makes it clear that a change in the law is required, because administrative measures may be altered at any time by the administration;

(e) inadequate implementation in practice.

This last type of non-compliance arises where a member state has passed all the legislation required to implement a directive, but there is no compliance in fact. For example, it could arise where a Member State fails to enforce the provisions of a law, or where standards laid down in a directive are not adhered to in practice. In Case C-337/89 *Commission* v *United Kingdom* [1992] ECR I-6103, the European Court of Justice effectively equated non-compliance in fact with non-compliance in law. It decided that, by failing to comply with the maximum admissible concentration of nitrate in drinking water in some supply zones, the UK government was in breach of Directive 80/778 on Drinking Water. This raises some important points, because in a decentralised country the national government is not necessarily the body that was actually responsible for the breach and, indeed, may not, in some cases, be in a very strong position to rectify matters. Nevertheless, it appears that the national government will be held responsible as a matter of EC law.

Each Member State will normally be required to send a 'compliance letter' to the Commission explaining the measures that have been taken to ensure compliance with a directive. These provisions are often stated in each individual directive, but have not always been adhered to rigorously in the past. Accordingly, Directive 91/692 relating to the harmonisation of provisions on reports on the implementation of environmental Directives was passed. This is increasing the Commission's ability to identify non-compliance, as to a limited extent is the creation of the European Environment Agency, though at present it is quite clear that complaints from environmental groups and individuals in Member States are the most significant sources of information on non-implementation.

Non-compliance: enforcement by the Commission

If a Member State does not implement a Directive properly, or maintains in force a law which is contrary to EC law, there are only a limited number of options. The main responsibility for ensuring compliance rests with the Commission, which has a discretion to start infringement proceedings. Its current policy is to start these automatically in cases where any failure to comply is alleged.

These infringement proceedings have various stages. The Commission will write to the state informally, asking it to explain its position. If a satisfactory answer is not received, a formal letter will be sent, and the state's observations will be formally required. If the Commission is still not satisfied that the matter can be settled, it will issue a Reasoned Opinion, explaining what it thinks are the main features of the non-compliance. Most cases are resolved at these preliminary stages, and there are obvious parallels with the graded procedures adopted in practice by most regulatory agencies when dealing with breaches of domestic environmental law.

Under Article 226 (ex 169), the Commission then has an absolute discretion to bring the Member State before the European Court of Justice. Another member state may join in Article 226 proceedings as a third party to argue for one side or the other (for example, Britain did this to support the Commission in the *Danish Bottles* case). If the Commission does not bring infringement proceedings, another Member State may bring them under Article 227, although this is very rare. An individual has no standing to bring infringement proceedings, or to compel the Commission to do so, but is limited to drawing an alleged non-compliance to the attention of the Commission.

The European Court of Justice is the ultimate arbiter of whether there has been compliance in law, and will give a decision on whether the state is in breach of EC law, but in the past it simply had declaratory powers. Nevertheless, states normally have complied as a matter of political necessity. Otherwise the Commission or another Member State can reinstitute the infringement proceedings (again this is rare). The Maastricht Treaty changed matters considerably. Under Article 228 (ex 171), the Commission may now issue a Reasoned Opinion if it considers that a Member State has not complied with a judgment of the Court. If the Member State then continues to fail to comply, the Commission can bring the case back before the Court, which may impose a fine. The level of financial penalty will depend upon the seriousness and duration of the violation and the need for a 'dissuasive' effect.

In addition to these factors, there is a degree of weighting which is applied taking into account the Member State's influence over the law which has been violated (i.e. the number of votes it has in the Council and its ability to pay (based on its GDP)). If all of these factors resulted in the maximum daily penalty it could lead to significant fines (well in excess of €500,000 in some cases), which could be a serious deterrent. The Commission began seeking fines in environmental cases in 1997 and the first such cases involving Art. 228 are now coming before the ECJ. The first decided case involved non-compliance by Greece with two waste directives (Case C-387/97 *Commission* v *Hellenic Republic*, 4 July 2000, unreported). The ECJ imposed a daily fine of €20,000, judging the failure to implement management plans for toxic waste as serious a breach as actual unlawful disposal of non-toxic waste. It is too early, however, to say what effect the Art. 228 procedure will have in practice. The Commission has also discussed the possibility of withholding EC funds provided for environmental matters in the event of non-compliance.

Non-compliance: individual remedies

In addition to these formal infringement procedures, the Court of Justice has used the concept of the supremacy of Community law to develop various strands of case law which relate to the question of compliance with EC law. Two of these — the doctrine of direct effect and the interpretation principle established by *von Colson* and *Marleasing* (known as 'indirect effect') — have already been mentioned above. But it is worth summarising them again because, when these judicial developments are all taken together, they ensure that a lot of pressure can be exerted on Member States to implement directives properly and in full.

(a) Direct effect

The doctrine of direct effect is of great importance, since directly effective EC laws can be relied upon in the courts of Member States without the need for implementation: any incompatible national law can simply be ignored. If a national court is unwilling to accept that a directive is directly effective, the applicant may ask it to refer the question to the European Court of Justice under the Article 234 procedure. However, the doctrine has its limitations. First, because the obligations must be sufficiently clear and precise, there are difficulties with directives that seem to impose more general obligations to achieve results. For example, in Case C-236/92 *Comitato di Coordinamento per la Difesa della Cava* v *Regione Lombardia* [1994] ECR I-483, the European Court of Justice found that Article 4 of the Waste Framework Directive (75/442) did not have direct effect. This was because the Court held that it only laid down a general objective to be pursued, and general measures to do so, rather than anything more concrete and binding (see further below). On the other hand, in *R* v *Bolton Metropolitan Council, ex parte Kirkman* [1998] Env LR 719, the Court of Appeal held that an individual could, in challenging a planning permission for an incinerator, bring an argument based on essentially the same provision of the Waste Framework Directive. The provision had been transposed almost word for word in the Waste Management Licensing Regulations 1994 (SI 1994/1056), creating a sufficiently absolute obligation on the local planning authority that could be enforced by a judicial review, but only because the planning authority had not considered it. From this it is clear that whether a provision is sufficiently precise depends in part on the context in which the question is being asked. In many other cases, however, the ECJ has stressed the *lack* of discretion that Member States have at the implementation stage. This can be seen most clearly from a series of fairly robust judgments in relation to the Directives on Wild Birds (79/409) and on Environmental Assessment (85/337) (these cases are discussed in detail on p. 359 and p. 642 respectively). This doesn't mean that in every case these directives will be directly effective, but it does show, e.g., that decisions by Member States about when to apply directives (i.e. in which particular areas, or over which particular projects) can be seen as unconditional (the third limb of the test for direct effect).

Secondly, there is some doubt as to whether directives which allow Member States to set stricter standards can be directly effective. The view of the Advocate General in Case C-168/95 *Arcaro* [1996] ECR I-4705, a case about a daughter directive to the Dangerous Substances Directive (76/464), was that this would prevent the directive from being directly effective. The Court did not consider this part of the judgment. However, it is now clear that under both Articles 95 and 175 of the EC Treaty, Member States have a certain amount of room to introduce stricter measures beyond those contained in *any* directive. If the reasoning of the Advocate General was followed, therefore, no environmental directive could have direct effect. From the point of view of asserting individual rights and enforcement more generally, this is a most unattractive proposition to say the least. It must be hoped, however, that in the interests of ensuring compliance with EC law, the Court of Justice would not follow this line of reasoning, and would hold that directives could be directly effective up to the level of the standards which they contain (and which the Member States must give effect to).

Thirdly, a potential drawback of direct effect is that it only applies 'vertically' against central government or other 'emanations of the state', such as public bodies like the Environment Agency or local planning authorities. It has always been an area of some uncertainty whether a challenge by one individual effectively alleging breach of a directive by another private party (e.g. a company) would fall foul of the rule prohibiting directives having 'horizontal' effect. This issue has now come before the UK courts in a case involving a challenge by a local resident to the grant of a planning permission for quarrying by a private company which had been given without an environmental impact assessment under Directive 85/337 (*R v Durham CC, Sherburn Stone Company Ltd & Secretary of State for Environment, Transport and the Regions, ex parte Huddleston* [2000] JPL 409). Although the case was brought as a review of the local planning authority's decision, the developer argued that the effect would be to impose obligations on it, including possible criminal liabilities for mining the site without permission.

The Court of Appeal, however, rejected this line of argument, and held that there was a distinction between effectively imposing legal obligations as between individuals, and imposing conditions upon an individual's right to secure a benefit from the state. Sherburn's situation, it said, fell into the latter category. In a forceful judgment, Sedley LJ held that an individual could not be prevented from enforcing a directive against the state just because of its impact on other individuals. If this approach is followed, the number of cases where arguments about horizontal effect would invalidate challenges to EC environmental directives would be significantly reduced, since actions could be taken against regulatory agencies for failing to comply with their obligations (so long as these were clear in the way that the need for an environmental assessment in *ex parte Huddleston* was not in question).

Finally, there is the thorny question of whether an individual right must be breached for a directive to have direct effect. Unlike state liability claims (see below), it is still not clear whether individual rights need to be breached. There is a line of authority which suggests that they do but much of this comes out of actions brought by the Commission for non-compliance, and does not address the question directly. There is some support for the proposition that a directive can be directly effective if not doing so would compromise the effectiveness of EC law (a similar approach to that taken by some judges in the national courts that it is not so much an individuals standing to challenge a public law decision that matters so much as the interests of good administration; see further p. 77) although another view is that what is going on here is not 'direct effect' but perhaps a new remedy entirely, which could be particularly useful in environmental cases.

(b) Indirect effect

The indirect effect doctrine established in *von Colson* and *Marleasing* (that national laws should be interpreted so as to comply with EC law) avoids one of the limitations of direct effect by allowing horizontal actions. But it can be criticised for imposing unfair burdens on private bodies, since they will often have relied on the provisions of British law in carrying out their activities, only to find that their expectations are not met when the law is interpreted in a wider manner. It remains to be seen how far this doctrine will have an impact in British law, since it ultimately depends on the willingness of UK judges to adopt the EC interpretation and on the existence of some national law that can plausibly be 'interpreted' in the appropriate manner.

(c) State liability

The third development stems from the decision of the European Court of Justice in Cases C-6 and 9/90 *Francovich and Boniface* v *Italy* [1991] ECR I-5357 which developed a judicial damages remedy for certain breaches of EC law by Member States. As developed in later cases the state liability principle applies where:

(i)   the rule of law is intended to confer rights on the individuals concerned;

(ii)   the breach is sufficiently serious; and

(iii)   there is a direct causal link between the breach of the obligation resting on the state and the damage sustained by the injured parties.

The development in the case law has come in relation to the second criteria. While *Francovich* was a case of failure to implement a directive, in later cases the Court has held that there may be liability for incorrect transposition where the Member State has 'manifestly and gravely disregarded' the limits of its discretion. What will constitute this includes, for example, persisting with a breach in the face of a contrary ECJ ruling or other settled case law. It will also depend on the breadth of discretion given to the state. (In this respect, contrast the very prescriptive Drinking Water Directive 80/778 with, e.g. the Waste Framework Directive.) Complete failure to implement a directive, or failure to take any measures to achieve the objectives of the directive, will always be a serious breach. In the case of environmental directives, it is interesting to consider what degree of non-implementation in practice (e.g. through non-enforcement of the law) would amount to a sufficiently serious breach.

Requirements (i) and (iii) also raise difficulties in an environmental context. While it is clear that directives such as the Drinking Water Directive or the Environmental Information Directive (90/313) give rights to individuals, in many cases the directive is primarily directed towards protection of the environment. However, it is suggested that most directives laying down standards can be interpreted as conferring implied rights on individuals. This conclusion is supported by decisions of the European Court of Justice, such as in Case C-131/88 *Commission* v *Germany* [1991] ECR I-825. In addition, directives which have as their legal base Articles 100 or 100A (now Articles 94 and 95) and are justified in part on competition grounds may confer individual rights. This was the view of the Court of Appeal in *Bowden* v *South West Water Services Ltd* [1999] Env LR 438, which held that it was at least arguable that a shellfisherman had a state liability claim where his economic interests were harmed following alleged failures in the implementation of the Directive on Shellfish Waters (79/923). However, similar claims made under the Directives on Bathing Water (76/160) and Urban Waste Water Treatment (91/271) were struck out, because the claims were for losses of income from the claimant's business. The Court did, though, keep the door open to a potential claim under the other directives by holding merely that the claimant was not directly affected as a bather or by waste water. The causation issue is also tricky, since in most situations the harm will be caused by an operational failure rather than by the government's faulty implementation. But in its favour the action is against the state, and the liability of individual polluters need not be shown.

(d) National Procedural Rules

The final area worth mentioning is the extent to which national procedural rules must be set aside to give effect to EC law. The basic principle is that procedural matters are for the Member States to decide, and will not be interfered with so long as they do not make it impossible or excessively difficult in practice to obtain a remedy (Case C-188/95 *Fantask* [1998] All ER (EC) 1). An example of where it was held that national rules had to be set aside is Case C-213/89 *R* v *Secretary of State for Transport, ex parte, Factortame Ltd* [1990] ECR I-2433, where English law rules on granting interim relief were set aside so that EC fisheries law could be effective. However, there is something of a balance to be struck here between making EC law effective and respecting very different national procedural rules. In a sense, while *Francovich* liability (state liability) has been imposed as a common remedy across the Member States in limited situations, the pendulum seems to be swinging away from requiring courts to set aside national rules, both on remedies and on procedures.

To illustrate this issue: although standing to bring judicial review actions may not be the hurdle it once was (see p. 77), other procedural restrictions may prevent actions being taken, e.g. the need to have a recognisable interest to bring an action in nuisance (see p. 262). Moreover, in a number of important recent cases, applications for judicial review have been rejected as being out of time (see p. 79). Many of these cases have involved allegations of a breach of mandatory EC rules. This is an area where the courts have discretion, and thus it is impossible to say with certainty what approach a court will take. Nevertheless, there are a number of recent examples where the courts have refused to use their discretion to extend basic time limits where this would be necessary to give effect to a mandatory obligation under EC law. This was the case, e.g. in two decisions of the Court of Appeal concerning the lack of an environment impact assessment under Directive 85/337; see *R* v *London Borough of Hammersmith and Fulham, ex parte CPRE* (21 December 1999, unreported) and *R* v *North West Leicestershire District Council and East Midlands International Airport Ltd, ex parte Moses* (12 April 2000, unreported) (see further p. 362). On the other hand, in *R* v *Secretary of State for Trade and Industry, ex parte Greenpeace (No. 2)* [2000] Env LR 221, one reason why the judge allowed the application to proceed out of time was the seriousness of the breach of the Habitats Directive (92/43) (see p. 80).

These various developments set in motion by the ECJ to improve compliance with EC law give rise to a range of propositions. For example, if a consumer were to become ill as a result of drinking water from the public supply that did not comply with the standards laid down in the Drinking Water Directive (80/778), it would seem that there is a claim either directly in tort, relying on the direct effect of the Directive, or under the *Francovich* doctrine, even if the water did comply with national standards. A more far-reaching example might be where an environmental group wished to challenge the non-implementation of a directive (or even a failure to enforce it, since the two are arguably the same thing in practice). In addition to making a complaint to the Commission, it could seek a declaration claiming that directly effective standards were not being enforced, and argue that the rules on standing or delay should not be used to deny it access to the courts. It might even carry out a clean-up operation and claim its expenses under *Francovich*, even though such a claim would be bound to fail if only national laws were used. As can be seen, some of these very interesting propositions are beginning to be tested in the courts and can be expected to be tested further in the years ahead.

Non-compliance: the Commission's proposals

The need to improve the enforcement of existing legislation has been an aim of the Commission for several years. In a Communication to the Council and European Parliament on Implementing Community Environmental Law, the Commission reported that at October 1996, in relation to environmental matters, there were over 600 outstanding infringement cases against Member States with over 85 awaiting determination by the ECJ, with further cases being registered with the Commission at the rate of over 250 a year (over 20 per cent of all infringement cases). This is probably the tip of the iceberg as only the most serious cases will be reported to the Commission and these will not involve the thorny question of under-enforcement (i.e. where there has been formal compliance in terms of the transposing legislation but no implementation in practice).

The suggestions for improvement put forward in the Communication included:

(a)   The development of standards for inspection tasks by authorities in the Member States which would ensure that annual reports were compiled. These reports would enable the Commission to arrive at an informed view of the successful transposition and implementation of European legislation.

(b)   The creation of an official grievance procedure in each Member State, possibly by means of a 'European Ombudsman'. This would ensure that complaints were handled swiftly at a local rather than Community level.

(c)   Increasing the opportunity for environmental cases to be dealt with by national courts through broader access to justice on Community environmental issues. This might involve relaxation of the rules on standing to include recognised environmental non-governmental organisations (which would fall in line with the decision of Otton J in *R* v *Inspectorate of Pollution, ex parte Greenpeace Ltd (No. 2)* [1994] 4 All ER 329, see p. 77). Access to justice is a central feature of the 1998 Århus Convention (see p. 222) which the EC as a bloc is likely to ratify eventually.

The role of the European Environment Agency and associated organisations, such as IMPEL, is likely to develop as coordination and cooperation between Member States improves. This in turn could give rise to even more infringement proceedings if the Agency's monitoring powers mature.

The Commission's work on implementation has also led to a wider focus on the nature of the whole 'regulatory chain': 'the whole process through which legislation is designed, conceived, drafted, adopted, implemented and enforced until its effectiveness is assessed . . . a methodological tool allowing for a 'holistic' approach to address instruments of environmental policy.'.

Future directions in EC environmental law and policy

In addition to the impact of subsidiarity and greater flexibility, and greater emphasis on enforcement, there are a number of trends in relation to the future of the EC's environmental policy which may be picked out.

(a)   Future policies are increasingly likely to be preventive in nature, emphasising sustainable resource use. The focus of attention in environmental and safety matters is shifting from straight regulation of activities to preventive and precautionary measures, such as addressing waste management problems by requiring waste reduction and recycling (e.g. Directive 94/62 on Packaging and Packaging Waste, and other initiatives on producer responsibility such as advanced proposals for an End-of-life Vehicles Directive, as well as for certain electrical goods). The polluter pays principle also impinges on these questions of producer responsibility, recognising that the polluter is as much the manufacturer of the good as the user.

(b)   Cross-media approaches to pollution control are likely to be encouraged, along the lines of integrated pollution control in this country. Most of the existing directives have tended to concentrate on one particular sector, whether an industry, a substance or an environmental medium. The IPPC Directive is a major step towards a more integrated approach (see p. 380).

(c)   The integration of environmental matters into other policies, as now required by Article 6, is likely to be of considerable importance, with attention already focused on the sectors identified in the fifth Action Programme (see p. 130). However, the modest attempts to 'green' the big spenders in the Community — the Common Agricultural Policy and the Structural and Cohesion Funds — indicate how far there is to go. In the case of the latter, criticism of the lack of attention to the environmental impact of funded infrastructure projects has come from a broad spectrum of interests, as well as the Court of Auditors.

(d)   'Post-regulatory' law is likely to be emphasised. Ancillary measures, such as freedom of information, the encouragement of public participation in decision-making, and the creation of environmental rights are likely to be stressed, following the lead of Directive 90/313 on Freedom of Access to Information on the Environment and Directive 85/337 on Environmental Impact Assessment, which encouraged openness in the planning of environmentally significant developments. This is crucial to the success of many of the EC's programmes, since consumers can only take responsibility for environmental affairs if they are given sufficient and accurate information on the environment and the environmental performance of polluters. This move away from 'command and control' mechanisms can also be seen in somewhat modest proposals for environmental covenants and agreements.

(e)   This previous point links to the need for an increased democratisation of the EC's decision-making processes, and greater transparency. At present, efforts in this regard are effectively channelled into the granting of greater powers to the European Parliament. Arguably, the development of some form of European environmental citizenship may be productive. For the time being, efforts are being channelled into including an environmental dimension into the Charter of Fundamental Rights presently under discussion.

(f)   Action on international problems, such as global warming, acid rain, ozone depletion and oil pollution, will continue to be taken, since the EC is well placed to tackle these problems. The role of the EC has been significant in coordinating a European-wide response and this will continue. In particular, the EC stressed in *Towards Sustainability* the role that it can play in combating climate change. It may well be that the main contribution that the EC will make in this area is the development of some form of 'carbon tax', although this is a matter which is currently fraught with political difficulties, and an EC 'emissions trading' regime may emerge. The EC also acts, in some ways, as a 'testing ground' for the legal and policy status of many environmental principles. Finally, the role of the EC in acting as a conduit for new environmental norms and standards from international law should also be noted (e.g. in conservation law the CITES and the Berne Convention). The dynamic and reciprocal nature of EC-international relations is likely to continue.

(g)   As on the domestic scene, there may be a greater use of economic and fiscal instruments. The Environment Council accepted this idea in principle at its meeting in October 1990, and the commitment was a major part of *Towards Sustainability*. However, as the Commission itself recognises, developments in this area at EC level have so far been 'disappointing' (see COM(99)543 final), which it attributes to the need for unanimity amongst the Members States when environmental measures of a fiscal nature are agreed (see Article 175(2) EC). This has so far proved fatal to proposals for carbon taxes and taxes on energy products. Even where unanimity is not required, however, progress has been slow; attempts to adopt an EC-wide civil liability regime have dragged on for many years, and only recently has a loosely worded White Paper emerged (see further p. 287). In this sense, the wider, positive use of economic instruments remains a vision rather than a reality, although there are clear signs that the environmental impacts of subsidies in areas like agricultural support and regional funding is now being addressed, albeit slowly.

(h)   Instead of economic instruments, we may see greater use of more self-regulatory and market-*based* instruments. For example, there are proposals for some form of EC emissions trading scheme as a mechanism for combating climate change, which would see trading either between the Member States or, more likely, individual companies emerging (see

COM(2000)87). However, it is notable that although the Commission entered into voluntary agreements with the car industry in relation to vehicle emissions and fuel quality (see COM(98)495 final and COM(99)446 final, agreements with European and Far Eastern car manufacturers respectively) there are signs that the Commission may propose binding legislation in the same areas, which suggests some limitations of more informal rule-making.

(i) Despite this wider theoretical focus, however, it is clear that as things stand, the Commission continues to focus on improving its enforcement record (which is borne out at least by the number of infringement proceedings it has initiated recently). This is on the basis that environmental legislation has not been enforced vigorously enough to be able to assess this particular link in the regulatory chain, and thus the process overall. Improving compliance with existing EC environmental law is likely to be a major theme of the Sixth Environmental Action Programme.

EC environmental law and Britain

There is little doubt that the EC's environmental policy and the various directives and regulations adopted in pursuance of it have had an important influence on British environmental law. They have led directly to new legislation, new standards being adopted, significant changes in government policy, and also a general reassessment of the whole British approach to pollution control. It is not practical to provide an exhaustive list, but the following examples should give a flavour of the impact of EC environmental law. Further examples are covered at relevant places elsewhere in the book.

(a) Legislation
(i) New domestic legislation has been passed in relation to: environmental assessment (see the Town and Country Planning (Environmental Impact Assessment) (England and Wales) Regulations 1999 (SI 1999/293)); drinking water quality (see the Water Supply (Water Quality) Regulations 1989 (SI 1989/1147)); the protection of important natural habitats (see the Conservation (Natural Habitats etc.) Regulations 1994 (SI 1994/2716)); the definition of waste (see the Waste Management Licensing Regulations 1994 (SI 1994/1056), sch. 4); the recovery and recycling of packaging waste (see the Producer Responsibility Obligations (Packaging Waste) Regulations 1997 (SI 1997/648); and access to environmental information (see the Environmental Information Regulations 1992 (SI 1992/3240)).

(ii) New standards have been adopted for such things as air quality (see the Air Quality Standards Regulations 1989 (SI 1989/317)), emissions from cars (e.g. in relation to lead and carbon dioxide) and bathing waters (in order to reflect the standards laid down in Directive 76/160). In addition, consents for discharges to controlled waters incorporate standards laid down in EC directives, as do the water quality objectives which underpin many decisions on the control of water pollution.

(iii) In the making of legislation, the move away from unanimous voting to qualified majority voting has undoubtedly forced the UK to agree to some measures it might not otherwise have done, although probably less than might be expected. Although the influence has not all been in one direction, it is notable that nearly all of the measures which the UK objected to in the early 1990s (e.g. on landfill) have now been adopted. One explanation for this, of course, is that EC environmental legislation is becoming more flexible in the style of the characteristically 'British approach'.

(iv) There has been far less direct impact in relation to establishing environmental principles as legislative principles. The environmental principles in the EC Treaty are essentially policy principles, and not directly enforceable, and while they may be having an indirect effect on national policy formulation, there is little sign that they are yet crystallising into legislative principles (see further p. 48). The classic example of this remains *R v Secretary of State for Trade and Industry, ex parte Duddridge* [1995] Env LR 151, where the Divisional Court refused to apply the precautionary principle, listed in Article 175 of the Treaty, as a matter of English law. The Court held that the principle did not impose any immediate obligations on Member States. While this was not surprising, the fact that the court also described the proposition that the principle should be adopted as 'startling' does, perhaps, illustrate that British judges may struggle when it comes to developing principles of environmental law and policy to cope with the peculiarities of environmental litigation and good administration.

(b) Policy

The impact on policy can be seen clearly in the case of the privatisation of the water industry. The then government originally intended to privatise the whole industry, including the regulatory aspects, but was forced to create a public regulatory agency (in the form of the National Rivers Authority) when it became clear that a private regulator would not fulfil the requirement for a 'competent authority' to have responsibility for overseeing the directives on water pollution. A different example is that Directives 91/271 on Urban Waste Water Treatment and 76/160 on Bathing Waters have led to important changes in capital spending programmes in the water industry. It is also arguable that the partial shift in British policy from basing controls on the impact on the receiving environment to using concepts based on best available techniques has been strongly influenced by the EC. Finally, the existence of EC standards has been of great importance for environmental groups, who have something with which to compare British practice when publicising alleged deficiencies in environmental performance.

(c) Practice

As noted earlier, one of the key effects that EC legislation has had in the UK is that, at least for certain directives, failure in practice to achieve minimum quality standards has been equated by the European Court of Justice with non-implementation as a matter of law. An example of this is Case C-56/90 *Commission v UK* [1993] ECR I-4109, a case concerning the quality of bathing waters at Blackpool and Southport beaches. The ECJ held that it was not enough for the UK to take all necessary steps to achieve compliance; what was required was compliance with the quality standards in the Directive. Because it did not fall within any of the recognised exceptions in the Directive, the UK was in breach of its obligations. Given that Member States can now be fined for non-implementation, this strict approach to implementation is obviously important. Even if the ECJ had not taken such a strict line, however, it is arguable that as a matter of practice, not meeting the required standards would be seized upon by pressure groups, who would have a benchmark against which to argue that public health was being compromised or environmental damage being caused.

(d)   The drinking water litigation: a case study
A good illustration of the impact of EC environmental law can be seen in the national experience of implementing the Drinking Water Directive (80/778). This has given rise to the two other occasions when, following action by the Commission, the UK has been held by the Court to have breached EC environmental directives. In the first case, Case C-337/89 *Commission* v *UK* [1992] ECR I-6103, the European Court of Justice decided that there had been a failure to implement the Directive by (i) failing to ensure that water used for food production purposes was covered by the implementing regulations (a failure now rectified), and (ii) failing to comply with the maximum admissible concentration of nitrate in some supply zones. This second part of the decision held the duty to comply with maximum admissible concentrations to be an absolute one, thus effectively treating non-compliance in practice in the same way as formal non-compliance and opening the way for future infringement proceedings based on a failure to enforce EC standards properly in practice. In Britain this is of importance because of the way that much of the practical implementation of the law is delegated to independent agencies and quangos.

In this context, the Court of Appeal decision in *R* v *Secretary of State for the Environment, ex parte Friends of the Earth* [1995] Env LR 11 is instructive. The case arose out of the first European Court of Justice decision on Directive 80/778 on Drinking Water referred to above. The Court of Justice had decided that the duty to comply with the standards laid down in the directive is absolute, rather than simply to take all practicable steps to comply, as had been argued by the UK Government. When it later transpired that certain water companies were supplying water that was in breach of the pesticide standards set out in the Directive, the Secretary of State had accepted undertakings from them about their plans to remedy the situation, rather than making an enforcement order. This was challenged by Friends of the Earth, but the Court of Appeal accepted that, whilst the *primary* duty imposed by the Directive on the government was absolute, this then gave rise to a *secondary* duty to comply with the judgment. lt appears that this secondary duty is not absolute in the same way, but is capable of being qualified by practical considerations.

Subsequently, the Commission took further infringement proceedings against the UK, alleging that the use of these undertakings (which in practice are drafted by the water companies and then agreed with government) breached the Directive. However, the undertakings were argued to be a reasonable and legitimate response to remedying the problem after it was recognised that the deadline for complying with the Directive had been breached. The Court of Justice, though, supported the Commission (see Case C-340/96 *Commission* v *UK* [1999] ECR I-2023). This decision was not really surprising, since the Water Industry Act 1991, under which the undertakings are made, does not specify the kinds of things to be covered in the compliance programme, nor indeed the speed with which compliance should be attained.

The second infringement action does show, however, the rather different approaches taken by the European Court of Justice and the national courts. For the latter, in the *ex parte Friends of the Earth* case, there was an obvious reluctance to interfere with the undertakings that had been accepted by government. For the ECJ, however, the undertakings were clearly incompatible with its established case law on implementation and the need for effective EC legislation. Following the second infringement case, it is interesting to note that the Drinking Water (Undertakings) (England and Wales) Regulations 2000 (SI 2000/1297) have been enacted. These are an explicit response to the ECJ's judgment, and in effect require undertakings to be entered into only for the shortest possible period and only if no reasonable alternatives exist. It is unlikely that they really bring national law into compliance with EC law, but they are probably the least worse option politically (and probably enough to head off any action by the Commission under Art. 228); at any event a further example of formalism in response to EC law.

(e) Transposing directives

Two related issues arise in relation to transposing directives into national law. First, in response to worries about the formal transposition of directives into British legislation, the tendency nowadays is for implementing regulations to repeat the wording of the relevant directive and to make little attempt to 'translate' what are often unclear terms into the sort of precise language that is normal in British legislation. The regulations implementing the Directives on Freedom of Access to Environmental Information (90/313) and on Habitats (92/43) illustrate this point perfectly. The result is that the meaning of the regulations remains unclear and that fuller enlightenment must await either administrative guidance (which gives undesirably wide powers to the administration and is, in any case, not conclusive), or a decision by the courts (normally this would involve a judicial review action, with all the difficulties and expense that entails). For example, it is unclear exactly which bodies and what categories of information are covered by the Environmental Information Regulations 1992, but conclusive answers to these points will only be given should an aggrieved party bring a challenge against a body which it believes has failed to comply with the regulations. Such a roundabout method of discovering the scope of the law is most undesirable.

The second issue is that regulations to transpose directives are usually enacted under the European Communities Act 1972, which means that matters not covered by the directive cannot be legislated on at the same time (see e.g. the environmental assessment of projects not covered under Directive 85/337, discussed at p. 346). Given the limitations on Parliamentary time, this may have the practical effect of restricting the passage of environmental legislation in some situations. One way to avoid this difficulty is to enact framework statutes which allow for both EC and national measures to be passed. This is the case with the Pollution Prevention and Control Act 1999 which, although criticised for the width it gives the Minister to make regulations, allows for regulations to be made that go beyond simply transposing the IPPC Directive (96/61).

(f)   Direct effect and judicial attitudes
An illustration of official attitudes in the UK towards EC environmental law is the response of the national courts to the question of whether environmental directives can have direct effect. There have been some welcome, if tardy, developments. Thus, in *R v London Boroughs Transport Committee, ex parte Freight Transport Association Ltd* [1990] 3 CMLR 495, the Court of Appeal held that a requirement in Directive 70/157 on Noise from Vehicles was directly effective; and in *R v Secretary of State for the Environment, ex parte Friends of the Earth* [1995] Env LR 11, the Court of Appeal accepted implicitly that the standards laid down in Directive 80/778 on Drinking Water were directly effective (as, indeed, was clear from the European Court of Justice decision in Case C-337/89 *Commission v UK* [1992] ECR I-1603). More recently, the High Court has made it clear that it would have held the Habitats Directive (92/43) to be directly effective, if it had been required to do so (*R v Secretary of State for Trade and Industry, ex parte Greenpeace (No. 2)* [2000] Env LR 221).

The response of the courts to whether the Environmental Assessment Directive (85/337) can have direct effect nicely illustrates changing attitudes. In essence, early judgments on this point rejected the possibility of direct effect, either because of a cautious approach to environmental legislation or, worse, misunderstanding of accepted jurisprudence of the ECJ (we discuss all the key cases on environmental assessment and direct effect on p. 349). Only in response to rulings from the ECJ have national courts taken the view that the Directive can be directly effective (see e.g. *R v St Edmundsbury Borough Council, ex parte Walton* [1999] JPL 805).

It might also be added that at no point was there a reference from the national courts to the ECJ (under what is now Article 234) on the EIA Directive, a rather curious fact given the extent to which the national judgments were themselves inconsistent and there was no ECJ case law to be guided by. This, however, is typical of a more general reluctance to refer environmental law cases to the ECJ. A clear example is the Court of Appeal's decision in the *Lappel Bank* case where, although the judges were split on the interpretation of Directive 79/409 on Wild Birds, they declined to make a reference, although the House of Lords later rectified this by referring the case (see further p. 642). Since then, however, the High Court has begun to make references, although only in a couple of cases so far (see Case C-293/97 *R v Secretary of State for the Environment, ex parte Standley* [1999] ECR

I-2603, a case on the Nitrates Directive 91/676, and Case C-371/98 *R* v *Secretary of State for the Environment, Transport and the Regions, ex parte First Corporate Shipping Limited*, a case on the Habitats Directive 92/43 which the ECJ is expected to rule on sometime in 2000). Whether this lack of references is a product of a general lack of familiarity with EC law, an undue confidence in the judges ability to determine tricky points of EC law, or a hostility to procedural measures which go against the grain of national decision-making procedures, is hard to tell.

The drinking water litigation mentioned above is a good example of the extent to which the performance of the British courts in interpreting EC environmental law compares unfavourably with the more robust approach to interpretation of the law taken by the ECJ. For example, the Court of Justice has been willing on a number of occasions to interpret the somewhat vague provisions of environmental directives as laying down clear objective criteria (see, for example, case C-56/90 *Commission* v *United Kingdom* [1993] ECR I-4109, where it stated that the criteria for designation as a traditional bathing water were objectively clear from Directive 76/160, and Case C-355/90 *Commission* v *Spain* [1993] ECR I-4221, where it held that the requirements for classification as a special protection area for birds were objectively clear from Directive 79/409).

Yet the British courts have usually managed to find some hurdle to explain why the applicant should not succeed. One example of this, arguably, is the approach taken to the question of delay (see further p. 79). Another good illustration is the general approach to interpreting general obligations under EC law to pursue environmental objectives, for example by minimising the impact of pollution. For example in *R* v *Leicester County Council, Hepworth Building Products Limited and Onyx (UK) Ltd, ex parte Blackfordby and Boothcorpe Action Group Ltd* (15 March 2000, unreported) the legal status of the general objectives laid down in Article 4 of the Waste Framework Directive were at issue (the same duties as in the *Lombardia* and *ex parte Kirkham* cases mentioned on p. 139 above, although in a different context). The approach of Richards J was to reject any suggestion that these should be given any special weight by the decision-maker. On this reasoning, it is enough that decision-makers take these objectives into account; they do not need to do all they can to achieve them. This gives them little more than the status of 'material considerations' as found in town and country planning law, i.e. that the decision-maker must have regard to them, but the weight that he gives any consideration is a matter of judgment which will not be overturned by the courts (see further p. 324). For all the changes described above, therefore, there are still some very significant limitations to realising some of the objectives of EC environmental law in the real world of decision-making, where the courts tend to resort to traditional ways of supervising discretion rather than develop new approaches to meet new challenges.

SIX

The administration of environmental law and policy

The administration of environmental law and policy is carried out by a diversity of bodies. There are bodies at the international, European and national level and their status can cover the spectrum of formality from powerful international bodies (e.g. the European Commission) through to ad hoc groups which are formed for a specific task and then disbanded. Their functions range from rule- and policy-making through implementation (e.g. by way of decision-making) to enforcement and the imposition of sanctions. International and European bodies are covered in some detail in the chapters dealing with those areas (Chapters 4 and 5 respectively) and therefore the emphasis in this chapter is placed upon the national bodies involved with the administration of environmental protection.

The large number of bodies with responsibilities, duties and powers in relation to the protection of the environment reflects some of the difficulties in drawing up boundaries for a subject which could cover every aspect of political, social, economic and legal life. There is an increasing understanding that the decisions and actions of many bodies which do not necessarily have any direct interest in the environment can have an indirect environmental consequence. Thus, although this chapter concentrates on those bodies which are traditionally associated with environmental protection (including the Environment Agency and the Department of the Environment, Transport and the Regions), some consideration has to be given to these wider issues.

Scotland, Northern Ireland, Wales and the regions

As there are separate legal systems in Scotland and Northern Ireland, there have always been slightly different administrative and regulatory arrange- ments in these two countries (although it should be pointed out the private law mechanisms in Scotland are much more distinctive). These differences, in so far as the system of regulation is concerned, are more structural and procedural than substantive (reflecting the fact that many new laws are the result of EC or international influences which apply to the United Kingdom as a whole), although some minor differences do occur. It is possible that these differences will increase as a result of devolution which transfers substantive law-making powers to new national legislatures in Wales, Scotland and Northern Ireland. The constitutional changes brought about by devolution will shift responsibility for most matters of environmental protection to the national assemblies.

The creation of distinct models of government in Scotland, Wales and Northern Ireland brought about by devolution will, therefore, have some impact upon the administration of environmental protection in the United Kingdom. It is, however, important to note that the fundamental differences in environmental laws will not necessarily be that great for a number of reasons:

(a)   The devolution of primary law-making powers is not comprehensive. Whilst the Scottish and Northern Ireland assemblies will have the powers to pass primary legislation in certain areas (including the environment), Wales only has the power to pass secondary legislation.

(b)   The power to pass any new environmental legislation is constrained by the need to comply with EC law or international obligations. As the United Kingdom is the Member State, it has the responsibility to ensure that there is overall compliance with any obligations imposed in each country (historically, this has led to problems of non-implementation and non-transposition of directives particularly in the case of Northern Ireland). There are powers available to UK authorities where there has been any failure to give effect to EC law in each country, whether it be the country passing incompatible legislation or failing to transpose EC measures (see e.g. Scotland Act 1998, s. 35).

(c)   The need to comply with European/international obligations raises another issue. As the obligations fall upon the United Kingdom as a whole, they are negotiated on behalf of the UK and none of the devolved parliaments formally has a say in the formation of those laws or policies. Thus the uniformity of obligations as between different countries of the UK will continue. It should be noted, however, that EC law and policy is becoming more sensitive to regional environmental differences which could mean that in future, the nature of the obligations may vary in emphasis.

(d)   Control over certain aspects of law-making have not been devolved. For example, most aspects of revenue raising by way of taxes or duties do not fall under the control of the new assemblies. Thus any economic instruments such as the landfill tax could not be introduced or altered. Other areas including transport, energy and consumer protection have been transferred to a greater or lesser extent.

In the light of the above restrictions, these constitutional changes do not appear to create many opportunities for wholesale amendments to environmental law in each country. That is not to say, however, that the introduction of national parliaments (and the executives which hold power) could not be used to bring about different styles of environmental regulation. In particular, there is an opportunity (within the constraints mentioned above) to construct and scrutinise environmental legislation from the very different cultural perspectives of each country. There is also scope to alter the terms of secondary legislation to take into account national concerns. For example, it is not too difficult to envisage a situation where statutory exemptions from pollution control licensing might vary from country to country. Over time, the aggregation of these minor differences could result in distinct bodies of law with national characteristics. Indeed, in relation to Scotland and Northern Ireland at least, there are sufficient substantive differences already to warrant individual text books on national environmental law which are referred to in the bibliography.

Although the differences which devolution will make to new environmental legislation may take some time to gain real significance in the UK context, it is perhaps more likely that individual policy areas in the devolved countries will provide an interesting contrast. It is quite clear that each country has its own priorities and problems in relation to environmental issues. For example, nature conservation sites cover a greater proportion of land in Scotland than in England and Wales and different policy approaches to the management of such sites are already being pursued (see further Chapter 21). In addition, rural issues such as the environmental impact of agriculture and forestry will have a greater significance than, for example, pressure to release green belt land for housing or economic development. This raises questions of uniformity and consistency in the application and implementation of national and international obligations in the UK. The dangers of inconsistency of application can be seen in the debate over the separation of nature conservation responsibilities under the EPA 1990. It is not inconceivable that an increase in distinct national approaches to other environmental issues could give rise to inequalities across the United Kingdom (although it could be argued that these existed under arrangements where policy- and rule-making were more centralised).

The changes in law-making powers are part of a wider attempt to decentralise certain aspects of government and can be viewed in tandem with other attempts to regionalise facets of environmental policy-making. The Regional Development Agencies Act 1998 created English Regional Development Agencies to match similar agencies in Scotland (Scottish Enterprise) and Wales (Welsh Development Agency). Whilst these bodies are not directly concerned with environmental protection policies, they have a remit to consider economic and social issues in a regional setting which will have inevitable consequences for the pursuit of sustainable development (see s. 4(c)).

The substantive and procedural differences are such that trying to accommodate coverage of each jurisdiction in a book of this type is impossible. There are some brief details of the administrative arrangements below but the majority of this book will cover the law and administration of environmental protection in England.

Central government

The main policy- and rule-making powers in environmental matters lie with central government. Although the focus of these activities is the Department of the Environment, Transport and the Regions (DETR), which was created by the Labour Government in May 1997 (with the amalgamation of two separate departments, Transport and Environment), there are three further areas where Central Government plays a part in environmental matters. First, there are bodies which have powers to set policy (and make rules) in relation to environmental issues. Government departments such as the Ministry of Agriculture, Fisheries and Food (MAFF) (e.g. in relation to agriculture), the Department of Trade and Industry (DTI) (e.g. in relation to energy), and the Treasury (e.g. in relation to economic instruments such as the landfill tax), exercise enormous influence in their own fields. Similarly, the Executive in Scotland, Wales and Northern Ireland will exercise an increasing control within their own geographical areas. Secondly, there are bodies which are bound to take into account environmental considerations in relation to the exercise of their policy-making functions (or may be required to take such considerations into account by operation of statute). For example, a number of pieces of legislation now include general requirements to take the environment into account. These include the Countryside Act 1968, s. 11 which states 'in the exercise of their functions relating to land under any enactment every Minister, government department and public body shall have regard to the desirability of conserving the natural beauty and amenity of the countryside'. Although these general duties can be so vague as to be meaningless (other than in cases where the duty has been completely ignored), they do provide certain formal requirements which can have a positive longer term effect upon the policy- and rule-making process.

The third way in which central government plays a part in environmental matters reflects this wider role for environmental appraisal in all forms of policy- and rule-making which can be seen in the revitalised 'Greening Government' initiative which was launched by the Labour government shortly after entering power. This initiative followed the Conservative Government's attempts to nominate a Minister in each government department who was responsible for considering the environmental implications of its policies and programmes and to introduce some form of wider environmental appraisal of policies. The Greening Government initiative is somewhat broader than this and includes a range of different bodies which are considered below.

(a) The House of Commons Environmental Audit Committee

This committee was set up in November 1997 to act as a 'watchdog' over Central Government departments and their attempts to broaden the base of environmental appraisal, in the same way as the Parliamentary Accounts Committee checks public spending. The committee has produced a number of reports including annual reviews of the progress of the Greening Government initiative, in particular drawing unfavourable comparisons between the relative unimportance of this initiative as compared with other cross-departmental policy measures and criticising the lack of leadership from Ministers in each department.

(b) The Cabinet Committee on the Environment

This committee, established in 1990 under the Conservative Government, is currently chaired by the deputy Prime Minister and provides a high level, inter-departmental strategic forum for the discussion of government policy on sustainable development and environmental protection issues. Unfortunately, it is difficult to find out what it actually does as its proceedings are undisclosed and infrequent. Indeed, this Cabinet Committee acknowledged that it conducted most of its business by correspondence. The Audit Committee identified the Cabinet Committee as being the body which was so poor at providing adequate leadership on many cross-departmental environmental issues.

(c)   Green Ministers Committee

The purposes of the Green Ministers Committee have altered since its birth under the Conservative Government. The Green Ministers' main remit is to ensure that each department uses environmental best practices and to establish an effective programme of policies which will combine to help achieve the goal of sustainable development. In this sense they are supposed to identify and promote specific measures to support and implement the strategic decisions taken by the Cabinet Committee. The identification of each Green Minister is a matter for the department concerned and their role within each department can differ accordingly.

(d)   Greening operations

In conjunction with the Green Ministers, departments are subject to setting targets for environmental improvement in areas such as waste production, energy consumption and transport. Although these central initiatives provide some form of institutional structure which should enable environmental issues to be integrated into the wider policy arena, the evidence is not convincing. For example in the Environmental Audit Committee's Sixth Report (Session 1998–99, *The Greening Government Initiative*), only eight government departments were able to set out policies which had been subjected to some form of environmental appraisal, with many departments acknowledging that they did not even have the systems in place to undertake such an appraisal.

Parliamentary select committees

Parliamentary select committees may be said to perform the functions of scrutinising the day-to-day activities of government. In the area of environmental law and policy the select committee plays an important role in helping to inform the public debate outside Parliament and therefore increasing the accountability of and accessibility to the policy and rule makers in the DETR and elsewhere. In the House of Lords, the European Communities sub-committee has been especially important in analysing the potential impact of proposed EC legislation. In the House of Commons, the select committees are organised so as to mirror government departments. Thus, there is a House of Commons Select Committee on the Environment, Transport and Regional Affairs. This body has had a large impact on the direction of environmental policy in the recent past, arguably constituting the loudest

Parliamentary voice for a greater role for environmental regulation. The issues considered by the Environment Select Committee reflect the remit of the government department and therefore include areas outside the traditional boundaries of environmental protection (including such things as local government, housing and transport). Since 1983, when the committee was chaired by Sir Hugh Rossi, there has been a significant concentration on environmental issues, with the committee conducting inquiries into such matters as acid rain (1984), the operation and effectiveness of Part II of the Wildlife and Countryside Act 1981 (1985), pollution of rivers and estuaries (1987), air pollution (1988), toxic waste (1989) and the government's proposals for an Environment Agency. The broadening of the remit of the department in 1997 has led to a slight reduction in the number of environmental inquiries but there have still been important reports such as sewage treatment and disposal (1998); the operation of the landfill tax (1999); and the work of the Environment Agency (2000).

There is little doubt that the reports of these inquiries, all of which have been unanimous on a cross-party basis, have an influence on government policy and legislation. As an example, the Report on Contaminated Land (1990) recommended (amongst other things) the creation of public registers of contaminated land, a recommendation that was implemented in the EPA 1990. The fact that these provisions were repealed without ever coming into force reflects one of the criticisms which could be made of the select committee process. The proposals for the registers were condemned by many involved in the property industry and elsewhere (see Chapter 18) which suggests that the evidence which was considered by the Select Committee did not represent a true sample of views on the topic. As the select committee is reliant upon the evidence which is given at any inquiry, its views will be shaped by what is a relatively select group of witnesses (which nevertheless comprises experts in the field). There is little attempt to elicit wider views or public values. Having said this, however, the introduction of the controls over the clean up of historically contaminated land in the Environment Act 1995 owes a lot to the Select Committee's inquiry and report.

Royal Commission on Environmental Pollution (RCEP)

This is a rather rare beast, a standing Royal Commission with its own secretariat. It has been in existence since 1970 and has produced 22 reports on a variety of matters. These reports have enormous authority in relation to the subject matter discussed and exert a significant influence on the direction of future policy, although by no means all the recommendations of the Royal Commission are implemented. The Royal Commission has been a particularly strong supporter of the widening of access to environmental information, and can also claim to have popularised the concept of 'Best Practicable Environmental Option'. Important reports have been the fifth report, *Air Pollution Control: An Integrated Approach* (Cmnd 6371, 1976), the tenth report, *Tackling Pollution — Experiences and Prospects* (Cmnd 9149, 1984), the eleventh report, *Managing Waste: The Duty of Care* (Cmnd 9675, 1985) and the twelfth report, *Best Practicable Environmental Option* (Cm 310, 1988). The most recent reports are the twentieth report, *Transport and the Environment — Developments since 1994* (Cm 3759, 1997), the twenty-first report, *Setting Environmental Standards* (Cm 4053, 1998), which considers the purpose and mechanism of environmental regulation and is highly recommended as an introduction to the area, and the twenty-second report, *Energy — The Changing Climate* (Cm 4749, 2000), which considers the sustainable use of energy in the context of climate change.

Other advisory bodies

In addition to the RCEP, central government has established a number of other non-statutory advisory bodies with various roles. In particular, three bodies established in 1994 as a result of the publication of the UK's strategy on sustainable development assist with the consideration and implementation of environmental policy and the strategy. The UK Round Table on Sustainable Development consists of 30 members from a selection of bodies, including non-governmental organisations, business, local government and the Churches. The Round Table has identified a small number of discrete areas for discussion which have included sustainable transport, energy policy and environmental auditing. The Government's Panel on Sustainable Development is made up of five members, reports directly to the Prime Minister and advises upon issues which arise from the sustainable development strategy. These have included more general topics such as the use of economic instruments in environmental policy; sustainable development and employment; environmental issues and the European Union; and community and indigenous peoples' intellectual property rights over biological resources. These two bodies will be replaced by a Sustainable Development Commission some time in 2000. It is anticipated that the Commission will have more of a monitoring and reporting role than the existing bodies and will help to identify priority areas for action rather than considering discrete topics.

Department of the Environment, Transport and the Regions (DETR)

Central control of the majority of environmental matters falls to the 'super ministry' created by the Labour Government in May 1997. As the name suggests, the department is also responsible for transport policy and the decentralisation of certain aspects of decision-making and policy to the regions (in England — Scotland, Wales and Northern Ireland are dealt with separately).

Control is mainly manifested at the level of policy, but since environmental law is essentially about the taking of discretionary, political decisions, this means that the DETR has an enormous impact, even if this is not always apparent from a bare statement of the law. However, a number of important qualifications must be made about the role of the DETR.

First, it could be argued that the DETR is not a particularly strong department within central government, even in relation to environmental matters. For example, as certain controversies have shown (such as the planting of genetically modified seeds), the DTI often carries greater weight in inter-departmental disputes.

Secondly, it has few operational powers relating to environmental protection. Those that it does have are often delegated to others. For example, although planning appeals are made to the Secretary of State, in the vast majority of cases they are decided by members of the Planning Inspectorate, which has been an executive agency of the DoE (and now the DETR). Indeed, since that time the Inspectorate has become responsible for a wide range of appeals in relation to environmental matters, including appeals concerning waste management licences, water pollution discharge consents and local air pollution control authorisations.

Thirdly, it is not concerned simply with environmental protection. It has a very wide portfolio, which includes responsibility for local government (including the vexed question of local government finance), housing, transport infrastructure and the water industry. It is fairly clear that some of these areas not only take priority over environmental protection but are often in direct conflict with environmental aims.

Some of these points require amplification. The Secretary of State has very wide legislative and quasi-legislative powers which stem from the framework nature of the main environmental protection legislation, and also from the need to update legislation in the light of EC requirements. Very wide discretionary powers are also granted: for example, the decision to give the Environment Agency a specific or general 'direction' to do something, is virtually an unfettered discretion given to the Secretary of State.

There are also very wide powers in relation to appeals against decisions made by the regulatory bodies. This is most obvious in the planning area, but an appeal to the Secretary of State is a common feature of many of the regulatory systems covered in this book. This reflects the political (i.e. policy-based) nature of much of this area of law. For example, it is significant that the Planning Inspectorate has always been kept within the DETR, rather than being moved to the Lord Chancellor's Department. This reflects the fact that the important feature of its decisions is that they are based on policy rather than on any notion of judicial fairness, despite the increasing formality of planning procedures.

The DETR may impose its policies in a number of ways. One is by changing the law (a feature of the British system of government is that the government is rarely defeated in Parliament). Another is through exercising powers granted under the legislation. This may include the making of directions, the power to approve actions of regulatory bodies, the power to make appointments to the various regulatory bodies, or the power to hear appeals. Interference has been at its clearest in town planning, where there is the greatest opportunity to disagree over matters of policy. Although the DETR has reserved the main legislative powers in the Environment Act 1995, the transfer of a variety of powers to the Environment Agency (see below) has been viewed suspiciously by some observers. A third method is by the manipulation of available resources. The DETR and the Treasury have complete responsibility for the budgets of a number of the regulatory agencies (e.g. the Countryside Agency and the Nature Conservancy Councils). They also control local government finances very tightly. One avenue for future development here is the way that regulatory agencies are being encouraged to acquire some financial independence by charging for parts of their work. This theme has been developed strongly in the Environment Act 1995, with a range of revenue-raising measures (see p. 201).

Given the importance of independent regulatory agencies in environmental law, it is also significant that the DETR is the channel through which Parliamentary accountability of a number of these agencies, such as the Countryside Agency, is provided.

Regulatory agencies

The day-to-day implementation and enforcement of environmental law and policy lies in the hands of a variety of regulatory bodies. In England and Wales, primary control over pollution is carried out by a single body, the Environment Agency, although, as explained below, the administrative arrangements are far from simple and there is a degree of overlap in institutional responsibilities. Indeed, even within the Agency itself, there are different sections carrying out separate functions and the true integration of the pollution control functions is perhaps clearer in theory than in practice.

For many years prior to the creation of the Environment Agency, the number of different agencies involved in environmental protection reflected the fragmented nature of policy and law enforcement in this area. The creation of the Agency, in April 1996, saw the amalgamation of three of the four main regulatory agencies at the time: the National Rivers Authority in relation to water quality and other operational functions; the Waste Regulation Authorities in relation to the regulation of waste management; and Her Majesty's Inspectorate of Pollution primarily in relation to controls over emissions from industrial processes. The creation of the Agency has been accompanied by a recentralisation of many regulatory powers, certainly within England and Wales, for example with national strategies on waste and air quality and centralised guidance on such things as IPC, IPPC and contaminated land. Whilst individual decisions will continue to be made on a case by case basis, reflecting individual conditions, there has been a shift away from local control probably on the basis of improving the quality and consistency of decision-making. A side-effect of this recentralisation is the consequential loss of accountability. A distinction needs to be drawn between those bodies with and without electoral accountability. The Environment Agency is a creature of statute with no direct public accountability. In the light of the wide discretionary powers which the agency exercises and the policy and rules which it is responsible for, this remains a central issue.

As mentioned above, the institutional arrangements in Northern Ireland and Scotland are different from England and Wales. During the Parliamentary debates on the Environment Bill there were strong arguments put forward in favour of creating separate agencies for England and Wales. This was rejected on the basis that there were geographical (e.g. river catchments) and institutional (e.g. the National Rivers Agency's personnel) overlaps which suggested that integrated management across national boundaries was to be preferred. Provisions were made, however, to ensure that the Welsh national interest was furthered by creating one place on the Environment Agency Board for Welsh interests and setting up an Advisory Committee for Wales (s. 11, Environment Act 1995). It is, however, possible that further separation of the Agency in these two jurisdictions may result after the effects of devolution become clearer.

Regulatory agencies — Scotland

Prior to the implementation of the Environment Act 1995 there were a variety of regulatory bodies responsible for environmental protection in Scotland. The river purification authorities were responsible for the control of water pollution, and integrated pollution control was regulated by Her Majesty's Industrial Pollution Inspectorate (HMIPI). The local authorities (the district and island councils) acted as waste regulation authorities (although there was no separation of regulatory and operational functions as in England and Wales) and as enforcing authorities for air pollution control under Part I of the EPA 1990.

The Environment Act 1995 introduced a unified agency for Scotland known as the Scottish Environment Protection Agency (SEPA). The range of powers, functions, aims and duties applicable to SEPA broadly reflect the position of the Environmental Agency (as to which, see below). There is, however, a narrower regulatory focus on fundamental pollution control matters without the wider issues of water resource management which were transferred from the National Rivers Authority (NRA) to the Environment Agency. This focus is reflected in the title of the agency (with the significant omission of the word 'protection' from the Anglo-Welsh agency) and the fact that there are some minor variations in the legislative provisions which could become more significant with the passage of time (e.g. SEPA does not have a 'principal aim' as specified under s. 4 of the 1995 Act for the Environment Agency (see below)).

There are two major differences in the scope of the powers of the two agencies. First, SEPA has control over all prescribed processes under Part I of the EPA 1990, whereas in England and Wales control remains divided between the Environment Agency and the local authorities. Secondly, as mentioned above, SEPA has none of the non-pollution-related water management functions. The majority of these remain with the new unitary local authorities created by the Local Government etc. (Scotland) Act 1994. The position of the water and sewerage undertakers is also different in Scotland. Unlike England and Wales, which has privatised water companies, Scotland has three public, non-departmental water authorities created under the provisions which led to the local government reorganisation referred to above.

Regulatory agencies — Northern Ireland

The current administrative set-up in Northern Ireland is somewhat different from the rest of the UK reflecting the fact that, in many ways, the institutional arrangements could be said to be about ten years behind the other countries. For example, operational functions for water and sewerage matters fall within the same department as the regulatory functions in relation to water pollution (a position which was altered in 1989 in England and Wales under the Water Act 1989). In other ways, however, the administrative arrangements are much more integrated than elsewhere in the UK with a broader range of environmental issues brought within the control of one body (although each area of control is theoretically autonomous within the department).

Under existing arrangements, regulatory controls for many environmental matters fall under the control of an executive agency of the Department of the Environment for Northern Ireland, namely the Environment and Heritage Service. This body has similar responsibilities to SEPA and the Environment Agency, including the general pollution control matters (e.g. the regulation and protection of water quality, air quality, radioactivity and waste management). It also has control over nature conservation matters and wider countryside issues. The provision of sewage treatment and control over drinking water quality is undertaken by the water service of the department.

The Environment Agency

The history of the Environment Agency (EA) is long and tortuous. In 1989 the House of Commons Select Committee on the Environment, in its Report on Toxic Waste, recommended that an Environmental Protection Commission should be established with responsibility for the whole range of pollution control matters. This recommendation was rejected by the government of the time, a stance that was reiterated in the White Paper, *This Common Inheritance* (Cm 1200, 1990). One reason given was that there had been many changes in relation to environmental protection in recent years, and that such a major change might have to wait until things had settled down. The White Paper did suggest, however, that consideration would be given to the establishment of an umbrella body overseeing the work of HMIP and the NRA. It also proposed that HMIP should become a separate executive agency within the government (i.e. a 'Next Steps' agency) 'as soon as possible', although it would still remain part of the (then) DoE. This mechanism was popular with the Conservative government as a means of providing regulatory agencies with a degree of independence, whilst at the same time injecting some basic management principles and subjecting the agencies to some of the rigours of the marketplace.

However, in an important reversal of policy, in July 1991 it was announced that it was the government's intention to create a unified environmental protection agency, a move that had already gained the support of all other political parties. Details of what was intended gradually emerged. There were two main points of argument which led to a significant period of delay. One was whether the waste regulation duties of the local authorities should be included within the agency's ambit — to do so would create a uniformity of practice that was lacking, but would obviously reduce local accountability. The other was whether the NRA should be brought within the agency *en bloc*, or whether only its pollution control functions properly belonged there. The Minister of Agriculture argued strongly for the NRA's non-pollution control functions to be devolved to the Ministry of Agriculture, Fisheries and Food, but that was strongly opposed by environmentalists and the NRA itself, who argued that the need to retain integrated catchment management was at the heart of everything that the NRA did.

After some discussion and consultation the government accepted that the EA would take over all the powers and functions of HMIP and the NRA, together with the waste regulation duties of the local authorities.

The Environment Agency: an overview

The name of the Agency is misleading. It does not have control over all environmental regulation. Despite government statements made during the discussion which led to the creation of the EA, the Drinking Water Inspectorate is not included (although there is an outstanding Labour Party commitment to reverse this); nor are any direct functions relating to nature conservation (although there are a number of general duties relating to sites which are of nature conservation interest). These omissions (when coupled with the areas of environmental regulation which remain with local authorities) meant that at the time of its creation, the EA was effectively a pollution control authority with a large number of water-related functions such as land drainage and flood defence (with the interesting side effect that the number of staff in these areas outnumber those in pollution control).

The functions of the EA largely reflect the pre-existing functions of the NRA, HMIP and the waste regulation authorities. A detailed description of each of these areas of responsibility can be found in Part II of this book. They include:

(a) *Water-related functions.* The EA has responsibility for a wide range of matters relating to water and water resources (see further Chapter 19), including:

(i) the control of pollution of water resources under Part III of the Water Resources Act 1991 (e.g. the setting of water quality objectives, the use of powers to prevent pollution and the enforcement of pollution control);

(ii) management of water resources (e.g. abstraction licensing, drought orders and powers to secure adequate supplies from the water companies);

(iii) supervision and administration of flood defences;

(iv) fisheries regulation;

(v) navigation, harbour and conservancy duties.

(b) *Waste management-related functions.* The EA has responsibility for a range of waste management functions (see further Chapter 17), including:

(i) licensing waste management facilities (including supervision of waste management activities and taking action against breaches);

(ii)   the registration of activities which are exempt from the waste management licensing system;

(iii)   the registration and regulation of waste carriers and brokers;

(iv)   the administration of the surrender of waste management site licences;

(v)   the enforcement of the duty of care under the EPA 1990, s. 34.

(c)   *Industrial processes.* The EA has responsibility for the control of all emissions from industrial processes under Part I of the EPA 1990 which are prescribed for central control (see further Chapter 13). It will continue to maintain this control for IPPC installations under the Pollution Prevention and Control Act 1999 and associated regulations.

(d)   *New functions.* In addition to the functions which have been transferred from the pre-existing agencies, the Environment Act 1995 created a range of new functions for the agency, including:

(i)   the role of enforcing authority in relation to 'special sites' under the provisions in Part IIA of the EPA 1990 concerning the regulation of historically contaminated land;

(ii)   the administration and regulation of the producer responsibility initiative under ss. 93 and 94 of the Environment Act 1995;

(iii)   the issuing of guidance in relation to various matters including IPC processes and contaminated land;

(iv)   the carrying out of research and the provision of information on the environment (including the setting up of public pollution control registers);

(v)   being statutory consultees in relation to such things as the National Air Quality Strategy and the National Waste Strategy.

(a)   Structure of the Agency

The EA is an independent corporate body (Environment Act 1995, s. 1(1)) and does not have Crown immunity, although partial immunity can be granted where the Agency exercises its functions under an agreement to carry out a Ministerial function (s. 38). In order to assist with the carrying out of its functions, the Agency is under a duty to establish an Environment Protection Advisory Committee (EPAC), made up of people with a 'significant interest' in the Agency's functions. An EPAC is established for each Agency region. Once established, the Agency is under a duty to consult the committee and consider any representations made by it.

The regional structure of the Agency was the subject of much debate as a result of the very different administrative boundaries used by the NRA, HMIP and the waste regulation authorities (WRAs). Whereas the NRA and HMIP were split into regional sections (eight and three, respectively) the WRAs were split on the basis of local authority areas. In the end, the EA was organised on a regional basis, but the water management boundaries remain based on the NRA's river catchment areas, whilst the pollution control functions are organised largely on the basis of county authority boundaries (in the case of water management areas the district boundaries are sometimes used where they provide a convenient 'match').

(b)   General powers and duties

The Agency is subject to a complicated framework of principal aims, other duties and objectives. Some of these have been transferred from the NRA, but most are either new in substance or scope. Some of these objectives were subjected to a good deal of Parliamentary scrutiny during the passage of the Environment Bill (which led to the introduction of the 'principal aim' of meeting the objective of sustainable development under s. 4), but there is still a lack of clarity in many of these statutory aims and objectives.

These aims and duties are designed to underpin the policy decisions of the Agency, but do not fetter that discretion unduly. The duties are expressed in a variety of ways (see below), with the Agency being required to 'have regard to' some duties whereas others have to be 'taken into account'. When it comes to individual decision-making, the Agency has a wide discretion and the weight which attaches to each duty will be variable. Therefore, it would be difficult to challenge legally any decision made by the Agency on the basis that it had failed to carry out the duty unless the Agency had acted unreasonably in the *Wednesbury* sense.

It is important to bear in mind that the aim, objectives and duties are not framed in a statutory vacuum. In addition to the general matters set out in the Environment Act 1995 there is an increasing range of specific statutory objectives which are set out in relation to individual functions of the Agency. Many of these have been imposed as a result of the need to meet EC legislation which favours the use of such specific targets. For example, the Agency must seek to achieve water or air quality objectives when exercising its functions in determining authorisations and consents and in doing so it must place those objectives above the general aims and duties.

(c)   Principal aim and objectives of the Agency

Section 4 of the Environment Act 1995 defines the principal aim for the Agency: in discharging its functions the Agency is required so to protect or enhance the environment, taken as a whole, as to attain the objective of achieving sustainable development. Although this may be the first time that such an overarching duty has been imposed upon an environmental agency, the extent to which this section creates a legally enforceable obligation upon the Agency is a little uncertain. A number of factors, set out in s. 4, are designed to influence the implementation of the duty in practice.

First, the Agency must take into account the likely costs of achieving the principal aim. This was inserted into s. 4 to ensure that environmental considerations are not paramount when pursuing the aim of sustainable development, and the cost of the pursuit of the principal aim is to be taken into account. This reflects the policy distinction between the aims of sustainability and sustainable development (see Chapter 2).

Secondly, the principal aim is to be pursued in relation to the conservation and enhancement of the environment 'taken as a whole'. This was introduced to ensure that the decision-making process was not overburdened by detailed consideration of impacts on individual environmental media. Instead the government suggested that there should be an integrated analysis of all impacts, and decision-making should take into account these overall factors. Another interpretation of this provision could be used to justify attaching less weight to any one individual factor on the basis that the factors 'when taken as a whole' lead to a particular conclusion.

Thirdly, the principal aim has to be viewed in relation to all of the other objectives which apply to the Agency (surprisingly there are no other statutory 'aims' — which rather begs the question over the use of the word 'principal'). The 'principal' aim will only take precedence over other statutory objectives where there is a direct conflict between the two. Thus it would appear that in a situation where the Agency is making a decision to act and it cannot meet both objectives, the principal aim would take precedence. Confusingly, however, the aim is stated to be 'subject to' other provisions of the Act, which would include the other objectives. This confusion over the hierachy of the principal aim and the other statutory objectives underlines the difficulty of introducing a principal aim which does not actually create any legally enforceable rights. It rather defeats the purpose of a 'principal aim' when it is subject to the myriad of other statutory objectives and functions.

Finally, the Agency must have regard to guidance issued by the Secretary of State when discharging its functions (s. 4(3)). Guidance on the principal aim was issued in November 1996. The guidance is contained in two short, relatively bland, sections which do little more than express very general objectives and strategic aims. The emphasis on the Agency's contribution to sustainable development centres on the need to take a holistic approach to the protection and enhancement of the environment; to take a long term perspective of the implications and effects of carrying out its functions; to enhance and protect biodiversity; to discharge, where possible, its regulatory functions in partnership with regulated organisations; to develop a close and responsive relationship with the public; and to provide high-quality information and advice on the state of the environment.

The role of guidance is central to meeting the principal aim. One of the inherent dangers of using such guidance to flesh out such a statutory provision is that it is capable of change without recourse to legislation. This could have a significant impact upon the manner in which the Agency carries out its functions without the scrutiny which is afforded to legislative proposals. There are two safeguards to prevent the abuse of this process. First there is a duty on the Secretary of State to consult before issuing such guidance and secondly a draft has to be put before both Houses of Parliament with rights of veto available if either House resolves to do so (s. 4(5)–(7)).

On any analysis (legal, philosophical or even semantic), the complexities of the principal aim obscure the nature of the legal obligation which is created. Whilst the creation of a policy framework is long overdue, the real issue which remains to be clarified is the way in which this principal aim will be taken into account in relation to individual decision-making and the setting of strategic goals or targets. There is a real danger that the width of the discretion given to the Agency when merely having regard to the guidance will mean that the principal aim is little more than a statement of intent which will not be subject to judicial scrutiny. Notwithstanding the uncertainty over the nature of the legal obligation created by the aims and duties, they are still of importance in internal decision-making within the Agency and as political levers for environmentally sensitive decisions.

(d)   Other aims, objectives and functions
In addition to the principal aim of the EA, a range of other duties and objectives is set out in ss. 5–9 of the Environment Act 1995. These relate to the following areas:

(i)   *Pollution control functions.* Under s. 5 of the Act, the EA is under a duty to exercise its functions for the purpose of preventing or minimising, or remedying or mitigating the effects of, pollution of the environment. This section distinguishes between the Agency's pollution control functions and the other non-pollution powers and functions (e.g. flood defence and fisheries). This distinction is carried over in s. 7 which provides that the Agency, when formulating or considering any proposals, is to *have regard to* the desirability of conserving and enhancing natural beauty and the conservation of flora, fauna and geological or physiographical features. In relation to non-pollution powers and functions this duty is raised so that the Agency is required to *further* the conservation etc. This distinction reflects the fact that the Agency cannot be said to be furthering environmental conservation when it is issuing consents, authorisations or licences for activities which by definition will be polluting.

(ii)   *General environmental duties relating to water.* Section 6 of the Act provides for general environmental duties in relation to the water industry. The duties generally reflect some provisions of the Water Resources Act 1991, s. 16 (since repealed), and the Water Industry Act 1991, s. 3 (in relation to the water companies' environmental duties). The duties under the Water Resources Act 1991, s. 16 were transferred to the Environment Act 1995, s. 7 (see below). Under s. 6 the duties relate specifically to promoting the conservation or enhancement of the natural beauty and amenity of waters (including land associated with such waters) and the conservation of flora and fauna which are dependent on the aquatic environment. These duties are not particularly onerous, requiring action only when the Agency considers that it is desirable to do so. The desirability of carrying out this duty will be affected by the duties under s. 7 and the principal aim under s. 4.

Subsections (4)–(6) of s. 7 cover access to water, or lands associated with such water, for recreational purposes.

(iii)   *General environmental duties.* The Agency's general environmental duties are found in s. 7 of the Act. These duties also apply to the relevant Secretaries of State. The duties are divided into two. Subsections (1)–(3) cover environmental duties whereas subsections (4)–(6) cover the duties in relation to public recreational access to water. Once again these are adapted from the duties found within the Water Resources Act 1991, which applied previously to the NRA. The duties apply to the Agency when considering or formulating 'proposals'. Although there is no definition of 'proposals' within the Act, the term would include all strategic policy-making (such as the strategies on air quality and waste) and would arguably cover individual decision-making on licence applications.

These general duties are divided into duties which apply to pollution control functions of the Agency (see (a) above); duties which apply to the non-pollution powers and functions; and duties which apply to both.

In relation to non-pollution control functions the Agency is under a duty to further the conservation and enhancement of natural beauty and the conservation of flora, fauna and geological and physiographical features of special interest. In addition the Agency must have regard to a range of matters including the desirability of protecting heritage sites or public access to areas of natural beauty, the effect of proposals on the beauty of any area and the effect on the economic and social well-being of rural communities.

(iv) *Environmental duties with respect to sites of special interest.* There are specific duties in relation to notification and consultation in the case of any land of a special conservation interest which may be affected by any works carried out by the Agency or by any authorisation which it is considering (see further below).

The Secretary of State has the power to issue codes of practice under s. 9 of the Environment Act 1995 to assist the EA in carrying out any of the duties referred to above. This power has been exercised in the issue of the Water and Sewerage (Conservation, Access and Recreation) (Code of Practice) Order 2000 (SI 2000/477) which gives practical guidance to the Agency (and water and sewerage undertakers) relating to their environmental and recreational duties. Contravention of the Code does not give rise to any criminal offence or civil right of action, but will be taken into account by relevant bodies in deciding whether to use any powers available to them.

(e) The cost-benefit duty
Probably the most controversial duty imposed upon the EA is the duty to take into account the costs and benefits of exercising its powers. Section 39 of the Environment Act 1995 provides that the Agency:

(a)   in considering whether or not to exercise any power . . . or
(b)   in deciding the manner in which to exercise any such power,
shall, unless and to the extent that it is unreasonable for it to do so in view of the nature or purpose of the power or in the circumstances of the particular case, take into account the likely costs and benefits of the exercise or non-exercise of the power or its exercise in the manner in question.

'Costs' are defined as environmental as well as personal costs (s. 56(1)) and although 'benefits' are surprisingly (given the mutual relationship between the phrases) not defined, the term would arguably include environmental benefits in addition to any personal benefits.

There are two important restrictions on the application of the duty. First, it does not apply if it would be unreasonable in the circumstances of a particular case. The clearest example of this would be where emergency action was required by the Agency. Secondly, the duty does not affect the exercise of other mandatory obligations such as complying with environmental quality objectives. In such circumstances, the decision-making discretion of the Agency is constrained within the pursuit of the specific objective and the costs and the benefits become less relevant. The general cost-benefit duty does, however, apply where the Agency can select from a range of potential options when seeking to achieve these objectives and the costs and benefits of each of those options can be considered when selecting which is the most appropriate.

The main controversy over this section was centred around the extent to which it could be used to challenge a decision of the Agency on the basis that the benefits of a proposed action or strategy could not be shown to outweigh the costs. Thus, the exercise of any regulatory power by the Agency, including powers to investigate, prosecute or require preventive or remedial measures, could be challenged where the duty was not carried out. The danger of challenge could, in turn, lead to excessive bureaucracy as each decision would be subjected to detailed scrutiny by the Agency and those affected by the decision alike.

These dangers do not reflect the essentially discretionary nature of the decision-making power of the Agency. Taking account of costs and benefits does not necessarily mean that the Agency has to demonstrate that the costs outweigh the benefits (or vice versa) or even that, once it has carried out such an appraisal, it must act in accordance with the conclusions. A requirement to take account of costs and benefits arguably does no more than raise an evidential presumption that they will be considered. In classic administrative fashion it does not prescribe the weight which should be attached to such costs or benefits and therefore any decision based on such an analysis will be difficult to challenge.

The Secretary of State has issued non-statutory guidance on the cost-benefit duty as part of the explanatory document which accompanies the statutory guidance on the principal aim of the Agency. The guidance emphasises the importance of carrying out environmental appraisals before exercising decision-making powers. In addition, the guidance points out the difficulties in quantifying environmental costs, benefits, and places, and sets out a number of factors which may be relevant in reaching a decision. Arguably the most important section of the guidance stresses the fact that in many situations, the application of the duty will require the exercise of judgment by the Agency — a judgment which is likely to be unchallengeable in the courts.

In addition to this general duty under s. 39, the Agency has to consider the costs associated with other duties. Thus there is a duty to consider 'any likely costs' when seeking to achieve its principal aim under s. 4 (see above) and the Agency must set out the costs and benefits for exercising its options under the pollution control functions in s. 5.

(f) Unification of administrative and regulatory powers

In addition to the general aims and objectives, the Environment Act 1995 unified a variety of the powers which were previously found in disparate legislation. The aim is to provide consistency and uniformity in a range of areas, including inspection, entry, enforcement and fees and charges.

(g) Inspection, entry and enforcement powers

The EA has a range of inspection and enforcement powers. These powers are exercised for the purpose of: determining whether any environmental legislation is being complied with; exercising or performing any of the agency's pollution control functions; determining whether or how a pollution control function should be exercised (s. 108(1)).

Section 108 of the Act provides that an officer appointed by the Agency can, when there is no emergency:

(a) enter premises at any reasonable time (s. 108(4)(a));
(b) be accompanied on to premises by a police constable should the officer apprehend that they will be obstructed in their duty (s. 108(4)(b));
(c) make any investigation as necessary including: measurements, taking samples, photographs and questioning individuals (answers given to such questions will not be admissible in any prosecution brought against *that person* although they can be, and in practice are used against another person, for example an employer) (s. 108(4));
(d) carry out experimental borings and install and maintain monitoring equipment (with at least seven days' notice) (s. 108(8)).

Where occupants are likely to refuse entry, the officer can seek a warrant prior to entry onto premises. Documents which are subject to legal professional privilege are exempt from the above requirements (s. 108(13)). In cases of emergency entry can be gained at any time, with force if necessary (s. 108(4)(a)). In such circumstances no prior notification is required when setting up monitoring equipment or carrying out experimental borings. Under s. 110 it is an offence to obstruct intentionally an authorised officer in the exercise of his or her duties.

In addition, there are specific powers to requisition information in writing in relation to individual functions (e.g. EPA 1990, s. 71, in relation to waste management offences). The answers to such requisitions are not subject to the rule against self-incrimination (referred to in s. 108), as the section impliedly excludes this protection on the basis that the purpose of the legislation would be defeated if a person could refuse to answer written requisitions (see *R v Hertfordshire County Council, ex parte Green Environmental Industries* [2000] 2 WLR 373).

Schedule 22 to the Environment Act 1995 has amended the provisions relating to enforcement powers for individual functions (e.g. waste management and pollution of controlled waters) so that there is no significant imbalance in the powers which are available to the agency for each of these functions. For example, ss. 90A and 90B of the Water Resources Act 1991 (as inserted by the Environment Act 1995) give the Agency the power to serve an enforcement notice where there has been, or is likely to be, a breach of a condition of a discharge consent. This is a new power which widens the range of enforcement options in relation to water pollution.

(h) Fees and charging schemes

It is intended that the EA should seek to operate on a cost recovery basis (i.e. the amount of money it receives in charges and fees should cover its administrative expenses). Sections 41 and 42 of the Environment Act 1995 provide the power to introduce charging schemes for all forms of environmental licensing. The Agency can exercise this power itself, unlike some of the previous powers to raise fees and charges which were exercisable by the Secretary of State (e.g. waste regulation and IPC under the EPA 1990). To ensure that the schemes are subject to proper scrutiny, each must be published in draft and approved by the Secretary of State and the Treasury before it can come into operation. Furthermore, the scheme must be made by statutory instrument and can be annulled by either House of Parliament.

There are no restrictions on the amount which can be charged nor on any differentials in charging to reflect the administrative burden of each individual application. At present, all charges are levied on a fixed basis with variations for certain classes of licences. This does not, however necessarily reflect the amount of administrative effort involved in the processing of each individual application. There have been some suggestions that charging schemes should be developed which would accurately reflect the amount of work required.

There are separate annual charging schemes for IPC (and IPPC) and the waste management licensing system. The scheme in relation to discharge consents has effect for a five-year period with annual revisions of the fee levels.

In addition to this specific power, the Agency has general powers to charge for any services provided in connection with environmental licences under s. 37(7) and (8) (there are further incidental powers under s. 43). This would cover any advice or assistance provided to applicants when preparing applications. The use of this power would enable the Agency to introduce charging rates which more accurately reflect the administrative burden without necessarily complicating the existing charging schemes.

(i) Directions from the Secretary of State
The Secretary of State has a wide range of powers to issue directions to the Agency. These directions can be of a specific or general nature. In relation to individual functions they include:

(i)   directions requiring the inclusion of specific conditions in IPC or waste management licences (see EPA 1990, ss. 7(3) and 35(7));
(ii)   directions requiring the Agency to take specific enforcement action in relation to IPC and waste management licences (EPA 1990, ss. 12–14, 37, 38 and 42);
(iii)   directions requiring the Agency (amongst other things) to carry out surveys of waste arisings in relation to the national waste strategy (s. 44A);
(iv)   directions made in the interests of national security or mitigating the effects of a civil emergency (Water Resources Act 1991, s. 207).

The Environment Act 1995, s. 40, gives the Secretary of State a further general power to issue any directions of a specific or general character. This power is exercisable under the Secretary of State's discretion and represents a formidable tool to centralise certain aspects of the Agency's activities.

(j) Overlap with other agencies

Although the EA has primary responsibility for the majority of powers in relation to pollution control, there are still a number of other bodies with direct responsibility for specific aspects of pollution control and wider areas of environmental protection. In particular, local authorities play an important role in regulating the clean up of historically contaminated land, statutory nuisances, noise, air quality (including smoke control and other atmospheric emissions) and planning. In addition, the privatised water companies act as sewerage undertakers, controlling discharges to sewers (see Chapter 20). There is a good deal of overlap in these areas which covers both substantive law and administration. An outline of these overlaps is given in each of the relevant chapters in Part II.

In the area of nature conservation and countryside matters, the EA has responsibilities which overlap with the relevant statutory bodies. English Nature, the Countryside Council for Wales, the National Parks Authorities and the Broads Authority are under a duty to inform the EA of the identity of any land which may be affected by the Agency which is of special nature conservation interest because of its flora, fauna or geological or physiographical features (s. 8). Where the Agency has been notified of the identity of such land, it is under a duty to consult the relevant body before carrying out or authorising works which would destroy, damage or significantly prejudice those features notified. This applies to all authorisations which are regulated by the Agency. Although nature conservation bodies have always been consultees on applications for regulatory consents previously, this duty to consult is considerably wider and would include not only actions carried out by the Agency itself but enforcement actions which would require remedial measures to be undertaken by third parties.

Sewerage undertakers

In relation to discharges to sewers, the licensing body is the privatised sewerage undertaker, which grants what are called trade effluent consents. This is an unusual example of a private body undertaking an environmental regulation function, although it is arguable that a sewerage undertaker is in reality doing little different from a private waste disposal contractor in providing a method of waste disposal through privately owned facilities. Appeals against trade effluent consent decisions are heard by the Director General of Water Services (Ofwat), who is appointed under the Water Industry Act 1991 and whose main functions relate to the regulatory control of the newly privatised water industry. For a further explanation of the water industry and trade effluent consenting see Chapter 20.

Countryside bodies

Within the countryside, the absence of a controlling 'Department of Rural Affairs', such as many other countries possess, is crucial. In the past the dominant force has tended to be MAFF, simply by virtue of the weight of resources available to it. This has traditionally been a very insular Ministry, although under the Agriculture Act 1986, s. 17, the Agriculture Ministers are now required to seek to achieve a balance between the interests of agriculture, the economic and social needs of rural areas, and conservation and recreation. In addition the enhanced integration duty in the EC Treaty should lead to a cultural change within the Ministry through external forces.

There are, however, other independent agencies within the government responsible for specific matters. In England there is a Nature Conservancy Council for England (known as English Nature) and a Countryside Agency, which have responsibilities for nature conservation and for recreation, landscape and amenity respectively. This division of responsibility reflects a split in functions decided upon as long ago as 1949 and some reasons behind this are explained in Chapter 21. The Nature Conservancy Council was organised on a Great Britain basis until 1 April 1991 when, for largely political reasons, it was split into three separate national bodies by the EPA 1990. (In this book, for ease of reference, these are referred to generically as the Nature Conservancy Councils.) In Wales, the nature conservation functions were amalgamated with the amenity functions in a new Countryside Council for Wales. In Scotland, a similar body called Scottish Natural Heritage was established under the Natural Heritage (Scotland) Act 1991, which also combines the two functions. There is no intention at present to combine English Nature and the Countryside Agency.

Local authorities

There has been a great deal of restructuring in local authorities in England over recent years. In 1986, the abolition of the metropolitan county councils led to the creation of two separate structures for local government in England (with slight variations in the case of London). As a result of further local government reorganisation under the Local Government Act 1992, there are now three main types of local authority:

(i) *Single-tier London boroughs and metropolitan districts.* In metropolitan areas, there is a one-tier system, the metropolitan district councils. These obviously have responsibility for all matters, although some functions (police, fire and transport) are run by joint boards of the councils.

(ii) *Non-metropolitan areas.* In non-metropolitan areas, there is a two-tier system of county and district councils. In constitutional terms these two tiers are equal, but they have differing responsibilities. County councils have responsibility for the police, fire services, personal social services, transport, highways, education, libraries, strategic planning and development control in certain prescribed 'county matters' including waste disposal and minerals development. District councils have responsibility for housing, general development control, recreation, environmental and public health.

This split causes problems for the public which often finds it difficult to identify which tier is responsible for any particular matter. The problem is particularly acute in the environmental sphere because of the overlapping powers of the two tiers (e.g. in town planning). This confusion was cited as one of the factors which led to the reorganisation of local government and the introduction of unitary authorities.

(iii)   *Unitary authorities.* This third class of local authority was created after a review of local government considered a large number of proposals to introduce more single-tier authorities to replicate the powers of the metropolitan district councils.

At present, in England there are 35 metropolitan district councils, 33 London borough councils (including the City of London), 36 county councils, 264 district councils and 25 unitary authorities. All undertake a wide variety of tasks in relation to environmental protection. There are six main areas to consider:

(a)   Town and country planning
The local authority is normally the local planning authority. This means that it is responsible for the making of development plans and for the control of development. The powers also incorporate responsibility for related matters, such as tree preservation orders, listed building protection, conservation areas, hazardous substances consents, the control of derelict land, and the protection of the countryside. As explained above, planning functions are split between county and district councils, with county councils being responsible for strategic planning (at the Structure Plan level) and for minerals and waste disposal matters, whilst district councils have responsibility for other development control decisions and smaller scale development planning in local plans.

(b)   Public health matters
Local authorities have always had responsibility for a very wide range of matters under the Public Health Acts. In particular, this involves duties in relation to the control of statutory nuisances, the law on which was remodelled in the EPA 1990, Part III (see Chapter 15).

(c)   The control of noise
Local authorities have primary responsibility for the control of noise from premises. In the past these provisions had been separate from those relating to statutory nuisance, but in the EPA 1990 the two sets of powers were treated together (see Chapters 15 and 16).

(d)   Air pollution
Local authorities have long had responsibility for the control of smoke, dust, grit and fumes under the Clean Air Acts and related legislation. In the EPA 1990, Part I, they were given more complete powers to control air pollution from plants which are not the responsibility of the EA under integrated pollution control. In addition to these specific controls over emissions, the Environment Act 1995 gave local authorities greater responsibilities for establishing strategic control over air quality matters. This includes a duty to review air quality in an area in order to assess compliance with air quality standards, a duty to designate air quality management areas where those standards are not being met and a duty to prepare an action plan to address the problems of air quality.

(e) Waste collection and disposal
Perhaps the biggest change for local authorities brought about by the Environment Act 1995 was the transfer of waste management regulation from county and metropolitan authorities to the EA. Although the regulatory functions were removed, responsibilities for waste collection and the arrangements for the disposal of waste remain with local authorities under the waste collection and waste disposal authorities. Indeed there is a growing recognition that local authorities will play an important role in ensuring that waste reduction and recycling targets can be achieved as they control a large proportion of the waste arising at the place of production.

(f) Contaminated land
The introduction of the regime to deal with the clean up of historically contaminated land under Part IIA, EPA 1990 has given local authorities a range of new duties, powers and obligations. As the legislation was supposed to mirror the existing controls under the statutory nuisance regime, it was considered to be appropriate to give local authorities the major task of inspecting and identifying land within their area for the existence of contaminated land and to take action against the person responsible for the contamination or the owner/occupier of the land. These responsibilities are shared (in some respects) with the EA which is given corresponding powers and duties in respect of sites which are more heavily contaminated (known as 'Special Sites').

In addition to these areas, it is clear that local and regional policies on such things as transport provision, recreation and strategic planning specifically and all of an authority's functions generally all have a part to play in the protection of the environment and the pursuit of sustainability. Indeed, local authorities have a central role in sustainable development by developing local strategies involving businesses, voluntary groups and young people. These strategies, known as Local Agenda 21 Action Plans, implement on a local level the wider blue print for sustainable development (known as Agenda 21) which was agreed in 1992 at the Rio Earth Summit.

Decision-making in local authorities

Local authorities are elected bodies. In theory it is the elected councillors who make the ultimate decisions, usually through the appropriate committee. However, in practice, most actual decisions are taken by officers, with the committee rubber stamping them. The councillors are always free to disagree with the recommendation of an officer, but, in so doing, they must be careful to act only on grounds permitted in the relevant legislation, otherwise their decision will be capable of being challenged as *ultra vires*. The constitutional monopoly of the elected councillors has also been removed. The Local Government Act 1972, s. 101, provides that the local authority may delegate any of its powers (apart from a few that must be exercised by a resolution of the whole council, e.g. adopting a local plan) to committees, or to specified officers.

This structure makes councils accountable to the electorate. But it also means that the range of considerations taken into account by local authorities is necessarily wider than those which relate simply to environmental protection. Local authorities, because of their elected status, have a democratic right to balance the advantages of conflicting courses of action which is arguably lacking in many other bodies, even if it does occasionally mean that strange decisions are reached.

In addition, all local authorities are subject to rules on the ability of the public to attend meetings and to receive information about the council's activities. Originally, the Public Bodies (Admission to Meetings) Act 1960 gave members of the public a right of admission to meetings of local authorities. This was extended in the Local Government Act 1972, s. 100, to cover all committee meetings. That provision was itself greatly expanded in the Local Government (Access to Information) Act 1985, which added new ss. 100A to 100K to the 1972 Act. In essence, a member of the public has a right not only to attend meetings of the council and its committees and sub-committees, but also to have access to agendas, minutes, and background reports. This enables information to be obtained on such things as the grounds for a decision, or whether the councillors have diverged from the recommendation of an officer. This written information must be available at all reasonable hours at the offices of the council, and members of the public may make copies of it. Under the statutory provisions, the information must be made available to the public at least three clear days before a committee meeting and this is generally the practice of local authorities. There is, however, some authority to suggest that where the information is particularly complex it must be made available as soon as possible after the authority has received it (see *R* v *Rochdale Metropolitan Borough Council, ex parte Brown* [1997] Env LR 100).

There are limitations. There is a list of exempt information, and the council may resolve to exclude the public if publicity would be prejudicial to the public interest. This may cover meetings such as those to consider whether to recommend that enforcement action is taken on a particular issue, since it may be rendered useless if prior warning is obtained. However, in practice, many local authorities not only allow access to meetings, but permit objectors to address the meeting.

Unlike the questions of secrecy and access to environmental information covered in Chapter 8, the purpose of these powers is to show openness in decision-making and to give an impression of public accountability in what is accepted to be a political system. These powers should therefore be compared with the restrictions on access to meetings of most of the other regulatory bodies discussed (although the Environment Agency in particular has made some moves towards greater openess through its public board meetings and commitment to greater public participation in contentious decision-making).

Mention of local authorities would not be complete without a reference to their current finances. It is quite clear that with restrictions on spending they are unable to carry out properly many of the tasks entrusted to them in the environmental area, thus calling into question the effective enforcement of parts of environmental law.

SEVEN

The regulation of environmental protection

In Chapter 3 it was argued that there are many different sources of environmental law. Indeed, the diversification of regulatory 'tools' has increased dramatically over the last 30 years, reflecting not only the growth in the complexity of laws and regulatory systems generally but also the continuing development of the understanding of how to address environmental problems through legal means. In addition to the diversity of domestic sources of law, there is an increasing 'layering' of laws with different instruments having differing legal effects at international, European and national and even regional levels.

Despite this proliferation of legal mechanisms and in particular the current vogue for suggesting economic or fiscal mechanisms for combating environmental problems, the system of regulation by public bodies remains the prime tool for environmental protection in this country. There has been a spate of environmental taxes which have been promoted by the Government (on such things as pesticides, minerals and the discharge of effluent) but whatever the political rhetoric, the use of taxation and subsidies will always be secondary to regulation in its widest sense.

What does regulation mean in this sense? At one level all the word means is the use of rules to control activities. Under this definition these could include criminal law rules, civil law rules or private non-legal rules operated by a body such as a trade association, or maybe even the 'rules' of the free market. In Chapter 3 there was some discussion of the wide range of environmental rules which might fall within this definition. In this book, however, the word 'regulation' is generally used as shorthand for administrative or bureaucratic regulation (i.e. the application of rules and procedures by public bodies so as to achieve a measure of control over activities carried on by individuals and firms).

Other means of controlling activities, such as criminal law or civil law and the use of the market, will be considered later in this chapter, but since these are often subsidiary to administrative regulation, this will be explained first.

Administrative regulation

Administrative regulation is far more than just the setting of rules on what can and cannot be done. It denotes a coherent *system* of control in which the regulating body sets a framework for activities on an ongoing basis, with a view to conditioning and policing behaviour as well as laying down straight rules.

The advantages of such a system include the ability to provide uniformity, rationality and fairness between those who are regulated. Some form of public accountability is also produced by having a public body responsible for regulation. In particular, one advantage over the criminal law is that a coherent link can be made with other policies, so as to balance all relevant factors. This is often seen as an important part of the 'British' approach to regulation: that it involves an explicit balancing of environmental factors with such things as economic and social considerations.

British regulatory systems can be said to exhibit a pragmatic and flexible approach. The same mechanism is not used for each situation. In some cases the reason is simply that it is recognised that a control mechanism that works for one problem is unlikely to work for a different one. This is a good illustration of the use of law as a tool or a technique to help to solve particular problems. In other cases, there are historical reasons, since one of the features of having a long history of environmental control is that the administrative structures have built up piecemeal and in response to problems as they arise. For example, many controls have in the past been given to local authorities purely because they happened to be dealing with similar matters already, or because there was no other relevant body around at the time.

The processes of regulatory decision-making

Before looking at the main features of regulation in this country, it is necessary to summarise the main processes or stages in regulatory decision-making. These are:

(a)   the establishment of general policies;

(b)   the setting of standards or specific policies in relation to the environmental issue concerned;

(c)   the application of these standards and policies to individual situations;

(d)   the enforcement of standards and permissions;

(e)   the provision of information about the environment and the regulatory process; and

(f)   the utilisation of iterative or 'feed-back' mechanisms to monitor and improve the decision-making processes associated with the regulatory system.

(a)   The establishment of general policies

The process of establishing general policies is not really part of the regulatory system, but a necessary precondition for any system of environmental control. Having said that, one of the most obvious features of the British political system is the absence of formal national policies in many areas (although national strategies are emerging in some areas — air, waste, sustainable development — which could be said to be the start of a new era of environmental planning). Even where there are local or sectoral plans, there is often no national plan, or, if there is, it is made up of somewhat imprecise and flexible policies laid down in a variety of documents. A good illustration of the flexible nature of policy-making in Britain is provided by the town and country planning system, where the 'national plan' is to be found scattered amongst numerous Circulars, Planning Policy Guidance Notes, Ministerial decisions, White Papers and other assorted policy statements.

Given the essentially political nature of much of environmental law, the general tenor of the policies tends to be decided by central government. The presumption in favour of development in town planning is one example, but general decisions on energy and transport policy, such as the favouring of road transport over rail, or the retention of a nuclear power programme, are others. Certain political philosophies may also be imposed by central government; good examples are the principle of voluntariness in relation to controlling agricultural activities, or the policy of privatisation. However, because of the decentralised nature of much of pollution control, some general policies are effectively decided by bodies other than the elected central government. Other policies stem from general assumptions about the nature of the regulatory system itself — which we later refer to as the 'British approach' to environmental regulation (see p. 191).

A final factor is that the shape of many policies is now decided, or at least affected, by the EC. Arguably some of the most significant impacts on the environment in the next few years will follow from the process of integrating environmental policy into other, more general areas of EC policy (under Art. 6 of the amended Treaty).

(b)   The setting of standards or specific policies in relation to the environmental issue concerned

Any system of control must have some objectives that are set for it, otherwise it runs the risk of ceasing to be rational, uniform or fair. These may be fairly explicit objectives, such as air quality standards with specific maximum concentrations for a range of pollutants, or they may be far more vague, such as a water quality objective to the effect that a river should be capable of supporting fish.

In the past reliance has usually been placed on rather vague standards, such as the test of nuisance at common law, or the idea that best practicable means should be used to reduce gaseous emissions to the atmosphere. In addition, standards were often set in an informal manner, as used to happen with non-statutory water quality objectives. More specific and more formal standards are becoming the norm rather than the exception, a good example being the publication of Process Guidance Notes for processes covered by Part I of the EPA 1990. In the development control system, policies of this type are set out in development plans and in Planning Policy Guidance Notes. There is often overlap between this stage and stage (a) above.

(c)   The application of these standards and policies to individual situations
This is often seen as the central part of the regulatory process. There are numerous examples where a permission, authorisation, consent or licence is required from a public body. (Different pieces of legislation use different words but they all mean essentially the same thing.) Whether one is granted, and the nature of any conditions attached, will normally be a discretionary decision, but one that is made by reference to the general standards established at stage (b). The application of standards may also be seen in such processes as court actions for nuisance and the specific application of whether best practicable means or best available techniques are being used.

(d)   The enforcement of standards and permissions
In practice, one of the most important areas of environmental law is whether the legal instruments that are available are used, since there is often considerable discretion given to the regulatory body. 'Enforcement' covers a far wider range of matters than the single question whether to prosecute for breaches of the law. In any regulatory system, there is normally a whole range of administrative and other remedies available in addition to prosecution. The question of which remedy to use is also tied up with how the regulator should proceed. There is a wealth of evidence to show that informal methods of enforcement are often preferred, and that regulators normally adopt a 'compliance strategy' towards enforcement, rather than a 'sanctioning strategy' (i.e. one based on confrontation, see Chapter 9). Questions of inspection and monitoring also arise as part of the enforcement process.

(e)   The provision of information about the environment and the regulatory process
A theme which runs through the regulatory process concerns the openness of the system. This includes such questions as the production of official information on the state of the environment, the availability of public registers, and the publication of information about how the regulatory system itself works. Britain's traditionally secretive administrative processes are slowly becoming more open (see Chapter 8). This is most obvious in relation to stage (c), but is also apparent in the extension of public registers, enabling more information to be available for enforcement purposes. It may also be seen in the increased willingness of the government to issue consultation papers before changes in the law and practice are adopted.

(f)   The use of feedback mechanisms to monitor and improve decision-making
The final stage of the regulatory process links back into the first. An efficient regulatory system needs to be responsive to practical operational experience and shifting collective values. Thus, there is a need to monitor and review the operation of environmental rules to feed back into the revision of existing rules and policies and the establishment of new rules and policies. These iterative mechanisms work on a number of levels. First, there are broad

requirements to report on progress in relation to the implementation of EC directives and to revise the terms of such directives in the light of experience. This facilitates reflection and improvement and perhaps more importantly changes in direction in policy terms. Unfortunately, this formal commitment to review is often more honoured in the breach. When it does take place it can be mechanistic rather than purposive, involving the publication of reports from Member States without any analysis of the consequences or implications of the data. In contrast there are few examples of formal monitoring of environmental laws in the UK. Indeed, the most obvious illustration of this is in the move to deregulation where existing laws are reviewed in order to repeal them if they are obsolete. This does not mean that there is *no* review or monitoring of existing policies and rules, rather that it does not take place on any formal basis.

Secondly, on an individual level there are general requirements to keep up to date with advances in pollution abatement technologies under IPC legislation or to supervise and vary pollution control permits/authorisations at certain specified periods. Finally, there are other methods of monitoring the operation of environmental laws through informal mechanisms (e.g. there have been some major steps taken to improve the process of environmental assessment in the light of academic research which has focussed upon 'best practice').

Anticipatory and continuing controls

Regulatory mechanisms may be divided into two general types, anticipatory controls and continuing controls.

(a)   Anticipatory controls

These are measures in which controls are imposed on an activity at its commencement in order to forestall potential environmental problems. Usually the objective is to prevent the activity unless certain requirements or conditions are met. The category includes a wide range of licensing-type controls, where permission of some sort is required before an activity may be started or carried on. These are normally complemented by a combination of criminal and administrative sanctions if the activity starts without permission, or if the permission is contravened.

The range of possible anticipatory controls is quite wide. It includes:

(i)   An outright ban (e.g. the ban on the use of CFCs in products, or the ban on the dumping of sewage sludge at sea). Of course, there is no *necessity* for a public regulatory body to be involved here, but someone will need to police the ban.

(ii)   A prohibition on an activity unless a particular body is notified in advance (e.g. the requirement under the Wildlife and Countryside Act 1981, s. 28 that owners and occupiers of a site of special scientific interest notify the relevant Nature Conservancy Council of any intention to carry out a potentially damaging operation, thus forewarning the Council of a possible need to take further protective steps).

(iii)   A prohibition on an activity unless it is registered, registration being something that cannot normally be refused by the registering body (e.g. there is a requirement that carriers of controlled waste register with the Environment Agency).

(iv)   A prohibition on an activity until a licence, permission, authorisation or consent is obtained, where the granting of the permission is at the discretion of the regulating body.

In relation to this last type, there are two distinct categories of permission or consent. Some are one-off permissions which, once granted, create what are in effect permanent rights because it is difficult to vary or revoke them. A good example is the granting of planning permission, where revocation entails the payment of compensation. Others provide for variation or revocation in the light of future circumstances. Most pollution control consents fall into this category, examples being the requirement to obtain an authorisation/ permit from the Environment Agency for carrying on a prescribed process, or a consent for a discharge to controlled waters.

(b)   Continuing controls

These are measures where the carrying out of an activity is controlled on a continuing basis. Typically they relate to the way an activity is carried on, so another way of referring to them would be as *operational* controls. An obvious example is the ongoing duty to comply with the terms of a consent, licence, authorisation, or permission granted by a pollution control authority, which will normally be combined with a range of other regulatory controls relating to monitoring and enforcement. The distinction between anticipatory controls and continuing controls is thus that one relates to *whether* an activity should be carried on in the first place, whilst the other relates to *how* it is carried on once it has started.

Of course, anticipatory and continuing controls are mutually supportive and most regulatory systems combine the two types of mechanism. Anticipatory controls still require some monitoring to ensure that the prohibited activity is not being carried on. Conversely, most continuing controls rest on the need for some initial permission before an activity may be started; indeed, the threat of withdrawal of the initial permission may well constitute the strongest inducement to comply with continuing regulatory requirements. For example, planning permission is required before a new activity is started, but that permission will often include conditions that require some adherence to defined standards over a period of time, such as permitted working hours or noise limits. Similarly, consents, authorisations and licences obtained from pollution control authorities normally combine the initial need for a consent with an ability to vary the requirements as the situation changes. This mutually supportive position is reinforced by the fact that many activities are subject to the requirements of more than one regulatory system.

Planning and prevention

The town and country planning system is the major system of anticipatory control in environmental law. To a large extent this stems from the very nature of planning control. It involves the preparation of plans, which may then guide future behaviour. The controls are necessarily imposed at the outset, whilst most pollution control mechanisms basically assume a continuing activity. Planning also mainly concerns land use, siting and locational issues that logically pre-date the operational controls.

A further reason results from practice. In these other systems, it is rare for the initial consent to be refused or revoked (although this power does remain as a threat for those who contravene the continuing controls). For example, it appears that no instance was ever recorded of a certificate of registration being refused under the Alkali Acts, either at the outset or on renewal (see Wood, *Planning Pollution Prevention*, Butterworths, 1989). In other areas of pollution control, the record may be slightly different, but there are still few examples of a consent from a pollution control authority actually being refused where there is already a planning permission.

One result is that the main burden of deciding whether a particular plant should go ahead normally falls upon the local planning authority. By way of example, a new factory will require planning permission as well as consents for emissions from the EA, and maybe the sewerage undertaker and local authority (in its capacity as regulator of air pollution) as well. It will be the local planning authority that decides whether to have the factory in that particular place. The pollution control authorities tend to see their task as setting limits on what is acceptable in terms of pollution from the site proposed rather than as stopping the development going ahead at all. Traditionally, these authorities have had little scope for saying, 'this development would be better somewhere else', though that is a matter they could raise when consulted by the local planning authority over the development proposal. (For an analysis of the relationship between the systems of planning and pollution control, see *Gateshead Metropolitan Borough Council* v *Secretary of State for the Environment* [1995] JPL 432 discussed at p. 391.)

This is perhaps inevitable given the differences in nature between local planning authorities and other regulatory bodies. A local planning authority has a specific remit under the Town and Country Planning Act 1990, s. 70 to consider *all* material factors relating to a development, whilst other bodies often have a more limited range of relevant factors to consider in making their decision (factors which should relate to pollution control issues alone i.e. not economic, spatial or social). It is also an elected body, where ultimate power resides with elected members, and therefore has greater legitimacy in terms of making a balanced policy decision to refuse a development.

Standards in environmental law

Most environmental controls rely on some form of measurable standard. This standard may be used as a guideline (i.e. an objective) or it may be used as a means of defining what an individual or firm may do. Indeed, one of the distinctive features of environmental regulation is that the regulatory body often has responsibility for defining the standard as well as enforcing its application.

There are a number of different types of standards, but a crude division can be made into those which are set by reference to the *target* which is being protected and those which are set by reference to the *source* of the pollution. Source-related standards may be further divided into emission standards, process standards and product standards. There are other factors that have a significant impact on the nature of a standard, such as whether it is centrally or locally set, uniform or flexible, precise or imprecise.

The following summary is not intended to be an exhaustive list of the various types of standard (from the list of variables above obviously the number of potential types is very great), but is an attempt to introduce a basic vocabulary of terms. It also aims to illustrate some of the more common methods used, together with some thoughts on their relative strengths and weaknesses. In a sense, these are the tools available to the legislator in deciding how a regulatory system is to work.

(a)   Environmental quality standards (target standards)

Some standards concentrate on the effect on a particular target. In many cases, the protected target may be human beings and the standard is accordingly set by reference to the effect on them (e.g. the control of noise levels from machinery). However, since this is a book about environmental protection, it will mainly concentrate on situations where the protected target is the environment, or part of it (with Chapter 16 on noise being the primary exception). The phrases 'target standards' and 'environmental quality standards' will therefore be treated as interchangeable.

The effect on the target may be measured in different ways. It may relate to a biological effect, thus channelling all information directly into a consideration of the actual impact of a pollutant (e.g. a standard requiring that a discharge to water is not harmful to fish or aquatic animals). Alternatively, it may relate to the exposure of the target, from which certain biological or other effects may be presumed. In the environmental field, however, it will more usually relate simply to some measurable quality of the receiving environment, such as the level of a particular pollutant.

An environmental quality standard can therefore be defined as a standard where conformity is measured by reference to the effect of a pollutant on the receiving environment. It is unusual for the selected target to be the whole environment. More commonly a particular medium will be chosen as the reference point, such as air or water. In order to retain flexibility, there will frequently also be a geographical limitation: the standard may thus be set by reference to a particular river or area, or may be even more specific, such as where air quality or noise levels are fixed within factories or any other enclosed area.

Examples of environmental quality standards include:

(i)   setting air quality standards for the maximum or minimum concentration of any specified substance in air (e.g. the Air Quality (England) Regulations 2000 (SI 2000/928) set mandatory standards for sulphur dioxide, nitrogen dioxide, lead, carbon monoxide, benzene, 1.3 butadiene and small particles (PM_{10}));

(ii)   setting water quality standards for the concentration of specified pollutants in 'controlled waters';

(iii)   the nuisance test at common law, under which property owners are entitled to the enjoyment of their property without unreasonable interference from neighbours.

It will be clear that these standards may be set by reference to any number of parameters. For example, a water quality standard could be set specifically for the maximum concentration of zinc, or a whole range of parameters may be used, as is the case for drinking water. It will also be clear that the standard can be precise or imprecise — the nuisance standard is a good example of an imprecise standard.

(b)   Emission standards

An emission standard can be defined as a standard where conformity is measured by reference to what is emitted rather than the effect on the receiving environment. Emission standards thus tend to concentrate on wastes produced. For example, the content of a discharge from a pipe or chimney could be controlled by reference to an emission standard.

Examples of emission standards include:

(i)   the maximum content of a particular substance in a liquid discharge from a pipe to a sewer or 'controlled waters';

(ii)   the noise level measured as it emanates from a piece of machinery;

(iii)   the maximum content of a particular substance in an emission from a chimney or exhaust pipe.

(c)   Process standards

A standard may be imposed on a process either by stipulating precisely the process which must be carried on, or by setting performance requirements that the process must reach. In the second case there would be a choice as to how to reach these requirements. These standards may relate to the whole of the process or, alternatively, to a part of it, such as the way that a product is made or the way effluent is treated. They may include requirements about the technology that is used, the raw materials, or operational factors such as whether the process is being carried out properly.

Examples of process standards include:

(i)   a requirement that a particular pre-treatment plant for effluent be used;

(ii)   a stipulation on the height of a factory chimney;

(iii)   a stipulation about the use of a particular grade or quality of fuel;

(iv)   a requirement that the 'best available techniques' are used to prevent environmental harm, though the general requirement is often translated into a set of emission standards in practice;

(v)   conditions attached to the operation of a landfill site or incinerator.

It is clear that current practice is to emphasise the use of process standards, and this is illustrated by their use in the pollution prevention and control legislation (see p. 396). They are a good means of preventing harm to the environment arising in the first place.

(d)   Product standards

Product standards may be defined as where the characteristics of an item that is being produced are controlled. This may be done with the aim of protecting against damage the product may cause whilst it is being used, or when it is disposed of, or even during its manufacture. Examples include:

(i)   a requirement that all new cars are capable of running on unleaded petrol;

(ii)   a requirement that cars are fitted with catalytic converters;

(iii)   it may even be thought that requirements on the labelling of goods are a type of product standard.

(e)   Use standards

Another form of standard which is closely related to product standards is a standard which relates to the use of a product. As the name suggests, whilst product standards are primarily concerned with characteristics or concentrations, use standards relate to the marketing or use of the product. Examples include the restrictions on the use and marketing of new chemical substances, pesticides, veterinary medicines and, most controversially, genetically modified organisms. These standards are concerned with the measurement of any risk associated with the consequences of the use of such products rather than any restrictions on the product itself.

Interrelationship of standards

Of course, these five types of standards are not exclusive of each other. An emission standard will often be set so as to achieve an environmental quality standard. Product standards for a car will include many matters relating to the emissions from it, such as lead, carbon dioxide or noise. In addition, the cumulative effect of these emissions will have an impact on the attainment or otherwise of any environmental quality standard.

Taking one particular toxic pollutant, lead, environmental concentrations may be controlled in a number of ways:

(a)   Environmental quality standards may be set, stating that levels of lead should not rise above a certain level in the air, in water, or in the soil.

(b)   Emissions of lead may be controlled, so that any emission, whether into air or water or on to land, should not include more than a specified concentration of lead, to be set in some form of permission or consent.

(c)   Processes may be regulated to reduce the use of lead, or to reduce by good design possible emissions and escapes of lead into the environment.

(d)   Products likely to include lead may be regulated, either to ban its use (e.g. lead fishing weights) or to limit the use of lead (e.g. setting maximum amounts of lead in leaded petrol or in drinking water).

Other characteristics of standards

As stated earlier, a number of other matters are also important in relation to the nature of a standard. The standard may be a precise one, such as one set by reference to a quantifiable maximum or minimum — often a numerical value. Alternatively, it may be an imprecise one, such as a requirement that 'best practicable means' (BPM) or 'best available techniques' (BAT) are used, or one applying the common law test of nuisance.

The standard may be a uniform one across the country (or the EC), or it may vary from area to area. Indeed, it may be set on an individual basis. Certain matters demand uniform standards. For example, uniformity is normally desirable for emissions from mobile sources such as cars, otherwise problems are caused at boundaries. For similar reasons, most product standards are set on a uniform basis. It is strongly argued by some that uniformity creates equality, a particularly important consideration in the context of the EC and the single internal market. Limit values, as used by the EC in a number of directives, create a special form of uniformity. They require that a certain standard is reached, but allow Member States to impose more stringent standards if circumstances require (see p. 132).

The standard may be set centrally or locally. This distinction tends to reflect the same division as that between uniform and individualised standards, since centrally set standards will usually be uniform whilst locally set ones will vary with the discretion given to the decision-maker. In this context, it must be remembered that traditionally, few standards in Britain have been set by legislation. Often this exercise was left to local bodies, although this is changing as EC standards permeate domestic environmental law.

Strengths and weaknesses of different types of standards

Obviously it is not possible to cover all types of standards, but it is possible to see the relative strengths and weaknesses of the more commonly used examples.

Environmental quality standards, by concentrating on what it is that requires protection, are able to deal with inputs to the environment from all sources and via all potential pathways, whilst the other mechanisms, used on their own, tend to permit cumulation of any particular pollutant. For the same reason, environmental quality standards can also cater for potentially harmful combinations of substances on the environment. They can thus enable a policy-maker to identify areas where work is needed, and channel resources effectively. They can also be tailored for particular circumstances, for example by being more stringent in sensitive areas than in others.

However, there are a number of limitations to environmental quality standards. They require constant monitoring of the environment, which may prove to be impractical or expensive. Enforcement poses difficulties, since failure to reach a standard may alert us to the existence of a problem, but does not necessarily tell us the cause or how to remedy it. For example, in order to clean up a river which is chronically contaminated with organic wastes, a regulator would first have to identify the causes of the pollution and then find some method of restricting inputs that was fair and enforceable. A further problem of environmental quality standards is that they may give no incentive to polluters to improve their performance in areas where the standard is already being met.

The very nature of environmental quality standards is that they tend to be set as *objectives* rather than as legal requirements, except in those situations where there is a limited number of sources and targets, such as enclosed work environments. This use as objectives makes them useful at the strategic and planning stages of the regulatory process. For example, development plans often set environmental quality standards, even if they are frequently very imprecise, such as a policy that developments liable to cause a nuisance should not be permitted in a defined area.

By contrast, the strength of emission standards is that they are relatively easy to control and monitor by sampling at the point of emission. Enforcement is also easier because of the simplicity of the causation requirements where there is a point of discharge. In addition, an emission standard may be tightened progressively to encourage a discharger to improve the process, whilst still retaining choice as to how this is done.

A main drawback of emission standards relates to the difficulty of controlling diffuse (or non-point) emissions, such as fertiliser or pesticide run-off, by these means. There is also the difficulty (shared with process standards and product standards) of organising a system that can cope with an accumulation of similar emissions in one area, such as car exhausts in Los Angeles or similar industrial concerns in one water catchment area. This second difficulty is not an insoluble problem, however. It may be tackled by setting very strict local emission standards, by linking them explicitly to an environmental quality standard, or by applying the 'bubble' approach (i.e. by aggregating together all emissions in a particular area and permitting a total amount of emissions for that area).

Process standards are obviously limited to where there is a process to control and thus tend to apply mainly to the manufacturing industry. Their main strength is that they may be set so as to prevent a problem arising in the first place. They may also help to pool resources for research at a central level. There is a potential disincentive for producers to find more effective ways of reducing pollution, unless the standards are made progressively stricter, or are periodically altered, or are set at levels that force the producer to develop the technology so as to reach the standard (so-called 'technology forcing' rules).

Product standards are similarly limited to where there is a product and have similar strengths and weaknesses as process standards. As stated above, both categories also have difficulty in catering for the cumulative effect of pollutants on their own.

Locally set and centrally set standards: Britain versus the EC

It has often been noted that Britain and the rest of the EC do not seem to see eye to eye on pollution control. This is sometimes translated into a conflict between a British preference for locally set and variable (i.e. non-uniform) emission standards, set by reference to local environmental quality, and an EC preference for centrally set uniform emission standards. Haigh (in *EEC Environmental Policy and Britain*, Longman, 1989) points out that any conflict on these grounds has been much exaggerated (see below).

Nevertheless, these two types of standards provide an excellent opportunity for a case study on their relative strengths and weaknesses.

(a)   Locally set and variable emission standards set by reference to local environmental quality

Each of the features of this combination of ideas merits some mention. Referring everything to environmental quality can be said to target controls where they are needed — at the protection of the environment. In this way, the impact of non-point emissions and background levels of pollution may be taken into account, as well as discharges from pipes and chimneys. The fact that neither the emission standards nor the environmental quality standards are uniform provides flexibility. This enables more sensitive areas to be protected more strictly, or polluters who are seen as more useful to the community to be treated more leniently. In all cases, a great deal of discretion is granted to decision-makers. It is also argued that, since standards can be varied to take account of local circumstances, the mechanism is economically efficient. For example, greater pollutant loads could be permitted in remote, unpopulated areas or where the self-cleansing properties of the local environment are greater.

(b)   Centrally set uniform emission standards

These have obvious advantages. Uniform standards are easily imposed, easily implemented and easily monitored. They are fair between polluters since all are treated the same, and they avoid difficult problems about allocating the right to pollute amongst different polluters. As a result they may be relatively cheap for the regulator to operate, because they involve less administrative discretion than variable standards. They also fit in well with the economic principles of the EC's common market.

On the other hand, they can be said not to allow local conditions to be taken into account, because there is no flexibility (although this can be provided at the enforcement stage). They are meant to be unable to deal with the situation where there is a number of polluters in one area, since there is no jurisdiction to reduce the emission standard to fit local conditions. They are also sometimes said to lead to the possibility of a uniformly polluted country if there is one relevant discharge in every area. These last two criticisms are rather too general, since good use of preventive controls would help in both cases.

Why Britain and the EC differ

It is not difficult to think of reasons why Britain may differ from other Member States within the EC. As an island, mainland Britain has no frontiers. Thus, the argument about fairness has never had the impact that it has in France and Germany, which share the Rhine as a border, and where the inequality of one factory being allowed to discharge more than another on the other bank is obvious. Other factors stem from the 'British approach' to pollution control, such as that Britain has a tradition of discretionary, local decision-making and a system based on pragmatism, in which the effects on the environment are balanced with social, economic and political factors.

But the main argument for the British position probably stems from self-interest. With its rainy climate, fast-running streams, ample coastline and relative remoteness, Britain can claim a comparative advantage when it comes to pollution. Put very crudely, the same discharge is supposed to cause less pollution in Britain than in other countries, because of its lesser effect on the environment. When it comes to setting standards, some people in Britain do not see why stringent uniform standards should apply across the EC if they have no justification in terms of environmental protection in the British context, even if they provide that protection elsewhere.

As stated earlier, the differences have been exaggerated. Even discounting the influence of EC legislation, there are many examples of uniform emission standards applying in Britain, although this is sometimes hidden by being the product of administrative practice rather than legislative action. This is especially the case in relation to dangerous substances, where no amount of discretionary balancing with other factors will make them safe. Also the differences set out above relate mainly to water pollution, which is, arguably, the area where Britain has the greatest comparative advantage. Even in relation to water pollution, the differences have mainly surfaced over one particular directive — the framework Directive 76/464 on Dangerous Substances in Water. It was in relation to this directive that Britain's position led to alternative regimes being adopted for the control of dangerous substances (see p. 565). But, as Haigh points out, it seems that what the other EC Member States saw as cause for concern was not the use of environmental quality objectives to define the context for the setting of variable discharge consents, but the fact that these quality standards were, at the time, informal, unpublished, and set by regional authorities. It is not hard to imagine that other Member States thought they were being told that the British approach to controlling dangerous substances was that 'it all depends on the circumstances'.

In addition, it should be observed that in any case Directive 76/464 did *not* lay down uniform emission standards. It laid down limit values, and many of the arguments against uniform emission standards do not apply to these, because there is the flexibility to have a stricter standard if desirable. As a final point, it is interesting to note that these sorts of arguments have been taken into account and dealt with in the proposed Water Framework Directive, which will replace Directive 76/464 at a national level (see further p. 570).

The 'British approach' to regulation

Since administrative regulation can take many forms, it is important to establish the distinctive features of the British style or approach. In other words, what types of rules and standards are employed? How are they set and by whom? How are they enforced and by whom? What role does the public play in these processes?

In *National Styles of Regulation* (Cornell UP, 1986), Vogel identifies a number of characteristics of the British style. The book claims to be 'an examination of British environmental policy as seen through the eyes of a student of American politics', and consists of a comparison of approaches to environmental regulation in Britain and the USA. Vogel writes that Britain's regulatory style is characterised by flexibility and informality, and summarises the system as involving:

> An absence of statutory standards, minimal use of prosecution, a flexible enforcement strategy, considerable administrative discretion, decentralised implementation, close co-operation between regulators and the regulated, and restrictions on the ability of non-industry constituents to participate in the regulatory process.

At the risk of producing an unmanageable list, to these points could be added others, such as delegation of decision-making to autonomous quasi-governmental and non-governmental bodies, extensive use of industrial self-regulation, a limited availability of legislative and judicial scrutiny of regulators, a gradualist approach to change, reliance on scientific knowledge for decision-making and habitual reference to economic factors before decisions are made.

Vogel compares this approach with that of the USA, which he characterises as rule-oriented, normally employing rigid and uniform standards, and making little use of industrial self-regulation. In addition, less use is made there of administrative discretion, prosecution is much more common, there is great executive and judicial scrutiny of regulators and technology-forcing rules are favoured. All of these features lead to conflict between regulator and regulated and to an adversary mentality.

Of course many of these differences are not unique to environmental regulation in the two countries, but are a matter of general political culture. They probably stem from different attitudes towards regulation engendered by different population densities and degrees of cultural homogeneity. In Britain the need for a balancing process is all too clear, whilst in the USA the 'frontier mentality' is understandably more prevalent.

At this point a warning should be given. Since the 1960s the situation in the USA has changed dramatically, and what Vogel describes in the 1980s is quite different from what happened before. Similarly, the British approach has been undergoing a process of change over the last 20 years. The informal and flexible basis remains, but the approach has undoubtedly got more open, more centralised, more legalistic and more contentious, especially in the last 10 years or so. The changes in legislation have been substantial, but there have also been more disguised internal changes of practice by regulators. As a result, Vogel's analysis is now somewhat outdated.

One crucial factor in this change is the attitude of the EC. The British approach has tended to conflict with that adopted by other Member States and has had to be modified to fit in with that. At the same time, the increased profile of environmental issues, particularly international ones requiring common responses, has led to some changes of style out of political necessity. A further factor which has influenced the change away from the traditional British approach has been the changing political landscape within a period of radical change in the regulation of environmental protection. This commenced with the Conservative government in the early 1980s and has been adopted (to a greater or lesser extent) by the Labour Government of the late 1990s. The major policy features during this time included the rejection of long-term planning in favour of market forces, deregulation of unnecessary bureaucratic controls, privatisation of public services, imposition of strict spending controls on public bodies, the general weakening of local authority power and the use of voluntary controls allowing choice wherever possible.

The following sections will explore some of the manifestations and implications of the British approach, and will seek to illustrate just how it is changing and in what direction. However, it must be stressed that this is only a general approach. No one would suggest that all these symptoms are displayed by each of the various regulatory processes in the country, merely that these are recognisable general features.

The implications of the British approach also vary at the different stages identified earlier, with the result that, for example, general policy-making remains mainly a central function, rather than being particularly decentralised (although many of these general policies are now in practice agreed at international or EC level). Nevertheless, the general features of the regulatory system can be illustrated by considering a number of key issues.

Decentralisation

Decision-making is decentralised in three ways: by being given to a wide range of bodies, by significant use of delegation, and by geographical decentralisation.

There are a range of bodies exercising environmental responsibilities (see Chapter 6). Although the creation of the Environment Agency unified a variety of pollution control functions, Britain still has a large number of autonomous or semi-autonomous environmental agencies, such as the Nature Conservancy Councils, the Health and Safety Executive, the Nuclear Installations Inspectorate, and the Countryside Agency. Local authorities also have wide-ranging environmental protection powers in relation to such things as air pollution, contaminated land, noise control, town and country planning and environmental health. Traditionally, there has also been decentralisation within central government. For many years the nominal responsibility for environmental policy has been located with the Department of the Environment (and its variants). This has obscured the fact that many decisions and policies which have important environmental effects have been made by other Departments including the Department of Trade and Industry (e.g. on power stations and transmission lines), the Department of Transport (e.g. on emissions from vehicles and the routes of new roads) and the Ministry of Agriculture, Fisheries and Food (e.g. on agricultural support schemes). The diversity was compounded by the tendency to have separate bodies in Wales and Scotland. Under the Department of the Environment, Transport and the Regions (DETR), there has been some acknowledgement that there is a need to re-integrate certain aspects of environmental policy and the introduction of the Environmental Audit Committee should ensure that the environmental implications of all decision-making are at least considered. Although these moves suggest a greater use of centralised policy-making powers, these must be balanced against the re-emphasis of regional policy-making and devolution for Scotland and Wales.

Even within the DETR matters are often delegated. For example, appeals against refusals of planning permission are normally dealt with by the Planning Inspectorate Executive Agency, although this remains formally part of the DETR.

Over the years this decentralisation of power has tended to result in a rather incoherent environmental policy, with very little uniformity across the country. Even such a central function as the monitoring of the environment has tended to be done in an uncoordinated way but there have been a number of changes which have altered matters. For example, the regulation of water pollution was organised on a regional basis until 1989, when the NRA was established as a national body covering England and Wales. HMIP was created in 1987 to draw together a number of inspectorates at that time operating separately within the Department of the Environment and the Health and Safety Executive. Both these institutional changes clearly fostered uniformity in decision-making. The Environment Act 1995 created the Environment Agency for England and Wales and the Scottish Environment Protection Agency for Scotland, thus continuing the process of producing a more coherent and uniform institutional structure.

Decisions are also commonly made locally. Local authorities have the wide powers referred to above, whilst many of the inspectorates and other agencies operate on a regional basis, granting some discretion to local decision-makers. There is a philosophy underpinning this, of course. The British approach is geared pragmatically towards the protection of the receiving environment, so it is sensible that decisions are taken by people or bodies with a knowledge of local conditions, whether environmental, social or economic.

An important change has been the centralisation of policy decisions in recent years. This has been most marked in relation to matters where there is conflict between central and local government. For example, in the town and country planning system, increased intervention in local decisions by central government was the major issue of the 1980s. It was manifested mainly through hard-hitting and directory Circulars, which were applied on appeal so as to alter the policy context of most planning decisions, though there were also changes to the law and in institutional structure designed to reduce local control, through such creations as urban development corporations. However, centralisation is also a reality in relation to pollution control. For example, local authorities have lost a significant amount of discretion in relation to air pollution as a result of the implementation of Part I of the EPA 1990, whilst the EA has taken over the waste regulation functions previously carried out by local authorities. Even in an area where local authorities have been given new powers, such as in the regulation of historic contamination under Part IIA of the EPA 1990, they are obliged to act in accordance with central guidance or are subject to technical advice from the EA.

Centralisation may also be seen at work in the control of public spending. The regional water authorities were severely limited for many years in their ability to make capital expenditure decisions, and the same is true for local authorities. For bodies such as the Countryside Agency which rely almost entirely on government grant, the position is even clearer.

Finally there is a very significant element of centralisation involved in the relationship between Britain and the EC. Not only is EC decision-making essentially secret, but there is little formal input to it by local or regional bodies in Britain. However, the crucial point is that EC law is binding on Member States. The requirement to conform with it, coupled with the policy goal of harmonisation throughout the EC, means that power is taken away from local and non-governmental bodies and given to central bodies. This is clearly true in relation to the first two stages of the regulatory processes identified earlier (the policy-making and objective-setting stages), and it is becoming increasingly true for the third stage (the operational stage of setting individual consents) as well.

Discretion

The amount of discretion is great at all the stages of regulatory decision-making. Parliament rarely sets firm policies and standards in legislation, allowing for these to be defined in delegated legislation or through administrative guidance. For example, in the town and country planning system the nature of central guidance is nowhere dictated in the legislation, but is set out in government Circulars and Planning Policy Guidance Notes, which may be altered at any time.

At the standard-setting and consent-setting levels the discretion is usually given to the relevant regulatory body. As examples, local planning authorities have the ability to grant or refuse planning permission as they think fit (subject mainly to the Secretary of State's control over policy on appeal), the Environment Agency has discretion over the setting of standards for discharges to water and in the definition of 'best available techniques not entailing excessive cost' (BATNEEC).

A similar wide discretion can be seen at the enforcement stage. There are few statutes which lay down duties to enforce the legislation, or which set out statutory factors to take into account, and usually the decision whether to take action is taken by the regulatory body on the basis of practical and political factors which are not mentioned in the legislation. Since many of the most important remedies are administrative remedies which are unavailable to individuals, this discretion is of enormous practical importance. Enforcement is discussed in greater detail in Chapter 9.

Judicial interference is frequently limited by the width of discretions given in legislation. This is best illustrated in the town and country planning legislation, where there is a clear policy of judicial non-intervention in decisions about the weight to be attached to material considerations. An example of this policy was shown in *London Residuary Body* v *Lambeth London Borough Council* [1990] 1 WLR 744, where the Secretary of State's decision to grant planning permission for office development in London County Hall was held to be unchallengeable by the House of Lords. This was so even though he had accorded overriding weight to the presumption in favour of development where there was nothing else in favour of the development and some grounds against. As a result of all these factors, and also the general British preference for variable rather than uniform standards, the British system of environmental control has become characterised by flexibility and lack of uniformity.

Although there is a wide discretion granted to decision makers, this is not completely unfettered and the courts have intervened in cases which demonstrate that the exercise of discretion can be challenged over and above the level of individual decisions. Thus, there have been a number of cases where both the European Court and the High Court have rejected discretionary decisions which have been based upon incorrect criteria.

In particular, this has been the case when dealing with the relative importance of economic considerations over environmental factors. For example, the courts have held that economic considerations were afforded too much weight when the Secretary of State drew the original estuarine limits for the purposes of the Urban Waste Water Treatment Directive (91/271), see *R* v *Secretary of State for the Environment, ex parte Kingston upon Hull City Council* [1996] Env LR 248. This case can be contrasted with the decision in *R* v *National Rivers Authority, ex parte Moreton* [1996] Env LR 234 in which Harrison J held that the NRA was entitled to take into account economic considerations (i.e. the investment budget of the local water company) in addition to the achievement of water quality standards when deciding whether or not to grant a discharge consent (perhaps illustrating the distinction between the exercise of general discretion in *Hull CC* compared to individual decision making discretion in *Moreton*). Other examples of the limits of discretion in relation to establishing boundaries can be seen in various nature conservation cases (e.g. *R* v *Secretary of State for the Environment, ex parte RSPB* [1997] QB 206 and further p. 645).

Gradualism and reliance on scientific evidence

The place of these ideas as two of the key tenets of British pollution control is emphasised in Department of the Environment Pollution Paper No. 11,

Environmental Standards — The UK Practice. This very readable document was published in 1975 and is now somewhat out of date, but it has great significance in terms of explaining the British approach to pollution control, since it is effectively a justification of that approach in the face of alternatives being put forward within the EC.

The philosophy of gradualism is that pollution controls should be strengthened gradually as economic circumstances, the goodwill of producers and scientific abilities allow. This links very strongly with the related idea that decisions should be taken on the basis of a reliable scientific base, although it should be recognised that science does not necessarily produce facts in the environmental sphere, but estimates of risks or probabilities. There is accordingly always a political factor involved in whether to accept a risk or not (see below).

One major effect of these two ideas has been that environmental controls have tended to be reactive rather than anticipatory. They have rarely been concerned with laying down a framework in advance, leading to the fragmentation of the system and to its lack of uniformity. A more specific effect is that time is normally given for changes to be made in order to give industry time to adjust capital programmes and work methods. In relation to the requirement that best practicable means be used, it was normal practice to allow any process to continue for its operational life (often 10 years) before declaring it in contravention of the requirement, even though it may have been superseded before then. Similar approaches were taken in relation to IPC and BATNEEC and the IPPC Directive's requirements.

The extended time scale for implementing the EPA 1990 (full implementation did not take place until 1996), apart from being a comment on the complexity of the new requirements, is a further example of the gradualist approach. Interestingly, the timetable for the introduction of Part I of the Act was laid down after an undertaking was given in Parliament to do so, thus attempting to avoid a re-run of the non-implementation of the Control of Pollution Act 1974. At the EC level, this approach is also reflected in the time scale allowed for implementation of directives, which is normally at least two years, and often five years. A final example is that the British have frequently rejected the use of 'technology-forcing' rules. These represent the setting of a rule which is stricter than currently achievable, though with a time scale for its achievement. The theory is that producers will thus be forced to adapt their current technology to meet the requirements. This concept is much used in the USA, but in Britain the potential cost to industry, and benchmarking against best practice at national or international level, is more frequently used to argue for a gradual change.

The importance of context

In establishing environmental controls, importance is nearly always attached to economic and other factors. As Pollution Paper No. 11 put it:

> The tendency in setting standards in the UK is less to seek an absolute scientific base than to use scientific principles and all relevant and reliable evidence, then to try and progressively reduce emissions in a way that is

consistent with economic and technological feasibility and with what at any one time is thought to be an acceptable ultimate objective.

It is difficult to separate the reasons for this policy from its effects. One reason is undoubtedly the historical influence that the town and country planning system, with its explicit requirement to balance all material considerations, has had on the development of the law, but a major reason must relate to the definition of pollution and the objectives of environmental controls.

Pollution has been defined as a relative concept, in the sense that there is no absolute rule about what amounts to pollution. The same applies to other forms of environmental change, such as urban or agricultural development. It is not possible to eradicate pollution, merely to reduce it. It follows that, at some stage, a choice has to be made about what is, and what is not, permissible. This is ultimately a political question, and involves a balancing of various factors. However, there are two possible objectives of pollution control. One is to aim to reduce pollution to 'acceptable' levels. An alternative is to aim to reduce pollution as far as possible. In Britain the first approach is implicitly adopted in relation to most substances. This explains the inevitability of a political balancing process, and also the preference for variable environmental quality standards. The second approach tends to lead to a reduction in discretion and to greater reliance on uniform standards, because if one producer can reduce to a particular level others should be able to do so as well.

The contextual approach accepts, therefore, that there is always going to be a trade-off between environmental protection and other factors, such as cost. This is fundamental to most British environmental controls. For example, it is reflected in the phrase 'best available techniques not entailing excessive cost' (BATNEEC) which was the cornerstone of Part I of the EPA 1990. The best available techniques part of the formula suggests that every step should be taken to protect the environment, but the not entailing excessive cost part qualifies it by reference to economic factors. This trade-off is reflected with the European context by the test of proportionality which means that although the concept of 'best available techniques' (BAT) within the IPPC Directive lacks any explicit reference to costs, there is still a degree of flexibility in carrying out the balancing exercise.

This philosophy of balancing environmental protection with material welfare is apparent in most areas of the law. It explains the wide discretions given to decision-makers, the emphasis on decisions being taken by reference to local factors, and the practice of defining some concepts after consultation with the industry involved. The emphasis on balance also explains such fundamental features of British law as the preference for flexible environmental standards rather than uniform ones, and the flexible and cooperative enforcement strategies that are employed by regulatory agencies.

Are things changing?

As the previous section suggests, a number of things appear to be changing in relation to the traditional British approach to regulation. In particular, there is an increasing tendency for standards to be set centrally (which often goes hand in hand with more uniform standards), and a further tendency for them to be set out more explicitly in legislative instruments or formal policy documents.

A number of examples could be used to illustrate the point. Perhaps the clearest relates to the way that EC standards are imposed through directives, thus effectively replacing local discretion with central prescription, but there are also examples from domestic legislation. In relation to water pollution, a major change over the next few years will be the setting of statutory water quality objectives by the Secretary of State for stretches of controlled waters. The Environment Agency is under a duty (under the Water Resources Act 1991, s. 84) to exercise its powers so as to ensure, as far as it is practicable to do so, that the statutory water quality objective ('SWQO') is achieved at all times. This covers, amongst other things, its powers in relation to setting discharge consents and clearly entails the whole process becoming more open and predictable. It should be noted that this shift towards centralism and formalism does not necessarily imply that SWQOs will be set uniformly nor that individual consents will be set in a blanket fashion. There will continue to be a considerable measure of local differentiation and local input in the setting of discharge consents. It is, however, the *shift* from secretive, flexible, subjective and individualistic approaches, to more open, formal, objective and collective forms of decision-making which is significant. A similar process can be seen at work in the town planning requirement (in the Town and Country Planning Act 1990, s. 54A) that decisions are to be made in accordance with the provisions of the development plan, unless material considerations indicate otherwise (see p. 322).

As well as centralising decisions and reducing discretions, this new formalism also increases the potential role of the courts. It has already been noted how the courts have played a lesser role in the development of environmental policy in this country than in, for example, Germany or the USA. This is probably because of the wider discretions provided in the legislation, which are often unchallengeable. However, the development of more explicit standards, coupled with clear operational duties imposed on the regulatory agencies, means that a greater number of decisions may potentially be challenged through judicial review. An example is the duty imposed on the Environment Agency under the Water Resources Act 1991, s. 84, referred to above: it is quite possible that this could be used in the future to compel the Agency to adopt a certain course of action. The likelihood of the courts playing an increasing role in the development of environmental law is further increased by developments in relation to judicial review and EC law. For example, the concept of the supremacy of EC law has been used to develop various doctrines with the aim of ensuring not only that legislation is passed to implement EC directives, but also that the laws that are passed are implemented and enforced in practice (see p. 136).

Of course, much of this discussion is only of real relevance to regulatory systems. If, as may be the case in the future, market mechanisms are preferred to regulation, they may represent a force moving in the opposite direction.

One of the potential results of deregulation and a shift towards the use of market mechanisms is a decentralisation of decisions from government to consumers and industry.

There is another general change that can be identified, which is that there is a discernible shift away from reliance on flexible standards based on the impact on the receiving environment towards standards based on the use of the best available techniques. This is seen at its clearest in relation to Part I of the EPA 1990 and the provisions of the Pollution Prevention and Control Act 1999, where the conditions attached to authorisations are set by reference to BATNEEC and BAT respectively, but it is also an inevitable by-product of a more centralised and formal system. It also follows from the increased involvement of lenders, insurers and other stakeholders in decisions on environmental management, since they are likely to insist on the use of the best available techniques as a protection against liability or loss of their stake.

Deregulation

This term appears to carry three separate, but overlapping, meanings. One refers to the so-called 'war on red tape': in other words that excessively bureaucratic procedures and practices should be removed and simplified. A second meaning relates to the general disinclination to use regulatory mechanisms unless they are necessary, which often translates into favouring voluntary and market-style mechanisms. A third meaning can be discerned in terms of a policy not to interfere with the operations of business.

The origins of the deregulation initiative can be traced back to the Conservative Government and in particular a formal programme which was commenced in 1993 which resulted in the active search for examples of perceived over-regulation by government departments. More recently, the concept has been adapted by the present administration and rebranded as a 'better regulation' initiative with the production of the White Paper, *Modernising Government* (Cm 4310, 1999) and the setting up of bodies such as the Better Regulation Task Force (with a remit to reduce unnecessary regulation, reflecting the first definition) and the Cabinet Office's Regulatory Impact Unit (with a role in overseeing new domestic and European proposals).

The main statutory basis for the deregulatory push is the Deregulation and Contracting Out Act 1994 (and there are proposals to extend the effect of this Act in the future under a Regulatory Reform Bill put forward in the Queen's Speech in 1999). It includes a general power for any Minister to amend or repeal legislation by means of a statutory instrument if they are of the opinion that the measure imposes a burden on any trade, business or profession, and that the amendment or repeal will reduce that burden. There are some limited consultation and procedural requirements that temper this very wide power, but it is clear that it could be used to reduce the impact of environmental protection legislation. In addition, s. 5 of the 1994 Act empowers Ministers to 'improve' various enforcement procedures (a term which includes such things as revocation and variation of a licence, as well as criminal prosecution) by statutory instrument.

One of the main deregulatory initiatives in relation to environmental law and practice was introduced by way of a Code of Enforcement Practice issued by the Environment Agency which (amongst other things) gave businesses the right to object to proposed enforcement actions and the right to be notified in advance of such action being taken. Ironically, these deregulatory moves were reversed in 1998 when a revised *Enforcement and Prosecution Policy* was adopted on the back of the move towards 'better regulation'. Other changes brought about by the initiative include amendments to the Water Resources Act 1991, made by the Environment Act 1995, which: removed tripartite sampling (paradoxically making life easier for the EA when bringing prosecutions); reduced public participation in setting discharge consents; and extended the period for varying discharge consents from two to four years. In addition, the repeal of the Alkali Act 1906 was claimed to be part of the results of the deregulation drive although in truth it was inevitable given the full implementation of the IPC system under the EPA 1990.

Given that there are moves to extend the scope of the Deregulation and Contracting Out Act 1994, the position in relation to the impact of deregulation on existing environmental laws is somewhat equivocal. There is, however, some evidence that legislation will be amended in response to complaints of industry (see e.g. the legislation in relation to packaging waste where the turnover threshold for companies which are regulated under the legislation was doubled to exclude smaller companies who would be unfairly burdened). The real justification behind most of these amendments appears to be in accordance with the third meaning discussed above: i.e. no interference with the operations of business.

Market mechanisms or the use of economic tools

These rather general phrases are meant to encompass all approaches which seek to use prices or economic incentives and deterrents to achieve environmental objectives. This could be done, for example, by encouraging pricing systems that signal the true environmental costs of products to consumers, thereby making 'environment-friendly' items cheaper than those that pollute or waste natural resources. In a sense, therefore, these economic tools or instruments are the exact opposite of using the free market, since they normally involve an interference or intervention in the free market for the purpose of environmental protection. However, they do involve the use of the market in the sense that they are normally designed to allow consumers and industry to make choices about their actions. By way of contrast, many people would argue that most, though certainly not all, regulatory systems tend to operate so as to remove choice.

There is thus a potential confusion in referring simply to 'using the market' for environmental protection ends, since that runs together the policy of allowing an unrestricted free market to allocate resources on the assumption that that is somehow more efficient, and the separate policy of intervention in the market for protective purposes. As Nicholas Ridley, a devoted free marketeer, wrote in an explanation of the Conservative government's environment policy whilst Secretary of State for the Environment: 'It is an essential part of the free market philosophy that regulation by Government is necessary to secure the public interest in environmental protection' (*Politics Against Pollution: The Conservative Record and Principles,* Centre for Policy Studies, 1989).

Annex A to the White Paper, *This Common Inheritance* (Cm 1200, 1990) discusses a range of different ways in which economic instruments may be used to further environmental protection. These build on five general categories identified by the Organisation for Economic Cooperation and Development, namely: charges, subsidies, deposit or refund schemes, the creation of a market in pollution credits and enforcement incentives. It is accepted in the White Paper that charges and subsidies have constituted the main uses of economic instruments so far although there is an increasing adoption of more complex and sophisticated measures. It also becomes clear that some of the mechanisms are self-standing whilst others, such as most charging schemes, require a regulatory framework and proper policing, so they must be seen as additional to, rather than separate from, regulatory systems.

In addition to direct economic instruments there are some examples of legislative schemes which have the indirect effect of creating a market which has environmental benefits (theoretically most of these fall within the class of the creation of a market in pollution credits, see below). Indeed, although they do not involve any direct taxation, many of those affected by the legislation view the effects in that way. For example, the legislation dealing with the obligation imposed on producers of packaging to meet certain recovery and recycling targets has effectively created a market in packaging waste recovery notes (PRNs) by compelling producers to demonstrate compliance with the statutory targets through the purchase of PRNs from authorised reprocessors (see further p. 480). This, in turn, should act as a direct financial incentive to reduce the amount of packaging in circulation. The creation of the market in tradeable certificates is, of course, an indirect effect of the legislative provisions (indeed the concept of PRNs cannot be found anywhere in the primary or secondary legislation), but it is nevertheless an intended effect. Similar points could be made about the legislative scheme dealing with contaminated land — the use of a legislative scheme to drive the market and to act as an incentive to promote the cost-effective remediation of contaminated land has appeal as it provides the certainty of regulation in addition to the political acceptability of the use of the market.

A selection of economic tools or instruments is considered below.

(a)   Charges for the administrative cost of operating the regulatory system

This now goes under the title of 'cost recovery charging' and has been adopted in relation to a number of regulatory activities. The idea is to recover the regulatory costs that are incurred in granting applications or consents, or in such things as inspecting, monitoring or policing those consents. The current policy is not to charge for the general costs of operating the whole regulatory system, but to limit the charge to the amount which can be referable to each consent or discharge. In the interests of administrative simplicity, the charges are normally arranged in bands, rather than being worked out individually.

For example, in relation to water pollution, a scheme of charging for applications for consent was introduced in October 1990. This was intended to recoup the costs of administering the application procedures for discharge consents. More significantly, annual charges to recover the cost to the NRA (and subsequently the EA) of policing any discharges to controlled waters were introduced on 1 July 1991 (see the *Scheme of Charges in Respect of Applications and Consents for Discharges to Controlled Waters*). These are set so as to recoup the costs associated with inspecting and monitoring discharges, not the full cost of monitoring water quality, which will still be paid for by the taxpayer (see p. 580).

Similar schemes were introduced from 1 April 1991 for applications and authorisations for operating a process subject to integrated pollution control (*HMIP Integrated Pollution Control Fees and Charges Scheme (England and Wales)*) and for local authority air pollution control (*Local Enforcing Authorities Air Pollution Fees and Charges Scheme (England and Wales)*). In the Integrated Pollution Control Scheme, the various processes subject to integrated pollution control have been divided into components and a flat rate is payable for each component. This is an attempt to cover the approximate cost to the EA of granting and monitoring an authorisation. A further scheme has been introduced for waste management licences.

Cost recovery charging systems may be progressive and thus have a beneficial environmental effect. For example, the charging schemes referred to involve higher charges for discharges which cost more to monitor, and these are often those which cause more pollution.

There always has been a rather different system of charging for discharges to sewers. This involves a rate for domestic consumers which is normally linked to property value, and a variable rate for trade dischargers linked to the volume and strength of the discharge as measured by Chemical Oxygen Demand. This produces a relatively unsophisticated method of charging for the cost of sewage treatment according to the demands made upon the system by the discharge. An incidental effect of concentrating on volume is, however, to reduce the level of water used and the level of waste, and thus to encourage both conservation of resources and recycling.

(b)   Charges reflecting the full environmental cost of an activity

The system of charging for sewage discharges shows the potential for use of charging systems which aim to charge for the full environmental cost of an activity. Such systems may be seen as the true environmental or pollution taxes referred to by Pearce, Markandya and Barbier in *Blueprint for a Green Economy* (Earthscan, 1989). The most controversial example is the so-called 'carbon energy tax' (also referred to as the Climate Change Levy). The objective behind this idea is to raise the price of fossil fuels to reflect their true (and hitherto uncosted) environmental effect, thus curtailing their use and reducing the greenhouse effect (see further p. 412). There are distinct problems with such an idea. One is obtaining sufficient information about the discharge or process to make the taxes work properly. This would seem to demand a strong regulatory structure to police the system, although self-monitoring methods may have a large part to play in this respect. Another is the problem of obtaining accurate information about environmental effects on which to base the tax levels.

There is no doubt that this is an idea which is going to be greatly used in the future, and the government has promised to consider it for discharges to 'controlled waters'. However, despite the recommendation of the Royal Commission on Environmental Pollution in its Sixteenth Report, *Freshwater Quality* (Cm 1966, 1992), that a system of charges reflecting impact on the environment should replace the present system of cost-recovery charges in order to act as an incentive to clean up environmentally harmful discharges, little has yet happened beyond the ritual consultation document. It is significant that powers to introduce such environmental charges were not included in the Environment Act 1995. The proposed Water Framework Directive has raised the prospect of a system of cost-recovery charges again, and we can expect a continued debate on the issue over the next few years (see further p. 570).

(c) Charges to finance environmental or pollution control measures
A number of examples may be given here. The EA may, under the Water Resources Act 1991, s. 161, pass costs incurred in preventing or remedying water pollution back to the person who caused it. The EA may also recover costs incurred in cleaning up unlawful deposits of waste from the occupier or the person who made the deposit (EPA 1990, s. 59). In relation to statutory nuisances, there are similar clean-up and cost-recovery powers available to local authorities in EPA 1990, s. 81.

Fines levied in court for offences may also be seen as a form of environmental charge. Indeed, given the nature of environmental offences and the limited moral blame often attached to them, many people treat fines as administrative penalties rather than as true criminal sanctions. The typically low level of fines means that their economic effect is limited, though levels are rising steadily, for example, the maximum fine for many environmental offences was raised to £20,000 on summary conviction by the EPA 1990. More recently, in an appeal related to the *Sea Empress* prosecution, the Court of Appeal has made it clear that fines should be set by references to the principles established for Health and Safety offences (see p. 247). Although this should see overall fine levels rise, there is still no direct connection between the penalty and the environmental damage caused (primarily because there is no way of ensuring that fines are actually used for environmental benefit) as borne out in the *Sea Empress* prosecution where the fine of £750,000 bore no relation to the clean up costs which were estimated at £60 million. One interesting development in this respect is the decision in *Herbert v Lambeth London Borough Council* (1991) 90 LGR 310, that a compensation order may be made under the Powers of Criminal Courts Act 1973, s. 35, where damage has been caused by a statutory nuisance, although there is a statutory limit of £5,000 on the sum which may be awarded.

Civil law remedies may also be seen as achieving the same objectives. Many statutes now include civil liability for damage to people or their property, and the creation of a remedy of breach of statutory duty may act as a potent method of reallocating costs. The drawback at present is that few civil actions recognise fully the costs involved in environmental damage. The law has never developed any concept of 'environmental rights', with the result that the only possible civil law claimants are people with private rights. Put more simply, animals, birds and plants do not have civil law rights. The debate on the introduction of liability for environmental damage is likely to intensify with the European Commission pressing for a unified liability scheme amongst Member States with its latest proposals in the White Paper on Environmental Liability (see p. 287).

(d) Charges levied on polluting materials or processes

Instead of a charge being levied on the results of pollution, it could be levied on a process or a product. The best example is the landfill tax which was introduced in October 1996. The idea is that a tax is payable on all waste that is disposed of to landfill. It is expected that the amount of the tax will be passed back by the operators of the landfill site to the originators of the waste, thus increasing the cost of landfill and acting as an incentive to reduce the amount of waste produced. The potency of the incentive relates to the level of the tax. Originally, it was proposed by the government that the tax should be based on the value of the waste, but it was pointed out by many commentators that this might lead to cost-sensitive producers of waste sending it to cheaper sites, which are likely to be precisely those sites where environmental standards are lowest, and lead to undesirable transportation of wastes in an attempt to find a cheaper site. It was subsequently announced that the tax would be based on the weight of the waste, with inert wastes (such as demolition wastes) subject to a lower rate to reflect their lesser environmental impact. Landfill operators are able to obtain rebates from the tax by setting up environmental trusts which promote sustainable waste management practices (see further p. 476).

This use of tax income is somewhat of a breakthrough since, although it has been appreciated for some time that taxes could be used to combat pollution and contamination problems, little has been achieved. However, the Treasury has always vigorously opposed any attempt to earmark taxes and charges for specific spending purposes (a process known as 'hypothecation') and, without that, a subsidiary aim of environmental taxes, which is that they should be linked directly to environmental spending, will not be achieved. For example, the proceeds from the landfill tax could be used to fund the clean-up of 'orphaned' closed landfill sites (i.e. those where the original operator cannot be found or does not have the resources to afford the clean-up), although the environmental trust funds may also be used in the same way. Nevertheless, the introduction of a landfill tax may well herald a faster development of environmental taxes in the future.

An alternative is that a charge may be reduced for relatively environment-friendly activities. The most obvious example was the reduced tax payable on unleaded petrol compared with leaded petrol. This led to a significant rise in the use of unleaded petrol over the last few years. A further example is the EPA 1990, s. 52, which introduced the concept of waste recycling credits for authorities or others who retain waste for the purpose of recycling it.

(e) Subsidies and grants

These are commonly used for environmental ends, although their use within the EC is restricted by the rules on illegal state aids. For example, subsidies are available for the construction of facilities for the improvement of the treatment of agricultural water and silage effluent — both particularly potent, and common, causes of pollution. Care has to be taken that the subsidies achieve the result intended. Some subsidies on forestry and agriculture, for example, have been accused of having detrimental environmental effects because of their inability to select between beneficial and non-beneficial projects.

Compensation payments for environmentally sensitive activities may also be seen in this category. The prevailing policy in relation to countryside protection has tended to be one of voluntariness, whereby farmers and landowners are compensated for agreeing to forgo certain advantages in the interests of the environment. Sometimes this is through the payment of direct compensation and sometimes through the negotiation of management agreements. For example, management agreements may be agreed in relation to the protection of national nature reserves or sites of special scientific interest, and similar methods are being used in other designated areas such as environmentally sensitive areas and nitrate sensitive areas (although there may be some changes under the Countryside and Rights of Way Bill, see further p. 640).

(f)   The creation of a market in pollution credits

A further instrument is the use of tradeable quotas, or emissions trading. These are methods of creating a market in the right to pollute. For example, a total for emissions of a specified substance may be set for a particular area. Firms may then bid for the right to take up a part of that total. Prospective or new polluters would have to buy the rights of existing holders if there was no spare capacity. By restricting the available emissions, prices would be driven up, providing an incentive to reduce emissions or to develop alternatives.

The idea is most developed in the USA, but the groundwork for its use in Britain is laid in the EPA 1990, s. 3(5), which allows the Secretary of State to establish total emissions of any substance either nationally or for a limited area, and to allocate quotas, with power progressively to reduce the total allowed. This provision has been supplemented with a power to introduce emissions trading schemes under the Pollution Prevention and Control Act 1999 (see sch. 1, para. 1). This power can cover all emissions (including release to water and land) although the first target is most likely to be carbon dioxide emissions in order to meet internationally agreed reduction targets which have been set to combat climate change.

There is a slight variation of the emissions trading scheme in the waste management system. In circumstances where there is a need to increase the capacity of the recycling and recovery industries a system of trading certificates has been employed. For example, under the packaging waste legislation, companies who recover or recycle packaging waste produce certificates which are then sold to companies who have an obligation to demonstrate that certain amounts of packaging waste have been recovered or recycled. The money raised by this sale is then (theoretically) channelled back into the recycling and recovery industry to provide more facilities and thereby increase capacity in order to achieve statutory targets at the lowest possible price to industry. Similar systems have been proposed in relation to the supply of renewable forms of electricity (with suppliers obliged to supply renewable energy or purchase evidence of renewable supply from others) and waste electrical and electronic equipment.

(g) Deposit and refund schemes
Although deposit and refund schemes are clearly severe interferences with a free market, it is also clear that they may have an enormous impact on the amount of waste produced. Traditionally, the Conservative administration favoured voluntary mechanisms here, rather than ones imposed by law. By way of example, the UK government intervened in the *Danish Bottles* case (case 302/86 *Commission* v *Denmark* [1988] ECR 4607) in the European Court of Justice, supporting the EC Commission's argument that a Danish law requiring drinks containers to be returnable was contrary to the free market principles of the EC. The Court of Justice upheld most of the Danish scheme despite its clear anti-competitive effect, on the grounds that the aim of environmental protection justified some interference with the operation of the single internal market within the EC (see p. 135).

Future uses of economic instruments

The above summary is not intended to be an exhaustive list of those mechanisms which might be tried, or even of those which are already in use, but to give an idea of the type of instrument that may be available. As stated before, there is little doubt that market-related instruments will increasingly be used in the future. Indeed, they could currently be said to be 'flavour of the month' as far as environmental regulation is concerned.

One reason for this is that market mechanisms have a degree of political acceptability which crosses current party political ideological boundaries. There is a strong link with the principle of choice, the idea that people should be given a choice of how to act, as long as their actions do not breach some generally accepted limits. This idea is seen most strongly in the realm of town and country planning where the importance attached to market forces is made explicit in much of central government policy advice. The principle is also seen in relation to such things as the adoption of voluntary methods of protection in the countryside (see Chapter 22) and the preference for pollution control systems which set objectives whilst leaving producers to work out for themselves how to achieve them. There is also a strong link with the related policy of deregulation pursued throughout the 1980s and 1990s and explained in White Papers such as *Lifting the Burden* (Cm 9571, 1985), *Building Businesses, Not Barriers* (Cm 9794, 1986) and latterly, *Modernising Government* (Cm 4310, 1999). Amongst other things, this policy amounts to a rejection of imposed restrictions in favour of agreed ones and a removal of unnecessary state powers.

Within the EC, the Commission has also suggested a shift in EC environmental policy towards the greater use of economic instruments rather than the administrative regulation approach. Although the Commission's proposals have seen little positive action, it is clear that European initiatives are likely to become more prevalent in the coming years with the likely introduction of full cost-recovery charging under the Water Framework Directive (see p. 570) and proposals for an EC climate change emissions trading system.

The polluter pays principle

The EC can claim another important contribution to the development of economic instruments; its environmental policy has always included the adoption of the 'polluter pays' principle, although it was probably the Organisation for Economic Cooperation and Development (OECD) which first popularised the idea in the early 1970s (see OECD, *The Polluter Pays Principle*, 1975). The principle basically means that the producer of goods or other items should be responsible for the costs of preventing or dealing with any pollution which the process causes. This includes environmental costs as well as direct costs to people or property. It also covers costs incurred in avoiding pollution, and not just those related to remedying any damage. There is a very strong link between the principle and the idea that prevention is better than cure. It will also be clear from the foregoing discussion that these costs should include the full environmental costs, not just those which are immediately tangible.

The relevance of this principle to the discussion of economic instruments is obvious, since a producer will have to pass on any costs in the price of goods to the ultimate consumer. However, this is only a principle, it has no legal force and there is no agreed definition that has anything approaching the precision of a statute. On the contrary, there has frequently been dispute over its exact scope, especially over the limits on payments for damage caused. Even when the question of payment is relatively settled, there is a further issue as to the identity of the polluter. For example, under the Nitrates Directive (91/676) there was a significant degree of discretion given to Member States to set up schemes to prevent water pollution from nitrates. This discretion was, however, constrained by a need to show a 'significant contribution' by the polluter. The categorisation of polluters into 'significant' and others raises questions of definition and fairness which were considered in *R v Secretary of State for the Environment and Minister of Agriculture, Fisheries and Food, ex parte Standley* [1999] Env LR 801 (see further p. 604). Similar issues arise within the context of the contaminated land regime under Part IIA, EPA 1990. In any case where certain polluters are targeted or excluded for administrative or other purposes, the principle is watered down to 'some polluters pay' which weakens the legitimacy and application of the general principle. It is essentially a guide to desirable courses of action, but it is fairly clear that it has rarely been fully satisfied in either EC or British environmental legislation.

As a result the principle has sometimes seemed to be all things to all people, and has even been used to justify views with which it has little connection, for example the suggestion that producers may pollute as long as they pay for it. That is a complete misunderstanding of the principle's true meaning, and the potential abuse of such an imprecise phrase should be appreciated.

Self-regulation as a tool for environmental protection

One of the consequences of the deregulatory move away from direct methods of regulation has been the upsurge in interest in developing effective mechanisms based upon voluntary action. Such action can be termed 'self-regulation'. Although this term can have more precise definitions (e.g. where a group is responsible for the action of its members without any form of governmental or regulatory supervision), for the purposes of this discussion the common identifying factor is that self-regulatory mechanisms are underpinned by voluntary action rather than compulsion. The triggers for such action may be diverse, including the threat of compulsory action, commercial benefit (e.g. through cost savings or green marketing initiatives), or even a shift in values which attaches greater importance to environmental protection.

These examples indicate that there are factors other than legal factors which can be influential in changing behaviour. Thus, economic benefits which accrue from increasing sales of so-called 'environmentally friendly' goods or the social benefits (e.g. employee satisfaction or enhanced public image) which result from environmental improvement can act as regulatory controls. Moreover, these triggers suggest that there are very few occasions where actions are purely 'voluntary'. Indeed, there is a broad spectrum of mechanisms which can fall within this definition of self-regulation, ranging from the purely voluntary (i.e. no form of compulsion at all) through to mechanisms which use a mixture of direct regulation and self-regulation (see e.g. the position of compliance schemes in relation to the producer responsibility legislation or the relationship between the links in the waste management chain under the duty of care).

The strengths of self-regulatory mechanisms are clear, in that they are quick, flexible, non-interventionist and therefore more acceptable to the companies which are regulated. Perhaps most importantly, it encourages a sense of environmental responsibility within the regulated companies which should promote environmental improvement not as a reaction to legislation but as part of corporate development generally. The disadvantages are that the voluntary nature of the mechanisms often means that there are no explicit enforcement mechanisms; there are problems of so-called 'free-riders', i.e. companies which do not adopt self-regulation and therefore possibly gain an advantage over competitors whilst employing lower environmental standards; there is a lack of transparency and accountability; and there is the problem of setting standards which are at the lower end of what is achievable rather than setting goals which might not be attained.

Given that the range of mechanisms is wide and the suggested definition of self-regulation imprecise, it is possible to set out a selection of self-regulatory mechanisms below.

(a) Management standards

Theoretically, management standards could have been included in the list of environmental standards which were discussed earlier in this chapter, or within the discussion of economic instruments above as they can have a direct economic impact. It is, however, arguably most appropriate to consider such standards within the context of self-regulatory tools as they are voluntary and there are no specific legal sanctions for either failing to adopt the standards or comply with them once adopted. At its widest, the term 'environmental management standards' can be said to cover such things as the technical competence and financial security of a regulated operator (which, for example, would include the test of 'fit and proper person' in relation to waste management). The more common use of management standards, however, relates generally to the system of measurement by which environmental performance and improvement of a company can be measured.

The use of environmental management systems and the associated concept of environmental auditing is a rare area where the UK can claim to lead the world in the development of a form of environmental regulation. Many firms are now tackling the increased pressures and potential liabilities imposed by environmental laws by adopting systems and procedures for assessing environmental performance. The driving forces behind these moves stem from the requirements of customers (both individual consumers and corporate buyers of goods and services), financial institutions and insurers.

Environmental management systems (EMSs) are simply systems and procedures which are put in place to measure environmental performance and provide a benchmark for future improvements. The systems are backed by a certification procedure which provides a method of formal and objective verification for the system. The first EMS was introduced as a British standard, BS7750, in 1994, and the general requirements of this standard have provided the framework for others which have been adopted more widely. BS7750 was based on a quality management approach with the result that no specific levels of environmental performance were stipulated in the EMS itself. The setting of environmental objectives was a matter for the company itself. These objectives were measured against a publicly produced environmental policy which included a minimum commitment to complying with all legal standards whilst improving environmental performance. This commitment required the company to understand the environmental effects created by the business; to set both broad and detailed goals for environmental performance with specific targets; to set up an active programme for managing the environmental performance which was designed to achieve these goals and targets; and a system for auditing the EMS. Adherence to the requirements of the EMS was verified on an annual basis by accredited independent verifiers.

BS7750 was to influence the establishment of other EMSs including an international standard ISO 14001 (the introduction of ISO 14001 saw the subsequent withdrawal of BS7750 in March 1997) and the EC Eco-Management and Audit Scheme (EMAS) (under Regulation 1836/93) which both more or less follow the management framework set out above. The ISO standard is less prescriptive than BS7750 and also commits companies to a goal of 'pollution prevention' rather than environmental improvement, but mostly reflects the requirements of the British standard. The EMAS scheme also requires companies to establish procedures to protect the environment and to commit themselves to continuous environmental improvement.

The most significant difference between EMAS and ISO 14001 is that EMAS requires a company to publish a report setting out its environmental performance every three years and to have that report verified by an independent body which has been accredited for that purpose. The aim of such a report is to enable stakeholders such as members of the public to assess whether the company is meeting the requirements of the EMAS standard.

The uptake of the standards has been steady rather than spectacular with an emphasis on those industries which have come under contractual pressures from customers, particularly in the global marketplace. Although the standards for the measurement of environmental performance can ensure that there is a degree of transparency (and objectivity) of assessment, it could be argued that the use of EMSs as a trigger for environmental improvement has been less successful. One of the main defects in the system is the subjective nature of the setting of improvement goals. It is perfectly possible for a company which achieves compliance with legal requirements to set very low targets and still achieve certification. On this level, an EMS is little more than an objective statement of keeping within the law.

(b) Information based mechanisms

Although there are legal requirements to make certain environmental information available to the public through the systems of pollution control registers (see further Chapter 8) there are other voluntary mechanisms whereby environmental information is made available to the public on wider issues. Companies have, for example, incorporated environmental information into annual reports. Corporate environmental reporting has been patchily adopted by UK companies with a wide variety of both quality and quantity of information and an emphasis on industrial sectors which carry out particularly sensitive environmental operations (e.g. mining and energy). There is some pressure to standardise reporting requirements and the government has suggested that if the voluntary approach does not produce consistent results, direct regulation will be introduced.

Other information based mechanisms include eco-labelling or certification processes which give consumers of products information about the environmental impacts of goods and products. There is an EC regulation on the subject (880/92) which set up the EC eco-labelling scheme. This scheme has had only limited success as it has proved to be administratively cumbersome with the consequence that relatively small numbers of products have been considered and the market credibility of the scheme has been undermined. The scheme is to be revised in order to streamline applications for eco-labels and the adoption of product criteria. The fundamental aspects of the scheme will, however, remain unchanged. Criteria are developed by the European Commission to enable the environmental impact of a product to be analysed by taking into account the whole of its life cycle. Product groups which have been covered under the scheme include light bulbs, paints, personal computers, footwear, textiles and washing machines. The regulation was originally implemented in Britain through the establishment of an Eco-Labelling Board in November 1992. This Board was, however, abolished in 1999 as part of a move towards an integrated products policy which places eco-labelling in a curtailed role in reducing the environmental impacts of consumer products. Although the European wide system would continue to operate, the prospects for a national eco-labelling scheme appear to diminish. There is likely to be greater emphasis placed upon the top of the supply chain, i.e. the manufacturers of products providing information on the environmental impacts rather than the provision of general labelling criteria.

(c) Private agreements

The use of private agreements in environmental regulation ranges from the formal statutory mechanisms found in planning legislation (Town and Country Planning Act 1990, s. 106, see p. 330) and nature conservation legislation (Countryside Act 1968, s. 15, see p. 636) to the more informal agreements which have been negotiated between government or the regulator and individual companies or industry sectors. Although the uptake of these more informal agreements has traditionally been more prevalent in other countries (particularly the US and the Netherlands), the UK has started to adopt this mechanism with an increasing frequency. The nature of these agreements differs widely and is dependent upon the parties to the agreement (e.g. the European Commission, national governments, regional bodies or regulatory agencies on the one side and industry sectors or individual operators on the other) and what is required (e.g. general or specific targets for reducing pollution).

At a European level, the Commission has produced guidelines on the use of such agreements between public authorities and industry (see COM(96)561 final). Examples of such agreements include an agreement between the Commission and European car manufacturers to cut average carbon dioxide emissions from new cars by 25 per cent by 2008. On a national level, there have been agreements with newspaper publishers to increase the proportion of waste paper in newsprint to 40 per cent by 2000 and the Chemical Industries Association to reduce its members' energy consumption per tonne of product by 20 per cent between 1990 and 2005. This latter agreement is the precursor of further initiatives in relation to the Climate Change Levy whereby energy intensive sectors have been offered tax reductions on the basis that they enter into voluntary agreements to improve energy efficiency.

There are many criticisms of such voluntary agreements. Many of these reflect the criticisms of self-regulatory mechanisms generally (e.g. lack of transparency or accountability, no public participation, lack of satisfactory enforcement mechanisms), but most of these stem from the fact that the status of many of these agreements is uncertain given that they are neither private contracts nor agreements made under statutory powers. It would appear that the role of these agreements is to provide a further mechanism which is complementary to direct regulation. They allow government or regulators to set targets and goals which go beyond that which could be required under the legislative scheme.

The civil law as a tool for environmental protection

The detailed role of the civil law is considered in Chapter 10. However, as pointed out in the section on charges, the civil law can be seen as a form of market mechanism, so it is worth making a few general comments about civil liability in this chapter. There is little doubt that the last few years have seen a great increase in interest in the use that can be made of civil law mechanisms — by policy-makers as well as by lawyers. Recognising that civil liability appears to fit in well with the basic principles of EC environmental policy, such as the polluter pays principle, the EC has pursued proposals to introduce an EC wide system of civil liability since 1993. The latest version, issued early in 2000, is discussed on p. 287. The long delay and relative weakness of the current proposals reflect the fundamental controversies surrounding rules which attempt to merge different approaches to environmental liability across Member States.

The imposition of civil liability has other effects as well as simply sorting out the question of liability for specific incidents. It acts as an incentive to act in a particular way, because of the high possible risks. In so doing, it fulfils the precautionary principle and fits in well with the current EC emphasis on shared responsibility, since producers will act so as to reduce and manage risks themselves. It thus acts as a stimulus to integrate risk management principles into all levels of business decision-making, as there is little doubt that the threat of civil action is a potent one, especially in an age when insurance against such risks is hard to obtain.

The criminal law as a tool for environmental protection

The criminal law can be used either to provide direct criminal sanctions for environmental harm, or in a subsidiary and complementary role within a regulatory system. It tends to be of greater use in the second way. This is because the main purpose of the criminal law is to punish clearly identified wrongs. Yet, in relation to many environmental matters, it is often impossible to identify wrong without reference to other factors. For example, it is clearly desirable to have industry and many other activities which may cause pollution. The question is not a simple one of whether to have them, but a more difficult one of how much pollution is acceptable (see also the definition of pollution on p. 25). That requires a balancing of the various factors involved against what is reasonable — a discretionary, political process, for which the regulatory system is well-suited. The criminal law is rather inadequate for such a balancing process, and thus tends to be used mainly to deal either with clear acts of environmental vandalism, or to support the regulatory system once it has decided what is and what is not acceptable.

There are a number of examples of offences which stem directly from environmental harm. Under the EPA 1990, s. 87, it is an offence to drop or deposit litter in a public or other specified place. In the Water Resources Act 1991, s. 85, there is a general offence of causing or knowingly permitting any poisonous, noxious or polluting matter to enter controlled waters. It is not always necessary to show actual harm to the environment, (e.g. see, in the case of water pollution, *R* v *Dovermoss Ltd* [1995] Env LR 258): in some cases an activity may be prohibited because harm can be assumed to follow or because the risk of harm is too great to take. For example, under the Clean Air Act 1993 it is an offence to emit dark smoke from premises.

However, even in these cases, enforcement is often left to a public body. One reason for this is practical, given the difficulty in some situations of identifying and proving environmental harm. Another reason is that the right of prosecution has often been restricted in English law. This is becoming less common, but a good example is the restriction in relation to water pollution. Under the Rivers (Prevention of Pollution) Acts 1951 and 1961, which established a system of consents for discharges to water for the first time and also a general pollution offence in similar terms to the Water Resources Act 1991, s. 85, it was provided that a prosecution could only be brought by a water authority, or with the consent of the Attorney-General. This restriction was removed by the Control of Pollution Act 1974, with the result that there is now a right of private prosecution for all the basic water pollution offences.

A third reason for enforcement being left to public bodies is the lack of available public information relating to pollution. Under the Rivers (Prevention of Pollution) Acts, there was no public register of consents, samples taken of water quality, or samples taken of discharges; indeed it was an offence for water authority officers to disclose such information gained in the course of their duties. Under the Control of Pollution Act 1974, a system of public registers was first established, which has largely removed the secrecy of earlier years. Similar limitations on private prosecution and access to information have been present in most areas of environmental law over the years.

The most frequent use of the criminal law is therefore in a subsidiary capacity to administrative controls (i.e. to the regulatory system). Many criminal offences consist not of committing a direct act of pollution, but instead of ignoring the dictates of the regulatory body. Under the Water Resources Act 1991, s. 85, it is a criminal offence to discharge trade or sewage effluent without, or in breach of, a consent from the EA. In relation to town and country planning, the offence consists not of breaching planning control but of ignoring an enforcement notice. This makes the criminal offence truly subsidiary to the regulatory process, since only the local planning authority may issue an enforcement notice, thus taking the possibility of enforcement away from the public. The scope of these offences has been widened with the unification of enforcement powers within the Environment Agency

All of these matters have an effect in decriminalising the law. The offence is not directly linked to the environmental harm, but to an administrative process. Enforcement is normally by an administrative body and often for breach of an administrative requirement. The message that is given is that these things are truly related to administrative processes rather than the criminal law. In addition, the low sentences that are often imposed (sometimes because only low sentences are available), the marked reluctance to prosecute, the limited amount of moral censure that has traditionally been attached to environmental offences, the lowly status of many who are selected for prosecution and the escape of many major industrial polluters from prosecution (all factors which are discussed elsewhere in this book) tend to emphasise the decriminalisation of the laws. Once again, however, there is no doubt that things are changing as a result of changes in the perception of the general public. One development in the future may well be the making of an overt distinction between 'administrative' offences against the regulatory system and true environmental crimes, with higher personal penalties being available in the latter category.

EIGHT

Access to environmental information

In Chapter 7 we made the point that the provision of information about the environment and the regulatory process was an integral element of the regulation of environmental protection. In this chapter, we explore this idea in greater detail, looking at some of the reasons for giving greater access to environmental information; the types of environmental information which are available; the use of environmental information as a regulatory instrument; international and European initiatives; and past, present and future approaches to access to environmental information in Britain. There is also a brief outline of the different types of environmental and pollution control registers which are available to the public (there is more detailed coverage of some of these in the relevant chapters in Part II of this book).

The underlying themes

As the environmental regulatory system matures, we have seen a steady increase in openness and access to information. The reasons for this growing emphasis on access are many and varied (with European legislation and international initiatives playing a significant part in the process, as with other areas of environmental regulation) but it is possible to identify a number of overlapping themes which reflect some of the influencing factors. These themes include the following:

(a)   Improving regulation by increasing public participation
In Chapter 2, we identified the role that values played in the formation of environmental law; the need to ensure that such values are taken into account in environmental decision-making; and the way in which informed debate can draw out those values. The quantity and quality of information on the environment is the essential 'fuel' which powers the decision-making process and informs the debate. Increased access to good quality environmental information increases the accountability of the decision-maker and makes the process more legitimate in the eyes of the public. Examples of this would

include the requirements for publicity and consultation in relation to individual planning or pollution control applications or strategic development plans.

(b) Monitoring the effectiveness of regulation
In many areas of environmental law, the regulatory system is designed to reduce pollution or the environmental effects of an activity (as opposed to merely controlling a rise in aggregated pollution). For example, one of the policy aims of the waste management system is to reduce the environmental impacts of waste by increasing recycling and reducing the amount of waste being sent to landfill. One of the ways in which the effectiveness of the system can be monitored is to produce 'benchmarks' for performance (e.g. to gather and publish data on waste going to landfill and recycling rates). Greater access to this sort of information allows those who are regulated and the general public to assess the effectiveness of the legislation. This legitimises the introduction of new laws, ensures that existing laws are actually achieving the aims which they were designed to meet and ensures that ineffective laws are replaced.

(c) Environmental information as a self-standing regulatory instrument
As the complexity and the number of different types of regulatory instrument grows, environmental information can be employed as a complementary mechanism to the more traditional instruments. The use of eco-labelling to provide consumers with information which enables them to make informed purchasing decisions is an example of this.

(d) Environmental information and sustainable development
The provision of environmental information can assist in attaining the goal of sustainable development by influencing the behaviour and decisions of private individuals or companies. Making information available on a wider scale can be the catalyst in changes in behaviour or can increase the effectiveness of other instruments. For example, publishing information on energy efficiency and the associated environmental benefits can be used in conjunction with grants and subsidies to encourage people to reduce their consumption of energy (e.g. by installing energy efficient boilers or by turning the heating down).

(e) Improving enforcement
Most environmental offences involve the carrying out of unauthorised activities. These may arise from the breach of a condition in an authorisation or they may be entirely unauthorised actions. To assess levels of compliance, either generally or in relation to an individual authorisation, the public require access not only to information concerning the details of an authorisation/consent but also to monitoring data.

Although the enforcement of pollution control regulations is carried out mainly by statutory agencies, there is a role for the public as the traditional restrictions on private prosecutions have been removed. There are a variety of reasons why the public do not take action, including cost, apathy, and ignorance but even if those difficulties can be overcome there must be access to the information which forms the basis of enforcement action. Without adequate information, public rights to enforce environmental laws have little value. This includes basic information on the identity of polluters, where they are polluting and how much is being emitted.

(f) Informing the public about environmental risks

Where information is difficult to obtain, the perception of risks associated with an activity (whether in relation to human health or the environment) may be misconceived. The RCEP commented that 'secrecy — particularly the half kept secret — fuels fear'. It is, therefore, necessary to create much greater disclosure to enable informed debate not only about the risks to the public and the environment but also about the steps which might be taken to minimise those risks. In its Eleventh Report, the RCEP commented on the role of greater access in relation to risk assessment:

> A proper evaluation of the risk requires access to information and its interpretation, and the public will not be reassured by the interpretations provided by the putative polluter who has an interest.

Thus, where information is truly available, it enables informed debate by allowing the widest possible range of interpretations of the raw data rather than relying upon the assertions of interested parties (although in reality, greater access merely enables the views of different interested parties to be placed in the balance).

(g) A fundamental 'right' to environmental information

One of the basic features of environmental law is that, on a theoretical level at least, everyone has a 'stake' in the interests which the regulatory system is designed to protect (i.e. the environment). Whilst it is possible to take a narrow view that the 'stake' might be restricted to a proprietary interest (e.g. in the land a person 'owns'), a broader view would suggest that the interest is a general one held by everyone, both for themselves and on behalf of future generations. This stake in the environment competes with other interests such as industrial operations. In these circumstances, every attempt should be made to balance out conflicting interests by, for example, allowing access to information on the consequences of industrial activities, so that all relevant factors are taken into account. This has led the RCEP to talk of a general public 'right' to environmental information:

> the public must be considered to have a right, analogous to a beneficial interest, in the condition of the air and water and to be able to obtain information on how far they are being degraded.

There is a clear link here between the provision of environmental information and the achievement of the goal of sustainable development referred to above.

In order to understand the consequences of our current actions in terms of the legacy which is being passed on to future generations there is a need to ensure greater access to information on those consequences.

Arguments against access to environmental information

Although there are many arguments in favour of greater access to environmental information, the development of the legislation which has brought about this access has been the subject of a vigorous debate, with opposition coming mainly from industrial organisations. The counterarguments employed have largely been rejected by government. There is, however, some residual relevance as the statutory exceptions which are found in the current legislation dealing with access to environmental information have their origins, in part, in these objections.

(a)   Commercial confidentiality
The main objection to full public disclosure of environmental information was that such disclosure would detrimentally affect the viability of business by breaching commercial confidentiality. Concern stemmed from the belief that industrial competitors would be able to use the data released to gain access to commercially confidential information. The RCEP rejected these objections in its Seventh report (Cmnd 7644, 1979) and Tenth report (Cmnd 9149, 1984). In doing so, it was suggested that industry's refusal to disclose information on the basis of commercial confidentiality was often a 'reflex action' which did not reflect the commercial risk involved and that the emphasis which was given to such confidentiality was 'disproportionate and misconceived'.

There are cases where commercial confidentiality is, however, a legitimate interest which needs to be considered and most legislative schemes which promote greater access to environmental information have provisions which exclude commercially confidential information. Crucially, the decision on whether environmental information falls within the category of commercially confidential generally remains with the statutory enforcement body rather than the affected operator (this is subject to the operator's right of appeal, see below e.g. in relation to IPC).

Perhaps the greatest indicator that moves towards freer access to information are institutional as well as legislative (i.e. that moves towards openness are embraced within the changing culture of enforcing authorities) is that practical experience of the operation of such provisions would suggest that although there continue to be numerous attempts to exclude information, only a minority of the applications are successful (e.g. in 1992, only 14 out of 53 of the applications were granted).

(b)   Cost
Another fundamental objection put forward historically by industry was that the administration costs of such an exercise would be disproportionate to the public benefit which would accrue. The underlying argument that secrecy

would be cheaper than access is probably accurate. Whether 'cheaper' means 'more effective' is perhaps more contentious. The House of Lords Select Committee, when considering this objection, dismissed it summarily by stating that: 'information should in no circumstances be protected by price'.

(c) 'Misuse' of information and 'green nutters'

The final main objection to greater disclosure was that openness would lead to mischief-making and an unacceptable level of interference by activists. In 1984, the CBI referred to the access to information provisions of the Control of Pollution Act 1974 as a 'busybody's charter'. Other predicted consequences of greater disclosure put forward by MPs included the disappearance of the chemicals industry from Britain and 'an endless stream of prosecutions'. During the passage of the Environmental Protection Bill through Parliament, one MP alleged that greater access to information and broader rights of prosecution would 'allow the "green nutters" to get on parade and have a field day of litigation against industry on entirely inconsequential grounds'. With hindsight, these predictions appear to be unduly alarmist. Although the information has been used by environmental interest groups (see e.g. Friends of the Earth's 'Factory Watch' web site at *www.foe.co.uk/ factorywatch/index.html*), this has not been for the purpose of taking unreasonable enforcement action against industry.

The history of access to environmental information

The roots of environmental secrecy can be traced back to the mid-nineteenth century and the age of industrialisation when the Alkali Inspectorate adopted a policy of keeping any information secret unless publication was demanded by a particular statute or was permitted by the owner/operator of the process to which the information related. In its very first report, the Inspectorate stressed the importance of keeping information from the public, stating:

> Of course, all information regarding any work must be considered private unless publication is demanded by the Act or permitted by the owner.

The reason for the adoption of this policy is unclear; however it is likely that one of the most influential factors was the implementation of the cooperational approach between enforcement agencies and polluters and the desire of the alkali industry to keep sensitive information about the effects of the emissions from the operations private.

This unofficial policy was formalised with the introduction of the Official Secrets Act 1911. Section 2 of that Act provided that the unauthorised disclosure of information held by central government was a criminal offence. Although central government has never held large amounts of detailed information on the environment, this ban on disclosure covered important areas including the making of policy and individual decision-making. As environmental law was developing through an administrative regulatory system, the Official Secrets Act 1911 set the scene for more specific bans on disclosure.

Examples of environmental secrecy

Historically, secrecy has been endemic in environmental legislation. Many environmental statutes contained specific sections forbidding the disclosure of information relating to environmental releases. Even if there were no explicit sanctions for disclosure, access to information was prohibited unless another statute required that it be made available to the general public.

In the case of water pollution, the Rivers (Prevention of Pollution) Act 1961 restricted the public right of access to information concerning applications, discharge consents or effluent samples taken by the enforcing authority, unless the person/company making the discharge permitted its disclosure or there was a further statutory requirement to disclose.

In the case of air pollution, the Alkali Inspectorate's unofficial policy was transposed into legislation in the Health and Safety at Work etc. Act 1974, s. 28, which prohibited the disclosure of any information relating to recordings or measurements taken during the exercise of the Inspectorate's duties. Under the Clean Air Acts of 1956 and 1968, local authorities were given a power to disclose information, through the setting up of public registers containing details of non-domestic emissions. There were, however, a number of procedural hurdles (e.g. the creation of a committee to discuss the proposals for disclosure and an appeal mechanism for operators affected by disclosure) and the lack of resources to assist with the implementation of the system meant that very few registers were ever set up (figures in 1982 suggested that only five local authorities had bothered to set up a register and the emissions from only eight premises were publicised).

The role of the Royal Commission on Environmental Pollution

The Royal Commission on Environmental Pollution has examined the need for greater access to environmental information in a series of reports. In total, five reports have addressed the issue in one way or another. In its second report, in 1974, it concluded that it was in the public interest to make environmental information more widely available to anyone who would use it to improve the environment. This view was maintained throughout the subsequent reports. The RCEP consistently concluded that the public were entitled to know of the risks that they faced from environmental pollution and that there were few good arguments in favour of secrecy. In doing so, the RCEP adopted its 'guiding principle' which suggested that there should be a presumption in favour of unrestricted access to information which the pollution control authorities obtain or receive by virtue of their statutory powers, with protection for secrecy only in those circumstances where a genuine case could be substantiated (10th Report, Cmnd 9419, 1984).

Moves towards greater openness — the 1970s and 1980s

There were moves towards greater openness in the 1970s, in part in reaction to the RCEP's recommendations but also as a response to the findings of the

Franks Committee in 1972 and a subsequent White Paper on general freedom of information in 1978. In particular, provisions in the Control of Pollution Act 1974 introduced public registers dealing with information on water pollution (although there was a characteristic delay of over 10 years in the implementation of this part of the legislation as a result of industry pressure to delay disclosure even further). Other areas either remained secret or, in the case of the Health and Safety at Work etc. Act 1974, moved away from informal policies to more formal statutory non-disclosure powers.

In 1986, the Government in *Pollution Paper 23*, the product of an inter-departmental Working Party, responded to the RCEP's criticisms by embracing the 'guiding principle' whilst rejecting the recommendations to move towards a uniform regime of public access to all environmental information. When the first draft of the Environmental Protection Bill was produced in 1989, it showed that there were to be no general obligations of disclosure. Within a short space of time, however, there was a policy change and access to some areas of environmental information were covered in the Environmental Protection Act 1990 (waste management, IPC and APC). More general provisions on access were included in the Local Government (Access to Information) Act 1985 (in relation to environmental matters dealt with by local government, see further below) and the Official Secrets Act 1989 (with reforms to the 1911 Act which had the effect of narrowly protecting only certain limited classes of central information, excluding environmental matters).

A system of access to comprehensive environmental information — the 1990s and beyond

These progressive attempts to broaden access to environmental information reflected the growth of environmental law generally in that they were piecemeal and reactive. The use of public registers as the means of promoting greater access meant that there were restrictions in the categories of information (generally limited to pollution control and planning) and on the type of information (generally site specific or individual and therefore not aggregated).

The first attempt to establish a universal freedom of access in the UK was in response to European legislation in the form of the 1990 Directive on Freedom of Access to Information on the Environment (90/313). This Directive required a major change in the approach to disclosure of environmental information in that it required unrestricted access, on request, to all 'information relating to the environment' subject to certain exceptions. The breadth of this requirement created a number of problems for the UK government most of which were dealt with by delegating many of the critical issues to other relevant public bodies (which in turn created implementation problems, particularly in relation to consistency of application — see below). The requirements of the Directive were finally transposed in the Environmental Information Regulations 1992 (SI 1992/3240) (see further below).

In 1997, the Government produced proposals for a Freedom of Information Act in a White Paper, *Your Right to Know* (Cm 3818, 1997) which would have radically overhauled the right of access to information generally and many of the aspects of the 1992 Regulations in particular. The Freedom of Information Bill was finally published in 1999 and although some of the key changes remain, many of the provisions had been watered down (see further below). It is likely that the Bill will be passed in the 1999–2000 Session. In particular the Act, when passed, will repeal the 1992 Regulations and implement the UK's international obligations under the 1998 Århus Convention on Access to Information, Public Participation in Decision-Making and Access to Justice in Environmental Matters. A further complicating factor is the implementation of the Human Rights Act 1998 and the effect that this will have on the interpretation of any Freedom of Information Act and other statutory provisions on access to environmental information.

International approaches to access to information

The importance of a right of access to environmental information at all levels is emphasised by the weight which greater disclosure is given in international law. In particular, the role of information in meeting the goal of sustainable development is acknowledged in the Agenda 21 document which was agreed at the 1992 Earth Summit at Rio which stresses the importance of ensuring that all stakeholders in the environment have access to relevant environmental information relating to products or activities which have an environmental impact. This general commitment to greater access is specifically implemented in various international conventions including the Climate Change Convention (see Art. 6) where the exchange of public information on climate change is considered to be a pre-condition to the successful implementation of the other substantive provisions of the Convention.

The need to ensure greater consistency and transparency of public access to environmental information within international law led to the adoption of the UN/ECE Århus Convention on Access to Information, Public Participation in Decision Making and Access to Justice in Environmental Matters. In relation to access to environmental information, the Convention mirrors the European Directive on Access to Environmental Information (90/313) although it is somewhat broader in its effect covering such things as health and safety and economic analysis of environmental issues

One other matter which should be considered within the international context is the effect of the incorporation of the European Convention of Human Rights into domestic legislation by way of the Human Rights Act 1998. In particular, the European Court of Human Rights has interpreted certain articles of the Convention (in particular, the right to privacy, home and family life under Article 8) in a way which should mean that statutory provisions on access to information (including any Freedom of Information Act) might have a much wider application than has been the case previously.

For example, in *Guerra v Italy* (1998) 26 EHRR 357, the Court held that public authorities were under an obligation to supply information about the risks involved in living in close proximity to an environmentally sensitive use. The Court considered that the local authority was under a positive obligation to supply information which enabled the residents to assess the risks from the factory. On a broad interpretation it would not be possible for an authority to reject a request on the basis that it did not have the information (see also *McGinley and Egan* v *UK* (1999) 27 EHRR 1 and *Lopez Ostra* v *Spain* (1995) 20 EHRR 277).

European approaches to access to information

A distinction needs to be made between access to environmental information at Member State level and access to information about the decision-making process operated by European bodies, and in particular the European Commission and Council. Historically, the processes of decision-making within the European Commission and the Council were shrouded in secrecy. For example, documents relating to infringement proceedings against Member States were secret. Moves towards greater openness were formalised in 1994 with the publication of a Code of Conduct on Public Access to Commission and Council Documents (see Decision 94/90/ECSC, EC, Euratom). The Code of Conduct is subject to a general principle that the public should have the 'widest possible access to documents held by the Commission and the Council' although there are mandatory (protecting the interests of third parties or the general public, e.g. commercial confidentiality) and discretionary (protecting the institutions' interests alone) exceptions to the general disclosure rule. The ECJ has held that although the Code of Conduct is a voluntary document, it is capable of conferring rights on third parties and that the exceptions should be construed in a manner which did not override the general principle. In addition, the applicability of the general principle was such that the exceptions could not be used as a 'blanket ban' on the disclosure of documents and each request for documents would have to be assessed individually with specific reasons given for a refusal to disclose (see Case T-105/95 *WWF* v *EC Commission* [1997] Env LR 242).

One final source of European information comes from the European Environment Agency. One of the reasons for the setting up of the Agency was to provide Member States and the European public with objective and reliable information on the state of the environment within the EC. The Agency has adopted a Code of Conduct on access to its documents which is similar to the Codes dealing with the Commission and Council's documents. It also produces periodic reports on the state of the European environment which are available from its web page (*www.eea.eu.int*). The Agency is closely involved with the European Environment Information and Observation Network (EIONET) which connects national environmental information organisations within Member States and includes some countries outside the EC and other organisations such as the European Free Trade Association.

Given the historic secrecy of the workings of the Commission and the Council it is perhaps ironic that the disclosure of environmental information at member state level has been a significant part of EC environmental policy since the drawing up of the First Environmental Action Programme in 1973. Although a wide range of environmental directives had provisions for access to individual elements of environmental information, the first general legislative measure was adopted during the Fourth Action Programme. Directive 90/313 on the Freedom of Access to Information on the Environment was adopted in 1990 and came into force at the end of 1992.

The Directive does not impose any requirements in terms of practical arrangements for access, leaving that to the discretion of the Member States. It applies to any 'information relating to the environment' held by 'public authorities' and certain other bodies under their control (see arts. 1 and 6). The information included under the directive covers the 'state of air, water, flora, fauna, soil and natural sites'. There are two levels of exemptions from the requirement to disclose. The first in article 3.2 lists exemptions which Member States can make mandatory or discretionary. This includes information which would affect commercial confidentiality, national security and information which relates to legal proceedings. The second level in article 3.3 lists exemptions which must be discretionary. A request must be responded to as soon as possible or in any event within two months (art. 3.4). Finally, public authorities may make a reasonable charge for the supply of requested information.

The Directive is worded in a broad manner with a number of the key provisions being open to further interpretation. The ECJ has taken a purposive approach to the interpretation of the Directive. In *Mecklenburg* v *Kreis Pinneberg — Der Landrat* [1998] ECRI-3809, a member of the public asked his local authority for a copy of a document which set out the countryside protection authority's views on a local road project. The authority refused on the basis that the information was not 'information relating to the environment' and that it was exempt within the terms of the Directive. The ECJ held that the concept of 'information relating to the environment' was broad and it included documents which could be influential in determining the outcome of the decision-making process in relation to the road project. On the question of whether the information was exempt, the ECJ took the view that exemptions should be viewed narrowly and in accordance with the aims of the Directive (reflecting the approach to the Code of Conduct in the *WWF* case above).

Britain's evolving approach to access to information

As the outline of the legislative history described above shows, Britain's approach to access has had three identifiable phases, from an initial approach which was based upon a presumption against disclosure through the establishment of a system of pollution control registers to more recent attempts through the implementation of Directive 90/313 to open up all environmental information with restricted classes of exemptions in the Environmental Information Regulations 1992. The basic practical distinction between these last two approaches is in the nature of the access. In the case of public registers, the information is held by public authorities specifically for the purpose of public access. In the case of broader access, the information is disclosed only where a request is made (although the provision of information on registers is included within this). Although these approaches characterise the approach to disclosure of pollution control information, there are other more sophisticated information instruments which are discussed further below.

The Environmental Information Regulations 1992

These regulations were brought into force on 31 December 1992 and will be repealed by the Freedom of Information Act. The regulations were made under the European Communities Act 1972 and therefore purport to follow the wording of the Directive closely. As with other cases of direct transposition, however, there are some areas where there are significant differences between the two pieces of legislation.

Under the regulations, public authorities with responsibilities for the environment must make information which 'relates to the environment' available to every person who requests it. The phrase 'environmental information' is defined widely in accordance with the directive definition, It includes information on the quality and state of air, water, soil, flora, fauna, habitats and other land (reg. 2(2)(a)). It also covers activities which adversely affect these areas and the measures which are used to protect them (reg. 2(2)(b)). Although this is an extensive list, there have been certain areas such as information on operational matters (e.g. water leakage rates) and financial records (e.g. investment plans of the water companies) where there has been some doubt as to the applicability of the definition.

The regulations apply to all public authorities with 'responsibilities in relation to the environment' (reg. 3). This clearly covers such bodies as the Department of the Environment, Transport and the Regions, local authorities and the Environment Agency. There is, however, no further definition of this phrase in statute (although there is some discussion of the phrase in guidance) leaving the decision as to whether an authority comes within the regulations to the discretion of the authority itself. This delegation of responsibility for the applicability of the Directive has been criticised by the House of Lords Select Committee on the European Communities on the basis that it provides a ready excuse to evade the duties under the regulations (see 1st Report, Session 1996–97: *Freedom of Access to Information on the Environment*). In particular, the privatised utilities including the water companies hold the view that the regulations do not apply to them (notwithstanding that the equivalent public bodies in Scotland and Northern Ireland were covered) — a view described as 'bizarre' by the Select Committee.

When a request for information is made, there must be a response as soon as possible, and in any event, not more than two months from the date of the request (reg. 3(2)). Any refusal must be in writing with reasons (reg. 3(2)(c)).

There is a long list of exceptions to the right to information. These are divided into two classes. The first class of exceptions covers matters which *must not* be disclosed (i.e. mandatory confidentiality). This includes personal information contained in records held in relation to an individual; information which would breach any statutory provisions or agreement if disclosed; information which would increase the likelihood of damage to the environment if disclosed; and information which has been voluntarily supplied by a third party (reg. 4(3)). The second class of information covers matters which *may* be disclosed (i.e. the determination of confidentiality falls within the discretion of the relevant authority). This includes information affecting national security; commercially confidential information; information relating to legal or other proceedings; and information relating to any internal communication or unfinished documents (reg. 4(2)). The Select Committee criticised the breadth of these exceptions to disclosure. In particular, it took the view that the lack of any overriding public interest which would outweigh the legitimate exceptions was a 'serious weakness'.

There are other grounds upon which an authority can refuse to disclose information. The authority may argue that it does not have 'responsibilities in relation to the environment'; the information may not 'relate to the environment'; or the request may be too vague or manifestly unreasonable (reg. 3(3)).

'Information' covered under the regulations includes anything contained in records, registers, reports and computer records (reg. 2(4)). A charge can be made in respect of the costs attributable to the supply of the information, and such a charge can be levied as a condition of the supply of the information (reg. 3(4)). There is no standardised system of charging and evidence suggests that there are significant inconsistencies in relation to the basis of charging adopted by different authorities for the supply of similar types of information (see the House of Lords Select Committee's Report).

The regulations do not prescribe any practical arrangements for access, leaving this to the discretion of the relevant authority. In the light of this and the very wide and vague statutory definitions, perhaps the most significant failure of the regulations is the lack of a right of appeal against any refusal to supply information. The only avenue of redress is by way of judicial review in the High Court. The expense and the procedural and substantive uncertainties of such an action mean that a refusal to disclose will only be challenged in the rarest of circumstances, as is borne out by the tiny number of cases taken to a conclusion (although the threat or actual commencement of proceedings can secure the desired disclosure).

Freedom of Information Bill

Some of the flaws in the Environmental Information Regulations 1992 are to be addressed in the Freedom of Information Bill which is scheduled to be passed in the 1999-2000 Parliamentary session (and therefore, at the time of writing, subject to amendment). In particular, the definition of 'public authorities' will be fleshed out by a comprehensive statutory list of public bodies to whom the Act applies with amendments and additions to the list being made by order. The Act will require public authorities to adopt and maintain 'publication schemes' setting out practical access arrangements and there will be a method of enforcing the Act with the appointment of an Information Commissioner to oversee the implementation of the Act; a code of practice setting out guidance on the implementation of the system; powers of enforcement to secure compliance; and a system of appeals for persons aggrieved.

Public registers

The traditional format of disclosure of pollution control information is through the system of statutory public registers. It is not possible to set out the detailed contents of each register in a book of this type. The most significant environmental registers are listed below.

(a) Water

Registers are kept in relation to the system of discharge consents (see the Water Resources Act 1991, ss. 190, 191 and the Control of Pollution (Application, Appeals and Registers) Regulations 1996); statutory water quality objectives (Water Resources Act 1991 s. 105); the water industry and the trade effluent system (Water Industry Act 1991, ss. 195, 196); water abstraction licences (Water Resources Act 1991, s. 189); and drinking water quality (Water Supply (Water Quality) Regulations 1989).

(b) Industrial processes

Registers are kept in relation to integrated pollution control and air pollution control authorisations (see the Environmental Protection Act 1990, ss. 20–22 and the Environmental Protection (Applications, Appeals and Registers) Regulations 1991); they will be kept in relation to integrated pollution prevention and control permits (see Pollution Prevention and Control Act 1999, sch. 1); and in relation to information about risks and hazards from major industrial sites (see COMAH Regulations 1999 (SI 1999/743)).

(c) Planning

Planning registers contain information on planning applications, enforcement and environmental impact assessments (see the Town and Country Planning Act 1990, s. 69, the Town and Country Planning (General Permitted Development) Order 1995, arts. 27–28 and the Town and Country Planning (Environmental Impact Assessment) (England and Wales) Regulations 1999, regs. 20, 21).

(d) Waste management

There are public registers which hold information in relation to the waste management system (see the Environmental Protection Act 1990, ss. 64–6 and the Waste Management Licensing Regulations 1994, regs. 10, 11). Other details are kept in relation to special waste sites although these are not held on public registers (see p. 521 and the Special Waste Regulations 1996, regs. 15–16). Information on land which has been identified as 'contaminated' is also held on public registers (see Environmental Protection Act 1990, ss. 78R–78T and the Contaminated Land (England) Regulations 2000, reg. 15).

Common features of public registers

Although the statutory provisions vary depending upon the area of concern, there are common features in most of the pollution control registers. In particular, the public registers holding information on IPC/APC, IPPC, waste management licensing and the discharge consent system are almost identical. In these cases the common features include the following.

(a) Availability of information

Generally, information must be available at all reasonable times for inspection by the public free of charge. Copies of any document can be taken on payment of a reasonable charge. The registers are held at the principal offices of the relevant local authority or the regional office of the Environment Agency (in relation to the location of the operation which is the subject of the authorisation or permissions).

(b) Nature of the information

The information on registers covers applications; details of permissions, authorisations etc. including the name and address of the operator; particulars of any enforcement action or criminal actions; appeals; and information provided by the operator in order to comply with conditions (this normally includes self-monitoring data and spot samples of environmental releases). Records can generally be kept in any form (e.g. electronically).

(c) Exemptions

There are exemptions for certain classes of information where disclosure would affect national security or commercial confidentiality. Commercial confidentiality is defined by reference to whether disclosure would prejudice to an unreasonable degree the commercial interests of the person concerned (see e.g. Environmental Protection Act 1990, ss. 22(11), 66(11), and 78T(10) in relation to IPC registers, waste management registers and contaminated land respectively and the Water Resources Act 1991, s. 191B(11)). Where information is excluded from the register on the ground of commercial confidentiality, there is a statement in the register which indicates the existence of the information.

(d) Rights of appeal

The preliminary determination of whether a particular piece of information is commercially confidential lies with the regulatory body (usually the Environment Agency). There is a right of appeal against that determination to the Secretary of State within 21 days of provisional notification and until the appeal is finally decided the information is kept off the register.

Public registers in practice

Although the system of public registers provides an easy source of information about polluting activities, empirical evidence suggests that they are underutilised by members of the general public (see e.g. Burton: 'Access to environmental information: the UK experience of water registers' (1989) JEL 192 and Rowan-Robinson, Ross, Walton and Rothnie: 'Public access to environmental information: A means to what end?' (1996) JEL 19). There are a number of potential reasons for this which are primarily connected to the accessibility of the registers themselves and the quality and comprehensiveness of the information found on the registers. For example, raw monitoring data, of the sort which is found in the registers, often shows the results of single samples without providing 'non-experts' with a clear picture of overall levels of compliance. In most cases, there is no information relating to general environmental quality standards or the cumulative effects of releases into the environment.

In recent years, however, there have been a number of attempts to make pollution control information more accessible and user friendly specifically via the internet (in particular the Environment Agency's 'What's in your backyard?' web site (*www.environment-agency.gov.uk*) which sets out environmental data in a national, regional and local context) and general aggregated sources (see below).

Different classes of environmental information

There is an increasing recognition that the use of information can be an integral part of an environmental regulatory system in more sophisticated ways than through the provision of pollution data on public registers. There are, therefore, a number of broad, overlapping instruments which could be classified as 'information based'. Although such classifications are crude in the sense that they tend to be 'soft' and ill defined (often as a consequence of their voluntary nature) they paint a picture of how information can slot in to various aspects of the regulatory system.

Environmental reporting

In addition to mandatory disclosure of information in the form of statutory public registers, many companies have developed a system of voluntary disclosure of environmental information through the provision of annual corporate environmental reports. Surveys amongst the top 350 FTSE companies suggest that about 70% publish some environmental information although fewer than 20% of these publish a stand alone environmental report. The Government has expressed an intention to see all of these top 350 companies publish a common format environmental report by the end of 2001 (with the threat of legislation compelling them to do so in the alternative). In the long term, the aim is to ensure that all companies with over 250 employees will report on their environmental performance.

One of the fundamental difficulties with corporate reporting is that there is no standard format for disclosure and the quality of the information can vary. The reports range from little more than one line references to the environment to detailed assessments of environmental impacts. Elements of a report could include a discussion of the environmental issues which are relevant to the business; legislative compliance and the result of any environmental audits of the business; information on releases to the environment (whether or not they are included on a public register); energy efficiency and other resource conservation issues; local issues; the setting of key performance indicators and targets for future environmental performance; a comparative analysis of performance within the relevant industrial sector; and the achievement of sustainable development targets. Many of these issues are covered in a rudimentary manner with more sophisticated analysis being dependent upon the development of environmental accounting which could place some of the matters covered into a corporate and financial context (e.g. by allocating a financial cost to the environmental impacts disclosed).

Environmental reporting has developed apace since the early 1990s. Part of the reason for this development has been external pressure from stakeholders (e.g. investors, environmental interest groups and the general public) although it should be emphasised that internal corporate environmental responsibility and the competitive advantage to be gained from demonstrating environmental compliance and improvement (in relation to corporate clients) also have had a part to play. There are moves to formalise both the content of and the requirement to report. The International Standards Organisation has published guidance on developing indicators of environmental performance (see ISO 14031) and the government has issued a consultation paper on company law reform which puts forward a suggestion that environmental reporting might be made mandatory (see DTI consultation paper, *Modern Law for a Competitive Economy: The Strategic Framework*, 1998, chapter 6). In the absence of formalisation of environmental reporting, the weaknesses inherent in this type of disclosure of environmental information remain. The lack of any formal structure means that companies can 'interpret' the raw data in any way they think fit or omit bad news entirely and the lack of any requirement for independent external validation of data can undermine the objectivity of any report.

Having identified some of the weakness of corporate environmental reporting as a means of disclosing information, it should be pointed out that there are also real benefits which can result from the process of voluntary disclosure. The most obvious benefit is that the public and other stakeholders have access to information about a company's operations which might not otherwise be disclosed. This might involve previously undisclosed qualitative (e.g. types of waste arisings) and quantitative (e.g. aggregated waste arisings) environmental information. In addition, the information will generally be in a format which can be easily communicated to and accessed by the public (e.g. via the internet).

The second main benefit is internal to the company compiling the report. The preparation of an environmental report means that a company must be aware of and address the environmental impacts which it creates. This preparatory work can assist the company in identifying areas where environmental performance can be improved and/or cost savings made.

The third benefit is that the publication of reports can set standards within an industry sector which others must follow. This could be on a simplistic level (e.g. the 'name and shame' policy adopted by government to isolate those companies which are not preparing environmental reports) or it could be more sophisticated in the sense that the presentation of comparative environmental performance indicators could set the standard within the industry sector.

In addition to this voluntary form of corporate environmental reporting there is a more formalised system of disclosing the environmental impacts of a business through the environmental management standard adopted under EC Regulation (1836/93) on Eco-management and Audit Scheme (known as EMAS). As part of the accreditation process, a business must publish a publicly available document outlining its environmental policy and targets for improvement. This written statement is subject to external and independent verification but there are potential weaknesses as a source of dependable environmental information (see further p. 209).

Environmental information to the consumer

Environmental information on products can assist consumer choice by facilitating a better assessment of the environmental impacts or costs which are involved in their production and thereby, on a theoretical level at least, internalise some of the external environmental costs (although there is a legitimate debate about the extent to which the consumption of consumer goods can 'benefit' the environment). The disclosure of information can, in conjunction with other instruments, (e.g. product standards or economic instruments such as taxes or subsidies) help with the process of 'market transformation' whereby there is an increase in the proportion of products which have lower environmental impacts whilst decreasing the proportion of products which bring about greater environmental harm (see DETR Consultation Paper, *Consumer Products and the Environment*, October 1998).

For example, a label could indicate the energy consumption of domestic central heating boilers. Secondly, there could be a ban on boilers with an energy efficiency rating below a certain standard. Finally, a financial grant could be made available to assist people who wanted to replace any boiler over 10 years old with a new boiler that came with a designated eco-label which indicated high levels of energy efficiency. The effect of these combined measures (the first and last of which are information instruments) would be to ensure that more energy efficient boilers were placed on the market.

The nature of this information can range from informal advertising information (often referred to as 'green claims') through more formal sectoral product certification schemes (e.g. timber products manufactured from sustainable managed timber certified by the Forest Stewardship Council, or the Marine Stewardship Council certifying sustainable fisheries) to official national eco-labelling schemes regulated by national authorities across a range of products with specific criteria for each product grouping (see below). Other matters which could be covered include information on the safe use, re-use, recycling and disposal of products.

(a)   Green claims

Once manufacturers recognised that environmental issues were a factor in purchasing decisions, they developed a range of green claims for their products which included meaningless and objectively immeasurable claims ('environmentally friendly') or statements which expressed a truism ('CFC free' in products after the implementation of the ban on CFCs). These sort of claims undermine the primary purpose of disclosure of this type of information to consumers (i.e. to differentiate objectively between different products). Although there are some safeguards against claims which are factually incorrect (under the Trade Descriptions Act 1968, s. 1 this would be a criminal offence), statements which are empty of meaning or axiomatic fall outside existing statutory control. The governmental response to this problem has been to rely on self-regulation by producing the *Green Claims Code*, a voluntary code of practice with all of the weaknesses that such self-regulatory systems possess.

(b)   Eco-labelling
One way of addressing some of the weaknesses of these green claims is to ensure that there is a consistent, objective, and identifiable symbol which can indicate to the consumer that a product has been assessed and approved against a set of approved criteria. The European eco-labelling scheme (under Regulation 880/92) was designed to provide such a label in the shape of a characteristic blue and green flower. The scheme was launched across Member States in July 1993 and applied first in the UK to eco-labels on dishwashers and washing machines later that year. The system of approval can be divided into three distinct phases. First, the European Commission classifies a product group after consulting and negotiating with interested parties (e.g. consumer groups, environmental interest groups and industry). Once the group is classified the criteria for the award are established (once again after consultation with stakeholders). The criteria for approval vary depending upon product groups but are generally associated with such things as raw materials consumption (e.g. water and detergent) in addition to a broader life cycle assessment.

The second phase sees the manufacturer applying to the national competent body for approval. In the UK, the Eco-labelling Board was set up to deal with these applications. In late 1999, however, it was announced that the board would be disbanded and that the award of eco-labels would be administered within the DETR. The third and final phase of the eco-labelling process is the revision of the product group criteria which, once again, is carried out by the European Commission.

The eco-labelling scheme has not been an overwhelming success either in terms of the quantity of the product groups which have been classified or the level of consumer or market interest. The scheme is perceived to be over-complicated, prescriptive in its criteria and too rigid (see the consultation responses to *Consumer Products and the Environment*, DETR, August 1999).

(c)   Other forms of product certification
There are other product certification schemes which have had greater levels of acceptance and success than the eco-label. For example, at the European level, there is an 'energy label' under Directive 92/75 with subsequent

daughter directives for particular appliances (see e.g. washing machines under Directive 95/12). At national level there are a number of sectoral labels such as the ones in the timber and fishing industries referred to above or a scheme designed to show the Volatile Organic Compound (VOC) content in paints promoted by the British Coating Federation. The main problem with this proliferation of schemes is that they tend to undermine the credibility and power of centralised labelling schemes with the inevitable consequences for the process of 'market transformation'

Information about pollution and the environment

For many years, the focal point of the debate about greater public access to information has been the system of pollution control registers as they provided the main form of access to environmental information. As mentioned above, research has demonstrated that the provision of information in public registers is notably unsuccessful in terms of access to and utilisation of the data. More recently there has been a shift towards different methods of communicating information about pollution levels and the provision of general information about environmental quality. The growth of information on the internet has given the general public easy access to a wide range of official and unofficial sources of sophisticated levels of information. This includes consultation papers and official policy documents from the DETR, the Environment Agency's Pollutant Inventory (see below) and the Friends of the Earth's register of local polluters (see the Bibliography for further details).

(a) General information
There is no statutory requirement to provide a comprehensive annual survey of the state of the environment. In recent years there has, however, been a move towards providing better wide-ranging information about the environment on a regular basis. Examples include *This Common Inheritance* and its consequent reports (Cm 1200, 1990) from central government; and *The Environment of England and Wales: A Snapshot* (1996) from the Environment Agency. More up-to-date information on the state of the environment can be found at *www.environment-agency.gov.uk*. Another source of general information on the annual work and achievements of the DETR can be found in the Department's annual report which is intended to inform Parliament of past and spending plans but also includes general environmental information. The Environment Agency is also under a statutory duty to draw up an annual report (Environment Act 1995 s. 52)).

Although there is no general statutory requirement to provide an overall summary of the state of the environment, a picture can be pieced together from other sources of information which must be prepared and made publicly available (commonly by the Environment Agency). For example, the Agency is under a statutory duty to gather information on the state of the environment (see Environment Act 1995 s. 5(2)) and make available any research carried out by the Agency or its behalf on the payment of a fee (s. 37(5)(b)).

There are requirements to prepare more detailed and specialised reports (e.g. in relation to the state of contaminated land; see Environmental Protection Act 1990 s. 78U) and the national strategies in relation to waste and air quality will also contain relevant information (Environmental Protection Act 1990 s. 44A and Environment Act 1995 s. 80).

Environmental information held by local authorities is available under the Local Government (Access to Information) Act 1985 and the Environmental Information Regulations 1992. The 1985 Act provides rights of access to minutes of council committee meetings, reports prepared for those meetings and any information which was used to compile those reports. This would include information relating to areas such as planning, waste disposal, statutory nuisances, contaminated land, air pollution and minerals matters (see further p. 176).

(b) Pollutant inventories

Whilst the details of the effects of individual operations are kept in a series of public registers, there have been relatively few attempts to provide this information on a national basis. The information on the public registers may assist with assessing individual compliance levels but it does little to enable a proper evaluation of the total effects of releases upon the environment as a whole. In order to address this issue and to implement a governmental commitment to increase access to information, the Chemical Releases Inventory (CRI) was created in 1990. Information on the CRI formed the basis of an annual report which set out figures for releases from the most polluting industrial sites (i.e. IPC processes). The CRI was criticised primarily because t did not provide an accurate picture of all releases and because it was inconsistent in the way that it reported data (it tended to concentrate on point source emissions).

As a result of these criticisms, the Environment Agency introduced a replacement for the CRI, the 'Pollutant Inventory'. The aim of the Pollutant Inventory is to provide information on annual mass releases of specified substances to air, water or land which arise from IPC processes. This includes specific releases (e.g. discharges to water from pipes or to air from chimneys) and non-point sources and fugitive emissions (e.g. from leaks or spillages). In order to facilitate this broader range of information, the Environment Agency varied every IPC authorisation to include a condition requiring operators to report annually on releases of certain substances. The annual report includes information on total releases and notifiable releases (normally this covers unauthorised releases made as a consequence of accidents, emergencies etc.). There are still weaknesses in the Pollutant Inventory. It does not include all sources of pollutants such as traffic, or landfill sites (which are a major source of methane). It also excludes releases from other regulated activities, in particular, Part B processes and the operations which are controlled under discharge consents.

There are other aggregated pollutant inventories which provide information about environmental releases. Examples cover air quality (see the National Atmospheric Emissions Inventory, *www.aeat.co.uk/netcen/airqual*, which also provides daily pollution forecasts and bulletins); and water quality (see DETR, *Water Quality: A Guide to Water Protection in England and Wales* at *www.environment.detr.gov.uk/wqd/guide/water.htm*).

From environmental data to information

The greater availability of general information about the environment is part of a general shift away from the mere production of environmental data on pollution to a broader communication of the implications of activities in terms that people can understand. One example of this can be found in the 'Pollution Injustice' information which is produced by Friends of the Earth (see *www.foe.co.uk*). This mixes otherwise one dimensional pollution data with other important variables such as poverty indicators and health statistics to produce a more informative (although arguably subjective) picture of the implications of pollution. The Strategy on Sustainable Development adopts a similar approach with its 'headline indicators' which show the progress (or otherwise) of environmental improvements (see further p. 43).

Although access to such information can communicate on a much wider basis, it still has its limitations in the sense that it does little to capture the social or cultural aspects of environmental values (see further p. 37). For example, aggregated indicators may suggest that the loss of natural habitats has fallen on a year by year basis, but this might conceal the fact that in one village, a particularly important green space which has cultural significance has been lost to development. This example merely illustrates that there will be some aspects of environmental protection which only gain significance when viewed within the local context and as such, are difficult to capture as general information.

NINE

The enforcement of environmental law

We have seen (in Chapters 3 and 7) how the environmental regulatory system is made up of layers of laws, rules and other instruments and how there are various statutory bodies which have been set up to administer these rules (see Chapter 6), but this only gives a partial picture of the way in which environmental laws work in the real world. The final piece of the regulatory 'jigsaw' is the manner in which these rules are enforced. Thus, this chapter is concerned with the enforcement of environmental law and the practical use of the rules as a technique to influence and control those who are regulated for the purposes of environmental protection. If rules can be described as the tools of the environmental lawyer's trade then enforcement is the selection and use of the right tools to prevent environmental harm.

Enforcement and enforceability

A distinction needs to be made at the outset between enforcement and *enforceability*. The latter is concerned with the potential hurdles which must be overcome before a 'tool' can even be selected. Reference has already been made to the fundamental unenforceability of international environmental law and the limitations on the enforceability of European law. These limitations include the doctrine of direct effect; the restrictions on the recovery of damages in relation to *Francovich* liability (see the discussion on the overlap between European and private law at p. 143); and the reluctance of the European Court of Justice to interfere with domestic rules on procedure (a reluctance which was emphasised when the Court of Appeal relied on the procedural ground of delay to reject an appeal relating to a substantive failure to undertake an environmental assessment, see *R v North West Leicester DC, ex parte Moses*, unreported, 12 April 2000 and p. 79).

There are also barriers to enforceability in relation to domestic environmental laws. These can be substantive such as a restriction on the right to bring a prosecution (e.g. for nature conservation offences) or more generally for administrative mechanisms. There can also be procedural hurdles such as the rules on standing or delay in relation to judicial review or other, broader difficulties in relation to access to justice (e.g. the funding of actions and the award of costs against unsuccessful public interest litigants). Other factors which affect the enforceability of environmental law include the need to gather technically complex evidence which can be expensive and uncertain; the role of policy in environmental decision-making which can mean that a successful legal challenge may simply result in a referral of the decision to the original decision-maker who, in turn, can reach the same final decision; and the slowness and inflexibility of the legal system. The existence of these hurdles means that although there are environmental laws which are enforceable in a technical sense, these may be ineffective tools in a practical sense. Many of the cases which come before the courts illustrate the unenforceability and ineffectiveness of environmental laws.

(a) Enforceability and injunctions
A good illustration of the distinction between enforcement and enforceability can be found in the use of injunctions to enforce environmental law. As an enforcement tool an injunction is theoretically a very effective way of preventing environmental harm. It has a number of advantages including speed (courts will often hear applications for injunctions at short notice and without giving notice to the affected party); the ability to prevent anticipated harm before it becomes irreversible (which is particularly useful in cases of habitat destruction); and the penalties for breach of an injunction are severe (it would be a contempt of court, which can be punished by imprisonment).

The *enforceability* of injunctions is, however, restricted by a number of factors. First, the ability to seek an injunction in relation to regulatory enforcement is not necessarily freestanding. There must either be a specific statutory power to do so (e.g. s. 24, EPA 1990), a private right to protect, or the action has to be referred to the Attorney-General under a relator action (although there is some evidence that courts will grant an injunction in favour of a body like English Nature on a public interest basis alone). Secondly, the decision to grant an injunction is discretionary and regulators need to demonstrate a good arguable case and that the 'balance of convenience' is in its favour. Thirdly, in non-statutory injunctions granted without notice, a regulator may have to give an undertaking in damages (i.e. a pledge to pay compensation should the final judgment go against it). Finally, in the cases of injunctions sought under statutory powers, the courts have stressed the need for enforcing authorities to exhaust all criminal remedies before seeking an injunction (see *Tameside MBC* v *Smith Bros (Hyde) Ltd* [1996] Env LR 316). These latter two points might suggest that although the use of injunctions appears to be an effective way of dealing with cases of potential harm, there are good practical reasons why such a remedy might be considered to be unattractive or impractical by enforcement agencies.

An example of the practical consequences of the unenforceability of injunctions can be found in *R* v *Secretary of State for the Environment, ex parte RSPB* [1997] Env LR 431, where the House of Lords refused to grant an injunction in relation to preventing the development of the Special Protection

Area at Lappel Bank pending the referral of the matter to the ECJ. The primary reason for this refusal was the reluctance of the RSPB to give a cross-undertaking in damages which would have tied up and risked millions of pounds of the RSPB's funds. Before the ECJ had an opportunity to give a final ruling, Lappel Bank was destroyed by the development in question. It is worth pointing out that although the ECJ did not deal with the issue of the refusal to grant an injunction at the hearing, it is unlikely that it would find against national procedural rules such as this.

(b) Enforceability and private prosecutions

Another noteworthy example of the distinction between enforceability and enforcement can be found in the availability and use of private prosecutions in environmental law. Unless a statute specifically restricts the right, anyone can bring a private prosecution (*R* v *Stewart* [1896] 1 QB 300). In the case of most environmental laws (with one of the notable exceptions being nature conservation offences under the Wildlife and Countryside Act 1981), an individual can prosecute an offence. As we shall see below, strict liability is imposed in relation to many environmental crimes which minimises the level of proof required to establish the offence. Notwithstanding this simplicity, private prosecutions are relatively rare, although not unknown (e.g. groups such as the RSPCA and the RSPB utilise private prosecutions in relation to animal cruelty offences). There are many factors which discourage private groups or individuals from taking action including funding and costs issues; the need to gather and present expert evidence; and the fear of the technical aspects of preparing and presenting a criminal case. In addition, many of the factors which influence the regulatory bodies in taking enforcement action, such as the relatively low penalties imposed by the courts, shape private attitudes to prosecution.

Although private prosecutions are unattractive because of the barriers to enforceability, they are still important as an enforcement tool. In a number of celebrated cases, the *threat* of private prosecution by groups such as Friends of the Earth and Greenpeace has acted as a trigger for action by the regulatory bodies. For example, in the case of the *Sea Empress* pollution incident, the threat of private prosecution by Friends of the Earth brought pressure to bear upon the Environment Agency which appeared to be reluctant to prosecute. The eventual successful prosecution by the Agency resulted in one of the largest ever fines for water pollution.

A definition of enforcement

In contrast to enforceability, the *enforcement* of environmental law is more concerned with the actual *use* of the tools rather than the factors which affect their effectiveness. When we talk of the enforcement of environmental law we run into the same problems of definition that we encountered in Chapter 3. With such a wide range of instruments which are capable of being utilised for environmental protection there is a corresponding breadth to the potential boundaries of defining the enforcement of those instruments. At its widest, the enforcement of environmental law could include *any* mechanism which could be used to secure compliance with a legal obligation which afforded environmental protection. This might involve the enforcement of private obligations (e.g. English Nature enforcing the terms of a management agreement to compel an owner to manage a SSSI either by injunction or for breach of contract; or a property owner bringing an action in nuisance to prohibit the operations of a nearby factory); the use of information by regulators or third parties (e.g. the 'naming and shaming' of polluters in the national press); or even the carrying out of a threat from the Secretary of State or regulator.

A narrower definition (and one which is adopted for the majority of this chapter) is concerned with the enforcement of environmental *regulation* and in particular the custom and practice of environmental regulatory agencies when it comes to such enforcement. Even within this narrower definition there is a range of actions which could come within the phrase 'enforcement'. These actions could include powers of prosecution which enable regulatory bodies to enforce against 'crimes against the environment'. These could be offences where there is direct environmental harm (e.g. polluting controlled waters; see the Water Resources Act 1991, s. 85); or the offence is indirectly related to harm (e.g. failure to comply with an enforcement notice; see s. 23 of the EPA 1990 in relation to IPC offences). Alternatively, enforcement could involve the right to take injunctive proceedings where statute permits it (e.g. s. 27, EPA 1990, dealing with integrated pollution control) or where private rights are affected.

The use of powers of prosecution and consequent criminal sanctions are, however, only one in a variety of formal enforcement mechanisms. There are alternative administrative powers which can control continuing activities. Unlike other European countries, Britain does not have a developed system of administrative courts which have the power to enforce and impose general sanctions. Pollution control legislation, however, typically provides for licences, authorisations etc. to be varied or revoked and for activities to be prohibited or enforced against without any reference to the criminal courts. Although the use of these powers does not impose any formal penalty in the same way as criminal penalties, there are other sanctions which are either explicit (e.g. the cessation or restriction of previously authorised activities) or implicit (e.g. they are steps which can lead to a prosecution). For example, the service of a statutory nuisance abatement notice or a notice for the requisition of ownership details under the Town and Country Planning Act 1990 are enforcement steps which can lead to prosecution although there is no element of direct punishment in taking such an action when taken in isolation.

Beyond these formal enforcement mechanisms there are other informal and more subtle practices which can be used to influence behaviour. These might include educating and advising the ignorant operator; imposing deadlines for the improvement of environmental performance; increased monitoring or inspection visits; or issuing verbal and written 'last warnings' prior to more formal enforcement action. As we shall see, these informal mechanisms play a central role in the enforcement practices of Britain's environmental regulatory agencies.

Understanding enforcement practices

Why do we need to understand the enforcement practices of environmental agencies? When the figures for formal enforcement action are considered it is clear that although there are significant numbers of breaches of environmental legislation, the proportion of prosecutions or other enforcement action is very low. This is the case for different environmental enforcement agencies including local authorities (e.g. only 16 authorities have brought prosecutions for local authority air pollution control (LAAPC) offences in eight years and Clean Air Act 1993 prosecutions form less than 1 per cent of the total number of statutory breaches, see DETR, *Local Authority Progress in Implementing the LAAPC Regime,* October 1998 and Chartered Institute of Environmental Health, *Environmental Health Report,* 1997/8 respectively); the Environment Agency (e.g. 270 prosecutions compared with 18,763 pollution incidents in the water sector and 17 prosecutions compared with 825 pollution incidents from IPC processes, see Environment Agency, *Annual Report,* 1998/9) and English Nature (e.g. 15 cases of 'formal enforcement' in 1997 with one prosecution). Although the figures for administrative enforcement (e.g. enforcement and revocation notices) are proportionately higher, there are still significant numbers of breaches of environmental legislation of all types which are not enforced against.

In trying to understand why this happens, we must explore the purposes of enforcing environmental law and the different styles of enforcement which might be employed to meet those purposes. On the basis of the published figures, many would argue that the enforcement of environmental law is inadequate and there should be a dramatic increase in the formal enforcement action taken against polluters (and those who take this view also tend to point to the leniency of the penalties which are imposed). This view does not, however, take into account the practicalities of enforcement such as the lack of resources (financial and in terms of personnel) or perhaps more importantly, whether such an approach would actually improve the protection of the environment.

Styles of enforcement

The central aim of the enforcement of environmental regulation is to *prevent* harm to the environment or human health rather than to detect and then punish those who cause such harm (although this is obviously one closely connected aim). Environmental enforcement is not, therefore, only concerned with punishment for breach of environmental laws but also with preventing those breaches occurring and assisting those who are regulated in doing so. These two elements of an enforcement strategy are linked with two different styles of enforcement; the compliance approach where there is an emphasis on all mechanisms other than prosecution in order to promote compliance with environmental laws; and the 'deterrence' approach which employs strict punitive measures, notably prosecutions to deter operators from future non-compliance.

(a) Compliance

The compliance (or conciliatory or cooperative) approach is typically characterised in environmental enforcement by the development of a continuing
relationship between enforcement agency and 'polluter'. At one extreme this
might involve a patient, persuasive, educative role for the enforcer almost
acting as an external advisor. In this case, mutual respect and trust can
develop which can be used to ensure compliance with laws or standards (e.g.
environmental quality standards). At the other extreme, the relationship
might be more detached with the regulator seeking compliance within strict
time limits (e.g. installing pollution abatement equipment or applying for a
requisite licence).

(b) Deterrence

The 'deterrence' (or confrontational) approach punishes those who are
responsible for causing environmental harm. At an extreme level, such an
approach would result in the punishment of every breach of environmental
laws. At first glance, this would not appear to meet the central aim of any
enforcement strategy, namely preventing harm to the environment. Compliance is, however, achieved through the desire to prevent future breaches and
thereby avoid any further enforcement action.

(c) Responsive regulation

If deterrence and compliance styles are seen as two ends of an enforcement
spectrum, a third approach has been identified as a 'pick and mix' blend of
different enforcement mechanisms with officers varying strategies in response
to whether the regulated are complying with their obligations (see Ayres and
Braithwaite, *Responsive Regulation,* OUP, 1992). Under 'responsive regulation' officers will use mechanisms of increasing formality and impact as the
regulated fail to meet their legal obligations. Thus an officer might progress
through verbal warnings of the consequences of non-compliance to more
formal enforcement notices to prosecution and even prohibition or revocation
notices. The other side of this approach is that there will be more informal
mechanisms used when the regulated come within compliance. The essence
of responsive regulation is that an enforcement officer will use the minimum
amount of formal regulation as possible in order to achieve compliance.

These styles of enforcement help us to understand why, for example,
prosecution rates are so low. The theoretical framework only gives us a
general overview, however, with many other factors having an influence over
decisions relating to individual enforcement action. Some of these factors are
connected to the British approach to environmental regulation, others relate
to the nature of the rules which are being enforced or cultural attitudes to
environmental offences and offenders.

The British approach to environmental enforcement

The British approach to environmental enforcement as exercised by administrative regulatory bodies is strongly underscored by the themes which

dominate Part I of this book. These include: the flexibility in the setting of individualised emission and process standards; wide definitions found in key statutory provisions; informal guidance on the interpretation of statutory rules; reliance on self regulation and voluntary compliance; and the use of discretionary powers rather than mandatory duties.

All of these factors (along with others) have a role to play in the style of enforcement adopted by the variety of environmental agencies. Whilst it is not possible to generalise across all agencies (indeed there will be variations of style between individual officers within the same agency), the British approach to environmental regulation facilitates the development of a flexible relationship between the regulator and regulated which is characteristic of the compliance style of enforcement. The amount of discretion given in setting the standards and in using enforcement powers means that enforcement officers can use the informal problem solving approach to breaches of environmental regulation rather than being forced to resort to formal sanctions such as prosecution.

There have been a number of empirical studies of the activities of environmental enforcement bodies in England (see Hawkins, *Environment and Enforcement*, Clarendon, 1984, and Richardson, Ogus and Burrows, *Policing Pollution*, Clarendon, 1988 in relation to the enforcement practices of the old style water authorities; and Hutter, *The Reasonable Arm of the Law*, Clarendon, 1983 in relation to local environmental health officers). Each of these studies tended to confirm the adoption of a 'compliance' style of enforcement, with officers often walking a tightrope between a cooperative approach and the effective enforcement of pollution control rules. In other areas of environmental regulation, such as nature conservation, where the emphasis has traditionally been on voluntary measures, the cooperative approach is even more important (see Chapter 21 and also Withrington and Jones, *The Enforcement of Nature Conservation Legislation: The Protection of SSSIs in Agriculture, Conservation and Land Use,* University of Wales Press, 1992).

These studies indicated that a hierarchy of enforcement mechanisms was utilised in order to maintain good relationships between the regulator and the regulated. The first stage of the enforcement process primarily focused on advice and education about the mutual 'problem' which was connected with the breach. If this was not successful in gaining compliance, further warnings both informal and formal were given with prosecution only an option where the offence was serious or the offender culpable. The development of an on-going relationship was central to the enforcement style. The work of environmental agencies was technically and scientifically based rather than founded on concepts of rules, sanctions and other penalties. Thus, education and advice were perceived as being more important than prosecution or other formal enforcement mechanisms. The continuing relationship with the operator/offender was designed to prevent harm and promote environmental protection and this could be achieved more effectively by cooperating with polluters rather than confronting them by adopting a 'deterrence' style.

Although the general characteristics of enforcement practices can be classified as a 'British' approach (e.g. the findings of Scottish research into enforcement practices broadly reflect the above studies, see Watchman, Barker and Rowan-Robinson, 'River pollution: A pragmatic approach to enforcement' [1988] JPL 764), there are variations certainly in relation to the Scottish approach and arguably in relation to the Northern Irish approach to enforcement. Mostly, these variations are associated with institutional differences. For example, in Scotland, prior to the creation of the Scottish Environment Protection Agency (SEPA), there was no dedicated environment agency and all prosecutions had to be brought by the Crown Office (i.e. effectively through the police), which lacked expertise in relation to the enforcement of environmental offences. In addition, the right to prosecute in Scotland is effectively held solely by the Procurator-Fiscal and thus, even with the creation of SEPA, the final decision to prosecute is determined outside the relevant agency. In Northern Ireland, the lack of uniformity of legislation with the rest of the United Kingdom often meant that actions which would have been considered to be an offence in, say, England were not illegal in Northern Ireland. For example, until the implementation of the Waste and Contaminated Land Order 1997, waste could be transferred from Northern Ireland to England without complying with the duty of care requirements. Other differences are not as stark, such as variations in sentencing (with average fines being even lower) which reflect different emphases placed upon some of the factors which are discussed below.

Most of the research referred to above dates back to the 1970s and early 1980s. Just as there has been a move away from flexible, discretionary styles of environmental regulation (see Chapter 7), there has also been a discernible shift away from the informal, cooperative approach to enforcement (e.g. notwithstanding the low percentages, there has been a rise in the total number of prosecutions for pollution control offences and agencies such as English Nature have been encouraged to use prosecution more readily). Although this shift can just about be perceived in the empirical data, this does not necessarily mean that a 'deterrence' style of enforcement has been adopted across the board. The subtle blend of influencing factors means that a decision about when and how to enforce against breaches of environmental law is becoming much more complex. Any list of the factors which influence enforcement could never be comprehensive as each individual case will have peculiar circumstances which shape the exercise of an enforcement agency's discretion. Certain factors can, however, be identified as having a general influence over styles of enforcement. These include legal, cultural, economic and political factors and are considered below.

Legal factors

When considering which enforcement style to employ, regulatory agencies are influenced by various legal factors. They may not be able to take certain action because the rules prevent them, or they may consider that a deterrence approach will ultimately be unsuccessful because the sentence which an offender will receive does not reflect the severity of the offence.

(a) The nature of the rules

One of the most important factors in any enforcement decision is the nature of the rules being enforced. For example, one of the great weaknesses of nature conservation legislation has been the relative narrowness of both the rules and enforcement options (e.g. any actions by third parties which cause damage to SSSIs cannot be enforced against and even owners and occupiers are only temporarily banned from carrying out damaging operations, see Chapter 21). On the other hand, the offence of causing the pollution of controlled waters under the Water Resources Act 1991, s. 85 is comparatively wide covering a broad range of potential polluters (e.g. holders of polluting substances can be prosecuted for pollution caused by the acts of trespassers, see p. 591). Moreover, there is a range of other enforcement mechanisms which can be selected to try to deal with any water pollution which has been caused (e.g. an enforcement notice under s. 191A or a works notice under s. 161A, Water Resources Act 1991 would be available).

These examples illustrate how, at one extreme, an officer working for English Nature has relatively few enforcement options available to deal with damage to a SSSI (indeed they might not be able to do anything at all), whereas the Environment Agency officer has the ability to select from an assortment of formal enforcement powers and possibly even from a list of potential polluters.

As discussed in Chapter 6, the Environment Act 1995 amended existing legislation to ensure that the Environment Agency was given a wider range of administrative powers to deal with different aspects of the enforcement of its pollution control functions. The main changes were made to the powers under the Water Resources Act 1991 dealing with water pollution.

(b) The nature of the liability

Another relevant legal factor is the nature of the liability. Although there are some notable exceptions (e.g. in relation to waste management there are Duty of Care and packaging waste offences which only cover 'unreasonable' behaviour), in most cases environmental enforcement powers operate upon the basis of strict liability, which means that there is no need to prove any negligence or fault on the part of the defendant/operator. Strict liability applies to all administrative enforcement but also for the vast majority of environmental crimes. A good example of strict liability in environmental cases can be found in *CPC (UK) Ltd* v *National Rivers Authority* [1995] Env LR 131, where the defendant company was found guilty of polluting controlled waters from a fractured pipe notwithstanding that the defect in the pipe was latent and the company did not and could not have known about the situation. Under strict liability, every breach could be subjected to enforcement, either as a criminal offence or under administrative powers.

Although there are good policy justifications for the imposition of strict liability for environmental crimes (in particular the criminal courts have accepted that there is a public interest goal inherent within environmental protection legislation), the intrinsic unfairness of such liability in certain cases is balanced by the availability of statutory defences. Typically these cover acting in accordance with a statutory consent (see e.g. the Water Resources Act 1991, s. 88); emergency situations (see e.g. s. 33(5), EPA 1990; s. 28(8)(b), Wildlife and Countryside Act 1981 and s. 89, Water Resources Act 1991 in relation to waste management, nature conservation and water pollution respectively); exercising due diligence in carrying out operations (see e.g. s. 33(7), EPA 1990 in relation to waste management or variations including BPM and BATNEEC); and having a 'reasonable excuse' (see e.g. the Wildlife and Countryside Act 1981, s. 28(7) and the EPA 1990, s. 80(4) in relation to nature conservation and statutory nuisances respectively). The courts have tended to construe these defences narrowly in order to protect the underlying aims of environmental legislation (see e.g. *Durham CC v Peter O'Connor Industrial Services* [1993] Env LR 197).

One of the interesting points to note in relation to these defences is that there is little consistency between the defences in relation to different areas of environmental law. When the Environment Act 1995 was passing through Parliament, there was a proposal to introduce a due diligence offence for water pollution offences under the Water Resources Act 1991, s. 85. Although the government rejected the amendment on the ground that it would be impractical for regulatory bodies to prove that a defendant did not exercise due diligence in carrying out activities, there is nothing obvious which would justify having such a defence in relation to waste management offences, for example (particularly in the light of the Duty of Care), and not in relation to water pollution. These sorts of inconsistencies are a good argument for the codification of environmental offences, certainly in relation to pollution control offences.

The main effect of the strictness of liability in environmental law is that it enables enforcement officers to use the threat or warning of prosecution and other formal action as part of a compliance strategy, even if it is only bluffing. On the other hand when a deterrence strategy is needed there is the comfort of a high probability of success in the selected enforcement action.

(c) Sentencing powers
The adoption of a particular style of enforcement can be influenced by the nature of the penalties or sanctions which are imposed as a consequence of breach of the law. Where penalties are low or the sanction insignificant, the impact of a deterrence approach is minimised, whilst the effectiveness of threats used as part of the compliance or responsive regulation styles is also reduced.

The empirical research on the use of enforcement powers has indicated that environmental regulators tended to have grave doubts about the level of criminal penalties used in sentencing for environmental crimes. The level of fines has traditionally been notoriously low and therefore not seen as an effective sanction when compared with the profits which were generated from activities which harmed the environment. In some cases the statutory maximum has been a restricting factor (e.g. in relation to damage to SSSIs, the maximum fine is currently a derisory £2,500 although it is likely to go up to £20,000 under the Countryside and Rights of Way Bill before Parliament).

More generally, low levels of fines have been imposed by the judiciary. This can be attributed to a number of factors including the lack of judicial experience in dealing with environmental offences (which is closely connected to a paucity of prosecutions); some of the conceptual difficulties in punishing strict liability offences referred to above; and the technical nature of some of the consequences of pollution which form the basis of the defendant's culpability.

The annual average fines have been in the region of £2,000 to £4,000 per offence in relation to water and waste offences, although the figures are often distorted by one or two very large fines. These low levels of fines have a knock-on effect in the sense that they tend to reinforce the view that environmental offences are morally neutral in the eyes of the judiciary. In the 1990s, the maximum level of fines in the magistrates' court was raised to take into account the need for the lower court to have wider powers to reflect the seriousness of the offences which do not merit being heard in the Crown Court. The EPA 1990 increased the level of fines for a number of pollution control offences from £2,000 to £20,000.

Although many environmental offences are triable either in the magistrates' court or the Crown Court, the option to try a matter in the Crown Court, with the opportunity to seek an unlimited fine and even imprisonment in the case of individual offenders has not often been taken. It is, however, becoming slightly more common for matters to be committed to the Crown Court for sentencing. Two significant examples are the cases of the prosecution of Shell (UK) in February 1990 and Milford Haven Port Authority in relation to its role in the *Sea Empress* disaster, both for water pollution offences under s. 85, Water Resources Act 1991. In each case the fines (£1,000,000 and £4,000,000 respectively although the latter was reduced to £750,000 on appeal) were huge in comparison with the annual average. Even though the imposition of significant fines has increased (e.g. there have been a few fines in the region of £150,000 to £300,000) they are still, however, very much the exception to the norm.

There are other powers of sentencing available to the courts in serious cases with individual defendants (as opposed to companies). These include community service orders and custodial sentences in the severest cases. These have been used sparingly in the past, though in keeping with other sentencing trends there has been an increase of these types of sentences, certainly in relation to imprisonment (e.g. a sentence of 18 months' imprisonment was passed for a waste management offence, although this was reduced to 12 months on appeal, see *R* v *Garrett* [1998] Env LR D2). It is interesting to note that the vast majority of sentences of imprisonment are passed in relation to waste management offences whereas in other areas (e.g. water pollution and IPC) the prevalent punishment is financial (i.e. a fine). The reason for this is closely connected to the identity of the polluter, with typical prosecutions for water and IPC offences involving major companies (with consequent restrictions on the nature of the sentence which can be passed) and a significant proportion of serious waste management offences being committed by single 'cowboy' operators (see further the discussion of corporate liability below).

The general concern about the levels of sentence for environmental offences has recently resulted in the Sentencing Advisory Panel issuing proposals to the Court of Appeal to frame sentencing guidelines for environmental offences. Although these are restricted to certain offences (e.g. in relation to waste management, water pollution, packaging waste and water abstraction), it is likely that they would be adopted for other environmental offences.

The guidelines set out a series of aggravating factors relating to the culpability of the defendant (e.g. whether the actions leading to the harm were deliberate, reckless or that the defendant was motivated by profit or cost saving) and the seriousness of the offence (e.g. the nature and extent of the environmental harm caused). In addition there are various mitigating factors which reduce the seriousness of an offence (e.g. previous good environmental record, minor role in the commission of the offence, steps taken to remedy the harm).

There is also guidance on the appropriate level of fine which, for the first time, it is suggested, should reflect the means of the individual offender (implying that companies with a large turnover will receive a larger fine than an individual with limited means notwithstanding that the nature of the offences is identical). Such an approach follows sentencing case law in other related areas including health and safety legislation (see *R v F. Howe and Sons Ltd (Engineers)* [1999] 2 Cr App R(S) 37). The status of the guidelines is somewhat uncertain following the decision of the Court of Appeal in *R v Milford Haven Port Authority*, unreported, 16 March 2000 (the appeal against sentence arising out of the *Sea Empress* disaster) in which the Court neither rejected nor endorsed the Advisory Panel's views when reducing the overall fine imposed on Milford Haven Port Authority. Although the Court considered the guidelines, it relied heavily upon the material factors which had been previously endorsed in *Howe* (thus emphasising the judicial view that there is a degree of similarity between environmental and health and safety offences). The most obvious explanation of the Court's reluctance to adopt the guidelines is that the *Sea Empress* prosecution was so different from other environmental offences, that the application of generalised sentencing principles would have been inappropriate.

Whilst there are some overlaps between the approach to sentencing approved in *Howe* and the views of the Sentencing Advisory Panel (e.g. fines should reflect the means of the offender), the differences, particularly in relation to wider considerations, are significant (e.g. *Howe* refers to the seriousness of the risk of death or serious injury which are not necessarily relevant in cases of pure environmental harm). These anomalies should be dealt with by the Court of Appeal if and when a more appropriate case comes before it.

One final area of note which is considered under the guidelines is the use of compensation orders in environmental cases. Under s. 35 of the Powers of Criminal Courts Act 1973, the courts have the power to award compensation to anyone who has directly suffered as a result of an environmental offence. These powers have rarely been used. The Sentencing Advisory Panel has suggested that where there is a specific victim (e.g. an owner who has had to pay to clean up after an incident or to re-stock after a fish kill), a court should always consider a compensation order although not before imposing a fine. The significance of the use of compensation orders is, however, reduced as a result of the existence of many statutory powers of clean up and cost recovery available to regulatory agencies in defined situations (e.g. s. 59, EPA 1990 or s. 161A, Water Resources Act 1991) and the fact that there is currently a limit of £5,000 for each order.

(d)   The availability of other enforcement mechanisms
As pointed out above, the power to prosecute is used only sparingly and the availability of other sanctions can also be a factor in selecting the right enforcement tool. For example, the use of administrative powers such as enforcement or revocation notices can have a greater operational and financial impact on an operator than a fine if the requirements of the notice specify the implementation of expensive new abatement technologies. The use of such mechanisms has been adopted widely in the enforcement of the system of integrated pollution control under Part I of the EPA 1990. Whereas the prosecution rates for IPC offences have remained low (on average, about 14 a year), other administrative powers have been used in increasing numbers. The use of enforcement notices after a pollution incident or to deal with chronic breaches gives an operator some time to deal with the cause of the problems without the ignominy of a prosecution. The service of the notice is seen as part of the enforcement process without excluding the possibility of prosecution either for the breach of the enforcement notice or for any continuing breaches.

Financial factors — the availability of resources

The allocation of resources in terms of personnel and funding plays an important role in the enforcement of environmental law. Historically, environmental enforcement bodies have had to cope with cuts in funding and understaffing. Partly this has been connected to the source of funding from central government (e.g. by way of grant in aid), and the restrictions on raising extra revenue. The funding limits imposed on local government are well documented and similar issues arise with other centrally funded agencies such as English Nature. These problems have a knock-on effect in terms of enforcement and inspection. For example there is little point in employing a 'deterrence' style of enforcement if there are not enough people to investigate and prosecute environmental offences. Of course the lack of resources has other less direct impacts on overall enforcement style. The reliance on voluntary acts in the regulation of the protection of nature conservation is closely linked to the lack of resources in terms of personnel (i.e. a dependence on third party owners to manage sites) and funding (i.e. the inability to plan a programme of buying up and managing threatened sites).

The Environment Agency has a mixed approach to funding with part coming in revenue from charges and a declining part from central grant. The Agency has sought increases in funding which will pay for the recruitment of new staff and more inspection and enforcement. If approved these increases will see the Agency's budget rise by 17 per cent before 2002/3 with an extra 1,100 staff over a five year period (commencing in 1998). Notwithstanding these increases, there are still problems with the effectiveness of the monitoring of pollution control licensing with, for example, a reported 23 per cent cut in the number of water quality samples taken in 1998/9 (see ENDS Report 295 p. 5). These cuts in inspection when coupled with an increase in the use of self-monitoring requirements as an automatic condition of pollution control licences calls into question the role of the Agency in this important aspect of enforcement.

Cultural factors — attitudes towards environmental offences

One of the main problems with the enforcement of environmental law is the moral ambivalence surrounding regulatory offences in general and certain aspects of environmental crime in particular. The extent to which pollution or other environmental harm is viewed as a 'crime' by operators, regulators and the general public is a factor which will influence the enforcement actions which are taken. Attitudes to environmental harm generally and offences more specifically have shifted over the years. From a time when pollution was seen as an acceptable by-product of industrialised activity there has been a shift so that environmental damage with long term consequences is presumed to be morally unacceptable.

(a)   A historical perspective
Traditionally, pollution offences were regarded as morally neutral and part of the consequence of living in an industrialised society. Research has suggested that although enforcement agencies were enforcing the same standards for all polluters, they were not necessarily concerned with the breach of the standards nor the extent of the environmental harm caused. Instead they tended to be influenced by the intent, or lack of it, behind the act of pollution.

When exercising their discretion in taking enforcement action (i.e. selecting the right tool to use), enforcement officers are influenced by the moral opprobrium which they themselves feel about the activity and also the moral blame which is attached by the general public. Historically, the commission of environmental crimes by industrial operators was viewed as less heinous than 'normal' criminal offences. It was thought that pollution was a natural consequence of industrial activity and the operators made a positive contribution to the local and regional economy. When the different influencing factors were placed into the balance, the need to protect the environment did not outweigh the utility of providing jobs and investment and therefore no intervention was thought necessary. This would provide one possible explanation for the extremely low rate of prosecution, with enforcing authorities being reluctant to use the ultimate sanction of prosecution unless moral blame was at the top end of the scale, which could be equated with gross criminal negligence or actual intent on behalf of the offender. Most accidents were not viewed as morally offensive.

Other cultural factors have played a part. Traditionally, those who have polluted have been of high status in society and those affected by pollution of low status. Pollution was more commonplace in working-class areas of high industrial activity (e.g. one of the reasons that the 'west end' of cities tends to be more affluent than the 'east end' is partly connected to the historical transmission of pollutants from the west to the east either by prevailing winds or via rivers). Many of those living in the area were working in the factory which was polluting the area. The pollution was often seen as a way of life rather than a matter for complaint.

(b)   Changes in attitudes towards environmental offences

The changes in fundamental attitudes to the environment have started to have an impact upon the enforcement of environmental law. Underlying these changes is a basic shift in the way that environmental problems are perceived, not only by the public but also by the enforcement agencies and even the general category of 'polluters'. The acknowledgement that environmental protection is important in its own right has undermined previous assumptions about the benefits of activities which cause environmental harm.

As environmental issues have become more important in the public eye, there is a desire to ensure that environmental standards are maintained and environmental damage minimised. Moreover, when public interest in the environment and the understanding of the consequences of environmental harm increases, there is an equivalent escalation in the amount of moral opprobrium which attaches to environmental offences. The publicity which is given to pollution incidents and other notorious examples of environmental damage (even ironically where such damage might be lawful, e.g. the case of the destruction of Twyford Down) tends to amplify the view that such harm and pollution is caused by something more than mere administrative difficulties and should be dealt with severely. These changes have necessitated a shift from compliance-based strategies of enforcement to arguably a more ambivalent approach.

Cultural factors — attitudes towards the offender

There are characteristics which are common to the attitudes to environmental offences and the approach taken by regulators to those who commit such offences. The factors which have been discussed above, such as the moral ambivalence to 'white collar crimes', tend to have an impact upon the way in which offenders are viewed. Other aspects of the attitude to environmental offenders are considered below.

(a)   Overlapping functions

Historically, attitudes towards offenders were shaped by the many overlaps between the operational and regulatory functions carried out by environmental agencies. The two main examples of this dual role were in the control of water pollution under the regional water authorities and the control of the disposal of waste to land through the county-wide waste disposal authorities under

COPA 1974. Both of these authorities carried out activities which had to be policed by themselves. The failure to separate these two contradictory roles created great problems. Often the greatest breaches of environmental laws were caused by the operational arms of the regulatory bodies.

This, in turn, led the private sector to argue that it was inequitable for the enforcement agencies to enforce against private companies when their own operations were also in breach. In addition, it influenced attitudes towards offenders. Many officers within enforcement agencies empathised with those in the private sector and therefore were happy to adopt a compliance-based strategy. Where officers had experienced the discomfort of striving but failing to comply with environmental laws they were much more ready to be sympathetic as an educator and advisor rather than a policeman.

The shift in attitudes towards the offender has become marked since the move away from the dual-function approach of the administration of environmental protection. The creation of the National Rivers Authority under the Water Act 1989 and the formation of the new system of regulation in the waste disposal industry under Part II of the EPA 1990 allowed the new and separate enforcement agencies to adopt an arm's length relationship with operators. This in turn allowed, for example, the NRA to concentrate on a deterrence style of enforcement. This was evidenced by an increase in the incidence of prosecution with figures suggesting that water pollution prosecutions rose at least 25% each year in the initial years of the NRA's life. The creation of the Environment Agency in April 1996 has further redefined the relationship between enforcers and operators with the integration of the enforcement functions in relation to various pollution control responsibilities. Other steps have been taken to increase the distance between regulator and regulated including the adoption of transparent policies on enforcement and greater third party involvement in the setting of standards and drawing up of guidance.

(b)   The relationship between regulator and regulated

The compliance style of enforcement is largely based upon the continuing relationship which exists between regulators and the regulated. Research has shown that where there were problems with trade effluent discharges, offenders were far more likely to be subjected to formal enforcement action and prosecution if the relationship was threatened or made more difficult as a result of the actions of the regulated. The reverse was also true; if the offender had a good relationship with the regulator then the prospect of formal enforcement action was reduced.

The type of relationship was strongly influenced by the attitude taken by officers to individual operators. Certain offenders would be viewed as putting profit or their own interests before the environment and disobeying the law when it suited their interests to do so. In these circumstances, the enforcement agencies would adopt a strong deterrence style of enforcement. Another group of offenders would be viewed as breaching the law because the imposition of environmental controls were considered to be unreasonable in terms of the financial or technical burden. A further identifiable group would be viewed as well meaning but organisationally incompetent. In this latter situation, the regulators would adopt a compliance style of enforcement, in particular relying upon advice and education to overcome incompetence.

(c) Capture theory
It has been argued that the closeness of the relationship between 'polluters' and regulatory agencies can lead to the 'capture' of the agency, where the agency concentrates on the interests of the regulated to the exclusion of the public interest. A good example of the potential effects of 'capture theory' can be seen in the attitude of the Alkali Inspectorate to the disclosure of pollution information where the Inspectorate favoured the protection of private companies (through the maintenance of a secrecy policy) over public disclosure of information on pollution. There have been various explanations as to why 'capture' occurs, including the political influence which major industrial or other interest groups (e.g. the farming community) hold over the rule makers and the regulators, and the common interests which can be found in both regulators and regulated (e.g. some Environment Agency officers have worked for the industries which they regulate). There is a clear link between 'capture theory' and the adoption of a compliance style of enforcement because the closeness of a regulatory relationship militates against a deterrence style.

(d) Corporate liability
Generally in Britain, where companies commit environmental offences, prosecutions are brought against that company rather than any one individual who might have responsibility within that company. This is in contrast to some European countries (e.g. Italy) where it is far more common for individual managers of companies to be prosecuted. The British approach is not, however, restricted by law. Under many environmental statutes directors and managers can be prosecuted individually in certain circumstances.

Any director, manager, secretary or other similar officer of a corporate body can be prosecuted personally if the offence is committed with their consent or connivance, or is attributable to their neglect (see e.g. s. 157, EPA 1990, s. 217, Water Resources Act 1991, s. 331, Town and Country Planning Act 1990). Who can be liable under these sections? In *Woodhouse* v *Walsall MBC* [1994] Env LR 30, the general manager of a waste disposal site (along with his employers) was convicted of an offence under the EPA 1990. The High Court was asked to determine whether the defendant was of sufficient status to be personally liable under s. 157, EPA 1990. The court held that the important test was whether a defendant was in a position to control and guide the corporate body in terms of policy and strategy. This is, of course, a question of fact and degree in every case. Although it is still uncommon for individual prosecutions to be taken out against managers of corporate bodies, the Environment Agency has expressed an intention to use powers of prosecution against individuals where personal responsibility or neglect can be shown.

The position of companies' responsibility for the acts of their employees (i.e. vicarious liability) was considered in *National Rivers Authority* v *Alfred McAlpine Homes East Ltd* [1994] Env LR 198, where the defendant company was held to be vicariously liable for the acts of any of its employees, irrespective of whether those employees exercised control in terms of policy and strategy (see also *Shanks and McEwan (Teesside) Ltd* v *Environment Agency* [1997] Env LR 305 and p. 508 below). Interestingly, this decision can be contrasted with the approach to corporate liability taken in other areas where a company can only be held criminally liable for the acts of those who possess the 'controlling mind' of the company (see e.g. *Tesco Supermarkets Ltd* v *Nattrass* [1972] AC 153).

The activities which lead to breaches of environmental law are carried out by a diverse range of individuals and corporate bodies from huge multi-national corporations to solo fly-tippers. The identity of offenders can influence the enforcement style adopted by regulators. Partly this can be explained by reference to some of the other factors which have been discussed above. For example, it is much easier to classify environmental offences as 'white collar' or business crimes, and therefore as being morally neutral, where the defendant is a major corporation. On the other hand, in circum-stances where there is an individual who is responsible for the commission of an offence, there is likely to be criminal intent or negligence which makes, for example, prosecution much more likely.

Political factors — policies on enforcement

One of the findings of the different research projects carried out in the 1980s was that there were differing levels of enforcement in different geographical locations. For example, in *Policing Pollution*, it was shown that in a three-year period, one water authority brought 48 prosecutions for the contraventions of trade effluent consents (with 90 per cent coming from one area) whereas another did not bring any prosecutions during that time. There could be a number of explanations for regional variations in enforcement figures (e.g. a particular area might have a disproportionate number of breaches or 'difficult' operators), but it is primarily characteristic of the lack of uniformity created by a wide discretion. The research found that different officers were disturbed by this lack of consistency in enforcement practices. They favoured a more explicit policy applicable throughout different divisions. They were evidently anxious to ensure procedural reasonableness and the application of predeter-mined rules to guide the exercise of discretion.

The creation of new environmental agencies in the late 1980s saw the development of specific policies on enforcement which were designed to structure discretion and improve the consistency of enforcement style. Dur-ing its lifetime, the NRA had an enforcement policy which used prosecution as an active component and this approach has been adopted by the Environ-ment Agency which has a published *Enforcement and Prosecution Policy*. The Policy consists of a statement of the Agency's policies on enforcement and prosecution.

The Policy sets out four principles of enforcement. These are: propor-tionality in the application of law and in securing compliance; consistency of approach; transparency about how the Agency operates; and the targeting of enforcement action at activities which give rise to the most serious environmental damage or where the hazards are least well controlled. Prosecutions will 'normally' be taken in relation to incidents or breaches with significant environmental consequences; operating without the required licence, consent or authorisation; persistent or excessive breaches of statutory requirements; failure to comply with formal requirements to remedy environmental harm; 'reckless disregard' of environmental management or quality standards; and obstructing Agency staff in the gathering of information. Other influential factors are whether an incident was foreseeable, the intent of the offender, previous offences, and the deterrent effect of prosecuting.

In addition to the general policy on enforcement and prosecution, there are internal guidelines relating to particular offences and breaches. The so-called 'Functional Guidelines' are comprehensive, dealing with every aspect of the Agency's functions and set out the 'Common Incident Classification Scheme' (CICS) which is a national system for recording and categorising pollution incidents and assessing the appropriate level of enforcement response. The CICS classifies incidents in four categories from Category 1 (a major actual or potential environmental impact) to Category 4 (no actual or potential environmental impact). This general approach to categorising incidents is supplemented by different methods of enforcement in relation to each of the Agency's functions (i.e. environmental protection, water resources, fisheries, flood defence, and navigation). Each individual section includes details of: the purpose of enforcement for that function; the enforcement powers available; the factors determining enforcement action; enforcement for non-criminal non-compliance; and the various criminal offences and enforcement options.

Although these policies attempt to introduce some consistency to enforcement across the Agency, it is arguable that all they actually do is to formalise policies which had been used on an informal basis over a number of years. The policies are worded in such a way as not to restrict the Agency's enforcement discretion and it is doubtful whether any enforceable legal rights are created which can be relied upon by the regulated (e.g. a legitimate expectation that the Policy will be followed). This continuing discretion is reflected in the fact that there are still identifiable discrepancies in the numbers of prosecutions in different Environment Agency regions although this may be connected to the different ways in which a 'prosecution' is recorded in each region (which in turn makes the figures difficult to interpret because of inconsistencies in charging practices across the regions). The courts have made it clear that the decision to prosecute (or not, as the case may be) is essentially within the discretion of the regulatory authority and cannot be subject to challenge on anything other than on the ground of *Wednesbury* unreasonableness (see e.g. in relation to the decision to prosecute in general criminal offences, *R* v *Chief Constable of Kent and CPS, ex parte GL* (1991) 93 Cr App R 416 and *R* v *DPP ex parte Kebeline and others* (1999) 3 WLR 972 which suggested that in the absence of dishonesty, bad faith or other exceptional circumstance, a decision to prosecute was not amenable to judicial review).

In the light of the detailed nature of the internal and external enforcement policies of the Environment Agency, it is perhaps surprising to find that other bodies with environmental regulatory functions are not covered by such guidance. For example, local authority enforcement of the air pollution control system has been criticised as being inconsistent and 'ad hoc' (see DETR, *Local Authority Progress in Implementing the LAPC Regime*, October 1998). The Cabinet Office, through its Better Regulation initiative, has published an 'Enforcement Concordat' which local authorities have been urged to adopt. In the absence of more prescriptive guidance, however, it is likely that inconsistency and lack of transparency will continue.

The Enforcement Concordat is the latest stage of the development of deregulatory initiatives as an influence over enforcement policy. The move towards more complex environmental rules has led industry to argue that legislation is becoming too complex and compliance entails excessive expenditure in comparison with the environmental benefits which are produced. The introduction of the Deregulation and Contracting Out Act 1994 was considered to be an initial response to this alleged problem and the deregulatory thrust was continued into the Environment Act 1995 with general restrictions on enforcement such as the duty to consider the costs and benefits of taking enforcement action (s. 39) and other similar provisions (see p. 168). Ironically, the deregulation initiative which started out as a 'war on red tape' has now produced numerous administrative tests and policies which the Environment Agency is under a duty to consider before commencing enforcement action.

Future enforcement styles?

In some of the discussion of the various factors above, there is a suggestion that in recent years, there have been significant shifts in the institutional, legislative and cultural frameworks which help to shape the enforcement styles of environmental agencies. Although these changes are discernible, there has not been any notable shift in the incidence of enforcement actions in the case of the main environmental agencies (i.e. local authorities, the Environment Agency and English Nature). This raises questions about the development of enforcement style and whether the diverse factors make any real practical difference. One thing is certain — the factors governing any individual decision to enforce are still complex and differ on a case-by-case basis. It is, however, possible to identify a shift away from the traditional, historical views of the offender and the offence, and the publication of more formal policies on enforcement which bear out the redefinition of enforcement style.

Although decisions to prosecute or take other formal enforcement action are still made on a discretionary basis, there is much more public scrutiny of individual incidents and enforcement policy suggests that moral culpability is only one factor in determining whether to take action against an offender. It would be easy to overstate any shift in emphasis in enforcement style. The true picture is that cooperation between regulator and regulated has not broken down and in some cases, particularly where a voluntary approach is relied upon such as nature conservation, it is probably the case that the continuing relationship is vital to the effectiveness of the rules which are being enforced.

It is likely that the future style of enforcement will be eclectic with different approaches being taken in relation to different offenders. With more reliance on self-monitoring and inspection and voluntary performance indicators, such as accredited environmental management standards (e.g. ISO 14001), there will inevitably be a greater targeting of those who might be labelled 'free-riders' (i.e. allowing others to comply with legislative requirements whilst they evade responsibility). For example, the enforcement of packaging waste legislation has initially concentrated on those companies who have failed to register rather than monitoring those who have already registered.

This approach reflects the fact that the interpretation of enforcement practices is becoming more sophisticated. The brief coverage of the practical enforcement of environmental law in this chapter portrays only part of the process. For the sake of simplicity, enforcement is presented as a linear process whereby regulatory agencies seek compliance from the regulated. In fact, the European Commission and others have described enforcement as much more of a two-way process, akin to a chain where things can be learnt on both 'sides' of the enforcement fence. This means, for example, that where the Environment Agency identifies a problem with compliance rates in a particular area (e.g. packaging waste registrations), it can target that area until such time as compliance rates rise. Once this happens, there is less need to undertake enforcement and other areas of non-compliance can be targeted. A more general form of this two-way process involves the review of the reasons for non-compliance and the ineffectiveness of environmental regulation in the light of experience of the regulatory agencies and the regulated.

The logical conclusion of this targeted approach would be to differentiate between those offences which are 'regulatory' in nature (i.e. those where criminal intent or negligence is the cause), and cases involving serious harm to the environment or human health. Other jurisdictions such as the US use a greater selection of administrative or civil penalties including fixed fines to punish relatively minor breaches of the law. These have the advantage of freeing enforcement resources to concentrate on truly criminal activity. Although there are disadvantages which can be identified (e.g. giving the impression that environmental harm is 'routine' or allowing wealthy operators the right to pollute), these can be minimised by using cumulative penalties (e.g. the points system in motoring offences) and ensuring that when true environmental crimes come before the courts there are adequate powers to punish offenders.

Whatever style of enforcement is adopted in future, it is worth noting that there will continue to be incidents which cause significant pollution where no formal enforcement action is taken. The aftermath of the *Braer* oil pollution incident off the Shetland Islands is a good example of an event which caused significant environmental damage where no prosecution resulted. Perhaps this illustration is a postscript to the problems of enforcing environmental law in the real world: that there is no simplistic connection between criminal activity, environmental pollution and the imposition of appropriate enforcement mechanisms or sanctions.

TEN
Private law and environmental protection

The development of the law relating to the protection of the environment is not solely governed by the realm of public and administrative law. Although the spread of regulatory control has accelerated within the last 60 years, traditionally, at first glance anyway, private law has attempted to serve a similar function in controlling environmental damage. As we describe below, however, the similarity is often superficial: the essential characteristic of private law is to regulate relationships between individuals (as opposed to the public law which governs the activities of public bodies like the EA and regulates the relationship between the state and individuals) by the balancing of individual interests, such as competing uses of land, rather than environmental protection.

In this chapter we focus on the torts traditionally relied on in environmental litigation: private and public nuisance, trespass, negligence and the 'rule in *Rylands and Fletcher*'. We then outline some of the negative characteristics shared by these common law mechanisms, before offering a critique of the place of private law in modern environmental protection. After discussing some of the issues which arise when public law standards clash with private law rights, we discuss some possible future directions for private law, including placing civil liability on a statutory footing and the impact of human rights legislation.

The law of tort and environmental protection

This book does not attempt to give a comprehensive account of the law of tort which is more than adequately covered in specialist texts. However, the various torts and their general principles are outlined below, and illustrations given as to their usefulness in protecting environmental interests.

Private nuisance

The law of nuisance is concerned with the unlawful interference with a person's use or enjoyment of land, or of some right over or in connection with it. This definition illustrates one of the primary distinctions between nuisance and other torts in that the protection afforded is directed towards protecting proprietary interests rather than the control of an individual's conduct. The generality of the definition also means that private nuisance can take an infinite variety of forms (unlike statutory nuisance, which is restricted to quite a narrow range of nuisances; see Chapter 15).

The protection of proprietary rights can have the incidental effect of providing a general benefit to the wider community by achieving improvements in environmental quality. But there have been occasions where the effect upon the community has been a negative one. In *Bellew* v *Cement Ltd* [1948] IR 61, an interim injunction was granted to restrain the noisy blasting at a quarry. This remained effective for several months. The effect of this stoppage upon the supply of cement in Ireland was devastating as 80% of the cement used in Ireland was created by materials from the quarry and there was then a national housing shortage. Thus the court upheld the protection of the private right involved at the expense of employment and construction.

The basis for a claim in nuisance is founded upon a balancing exercise centred around the question of reasonableness. As was stated in *Sanders Clark* v *Grosvenor Mansions Co. Ltd* [1900] 2 Ch 373:

> . . . the court must consider whether the defendant is using his property reasonably or not. If he is using it reasonably, there is nothing which at law can be considered a nuisance; but if he is not using it reasonably . . . then the [claimant] is entitled to relief.

Thus, in attempting to assess liability in a nuisance claim, a balance is made between the reasonableness of the defendant's activity and its impact upon the claimant's proprietary rights. However, things like the everyday sounds of domestic life (e.g. normal conversations) cannot amount to a nuisance, since both parties would be committing a nuisance (*Baxter* v *Camden (No. 2)* [2000] Env LR 112).

(a) Balancing factors in private nuisance
In assessing where to strike the balance, a court will take into account a number of specific factors including the locality of the nuisance, the duration and extent of the nuisance, any hypersensitivity on the part of the claimant, and the defendant's conduct.

(i) The locality doctrine
The locality doctrine is usually traced to the decision in *St Helen's Smelting Co.* v *Tipping* (1865) 11 HL Cas 642. In the mid-nineteenth century, St Helens was the centre of the alkali industry. The average life expectancy was well under 25 and it had built up a reputation as one of the dirtiest towns in Britain. The physical impact of the works had left most vegetation in the area dead and adversely affected the health of cattle. Mr Tipping brought a claim in private nuisance. The court drew the distinction between actual physical damage to property and a nuisance which would only cause 'personal

discomfort'. In the latter situation, the locality of the nuisance would be a material factor in assessing the balancing exercise. In a famous quote in the case of *Sturges* v *Bridgman* (1879) 11 ChD 852, Thesiger LJ stated, 'What would be a nuisance in Belgrave Square would not necessarily be so in Bermondsey'. Or, as one commentator put it, 'Those who suffer most from the ravages of pollution are the least worthy of protection' (McLaren (1972) 10 Osgoode Hall LJ 505).

Although there is a distinction drawn between actual damage done to property and interference with the enjoyment of property, in practice there is often an overlap. It has been alleged that the economic effect of nuisance can be just as detrimental as physical damage to an interest in land. If, for instance, a house is situated by a pig farm, the smells emanating from that may well make the house less attractive to potential buyers, but under the locality doctrine it could be argued that in an agricultural area an owner has to expect such farmyard smells (see, however, *Wheeler* v *J.J. Saunders Ltd* [1996] Ch 19 discussed below at p. 284).

However, even in the most heavily industrialised areas, there is not an absolute freedom to produce polluting materials. An illustration was given in the case of *Rushmer* v *Polsue and Alfieri Ltd* [1906] 1 Ch 234, where Cozens-Hardy LJ said:

> It does not follow that because I live, say, in the manufacturing part of Sheffield I cannot complain if a steam-hammer is introduced next door, and so worked as to render sleep at night almost impossible, although previously to its introduction my house was a reasonably comfortable abode, having regard to the local standard; and it would be no answer to say that the steam-hammer is of the most modern approved pattern and is reasonably worked. In short, if a substantial addition is found as a fact in any particular case, it is no answer to say that the neighbourhood is noisy, and that the defendant's machinery is of first-class character.

In that case, there was an injunction sought against a printing press being operated in Fleet Street, even though there were many other printing presses in the area and others also operated at night. The House of Lords affirmed the decision of the Court of Appeal and granted the injunction.

An important issue is what, precisely, judges do in locality cases. In some cases, e.g. difficult questions may arise about the boundaries of the locality or the intensity of the activities carried on there. What judges may end up doing, therefore, may be as much about prescribing what activities can reasonably take place in any location as it is about reaching an objective judgment about the state of the area.

(ii) The duration and intensity of the nuisance
Not every interference with property will be actionable in nuisance (contrast trespass, discussed below). There must be some appreciable harm, even in cases of property damage. This rule applies more generally to all nuisance claims, and the courts will look among other things to the duration and intensity (or seriousness) of the activity complained of.

For a nuisance to be actionable it must be something which is more than temporary. Isolated incidents can give rise to a nuisance only where the use which gives rise to the risk of that isolated nuisance is of itself a continuing use. For example, a factory which produces fumes does not necessarily have to produce those fumes continuously over a period of years for there to be a nuisance. However, where there are isolated incidents occurring regularly then the use of the land for that purpose is of itself a nuisance. The more isolated the occurrence, however, the less the likelihood that the use being carried out is a nuisance. In *Harrison v Southwark and Vauxhall Water Co.* [1891] 2 Ch 409, the defendant was a water company which had dug a shaft to pump water from land adjacent to the plaintiffs. As the shaft was being sunk the pumps that were being used created a continuous noise. Mr Harrison brought a claim in nuisance to stop the noise. In finding against Mr Harrison the court held that the works were not actionable because they were temporary and that such temporary works would only be actionable if unreasonable methods were used, unless physical damage was caused. Vaughan Williams J said:

> For instance, a man who pulls down his house for the purpose of building a new one no doubt causes considerable inconvenience to his next door neighbours during the process of demolition; but he is not responsible as for a nuisance if he uses all reasonable skill and care to avoid annoyance to his neighbour by the works of demolition. Nor is he liable to [a claim], even though the noise and dust and the consequent annoyance be such as would constitute a nuisance if the same . . . had been created in sheer wantonness, or in the execution of works for a purpose involving a permanent continuance of the noise and dust.

Again, judicial thinking seems to have been affected by taking a realistic balance of the number and type of occurrences as against the utility involved in the operation itself.

It is unlikely that the former view that a nuisance must be capable of being sensed would now be upheld. Although in cases relating to the meaning of 'damage' it was once the law that damage could not be established by scientific evidence alone (*Salvin v North Brancepath Coal Co.* (1874) 9 Ch App 705) this view no longer holds. This can be seen in, for example, *Blue Circle Industries v Ministry of Defence* [1998] 3 All ER 385, a case on radiation contamination, discussed below at p. 286.

(iii)   The hypersensitive claimant

The test for assessing a nuisance has two elements. Not only must the use of land which is complained of be unreasonable, but also the use of the land to which the nuisance applies must be a reasonable use. If a potential claimant is particularly sensitive to one type of nuisance then it will not be actionable unless that nuisance would have affected a 'reasonable' person. In *Robinson v Kilvert* (1889) 41 ChD 88, the defendant let out part of his building to the claimant to be used as a paper warehouse. The defendant himself kept some of the space in the building for a particular use which required the air within the building to be kept hot and dry. This use had consequently heated the floor of the paper warehouse and damaged the paper kept there. Unfortunately, the paper stored in the upper rooms was of a particularly sensitive nature. Normal paper would not have been affected to such an extent. The defendant argued that the claimant had not told him of the intended use of the premises and in the particular circumstances the Court of Appeal held that there was no nuisance:

> A man who carries on an exceptionally delicate trade cannot complain because it is injured by his neighbour doing something which would not injure anything but an exceptionally delicate trade.

The effect of the rule laid down in that case is perhaps not as wide as first imagined. The principle only applies when the unreasonableness of the conduct is specifically the result of the hypersensitivity of the claimant. If there is an independent claim brought because of the inherent unreasonableness of the nuisance, then action can still be taken. In the Canadian case of *McKinnon Industries Ltd* v *Walker* [1951] 3 DLR 577, the defendants operated a motor car plant which emitted poisonous gases. The claimant grew orchids for sale and the gases killed off his stock. He brought an action in nuisance. The defendants argued that the growing of orchids was a hypersensitive activity and therefore any damage suffered was not as a result of the unreasonable use of land. The court disagreed and held that the nuisance was independent of the special sensitivity of the claimant.

Thus, in pollution cases, there will be very few occasions where this particular factor will be taken into account. Normally, the type of pollution complained of will be itself a cause of action which can cancel out any arguments put forward about hypersensitivity. In the case of possible contamination of organic crops by genetically modified pollen, however, it is not yet clear whether the claimant's use of his land would be seen as unduly sensitive, although there is a strong suggestion that it might be in *R* v *Secretary of State for the Environment and Ministry of Agriculture, Fisheries and Food, ex parte Watson* [1999] Env LR 310. Arguably, though, this view ignores the considerable increase in organic farming in recent times, although the issue does raise the interesting point as to whether government policy encouraging organic farming to reach a much higher market share makes any difference to whether the activity is sensitive.

(iv) Fault

The defendant's conduct will be a relevant consideration in those nuisance cases where the activity complained of has ceased. (Questions of fault, of course, do not arise in cases where the activity complained of is ongoing, and an injunction is being sought.) There are various factors that go to make up fault, including the forseeability of the damage caused and the cost of taking preventive action.

The view that liability in nuisance is 'strict', if it were ever true, has now receded with the decision of the House of Lords in *Cambridge Water Co.* v *Eastern Counties Leather plc* [1994] 2 AC 264. Eastern Counties Leather had for several years used particular solvents. Until 1976, the way that the solvent was delivered meant that there were often spillages. The solvent eventually found its way into underground strata and then into an aquifer from which the Cambridge Water Company abstracted water. In 1982 the water company began testing for the solvent in the water, because new drinking water standards under Directive 80/778/EEC, which included parameters for the solvent, were to come into force in 1985. The tests found high levels of solvent, traceable back to the leather works. The cheapest option for the water company was to close down the borehole and open a new source of supply. The water company sued the leather works in nuisance (and also negligence and *Rylands* v *Fletcher*, discussed below). The House of Lords overturned the decision of the Court of Appeal that liability was strict (based on *Ballard* v *Tomlinson* (1885) 29 Ch D 115) and held that liability depended on the foreseeability of the relevant type of damage occurring (i.e. the pollution of groundwater above the levels laid down in the Directive). In the only full judgment, Lord Goff argued that as regards foreseeability it would be unjust if liability for property damage under nuisance was stricter than liability for personal injury under negligence, at least in relation to the remoteness of damages. (Liability is still 'strict' in the sense that there is no need to prove that the defendant has been careless.) The water company's claim in nuisance was therefore unsuccessful. The costs incurred by the water company only arose because of the changes to the drinking water quality regulations, and the spillages had ceased before these came into force. (An interesting issue to consider is the fact that the Directive is based on World Health Organisation standards which date from 1970.)

It would seem that both the particular type of damage and the 'pollution pathway' must be foreseeable, although reference to the 'reasonable supervisor' and the actual staff at the leather company seems unduly restrictive of what it is that reasonable foreseeability requires. While the costs of preventing such a spill will not be a relevant factor — and to that extent also liability remains strict — investing in 'state of the art' pollution prevention technology and management systems may mean that liability is avoided because either the type of environmental damage caused or the way in which it is caused is unforeseen at the time. In this sense, adherence to current regulatory standards (e.g. an industrial process using BATNEEC) are likely to be directly relevant to whether there is liability in private law. In cases where the damage and its cause might be revealed not because of regulatory controls but if voluntary measures were followed — e.g. where a firm is seeking accreditation under the Eco-Management and Audit Scheme (see p. 210) — the position is less clear and seems inevitably to slide into questions of whether it would be reasonable for any particular industrial activity not to take such steps.

(b)   Who can sue (and be sued) in private nuisance?

Anyone who creates a nuisance, or anyone who occupies land from which a nuisance emanates and who continues or adopts the nuisance, may be liable. Occupiers will be responsible for the acts of their employees and even for acts of trespassers, and (although the basic rule is that tenants are responsible for their own nuisances) landlords may be liable in a number of situations. Importantly, a polluter may be sued even though they are only one of many contributing to the pollution. In *Graham and Graham* v *Re-Chem International Ltd* [1996] Env LR 158, although the claimants were ultimately unsuccessful, Forbes J accepted their argument that the defendant's dioxin emissions only had to amount to a 'material contribution' (a concept from the law of negligence, see below) to the damage to the claimant's cattle complained of.

The problem that has troubled the courts in recent years is who can bring a nuisance action. The issue has now been settled by the decision of the House of Lords in *Hunter* v *Canary Wharf Ltd* [1997] 2 WLR 684. In two separate actions, over 500 residents in London's Docklands brought actions against the developers of Canary Wharf and the London Docklands Development Corporation for nuisance arising out of interference with television signals from Canary Wharf Tower and damage from dust emissions from road construction respectively. The Court of Appeal had held that nuisance did not just protect property rights but anyone with a 'substantial link' with the enjoyment of the property as a home. This reflected the view that the old ideas of nuisance did not adequately protect the interests of those without legal interests in land, such as spouses and children. In the earlier case of *Khorasandjian* v *Bush* [1993] QB 727 there had been signs that the courts were now prepared to use private nuisance law to protect personal interests such as the right not to be harassed, and many had thought this marked the start of nuisance law developing in a way that might offer greater protection of wider environmental interests. But the House of Lords (by 4–1) rejected this approach, calculating the potential damages according to damage to the property interests. Damages, had they been awarded, would not have been dependent on the number of residents affected. (See further discussion at p. 276 below.) In doing so, the House of Lords strongly restated the view that the right to sue in private nuisance can only be exercised by those with rights to the land affected, usually freehold owners or tenants in possession.

(c) Defences to a claim for nuisance

There are a number of defences which attempt to restrict the scope of the law of nuisance. However, in practice, they are either so difficult to prove as to be useless, or of dubious merit.

(i) The defence of prescription

Although it is possible in principle to acquire a right to pollute as an easement through 20 years continuous use, there are so many caveats that the practical use of the defence is very restricted. For the defence to apply, the right to pollute must be exercised openly, continuously and not with any specific permission of the person against whom it is so acquired. It must also be the result of a lawful act, so a discharge in breach of a consent would not suffice. For example, in the case of *Sturges* v *Bridgman* (1879) 11 ChD 852, the defendant, a confectioner, had used a noisy pestle and mortar in his premises in Wimpole Street for more than 20 years. There had not been any complaints over that period but a doctor residing at the back of the site built a new consulting room close to the defendant's operational area. Consequently, the noise became a problem. The Court of Appeal held that the defendant in this case had not acquired a right to pollute by prescription. In the court's opinion, the nuisance had commenced only after the consulting room had been constructed, because previously the activities complained of did not give rise to any interference. When the consulting room was occupied, however, such interference began. Thus, the period of 20 years did not start to run until the construction of the consulting rooms.

(ii)   No defence to say that the claimant came to the nuisance
In *Bliss* v *Hall* (1838) 4 Bing NC 183, the defendant operated a business as a tallow chandler. This business had been operated for at least three years when the claimant moved in nearby. Unfortunately, the defendant's business created highly toxic fumes which were blown over the claimant's land. The defendant argued that, as he had been on the site before the claimant, the claimant should have realised the state of the premises nearby and should therefore not be able to bring a claim in nuisance. Tindal CJ said:

> The [claimant] came to the house he occupies with all the rights which the common law affords, and one of them is the right to wholesome air. Unless the Defendant shows a prescriptive right to carry on his business in the particular the [claimant] is entitled to judgment.

When this principle is combined with the principle contained in *Sturges* v *Bridgman*, it is clear that whenever an individual moves into an area there could be the creation of a new 'nuisance history' which negates the prescriptive rights principle because of the need to allow a further 20 years before a prescriptive right attaches. This might happen if there is a new development, or change to an existing use.

In practical terms, the principle that it is no defence for a defendant to allege that the claimant has come to the nuisance is very important. Many old factories constructed in early Victorian times have now been surrounded by new housing. These potentially antagonistic uses can give rise to conflict. On the one hand, industrialists argue that they have been carrying out polluting activities for a large number of years without complaint and anyone who moved into the area would fully know of any problems. Questions of locality, however, remain.

The courts have also held that a planning authority can grant planning permission for a new development even though this is likely to give rise to complaints from the new occupiers as a result of an existing incompatible use (see *R* v *Exeter City Council, ex parte J.L. Thomas and Co. Ltd* [1991] 1 QB 471).

(iii)   Statutory authority
There may be occasions where nuisances are caused by statutory or non-statutory bodies under statutory authority. Where a body can point to such

authority then this will amount to a defence if an action is brought against them for any reasonably consequential nuisance.

For example, in *Smeaton v Ilford Corporation* [1954] Ch 450, there were particular problems with the corporation's sewers. The nuisance complained of arose because the sewers in the area were overloaded as a consequence of many new houses in the area utilising their right to be connected to the existing sewer system. Unfortunately, the sewers were not able to cope properly with the amount of sewage. Furthermore, the local authority did not have powers to refuse to connect the houses to the existing sewer system. Upjohn J held that the overloaded sewers were not a nuisance, since the local authority had a statutory duty to take domestic sewage and could not refuse the amount that was causing an overflow. There is, of course, a degree of control over such difficulties by restricting the grant of planning permission for development of housing, or restricting housing development without proper provision being made for discharges to sewers.

Although most statutory obligations are expressly contained within the body of the statute itself, it is also clear that a defendant could claim the defence of statutory authority where there is a clear implication that such activities have been authorised by an Act. In *Allen v Gulf Oil Refining Ltd* [1981] AC 1001, the Gulf Oil Refining Act 1965 (a private Act of Parliament) gave the defendants power to acquire land for an oil refinery at Milford Haven. The oil refinery emitted smells, noise and vibration and a local resident brought a claim against Gulf Oil in nuisance. The claimant argued in that case that although the Act gave the defendant the power to acquire land for the construction of the refinery, it did not give any guidelines as to how the refinery should be operated. Therefore, when the defendant sought to rely upon the defence of statutory authority it was suggested that, as the Act did not specifically allow for the operating of the plant in a manner which gave rise to a nuisance, the defence was unavailable. The House of Lords held that the statute implicitly gave the defendant an immunity to every act inevitably flowing from the construction of the refinery. The only possible exception to this would be where the nuisance complained of was of a greater degree than was necessary or where such activities were carried out in a negligent manner.

It should be pointed out that, where private rights are interfered with, it is often the case that statutes themselves provide for compensation. For example, where a new road is being built, statutory compensation is payable where there is injurious affection to the enjoyment of property which is the direct result of the works carried out. There are, however, situations where the interference with private rights is not compensated. More general issues relating to where private rights clash with public interests (exemplified by recent cases on nuisance and planning permission but also seen in connection with human rights legislation) are discussed below (see p. 283).

Public nuisance

Although seemingly a close relative of private nuisance, the law relating to public nuisances contains some similar elements but as many distinguishing features. Public nuisance is primarily a crime involving nuisance affecting a section of the general public, although the law developed over time so that anyone suffering 'special damage' beyond that suffered by the public generally has a claim in tort. This need only be a different degree, rather than type, of harm, and may include purely economic losses. But in those environmental cases where all suffer equally, there would appear to be no remedy in public nuisance. Injunctions can be sought either by the Attorney-General or by local authorities, although individuals can take a claim with the Attorney-General's permission (a 'relator' action).

The case of *Attorney-General* v *PYA Quarries Ltd* [1957] 2 QB 169 shows the width of the class of persons that must be affected. The defendants operated a quarry. During operations they carried out various blasting activities. These caused vibration and noise over a wide area. In attempting to lay down guidelines, Denning LJ declined to specify what numbers would be required to show that a particular nuisance was public rather than private. But he did say (at p. 191):

> I prefer to look to the reason of the thing and to say that a public nuisance is a nuisance which is so widespread in its range or so indiscriminate in its effect that it would not be reasonable to expect one person to take proceedings . . . to put a stop to it, but that it should be taken on the responsibility of the community at large.

If the need to show an effect over a section of the public is set aside, there is a good degree of overlap with the factors that are taken into account when deciding whether or not there is a private nuisance. An example of a claim in public nuisance is *Gillingham Borough Council* v *Medway (Chatham) Dock Co. Ltd* [1993] QB 343 (see p. 284 below). Some would argue that nowadays public nuisance is something of an incongruous hybrid, relied on only in those cases where the deficiencies of other torts have been exposed. For others, it may represent the basis for developing an environmental tort action unconnected to land and capable of protecting wider community interests.

Trespass

Trespass is the direct interference with personal or proprietary rights without lawful excuse. Trespass is actionable *per se* (*Entick* v *Carrington* (1765) 19 St Tr 1029, 1066), that is, it does not require proof of damage. This is well illustrated in the use of trespass law by the League Against Cruel Sports to hamper deer hunting (*League Against Cruel Sports* v *Scott* [1985] 2 All ER 489). The League, which bought parcels of land on Exmoor, was successful in its action even though the hunt was not deliberately directed across its land. Simply walking over another's land without permission is sufficient basis under trespass for an injunction, even though no damage to property has been caused. By contrast, nuisance requires something consequential to the act complained of. For example, depositing waste on someone else's land will be a trespass, even if the waste can be removed without contaminating the soil or causing injury or disease. But if the waste is on other land but causing loss of amenity because of smells or is spreading disease, then the most likely remedy will be an action in nuisance, since the harm is a consequence of the deposit, not the deposit itself.

The need to show direct interference has been a problem in environmental disputes, as two cases illustrate. In *Esso Petroleum v Southport Corporation* [1956] AC 218 an oil tanker stranded in an estuary jettisoned oil to lighten the ship and to try to refloat. The oil drifted ashore and polluted the claimants' foreshore. The claimants (the Corporation) claimed for the costs of cleaning up the beach. Although trespass was not argued, two judges in the House of Lords thought that it would have failed since the pollution was not inevitable. This might be compared with a case like *Jones v Llanrwst UDC* [1911] 1 Ch 393, where the court did find that there was trespass when sewage was accidentally released and polluted the banks of a river downstream. In this case the interference was held to be direct, because of the natural flow of the river. By contrast, in the *Esso Petroleum* case, there was no inevitability about the deposit of oil on the foreshore, which depended on the action of the wind, waves and tide. Because of the requirement of directness, trespass to the *person* has not been properly developed in pollution cases, although in theory making someone inhale toxic fumes could give rise to an action.

If this requirement of directness is followed, it will be almost impossible to bring an action in trespass for air-borne pollution unless the pollutant is deposited directly over the claimant's property. In *Kerr et al v Revelstoke Building Materials Ltd* (1976) 71 DLR (3d) 134 (Alta SC), for example, the claimants could claim for damages to them and their livestock because the offending cropduster had passed directly over their farm. Had the plane only sprayed over its own property, and the chemicals been blown over onto the claimants' land, there would be no action in trespass, although arguably a nuisance action could be taken. For these reasons, a challenge to the spread of pollen from genetically modified crops would have to be taken under nuisance law, either where the pollen was blown in the wind or, most likely, if it was brought on to the claimant's land by bees.

Trespass must also be intentional or negligent. *McDonald v Associated Fuels Ltd* [1954] 3 DLR 775 illustrates the distinction well. Sawdust fuel was being supplied to the claimant's house. To deliver it, the defendants parked their truck and blew the sawdust into a bin inside the house by means of a blower unit. Unfortunately, the intake mechanism for the sawdust was too close to the truck's exhaust system, and both the sawdust and carbon monoxide fumes blew into the house. The occupants were overcome, one breaking a hip on collapsing. It is clear here that the trespass itself (i.e. the entrance of the carbon monoxide directly into the house) was not intentional, but the act which caused the trespass was.

Two further points can be made about trespass law. Both can be seen in *Monsanto v Tilly* [2000] Env LR 313, a case involving direct action by members of the campaigning group GenetiX Snowball to destroy genetically modified crops at trial farm sites. The first was whether Monsanto, by entering into an agreement with the farmer but not actually owning or occupying the site, had sufficient interest to bring a trespass claim. The Court of Appeal held that it did (although in another case it has held that a developer which just had a right of access on to land to carry out surveys did not have a right of possession to maintain a trespass claim against a protester; see *Countryside Residential (North Thames) Ltd* v *Tugwell* (*The Times*, 4 April 2000)).

The second issue was whether the trespass was necessary because, so the protesters alleged, destroying the crops was to protect third parties or the general public from harm. This line of defence is always difficult to rely on, and the Court of Appeal took a rather dim view of this, deciding that the protesters were really after publicity (they had arranged in advance for the press to be there, and in the event pulled up very few plants). In any event central government had responsibility for ensuring that the trials were carried out safely, so it would be difficult to justify third party intervention of this kind. Depending on how strictly this approach is taken it might mean, for example, that individuals could not cross another's land to stop water being polluted by escaping chemicals, since the Environment Agency has a range of powers to deal with this (although in practice the landowner would have little interest in suing for trespass).

Negligence

The law of negligence is a particularly large area of tort law, and this book does not try to outline any more than its rudimentary features. The degree of coverage is also related to the general lack of utility of the law of negligence in environmental protection.

The three main principles of negligence are that the claimant must establish that (a) a duty of care is owed by the defendant to the claimant; (b) that the defendant has breached that duty; and (c) there has been foreseeable damage to the claimant resulting from the breach. There is no need to show a property interest, and so anyone who suffers damage from an act of negligence can bring a claim.

A key drawback of negligence is that it is a fault-based system; to succeed, there has to be some fault of the defendant. Compared with nuisance, for example, what is at issue is not the reasonableness of the use of the land but the reasonableness of the defendant's actions. In nuisance, as *Graham and Graham* v *Re-Chem* (see p. 263) shows, it is no defence to argue that state of the art technology is being used. But in negligence this is likely to be a critical factor, and compliance with current regulatory standards will be sufficient to avoid liability. Negligence therefore tends to be relied on only where other common law remedies are not available. It is also necessary to foresee the type of harm that will result from an activity. In the *Cambridge Water Co.* case discussed on p. 261 above, therefore, the claim in negligence was dismissed at first instance because at the time of the spillages the reasonable supervisor could not have foreseen the changes to the drinking water regulations (and possibly also the pollution pathway). The House of Lords confirmed that it would not be sufficient to show that 'pollution' could have been foreseen, as that is too wide a category of damages.

But compared with trespass, for example, negligence (as with nuisance) requires proof that the defendant has caused damage to the claimant. Particularly in the so-called 'toxic tort' cases, this may be difficult, time-consuming and expensive. *Graham and Graham* and the Sellafield leukaemia litigation (*Reay and Hope* v *BNFL* [1994] 5 Med LR 1) are both prime examples of the evidential and technical difficulties involved in proving a case, the latter an especially chilling reminder of the problems of relying on epidemiological evidence. Claimants may also be in a quandary because of the rules on the time limits for bringing cases. Waiting for certain proof of actual damage runs the risk that the court may say that the damage actually began beyond the limitation period.

Despite the frequent use of negligence in everyday legal life, it is perhaps surprising to find just how little it has been used to try to control environmental pollution. This appears to be changing slightly, perhaps in part because of the actions of a number of campaigning lawyers prepared to take on toxic tort cases. An example of a successful negligence action in the environmental field is *Tutton* v *A. D. Walker Ltd* [1986] QB 61, which involved the use of insecticide. Farmers had been advised by the manufacturers and by central government that using a particular insecticide when oilseed rape was flowering could lead to the death of insects such as bees. Furthermore, they were told that the insecticide was most effectively used after the flowering period. But the defendant sprayed his crop whilst the rape was in flower and a number of bees owned by the claimant were killed. The farmer was held liable for negligent use of the insecticide.

There are also cases where a failure to warn about environmental damage has been found to be negligent. In *Barnes* v *Irwell Valley Water Board* [1930] 1 KB 21 there was held to be a common law duty of care on a water company to warn consumers of potentially unwholesome water and damages in negligence were recoverable. The application of this principle in relation to regulatory authorities can be seen in *Scott-Whitehead* v *National Coal Board* (1987) P & CR 263. The defendants discharged a chlorine solution into a river. Because the river was in drought there was insufficient water to dilute the strength of the pollutant. The claimant farmer abstracted water downstream, causing damage to his crops. The second defendant, the regional water authority, was held liable for failing to warn the farmer of the potential danger from the condition of the water it knew was being abstracted. Extending the principle in this case, it would be possible to bring an action against an environmental regulator in negligence if it could be shown that a failure to warn materially contributed to damage. However, there appear to be no reported decisions where this has happened, and any such argument would now have to overcome the general judicial reluctance to impose private law duties on public bodies, as seen in *X (Minors)* v *Bedfordshire County Council* [1995] 2 AC 633. In a fairly extreme case, the failure to warn of an environmental risk has been held to be a violation of the human right to home life (see *Guerra* v *Italy* (1998) 26 EHRR 357, discussed further at p. 222).

The rule in *Rylands* v *Fletcher*

The principle known as 'the rule in *Rylands* v *Fletcher*' was first established in the case of that name ((1868) LR 3 HL 330). The defendant constructed a reservoir on his land, but the contractors failed to detect and block off mine shafts so that, when the reservoir filled up, water entered the shafts and flooded the claimant's mine. The problem was that there could be no action in negligence as the law then stood (there was no relationship between the contractor and the mine-owner) and, because it was an isolated escape, a nuisance action was thought to be precluded. In the lower court, Blackburn J first expounded the principle:

> . . . that the person who for his own purposes brings onto his land and collects and keeps there anything likely to do mischief if it escapes, must keep it at his peril, and, if he does not do so, is prima facie answerable for all the damage which is the natural consequence of its escape.

(a)   Non-natural use
In the House of Lords, however, the qualification was added that there would only be an action where there was a 'non-natural use' being made of the defendant's land. Originally this may have meant that there would have been no liability if the water (in *Rylands*) had been a natural lake or naturally flooded area rather than an artificial reservoir. But in time it came to mean that the use had to be 'some special use bringing with it increased danger to others and must not merely be the ordinary use of land or such a use as is proper for the general benefit of the community' (*Rickards* v *Lothian* [1913] AC 263). Over the years this was applied to numerous activities, so that 'natural' became synonymous with anything for the general public benefit, no matter how *un*natural. The high point was perhaps reached in *Read* v *Lyons* [1947] AC 156. The defendants made high explosive shells for the government. Ms Read was an inspector in the factory in 1942 when there was an explosion in which she was injured. The defendants had not been negligent, but she argued that they were engaged in a manufacturing process known to be highly dangerous and that the rule in *Rylands* ought to apply. In the House of Lords, Lord Macmillan said:

> Every activity in which man engages is fraught with some possible element of danger to others. Experience shows that even from acts apparently innocuous, injury to others may result. The more dangerous the act the greater is the care that must be taken in performing it . . . one who engages in obviously dangerous operations must be taken to know that if he does not take special precautions, injury to others may very well result. In my opinion it would be impracticable to frame a legal classification of things as things dangerous and things not dangerous, attaching absolute liability in the case of the former but not in the case of the latter . . . accordingly I am unable to accept the proposition that in law the manufacture of high-explosive shells is a dangerous operation which imposes on the manufacturer an absolute liability . . .

This decision may well have been influenced by the ongoing war effort at the time of the accident. But what is more important is that the House of Lords explicitly refused to extend the doctrine into a general theory of strict liability for ultra-hazardous activities which, of course, would have had profound implications for the development of environmentally hazardous technologies. The House of Lords again took this approach in *Cambridge Water Co.* v *Eastern Counties Leather* (see p. 261). But by contrast to the judge at first instance, who had considered the location of the tannery to be an 'industrial village' and refused liability under *Rylands* on the ground of natural use, Lord Goff took a different approach and noted that 'the storage of substantial quantities of chemicals on industrial premises was an almost classic case of non-natural use'. No mention was made as to whether acting lawfully under a planning permission or environmental licence would have affected this view. In all the comment about the restrictions on the use of the rule following *Cambridge Water* (discussed below) it is perhaps surprising that more attention has not been paid to this part of the judgment which, although not necessary for Lord Goff to reach his decision, would in practice expand the scope of liability if followed in later cases. Nor has there been much attention given to the suggestion in Lord Goff's speech of a relationship between 'natural use' and the 'reasonable user' test in nuisance. Not all industrial activities are 'unreasonable', not least those which are operating properly under regulation. Elsewhere, however, he equates 'natural use' with 'ordinary use', which further muddies the waters.

The issue of the 'naturalness' of the activity is not unrelated to its dangerousness, i.e. whether it will do 'mischief'. Over the years the rule has been applied in relation to water, fire, gases, electricity, oil, chemicals, colliery spoil, poisonous vegetation and even a fairground chair-o-plane. As seen above, the courts are reluctant to attempt to define what a dangerous or hazardous activity is, and have resisted a general definition. In this sense the approach mirrors that taken to what might amount to a 'nuisance' at common law.

(b) Other features of the use of the rule

There are other features of the rule in *Rylands* which were not directly addressed in *Cambridge Water*. Unlike nuisance, it appears that the claimant does not need to have an interest in land to invoke the rule. In *Halsey* v *Esso Petroleum* [1961] 2 All ER 145, for example, the claimant recovered not just for damage caused by noxious acid smuts to his land but also to his car parked on the highway. And there is at least some doubt whether the rule applies in personal injury cases. It is probable that the effect of Lord Goff's insistence in *Cambridge Water* that the rule in *Rylands* is really just a part of nuisance law, combined with the decision of the House of Lords in *Hunter* v *Canary Wharf* (see p. 263) restricting the right to sue in nuisance cases to proprietors, is similarly to restrict the right to sue following incidences of one-off escapes. *Cambridge Water* probably also now means that *Rylands* can no longer be used to claim for personal injury losses. What is clear, however, is that the balancing act between relaxing 'non-natural use' and now stipulating the reasonable foreseeability of the damage allows the courts to continue to pay attention to the costs of preventing damage arising.

Some important restrictions should be noted. First, the effect of the escape must be felt beyond the defendant's land, although it need not be the substance accumulated which escapes. This can be seen in *Rainham Chemical Works Ltd* v *Belvedere Fish Guano Co.* [1921] 2 AC 465, where a munitions factory exploded. The claim did not fail just because it was the bits of the factory, rather than the dangerous substance stored, that escaped. But where damage is confined to the defendant's property, as in *Read* v *Lyons*, there is no escape and no claim. This seems to be as irrelevant environmentally as it is offensive socially.

(c) Defences

There are a number of defences to an action brought under the *Rylands* rule. Perhaps the most notable is that there is a defence where the claimant benefits from the harmful activity. Thus, where gas, electricity or water supplies have caused damage to the claimant's property, no liability will accrue. The reasoning would appear to be that the defence is simply an extension of the defence of consent (see *Attorney-General* v *Cory Brothers & Co.* [1921] 1 AC 521). But to take the defence so far that any utility provider enjoyed immunity from *Rylands*-based liability because of the general 'common benefit' (as suggested in *Dunne* v *North Western Gas Board* [1963] 3 All ER 916) goes too far, extending the principle from one of risk-sharing to risk-imposing.

As with nuisance, the defence of statutory authority may be argued (see *Smeaton* v *Ilford Corporation* [1954] Ch 454). It may also be argued that the escape was an 'Act of God', although in the nature of especially risky activities it must be the case that greater foresight and consideration is required than other situations where this defence can be argued. (If it were not covered by specific legislation, nuclear installations would be a prime example.)

The protection of riparian rights

There is a separate action for interference with the rights of owners of riparian land. Although this action has some similarities with private nuisance, it is in practice used far more frequently owing to the strength of riparian owners' natural rights to water. For further explanation see p. 607.

Breach of statutory duty

Where there is a breach of a statutory provision, so that a claimant suffers a loss, there may be a remedy in damages. Although there does not have to be any finding of negligence by the defendant, the tort is little used because the courts have held that a claim will succeed only if it can be shown that Parliament intended the claimant to have a civil remedy. Sometimes it is clear that Parliament specifically excludes this possibility, as is the case under the Water Resources Act 1991 (see s. 100(b)). Otherwise, if this is not spelt out in the statute, then it must be inferred, and if the statute involves general public law duties, then the broader the exercise of discretion involved the less likely will be a right of claim for breach of statutory duty (*X (Minors)* v *Bedfordshire County Council* [1995] 2 AC 633). Also, the statute must give rights to a limited class of persons rather than to the general public, which makes its application in relation to general pollution control legislation difficult. It is used most frequently in relation to industrial safety legislation, but one example of its use in an environmental context was following the incident at Camelford in 1988 when 20 tonnes of aluminium sulphate wrongly ended up in the public water supply. The water authority eventually ended up settling the case out of court on the basis of a breach of its statutory water supply duties (see also *Read* v *Croydon Corporation* [1938] 4 All ER 631, discussed at p. 574). The Camelford incident was one reason why there is now a specific offence of supplying water that is unfit for human consumption under the Water Industry Act 1991, s. 70.

The common view is that if the statute provides for criminal enforcement then this rules out civil claims. This is said to be because the criminal sanctions show that the interests of those affected are being taken seriously, although this would also support the view that this is precisely why civil claims for damages should also be available. Breach of statutory duty was argued before the High Court in *Bowden* v *South West Water Services Ltd* [1998] Env LR 445 and rejected, because the judge thought that the three directives concerned were all too general in their application. However, the overturning of this decision in relation to the Directive on Shellfish Waters for the purposes of a state liability claim under the *Francovich* principle — because the directive was for the direct benefit of a limited class of shellfisher-men — might suggest that a similar view could be taken in relation to breach of statutory duty ([1999] Env LR 438; see further p. 608). Ultimately, however, the point remains that legislation intended to protect general environmental interests and which gives public authorities some discretion in implementation (such as in determining a licence), is unlikely to lead to a successful claim for breach of statutory duty.

Other private law mechanisms

Although the most common application of private law remedies as used for environmental protection is that of the law of tort, there are other private law mechanisms that may be useful in this context. Centrally, the law relating to property ownership shows both advantages and disadvantages for environ-mental protection. Using property law to exclude others from encroaching or trespassing on land has often been relied on by voluntary organisations like the Royal Society for the Protection of Birds to protect habitats, or by bodies like the National Trust to protect cherished landscape features. However, the reverse of this is that, as a matter of property law, owners are in principle allowed to interfere with their land in any way they wish. So, wild plants can be uprooted and land contaminated so long as neighbouring landowners are not affected. Similarly, restrictive covenants may regulate future land devel-opment (see *Tulk* v *Moxhay* (1848) 41 ER 1143). This may help prevent damaging development, but preservation and 'doing nothing' are not always compatible with enlightened environmental protection and, in any case, their use is ultimately subject to statutory control.

Another example are planning obligations (see p. 330) which can provide both for negative restrictions or for positive environmental benefits. Although such obligations are the creation of statute, developers and local planning authorities are given considerable width to enter into them. When they do so, they are contacts between the developer and the planning authority, and agreements entered into after the Contracts (Rights of Third Parties) Act 1999 came into force might be enforceable by local residents for whose benefits the agreements are undoubtedly made.

More recognisably, contractual agreements are also used in the form of management agreements such as those made under s. 95, Water Resources Act 1991. These are essentially contracts between the Ministry of Agriculture, Fisheries and Food and individuals to restrict the use of certain agricultural activities to reduce water pollution by nitrates so that the nitrates used in farming will not pollute the waters in the areas (see p. 602). The agreements may be entered into voluntarily, and compensation is payable under them for any restrictions. These types of management agreements are not as wide-ranging as freehold or leasehold covenants as they are not necessarily binding on third parties (unless of course statute makes them so). There is some use of private agreements between industrial organisations (like the Chemical Industries Association) and government, but so far these are limited. Contracts will have to be used where, under an environmental management system, for example, the whole of the supply chain must operate to certain standards.

Civil law remedies

The use of the common law as a mechanism for environmental protection would be useless unless there were effective remedies once a cause of claim had been established. There are three main types of remedies that can be sought: preventive and compensatory remedies, and abatement (self-help). An injunction allows for actions creating environmental problems to be stopped by order of the court. Monetary damages act as compensation for any damage suffered but can also pay for any clean up costs involved in rectifying the damage. Finally, there are limited circumstances where claimants can take action without resort to the courts to abate activities causing environmental harm.

As can be seen below, common law remedies have both positive and negative features when it comes to protecting the environment. On the positive side, the courts tend to treat remedies as following directly from the right that has been infringed. That is, they do not engage in a further balancing exercise between the claimant's rights and the defendant's (or wider social) interests. This is seen most clearly in relation to the preference for granting injunctions rather than awarding damages. Negatively, remedies are available to benefit claimants' rights not environmental interests. So, for example, damages need not be spent on restoring the environment.

(a) Injunctions

The granting of an injunction is a discretionary remedy that can either prohibit or restrict a defendant from carrying on an environmentally damaging activity. Normally, either the activity complained of has to be continuing at the date of claim, or there has to be a threat that the activity will continue. Even where the activity has ceased at the time of trial, an injunction can still be sought if it existed when the claim was brought. Although injunctions are discretionary, however, the general principle in the two torts where continuing damage is likely — nuisance and trespass — is that claimants can expect to obtain an injunction unless the activity complained of is not of sufficient gravity or duration to justify stopping the defendant's actions. Turner LJ in *Goldsmith* v *Tunbridge Wells Improvement Commission* (1866) LR 1 Ch App 349 said:

> It is not in every case of nuisance that this Court should interfere. I think that it ought not to do so in cases in which the injury is merely temporary or trifling; but I think that it ought to do so in cases in which the injury is permanent and serious; and in determining whether the injury is serious or not, regard must be had to all the consequences which may flow from it.

This principle was affirmed in *Kennaway* v *Thompson* [1981] QB 88, a complaint about noise from powerboat racing. The Court of Appeal decided to award the claimant an injunction restricting the times the boats raced and the noise they made, notwithstanding the public interest in the sport. The importance of this decision is that it confirms that a party which causes a nuisance or trespass cannot simply 'buy off' the rights of those affected by paying an award of damages. In the case of multi-party claims, of course, it is debatable whether courts could ever properly assess the right amount of damages payable if damages were ever to be preferred to injunctions on economic efficiency grounds.

There are situations where it is possible to obtain an injunction before the occurrence of the event causing injury or damage. Such anticipatory injunctions do not require proof of environmental damage at all. However, there must be sufficient proof of imminent damage and it must be demonstrated that if the activity were to continue the damage accruing would be significant enough to make it difficult to rectify. Such injunctions are seldom granted.

Injunctions are rarely specific in nature; the court merely sets the standard for the defendant to meet and this standard can be achieved in any way possible. For example, it may be met either by closing down a particular plant which is causing environmental difficulties or by fitting new arrestment equipment. To give defendants time to make such changes, injunctions are often 'suspended' for a certain period before being enforceable (an example being *Pride of Derby and Derbyshire Angling Association Ltd* v *British Celanese* [1953] Ch 149, see p. 609).

(b) Damages

Unlike an injunction, a claimant can *demand* that the court award damages. The aim of such damages is to place the claimant as far as possible in the position they would have been in had the wrongful act not occurred. This could be calculated in two ways; on the cost of clean-up operations necessary to restore the property to its previous state, or the difference between the value of the property as it was after the pollution had affected it, and before. The approach of the courts now, however, is to calculate damages according to the latter method. So, where there has not been physical damage, damages will be based on the difference in possible rental value during the period of the nuisance (see *Hunter* v *Canary Wharf*). This means that damages will not depend on the number of people affected, in line with the idea that nuisance is a *land* tort.

However, if there is actual damage this will have to be compensated. An example of this is *Marquis of Granby* v *Bakewell UDC* (1923) 87 JP 105, the defendant operated a gas works which discharged poisonous effluent into a river over which the claimant had fishing rights, killing numerous fish. The claimant received compensation equalling the costs of restocking the river in addition to the loss of a large amount of the food supply for other stocks. The court also took into account the effects of the pollution on higher quality areas of the river and considered that the damages would be higher where environmental pollution was greater.

Damages for all *future* loss are only available in lieu of an injunction. This remedy is used only sparingly because of the ready availability of the more usual injunction procedure.

Lastly, exemplary or punitive damages can be awarded in specific instances. The basis of such an award is to deter the defendant and others from committing torts which may result in financial benefit to the person responsible. The scope for these damages is, however, limited to classes of tort which were the subject of an award of exemplary damages before 1964 (*A.B.* v *South West Water Services Ltd* [1993] QB 507) and cases where there has been oppressive, arbitrary or unconstitutional action by servants of the government, or where the defendant's conduct was calculated to make a profit which would exceed the damages payable (*Rookes* v *Barnard* [1964] AC 1129). Thus a claim for exemplary damages in public nuisance after the public water supply was polluted was rejected on the ground that public nuisance fell outside the above categories (*A.B.* v *South West Water Services Ltd*, above).

(c) Abatement

The remedy of abatement tends to be more of historic interest than practical use. The remedy involves the removal of a nuisance by the injured party without recourse to legal proceedings. The courts view this remedy unfavourably, and it now appears to be confined to simple cases where resort to legal proceedings would be inappropriate, or where urgent action is evidently needed. An example of the use of abatement is *Lemmon* v *Webb* [1895] AC 1, where action was taken to trim back the branch of a tree that encroached on land from a neighbouring site. Any damages subsequent to an abatement action are restricted to damages in respect of harm prior to the abatement.

The utility of private law for environmental protection

As the brief analysis above of the various private law mechanisms makes clear, there are a number of general limitations on the use of private law (especially tort law) to protect environmental interests. There is also the key issue of the affordability of private law claims and other practical difficulties in its use.

(a) Private law acts only as a protector of private interests

Both the land torts and the contractual mechanisms considered above aim to protect private interests rather than the more nebulous concept of environmental 'rights' or 'interests'. This has two important consequences. First, the level of environmental protection that flows from these mechanisms will be determined according to private rather than public interests. *Cambridge Water Co.* v *Eastern Counties Leather* (see p. 261) is a paradigm example, where the damages sought by the water company would, had it been successful, have paid for the relocation of its borehole to an unpolluted site. Whichever way the case was decided, the land and groundwater remained contaminated. Private law will only lead to the remediation of such sites if this is the cheapest way for the claimant to be compensated. Another negative example is the possibility that an easement to pollute a river might be acquired. It is arguable whether such a claim could ever be in the interests of the environment.

Secondly, the right to bring a claim is generally restricted in some way. For example, private nuisance claims are restricted in this way. On the other hand, under the Contracts (Rights of Third Parties) Act 1999, a third party can now sue on a contract and this means that local residents might be able to enforce agreements entered into between planning authorities and developers (see further p. 331). Although there are narrow rights for groups to take action in public nuisance, private law mechanisms serve narrowly drawn private interests. Even where a private right can be argued, the substance of the right may do little to improve the environment of those who would stand to benefit the most from such improvements, as the operation of the locality rule in private nuisance shows.

In both cases, effective environmental protection requires wider public interests to be taken into account, including both wider ecological interests and the interests of non-land owners and perhaps also of future generations. It is true, of course, that the exercise of private rights may coincide with the protection of wider ecological interests. But English private law seems a long way off accepting the idea that, for example, there should be scope to bring a claim on behalf of wild plants and animals rather as children bring claims through a guardian in family law proceedings.

(b) Private rights are based on imprecise or unduly absolute standards

As we have seen in Chapter 7, environmental regulation increasingly involves the setting both of specific target standards and then specifically worded licences to try to meet these standards. Often, both of these will be expressed as quantitative limits. One advantage of these is that they make enforcement easier as the detection of breaches can be accurately monitored and proper assessments made of any discharge. There are, of course, a range of more qualitative standards that are used. The BATNEEC standard in IPC authorisations is perhaps the best example, but even with BATNEEC there is quite detailed guidance given to operators as to what standards will be required. The effective regulation of many industrial processes can only be dealt with through quantitative standards and scientific monitoring.

Private law mechanisms meet neither criteria. Generally the common law is based upon standards which are either unduly tightly drawn or necessarily imprecise. Both have their drawbacks. For example, trespass law does not require any proof of damage, and therefore provides a fairly absolute protection of property rights. While this level of protection does have its environmental advantages (e.g. in conserving nature conservation sites) the more general problem is that trespass law does not allow for the kind of balancing which might be needed in other contexts and arguably over-regulates in some situations, which may not be in the wider public interest. It also has the drawback that the absolute protection afforded to landowners' interests might be judged by some to prevent a wider experience of nature (although to some extent this is being rectified in the Countryside and Rights of Way Bill which will establish a limited 'right to roam').

In the case of imprecise standards, as we see clearly in nuisance law, the law tries to balance competing private interests, looking to the reasonableness of the activities rather than restricting conduct to specified levels. What is reasonable depends on the circumstances of each case. While this may be necessary in order to deal with disputes over matters as subjective as some noise nuisances, it makes the outcome of a nuisance claim highly uncertain, especially where it involves amenity damage. Inevitably, this uncertainty discourages arguable cases from being brought.

(c)   Problems of proof

Environmental regulation typically involves the setting of standards which, if exceeded, lead to a punishable breach. Standards may either be breached without damage to the environment (this may happen with 'technical' breaches of process standards), or they are breached because some quantitative standard has not been met. The key point is that there will usually be some monitoring on the site recording the breach; only rarely does the regulator have to take samples from the environment and try to establish where the pollutant came from. This, however, is often what has to be done in environmental tort claims. For instance, it is the nature of airborne deposits that they could have originated from a site many miles from the area of the damage. Seeking to show that the damage emanates from a particular site in these circumstances is particularly difficult. In heavily industrialised areas the problem is even more acute.

The common law does go some way towards solving this problem. As we have seen, it will be enough in negligence and nuisance to show that the defendant 'materially contributed' to the damage caused, even where his or her own contribution was insignificant if viewed in isolation (see p. 263). This is an important rule, especially in those situations where it would be impossible to pin down the exact contribution of any one polluter, as with nitrate run-off. Nevertheless, it has its limits. First, it is not enough to show that the damage is of the kind generally associated with operators like the defendant, as *Cambridge Water Co. v Eastern Counties Leather* illustrates. Secondly, there are practical and evidential limits: there must be evidence linking the defendant's operations with the damage caused, and proving causation is often technically difficult and very costly. Thirdly, and rather obviously, the rule is of no practical use where environmental damage has a vast number of small contributors (e.g. low level ozone pollution from motor vehicles).

(d) Private law as a fault-based system

Although trespass gives rise to strict liability, in other circumstances the bringing of a claim under common law either requires some carelessness on behalf of the person creating the damage (negligence), or at least foreseeability of the damage caused (nuisance). But most pollution loading, and isolated pollution spills, does not occur because of deliberate actions by careless and unthinking individuals. Most pollution incidents arise because of a number of circumstances that would not normally be foreseeable but which give rise to damage. In the interests of doing justice to defendants, the common law does not always seek to redress any damage caused by such accidents. Clearly, this is contrary to the general thrust of the polluter pays principle.

(e) Reactive controls

Private law controls are generally reactive and compensatory rather than preventive. It is only very rarely that private law can be used to prevent environmental damage, although it is possible in limited situations to seek anticipatory injunctions. While the priority given to injunctions over damages in nuisance law is beneficial, private law does not offer continuing controls which might gradually improve standards over time.

(f) An environmental injustice?

Despite many negative features, the common law torts contain a range of general principles that ought in theory to have gone much further in protecting both human and wider environmental interests. Instead, the need for environmental regulation was recognised at a relatively early stage of industrialisation. In large part this was because of an under-utilisation of the common law, for a number of connected social, political and economic reasons.

Resort to the law in the nineteenth century was always a rich person's prerogative. Taking a claim to law was both lengthy and ultimately outside the reach of the vast majority of the population. Until 1875 a claim in nuisance seeking an injunction needed two claims to be taken, one through the common law and one through the Court of Chancery. Lack of access to technical knowledge and resources followed inevitably from poverty, and made monitoring almost impossible.

Also, as we have seen, bringing a claim in nuisance required a proprietary interest. In the mid nineteenth century it has been estimated that only around 15 per cent of the population were owner/occupiers. Thus, the vast majority of the population would have had great difficulty in even founding a claim. When coupled with the level of damages, notoriously low for interference with the enjoyment of land, there were considerable obstacles to taking legal action.

Moreover, what has subsequently been identified as a complex system of power relationships ensured that in the social context there was tremendous pressure not to 'cause trouble'. Few workers would wish to proceed against their bosses and it was clear that there was a certain degree of class solidarity amongst the industrialists themselves. The perceived economic benefits to the local community were inevitably to the fore in the minds of the local authorities, who were most reluctant to use their powers to prosecute for public nuisances, and indeed were often responsible for much pollution themselves. Moreover, many factory owners bought up large areas of land surrounding their own sites and constructed low cost, high density housing for their workers. This, coupled with the impact of industry on surrounding land prices, effectively meant that a factory owner could purchase the right to pollute the surrounding area very cheaply. (Of course, the landowner would be most likely to have lived upwind of the prevailing westerly winds, one factor behind the association of affluence with the 'West End'; see p. 250.

Furthermore, the relative expense of bringing private law actions is well illustrated by the Third Report of the Royal Commission on the Pollution of Rivers in 1867:

[Bringing a common law claim] is an expensive remedy. For the same money which is spent over a hard fought litigation against a single manufacturer, a Conservancy Board armed with proper powers, might for years keep safe from all abuse, a long extensive river with hundreds of manufacturers situated on its banks.

St Helens Smelting Co. v Tipping (see p. 258) illustrates some of these points well. Mr. Tipping was a rich cotton magnate who owned 1300 acres of land. He could afford to risk the backlash of industrialists because of the well-documented conflict between the cotton and chemical industries. The damages received in his case and also in other nuisance cases were appallingly low. And in Halsey v Esso Petroleum (see p. 271) the claimant received only £200 damages following five years of noise, dirt and commotion from the neighbouring oil storage depot. This raises another problem with nuisance claims, namely that the effect of the locality rule means that any damages that *are* awarded may be small, reducing the incentive to complain.

The future of private law as an environmental protection mechanism

Following *Cambridge Water Co.* v *Eastern Counties Leather* and *Hunter* v *Canary Wharf*, it is clear that the House of Lords, at least, is reluctant to see significant development of the common law as a mechanism for environmental protection. In *Cambridge Water* they stated explicitly that the rule in *Rylands* should not be developed further into a more specific common law rule about the control of hazardous substances. But this was wrapped up in more general language about private law and environmental regulation:

> . . . given that so much well-informed and carefully structured legislation is now being put in place for [the escape of hazardous substances], there is less need for the courts to develop a common law principle to achieve the same end, and indeed it may well be undesirable that they do so.

The approach taken by the House of Lords in *Hunter*, putting private nuisance law back to its original position of protecting only property rights holders, shows a similar cautiousness. As Lord Hoffmann said:

> . . . the development of the common law should be rational and coherent. It should not distort its principles and create anomalies as an expedient to fill a gap.

As Wightman ((1998) MLR 870) remarks, however, the distinction which the House of Lords in *Hunter* was eager to make — between damage to land and damage to persons — can be conceived of too simply. He uses the example of interference with the use of a public footpath across private land. There may be no reason for the landowner to litigate to prevent or remedy any damage to the right of way if there is no damage to his agricultural interests. But those who use the footpath are left without a private law remedy. This calls into question the 'privateness' of private law. There may therefore be an argument that the connection between nuisance and property rights is justified in so far as the holder of the right acts in his or her own interests. But if this feature is absent, and the litigant (perhaps an environmental organisation or conservation trust) acts in a custodial manner in pursuit of wider 'public' interests, the justification for the strict nexus with land loses force.

The more general point, however, is whether the judges should take such a conservative approach to the development of the common law as they have done recently. It is no answer to say that environmental regulation is to be preferred, whether this is through contaminated land legislation at national or EC level (*Cambridge Water*) or town and country planning law (*Hunter*, discussed more fully below). Indeed, it is trite to say so, and the general advantages of regulation over private law mechanisms have been explored above. The key point is that both private and public law controls must co-exist, even if this is through either (a) principles of private law that make statutory authority a defence to a claim in private nuisance, trespass or (probably) the rule in *Rylands*; or (b) statutory rules which determine the extent to which compliance with an environmental licence may be a defence to a common law claim (see, for example, s. 100(b), Water Resources Act 1991, discussed at p. 606). A recent illustration of this relationship, and the legal and policy issues raised, is the relationship between nuisance and the grant of planning permission.

Human rights law

Regardless of any judicial reluctance to develop tort law to provide for remedies in new situations, there is one important respect in which the courts may have to become less conservative in their attitudes. Although tort law is about relationships between legal persons (individuals, companies, etc), the courts are public bodies under the Human Rights Act 1998 (s. 6) and therefore bound to act in a way that is compatible with the rights protected by the European Convention on Human Rights. Although a deliberate feature of the 1998 Act is that it does not incorporate Article 13 of the Convention, which provides that parties to the Convention must give effective domestic remedies for violation of the Convention, in practice it is highly likely that in developing the common law the judges will do so in a way which is consistent with, or at least avoids clashing with, Convention rights. So, while the 1998 Act does not provide for a new tort of 'breach of the Convention' which one individual can rely on against another, unsettled areas in the common law leave space for the courts to give the Convention this kind of 'horizontal effect' between individuals in private law cases. Furthermore, courts developing the common law will henceforth also have regard to the 1998 Act itself to the extent that it forms part of the legislative background to the common law.

In cases where legislation is involved (such as under the Nuclear Installations Act 1965, or where a private law right comes up against a public law authorisation like a planning permission or environmental licence) the courts must 'read and give effect to' this legislation to make it compatible with the Convention if it is at all possible to do so. This might mean, for example, some relaxations to the strict approach to statutory authority authorising a nuisance taken in *Allen* v *Gulf Oil*, although it is likely that the limits which the courts have already placed on such rights so that those rights cannot be used to authorise any interference which is more than necessary or which is negligent, will go a long way to showing that a proper balance has been struck.

Whether Convention rights will be of use in practice is illustrated by the follow up to *Hunter* v *Canary Wharf*, which was argued before the European Commission of Human Rights in *Khatun and 180 others* v *UK* (1 July 1998, unreported). The Commission found that the right protected under Article 8 — to respect for private and family life, home and correspondence — applied to all the applicants whether they were property owners or merely occupiers. This got round one of the major obstacles to the claim re-erected by the House of Lords. But the case under Article 8 fell because of the regard that must be had to the fair balance to be struck between the competing interests of the individual and of the community as a whole. In this context, the UK had shown that the development was 'necessary', i.e. that the interference corresponded to a pressing social need and was proportionate to the aim

pursued, namely economic redevelopment. In a sense, the economic justification for the development legitimised what the planning permission alone
could not do. The UK's case was helped by the fact that the individuals did
not suffer health problems from the dust and that the interference was for a
limited time only. (See further *Powell and Rayner* v *United Kingdom* (1990) 12
EHRR 355, discussed at p. 455, and *López Ostra* v *Spain* (1995) 20 EHRR
277, a successful claim in relation to severe pollution coming from a factory
12 metres away from the applicant's home.) The applicants' argument under
Article 14 that as owners and occupiers of less expensive properties they were
effectively discriminated against (see McLaren's comments above, p. 259)
was rejected for the formal reason that there was no one treated differently in
the present case. Under the Human Rights Act 1998, the courts must have
regard to judgments and opinions of the European Court of Human Rights
or the Commission respectively. Paradoxically, therefore, what some regard
as a rather limited approach by these bodies so far to the use of human rights
law for environmental protection may in fact hinder the use of Convention
rights for this purpose.

Despite this decision, there are clearly other aspects of private law which
may come under close scrutiny in the years ahead. One example is the locality
rule in private nuisance, which might be thought to infringe the rights of
landowners to be given the same level of legal protection of their interests.

It should also be pointed out that the convention uses a 'victim' test, and
is therefore unable to provide a vehicle for protecting general ecological
interests. There is no 'right to nature'. This raises more general issues as to
whether an individual, rights-based approach is appropriate for pursuing what
are often, by their nature, collective interests (see further p. 110).

Private law, public regulation and 'the public interest'

There is often a conflict between private law and public regulation, in the
sense that an activity may be lawful under one regime but not the other.
Private law rights can clash with many regulatory controls, although most of
the case law has been about planning law. Many uses of land that give rise to
nuisances, for example, have the benefit of planning permission. In granting
a planning application it must be assumed that the local planning authority
has balanced the impact of the development upon private interests (e.g.
neighbours) with any competing public interests and concluded that the
public interests in allowing the development to proceed should prevail. But
two problems remain. First, what weight do planning authorities have to give
to private rights in the decision-making process? Secondly, how does the
grant of the planning permission affect such private rights?

On the first point, a planning permission can be granted which makes a
nuisance action by the new owner/occupiers likely (see *R* v *Exeter City
Council, ex parte J.L. Thomas and Co. Ltd* [1991] 1 QB 471). A public law
challenge to such a planning permission will have to do something more than
simply argue that private rights will be interfered with. Although environmental impact relating to land use will be a 'material consideration' to which

the planning authority is to have regard, the courts have given considerable discretion to planning authorities to decide how much weight to give such considerations (including no weight at all).

In relation to the impact of the grant of planning permission, recent case law has now confined the scope of the controversial ruling in *Gillingham Borough Council* v *Medway (Chatham) Dock Co. Ltd* [1993] QB 343. The local authority granted planning permission for dock development, but later took a public nuisance action following complaints about noise and vibration caused by lorries going to and from the port, especially at night. There were two readings of Buckley J's judgment refusing to grant an injunction restricting lorry movements at night. A broad reading was that planning permission was equivalent to the defence of statutory authority. This raised concerns that any activities engaged in under a planning permission could not lead to liability in nuisance, meaning that private rights would be extinguished without any redress or compensation contrary to established principles of English law.

But it is the narrow reading of the judgment that has prevailed. On this view, planning permission does not act as a *defence* to a claim in nuisance. Instead, Buckley J's decision went to the heart of the *definition* of a nuisance and the locality doctrine in particular. The question was whether the planning permission had so changed the nature of the area that the locality became a commercial area, making the lorry movements a reasonable user of the locality. This narrower view was upheld by the Court of Appeal in *Wheeler* v *J.J. Saunders Ltd* [1996] Ch 19. There, planning permission was granted for pig-weaning units to be built close to the claimant's land. The claimant successfully complained of smell nuisance that followed once the development was implemented. The Court essentially laid down three rules. First, the *Gillingham* case only decided that 'strategic' planning decisions, affected by considerations of public interest, could legalise certain nuisances by changing the nature of the locality. This might have been the case with the major port development at the Chatham Dockyard, but it was not the case with lesser developments like pig units. (Quite where the dividing line is was not elaborated upon.) Secondly, the *Gillingham* decision is restricted to those situations where the effects of the development make a specific change in the nature of the locality. Building pig units in the countryside is not such a radical change. Finally, the Court clarified that it is *actual* development, rather than development plans, which matters. This was sensible, not least because many developments earmarked in plans never materialise.

The basic approach taken in *Wheeler* was later upheld by the Court of Appeal in *Hunter*, and approved of in some of the speeches in the House of Lords in that case. What is perhaps most important about the law in this area is the way that it highlights a certain amount of unease amongst the judiciary about the overlap between the exercise of rights conferred by public law powers, and private law remedies. As Gibson LJ said in *Wheeler*, 'The Court should be slow to acquiesce in the extinction of private rights without compensation as a result of administrative decisions which cannot be appealed and are difficult to challenge'. To be sure, traditional compensation concepts apply rather uneasily in relation to concepts like environmental harm. The value of keeping open the private law claim may therefore lie more with the way in which its existence may influence decision-making by public bodies, providing a means of keeping regulatory systems open and accountable. Indeed, this appears to have influenced the judges in *Wheeler*, who clearly were troubled by what they thought to be an injudicious grant of planning consent, seemingly obtained on the basis of inaccurate and incomplete information and with little or no regard to the claimant's interests. On this line of thinking, protecting private rights furthers, rather than restricts, public interests.

The relationship between private law and public regulation is not confined to questions involving planning permissions, and can arise in relation to other environmental licences, e.g. waste management licences (*Blackburn v ARC Ltd* [1998] Env LR 469). In *Budden and Albery v BP Oil* [1980] JPL 586 a claim in negligence was brought against two oil companies based on their use of lead in petrol, even though the companies had adhered to regulatory standards. For the court, allowing the claim would mean that valid regulations prescribing the lead content in petrol would effectively be replaced by a lower, judicially-determined standard. The case illustrates the way that, especially in negligence cases, statutory standards may dictate common law standards. But the 'balancing act' quality to nuisance law provides for rather more flexibility, as the unsuccessful claimants in *Murdoch v Glacier Metal Co. Ltd* [1998] Env LR 732 found when their claim about noise levels exceeding World Health Organisation standards failed.

The way ahead? Civil liability in statutes and EC proposals

One of the obvious limitations of private law controls such as nuisance law is that they are essentially aimed at protecting individual rights, or rights relating to property. As cases like *Cambridge Water* and *Hunter* show, many judges are clearly reluctant to develop these mechanisms so that they are *directly* concerned with environmental protection. However, there are already some statutory regimes which try to overcome the inadequacies of ordinary private law in relation to problematic areas like pollution from international oil spills.

What links many of these statutory regimes (and any environmental liability directive that the EC might adopt) is the extent to which they might be directly concerned with environmental protection or remediation, and not just the protection of property. In this sense, these regimes can be said to follow on from measures such as those contained in Part IIA of the EPA 1990 relating to contaminated land, or the Water Resources Act 1991, s. 161 which allows for the clean up of polluted water. Although in practice both might *indirectly* benefit other property owners (who will avoid having to pay for the cost of clean up), and directly affect the person paying for the cost of clean up in a way which, for them, is probably indistinguishable from compensating another private party (the person whose brownfield site is cleaned up benefits from the other party by seeing an increase in the value of his or her land). However, their central concern is with the quality of the environment in its own right, which can be cleaned up, for example, so that ecosystems are restored.

The purpose of the following sections is to explore the possibilities of statutory civil liability regimes, which would obviously meet the objection made by Lord Goff in the *Cambridge Water* case that it is not for the courts to develop the common law in areas where rule- and decision-making is complex and involves many stakeholders. Readers are invited to draw their own conclusions as to the merits of statutory civil liability as against, for example, regulatory clean-up regimes.

(a) Statutory civil liability
In addition to the common law, there are a number of statutes that impose liability by means of private law remedies, rather than the more usual public law methods.

(i) *Nuclear Installations Act 1965*
The individual problems of nuclear installations are not adequately dealt with by the law of tort. As the Chernobyl incident demonstrated, the damage caused by nuclear actions can be widespread and not confined to a specific period of time. There are also difficulties of proving a causal link between the injury caused and exposure to radiation. Many diseases that are caused by radiation also occur naturally, and trying to establish whether or not there is an epidemiological link is frequently fraught with difficulties. To avoid these difficulties, the Nuclear Installations Act 1965 introduced absolute civil liability for all damage caused from certain occurrences (ss. 7 to 10). Not all loss from nuclear damage is covered under the Act. Economic loss can only be recovered where there is specific physical harm caused to the land. Thus in *Merlin* v *British Nuclear Fuels plc* [1990] 2 QB 557 a claim for loss in value of a house in the area of the Sellafield nuclear installation resulting from radioactive contamination was refused because the 'contamination' had not given rise to physical harm. The presence of raised radioactivity levels in the house was not sufficient to amount to such harm.

The decision in *Merlin* v *British Nuclear Fuels plc* was considered in *Blue Circle Industries* v *Ministry of Defence* [1998] 3 All ER 385, in which a claim arose out of the contamination of land (owned by Blue Circle) neighbouring the Atomic Weapons Establishment at Aldermaston. Although the MOD carried out remediation works on Blue Circle's land which effectively removed the radioactive material, sale of the land fell through due to blight resulting from the contamination. Blue Circle brought a claim to recover £5 million in damages arising out of the diminution in value of the estate. The court distinguished the damage in *Merlin* from the contamination at the AWE by linking the economic loss in Blue Circle's case to the actual physical harm caused by the radioactive contamination. In *Merlin* it was thought that there was no physical harm and the nature of the loss was purely economic and non-actionable. The distinction, it must be said, is unconvincing and it is probably better to see *Blue Circle* as simple taking a less restrictive approach to damage. In finding in favour of Blue Circle the court also found that the 1965 Act imposed liability where there was *any* injury or damage, irrespective of the contamination levels.

(ii)   Merchant Shipping Act 1995
In the wake of numerous oil disasters in the mid to late 1960s, international concern led to the introduction of legislation to compensate for damage from oil. This is now consolidated in the Merchant Shipping Act 1995, which applies to spills both from tankers and other ships. The Act imposes strict liability on owners of ships in relation to physical damage to property and personal injury from oil pollution (ss. 153 and 154). The financing of the majority of losses stemming from the Act is covered by a compulsory insurance scheme, although there is a further international fund for compensation which pays out when the ship-owner cannot afford to. This fund has paid out compensation following both the *Braer* (1993) and *Sea Empress* (1996) oil spills. There are a number of statutory defences covering circumstances such as war, intentional acts of damage by third parties, or poor governmental control of navigation or lighting (s. 155). The Act also makes provision for the eventual transposition of the 1996 International Convention on Liability and Compensation for Damage in Connection with the Carriage of Hazardous and Noxious Substances by Sea (the 'HNS Convention').

(iii)   Environmental Protection Act 1990, s. 73
Section 73(6) of EPA 1990 imposes civil liability for the unlawful deposit of waste (see p. 521).

(b)   EC proposals
A second consideration is the possibility of an EC directive on civil liability for environmental damage and the impact this may have as regards a privately initiated claim to protect the environment. A White Paper on Environmental Liability has recently been published (COM(2000)66). The key features of the proposed directive are:

(a)   Apart from traditional kinds of damage (to persons and property), there would be liability for damage to the unowned environment. However, this would be restricted to significant damage to habitats and species protected under EC conservation legislation (i.e. species and habitats in Natura 2000 areas; see Chapter 21), a particularly narrow view of environmental damage which does not even cover all areas protected under EC law (such as nitrate vulnerable zones) and falls short of what we already have at national level under the contaminated land regime, which extends to more general ecosystem damage (see Chapter 18). Damages for biodiversity loss raise important questions about valuation of environmental resources.

(b)   For dangerous and potentially-dangerous activities there would be strict liability, in part because those who develop hazardous new technologies or processes should bear any costs which they give rise to (a principle that is found in US law, developed there from the rule in *Rylands* v *Fletcher*).

(c)   For non-dangerous activities, liability would be fault based (no reason is given for this distinction).

(d)   Only hazardous activities which are regulated under EC law (e.g. processes subject to IPPC) would be covered. This approach makes sense if a future liability regime is intended to bolster EC environmental law and give polluters incentives to comply with environmental directives, but clearly there are many very potentially damaging activities which would not be covered (e.g. water pollution caused by a spill from a milk tanker). Because *all* activities affecting Natura 2000 areas are covered by the key EC conservation directives, however, the distinction between dangerous and non-dangerous would not be made for these areas.

(e)   The proposals take no firm view on whether there would only be liability where an EC-based standard was breached, or whether discharging substances in line with EC limits could also be actionable (which is the case in most Member States; see, e.g. Water Resources Act, s. 100(b), discussed on p. 606).

(f)   There might be some recognition of the evidential difficulties faced by claimants. However, the White Paper is rather less explicit than some of its drafts, which spoke of shifting the burden of proof where the claimant could show a plausible pollution pathway, so that effectively defendants would have to establish that they were not responsible.

(g)   Environmental interest groups would have standing to bring actions, but only if the state had failed to act or to act promptly (akin to what in the US are called 'citizen suits'). The difference between this and bringing a judicial review action might be that NGOs could give regulatory bodies a set period of time in which to take action, after which the NGO could act itself (thus avoiding some of the almost insuperable difficulties that exist when arguing that a public body has, for example, failed to prosecute for breach of a standard).

(h)   In urgent cases, NGOs would be able to ask the court to issue an injunction, or be reimbursed for reasonable costs spent in preventing environmental damage. One argument against this approach, however, is that it is precisely these kinds of high-profile cases where regulatory agencies may act of their own accord. Arguably, NGOs should also have powers where there is chronic, low-level violation of standards, of the kind regulators might not wish to enforce for fear of the consequences to the relationship with the polluter, although there would doubtless be hostility to this, both by regulators and by the courts.

(i)   It would be up to each Member State to decide which environmental interest groups would be able to bring actions, and presumably also decide which other procedural rules they must comply with. One thing that would obviously be important is whether these rules, e.g. on the speed with which cases should be brought, would follow the approach taken in public law (which has very strict time limits; see p. 77) or private law, where the rules are much more generous.

(j)   The emphasis is on remediation of environmental damage: damages awarded would have to be applied to environmental restoration, or to compensatory schemes where restoration is not possible.

(k)   Liability would apply only to future damage. But how this is defined is problematic. If a cylinder containing chemicals is dumped and, after some time, begins to leak, it is not clear whether the incident causing the damage is the date of dumping, or when the leakage begins. In other words, it is not clear how the proposals would apply to latent damage.

Formal proposals along these lines have been around for over ten years (see the earlier draft directive on civil liability for damage caused by waste (COM(89)282 final, modified by COM(91)219 final, now superseded). As can be seen, in key areas like defences the White Paper is effectively a discussion paper rather than a document containing firm proposals. No doubt this is a recognition of how difficult adopting a directive in this area will be, and a Directive is some years from being adopted (if indeed it ever is). Nevertheless, the proposals would result in a radical overhaul of many features of English private law's limited protection of the environment. However, the impact on statutory clean up regimes, such as the newly implemented regime for contaminated land under Part IIA of the Environment Act 1990, will be slight. Depending on how any restriction against imposing retrospective liability is interpreted, there would simply be no duplication with the provisions for historic pollution contained in Part IIA of the Environment Act 1990 (see further Chapter 18).

Finally, a directive in this area might have important knock-on consequences for public environmental regulation. For example, the White Paper suggests that, in certain cases, regulators might be liable where the damage was 'entirely and exclusively caused' by permitted emissions. This might result in a body like the Environment Agency imposing tighter standards on IPPC permits and discharge consents than it might otherwise do, to cushion it from the risk of being held liable in civil law. It might also force licensing agencies to take greater enforcement action against persistent, low-level breaches, and could also lead to demands for greater uniformity in licensing under EC law. Finally, it is not clear what 'caused' means here, i.e. whether a local planning authority could be said to have caused an emission from a polluting development, even if the licensing of the emission was in the hands of a specialist environmental regulator. There must be some doubt, however, whether Member States would agree to a directive which potentially imposed large civil liabilities on their own regulatory agencies.

PART II   SECTORAL COVERAGE OF ENVIRONMENTAL LAW

ELEVEN
Town and country planning

The British system of town and country planning is undoubtedly one of the most sophisticated systems of land use control in the world. It is exceptional in incorporating controls over the use of land as well as over the design and form of the built environment. Accordingly, it plays a central role in environmental law because of its enormous importance in relation to locational issues, as well as determining how much of any particular activity (such as house-building) is allowed and the intensity of such development. It is, as stated earlier (see p. 183), perhaps the pre-eminent example in this country of an anticipatory system of control. However, 'town and country planning' is not just about environmental protection. It has a wider role in organising economic development, but in balancing economic, political, social and environmental factors to do with development in a democratic context it ought to be a key mechanism for making development more sustainable.

For reasons of space, this chapter is restricted to looking at those general aspects of planning law of greatest importance for protecting the natural environment. For this reason, specialist regimes within planning law, such as the regulation of minerals extraction, are not covered in any depth; nor are the specific planning provisions concerning conservation of the built environment, such as listed buildings and conservation areas. Specific aspects of planning law relevant to other chapters within Part II of the book are summarised at the appropriate place, though some thoughts are offered here on the general nature of the relationship between town and country planning and environmental protection.

A final introductory point is that this chapter deals with town and country planning law, rather than the role of planning-type mechanisms in general. There is now quite a number of other plans relating to the environment, both formal (e.g. the national strategies for air and waste) and informal (e.g. Local Environment Agency Plans). The RCEP is due to report on this extended role for planning (including town and country planning) in 2001.

The main features of town and country planning

These are as follows:

(a)   The local planning authority draws up a development plan, which sets out the strategy for development in the area. This involves a measure of public participation. Development plans are permissive (i.e. they do not guarantee what is going to happen, but act as guides to future development) and must be taken into account in any decision.

(b)   All 'development', which is widely construed and includes changes of use as well as physical development, requires planning permission from the local planning authority before it may be carried out.

(c)   For some developments considered minor, planning permission is deemed to be granted, usually if they fall within prescribed limits. The breadth of the planning system is also relaxed by excluding certain changes of use from being 'development', where both activities have similar land use impacts. In this latter case, planning permission is simply not required.

(d)   Procedures are laid down for applications for planning permission. These involve consultation with other public bodies and some limited public involvement.

(e)   The local planning authority decides on grounds of planning policy whether to grant permission or refuse it, taking into account the development plan, central government policies and any other material considerations.

(f)   Unlike most other systems of town planning, which rely heavily on zoning of areas within which certain generalised rules will apply, in this country each case must be considered on its merits.

(g)   If permission is granted, it may be subject to conditions; indeed, this is the normal position. If permission is refused, no compensation is normally payable — the right to develop land was effectively nationalised in the Town and Country Planning Act 1947.

(h)   The applicant has a right of appeal to the Secretary of State against any refusal or conditions. This is a complete rehearing of the whole matter, including the policy issues, and thus enables the Secretary of State to exercise a stranglehold on policy by having the final say on it.

(i)   There is no right of appeal for third parties and no right to appeal against a grant of planning permission.

(j)   There is a further right of appeal from the decision of the Secretary of State to the High Court on what are essentially the same grounds as for judicial review. The courts thus exercise a supervisory jurisdiction over the procedures and the decisions taken. However, the courts will not intervene on grounds of fact or policy.

(k)   Enforcement of the law is through another discretionary procedure in which the local planning authority may serve an enforcement notice requiring specified steps to be taken. It is not an offence to develop without permission, but rather an offence to fail to comply with an enforcement notice. Once again, a right of appeal to the Secretary of State is provided and, as this may involve consideration of policy issues, it is in most cases deemed a retrospective application for planning permission.

(l)   Planning permission effectively gives a right to develop. Unlike most systems of pollution control, there is no power to vary a planning permission in the future (unless compensation is paid).

Town and country planning as a tool of environmental policy

There are thus three main areas with relevance to environmental law:

(a)   The system of development plans, which ensures that environmental protection is considered at the level of policy-making. These plans often set the basic ground rules for action on the environment in any particular area, although they must be read in conjunction with the policy guidance emanating from central government.

(b)   The development control process, in which planning permission is required from the local planning authority for acts of development. This ensures a strict anticipatory control over many activities before they start and normally involves liaison with the relevant pollution control and environmental agencies.

(c)   The power to impose conditions relating to environmental protection on a grant of planning permission. These are capable of creating some form of continuing control over activities.

The traditional conflictual model of a regulatory body regulating the applicant by granting or refusing permission is no longer really appropriate here. Modern town planning may be seen as a negotiative process in which consultation between the prospective developer and the local planning authority in advance of the application is the norm, and in which proposals are both made and considered in the light of local and national policies. The local planning authority and the developer often have a community of interest in carrying out a particular development: the developer gets its proposal granted and the local authority obtains the revitalisation of the economy of an area, or the creation of jobs, or some other economic benefit. (Indeed, developments by local authorities and developers in partnership with each other are now quite common.) In addition, arrangements between developers and local authorities in which 'planning gain' is bargained for are increasingly used to supplement the regulatory controls (see p. 331).

It should also be borne in mind that the impact of planning control is in many ways incomplete or inadequate. Planning permission is not required for all environmentally harmful activities, for example for mobile pollutants such as cars, or in relation to most agricultural activities. There are difficulties where some form of continuing control is required, because of the limitations on planning conditions, or where positive management is required, since it is mainly a preventive system. The system also tends to get circumvented in various ways where nationally important development is desired by central government.

A further point is that the planning decision is a political one, and thus environmental issues may be subordinated to other needs. As the Royal Commission on Environmental Pollution commented in its Fifth Report in relation to pollution prevention, 'Our concern is not that pollution is not always given top priority; it is that it is often dealt with inadequately, and sometimes forgotten altogether in the planning process' (Cmnd 6371, 1976).

Nevertheless, the planning system is of central importance in many areas of environmental law, especially when used in conjunction with other regulatory controls. This is seen clearly in relation to waste disposal, where planning permission for a waste disposal site is required before a waste management licence can be granted. In other areas, planning control is arguably of greatest importance where the enforcement of pollution control is inadequate, since non-enforcement at the operational end puts increased pressure on initial siting and design issues.

Town and country planning and some themes of this book

This brief summary of the town and country planning system shows how it illustrates a number of the major themes of this book. For instance, it is a good example of a sophisticated anticipatory regulatory mechanism and it emphasises prevention of harm. That also means that the predominant method of control is through negative, restrictive measures, rather than through positive mechanisms. Local decision-making dominates, although there has been some shift of power towards central government in recent years (see p. 300). It is a highly discretionary system, in which decisions are made on a case-by-case basis and it is a democratic system in which ultimate political control rests with elected members rather than with officers (on appeal responsibility rests with an elected Secretary of State), although in practice most decisions are actually taken by officers. It is a fairly open and public system, but with inevitable trade-offs between speed and participation.

Enforcement is under-emphasised, being almost exclusively the responsibility of the local planning authority and dependent on political and tactical factors as well as on adequate resources (which in practice are often not available).

But the most important point is that it is a highly political system of decision-making. Local planning authorities and the Secretary of State make discretionary decisions by balancing economic, political, environmental and social factors. It is therefore just as important to understand the prevailing policy in relation to a particular issue as it is to understand the relevant law.

The role of the law and the courts requires some explanation here. The planning system is one where the law exercises a supervisory, or review, function. It is there to define the various concepts used in the planning system (such as what development is, or what types of conditions are legitimate), to ensure that the correct procedures are used and to ensure that discretionary decisions are taken in the proper manner. The law is therefore ultimately about procedures, i.e. about ensuring that decisions are made correctly rather than that the correct decisions are made.

The planning legislation

As Lord Scarman stated in *Pioneer Aggregates (UK) Ltd* v *Secretary of State for the Environment* [1985] AC 132, 'Planning control is the creature of statute . . . Parliament has provided a comprehensive code of planning control'.

Although private law rights can be used for rudimentary development planning and control, statutory planning law is not based on common law foundations in the way that, for example, the law of statutory nuisance is (see Chapter 15). This means that it is a largely self-contained code as far as interpreting planning legislation is concerned.

Modern planning legislation is generally traced back to the Housing, Town Planning etc. Act 1909 (see p. 10). The notable features of this Act, with its focus on the urban environment and discretion to implement, characterised much early planning legislation. It was not until the Town and Country Planning Act 1947 that a uniform and mandatory country-wide system of development control — Lord Scarman's 'comprehensive code' — was introduced. One of the most remarkable things about planning is that, whilst there have been numerous detailed additions and amendments to the law, the basic structure of much of this system (apart from that relating to development plans) has remained unchanged since then, although the way in which it is operated has in practice changed quite radically.

The legislation is now consolidated in the Town and Country Planning Act 1990. Important changes were made under the Planning and Compensation Act 1991, but inserted into the 1990 Act as amendments or additions. Unless otherwise stated, therefore, wherever a section number is given in this chapter without reference to a particular Act, it refers to the 1990 Act. Frequent reference will also be made to subordinate legislation, which fleshes out much of the detail of the law: central here are the Town and Country Planning (General Permitted Development) Order 1995 (SI 1995/418), the Town and Country Planning (General Development Procedure) Order 1995 (SI 1995/419) and the Town and Country Planning (Use Classes Order) 1987 (SI 1987/764). The first two relate to the grant of automatic planning permission for a wide range of activities, while under the latter a significant number of changes in the use of land are declared not to be 'development' and so fall outside the planning system altogether.

What is town and country planning: a changing concept?

Town planning has been described simply as 'How much of what is put where'. As befits a political system, the question of what planning covers has, over the years, largely been left to those who make planning decisions. The result has been an expansion of the idea, beyond straightforward amenity, public health and land use issues towards taking into account the economic and social impact of decisions.

This widening of the scope of planning has received the support of the courts. In exercising their supervisory jurisdiction they have often had to ask the question 'What is planning?' in order to decide whether a power has been used legitimately. In doing so they have proved willing to decide that most things are within the scope of planning. The most commonly used legal test is given by Lord Scarman in *Westminster City Council* v *Great Portland Estates plc* [1985] AC 661, who suggested that town planning covers anything that 'relates to the character of the use of land'.

This general formulation, however, hides fundamental divisions over the legitimate role and scope of planning. Until the 1970s, town and country planning was a relatively uncontroversial topic in party political terms, with the exception of the questions of compensation for refusal of permission and taxation of profits resulting from a grant of permission. There was a degree of consensus over what planning should consist of and over the preferred policies. The role of the state as itself a major developer was accepted.

In the 1980s, there remained agreement that planning should include land use and amenity issues, such as the location and design of new developments, but the extent to which socio-economic issues should be a legitimate part of planning became contested. Some saw planning as one means by which a particular form of social development might be produced. Others wished to see planning restricted as much as possible on the grounds that it interfered unduly with the free market. The second view was effectively the one that was espoused by the Conservative governments of the 1980s, with their firm beliefs in deregulation, a minimalist approach to restrictions on commercial activity, the power of the market as a distributor of resources, and the consequent need for speed and certainty in any system of control.

This deregulatory approach took various forms. Of great importance was the reduction of red tape and delays. Significant relaxations were made in the General Development Orders of 1981, 1985 and 1988 and in the Use Classes Order of 1987 to cut out the need for planning permission in many situations, with the objective of encouraging the development of small businesses. The procedures for development plans were streamlined, so that they might be adopted more quickly, leading to a consequent reduction in public opportunities for participation in the process. Regular encouragement was given by circulars to speed up the process of dealing with planning applications. The politically suspect metropolitan county councils were abolished by the Local Government Act 1985, leading to the introduction of a new system of unitary development plans in those areas. More dramatically, in planning terms, various mechanisms were introduced that removed most or all planning controls in designated areas. Enterprise zones, simplified planning zones and urban development areas (see p. 315) all contributed to the deregulation of planning controls; in the case of enterprise zones, decision-making was given to centrally appointed urban development corporations. Less visibly, the planning system was avoided altogether through the use of the Private Bill procedure or technical procedures under the Transport and Works Act 1992. Arguably, one of the current challenges in sustainable development, therefore, is not just to give greater weight to the environment in planning, but to reassert the place of social objectives alongside planning's role in relation to economic development.

Many of these changes indicated a significant move away from upholding participation as an important objective of the planning system *in its own right*, a strong theme of the late 1960s and early 1970s, and from the more general notion that planning is above all a *process* through which decisions are made, rather than anything with an absolutely definitive subject matter. There is little sign that under the present government public participation will be enhanced in any meaningful way. The present government's review of planning, *Modernising Planning* (DETR, 1998), indicates that business and development interests will be to the fore, especially at regional level. A pre-election commitment to give third parties a right to appeal against the grant of planning permission (as is the case in the Republic of Ireland) has been abandoned, and no extension to participatory rights is envisaged. While local planning authorities may be given more flexibility in decision-making, however, there are signs that thinking is moving beyond town and country planning in favour of wider 'spatial planning'.

One thing that is worth mentioning, however, is the extent to which the present Government appears to be using the planning system to further its social and economic policies. This is through its adoption of planning guidance on *Housing* (PPG 3, 2000), which makes it clear that planning authorities should use the planning system to foster a diverse mix of residents in major new housing developments to make housing more affordable, in order to combat social exclusion. Clearly this is a considerable departure from the idea that planning controls should work with the grain of the market, and may herald further developments in planning policy to widen the nature of the planning system.

The centrality of planning policy and the Secretary of State

The deregulatory agenda operated both at a procedural and substantive level. There has always been some sort of presumption in favour of granting permission, and the statistics on planning permission show that of the large numbers of applications made each year, approximately 90 per cent are granted. The difference is that this presumption has changed in substance from the basic public law requirement that reasons be given for a decision affecting someone's right to develop, to a *policy* in favour of development that may have a great weight attached to it by the decision-maker (see further p. 321). This is just one example of the increased importance attached to planning policy in the system, notwithstanding the retention of the basic legal structure of the system outlined above. Increasingly, change has been brought about by administrative means, particularly by the concerted application of strong central government policy, often on appeal.

In the 1980s, policy guidance sought to increase the role of the free market in generating development. Landmarks in this regard were Circular 22/80, with its overt encouragement of small businesses and private housing, and Circular 14/85 which stated that 'There is always a presumption in favour of allowing applications for development, having regard to all material considerations, unless that development would cause demonstrable harm to interests of acknowledged importance'. Circular 1/85 also played an important role, emphasising that conditions should not be attached unless they could be justified on clear grounds.

Naturally, this pro-development approach was also taken by the Secretary of State on appeal, applying his own policies. Often these would carry so much weight that local planning authorities ignored them at their peril, knowing that developers could exercise their right to appeal. The result was that in the 1980s these explicitly directory circulars grew to have far greater importance than local policies such as development plans. The appeals process was used to support this shift in power from local to central government. By the mid 1980s the number of successful appeals brought against refusal of permission doubled to 40 per cent. Not surprisingly, the number of appeals also rose sharply, so that by the late 1980s a quarter of all refusals were appealed. A similar story was apparent in relation to appeals against enforcement notices.

In keeping with the policy of doctrinal neutrality on the content of planning policies, the courts did not interfere with these changes, except to preserve the rationality of the decision-making process by insisting that adequate reasons were given for decisions. In this respect it should be recognised that the planning system has always been pro-development to some extent. This stems from the prominence of property-based ideas within it and is evident in, for example, third parties and objectors not being given the same rights to appeal against the grant of planning permission as developers are when permission is refused. The result is that permission will be granted if *either* the local planning authority or the Secretary of State is in favour of it.

A change of direction?

In the 1980s the planning system became far more centralised, in two main senses: more decisions were taken at a central level and central policy pervaded every decision even at a local level. One effect was to shift power from local government to central government; another to increase the areas of conflict between the two levels. But, interestingly, at the same time the system became in a way *less* centralised. This was because the changes in policy were designed to increase the role of the market at the expense of the state, and to make the system more developer-led. The system moved away from the direct promotion of wider social, economic and environmental objectives; reflecting the shift from public to private development, it became more concerned with resolving a myriad of competing land uses in the wider public interest.

However, it is clear that in the 1990s these trends were to some extent reversed, with greater regard being paid to local decisions. The Secretary of State no longer has to approve all development plans and there is now a presumption in favour of development in accordance with such plans. But the general political climate is now also such that the activity of land use planning has become less contentious. There are no longer the same debates about the purposes of planning as there were up to the 1980s, and so less need to impose government policy on appeal. However, the importance of central government may be rising because, increasingly, planning policy contains ever more prescriptive 'guidance', more in the form of rules for local authorities to follow than best practice to be commended. In any event, evidence suggests that in areas of discretion, the main influence on the formulation of local planning officers' judgment is overwhelmingly central government guidance.

In some ways, the focus has shifted to the propriety of the planning system, especially the role of elected councillors; that is, from matters of substance to matters of procedure. The Third Report of the Nolan Committee on *Standards in Public Life* (Cm 3702, 1997), e.g. received more complaints about planning than any other activity of local government. One impact of this shift can be seen in Planning Policy Guidance (PPG) Note 1 (1997) which effectively puts an onus on elected members to justify decisions taken against the advice of officers' written reports.

More substantively, the 1990s saw the gradual acceptance of the contribution of the planning system to achieving sustainable development, and the continuing importance of policy guidance in this respect. A range of PPGs now make reference to sustainable development objectives, and policy guidance on transport and on retail development (especially out-of-town shopping centres) now emphasise ways in which the planning system can help meet environmental objectives, such as traffic reduction. This change marks a significant departure from the approach taken in the 1980s, when planning was narrowly restricted to land use issues only. But, ironically, it remains difficult to use central policy to *promote* environmentally friendly developments, since there always remains local discretion about whether to permit such development (as the case of wind farms indicates; see p. 325).

This shift towards promoting sustainable development can also be seen in the increasing importance of EC-driven measures. These have had a double-edged impact. On the one hand, EC provisions such as those relating to waste, environmental assessment and habitat conservation (see Chapters 12, 17 and 21 respectively), and more indirectly EC obligations filtering through government guidance, are putting new boundaries on the discretion of decision-makers (see Purdue, 'The Impact of EC Environmental Law on Planning Law in the United Kingdom', in Holder (ed.), *The Impact of EC Environmental Law in the United Kingdom* (Wiley, 1997)). On the other hand, the impact of the EC as regards things like regional funding or coastal zone management is likely to broaden the scope of planning guidance into what were previously regarded as non-statutory land use issues (see Tewdwr-Jones, 'Planning Modernised?' [1998] JPL 518).

Local planning authorities

Initial responsibility for most planning decisions rests with local authorities, which in this context are generically called local planning authorities. As a result of local government reorganisation under the Local Government Act 1992, there are three main types of local planning authority:

(a) Single-tier London boroughs and metropolitan districts.

(b) Non-metropolitan areas in which the planning function is split between county and district authorities by sch. 1 to the 1990 Act (see further below).

(c) Unitary authorities which are responsible for all the development control and related functions that were previously exercised by both county and district authorities, including the preparation of a structure plan and a

302   Town and country planning

local plan, unless the Secretary of State provides by order that the authority should prepare a unitary development plan (UDP) for the area. In certain cases it may be preferable to have a development plan which covers a wider area and the Secretary of State can order authorities to prepare a joint structure plan (see further Circular 4/96).

County councils (called county planning authorities) are responsible for:

(a)   structure plans;
(b)   local plans relating to certain county subjects, such as minerals planning and waste disposal;
(c)   county matters in development control (including minerals developments and any related works or buildings, waste disposal applications, and applications relating to land in national parks);
(d)   certain development control decisions where they are able to grant themselves planning permission;
(e)   county councils are also consulted by the district planning authority over certain large-scale developments, principally those which affect the structure plan or county matters, and over highway matters in their capacity as highways authorities.

District councils (called district planning authorities) are responsible for all other local plans and for all development control decisions, *except* those relating to county matters.

There are two special areas where different rules apply:

(a)   In national parks, as from 1 April 1997, all planning decisions are taken by autonomous planning authorities set up under the Environment Act 1995, s. 63. Thus each of the seven national park authorities established under that section are responsible for maintaining the structure and local plans for the area of the National Park.
(b)   In the Broads, the similarly constituted Broads Authority takes all decisions (Norfolk and Suffolk Broads Act 1988).

In England, the Regional Development Agencies do not have planning responsibilities, although clearly their establishment under the Regional Development Agencies Act 1998 is important in terms of shaping economic development at this level. They are unlikely to be given any powers to determine any kinds of planning application unless and until they have a democratic mandate and greater public accountability. It is also worth noting that the Greater London Authority is not a local planning authority, although it will play a strategic role in relation to development since it must develop a 'spatial development strategy'.

Wales, Scotland, Northern Ireland

Prior to devolution, planning policy in Wales largely followed policy set by the Department of the Environment in London, although by the mid 1990s certain tensions were evident, in part because of the ideological convictions of John Redwood, one of the more neo-liberal Welsh Secretaries, who at times seemed opposed to anything but very general policy guidance. In the end, more because of devolutionary pressures, there was a disapplication of PPGs in Wales from 1996, replaced by general guidance supplemented by Technical Advice Notes (in part because of reliance on research and policy development from England, these are not dissimilar to English PPGs). Following devolution, planning in Wales remains subject to the TCPA 1990, but powers in relation to delegated legislation, and powers of the Secretary of State, have passed to the Assembly. Given the extent to which planning law and policy depends on decisions made at this level, there is considerable scope for significant differences to emerge. Whether it does remains to be seen. Similarly, although the Planning Inspectorate will continue to hear most appeals, the Planning Decision Committee of the Assembly, established in January 2000, has the power to hear cases which have been 'called-in' or where jurisdiction to hear the case has been recovered. However, it is the First Secretary or the Environment and Local Government Secretary who decides whether these cases are referred to the Assembly, and who will therefore exercise considerable power, effectively acting as a 'gatekeeper' for decisions on the more complex or controversial cases. Having a smaller panel to decide appeals may meet concerns that giving powers to the full committee would lead to an inconsistent application of policy, although there will be some rotation of members to keep the political balance.

In Scotland planning legislation was consolidated in the Town and Country Planning (Scotland) Act 1997, which is broadly similar to the TCPA 1990. Planning cases decided by the House of Lords that have their origins in the Scottish courts are therefore usually equally important elsewhere in Britain, since analogous terms are being interpreted. One difference, though, was that there were often larger differences in the wording of policy guidance, contained in National Planning Policy Guidance notes (NPPG) and Policy Advice Notes, and certainly differences in when guidance came into effect. With devolution, responsibility for town and country planning passed to the Scottish Parliament. Because there is only limited EC involvement in planning law, there is considerable scope for Scottish law and policy to develop in its own direction.

Town and country planning matters in Northern Ireland are also governed by legislation which mirrors the TCPA 1990 (the Planning (Northern Ireland) Order 1991) although there are important differences, notably any direct equivalent of the legal presumption in favour of the development plan. There are also institutional differences that reflect direct rule: responsibility for planning lies mainly with the Department of the Environment (Northern Ireland), which determines planning applications (there is no central role for local authorities), while appeals and called in applications are decided by a separate Northern Ireland Planning Appeals Commission.

Forward planning: development plans

Local planning authorities are responsible for producing development plans on a continuing basis, which then guide or influence development in the areas covered. In this country, all development plans are permissive, i.e. they lay down policies, aims, objectives and goals rather than prescribe what is going to happen in an area. They have no immediate effect other than as a statement of what the local planning authority considers is desirable. They do not themselves give permission to develop (as is the case with zoning plans in many other countries) but they do have a great and growing importance in the decision whether or not to grant planning permission (see p. 322).

There is *no* national plan. The nearest equivalent is the central government policy set out in Planning Policy Guidance Notes and government circulars. There are also as yet no formal regional plans, although groupings of local planning authorities do produce general regional strategies, and there is formal regional planning guidance issued by central government, often based on advice from these regional groupings.

For most areas the existing system is to have two tiers of plan — structure plans and local plans, collectively referred to as the development plan. However, in metropolitan areas, unitary development plans are taking over this function. They were first required by the Local Government Act 1985 (a consequence of the abolition of the metropolitan county councils), and although they are still in the course of being made, will replace structure plans and local plans in those areas in the next few years.

Changes to the nature of development planning

The system of development plans has been one area within planning law where there seems to have been a constant state of change. The original development plans established under the 1947 Act were basically detailed, spatial, land use maps, drawn up by local authorities for all areas, but requiring central government approval. Delay was endemic both in making the plans and keeping them up-to-date, and public involvement was not properly catered for, with the result that the two-tier system of structure and local plans was introduced in the Town and Country Planning Act 1968. Increased public participation rights were added by the Town and Country Planning Act 1971.

Before these plans had much of a chance to prove themselves, they became unpopular with a government unconvinced by the need for strong forward planning and antipathetic to the power of local authorities. Structure plans in particular were downgraded by comparison with local plans by the Local Government, Planning and Land Act 1980 and plans of all types were accorded ever-decreasing weight in decisions compared with central government policies. This could happen because the law did not stipulate how much weight decision-makers should place on the plan and on other material considerations.

Ultimately, some important changes were enacted by the Planning and Compensation Act 1991, sch. 4, which remodelled the part of the Town and Country Planning Act 1990 dealing with development plans (Part II). The main changes, which came into force in February 1992, were as follows:

(a)   Despite some consideration having been given to their abolition, structure plans were retained. But they should now cover a more restricted range of topics than before.

(b)   The requirement that structure plans and modifications to them must be approved by the Secretary of State was removed.

(c)   It became mandatory for a local planning authority to make a *district-wide* local plan, something which few had done in the past, preferring to concentrate their plan-making activities on specific parts of their district.

(d)   Development plans for the area of a national park became mandatory for the first time, as did a local minerals plan and a waste local plan, the last being intended to complement the waste disposal plan required by the Environmental Protection Act 1990, s. 50, which has limited public involvement. In time any existing waste disposal plans will be replaced by the national waste strategy (see p. 474). Amendments to the Development Plan Regulations require local planning authorities to have regard to any future national waste strategy in formulating development plans (see the Town and Country Planning (Development Plan) (Amendment) Regulations 1997 (SI 1997/531). Any waste disposal plan or modification of such a plan under s. 50 of the EPA 1990, whose content has been finally determined before 1 April 1996, is to continue in force until the content of the national waste strategy is finally determined, notwithstanding the repeal of s. 50.

(e)   In relation to all these types of plan (and also to unitary development plans) the procedures were streamlined so as to reduce the delay between initial deposit and final adoption, though the main elements of public participation and consultation were retained.

These changes make it clear that plan-making has assumed a much greater importance — a fact that gains in significance when considered alongside the movement towards a plan-led system of development control and the consequent increase in practical importance of the plans. This increase in importance has, however, led to a marked slowdown in the formal adoption of development plans — leading to problems similar to those experienced with the original development plans under the 1947 Act. The procedure for adopting local plans and UDPs in particular has come under great pressure as developers, local planning authorities and the public have come to recognise the importance of the adopted plan and have therefore subjected the proposals within the plan to great scrutiny. Some public inquiries into development plans have lasted for well over a year. Consequently, the target of achieving complete development plan coverage by the end of 1996 has been missed by some way and by the end of 1998 only 87 per cent of local plans and UDPs had been adopted. If the plan-led system is to operate effectively, the approval and adoption procedures have to be streamlined.

(a)   Structure plans

A structure plan is a statement of general strategic policies set out in the form of a written statement supplemented by representative diagrams and a written memorandum (which is not a formal part of the plan). It will contain major strategic policies for the area of a county. PPG 12 (2000) sets out current government policy, which is to restrict the scope of structure plans to topics undeniably connected with land use. These are listed as housing, green belts, conservation, the economy (including major employment-generating development), strategic transport issues, minerals matters, waste treatment and disposal, land reclamation, tourism, leisure and recreation, and energy generation, including renewable energy.

There are also statutory duties to include policies in respect of the conservation of the natural beauty and amenity of the land, the improvement of the physical environment, and the management of traffic (s. 31(3)), and many structure plans now include policies on such topics as air pollution. These will set out general objectives for the area and act as a framework for land use decisions. It has been held that policies in a development plan which restricted development leading to unacceptable levels of pollution, could be used to justify refusing planning permission to an applicant with previous convictions for pollution offences (*Blake & Sons* v *Secretary of State for the Environment and Colchester BC* [1998] Env LR 309). This approach neatly side-steps the normal rule that only issues to do with the proposed land use, not the proposed user, are material.

All areas now have a structure plan, but there is a continuing duty for a county planning authority to keep under review matters affecting the development and planning of its area (s. 30), and the new PPG 12 envisages there should now be a formal review every 5 years. In addition, some counties have different structure plans for different parts of the county and are now required to prepare revised plans on a county-wide basis. The procedures for modifying the plan are set out in ss. 31–35C and the Town and Country Planning (Development Plan) (England) Regulations 1999 (SI 1999/3280), which allow for limited public involvement. In essence, the county planning authority produces and publicises reasoned proposals. It must consult with a wide range of interested bodies (including the various regulatory agencies with environmental responsibilities), send a copy to the Secretary of State and allow at least six weeks for members of the public to make representations. Unless the Secretary of State directs otherwise, an examination in public (a limited form of public inquiry at which there is no right to present a case unless invited to do so) must be held. This appears to be dispensed with in over half the cases.

In the past, a structure plan required the approval of the Secretary of State, giving him the final say on the scope and content of the plan and its policies. The power was often used to ensure that policies acceptable to central government were adopted rather than those originally proposed by the local planning authority. This requirement has now been dropped, but the Secretary of State has a power to call a plan in (s. 35A), and thus is able to exercise ultimate control over policy. Although this is sparingly used, the power under s. 35 to direct that a plan is modified has been used on a number of occasions to force county council to increase their housing provision. The unsuccessful challenge to this in *West Sussex County Council* v *Secretary of State for the Environment, Transport and the Regions* [1999] PLCR 365 indicates where power lies in the planning system; the direction would only be overturned if it was *Wednesbury* unreasonable. The plan should be in conformity with the Regional Planning Guidance produced by the Secretary of State.

(b)   Local plans

Local plans are more detailed, consisting of written policies and specific land use allocations by reference to a map, so their relevance to individual development control decisions is much greater. Thus, while a structure plan will determine the projected number of new houses needed, the local plan will identify specific areas deemed capable of catering for such development.

Despite their importance for development control, until the passage of the 1991 Act there was no requirement for all areas to have a local plan. Both through guidance (e.g. Circular 22/84) and through the appeals system, their making was actively discouraged during the 1980s. In line with the move to 'plan-led planning', however, there has been a distinct policy U-turn, and the making of local plans became mandatory under the 1991 Act. Each district planning authority is now under a duty to make a single district-wide local plan. (The delay in adopting local plans, noted on p. 305, means that some 'subject' and 'action area' plans adopted under the old rules might still be in force in some areas.)

Prior to the passage of the 1991 Act, the local planning authority had a discretion to include environmental measures in a local plan, but policies varied from the detailed to the non-existent. There is now a duty, analogous to that for structure plans, to include such policies. Moreover, the local plan must be in 'general conformity' with the structure plan (s. 46). However, if there is a conflict between the two, it is the local plan which prevails, unless the structure plan specifically lists the local plan as not conforming with it (s. 48).

The procedures for making or modifying a local plan are set out in ss. 36–52 and the Town and Country Planning (Development Plan) (England) Regulations 1999 (SI 1999/3280). In the past these procedures allowed for greater individual involvement than structure plans, but the initial procedures are now effectively the same for each type of plan. Objectors must be given at least six weeks notice and have a right to appear at the public inquiry (s. 42). The procedure is governed by a *Code of Practice on Development Plans*, published as an Annex to PPG 12. The local planning authority must consider the Inspector's recommendations and can adopt the local plan formally by resolution, unless the Secretary of State exercises the right to call in the plan for approval — a very rare occurrence (ss. 44 and 45). The local plan should be reviewed at least every 10 years.

(c)   Unitary development plans

The Local Government Act 1985 introduced unitary development plans (UDPs) to replace structure and local plans in metropolitan areas. This is being done gradually, but progress is as slow as with local plans, even though all metropolitan authorities have been directed to make one. Existing structure and local plans remain in force until the Secretary of State brings the new plan into force and existing local plans may be incorporated into it. The Secretary of State can also direct a new unitary authority to prepare a UDP.

The UDP consists of two parts: Part I in general corresponds to the structure plan and Part II to the local plan. The procedures for them are set out in ss. 12–28. Essentially they allow for a mixture of the current procedures used for structure plans and local plans, combining central supervision over strategic and regional matters with a commitment to some public involvement in more detailed matters. There is a provision for all or part of the plan to be called in for central approval, although it is not expected that this will be usual, even for Part I. The Planning and Compensation Act 1991 imposed a duty to include environmental matters in both Parts I and II.

Challenges to development plans

A challenge to a structure plan modification, or to the adoption of a local plan or UDP, can be made by any 'person aggrieved' within six weeks of the decision under s. 287. Two grounds of appeal are provided: that the plan is outside the plan-makers' powers, or that there has been some procedural error. In practice, the courts have held that these statutory grounds are to be equated with normal grounds for judicial review (see *Warren* v *Uttlesford DC* [1997] JPL 1130) and there is little difference in judicial review between a person aggrieved and someone with sufficient standing. The leading case remains *Westminster City Council* v *Great Portland Estates plc* [1985] AC 661. Amongst other things, this emphasises the need to include *all* land use policies in plans, not least in the interests of public participation. The case law shows that the courts impose a stricter duty on local planning authorities to give reasons when their development plan is being adopted than where planning permission is being refused (*Stirk* v *Bridgnorth DC* [1997] JPL 51).

Research by Purdue ([1998] JPL 837) indicates that developers or prospective developers bring most challenges, while costs rules force amenity groups to prefer Ministerial lobbying. Although the number of challenges has increased, a key finding is the relative lack of challenges being brought, bearing in mind the legal significance of the development plan after 1991. This may be explained by the fact that plans often simply legitimise national planning policies. Because of the procedural duties relating to the public local inquiry, a successful challenge to a local plan is more likely than for a challenge to a structure plan. Challenges to development plans under human rights law, especially Article 6 of the ECHR, are a distinct possibility.

Development plans: critique and future

As far as incorporating environmental considerations is concerned, the record appears patchy. Despite government guidance (*Policy Appraisal and the Environment*, DoE, 1991; *Environmental Appraisal of Development Plans: A Good Practice Guide*, DoE, 1993), many organisations have raised concerns about development plan coverage and content, especially about the lack of mention of nature conservation issues (see e.g. CPRE, *Environmental Policy*

Omissions in Development Plans, 1994). More detailed research also indicates the priority attached to economic interests. Local authorities may view the environment either as a commodity or service, or in aesthetic terms, with ecological references being largely rhetorical. Integration of the environment with other key sectors like transport may be lacking. Business interests, and elected councillors anxious to create jobs, exercise most power in determining development plan policies. This leads to an inevitable conclusion in those situations where, as is sometimes the case, the development plan indicates that trade-offs between environmental and non-environmental assets will be handled *through the planning system itself* rather than through any other system of assessing public benefits (see Davoudi et al (1996) 67 TPR 421).

Concerns about the speed of adopting local plans and UDPs have led to significant changes to the Development Plan Regulations 1999. These are aimed at having more targeted consultation, with formal rights of public participation being exercised later in the adoption process, and encourage negotiation with objectors. They will probably also lead to shorter, and arguably more imprecise, plans, giving planning authorities greater discretion when determining planning applications. On the other hand, there is now considerable pressure for development plans to serve as vehicles for sustainable development. This is a major theme of PPG 12 on *Development Plans* (2000), which includes guidance on sustainability appraisals of development plans, on the integration of transport and land use policies.

Perhaps the most notable development is the re-emergence of regional planning. Draft guidance envisages a central role for regional planning guidance, formulated by groupings of 'regional stakeholders', with the Secretary of State acting only as consultee. The proposal is clearly in line with government policy of establishing regional governance structures, but contains many novel features including compulsory environmental assessment and 'sustainability appraisal' for all plans.

Non-statutory plans and guidance

Local planning authorities frequently have other policies and drafts that have not gone through the statutory procedures. In practice, a large range of such 'non-statutory' material, ranging from draft local plans to design briefs and technical specifications, is used by local planning authorities in making decisions. But there are obvious problems in this practice, because it may be seen as subverting the statutory public participation requirements, and thus the democratic legitimacy of the planning process.

In *Westminster City Council* v *Great Portland Estates plc* [1985] AC 661, a distinction was drawn between different types of non-statutory guidance. The House of Lords required that all matters of *policy* should be included in the statutory plan and that only supplementary matters of detail, or those which relate to the implementation of these policies, should be put in non-statutory guidance. However, as long as this non-statutory material is not illegal (i.e. it must relate to the character of the use of land) it is a material consideration under s. 70(2) and must be considered alongside the statutory development plan, although perhaps not always accorded the same weight. The weight attached to it will depend on the circumstances in which it was produced.

The latest version of PPG 12 indicates that the use of this 'Supplementary Planning Guidance' will be encouraged by central government, which will place 'substantial weight' on it.

Development control: the meaning of 'development'

It is in relation to the system of development control that the town and country planning system has its greatest impact on environmental law. Planning permission is required for the carrying out of any development (s. 57(1)). The general approach is to define development very widely so that virtually everything is included initially, and then to relax the need to apply for planning permission, either by excluding activities from being 'development' (as is done under the Use Classes Order), or by deeming planning permission to be granted under some kind of development order (such as the General Permitted Development Order) or similar provision. This has the effect of shifting the focus in most practical situations from what is included to what is excluded (see further pp. 312 and 314).

Development is defined in s. 55(1), which provides that:

> Development . . . means the carrying out of building, engineering, mining or other operations in, on, over or under land, or the making of any material change in the use of any buildings or other land.

This definition has effectively remained unchanged since 1947, so past decisions of the courts, which are the ultimate interpreters of the meaning of the Act, are relevant. Decisions of the Secretary of State on appeal are also of importance in understanding the definition. Although these are not binding as legal authority, in practice they can have a prescriptive effect.

The courts have decided that the existence of development is a question of 'fact and degree' in each particular case. It is for the local planning authority (or the Secretary of State on appeal) to apply the relevant law to the facts of each case to decide whether there has been development. The courts limit themselves to supervising and reviewing these decisions under normal judicial review grounds.

There are two limbs to 'development' — operational development and development by a material change of use.

(a)   Operational development
This involves building, mining or engineering operations. 'Other operations' is a little discussed (or relied on) catch-all category apparently designed to ensure that matters such as waste disposal and drilling are covered.

(i)   Building operations
These are defined very widely in s. 336. 'Building' includes any structure or erection, and any part of a building as so defined, but does not include plant

or machinery comprised in a building. 'Building operations' include rebuilding operations, structural alterations of or additions to buildings, demolition of buildings and other operations normally undertaken by a person carrying on business as a builder.

Any significant works are included, such as rebuilding works, works of alteration, the building of an extension, and the erection of such things as shop canopies, walls, advertising hoardings and large sculptures. In one celebrated example, the erection of a model shark emerging from the roof of a house was held to amount to a building operation (though it ultimately received planning permission: [1993] JPL 194). It is normally considered that very minor alterations, such as the installation of ordinary TV aerials, are not significant enough to amount to development. Moveable structures like cranes may amount to 'buildings' depending on the degree of permanent attachment to the land and the ease with which they can be removed from the land (*Barvis Ltd* v *SSE* [1971] P & CR 710).

(ii)   Engineering operations
The Act gives little guidance on the meaning of this term. The test used by the courts is whether they are 'operations of the kind usually undertaken by engineers, that is, operations calling for the skills of an engineer' (*Fayrewood Fish Farms* v *Secretary of State for the Environment* [1984] JPL 267). There are many exceptions for public works in s. 55 and the General Permitted Development Order.

(iii)   Mining operations
These include all forms of extractive operation, such as mining, quarrying and the removal of materials from mineral deposits and waste tips (s. 55(4)). There are additional powers over minerals development, exercised by county planning authorities.

(b)   Development by material change of use of land or buildings
The power to control changes in the use of land is virtually exclusive to British town and country planning, and makes it peculiarly able to exercise detailed control over land use. In the debates on the 1947 Act, Lord Reid, then an MP but later a Law Lord, is reported to have said of material change of use, 'Nobody knows what that means'. And very little guidance is given in the Act on the meaning of this rather vague phrase. But over the years the judges have filled in any gaps by the creation of a number of important explanatory concepts. Nevertheless, this remains a somewhat flexible phrase, and flexibility is aided by decisions whether development has taken place in any particular case being a matter for the local planning authority, applying the law to the facts. What is important is that the change must be material in a planning sense, that is it must have:

(a)   a physical impact on the land;
(b)   a substantial impact; and
(c)   an impact that is relevant to town and country planning.

The unit of land to be considered when ascertaining whether there has been a change of use is called the *planning unit*. This is normally the unit of occupation prior to the change and it is unusual to aggregate together more than one unit of occupation, or to subdivide one, unless 'two or more physically distinct areas are occupied for substantially different and unrelated purposes' (*Burdle* v *Secretary of State for the Environment* [1972] 1 WLR 1207). Thus a factory is usually treated as one unit, allowing some internal shifting of activities between parts of the site.

The courts have also laid down further tests. Thus, an ancillary use will not normally be of any planning concern. But if it becomes a dominant use there has been a material change, such as where 44 dogs were kept in a dwellinghouse. In effect, the house had two main uses: residential and dog-breeding (*Wallington* v *Secretary of State for Wales* (1990) 62 P & CR 150). And an *intensification* of a use can also be a material change of use: the question the courts often ask is whether the intensified use is so different in nature that it could be given a different name (see *Royal Borough of Kensington and Chelsea* v *SSE* [1981] JPL 50). This might be the case where someone goes from repairing her own car in her garage to mending several cars on a commercial basis.

'Land' is defined as meaning any 'corporeal hereditament' (that is, the physical and tangible aspects of property, as opposed to any intangible rights), including a building. Whether there could be material change in the use of land by establishing a floating heliport on the River Thames was considered in *Thames Heliports plc* v *London Borough of Tower Hamlets* [1997] JPL 448. Although flowing water is not a corporeal hereditament, the Court of Appeal held that use of navigable water can be a use of land as the use of the navigable water related to a use of the river bed or channel. The judgment is notable for implying that 'material' means material to humans, but then seemingly giving this a wide interpretation to include environmental effects.

Exemption from the need to apply for planning permission

As noted above, the legislation exempts developers from having to apply for planning permission in one of two ways. First, some activities are deemed not to amount to 'development'. These include many activities with considerable environmental impacts, such as the use of land for agriculture. Secondly, certain activities are automatically granted planning permission.

One consequence of the distinction between these categories is that those activities that are not defined as development escape other controls which are important in environmental terms. These include the general Town and Country Planning (Environmental Impact Assessment) (England and Wales) Regulations 1999. Although impact assessment for some activities which are not development is separately provided for in regulations, there can be no general 'catch-all' provision. They also include key nature conservation controls which build on controls under planning law.

(a)   Activities which do not constitute development
The following operations and uses of land do not constitute development (ss. 55(2)(a)–(g)):

(a)   maintenance, improvement or alterations to a building affecting only its interior, or not materially affecting the external appearance;

(b)   certain works carried out by highway authorities to maintain or improve roads;

(c)   works by local authorities or statutory undertakers for the inspection, repair or renewal of sewers, mains etc., including breaking open streets;

(d)   the use of any buildings or other land within the curtilage of a dwellinghouse for any purpose incidental to the enjoyment of the dwelling-house as such;

(e)   a change of use within the same class of the Use Classes Order (e.g. change of use from a post office to funeral directors would not be development, as both are found in the same Use Class (Class AI Shops)) (see below);

(f)   the use of land for the purposes of agriculture or forestry (including afforestation) and the use for any of those purposes of any building occupied together with land so used;

(g)   the demolition of any description of building specified in a direction given by the Secretary of State to local planning authorities generally or to a particular local authority.

(b)   Use Classes Order
The Use Classes Order is used as a way of avoiding the need for planning permission for what are considered to be changes between uses that have a reasonably similar land use impact. The current Town and Country Planning (Use Classes) Order 1987 (SI 1987/764) is significantly more liberal than previous Orders, a legacy of the deregulatory strategy followed in the 1980s. More recent widening of the general industrial class (B2) to include what were formerly grouped together as special industrial uses (under SI 1995/297) were justified on the basis that control could be exercised effectively by pollution control agencies. But given the different impacts on amenity that some authorised changes may give rise to — e.g. change from an engineering use to a blood-boiling factory — this might be questioned.

Certain unusual uses (so-called '*sui generis*' uses) are not found in any Class, and neither are concurrent uses where the components are in different Classes. Non-listed uses include petrol stations, scrapyards and mineral storeyards, so a change to these uses always requires planning permission. Some uses of land, such as agricultural uses, are simply not mentioned in the Order, because the *use* of land for agriculture is not development.

(c)   Existing uses
Normally there is a right to carry on the existing use of a site, unless it is in breach of planning control. This is roughly equivalent to a property right attaching to the land and has a distinct value. Of course, when the occupier of land voluntarily changes the use, the existing use right switches from the old to the new use.

Existing use rights have been described as 'hardy beasts with a great capacity for survival' (Lord Scarman in *Pioneer Aggregates (UK) Ltd* v *Secretary of State for the Environment* [1985] AC 132), but they may be abandoned by a lengthy period of disuse (*Hartley* v *Minister of Housing and Local Government* [1970] 1 QB 413). It is also possible to lose the benefit of the existing use of a site by carrying out works or changes which effect a *radical change* to the site (*Jennings Motors Ltd* v *Secretary of State for the Environment* [1982] QB 541). This applies whether planning permission is obtained or not. If there is a planning permission, any limitations in it will be operative; if there is no permission, then *any* use of the site will be in breach of planning control. Otherwise, an existing use right can only be removed by a discontinuance order (s. 102), or an order revoking planning permission (ss. 97–100). In both cases compensation is payable.

It is not possible to abandon a planning permission, since it is a public right attaching to the land not the occupier. This is illustrated by *Pioneer Aggregates (UK) Ltd* v *Secretary of State for the Environment* [1984] 3 WLR 32, where a perpetual permission for quarrying was granted in 1950. Quarrying ceased in 1966 and, when it was recommenced in 1980, the local planning authority argued that the use had been abandoned. The House of Lords decided that the planning permission still applied to permit quarrying and any removal of that right would entail payment of compensation.

This position distinguishes planning control from most other areas of environmental control. As a matter of practice, the rules on compensation mean that there is little scope to vary a planning permission once it has been granted, even though variation and revocation are possible in theory (s. 97). Compensation must be paid even where the circumstances have changed radically in a way that was not foreseen at the time the permission was granted. This emphasises that a grant of planning permission is an irrevocable event, effectively creating rights for the landowner in a way that a consent from a pollution control agency does not.

In relation to minerals planning permissions, however, the position is rather different, and awareness of the environmental harm that can be caused by permissions granted many decades previously means that old permissions can now have environmental protection conditions attached to them (see Part III of the Act, as amended by the 1991 Act, and generally Hughes, *Environmental Law*, Butterworths, 1996, ch. 8).

'Development' activities for which planning permission is granted by statute

Certain activities are automatically granted planning permission under statute. Some use has always been made of a *general* development order. However, the 1980s saw the use of new ways of deeming planning permission to be granted in *specific* areas, a departure from the previously uniform approach and a key deregulatory mechanism designed to effect the regeneration of the inner cities.

(a)   Development permitted under the General Permitted Development Order
The Town and Country Planning (General Permitted Development) Order 1995 (SI 1995/418) (the GPDO) grants automatic planning permission for

33 classes of development, listed and defined in sch. 1. These are called 'permitted development rights'. There has been some relaxation of the GPDO in order to remove what were seen as unnecessary restrictions on development. In addition, the Town and Country Planning (General Development Procedure) Order 1995 (SI 1995/419) (the GDPO) sets out various procedural requirements connected with both permitted development and normal planning applications. Three general types of activity are exempted in this way:

(a) minor developments;
(b) developments carried out by a whole range of public services, such as drainage authorities and statutory undertakers; and
(c) favoured activities, especially agriculture and forestry.

The GPDO often includes thresholds above which development consent will still be needed. In the case of certain permitted agricultural and forestry buildings, however, local planning authorities have certain powers over their siting and design, and prior notification now also extends to mobile phone masts. And in some cases, permitted development rights are withdrawn for a number of developments including those which require environmental assessment (see the Town and Country Planning (Environmental Assessment) (England and Wales) Regulations 1999 (SI 1999/293); p. 347 below) or which are likely to have a significant impact upon certain areas of nature conservation value. Certain automatic rights are more restricted in national parks, areas of outstanding national beauty and conservation areas.

Under Article 4 of the GPDO, a local planning authority may restrict automatic rights by serving a direction withdrawing the automatic planning permission, in which case permission must be sought in the ordinary way. The direction may be general to a type of development or specific to a site. Such directions normally require the approval of the Secretary of State, must be made before the development is started and involves the payment of compensation to owners and occupiers, because effectively they take away the right to develop.

(b) Development permitted under a Special Development Order
A more specific version of permitted development is provided under s. 59. This process has been used for granting blanket permissions in new towns, urban development areas (a deregulatory product of the Local Government, Planning and Land Act 1980, now in the process of being phased out) and enterprise zones. The Thermal Oxide Reprocessing Plant (THORP) at Sellafield was also permitted in this way by the Town and Country Planning (Windscale and Calder Works) Special Development Order 1978 (SI 1978/523). In this case the Order followed a public inquiry and a Parliamentary debate, but neither is strictly required.

(c) Development in an enterprise zone
Enterprise zones were also introduced by the Local Government, Planning and Land Act 1980 to encourage business activity. The order establishing an

enterprise zone, made by the Secretary of State after some limited publicity, grants automatic planning permission for categories of development specified in the enterprise zone scheme (1990 Act, s. 88). However, the local authority draws up the scheme to cover those matters it wishes to permit. Thus, while enterprise zones are formally designated by the Secretary of State, local authorities decide what is to be permitted. They also remain the local planning authority for other development not covered by the scheme.

An enterprise zone normally lasts for 10 years and involves fiscal and administrative advantages for those in it, as well as the planning exemptions. Few new zones are now expected to be made, but development commenced before the expiry of the scheme retains the benefit of the automatic permission.

(d)   Development in a simplified planning zone

These were introduced in the Housing and Planning Act 1986. As with an enterprise zone scheme, a simplified planning zone scheme grants automatic planning permission for the matters specified in it, but there are no non-planning effects (TCPA 1990 Act, s. 82).

Every district planning authority has a duty to consider whether to impose a simplified planning zone in part of its area. It must prepare a scheme if satisfied it is expedient to do so. Anybody may request the making of a scheme and the Secretary of State may direct the making of one. There is no requirement that the scheme be approved by the Secretary of State, though it may be called in for approval. A simplified planning zone lasts for 10 years, but development commenced before the expiry of the scheme retains the benefit of the automatic permission. Despite the streamlining of the designation in 1992 (SI 1992/2414) only a handful have been made.

National parks, areas of outstanding natural beauty, conservation areas, sites of special scientific interest, and designated green belt cannot be the subject of a scheme. County matters are also excluded, as are matters covered by the need for an environmental assessment.

(e)   Developments authorised by a government department

If authorisation from a government department is needed for a development to be carried out by bodies like local authorities and statutory undertakers, then that authorisation also acts as a deemed planning permission (s. 90). This prevents a duplication of effort, but does result in the decision being taken centrally rather than locally. For example, applications for the construction of major projects such as nuclear power stations are dealt with like this, since permission for power stations is also required from the Department of Trade and Industry under the Electricity Act 1989 and operators are classed as statutory undertakers.

Special cases

Although not cases of 'deemed permission', streamlined procedures apply in the following cases:

(a) Where local authorities grant themselves planning permission (s. 316 and the Town and Country Planning General Regulations 1992 (SI 1992/1492)). The intention to acquire planning permission must be publicised, and representations taken into account. But any permission the authority resolves to grant itself is deemed to have been granted by the Secretary of State, so there is no right of appeal; it can be challenged only be judicial review. The possible conflicts of interest have led the courts to interpret the procedural requirements strictly (*Steeples* v *Derbyshire CC* [1985] 1 WLR 256).

(b) Where use is made of private or hybrid Acts of Parliament. These avoid any of the planning procedures and effectively give the decision to a small Parliamentary joint committee, with limited public scrutiny. An example with a significant environmental effect is the Channel Tunnel Act 1987. Nowadays, the Transport and Works Act 1992 tends to be used, principally for railways and tram projects such as the Leeds Supertram, but it can also be used for works which interfere with navigation, and so could be used for bridges. There will be a public inquiry and the Secretary of State can (and in practice will) consider granting deemed planning permission at the same time as any Works Order is determined.

(c) Crown land (land owned by the Crown and Government Departments, but not nationalised industries) is effectively excluded from the Act by the provision of immunity against service of an enforcement notice. Circular 18/84 states that Crown bodies have agreed to abide informally by the same procedures and requirements as apply to private developers, but this system is not legally enforceable. One exception is that Crown immunity has been removed from health authorities and NHS trusts by the National Health Service and Community Care Act 1990.

Is planning permission required?

There is a fairly simple mechanism for ascertaining whether planning permission is required. Section 192 provides that anyone may apply to the district planning authority for a certificate of lawfulness of proposed use or development, specifying the proposed use or operation. A certificate must be granted if the authority is satisfied that the use or operation would be lawful if subsisting or carried out at the time of the application. This is then conclusive of the legality of the development, as long as circumstances do not change before the development takes place. In other words, a certificate is the equivalent of a planning permission for what it covers.

The exact procedures for an application are contained in the GDPO. Since the application has to be specific, it is not possible to make one that relates to a hypothetical situation. Neither is it possible to apply after the development has taken place. In such a situation, the only way of discovering the position would be to seek a declaration in the High Court (a very expensive step), or to await the service of an enforcement notice and then appeal against it. The applicant may appeal under s. 78 to the Secretary of State against a determination under s. 192, or against a failure to make one within eight weeks.

Applying for planning permission

Anyone can apply for planning permission. It is not necessary to be the owner or occupier of the property, or even a prospective occupier. An application may even be used as a form of publicity stunt. For example, Friends of the Earth once submitted an application for an oversize replica of the Leaning Tower of Pisa to draw attention to the inadequacy of the UK Atomic Energy Authority's application for a nuclear reprocessing plant at Dounreay.

There are several types of permission the applicant may seek, including full permission or retrospective permission (s. 63(2)), and an application for the renewal of planning permission. In addition, a developer may apply for 'outline permission' only (see s. 92 and GDPO, art. 3). This allows developers to 'test the water' with the local planning authority to see whether a general type of development would be acceptable. 'Reserved matters' such as design and landscaping need not be submitted at this stage, but must generally be approved within three years (GDPO, art. 4). Outline permission may also be sought where the nature of the development means that it is difficult to know what it will eventually contain, e.g. retail parks (this has posed problems for developers where environmental impact assessment is needed; see further p. 356). Applicants can also ask for a condition of a planning permission to be discharged without putting the rest of the permission at risk (s. 73). This is an important means of removing outdated restrictions and providing a measure of continuing control over development.

(a)   Steps for the applicant to take

The applicant must apply on a form provided by the local planning authority. It must also notify owners and tenants of the land and submit a certificate to the authority stating that it has done so. This enables these people to be aware of the application and to make representations that the authority must take into account. It is an offence knowingly to issue a false certificate.

In *Main* v *Swansea City Council* (1984) 49 P & CR 26, the Court of Appeal decided that failure to carry out such procedures does not necessarily render a subsequent grant of planning permission void: it all depends on whether anyone with standing has been prejudiced as a result. This applies to most procedures under the Act. In any case, *R* v *Rotherham Metropolitan Borough Council, ex parte Rankin* [1990] 1 PLR 93 shows that an action to quash a permission must be brought without delay.

Fees are payable for all applications for planning permission and deemed applications in connection with an appeal against an enforcement notice. There are fixed charges for different types of applications. The categories are set out in the Town and Country Planning (Fees for Applications and Deemed Applications) Regulations 1989 (SI 1989/193 (as amended)). The local planning authority need not consider an application until the requisite fee has been paid.

The current rates (they are periodically increased) are set out in the Town and Country Planning (Fees for Applications and Deemed Applications) (Amendment) Regulations 1997 (SI 1997/37). For example, the rate is £190 for each house and for a material change of use, and £95 for extensions. At present the fees do not cover the full administrative cost to the local planning authoriy of processing applications but, in line with government policy, the level can be expected to rise in order to do so in the next few years.

(b)   Steps for the local planning authority to take

On receipt of an application, the local planning authority will consult with a wide range of public bodies as required for specified situations by the GDPO 1995, art. 10. These include highways authorities, other local authorities, parish and community councils, the Environment Agency, the Ministry of Agriculture, Fisheries and Food, and the relevant Nature Conservancy Council. There is a code of conduct governing this consultation procedure and those consulted have procedural rights in the event of an appeal. Any representations that are made are material considerations which must be taken into account by the local planning authority before it decides the application. However, it must not slavishly follow the advice of another public body, otherwise the decision will be challengeable for fettering of discretion.

The local planning authority must also publicise *all* applications (GDPO, arts. 6 to 8). This reflects a major change from the position prior to 1992, when there were no statutory publicity requirements other than for applications which did not conform with the development plan, applications relating to a listed building or in a conservation area (the duties in this respect still exist in addition to those explained below), applications subject to environmental assessment (see Chapter 12), and applications for a certain number of anti-social activities termed 'bad-neighbour' developments.

The rigours of the earlier position were mitigated by most local planning authorities including provision for publicity in a wider range of cases in their standing orders, as indeed they were encouraged to do by circular. For example, neighbours and others likely to be affected would often be informed of an application. The Local Government Ombudsman formalised some of these practices by deciding that, where a local authority had a policy of publicising applications, it would amount to maladministration not to follow that policy in any given case (see the case at [1983] JPL 613). However, this approach is of limited use since, while it may result in an aggrieved neighbour receiving an apology or some compensation for not being notified, an Ombudsman cannot quash the planning permission. Nevertheless, it remains an alternative course of action should the statutory requirements be ignored.

The publicity requirements set out in the GDPO split applications into three categories:

(i)   major developments, such as developments on sites of more than one hectare, the building of 10 or more houses, developments involving 1,000 square metres or more of floor space, and mineral and waste applications — in these cases an advertisement must be placed in a local newspaper and either a site notice posted or neighbours notified;

(ii)   applications covered by the need for an environmental assessment, or which do not accord with the provisions of the development plan, or which affect a public right of way — in these cases a newspaper advertisement and a site notice are required;

(iii)   in all other cases either a site notice or neighbour notification can be used.

In addition, the Town and Country Planning (Development Plans and Consultation) Directions 1992 require that certain applications which do not accord with the provisions of the development plan should be referred to the Secretary of State so that a decision can be made whether to call them in. On the basis of court decisions such as *Main* v *Swansea City Council* (1984) 49 P & CR 26 and *R* v *St Edmundsbury Borough Council, ex parte Investors in Industry Commercial Properties Ltd* [1985] 1 WLR 1168, it must be assumed that a failure to comply with these procedures may invalidate a decision, but would not necessarily do so because of the discretionary nature of judicial review.

Determining the planning application

The Secretary of State has an unfettered power to call in any planning application for determination (s. 77). This immediately transfers jurisdiction from the local planning authority to the Secretary of State. This power is used sparingly, usually only for matters of national or regional importance or of local controversy, such as significant developments in the Green Belt. There is a right to a public inquiry unless waived by the parties and the Secretary of State and one is normally held. The procedures are virtually the same as for appeals, suitably amended to provide for this being a first determination. There is no formal power to request the Secretary of State to call in an application: objectors should write to the Secretary of State putting their case for this to happen. The Secretary of State also has related powers to make directions to local planning authorities, for example to consult him before deciding an application (GDPO, art. 10(3)).

In the usual case, however, a local planning authority has eight weeks in which to decide the application (in accordance with the substantive rules outlined below), after which time the applicant can appeal as if the application were refused (GDPO, art. 20). Whether the application is called-in or not, the decision-maker may grant planning permission unconditionally, grant permission subject to conditions or refuse permission. The decision must be in writing and must include reasons for the decision and the imposition of any conditions. These are normally brief and it seems that a failure to provide reasons does not make the decision void. Public registers of all applications and decisions must be maintained (s. 69, and GDPO, art. 25). These, and the enforcement registers (see p. 338) are an invaluable guide to the planning history of a site.

Summary of rights of third parties

Third parties or objectors have limited specific rights under the legislation, although statutory publicity is now required for all applications and the Local

Government (Access to Information) Act 1985 ensures the right to attend council meetings (see p. 176). Any representations made to the local planning authority must be considered as a material consideration.

Since third parties have no right to appeal against a planning decision, they must apply for judicial review of any adverse decision. This entails having standing, acting without delay, and being able to afford the large costs involved, and has very little chance of success. Only local planning authority decisions can be subject to judicial review: decisions of the Secretary of State are immune from challenge except under s. 288 (see p. 336). If an appeal is brought by the applicant, third parties have wider procedural rights at that stage.

The local planning authority's discretion

Under s. 70(2), in deciding whether or not to grant permission, the local planning authority 'shall have regard to the provisions of the development plan, so far as material to the application, and to any other material considerations'. The Secretary of State is subject to the same requirements in relation to decisions on a s. 78 appeal, or which are called in under s. 77.

It is central to an understanding of planning law to appreciate the scope of s. 70(2):

(a)   It gives the local planning authority a wide *discretion* whether or not to grant permission.

(b)   This discretion must be exercised on grounds of *planning policy*.

(a)   The role of the Secretary of State and the courts

The principal means of controlling this discretion is through the appeals system. The Secretary of State (usually through an Inspector) considers afresh the whole application, and can form his own opinion on what planning policy requires, effectively exercising a stranglehold over the appeals process. He can consider both legal grounds (e.g. that the objections are not planning objections) and policy grounds (e.g. that too much weight was attached to objections).

By contrast, the courts will only interfere if there has been some illegality in the decision-making process, and ordinary principles of public law are applied (see p. 73). As long as the policies that are applied are lawful (i.e. relevant to planning), the courts do not interfere with their content. This is effectively a principle of non-intervention in policy matters. Accordingly, the *weight* given to any policy is a matter for the decision-maker, unless the decision is perverse. As Lord Hoffmann said in *Tesco Stores Ltd* v *Secretary of State for the Environment and others* [1995] JPL 581, 'If there is one principle of planning law more firmly settled than any other, it is that matters of planning judgment are within the exclusive province of the local planning authority or the Secretary of State'. However, it is impermissible to have an absolute policy, or to apply it rigidly, since this would constitute an unlawful fettering of discretion (*Stringer* v *Minister of Housing and Local Government* [1970] 1 WLR 1281). The courts thus see their role as ensuring that decisions are made rationally in the light of all planning considerations. This is ensured by the requirement that *reasons* must be given for decisions, something that has attracted a great deal of attention in recent cases.

As discussed previously, the 1980s saw a strengthening of 'developer-led' planning. This was encouraged by strongly worded policy guidance indicating that the onus was on local planning authorities to show why development could *not* be permitted. Unless specific restraint policies applied, such as in the Green Belt (see PPG 2), the guidance required development to be permitted 'unless the development would cause demonstrable harm to interests of acknowledged importance' (Circular 14/85, repeated in PPG 1 (1988)).

Such explicitly directory planning guidance could be used to great effect because of the Secretary of State's role in the appeals process. But it was also powerful because of the approach of the courts in refusing to prioritise the weight given either to the development plan or to other material considerations. The development plan was an important consideration, but need not be 'slavishly adhered to' (*Enfield London Borough Council* v *Secretary of State for the Environment* [1975] JPL 155). Unlike the situation in many other countries, a plan did not have to be followed; it was a statement of aims or objectives only.

The relevance of the presumption in favour of development was addressed by the House of Lords in *London Residuary Body* v *Lambeth London Borough Council* [1990] 1 WLR 744, which decided that the policy presumption must be taken into account and had the weight attached to it by the decision-maker. As a matter of interpretation, it was not limited to resolving a deadlock where the factors in favour of permission equalled those against, as suggested by the Court of Appeal. This decision, by confirming the principle of non-intervention in the contents of policies, allowed the government freedom to accord the presumption a very high value.

(b)   The presumption in favour of the development plan

This state of affairs has now changed. The first signs of any change were seen in a number of appeal decisions around the start of the 1990s which decided that where there was an up-to-date plan with clear policies that were in conformity with regional and national policies, then it was likely to be followed. Legislative recognition of this point was provided by s. 54A, which was inserted by the Planning and Compensation Act 1991. This states:

> Where, in making any determination under the planning Acts, regard is to be had to the development plan, the determination shall be made in accordance with the development plan unless material considerations indicate otherwise.

This section appears to introduce a presumption in favour of following the provisions of the development plan, because it replaces the existing duty to 'have regard to' the plan with a duty to act 'in accordance with' it. This is certainly the position espoused by government Ministers in all administrations since 1991, who have suggested that the period of 'market-led' or 'developer-led' planning has been replaced by 'plan-led' planning.

Initially, the courts appeared to hold that the presumption in favour of the development was not a strong one and could be rebutted fairly easily (at least as a matter of law, if not of policy — see further below) by other considerations, such as central government policy and the presumption in favour of development, as long as the reasoning was clear and rational (see *St Albans District Council* v *Secretary of State for the Environment* (1992) 66 P & CR 432). In *Loup* v *Secretary of State for the Environment* [1996] JPL 22, however, the Court of Appeal seemingly elevated the strength of the presumption in favour of the development plan by referring to part of PPG1 (subsequently revised — see further below) which referred to the planning system operating 'on the basis that applications for development should be allowed, having regard to the development plan and all material considerations, unless the proposed development would cause demonstrable harm to interests of acknowledged importance'. In doing so, the court acknowledged that the whole purpose of the plan-led system was to give certainty to the development plan, which in turn would lead to greater consistency in decision-making. The relative certainty created by the development plan could itself amount to an interest of acknowledged importance.

In what is now the leading case on s. 54A, the House of Lords has held that the presumption in favour of the plan is neither a 'governing' nor a 'paramount' one (*City of Edinburgh Council* v *Secretary of State for Scotland* [1998] JPL 224). Nor does a decision-maker have to follow any particular procedure; the plan and the other considerations can, if preferred, be taken together, and the plan need not be considered first in time. This judicial guidance, however, should not be confused with policy guidance on s. 54A which is now set out in the latest version of PPG 1 from 1997. Unlike the previous version, which was influential in *Loup*, this further downgrades the policy presumption in favour of development, saying only that 'those deciding . . . planning applications or appeals should always *take into account* whether the proposed development would cause demonstrable harm to interests of acknowledged importance' (emphasis added). This could once again lead to a watering down of s. 54A, on the basis that taking the harm into account (when considering the development plan as an interest of acknowledged importance) could mean that there is a return to the position which makes the presumption in favour of the plan rebuttable by fairly weak considerations.

The guidance on the basic approach that decision-makers ought to employ in determining applications or appeals is virtually unchanged in the latest version of PPG 1. The plan is said to be the starting point. If the proposal is in accordance with the plan, it will normally be granted permission. If the proposal is in conflict with it, the developer will normally have to produce 'convincing reasons' to show why the plan should not apply. If the plan is neutral, then the presumption in favour of development has a role to play as one of the material considerations. It is clear that importance will be attached to such things as the age of the plan, the strength of the relevant policies, how far they are consistent with other national and regional policies, and whether the Secretary of State had intervened during the making of the plan. On this last point, PPG 1 states that if there was no formal intervention at the plan-making stage, it may be assumed that the Secretary of State 'will attach commensurate weight' to the plan on any appeal.

In summary, it appears that the planning system has moved into an age that can still be characterised by the description 'plan-led', but that this is no guarantee that the plan will always be followed, since the weight to be accorded to the plan remains, untimately, a matter for the decision-maker. One point that has therefore acquired increased significance is the interpretation of development plans. In the past it has often been assumed that this is a matter of law for the courts to decide. This is undoubtedly correct, but it does not solve the question of whether the courts will impose their own interpretation or will be content to adopt the less interventionist method of reviewing whether the decision-maker's interpretation was a reasonable one. This is crucial to the extent to which the courts will interfere with decisions via s. 54A. Past experience suggests that they will continue with their normal, non-interventionist approach and adopt the second method, thus reinforcing the view that the real change in planning that was envisaged in the 1990s will result from actual changes in policy rather than from anything the courts require. Or, as Lord Hope puts it in the *City of Edinburgh* case, 'It would be a mistake to think that the effect of [s.54A] was to increase the power of the court to intervene in decisions about planning control'.

If present government reforms relating to local plans and UDPs are enacted and less precise plans are adopted in the future, this may give greater discretion to decision-makers in relation to determining what 'the development plan' requires, and thus even less scope for the courts to intervene.

(c)   Other material considerations

The key point as to the meaning of 'other material considerations' is that the Act gives no guidance on this term, which has fallen to the courts to be interpreted. To be material a consideration has to be material to planning, and material to the application. Certain matters will always be taken into account: non-statutory plans, government planning guidance such as circulars and PPGs (*Pye Ltd* v *West Oxfordshire DC* [1982] JPL 577), the results of consultations, and any representations made by third parties or objectors. Other matters, such as impacts on amenity, on the local economy, transport and highways considerations, the balance of land use in the area, will nearly always be material on the facts.

A range of other matters have also been held to be material in certain circumstances: the effect on private rights (*Stringer* v *Minister of Housing and Local Government* [1970] 1 WLR 1281); the existing use of the site (*Clyde & Co.* v *Secretary of State for the Environment* [1977] 1 WLR 926); the personal circumstances of the occupier (*Tameside Metropolitan Borough Council* v *Secretary of State for the Environment* [1984] JPL 180); the precedent effect of a decision (*Collis Radio Ltd* v *Secretary of State for the Environment* (1975) 29 P & CR 390); and the availability of alternative sites, which has great implications for objectors seeking to put forward the argument that another site elsewhere is more suitable for the development (see *Greater London Council* v *Secretary of State for the Environment* (1985) 52 P & CR 158). The achievement of a separate planning objective of the local planning authority can also be material. Protecting the Royal Opera House by allowing it to raise funds by carrying out office development which would not otherwise have been permitted has been upheld (*R v Westminster City Council, ex parte Monahan* [1988] JPL 557). This principle has been used to fund the conservation of wildlife sites, such as at Barn Elms in West London, by allowing a limited amount of otherwise unacceptable development on the site.

It should be noted that emerging plans (*R v City of London Corporation, ex parte Allan* (1980) 79 LGR 223) and whether the application is premature in the light of such plans (*Arlington Securities Ltd v Secretary of State for the Environment* (1989) 57 P & CR 407) are not 'the development plan' but material considerations to be weighed in the balance. The closer a plan is to being adopted, the more weight it will carry. Equally, supplementary planning guidance such as design briefs are not 'the plan' but material considerations. While the need for a development may also be material, it is not the job of the local authority to second-guess the financial viability of a scheme.

Environmental considerations as material considerations

In relation to environmental matters, it is clear that planning permission may be refused on a number of grounds. An industrial development may be refused because of possible pollution or safety problems (e.g. it is possible to prevent a plant handling dangerous substances, or a waste disposal site, from being sited near to a sensitive watercourse). A housing estate may be refused because of the inadequacy of the existing sewerage provision. The impact of noise on neighbouring properties will also be material, as may be the objective of pursuing the BPEO (*R v Bolton Metropolitan Council, ex parte Kirkman* [1998] Env LR 719). There are also a number of situations in which EC obligations will be material considerations in planning decisions. Often the mechanism used for bringing these to planning authorities' attention is government guidance. For example, PPG 9 gives advice on the extent to which nature conservation interests protected under EC law ought to be taken into account.

However, it must be remembered that these are only some of the matters that must be taken into account. The final decision involves a balancing of all the factors. A clear example of the discretion given to the local planning authority to decide that other factors outweigh environmental ones is *R v Exeter City Council, ex parte J. L. Thomas & Co. Ltd* [1991] 1 QB 471, considered in Chapter 10, where a decision to grant planning permission for a development that would be likely to lead to private nuisance claims by the future occupants of the new development was unchallengeable in public law.

The weight accorded to environmental considerations can be seen in *West Coast Wind Farms Ltd v Secretary of State for the Environment and North Devon DC* [1996] JPL 767. An application to construct two wind farms was refused. Although government planning advice (PPG 22) supports energy from wind, it also recognises the need to protect local environmental quality, and this latter factor was accorded more weight. The Court of Appeal held that there was no policy presumption in favour of such developments, even if they were a policy aim. Although such sources might be 'needed' in a general sense, each application still had to be decided on its merits. In such situations, of course, refusals can be appealed, and if the policy is genuine it can be enforced appropriately by the Secretary of State. The more difficult situation is where an obviously harmful activity is consented to because each individual contribution to it is minor when looked at in isolation.

The extent to which environmental risks, 'genuine' or perceived, amount to material considerations is considered in more detail below (see p. 342).

Planning conditions

Section 70(1) permits the local planning authority (and the Secretary of State on appeal) to impose such conditions 'as it thinks fit'. This wide discretionary power is limited by statutory guidance in ss. 72 and 75, judicial control over what is permissible, and central government policy.

Statutory guidance is limited and relatively unimportant. Section 72 states that conditions attached to other land under the control of the applicant, and conditions requiring commencement of the development within a specified time, are permissible. It also allows for temporary permissions, which can be used to grant planning permission on a trial basis. This has been used for fibreglass sharks on roofs (see p. 311), and more seriously for 'low impact developments' such as at Tinker's Bubble in Somerset. Section 75(3) enables new buildings to be used for the purpose for which they were designed, unless the permission expressly limits the use.

What are of greater practical importance are the legal tests for the validity of conditions developed over the years by the courts. In contrast with the decisions on material considerations, these have produced some rather restrictive results, possibly because the cases were mainly decided earlier, when a more overt policy of protecting private property rights applied. In the leading case of *Newbury DC v Secretary of State for the Environment* [1981] AC 578, the House of Lords laid down the following tests for valid conditions:

(a) they must be imposed for a planning purpose and not for an ulterior motive;
(a) they must fairly and reasonably relate to the development permitted; and
(c) they must not be perverse ('so unreasonable that no reasonable authority could have imposed them').

The courts have also held that a condition should not be 'hopelessly uncertain', although they have taken a broad view as to what this must entail so that there may be considerable scope for saying that the terms of a condition are ascertainable (*Alderson v Secretary of State for the Environment* (1984) 49 P & CR 307).

Ground (a) above goes to the nature and limits of planning itself. The courts have done this by concluding that certain matters of a social planning nature do not relate to town and country planning. For example, in *R v Hillingdon London Borough Council, ex parte Royco Homes Ltd* [1974] 2 QB 720, a condition requiring that houses be occupied by people on the local authority housing list, who should then be granted ten years security of tenure, was held to be illegal. The burden of housing people in need was placed by statute on the housing authority, not private developers. Whether the courts would take such a strict line now, in the light of the present Government's use of planning guidance to provide for Affordable Housing (see PPG 3), remains to be seen,

Such issues to do with the planning system and social exclusion make it arguable whether the nature and scope of the planning system today is the same as it was in 1974, not least because of the wider policy objectives of using the planning system to achieve sustainability, which necessarily involves going beyond issues of the mere use and character of land. In recent years, the courts have not been asked to rule on the nature of planning, which might be explained by the lack of anyone with sufficient practical interest to do so.

Ground (b) requires that conditions have some geographic and functional link to the site to which the application relates. So a condition requiring works to be carried out on land neither included in the application nor under the control of the applicant is illegal (*Ladbrokes Ltd v Secretary of State* [1981] JPL 427). Thus, a requirement to screen a site by planting trees on neighbouring land will be illegal unless the land is under the applicant's control. But it is possible to make development conditional on the completion of work off-site, such as requiring infrastructure works (roads, sewers, etc) to be satisfactory before development commences (*Grampian Regional Council v Aberdeen District Council* (1983) 47 P & CR 633) ('Grampian conditions').

Finally, a condition can be struck down if it is perverse (ground (c)). This test has normally been used to prevent conditions undermining private property rights without compensation. A prime example is *Hall & Co. Ltd v Shoreham-by-Sea Urban District Council* [1964] 1 WLR 240, where a condition was attached to a permission for industrial development which required an access road to be built on the developer's land at its expense and dedicated to the public. The Court of Appeal held the condition illegal, even though it accepted it was beneficial in planning terms since it created a usable access to otherwise inaccessible land. The position is no different if the developer suggests or accepts such an imposition (*Bradford Metropolitan Council v Secretary of State for the Environment* (1987) 53 P & CR 55). This approach effectively frustrated the use of conditions to secure 'planning gain' for local communities, leading to the rise in the use of planning agreements and obligations for this purpose (see below). But it will not be perverse to impose a 'Grampian condition' even where the condition precedent may be unlikely to occur (*British Railways Board v Secretary of State for the Environment* [1994] JPL 32).

Conditions and policy

On appeal the Secretary of State can add, omit or amend any conditions as part of the total rehearing of the issues. This can be done on legal, factual or policy grounds, so an understanding of the Secretary of State's policy on conditions is essential.

Circular 11/95 requires conditions to be (a) necessary, (b) relevant to planning, (c) relevant to the development permitted, (d) enforceable, (e) precise, and (f) reasonable. In addition, it lays down some very important general policy tests: 'As a matter of policy, a condition ought not to be imposed unless there is a definite need for it'; 'a condition should not be retained unless there are sound and clear cut reasons for doing so'; a condition 'requires special and precise justification' if planning permission would not be refused if the condition were omitted. The local planning authority should also consider whether the imposition of any conditions may render an otherwise objectionable development acceptable, so as to save the application from being refused.

These are not legal requirements, but a local planning authority ignores these tests at its peril because of the applicant's right of appeal. It also appears from *Times Investments Ltd* v *Secretary of State for the Environment* [1990] JPL 433 that a failure to have regard to these policies (e.g. not to demonstrate the harm that would be caused by omitting a particular condition) may render the decision illegal for failure to have regard to a material consideration. Once again, therefore, the Secretary of State's guidance imposes significant restrictions on the decisions that may be reached. Circular 11/95 notes types of condition that would normally be illegal and those that require exceptional justification. Appendix A includes a list of model conditions and Appendix B a list of unacceptable ones.

Planning conditions and environmental protection

One particular issue relates to the use of planning conditions to achieve continuing environmental objectives, especially pollution control. There is a slender but marked distinction between the policy tests laid down in PPG 23 (Planning and Pollution Control) and the relevant circulars and the legal tests laid down in *Newbury District Council* v *Secretary of State for the Environment* [1981] AC 578. One of the important differences is that the legal tests do not suggest that a condition will be unlawful if it duplicates other statutory controls. As long as the matter which is sought to be controlled has a planning purpose (a concept which seems to widen with the passing years), it is lawful.

On the other hand, government policy in Circular 11/95 (echoing the RCEP in its Fifth Report) makes it clear that planning conditions should not be used to deal with difficulties which are the subject of controls under other legislation. The justification for this approach is that it prevents an unnecessary duplication of control or any argument over the nature of the conditions that are to be imposed. Whether it is desirable in policy terms is another matter and local planning authorities will always be wary of imposing conditions which duplicate other controls as the Secretary of State will, more often than not, amend the condition on appeal.

The problems of overlapping conditions can be significant in pollution control. The Department of the Environment's report on *Planning, Pollution and Waste Management* (1992) found that there were two main circumstances where planning conditions were used in the control of pollution. (It should be noted — as Wood, *Planning Pollution Prevention* (Butterworths, 1989), describes — that in general terms the town and country planning system has, for a variety of institutional and other reasons, been relatively *under*used for environmental protection.)

First, there were occasions where the only (or in some cases the most straightforward) means of controlling pollution was by imposing planning conditions (e.g. the control of groundwater pollution from direct or indirect sources, such as storage tanks). Secondly, conditions were used to override existing pollution control systems in circumstances where it was argued that planning authorities had little confidence in the pollution control authorities and wished to maintain a degree of control to protect the amenities of the area. Examples included a condition to impose a release limit which would run with the land, rather than be associated with a licence to operate, and a condition to impose a release limit where the planning authority was concerned that the relevant pollution control authority would not enforce its own controls.

These types of conditions were, and still are, clearly contrary to policy but not unlawful. For example, an Inspector imposed an overlapping condition on sulphur dioxide emissions in the planning appeal involving Ferro-Alloys and Metals Smelter in Glossop (see [1990] 2 LMELR 176). There, the planning authority was concerned about the enforcement record of HMIP and by its remarks that it might revise its condition downwards or not enforce it, and this was accepted by the Inspector as good grounds for imposing the condition. Although the powers (and resources) of the Environment Agency have improved since then, the legality of the determination still appears correct. This is because cases such as *Gateshead Metropolitan Borough Council v Secretary of State for the Environment* [1995] JPL 432 (discussed in more detail at p. 391) and *R v Bolton Metropolitan Council, ex parte Kirkman* [1998] Env LR 719 go no further than to say that the existence of specialist (and effective) pollution control agencies is no more than a material consideration for the planning authority to weigh in the balance. Unless there are overriding obligations (in *Kirkman*, duties under the EC Waste Framework Directive were important), the courts will not say that the existence of such agencies means that matters within their powers cannot be considered by the local planning authority, as this would be unduly fettering discretion.

The practical position therefore appears to be that if a planning authority is generally in favour of a development it may be content to leave a wide range of pollution control and environmental protection issues to specialist regulators, deflecting attention away from its own powers. On the other hand, if the development is less central to the local economy, and of a kind which has caused concerns to residents, it may seek to impose conditions to prevent local environmental harm, knowing that such conditions may be overturned on appeal. This would allow it to enforce via, e.g. a breach of condition notice, rather than rely on enforcement by agencies less accountable to the local electorate. (For examples of the problems faced by local authorities when dealing with odour nuisances: see *Tameside Metropolitan Borough Council* v *Smith Brothers (Hyde) Ltd* [1996] Env LR D4 and *R v Secretary of State for the Environment, ex parte West Wiltshire District Council* [1996] Env LR 312.)

Planning obligations

The town and country planning legislation has always included powers under which a local planning authority could enter into an agreement relating to the development or use of land. Whilst for many years little use was made of these powers, in the 1970s and 1980s they came to be seen as a mechanism for the provision of some form of 'planning gain' (i.e. some gain to the community that would not necessarily have been obtained without the agreement). The increased importance of agreements illustrated the negotiative nature of modern town planning and showed that the concept of planning as a strict system of regulation in which the regulator imposes restrictions on a developer had become rather outdated. But it also gave rise to some concern. There was no need for approval of agreements by the Secretary of State, no provision for publicity or appeal, limited scrutiny of the content of agreements and limited potential for a successful challenge by a third party. As a result, there was a great danger that an agreement could be seen either in terms of the local planning authority 'selling' planning permission to the highest bidder or the developer offering a bribe in return for favourable treatment.

When the Town and Country Planning Act was consolidated in 1990, the provisions on agreements were included as s. 106. However, they were soon completely rewritten by the Planning and Compensation Act 1991. The main change was that developers were enabled to give binding unilateral undertakings as well as to enter into agreements. The phrase 'planning obligations' is now used to cover both agreements and undertakings. It appears that unilateral undertakings have not been used wholesale as a 'developer's charter', although they can be used effectively when the local planning authority is unwilling to agree terms. But their greatest advantage to developers is on appeal — a developer can offer an undertaking and the Secretary of State (subject to the tests detailed below) will have to take it into account in deciding whether to allow the appeal. Other changes made by the 1991 Act were that the various powers were set out far more clearly than under the existing legislation and that a new procedure was introduced in which an application could be made for the discharge or modification of an obligation.

As a result, the redrafted s. 106 represents the current law, though the old provisions continue to apply to agreements made before 25 October 1991. Planning obligations can only be created by deed and by a person who has an interest in the relevant land. They may include positive as well as negative obligations (s. 106(1)). For example, a developer could offer to build and maintain on the site some facility of benefit to the community or could agree that traffic flows on to the site would be regulated in a particular way. They are enforceable against successors in title (s. 106(3)) and are local land charges (s. 106(11)). Where there is a breach, they are enforceable by injunction (s. 106(5)), which is often a more attractive method of enforcement for a local planning authority than reliance on the enforcement notice procedures. The local planning authority has an alternative power to enter the land, carry out the appropriate operations and recover its costs, as long as it gives at least 21 days' notice of its intention to do so (s. 106(6)). Following the Contracts (Rights of Third Parties) Act 1999, there is the possibility that new obligations will be enforceable by the local residents in whose favour, in a sense, they are made.

The creation of a s. 106 obligation does not replace the need to seek planning permission in the normal way, but the existence of a valid obligation is definitely a material consideration that should be taken into account under s. 70(2). The local planning authority will normally link the permission and the obligation by imposing a condition on the permission that implementation depends on the acceptance of a planning obligation. Planning obligation can therefore enable the local planning authority and the developer to supplement a permission by achieving objectives which could not be achieved by planning conditions. Indeed, as the Court of Appeal in *Good v Epping Forest District Council* [1994] JPL 372 remarked, why else would there be provision for them?

Section 106A includes provisions on the modification or discharge of obligations. This may be done by agreement, but there is also a right to apply to the local planning authority for modification or discharge after five years, with an appeal against refusal to the Secretary of State provided by s. 106B. The Town and Country Planning (Modification and Discharge of Planning Obligations) Regulations 1992 (SI 1992/2832) provide the procedures for these sections, but it is clear that the right is narrower than that for discharge of conditions set out in s. 73, thus providing another good reason why local authorities may choose an obligation in preference to conditions. Agreements existing on 25 October 1991 are still covered by the old law on variation and extinguishment, which allows restrictive covenants to be looked at under the Law of Property Act 1925, s. 84.

Planning obligations: the case law

The lawful scope of planning obligations has caused difficulties, reflecting the tensions between *legal* tests and *policy* tests discussed above. In *R v Plymouth City Council, ex parte Plymouth and South Devon Co-operative Society Ltd* (1993) 67 P & CR 78 the Court of Appeal had to examine the legality of the offer by two superstore developers of planning gain — including such things as construction of a tourist information centre, provision of a bird-watching hide, a contribution towards a 'Park and Ride' scheme, and up to £1m for infrastructure works at another site. The Court decided that community benefits could be material considerations even where they were not necessary to overcome or alleviate planning objections. A planning obligation had to satisfy the three tests which applied to conditions, i.e. (a) it must have a planning purpose; (b) it must fairly and reasonably relate to the permitted development; and (c) it must not be perverse or grossly unreasonable. The Court decided that the proposed benefits satisfied these tests.

The House of Lords has subsequently refined this decision in *Tesco Stores Ltd* v *Secretary of State for the Environment* [1995] 1 WLR 759. Once again, the case involved competing superstore developers, one of whom had entered into a planning obligation offering planning gain in the form of private funding for a £6.6m new road, which was intended to relieve traffic congestion, in return for the grant of planning permission for their site. The Inspector placed considerable weight on the offer, and recommended permission be granted, but the Secretary of State disagreed and refused permission.

In the House of Lords it was argued that the offer of funding was a material consideration and that as the Secretary of State failed to have regard to it his decision was flawed. The House took a different approach from the Court of Appeal in *Plymouth* and distinguished the tests for the legality of conditions and planning obligations. In particular, Lord Hoffmann, in an erudite judgment, held that a planning obligation could be valid even where it would not satisfy the second test set out in *Plymouth* (above) in the sense that the connection to the development had only to be more than *de minimis*. Thus, a planning obligation only has to satisfy tests (a) and (c) above. Whilst accepting that it would be unlawful to take into account an obligation which had no connection *whatsoever* with the development, the weight to be attached to the obligation was entirely a matter for the decision-maker (and different decision-makers could take opposing views on the weight to attach to the same obligation). The court did not, however, give any guidance on the sufficiency of the connection between the development and the obligation, other than to infer that it must be 'material'. It is difficult to envisage many obligations which could not be linked to the development in some manner (albeit that specific examples could be tortuous). Moreover, Lord Hoffman commented that it was not necessary for the obligation to be proportional to the development, nor did it have to be necessary to allow the development to go ahead.

The decision in the House of Lords in *Tesco* re-emphasises the fact that the earlier reported cases confused the legal question of the legitimacy of obligations with the *policy* test laid down in Circular 16/91 and its predecessors. In particular, the requirement that the development relates to a planning purpose merely reflects the legal requirement to take into account material considerations under s. 70(2) of the Town and Country Planning Act 1990. Moreover, the third test of general reasonableness equates with normal principles of administrative law. On the other hand, the second test set out in *Plymouth* was a test of policy that was specified in Circular 16/91.

Planning obligations: policy and practice

The legal tests are amplified by policy guidance on what is permissible by way of planning gain now set out in Circular 1/97. Given that policy and practice have arguably been more important than law in this area in the past, the terms of the circular are of special significance. They suggest that s. 106 should not be used so as to require a developer to provide more than that which is linked to the development in issue in terms of scale and kind. This appears to mean, for example, that a developer may be asked to provide more sewerage than is needed for the works applied for, but not sewerage for the whole general area. But this limitation seems unenforceable in many cases, since neither the developer nor the local planning authority will wish to challenge an arrangement they have themselves reached. Indeed, such arrangements may be encouraged by the local plan, which was the situation in *Plymouth* (and see also *R v South Northamptonshire DC and others, ex parte Crest Homes plc* [1995] JPL 200).

Moreover, other objectors may well lack either knowledge of the agreement or standing to challenge it. It is significant that the reported cases on planning obligations nearly all concern claims by one developer that a rival is being given preferential treatment as a result of an offer of planning gain that is questionable in terms of law or policy. The low visibility of planning obligations was one aspect of 'planning gain' criticised by the Nolan Committee (Cm 3702, 1997), which found evidence of the buying and selling of planning permissions. The case of *Daniel Davies and Co. v London Borough of Southwark* [1994] JPL 1116 illustrates some of the transparency problems. There, the Court of Appeal held that if an agreement was merely 'regulatory', determining how premises would be used, then it was not necessary that objectors see the terms of the agreement before it was signed. There could, it was acknowledged, be extreme cases where this rule would not apply, but the Court did not enlarge on what these might be. In part such concerns about the openness of the system are addressed by government proposals to require details of obligations to be put on planning registers, but this would only be after they have been concluded (see [1999] JPL 133; for a review of reform proposals see Cornford [1998] JPL 731).

Nevertheless, it remains the case that effectively we now have two systems operating concerning planning obligations. Where a planning obligation is being *required of* developers, the Secretary of State ought to apply his necessity policy on appeal. But where the obligation is being *offered by* developers, the decision-makers are likely to give much more latitude to what developers put on the table, and the courts will intervene only on legal, not policy, grounds.

'Environmental planning gain'

The use of planning obligations to provide for environmental benefits, or at least to prevent net environmental losses, raises important questions about valuation of the environment, perhaps also the 'polluter pays principle' and wider questions about sustainable development in planning. These cannot be explored in depth here. But research suggests that the idea of such 'environmental planning gain' has proved a powerful factor in allowing for greater development of rural land, allowing commodification of nature into a series of discrete environmental assets which could be traded in the interests of maintaining or even enhancing welfare and the environment (see Whatmore and Boucher, in bibliography). However, its significance may rest more in its powerfulness as an idea rather than in practice.

There appears to be rather limited use of environmental planning gain in practice, although as Healey, Purdue and Ennis (see bibliography) point out, what there is tends to be compensatory rather than alleviating or preventing losses caused by the development. What is perhaps more important is the extent to which the use of 'planning gain' allows for matters about what is in the public interest (including environmental objectives) to be decided in negotiations between developers and planning authorities.

What is clear is that the issue will not go away: the present Government is keen to investigate the use of planning obligations in the context of exploring the wider use of economic instruments in environmental policy. Moreover, at local level we might see the use of planning obligations as a means of cleaning up certain contaminated sites. For example, development of a greenfield site could be linked, through a planning obligation, to the clean up of a brownfield site where, for example, the contaminated land was an 'orphan' site for which remediation would otherwise not be possible or paid out of public funds.

Planning appeals

Section 78 provides a statutory right of appeal to the Secretary of State (in Wales, to the Planning Decision Committee of the Welsh Assembly) against refusals of permission or the imposition of any conditions, and where the local planning authority has failed to determine an application within eight weeks. Only the applicant can appeal. An appeal amounts to a total rehearing of the application, and the Secretary of State can make any decision originally open to the local planning authority.

An appeal is thus not primarily a contest, but a forum in which all relevant information may be produced and tested so that the Inspector may make a rational decision. However, it is clear that, over the years, appeals have come to resemble the confrontational model of court proceedings far more than was originally intended although research has indicated that many users of the system are unhappy with it, and changes to reduce inquiry times have been proposed.

There is also a right to seek judicial review of local planning authority decisions, although as a general principle of public law either any alternative remedies must first be exhausted or it must be shown that they would be inadequate if relied on (see R v Birmingham City Council, ex parte Ferrero Ltd [1993] 1 All ER 530; see also R v Environment Agency, ex parte Petrus Oils Ltd [1999] Env LR 732). In any event, an appeal to the Secretary of State will encompass policy matters and be cheaper. A decision to grant planning permission, or a refusal to allow an appeal, can only be challenged through judicial review. Such action requires the person initiating the challenge to have standing which is fairly easily satisfied for those with some interest in the case (see R v Sheffield City Council, ex parte Mansfield (1978) 37 P & CR 1). Alternatively, the Attorney-General can be requested to bring a relator action on behalf of the applicant.

The number of appeals increased rapidly in the 1980s, with a figure of 32,281 being reached in 1989/90. This has now fallen to around 14,896 appeals brought in 1997/8 in England and Wales. The success rate is 36 per cent, a significant increase on the 1970s, but not as high as the peak of 40 per cent reached in the late 1980s. There is clear evidence that the appeals process has been politicised, with the opportunity being taken to impose central government policy unless there are strong and clear local policies applicable (e.g. in a local plan), or a clear restraint policy, such as the Green Belt, applies. There is also considerable fluctuation between types of development in terms of success rates on appeal — over 46 per cent of major retail and minerals applications are allowed compared with 26 per cent for minor dwellings.

Procedure on appeals

Either party (or the Secretary of State) has a right to a public hearing. In large cases this will be a public inquiry under ss. 320 and 321. In an attempt to address some of the criticisms of the public inquiry system, there has been a shift towards the use of informal hearings to resolve planning disputes. Circular 15/96 makes it clear that it is central government policy to use hearings in all suitable cases, and to that end the choice of the hearing procedure is made by the Planning Inspectorate in consultation with the parties. Previously, either party to an appeal could request a public inquiry.

In the vast majority of cases, however, an appeal is dealt with by way of written representations. The Town and Country Planning (Appeals) (Written Representations Procedure) Regulations 1987 (SI 1987/701) introduced statutory rules for such procedures for the first time and laid down time limits for the various stages involved. Third parties have some limited rights to make representations on written appeals. However, it is clear that it will be very rare for a decision to be quashed because of inadequacies in the procedures actually adopted.

Apart from a very small number of matters of national importance, the decision is normally taken by an Inspector (see p. 159). In the remaining cases, the Inspector's report goes to the Secretary of State, who then makes the final decision in the light of the recommendations.

If a public inquiry is to be held, there are two similar sets of rules: the Town and Country Planning (Inquiries Procedure) Rules 1992 (SI 1992/2038) and the Town and Country Planning (Determination by Inspectors) (Inquiries Procedure) Rules 1992 (SI 1992/2039). They are an attempt to solve previous criticisms about the delays and costs involved in a public inquiry by setting out formal rules on pre-inquiry exchanges of information and laying down timetables for the various stages. However, there is no remedy to ensure these time scales are kept, except an award of costs.

The inquiry must be public and anyone is entitled to attend. In general, the procedure to be followed is at the discretion of the Inspector, but the rules give the appellant and the local planning authority full participation rights, including access to evidence, calling of witnesses, and the right to cross-examine. A right to appear and present a case is also conferred on other people who have served a statement of case. However, since the rules are supplemented by the rules of natural justice, as indeed are the written representation procedures, an Inspector normally permits anyone with anything new and relevant to say to put their case properly. Proposed changes under which lengthier inquiries will be time-limited could mean that the extent of rights to examine witnesses may be squeezed (*Improving Planning Appeals Procedures*, DETR, 1999). The Inspector is entitled to make a site inspection at any time, but this is not the place for hearing submissions.

Reasons must be given for the decision. Again, this duty has been supplemented by the courts, which require the reasons to be adequate, intelligible and not self-contradictory. The conclusions should follow from the evidence and all the main points raised at the inquiry should be dealt with (*Givaudan & Co. Ltd v Minister of Housing and Local Government* [1967] 1 WLR 250).

Unlike normal civil litigation where the loser will usually pay all the costs of an action, parties to a planning appeal are expected to pay their own costs unless there has been 'unreasonable behaviour' (as defined in Circular 8/93) by one of the parties which justifies an award of costs against them. On the whole, costs can only be awarded where there has been a public inquiry. Costs can also be awarded in the case of a written representations appeal where a public inquiry is cancelled as a result of the withdrawal of one or more grounds of refusal, but the appeal proceeds by way of written representation. In all other cases costs in written representation appeals are irrecoverable. There has been an increase in the number of successful claims in the last few years. The majority of awards are against the local planning authority, rather than the appellant, and very limited use has been made of the power to make awards against third parties. 'Unreasonable behaviour' for the appellant includes making an appeal that has no reasonable chance of success (e.g. an appeal against a refusal prompted by a clear planning policy such as the Green Belt — see the award in the *Bricket Wood* case [1989] JPL 629), and uncooperative behaviour. For the local planning authority, unreasonable refusal of the application is the main ground for an award, which puts great emphasis on the reasons for refusal and the statement of case submitted before the inquiry (see Walker [1988] JPL 598).

An increasing number of cases are now heard by the less formal procedure of a hearing. Hearings are not normally imposed by the Planning Inspectorate where third-party evidence is expected, or there are disputed matters of fact, or complex matters of law or policy. The details are currently laid out in a code of conduct published as part of Circular 15/96, but the present Government has decided to put procedural matters into a statutory instrument. This may have an impact on the balance struck between speed and informality, and procedural rigour, which has been at issue since it was stressed in *Dyason v Secretary of State for the Environment and Chiltern District Council* [1998] JPL 778 that 'a relaxed hearing is not necessarily a fair hearing'.

Challenging the decision of the Secretary of State

The Secretary of State's decision can only be challenged under s. 288, owing to s. 284 which ousts all other challenges. Section 288 thus provides a statutory appeal: this must be distinguished from judicial review under RSC Ord. 53 (now to be found in CPR 1998, sch. 1; see p. 75). About 150 cases under s. 288 are brought each year. These are the main source of decisions on planning law.

The s. 288 grounds approximate to judicial review grounds. A decision can be challenged either if it is not within the powers of the Act , or if substantial prejudice has been caused by a failure to comply with the relevant procedures (e.g. the Inquiries Rules). These will cover bad faith, perverse decisions, failure to take account of relevant factors, taking into account irrelevant factors, mistakes of law, acting on no evidence, giving inadequate reasons, or a want of natural justice.

Under s. 288, the High Court is limited to quashing the decision of the Secretary of State and remitting the case. It cannot make the decision for the Secretary of State, but can make some fairly explicit directions as to the relevant law. Thus, even if an appeal under s. 288 is successful, there is no guarantee that the redetermination will be any more beneficial. The High Court also has a discretion whether to quash a decision and will refuse to do so if it considers that the defect made no difference to the eventual decision.

Any 'person aggrieved' by the decision can use s. 288. This includes all parties who appeared at the inquiry or made representations, as well as the appellant, the local planning authority, and owners and occupiers of the site (see *Turner* v *Secretary of State for the Environment* (1973) 28 P & CR 123). The time limit for a s. 288 appeal is six weeks from the Secretary of State's decision, after which the decision is unchallengeable, no matter what the grounds of complaint (*Smith* v *East Elloe RDC* [1956] AC 736).

Enforcement under planning law

Unlike most pollution control legislation it is not in itself an offence to breach planning law. As discussed elsewhere (see p. 213) the offence consists of failing to comply with a notice served by the planning authority about unauthorised development or breach of a condition. The reason for this is that unauthorised development is not necessarily harmful; it would be wasteful to punish activities that have some social benefit. There are four types of notices used: planning contravention notices, breaches of condition notices, enforcement notices and stop notices. Of these, planning contravention notices and enforcement notices are used most often (around 5000 a year), with around 1500 breach of condition notices and 200 stop notices being served annually. Injunctions can also be sought. All are discretionary mechanisms, in the case of enforcement notices and stop notices it being explicitly provided that they may be sought where the authority considers it 'expedient' to do so. Finally, local planning authorities have wide powers of entry to enter land at any reasonable time to ascertain whether there has been a breach of planning control and what remedial steps may be required (ss. 196A–C).

(a) Planning contravention notices
Where it thinks there *may* be a breach of planning control, a local planning authority may serve these notices on any owner, occupier or other person who

is using or carrying out operations on land, seeking information from them relating to its use or occupation (s. 171C). The authority must have some basis for serving the notice: it cannot be used for a 'fishing trip' (*R* v *Teignbridge DC, ex parte Teignmouth Quay Co.* [1995] JPL 828). It is a summary offence to ignore such a notice, or knowingly to provide incorrect information (s. 171D). Information about suspected breaches can therefore be gathered, enabling the breach to be remedied co-operatively without recourse to formal enforcement procedures. Clearly, the issuing of such a notice will warn the recipient that the local planning authority will take further action if necessary.

(b)   Breach of condition notices
These provide for a simple summary procedure whereby a local planning authority may serve written notice on a person responsible for non-compliance with a condition, or having control over the relevant land, requiring compliance in a period of not less than 28 days (s. 187A). Not complying with such a notice leads to a maximum fine of £1000. Continuation of the non-compliance constitutes a further offence.

(c)   Enforcement notices
An enforcement notice under s.172 may be served by a local planning authority in respect of unauthorised development. Notices must be served on all owners and occupiers of the relevant premises, including licensees. The enforcement notice must specify the alleged breach, the steps required to remedy it, the reasons for issuing the notice, and the relevant land. It also has to specify when it takes effect, which must be at least 28 days from the date of service, and a further period after that for compliance with its requirements. At the end of this compliance period, the owner of the land (or in some cases a person with control of, or an interest in, the land) commits a criminal offence if its requirements have not been met (s. 179). The maximum penalty for these offences is £20,000 on summary conviction, or an unlimited fine on indictment. In determining the fine, the court must have regard to any financial benefit accruing to the convicted person. There is no provision for imprisonment. The local planning authority also has a power to enter the land and remedy a breach at the owner's expense (s. 178). Compliance with an enforcement notice does not discharge it: it attaches permanently to the land (s. 181). However, an enforcement notice is a local land charge, so future purchasers of the land should find out about its existence. Each district planning authority must keep a public register of enforcement notices, stop notices and breach of conditions notices (s. 188).

(d)   Stop notices
Enforcement notices cannot require immediate action to remedy breaches of planning law. Accordingly, under s. 183, the local planning authority may serve a stop notice on anyone carrying on an unlawful activity. This makes it an offence to continue any activity which is specified in the notice once it has come into force, which may be between 3 and 28 days from service. The penalties are the same as for breach of an enforcement notice.

There are limits on the application of stop notices. A stop notice is parasitic on an enforcement notice; that is it must be served together with one or after one has been served, and automatically ceases to have effect if the enforcement notice is withdrawn or successfully appealed. It may not be served to stop use as a dwellinghouse, or where an activity has been carried on for more than four years. Most importantly, compensation is payable by the local planning authority if the enforcement notice or the stop notice is withdrawn, or if an enforcement notice appeal is allowed on any other ground than ground (a) of s. 174(2) — the policy ground (see p. 340 below). This threat of compensation has meant that stop notices have rarely been used. Figures indicate that changes under the Planning and Compensation Act 1991, limiting compensation so that it is not payable if the activity stopped is in breach of planning control, have had no significant impact on the number of notices served.

Injunctions under local government law

Under s. 222 of the Local Government Act 1972, a local planning authority has always had a power to seek an injunction against any breach of the law where it is considered 'expedient for the promotion or protection of the interests of the inhabitants of their area'. This power has been interpreted fairly widely in the House of Lords in *Stoke on Trent City Council* v *B & Q (Retail) Ltd* [1984] AC 754, with the result that an injunction may be sought not only where there has been a deliberate and flagrant flouting of the law but where the normal enforcement procedures prove inadequate to deal with the problem. Section 187B provides a specific power for the local planning authority to seek an injunction if it considers it necessary or expedient to restrain an actual or *potential* breach of planning control, thus removing the need to rely on the Local Government Act 1972. In *Kirklees MBC* v *Wickes Building Supplies Ltd* [1993] AC 227, the House of Lords established that any public authority exercising the functions of law enforcement does not always have to give a cross-undertaking in damages when seeking injunctions, thus removing a serious practical obstacle that had previously restricted their use.

The penalty for breach of an injunction is potentially far higher than for breach of an enforcement notice, since the developer is in contempt of court and imprisonment is a possibility. An injunction is a discretionary remedy and will not be granted by a court unless the circumstances warrant such a strong solution. This seems in practice to restrict their use to powers of last resort, although there is no requirement that other enforcement methods have been exhausted first.

Immunity from enforcement under planning law

There are time limits for what is called 'taking enforcement action', which means serving an enforcement notice or breach of condition notice (s. 171A). These provide immunity from the service of such a notice where:

(a)   four years have elapsed from the substantial completion of an operational development (s. 171B(1));

(b)   four years have elapsed from a change of use *to* a dwellinghouse
(s. 171B(2));
(c)   ten years have elapsed from any other breach of planning control
(s. 171B(3)).

Immunity is also granted:

(a)   where there is a certificate of lawfulness of existing use or development, a certificate of lawfulness of proposed use or development, or an
established use certificate granted under earlier legislation relating to the
alleged breach (see ss. 191 to 194). These certificates are conclusive as to the
lawfulness of the matters to which they relate;
(b)   in relation to development by, or on behalf of, the Crown on Crown
land (s. 294), although a special enforcement notice may be served on a
private individual who is occupying Crown land (s. 294(3)), a power that is
primarily available to control trespassers.

Appeals against notices

The Act has elaborate provisions for appeals against enforcement notices.
Any person with an interest in the relevant land (or an occupier with a written
licence) may appeal to the Secretary of State (in Wales, to the Assembly).
Appeals must be in writing and must be received by the Secretary of State
before the notice takes effect. Thus the period for lodging might be as short
as 28 days. Appeals suspend the enforcement notice until after the Secretary
of State's decision. This allows the determined operator scope to delay
the final operation of an enforcement notice for a considerable time,
although there are provisions which seek to prevent this in blatant cases (see
s. 289(4A), (4B) and (5C)).
There are seven grounds of appeal set out in s. 174(2):

(a)   planning permission ought to be granted for the development, or the
relevant condition ought to be discharged;
(b)   the alleged breach has not in fact taken place;
(c)   the matters alleged in the enforcement notice do not in law constitute
a breach of planning control;
(d)   the matters alleged in the enforcement notice are immune from
enforcement action;
(e)   failures to carry out the correct procedures in serving the enforcement
notice;
(f)   the steps required to remedy the breach are excessive;
(g)   the time allowed for compliance with the enforcement notice is
unreasonably short.

These grounds are very wide, and cover both policy and legal grounds.
Ground (a) is effectively an application for planning permission from the
Secretary of State, and the major 'policy' ground. Grounds (b) to (e) are

collectively known as the 'legal' grounds because they mix issues of fact and law. Ground (f) is also important. A local planning authority may not 'over-enforce', i.e. put the recipient of an enforcement notice in a worse position than before the breach took place. This relates mainly to ancillary uses; the local planning authority may not require a developer to cease a use which would always have been ancillary (see *Mansi* v *Elstree Rural District Council* (1964) 16 P & CR 153). The procedure is similar to that for planning Appeals and is governed by the Town and Country Planning (Enforcement Notices and Appeals) Regulations 1991 (SI 1991/2804) and the Town and Country Planning (Enforcement) (Inquiries Procedure) Rules 1992 (SI 1992/1903).

The Secretary of State may (a) uphold an enforcement notice and refuse the appeal; (b) quash it (often this involves granting retrospective planning permission); (c) vary its terms; or (d) amend it. In the last two cases any error in the enforcement notice may be corrected if it would not cause injustice to the appellant or the local planning authority.

Challenges beyond grounds (a) to (g) above must be brought through judicial review, e.g. if the notice is hopelessly uncertain or some essential procedural requirement has not been met (see *Miller-Mead* v *Minister of Housing and Local Government* [1963] 2 QB 196). Because of the detailed appeal mechanisms, the validity of an enforcement notice may not be challenged in a prosecution for breach (*R* v *Wicks* [1997] 2 All ER 801). By contrast, because there are no rights to appeal against a stop notice or a breach of condition notice, the courts have allowed challenges to their validity when prosecutions for ignoring them have been brought (see *R* v *Jenner* [1983] 1 WLR 873 and *Dilieto* v *Ealing BC* [1998] 2 All ER 885 respectively).

Enforcement discretion

Only the local planning authority may serve a notice, although the Secretary of State has a reserve power to serve an enforcement notice (s. 182). A number of studies in the 1980s found that the enforcement of planning law was given a very low profile in many local planning authorities (see, e.g. [1986] JPL 482). Many authorities had no one responsible for enforcement. Monitoring of compliance with conditions and agreements was *ad hoc* and not guaranteed. And the most common method of discovery of a breach was from a complaint from a member of the public rather than from investigation. When it came to taking action, informal methods of solving the problem were favoured, such as warning letters and requests for details of ownership of the land (an easily recognised threat of more formal enforcement action). Even if an enforcement notice was served, there was no guarantee that it would itself be enforced if ignored, with low fine levels discouraging the bringing of court action.

Concerns such as these prompted the Carnwath report (*Enforcing Planning Law*, DoE, 1989), from which many of the changes to enforcement made under the Planning and Compensation Act 1991 stem. These have provided a welcome broadening of the powers at planning authorities disposal. The courts, too, have contributed to changing the enforcement culture. *R v Sevenoaks DC, ex parte Palley* [1995] JPL 915 shows the extent to which the courts will scrutinise the planning enforcement process more than they might do elsewhere, in that case granting judicial review of a challenge alleging that the planning authority had not sufficiently investigated a complaint. On the other hand, 'under-enforcement', i.e. not requiring every aspect of the breach to be remedied, is specifically approved of in official planning guidance on enforcement. And recent years have seen a significant decrease in the numbers of enforcement notices issued under s. 172, and a reduction in the number of enforcement injunctions granted and (in 1997/8) a corresponding increase in the number of injunctions refused. The extent to which economic considerations influence enforcement can be seen by survey evidence that enforcement is more common in South East England than in depressed urban areas.

Powers where there is no breach of planning law

There are some courses of action available to the local planning authority where there is no breach of the planning legislation. Normally these require the payment of compensation for the loss of any rights which have been taken away, so they are little used. But they are of importance as reserve powers where there is something creating an environmental problem that may not be removed or controlled in any other way.

Under s. 102 a local planning authority may serve a discontinuance order, which may require that any use be discontinued or that any buildings or works be removed or altered. Under s. 97 a local planning authority may revoke or modify a planning permission that has already been granted. In both these cases there are provisions for a public local inquiry to be held and compensation to be paid. The Secretary of State must also confirm these orders before they have effect and has reserve powers to make either type. Indeed, in March 1991, the Secretary of State took the exceptional step of making an order revoking a planning permission which Poole DC had granted to itself for housing on land designated a site of special scientific interest (SSSI) on Canford Heath in Dorset (thus belatedly rendering unnecessary the litigation in *R v Poole Borough Council, ex parte Beebee* [1991] JPL 643).

The local planning authority may also conclude a planning agreement under s. 106 in order to remove an existing building or use, although obviously the owner will require something of benefit in return.

Planning, the environment and risk

The place of the town and country planning system amongst other tools for environmental protection has already been discussed in outline (see p. 295), as have some more specific issues concerning the relationship between the planning and pollution control regimes (see p. 183). But the planning system also has an important role to play as regards more general issues of environmental risk regulation.

In the first place, planning law helps to shape the way in which environmental harm is conceptualised. Its relative openness and participatory nature, and a number of high profile public inquiries such as Sizewell B, have certainly provided valuable opportunities for public expressions of environmental concern. But these features have also contributed to the framing of the public's terms of reference about development and its environmental costs and benefits. This latter role is especially important in the light of the attention that must be given to public perceptions of risk and uncertainty, regardless of their foundation.

Secondly, in relation to public fears it is important to distinguish between risks and uncertainties, i.e. between those matters that are feared because of some quantifiable risk, and things which are feared where the odds of something adverse happening are not even known. With the former, there was an indication in *Gateshead MBC* v *Secretary of State for the Environment* (1995) (see p. 391) that the courts would take a strict line, when Glidewell LJ stated that 'if in the end public concern is not justified, it cannot be conclusive'. But this view was disagreed with by the Court of Appeal in *Newport BC* v *Secretary of State for Wales and Browning Ferris Ltd* [1998] Env LR 174, which reaffirmed the view that public perception of risk, even where unsubstantiated, could be a material planning consideration. Both cases, however, turned on the policy requirement at the time that 'demonstrable harm' to an important interest must be shown if planning permission was to be refused, a test which has now been slightly diluted (see para. 40, PPG 1, 1997). In any event, one reason why the Secretary of State has the final say in planning matters is precisely to override local opposition if this is deemed to be in the national interest.

What the courts may be more willing to do is hold that a planning authority has illegally ignored the odds in some way and intervene. This was the case in *Envirocor Waste Holdings Ltd* v *Secretary of State for the Environment, ex parte Humberside CC and British Cocoa Mills (Hull) Ltd* [1996] Env LR 49, a dispute about different calculations of the likely occurrence of a waste transfer station tainting the produce of a nearby factory. In that case, it was possible for the judge to overturn the Inspector's decision, since there were various ways in which the Inspector's calculation of risk could not be sustained. A general difficulty, however, remains in that it may be difficult to distinguish between risk and uncertainty. There is often a gloss of certainty about some risk calculations, and many assessments of risks are little better than glorified value judgements. Conversely, with some small-scale developments, it may be that what are better seen as quantifiable risks are, because of lack of available data, presented as uncertainties. In cases where there is a regulatory view about the assessment of risk, however, this view may carry considerable weight. Indeed, in *R* v *Tandridge District Council, ex parte al Fayed* [1999] 1 PLR 104 the judge held that 'strong weight' should be given to any such assessment, especially where a particular issue of national policy was at stake such that there was a need for a national consistency of approach to decision-making. An appeal in this case was dismissed (see [2000] Env LR D23), although in the Court of Appeal both sides agreed that objective unjustified fears could be material.

As regards the ultimate response of the planning system to issues of risk and uncertainty, there are essentially three options: ignore the fear, grant permission subject to appropriate conditions, or refuse the application. An uncertainty might conceivably be ignored, but ignoring a risk will make any decision liable to be overturned. The real issue then is whether the risks of environmental harm are managed or avoided. Arguably, PPG1 (1997) takes the 'management' approach, advocating the prevention of harm through appropriate decisions about the siting of development and using the planning system to minimise impact (see Owens (1997) 68 TPR 293). Owens argues that this really combines the more traditional 'technical fix' attitude with a 'spatial fix' approach: if development goes in the least harmful place it is acceptable. This approach obviously runs counter to the notion of environmental carrying capacity which, in relation to natural environmental resources, a reformed planning system might be equipped to tackle.

Finally, the importance of taking a wider view on risk regulation cannot be avoided. In cases like *Envirocor*, if the waste transfer station was not built, this posed serious regulatory problems for waste management in the area. More broadly, in relation to house building, for example, environmental concerns are not exhausted by the location of the 3.8 million projected new households, but also include concerns about the impact of a doubling of aggregates extraction which may be needed to satisfy such a demand. Regulating this calls for strategic assessment, something which can only really be tackled at a level above that even of development plans. However, effective and legally binding strategic environmental assessment is still some way off (see p. 371).

Planning and hazardous substances

The storage of hazardous substances was traditionally dealt with under normal planning procedures. There were, however, many occasions when the storage of large amounts of hazardous materials fell outside the scope of existing controls as it was either permitted automatically under the then General Development Order or did not amount to development at all (under the Use Classes Order or the general definition of development). Thus, it became necessary to control the siting of hazardous materials under a separate but complementary set of controls.

The Planning (Hazardous Substances) Act 1990 came into force on 1 June 1992. It requires hazardous substances consent to be obtained if hazardous substances are present on, over or under land in an amount at, or above, a controlled quantity. The Act gives hazardous substances authorities (HSAs), usually the same body as the local planning authority, the opportunity to consider whether the proposed storage or use of the substance is appropriate for the location, having regard to the risks arising to persons in the surrounding area, the wider implications for the community and other material considerations.

The provisions are not intended to duplicate the effect of other statutory controls. Thus the Act does not apply to controlled or radioactive wastes. Also, the controls do not apply to explosives, the location of which is controlled by licences issued by the Health and Safety Executive (HSE). The Planning (Hazardous Substances) Regulations 1992 (SI 1992/656) outlines the categories of substances regulated under the Act and the level at which they become subject to its provisions.

The Act operates by requiring any person wishing to store any listed substances at or above prescribed levels to obtain prior consent from the HSA. The conditions attached to any consent granted will be strongly influenced by the opinion of the HSE, which must be sought alongside other statutory consultees (under the GDPO). There is in effect a strong presumption in favour of the HSE's views. Non-compliance with a consent, or acting without a consent, is an offence punishable by a fine, and regard must be had to any financial benefit which has accrued or is likely to accrue to the defendant as a result of the offence (s. 23). There are defences where the defendant took all reasonable precautions and exercised all due diligence to avoid committing the offence, or did not know and had no reason to believe that an offence had been committed. Every HSA must keep a register of all applications, information about certain deemed consents, enforcement action and decisions of the HSA and directions of the Secretary of State (see s. 28, Planning (Hazardous Substances) Act 1990 and regulation 23).

Amendments to the regime have recently been made to give effect to Directive 96/82 on the control of major-accident hazards involving dangerous substances ('Seveso II'). The Planning (Control of Major-Accident Hazards) Regulations 1999 (SI 1999/981) make minor changes to the basic preventive approach already followed, including a requirement that the relevant Nature Conservancy Council is consulted where there is risk to an area of 'particular natural sensitivity or interest'. This suggests a prioritisation here of nature conservation interests over important landscapes. The revised Development Plan Regulations 1999 also include provisions which require development plans to have regard to preventing major-accident hazards.

TWELVE
Environmental impact assessment

The assessment of the environmental effects of a development has always been an implicit part of the decision-making process in the system of town and country planning operating in Britain. Indeed, there have also been explicit examples where detailed assessments of the environmental effects of developments have been carried out, for instance in relation to power stations and motorways. Environmental harm has always been a material consideration when deciding whether or not to grant planning permission and there are many developments which have had planning permission refused because of their detrimental environmental effects.

This implicit mechanism was raised to a more formal level with the adoption of EC Directive 85/337 on the Assessment of the Effects of Certain Private and Public Projects on the Environment. This Directive established the need for consideration of information about the effects of a development on the environment as a mandatory component of the decision-making process in relation to certain specified projects.

The Directive was the subject of fierce debate between the Member States (and has remained controversial ever since). After much discussion, and some alterations, the directive was implemented in England and Wales by the Town and Country Planning (Assessment of Environmental Effects) Regulations 1988 (SI 1988/1199) (there are similar regulations which apply in Scotland). These regulations were enacted in Britain under the European Communities Act 1972 and were specifically limited, therefore, to the categories of development listed in the Directive. Section 15 of the Planning and Compensation Act 1991 inserted s. 71A of the Town and Country Planning Act 1990, which provides the Secretary of State with the power to make regulations extending the categories of projects which are to be the subject of environmental assessment, and consequently environmental assessment now has a place in primary legislation. This power was used for the first time when the Secretary of State extended the classes of project which are subject to environmental assessment within the Town and Country Planning (Assessment of Environmental Effects) (Amendment) Regulations 1994 (SI 1994/677). This extended the requirement for environmental assessment to wind turbines, motorway service areas, coast protection works and financed toll roads (although it is only in the latter case that an environmental assessment is mandatory).

In the light of experience, the 1985 Directive was amended by EC Directive 97/11, which came into force on 14 March 1999. The necessary changes have been made by the Town and Country Planning (Environmental Impact Assessment) (England and Wales) Regulations 1999 (SI 1999/293) which cover projects that require planning permission and are listed in the Directive (for this reason, the regulations are made under the European Communities Act 1972). Those projects that do not require planning permission but are dealt with under separate consent procedures will continue to have separate specific regulations. These include such proposals as afforestation, highways, harbour works, marine salmon farms, power stations and overhead transmission lines. These separate regulations all follow the framework of the general planning regulations. Helpfully, the 1999 Regulations consolidated a number of regulations enacted over the years to plug various gaps in national implementation of the directive. The rules relating to the assessment of various projects which would otherwise avoid the need for planning permission because they are permitted development or do not amount to development, are now generally found in the 1999 Regulations. Under the 1999 Regulations, the previous terminology of 'environmental assessment' is replaced with 'environmental impact assessment' (EIA), bringing it into line with other Member States.

What is environmental impact assessment?

On a simple level, EIA is merely an information-gathering exercise carried out by the developer and other bodies which enables a local planning authority to understand the environmental effects of a development before deciding whether or not to grant planning permission for that proposal. On this level, however, there is little to distinguish this concept from the normal planning process under which environmental effects are a material consideration. The innovation behind the formal EIA process is the systematic use of the best objective sources of information and the emphasis on the use of the best techniques to gather that information. The ideal EIA would involve a totally bias-free collation of information produced in a form which would be coherent, sound and complete. It should then allow the local planning authority and members of the public to scrutinise the proposal, assess the weight of predicted effects and suggest modifications or mitigation (or refusal) where appropriate.

Thus, EIA is a technique and a process. It is inanimate rather than tangible. The key point is that strictly the 'assessment' is undertaken by the local planning authority on the basis of *environmental information* supplied to it. This information consists in part of an *environmental statement* prepared by the developer (or more likely, by hired consultants) which details at least the main environmental impacts of the project and any mitigating measures which are proposed to reduce the significance of those impacts. But just as importantly it also includes other information supplied by various statutory consultees (e.g. EA, English Nature), independent third parties (such as local conservation and amenity groups), members of the public and even the local planning authority itself.

Crucially, EIA is an inherently procedural mechanism. Although it is intended to be preventive (and, some would argue, also precautionary), there is nothing that requires the decision-maker to refuse a development project because negative environmental impacts are highlighted by the EIA, or even to impose conditions to mitigate any such impact. It should also begin as early as possible when projects are being planned. A further, and crucial, point is that EIA should be an *iterative* process, where information that comes to light is fed back into the decision-making process. Ideally, this would also involve some kind of post-project monitoring, but neither the Directive nor the 1999 Regulations currently require this.

The Environmental Impact Assessment Directive

Directive 85/337 as amended by Directive 97/11 requires Member States to ensure that public and private projects likely to have significant effects on the environment by virtue of their nature, size or location are assessed with regard to their environmental impact before development consent is given. Projects are categorised into Annex I (where EIA is compulsory) and Annex II (where EIA is only needed if there are such significant effects).

Whereas the term 'project' is defined as the execution of construction works or of other installations or schemes (which would equate roughly with the concept of 'development' in English planning law), 'development consent' is defined as the decision of the competent authority which entitles the developer to proceed with the project. There is some difficulty with the definition of 'proceeding with the project'. This does not necessarily equate with planning permission, as other statutory consents could be required. Whilst certain developments could be built they could not be operated without other licences.

On one interpretation therefore, it could be argued that, under the terms of the Directive, the Environment Agency (for example) could request an EIA when considering an application for a waste management licence where the local planning authority had failed to require an assessment. Although this is not the case in UK legislation it could be since the Directive has direct effect in some situations (as to which see below).

The Directive goes on to set out the detailed requirements for an assessment, which should include direct and indirect effects of a project on a variety of factors, including human beings, fauna, flora, the environment and material assets and the cultural heritage.

The developer must then submit certain specified information to the authority dealing with the application (see below for the contents of an environmental statement). There are also provisions for consultation with both the authorities likely to be concerned with the project and members of the general public, although the detailed arrangements for consultation are left to individual Member States.

Amendments to Directive 85/337

The provisions described below are those of Directive 85/337 as amended under Directive 97/11, but it is useful to appreciate the key changes that have been made and the reasons for these. This is important, of course, because all the case law discussed was decided under Directive 85/337 and earlier regulations.

A major criticism of Directive 85/337 was the significant inconsistencies in its application in different Member States when it came to the need for Annex II projects to be assessed. While some Member States appeared to use quite strict standards, others were more lenient (see generally COM(93)28). This had an obvious impact on the extent to which the Directive was creating a level playing field for developers (Directive 85/337 was adopted partly as a harmonising measure). As a result, some Annex II projects have been moved into Annex I, while more specific criteria have been written into the Directive to guide decision-makers on when EIA is needed for what is now an enlarged list of Annex II projects.

Further changes to the Directive that are of note here are that developers can now formally request guidance from the decision-maker on what things the environmental statement should cover ('scoping'); the developer must now provide information on alternatives studied; and the decision-maker must now give the main reasons for granting, or refusing, permission following an EIA. While some of these have always been best practice, other changes are more significant. For example, the duty to give reasons in some situations is a notable change from the previous position, where reasons were only required where planning permission was refused. The Directive also now allows for a single procedure to deal with the granting of development consent and pollution control authorisation under the Integrated Pollution Prevention and Control Directive (see p. 391), although this option has not been taken up in the UK.

The EIA Directive and direct effect

Unlike later directives (e.g. on Access to Environmental Information (90/313), Habitats (92/43) and Waste (91/271)), Directive 85/337 was not 'copied out' into UK legislation. Also, most Member States (including the UK) failed to implement the Directive on time. This led to a number of challenges to decisions made about projects that purportedly fell within the terms of the Directive but were not assessed. A central issue in all cases was whether the Directive had direct effect within UK law (for a general discussion of direct effect see p. 138). The amended Directive has similarly not been translated 'literally' into UK law, although arguably there is a closer fit between the two.

The key point, however, is that there may be situations where the words of the Directive will be relied on before the courts. At least for the main 1999 Regulations, this will not be because of late implementation, but some of the more specific regulations, such as on land drainage, missed the 14 March 1999 deadline for transposing the amended Directive and there is still no sign of regulations which, arguably, are needed to transpose our obligations to assess various agricultural operations listed in Annex II. For the 1999 Regulations, the question of direct effect is more likely to come into play when it is argued that there has been incorrect transposition of some procedural obligation, or that a discretion given under the Directive has been construed unduly narrowly.

(a)   The early British cases
The initial response of the UK courts to possible direct effect of Directive 85/337 was, at best, mixed, and at worst displayed an alarming ignorance of general principles of EC law. The direct effect of the Directive in relation to all projects was at first accepted (*Twyford Parish Council* v *Secretary of State for the Environment* [1993] 3 Env LR 37), then rejected for Annex II projects (*Kincardine and Deeside District Council* v *Forestry Commissioners* [1993] Env LR 151) and then rejected for all projects on the grounds that some of the directive's provisions were not sufficiently precise and unconditional (*Wychavon District Council* v *Secretary of State for the Environment* [1994] Env LR 239). As a matter of EC law, the decision of Tucker J in *Wychavon* was clearly wrong when compared with other directives where some, but not all, provisions have been held to have had direct effect (compare, e.g. Case 152/84 *Marshall* v *Southampton and South West Hampshire Area Health Authority (Teaching)* [1985] QB 401, and Case 14/83 *Von Colson* v *Land Nordrhein-Westfalen* ([1984] ECR 1891). But it left three separate judicial views on the direct effect of the directive, none of which referred to the others and one of which was based on an interpretation of EC law that was clearly contrary to the view of the European Court of Justice. Somewhat depressingly, in no case was there a reference to the ECJ.

(b)   Judgments of the European Court of Justice
However, the ECJ has now directly considered the direct effect of the Directive in two cases which illustrate a greater confidence in allowing the courts to review Member States' exercising of discretion. The first case, Case C-72/95 *Aanemersbedriff P K Kraaijeveld BV* v *Gedeputeerde Staten van Zuid-Holland* [1996] ECR I-5403, concerned a failure to assess the construction of Dutch dykes. Specifically, the ECJ was asked to rule on the question of the direct effect of Article 4.2 of the Directive, which makes provision for the assessment of Annex II projects. The applicants challenged the modification of a zoning plan which dealt with the reinforcement of dykes. They argued that the works were subject to EIA under the terms of the Directive. The projects fell within Annex II of the Directive but the modification fell below the threshold set out in the domestic legislation. The UK and Dutch Governments argued that the Annex II procedures were not sufficiently precise to have direct effect. The ECJ did not deal with the issue explicitly, as it phrased its decision in terms of the national court's ability to consider whether a member state had exceeded the limits of its discretion as to the form and method of implementing the Directive. The ECJ held that anyone concerned with the implementation of the Directive could raise the issue of an improper use of discretion in selecting the method of transposition. Moreover, a national court may be obliged to consider whether the Member

State has exceeded its discretion, even if the matter is not raised by the parties.

Subsequently, in Case C-435/97 *World Wildlife Fund (WWF) EA and others v Autonome Provinz Bozen and others* [2000] 1 CMLR 149, the ECJ was asked to consider a challenge to a decision not to require an EIA for redevelopment at Bolzano airport. The project would have changed the use of the airport from military to civilian and cargo flights, requiring some new development and intensifying effects from things like noise. The Court followed the *Kraaijeveld* case in holding that the key test in relation to Annex 2 projects was whether such projects were likely to have significant environmental effects because of their size, nature or location. If this was the case, then the relevant authorities were under a duty to ensure that the project in question was assessed.

(c)   Recent British case law

Experience from the UK courts suggests that the decisions in *Kraaijeveld* and *Bozen* are having an effect. Although there may be other obstacles to ensuring compliance with the Directive (e.g. national procedural rules on bringing cases promptly; see p. 142), the 'direct effect' of the Directive in relation to Annex 2 projects is no longer an issue (see, e.g. *R v St Edmundsbury Borough Council, ex parte Walton* [1999] JPL 805). This is interesting because on a strict view the ECJ has not said that individuals have rights to insist on EIA. Instead, the ECJ has focused on the *remedy* of correcting non-implementation of the Directive, probably because finding individuals had 'rights' under the Directive might open up *Francovich* claims.

The cases discussed above have all involved 'vertical' direct effect, that is claims by individuals against public bodies on the basis that the state has failed to implement the Directive correctly. In *R v Durham CC, Sherburn Stone Company Ltd and Secretary of State for Environment, Transport and the Regions, ex parte Huddleston* [2000] JPL 409, however, it was argued that a challenge to a deemed grant of mineral planning permission at a quarry was, in effect, a challenge based on 'horizontal' direct effect, i.e. that even though the claim was a judicial review against the planning authority, the challenge was in reality between the objector and the quarrying company. Because the planning permission was deemed to be granted, there had not been an opportunity for the applicant to be consulted in the way required by the EIA Directive. Although the High Court held that the challenge was an impermissible horizontal challenge, the Court of Appeal overturned this, which removes what might have been a significant hurdle since in every EIA case it could be argued that the applicant is really trying to deprive the developer of rights which they have been granted (see further p. 140).

Is the project subject to EIA?

The process of EIA can be broken down into a number of discrete stages. The first stage is to determine whether or not the project falls within the criteria for the requirement of EIA. The projects which should be subject to EIA are listed in a variety of regulations, the main ones being the Town and

Country Planning (Environmental Impact Assessment) Regulations 1999 (the 1999 Regulations). As mentioned above, there are developments which fall outside the control of the Town and Country Planning Acts which are dealt with in specific regulations. For the purposes of this chapter, reference will be made only to the 1999 Regulations.

The 1999 Regulations apply to the main groups of projects under what are known as schedule one projects and schedule two projects. Projects falling within schedule one to the 1999 Regulations *must* be the subject of environmental assessment, whereas projects falling within schedule two to the 1999 Regulations only require environmental assessment where there are *likely to be significant environmental effects.*

(a)   Schedule one projects: mandatory EIA

As might be expected, the projects falling within schedule one to the 1999 Regulations include major infrastructure projects. The list includes crude oil refineries, thermal power stations, integrated chemical installations, motorways and major roads. Following Directive 97/11, the list now also includes such projects as pig and poultry units and groundwater abstraction schemes. The ECJ has held that modifications to Annex I projects may, judged objectively, also fall within Annex I, if the modification itself exceeds the thresholds for Annex I projects (see Case C-431/92 *Commission* v *Germany* [1995] ECR I-2189).

This list of examples for which EIA is mandatory is not particularly surprising. Indeed, most of these types of projects will have been the subject of some form of EIA before the introduction of the 1999 Regulations. Projects of this type have always been subject to thorough scrutiny and are usually considered at major public inquiries which involve many months of preparation and a vast range of documentation. It is fair to say that until recently the public was largely excluded from the technical debate unless they had the financial resources to instruct experts to act on their behalf. If the EIA process operates satisfactorily in disseminating information in intelligible terms, then the public may be able to play a more effective role in these inquiries.

For most projects falling within schedule one, the definition of the project is self-explanatory. There are, however, in certain instances, thresholds which seek to define further the types of project to which mandatory EIA applies. For instance, a thermal power station other than a nuclear power station is subject to mandatory EIA only where it has a heat output of 300 megawatts or more. Where there is any degree of uncertainty over whether or not a project falls within schedule one, a ruling on the need for an assessment can be obtained from either the Secretary of State or the local planning authority (see p. 358).

(b)   Schedule two projects: EIA only when there are significant environment effects

The projects within schedule two to the 1999 Regulations are, by and large, the types of development that are less sensitive in nature. Examples include ski-lifts, motorway service areas, metal processing, food manufacture, holiday villages, knackers' yards, golf courses, tanneries, paper manufacture and urban development projects such as multiplex cinemas. The list also includes schedule one projects below their thresholds (e.g. a thermal power station with a heat output of less than 300 megawatts), and modifications to schedule two projects (something that the ECJ in *Dutch Dykes* had already decided should be subject to assessment). Notably, the significant effects need not be negative; an urban regeneration project specifically intended to improve the environment might also need to be assessed.

That a project falls within schedule two does not mean that EIA is necessarily required. EIA is only needed when the project is 'likely to have significant effects on the environment by virtue of factors such as its nature, size or location'. Under the previous provisions, decisions were taken on a case-by-case basis in accordance with general and indicative criteria laid out in DoE Circular 15/88. These were (a) whether the project was of more than local importance in terms of its size and physical scale; (b) the sensitivity of the location (such as a site of special scientific interest); and (c) whether it would give rise to unusually complex and potentially adverse environmental effects (e.g. from a polluting discharge). In addition, the guidance provided mostly quantitative indicative criteria for some, but not all, project classes.

Following important changes under Directive 97/11, the 1999 Regulations contain much more explicit guidance on when an EIA will be required. Schedule three now contains selection (or 'screening') criteria to which the decision-maker must have regard. These are grouped together under general headings of (a) the characteristics of the development; (b) the location of the development; and (c) the characteristics of the potential impact. Under the first of these, e.g. the size of the development, its use of natural resources and its waste production must all be considered. (These criteria are basically 'copied out' from Annex III of the Directive.)

More specifically, however, the 1999 Regulations take advantage of the option under the Directive of using thresholds to rule out the need for EIA in advance. Relatively low-level 'exclusive' thresholds are used for many schedule two developments, their use being to lighten the regulatory burden. For example, any golf course larger than one hectare will need to be screened, effectively requiring EIA for anything other than a pitch and putt. But these thresholds do not apply in 'sensitive areas', which includes SSSIs, European sites under the Conservation (Natural Habitats etc.) Regulations 1994, National Parks, World Heritage sites and AONBs (see reg. 2(1)). Exceptionally, projects falling below the relevant 'exclusive' threshold may still require an EIA.

The three general criteria under Circular 15/88 noted above, however, are still found in the new guidance (Circular 2/99), but their status is now rather different, since they flesh out the Secretary of State's interpretation of those situations where the schedule three screening criteria will result in an EIA being needed. An Annex to Circular 2/99 also gives guidance on specific projects. For example, any motorway service area in a sensitive area, or above 0.5 hectares, must be screened, but government advice is that EIA is 'more likely' on greenfield sites and if the proposed development would be above five hectares in coverage. The guidance also gives further locational factors which might be relevant, such as a Local Biodiversity Action Plan or the effect of the development on places like Air Quality Management Areas and designated bathing waters. Small developments, and even minor modifications, may have major impacts, such as where a small airport runway is extended to accommodate much larger planes.

A final point here is that early research carried out for the DoE showed that 50 per cent of local planning authorities who had not received any environmental statements had planning applications on their planning registers which were above the relevant thresholds for schedule two projects and which could have been suitable for environmental assessment. When questioned further the local planning authorities admitted that a principal cause of these discrepancies was their unfamiliarity with the then current regulations. This suggests that something more than a tightening of the screening criteria will be needed to ensure effective implementation of the Directive.

'Salami-slicing' of projects

The possibility that EIA might be avoided by breaking up a development project into several small projects, none of which individually require EIA, has been considered by the courts and in guidance. In *R v Swale Borough Council, ex parte Royal Society for the Protection of Birds* [1991] 1 PLR 6, permission was granted for 'land reclamation' on an area of mudflats near the mouth of the River Medway. The application was necessary to undertake dredging, which was the precursor to development of the area for further dock use and a business park. No environmental assessment took place. The RSPB argued that the application could not be viewed in isolation but was part of an integrated development strategy. As such it was either a schedule one project (i.e. a trading port), or a schedule two project with significant environmental effects. Simon Brown J held that it was appropriate for a planning authority to look beyond what was being applied for if the reality was that the application was part of a more substantial development (see also *R v Secretary of State for Transport, ex parte Surrey County Council*, 1993, unreported, a case about the widening of stretches of the M25 motorway), although the planning authority did not need to speculate on what future schemes the present development project would, or could, lead to. The RSPB's application for review, however, failed because the judge held that the decision whether a project fell within schedule one or two was essentially a matter of fact and degree for the determining authority (see further discussion below at p. 359).

The ECJ has yet to pronounce on the extent to which competent authorities may or must consider actual or likely projects beyond that under consideration, where the project forms part of a larger project: see Case C-396/92 *Bund Naturschutz in Bayern & Others v Freistaat Bayern* [1994] ECR I-3717. However, the Advocate-General in that case does make reference to the inclusion of projects within 'current plans'. This approach may have influenced the Secretary of State's decision in 1997 not to grant planning permission to UK NIREX Ltd, the government's nuclear waste agency, for a testing facility near Sellafield in Cumbria. NIREX acknowledged that the development was a necessary step in determining the suitability of the site for a nuclear waste repository. The Secretary of State said that any similar application in future would only be considered in the light of the environmental effects of the waste repository.

The effect of such decisions has been a toning down of the guidance, so that local planning authorities are not just advised to have regard to possible cumulative effects, but where appropriate to consider together more than one application for development to determine whether or not EIA is required (Circular 2/99, para. 46). Arguably, this is a very small step in the direction of strategic environmental assessment (on which see p. 371).

EIA and permitted development

Some activities are permitted development for which planning permission is deemed to be granted (see p. 314). These are usually minor developments, or developments in the public interest by statutory undertakers, but until changes to the law were made in 1995 (at the urging of the EC) they effectively fell beyond the reach of environmental assessment. The rules on EIA and permitted development are now contained in the 1999 Regulations and in changes to the Town and Country Planning (General Permitted Development) Order 1995 (SI 1995/418).

The basic position is that schedule one projects cannot be permitted development, and will always require submission of a planning application and an environmental statement. Schedule two projects will only be permitted development if the decision-maker determines, after screening, that EIA is not required, or if the Secretary of State uses his exceptional powers to direct that the development is exempt from EIA. Otherwise, permitted development rights are withdrawn and a planning application must be submitted together with an environmental statement. Those developments that are permitted but subject to separate control regimes, such as forestry operations, are covered by separate regulations.

Given the often uncontentious nature of much permitted development, it is unlikely that there will be many projects which require EIA, but there may be a few situations where the ability of a planning authority to investigate the impact of a development which would otherwise have automatic permission could prove to be decisive.

What is a 'project'? And what is a 'consent'?

The changes made in 1995 to make permitted development subject to environmental assessment went a long way to satisfying the EC that all developments listed in Annexes I and II should be subject to assessment, regardless of the national position in relation to automatic development consent. This interpretation of the Directive was clarified by Directive 97/11, which makes clear that *all* such projects *must* obtain development consent, i.e. that EIA also applies to projects where consent is not needed because the project is not 'development', or the development is permitted by a development order.

The more fundamental problem, however, is that EIA under the Directive is a *project*-based mechanism, with 'project' being defined as the execution of construction works or of other installations or schemes, and other interventions in the natural surroundings and landscape including those involving the extraction of mineral resources, and 'development consent' being the decision which entitles the developer to proceed with the project (Art. 1(2)). But UK planning law has traditionally been concerned with the control of 'development' through planning permissions. A good example of how this can give rise to difficulties is *R v North Yorkshire CC, ex parte Brown* [1998] Env LR 623. There, an old permission from 1947 for quarrying at Preston-under-Scar in North Yorkshire was registered under changes made by the Planning and Compensation Act 1991. Conditions were then attached, but no EIA was required. Lord Hoffmann in the House of Lords took a purposive construction of the 1988 Regulations in the light of the Directive, and held that it was the decision on the conditions that allowed the project to proceed. The whole point of the 1991 Act, uniquely, was to implement a statutory scheme under which permissions granted decades previously could be made acceptable for modern conditions, especially as regards environmental impact. The imposition of the conditions was a distinct event from, for example, the attaching of conditions to a planning permission. (For a similar case involving consent originally granted pre-1988 under a zoning plan, but where a fresh consent procedure was initiated after 1988, see Case C-81/96 *Burgemeester en welthouders van Haarlemmerliede en Spaarnwoude and Others v Gedeputeerde Staten van Noord-Holland* [1998] ECR I-3923.) *Ex parte Brown* could therefore be distinguished from a case like *R v Secretary of State for the Environment, ex parte Greenpeace Ltd* [1994] 4 All ER 352, which concerned the THORP plant at Sellafield. In that case, Potts J rejected an argument that authorisation under the Radioactive Substances Act 1993 — without which the plant could not operate — was something for which a separate development consent was required. The construction of the plant and its use for disposal of nuclear waste were all part of one project for which consent had been given before the directive came into force.

Finally, there is a particular difficulty in UK planning law which derives from the definition of 'development consent' as being the decision which entitles the developer to proceed with the project. This is that, in town and country planning law, many major developments effectively involve a two-stage approval process, whereby outline planning permission is first sought for the development, and then 'reserved matters' are approved by the local planning authority at a later date (for more discussion on this see p. 318). This raises the question as to what stage the ES has to be submitted.

The view of the courts seems to be that this must be done when outline planning permission is applied for, since at the reserved matters stage the local planning authority cannot raise objections to the principle of the development. In *R* v *Rochdale Metropolitan Borough Council, ex parte Tew* [2000] Env LR 1, there was a challenge to a 'bare outline' planning permission for a large business park, where there was only an illustrative plan of the kinds of activities that would eventually be included in the park in the 10–15 years. In the High Court, the permission was quashed because it was impossible for full environmental information about the project to be available for public scrutiny, since information about the size and scale of the eventual development could not be provided. The judgment suggests that, where EIA is needed, it will be difficult to submit outline planning permissions unless only minor matters are reserved, because of the lack of public participation when reserved matters are approved. Clearly, as the judge recognised, this is a major problem for developments like business parks or urban development projects which are demand led, and it may mean that developers may have to be clearer about the kinds of developments that go to make up these kinds of projects. Paradoxically, this may also be an impediment to developments which aim to have positive environmental effects such as urban regeneration projects.

If a proposal requiring EIA has reached the 'reserved matters' stage, however, does this mean that it will be too late to challenge the development? This seems to be view taken so far. Thus, in *R* v *London Borough of Hammersmith and Fulham, ex parte CPRE* (21 December 1999, unreported), the Court of Appeal refused to hold that there should have been an EIA in relation to reserved matters relating to a large retail development in the White City area of London, since this was not the stage in the planning process which entitled the development to proceed; the outline permission performed that role. This approach was also taken by the High Court in *R* v *London Borough of Bromley, ex parte Barker* (3 April 2000, unreported), a challenge to the lack of an EIA for a major cinema and leisure development at Crystal Palace Park. In both cases, however, there was also a challenge, using the judgment in *ex parte Tew*, to the outline planning permission, on the basis that this should have had an EIA. On a strict reading of *Tew*, this would have to follow. Both of these challenges, however, were held to be taken too late; for example in *ex parte CPRE* there had been a delay of three and a half years since the grant of outline planning permission, while there had been a delay of over a year in *ex parte Barker* where, arguably, the environmental impact of the project was lesser.

It is difficult, therefore, to say that the courts will always require outline permissions to be assessed (where this is required) while rejecting out of hand complaints raised at the stage of reserved matters. Taken together, the cases suggest that while the courts are taking a more *purposive* approach to the Directive, this falls short of a *principled* approach, in the sense that practical reasons may mean that an EIA might not be required. As with the case law where there has not been an ES submitted but the planning authority might be said to have otherwise considered possible environmental impacts (see the *Berkeley* case, discussed below), the courts will look to see whether allowing the complaint to succeed might prejudice good administration, or expose developers to lost profits or wasted expenditure. It is clear that the courts in

Barker and in *CPRE* were distinctly unimpressed by the delay between the outline permission being granted and the judicial review being taken. The difficulty, however, is that the discretion which Member States have to use ordinary procedural rules on things like standing to bring cases and time limits (see p. 77) is rather more difficult to justify when the EC law that is in question is *itself* procedural in nature, as with the EIA Directive.

Pre-application procedures for establishing the need for EIA

With the subjectivness of the indicative criteria for schedule two projects and the uncertainty of interpreting the definition for schedule one projects, there are a number of pre-planning application procedures which establish whether or not EIA is required. Many developers of major projects will need to know at an early stage of the development process whether or not an EIA is required, as the potential for delay and expense is great once a planning application has been submitted.

A developer can simply decide that an environmental statement must be submitted. Otherwise, under reg. 5(1) of the 1999 Regulations, it is open to an applicant at any time prior to making a planning application to seek an opinion from the local planning authority as to whether or not a proposed development falls within schedule one or schedule two, and whether it exceeds thresholds or is in any other way suitable for EIA (a screening opinion). This request is made to the appropriate planning authority dealing with the application, whether it be the county authority, district authority or metropolitan authority.

When making an application for an adjudication the applicant must provide some basic minimum information about the proposal, including at least:

(a)   a site plan;
(b)   a description of the development and its nature and purpose;
(c)   its possible effects on the environment.

Local planning authorities can request further information if they consider it to be necessary (reg. 5(3)). They must determine the request within three weeks or any longer period as the developer may agree. If the authority determines that environmental information is required it must give clear and precise reasons for its opinion (reg. 4(6)). All documents relating to the request, including the opinion of the local planning authority and the accompanying statement of reasons, are placed on the public register (reg. 20(1)).

If the local planning authority either fails to give an opinion within the determination period or requires the provision of environmental information before granting planning permission the developer may refer the matter to the Secretary of State for a direction (reg. 5(6)).

As with development permitted under the GDPO, the adoption of a screening opinion that EIA is not needed is necessary before development permitted by a simplified planning zone scheme or an enterprise zone order can be granted.

Pre-application directions from the Secretary of State

Where developers wish to challenge the local planning authority's determination they must send a copy of all the relevant documentation, including any representations made in the light of the local planning authority's opinion and statement of reasons, to the Department of the Environment, Transport and the Regions (in effect an appeal of the screening opinion). The Secretary of State will then give a 'screening direction' concerning the requirement for EIA within three weeks of the date of the application (reg. 6). Where the direction states that an EIA is required, it must be accompanied by a statement of reasons, giving a full explanation of the Secretary of State's view (reg. 4(6)). The Secretary of State also has a residual power under reg. 4(4) to direct that a particular form of development is exempt from EIA, or requires assessment not-withstanding that it does not fall within the general definition of 'EIA development'.

Challenges to the decisions of local planning authorities or the Secretary of State

Despite the changes to screening made under Directive 97/11, there remains a considerable amount of discretion over whether or not an EIA is required. Usually this question arises in relation to Annex II projects, although it is conceivable that it might also arise in relation to Annex I project, e.g. where there is a dispute whether a development project in fact falls within one of Annex I categories. Both the national courts and the ECJ have considered the nature of this discretion.

(a)   The decision-maker's discretion
The ECJ has put certain restrictions on the exercise of this discretion. In Case C-133/94 *Commission* v *Belgium* [1996] ECR I-2323 it laid down the general rule that Member States could not set thresholds so lax that Member State could, in advance, exempt whole classes of projects listed in Annex II. This same issue has also arisen in relation to the question of direct effect (discussed further on p. 350). Thus, the *Dutch Dykes* case, and more recently the *Bozen* case, show that the ECJ is prepared to accept that the discretion given to the Member States is limited by the overriding need to assess all projects in Annex II if they are likely to give rise to significant environmental effects because of their size, nature or location. While this provides for a base-line of consistency in national legislation, the question remains as to how decision-makers exercise discretion using lawful criteria in individual cases.

At national level, the judge in *R* v *Swale Borough Council, ex parte RSPB* [1991] 1 PLR 6 held that whether a project fell within a particular schedule of the Regulations was simply a matter of fact and degree for the determining authority. The court would only intervene if any decision was unreasonable in a *Wednesbury* sense. This approach, which was criticised by commentators who said that the issue was a straight question of law, was followed in *R v Metropolitan Borough of Wirral and another, ex parte Gray* [1998] Env LR D13. It also appears to have been followed in *R v St Edmundsbury Borough Council, ex parte Walton* [1999] JPL 805, though to say the least the judgment of Hooper J is less than clear on this point. In that case, a planning officer had recommended that an application by the Greene King brewery be refused planning permission because of impact to, among other things, water meadows. But he had not required an environmental statement to be submitted. As it stands, the case therefore suggests that the mere view that development should be refused on environmental grounds is not in itself enough to show 'significant' environmental impact such as to require EIA. (The applicants did, however, succeed, because the decision on 'screening' was judged to be too important to leave to a planning officer without formal delegation, which does at least send out some positive signals about the importance of EIA.)

(b) Mitigating measures

Ex parte Walton also deals with the issue of whether mitigating measures should be taken into consideration when deciding whether EIA is required. The judge held that they could be, a view also taken shortly afterwards in *Swan v Secretary of State for Scotland (No. 2)* [2000] Env LR 60. In that case, the Minister had not required EIA of a forestry proposal. One of the applicant's arguments was that the developer should be required to submit an environmental statement if his original application would lead to significant environmental effects. As it transpired, the original application was modified before the decision on whether EIA was required was taken. The argument was that the participatory purpose of EIA could be frustrated, because developers and decision-makers (and perhaps also some of the consultees) could, through prior and private negotiations, ensure that the proposal contained sufficient mitigation measures that it would fall below the thresholds for schedule two projects. But Lord Macfadyen considered that it would be 'wholly artificial' to do otherwise: 'the provision for public participation has not been nullified. The situation in which such participation is required has simply not arisen'. This may be correct in law, but it does beg questions about whether the EIA process can always ensure that the *best* advice about mitigating environmental impact emerges (which would be in line with the preventive nature of the Directive), not simply advice that is *sufficient*.

(c) What if impact has been considered without formal assessment?

Even if the courts are prepared to intervene and hold that the development is of a kind for which an environmental statement *should* have been submitted, the question remains whether they will order an EIA to be undertaken. So far the short answer to this has been 'no'. In *R v Poole Borough Council, ex parte Beebee* [1991] JPL 643, the Council granted itself planning permission without considering whether or not an environmental assessment was required. Schiemann J took the view that the purpose of an environmental assessment was to draw to the attention of the decision-maker any relevant information that would assist in reaching a decision. On the facts, he thought that the local planning authority had all the relevant information before it and therefore an environmental statement would have been superfluous. All the information that might have been gleaned from a formal statement had already emerged and ensured that the council had not arrived at an irrational decision.

As the purpose of EIA is to produce a systematic approach to the consideration of environmental effects using best practicable techniques and best available sources of information, it is bold to assert that the local planning authority had all the necessary environmental information for an EIA. Indeed, the transcript of the case suggests that the officers' reports to the decision-making committee had a number of omissions, which would imply that there were deficiencies in the local authority's decision.

Nevertheless, the Court of Appeal has taken a similar approach in *Berkeley* v *Secretary of State for the Environment and Fulham Football Club* [1998] Env LR 741. In that case, there had been no formal EIA of proposals to develop the ground of Fulham Football Club, which involved some encroachment onto the River Thames. The *Berkeley* decision is important because the Court directly considered the impact of Case C-431/92 *Commission* v *Germany* [1995] ECR I-2189. In that case, the ECJ held that there was an 'unequivocal obligation' to subject certain projects to EIA, but effectively put the onus on the Commission to point to specific instances where the procedures adopted by Germany failed to equate to the need for formal EIA. The Court of Appeal thought this was sufficient to justify what seems to be a general equivalence test. (At the time of writing, a decision by the House of Lords in *Berkeley* is awaited.)

The problem with this approach is that the Courts end up trying to prove negatives; that neither more nor better information would come to light if a formal EIA happened. It also means that the educative value of EIA as a process is diminished. There must also be some doubts about how inclusive the process is. A good example is the enforcement action the Commission brought against the UK concerning, amongst other things, the lack of EIA at Twyford Down. The High Court in *Twyford Parish Council* v *Secretary of State for the Environment* [1993] 3 Env LR 37 would not find that the 322 page Inspector's report could not amount to a non-technical 'summary', and the Commission complaint into this was also dropped on the somewhat extraordinary grounds that the report could amount to the 'equivalent' of such a summary.

(d) EIA and national procedural rules
As discussed above (see p. 142), one of the problems which stands in the way of bringing cases based on alleged breaches of EC law is the amount of discretion which the national courts have to decide their own rules of procedure. Most importantly, these include rules on standing and on delay, i.e. whether cases are brought with sufficient speed. When major development projects are at stake, the need to bring claims quickly is particularly important, since as time passes the developer is likely to be incurring costs at the site, and these costs will be a relevant factor for the court to consider if the case is not brought promptly.

In EIA cases, a key issue is whether the strictness of the legal duty to assess certain types of projects means that national procedural rules must bend to accommodate this. In two recent cases decided by the Court of Appeal, the applicants have argued that the decisions of the ECJ in the *Kraaijeveld* and *Bozen* cases mean that national courts must set aside any national rule which would prevent the mandatory obligation to assess projects from being realised. In both cases, however, the Court has rejected this argument, firstly in *R v London Borough of Hammersmith and Fulham, ex parte CPRE* (21 December 1999, unreported, see above) and then in *R v North West Leicestershire District Council and East Midlands International Airport Ltd, ex parte Moses* (12 April 2000, unreported), a case concerning extension to a runway at the airport, where there was also considerable delay in bringing the claim. In the latter case, the EC principles of legal certainty and proportionality were invoked by the applicant. But the Court of Appeal turned these principles around:

> There comes a point, however, when these principles support the rejection rather than the admission of long delayed challenges where third parties have acted in reliance on apparently valid decisions. That point has long since been reached in this case.

However, in *Swan v Secretary of State (No. 1)* [1998] Env LR 545, the Scottish courts did establish the important point that a developer can still be required to submit an environmental statement, even though the development to which it relates has begun. In that case, the effects of the afforestation would be continuing, but there was insufficient evidence to suggest that an EIA was no longer possible.

(e) Summary
For the ECJ, therefore, the main concern has been to prevent Member States from putting an unduly light burden on their own developers (and administrators), and in so doing frustrate one of the key aims of the Directive: harmonisation. For the national courts, however, the concern has tended to be to avoid being dragged into arguments about the merits of whether EIA should or should not be required, and maintaining the position that matters of discretion, and rules of procedure, are generally not interfered with, even where EC case law suggests that they should exercise a closer degree of scrutiny.

Other procedures for determining the need for EIA

Although the pre-application procedure will be utilised in most cases, where there is uncertainty over the requirement for an EIA there are a number of alternative methods which can be used.

First, it is open to a developer to volunteer an environmental statement and to state expressly that the document is to be viewed as being an environmental statement for the purposes of the (now) 1999 Regulations. This in turn means that the local planning authority has to carry out the other information-gathering exercises for the EIA process. This has led to the growth in the submission of quasi-environmental statements. These documents contain the information which would normally be contained within an environmental statement, but are not submitted as formal statements for the purposes of the 1999 Regulations. In such circumstances, if there is any doubt as to the need for EIA the local planning authority can gather the information from one source (i.e. the developer), but is not obliged to go through the whole EIA exercise. One of the consequences of this approach has been that there is a tendency to concentrate on the subjectivity of the developer's assessment of the environmental effects. Thus, the whole purpose and concept of the EIA can be undermined unless this quasi-assessment is carried out thoroughly.

If an environmental statement is submitted and it is not referred to as a statement for the purposes of the 1999 Regulations, the local planning authority should consider whether a formal EIA should be undertaken. If it decides that it should be carried out, the statement can be considered as the environmental statement for the purposes of the 1999 Regulations. If the authority takes the view that EIA is not required, it is still required to take the information into account when deciding the planning application.

(a) Post-planning application determinations on the need for EIA

Where a planning application has been submitted without an environmental statement, and without a screening opinion or direction, the local planning authority should consider whether the application falls within one of the schedules to the 1999 Regulations (reg. 7). Additionally, it should check to see if the Secretary of State has made any directions, or if the authority itself has made any prior determinations on the relevant project.

Where the local planning authority considers that the project falls within one of the schedules, it must inform the applicant within three weeks of the need for an environmental statement to accompany the planning application, giving its full reasons for doing so. Thereafter, the applicant can either ask the Secretary of State for a direction within three weeks (reg. 8), or supply the environmental statement. Failure to do so would mean that the application could not be decided until a statement had been submitted, unless the local planning authority was minded to refuse the application.

(b) Appeals and called-in applications

There is even scope for the Secretary of State to request an environmental statement after he has called in an application or it has gone to appeal (reg. 9). Where there is a direction that an EIA is required, the Secretary of State or an inspector cannot grant planning permission on appeal or after a call-in unless the environmental statement is submitted.

The environmental statement

A key component of any EIA is the environmental statement (ES). The basic position is that any application that needs EIA must include an ES. If it is not included, then the application is treated as if a screening opinion or direction is being sought (reg. 7). There is no statutory provision as to the form of an ES, but it *must* contain at least the following information (reg. 2(1) and Part II, sch. 4):

(a)   a description of the development comprising information on its site, design and size;

(b)   a description of the measures envisaged in order to avoid, reduce and, if possible, remedy significant adverse effects;

(c)   the data required to identify and assess the main effects which the development is likely to have on the environment; and

(d)   an outline of the main alternatives studied by the applicant or appellant and an indication of the main reasons for his choice, taking into account the environmental effects.

In addition, the ES must include certain information as is reasonably required to assess the environmental effects of the development and which the applicant can, having regard in particular to current knowledge and methods of assessment, reasonably be required to compile. In some respects this merely duplicates the categories mentioned above (e.g. mitigation and re-mediation measures, and the main alternative studied). But beyond this, more detailed information may need to be provided (Part I, sch. 4) under such heads as:

(a)   the description of the development, including for example the main characteristics of the production process such as the nature and quantity of the materials used;

(b)   a description of the aspects of the environment likely to be significant-ly affected by the development, including population, fauna, flora, soil, water, air, climatic factors, material assets, including the architectural and archae-ological heritage, landscape and the inter-relationship between these factors;

(c)   a description of the likely significant environmental effects, covering the direct effects and any indirect, secondary, cumulative, short, medium and long-term, permanent and temporary, positive and negative effects of the development, resulting from

(i)   the existence of the development;

(ii)   the use of natural resources; and

(iii) the emission of pollutants, the creation of nuisances and the elimination of waste, together with a description of the forecasting methods used; and

(d)   an indication of any difficulties (technical deficiencies or lack of know-how) encountered by the developer in compiling the required informa-tion.

For all of the above items of information, a non-technical summary of any information supplied must also be provided, enabling non-experts to understand its findings.

The important change made under the 1999 Regulations (following changes to the Directive) is to make much more information mandatory. This was to address concerns that information being supplied was, at worst, framed as little more than a piece of advocacy on behalf of the developer. There are, however, still limits.

An example is the question of alternatives. Only alternatives studied by the developer need to be included in the ES. In theory, therefore, only good practice requires alternatives to be studied as a matter of EIA law. Circular 2/99 states, however, that it would be open to a planning authority to decide that the absence of alternatives, or the known availability of better alternatives, was a material consideration that justified refusal. (These may be material even if the Circular did not mention it.) For example, where the proposal is for a nuclear power station there would be a significant obligation to undertake a thorough search for the best available site. This would involve at least a regional, if not a national, investigation. Alternatively, if the proposal is to establish an intensive pig-rearing unit there would not be the same degree of obligation. Notwithstanding this, if the unit is large enough there would be an expectation that the site identified for the unit would be the site giving rise to minimal environmental effects.

Reference to 'indirect effects' means that, for example, a developer of a brownfield site could refer to the saving of greenfield land. In theory, it would also be open to objectors to refer to negative indirect effects such as effects on climate change, although the environmental statement is not supposed to be, unlike in the US, a document over which there is specific litigation.

(a)   Scoping: opinions, directions and good practice

Following Directive 97/11, there are new provisions in the 1999 Regulations which give developers the chance to ask the local planning authority, before submitting an application, for its opinion on the information to be provided in the ES (reg. 10). Such 'scoping opinions' must involve consultation bodies, and be given in writing to developers, usually within five weeks. Screening and scoping opinions can be requested together. Where the planning authority does not reply in time, there is a right to request a scoping direction from the Secretary of State (regs. 10(7), 11). But unlike screening opinions there is no right to appeal a scoping opinion. This reflects the extent to which formal scoping is seen as less critical in the UK, which helps explain why the UK has chosen not to require mandatory scoping, as it could do under the Directive. Even where a scoping opinion or direction has been issued, the decision-maker can still request further information at a later date (regs 10(9), 11(6)).

It should be stressed that scoping has always been considered a key aspect of good practice in the preparation of ESs. Research suggests that the quality of ESs has improved over the years in part because of greater attention to informal scoping, such as by the holding of preliminary meetings with the local planning authority and other relevant consultees and in some cases also the local community.

(b)   Criticism of environmental statements

Around 300 to 350 ESs are submitted every year in the UK, around 65 to 70 per cent being made under the main regulations. This figure is expected to rise following the 1999 Regulations. Since 1988, considerable attention has focused on the quality of ESs submitted. Early research indicated considerable failings, with most academic commentators finding less than half of all statements studied to be of acceptable quality. Most of these deficiencies were to be found in the assessment of the environmental impacts of the project. This was not helped by the lack of formal scoping, and early research showed that as many as 50 per cent of local planning authorities were not consulted at the scoping stage. To aid consistency, the EC Commission produced *Environmental Impact Assessment: Guidance on Scoping* in 1996.

At national level, an initial problem was that few planning officers had any experience of judging the adequacy of ESs, and developers (through the retention of consultants who built up a greater experience of EIA) always possessed an information advantage over the authorities. To some extent this problem is decreasing: the chances that a planning authority has not dealt with an EIA application is receding, and many authorities now themselves engage consultants to review the adequacy of statements received. The result, however, is not clear. Though many studies record a gradual improvement in quality over time, others indicate no discernible differences. All indicate significant room for improvement. None of these studies, however, includes data following the issuing of central government guidance, both to developers and to decision-makers (see *Evaluation of Environmental Information for Planning Projects*, DoE, 1994, and *Preparation of Environmental Statements for Planning Projects that Require Environmental Assessment: A Good Practice Guide*, DoE, 1995), which may have improved matters. The guidance emphasises the need to differentiate between scientific calculation of impacts and the evaluation of the significance of the impact, which is at best an informed judgment (but see p. 53 above).

A problem was (and remains) that there are no agreed 'standards' for ESs, although academic bodies have developed their own criteria. Calls from several quarters for an independent 'Council for Environmental Assessment' which would be involved with scoping and quality review have not been taken up in the UK, although interestingly in the Netherlands there is an EIA Commission which carries out the scoping of all assessments.

Many have argued that improving the quality of ESs is central to improving the quality of the EIA process as a whole. But it is at least arguable that too much attention has been paid to the adequacy of ESs at the expense of the overall treatment of environmental information. Research suggests that planning officers and consultees generally believe that the results of the consultation process have a more significant impact on planning decisions than the content of the ES does.

(c)   Consulting on the environmental statement

As part of the scoping process, in gathering information developers are not only expected to consult local planning authorities; they may also seek views from the statutory consultees and possibly non-statutory consultees.

Ordinarily, the developer will go to the local planning authority first to discuss the project. At that stage the local planning authority may wish to identify the bodies with whom consultations should be undertaken. Such consultees will often extend beyond the range of those specified in the 1999 Regulations as statutory consultees. Regulation 13 provides that the statutory consultees should include those bodies which the local planning authority is required by Art. 10 of the Town and Country Planning (General Development Procedure) Order 1995 to consult on the determination of a planning application. These include, where appropriate, the HSE, the highway authority, English Heritage, the NCC and the Environment Agency. The width of consultation depends precisely upon the type of development proposed. In addition the NCC and the Countryside Agency should be consulted if they would not otherwise be consulted as a matter of planning law.

It is the developer's responsibility to approach the statutory consultees. Regulation 12 imposes a duty on the statutory consultees to make available, on request, any information in their possession which is relevant to the preparation of the environmental statement. This does not, however, require the public bodies to obtain information they do not have or to disclose confidential information. The consultees can levy a reasonable charge for making such information available.

The information which it is envisaged would be made available would include specialised information, such as the results of ecological monitoring, which would help the identification and assessment of the environmental effects.

Furthermore, there may be non-statutory consultees who could assist with this information. Developers can consult with these bodies where they offer some particular expertise or local insight. This type of non-statutory consultee could include such bodies as the RSPB, CPRE, local nature groups and members of the general public.

The consultation exercise (often extensive) forms the backbone of the whole EIA process and produces a number of advantages. First, quite often in development projects some environmental issues are obvious. The benefit of the consultation exercise, however, is that it identifies those issues which are perhaps not so clear. Secondly, a methodical, even approach to the objective analysis of environmental impacts enables alterations to be made to a project at an early stage without great expense or inconvenience. These alterations can mitigate or eliminate adverse effects. Thirdly, where a full and adequate consultation is carried out before a planning application is submitted, the amount of time taken by the local planning authority and other consultees to consider the application when submitted will be greatly reduced. Finally, the consultation process affords the developer the opportunity of communicating with all parties who are likely to have an interest in the project. Misunderstandings can be cleared up on both sides. This then enables the developer and the local planning authority to concentrate on the relevant issues.

Determination of the planning application

The developer is responsible for the content of the environmental statement which is finally submitted. Where the local planning authority considers that the information given is insufficient to allow for proper consideration of the environmental effects of the development, further information can be requested (reg. 19). Where the process of consultation has been carried out properly this should not arise.

Once an environmental statement has been prepared and submitted together with the planning application, there are further procedural steps which closely follow the standard procedure for planning applications. The two main differences are that the determination period for the application is extended to 16 weeks (reg. 32) and there are increased publicity requirements to ensure that the planning application including the environmental statement is advertised in the local newspaper and in a site notice. If the ES is submitted after the planning application, the developer must publicise.

Additionally, each statutory consultee is entitled to a copy of the ES free of charge, and a reasonable number of copies should be made available for sale to the public at a reasonable charge which reflects their printing and distribution costs (regs. 17 and 18).

The local planning authority then notifies the statutory consultees of the application (if this is necessary) and they have a minimum of 14 days to comment on the environmental statement. These requirements also apply where the local planning authority is itself the applicant for planning permission (reg. 22).

It is not open to the local planning authority to invalidate an ES because of its view of the inadequacies of the information supplied. Should it take the view that the ES is inadequate, it should use its powers to seek further information under reg. 19. Where the developer fails to provide further information and the local planning authority decides to refuse planning permission, or fails to determine the application within the 16-week period, the developer has the usual right of appeal to the Secretary of State.

(a)   The duty to give reasons
Following Directive 97/11, whether the outcome of an EIA application is to grant or refuse development consent, reasons must be given by the local planning authority to the Secretary of State and to the general public via a newspaper notice and through the planning register. Previously, such reasons were required only where the Member States' legislation so provided. Thus the previous rule in the UK, that reasons need be given only where planning permission is refused, no longer applies where an EIA has been undertaken. Reasons are to include (i) the content of the decision and any conditions attached; (ii) the main reasons and considerations upon which it is based; and (iii) a description where necessary of the main mitigating and remediation measures employed.

These new provisions, however, do not provide a general duty to give reasons in relation to EIA applications. There is, as we have seen, a duty to give clear, precise and full reasons why EIA is required (reg. 4(6)). But often, information will be sought about the reasons why no EIA was required in the first place. This was the background to *R v Secretary of State for the Environment, Transport and the Regions and Parcelforce, ex parte Marson* [1998] JPL 869, a judicial review about the lack of environmental assessment of proposals by Parcelforce to build a large sorting facility adjacent to Coventry airport. Although the project fell within schedule two, the Secretary of State did not think that it would give rise to significant environmental effects. No further reasons were given. The Court of Appeal held that there was nothing in national or EC law that required more information than had been provided. One rather worrying aspect of the decision is that the Court thought that reasons had been given 'albeit in summary form', when all that the Secretary of State noted was the bare statement that there would not be likely significant effects. To say the least, this is a circular argument that does not give any explicit reason for its own conclusions. The matter is likely to proceed to the European Court of Human Rights.

Transboundary effects

Directive 85/337 has always contained provisions requiring consultation between Member States where development is likely to have significant environmental effects in other Member States. These were never transposed into the first wave of implementing regulations. This might be excused because of limited scientific knowledge of such impacts at the time (a weak argument at best), but is less easily excused in relation to the regulations implementing the Directive into planning law in Northern Ireland! Following the 1991 Espoo Convention on Environmental Impact Assessment in a Transboundary Context (in force 1997), the Directive now contains more detailed provision on this issue (Art. 7) and these provisions are now transposed into the 1999 Regulations (regs. 27 and 28).

Where significant transboundary effects are likely upon another member state, that state must be notified in outline of the project. If the other state wishes to participate in the EIA, it must be sent the application and the ES and information about the assessment process. This provision is not restricted to projects located on or near national frontiers (Case C-133/94 *Commission v Belgium* [1996] ECR I-2323, para. 53). The Secretary of State must give the other country a reasonable time to decide whether to get involved. The information required must also be made available within a reasonable time to the national environmental authorities and the public concerned in the affected state. There must be consultation on the impact of the project and any mitigating measures, as well as agreement on a reasonable length of time for the consultation period. The other state must be informed of the ultimate decision reached, in line with the duty to give reasons noted above. There are also analogous provisions where projects in another member state are likely to have significant impacts in England and Wales.

It is important to note that this procedure does not confer rights upon individuals within an affected bordering state, but only apportions rights and duties at the national level. Also, the 1999 Regulations refer only to effects on, or from, other Member States, but there are parties to the Espoo Convention which are not members of the EC. Thus, the UK has obligations under international law to engage in transboundary EIA with signatories such as Norway and Poland.

EIA: an overall assessment

The original environmental assessment Directive has been described as the most important EC environmental directive. In part this is because it heralded the use of procedural law for environmental protection at EC level. But it is also because the Directive was the first to provide for the integration of environmental concerns into decision-making — a hallmark of sustainable development. That the Directive has been the subject of more complaints to the Commission about non-implementation than any other EC environmental measure is an indicator of its impact.

Initial fears about the costs to developers appear not to have been realised. Indeed, many commentators would question whether EIA is such a burden that developers would be particularly worried whether it was required for their projects, and concerns about costs seem to have receded over the years. As a research study examining the relative costs and benefits associated with implementation of the 1985 Directive in Greece, the Netherlands, Spain and the UK found, costs in excess of 1 per cent of total capital expenditure were the exception. They also tended to occur in relation to particularly controversial projects in sensitive areas, or where good EIA practice had not been followed. Costs as a proportion of total capital expenditure may be as low as 0.2 per cent, with the EA component being lowest for the largest projects (see European Commission, *EIA in Europe: A Study on Costs and Benefits*).

Moreover, the research recorded a high percentage of respondents (which would appear to be developers and decision-makers only) identifying a number of benefits to them or to the development proposal arising from the conduct of the assessment process. This included a finding that the environmental credibility of the developer had been enhanced in 61 per cent of cases. This is backed up by recent UK research which suggests that both planning officers (88 per cent) and developers/consultants (76 per cent) felt EIA to have been a net benefit in cases in which they had been involved. Such statistics may be seen as supporting the view of EIA as operating as a developers' charter, 'being used by developers to advance their projects in environmental terms' (Elworthy and Holder, *Environmental Protection: Text and Materials*, Butterworths, 1997, p. 418). The views of consultees and third parties tend to receive less attention, although it is notable that, in general, planning officers take a more positive view of the quality of ESs than researchers, while consultees tend to take a more negative view.

As to substantive criticisms, the lack of real powers to prevent biased statements still gives cause for concern. But if anything, the centrality of the

ES is diminishing, and the *assessment* process elevated. So far, this shift has not been recognised in significant changes to the law, either at EC or national level, although the new duty to give reasons for any decision on an application that has been assessed is certainly a positive step. The continued absence of any requirement for post-project monitoring, however, continues to detract from the iterative nature of EIA, arguably depriving EIA of a crucial learning tool.

Finally, it is notable that most planning officers feel that EIA probably makes no difference to the decision to permit or refuse any particular application. Of course, this may be because greater attention is given to mitigating measures, either agreed early on or eventually required under planning conditions or obligations. On the other hand, it might suggest that the boundaries within which individual decisions are taken leave relatively little scope for a significantly different resolution of the balancing of environmental and other objectives than would otherwise have occurred where environmental impact was considered as a material consideration in town and country planning law.

Towards strategic environmental assessment?

For some years the limitations of project-based assessment have been apparent. Indeed, the US law from 1969 that inspired the 1985 Directive covered all major federal *actions* and early drafts of the Directive extended to wider strategic assessment. In 1991, proposals for a draft directive on strategic environmental assessment (SEA) surfaced. Moves to adopt a directive in this area were strengthened by the review of the EIA Directive in 1993, which found that the evaluation of many projects was taking place far too late in the development planning process. Initially, the proposals for SEA extended to plans, policies, and programmes, but the inclusion of policy assessment in particular was the subject of significant objections from various Member States. The Council has now adopted a Common Position on the proposals. This gives a good indication of what any Directive will look like, although use of the co-decision procedure means that the European Parliament must reach a decision on this version of the text (for the original proposals and first revisions see COM(96)511 & COM(99)73).

The draft Directive applies to all plans and programmes which are prepared for the following sectors — agriculture, forestry, fisheries, energy, industry, transport, waste management, water management, telecommunications, tourism, town and country planning or land use — and 'which set a framework for future development consents' of projects listed in Annexes I and II to the revised EIA Directive. Also covered are plans and programmes which require an assessment under the Habitats Directive (92/43). In both cases, an exception is made for minor plans and programmes, which only need to be assessed if they are likely to have significant environmental effects. Beyond these, Member States must determine whether other plans and programmes which set the framework for future development consent of projects are likely to have significant environment effects; if they do, they must be assessed.

All of this is a significant change from the 1996 proposals, which were restricted to the town and country planning sector. However, deliberately linking SEA to EIA might create problems since, e.g. not all aspects of development plans or waste plans will relate to matters governed by EIA. In practice, it must be assumed that the EIA-related aspects of plans and programmes will not be looked at in isolation, and that for convenience (and regulatory coherence) all aspects of these types of plans, e.g. the whole of the national waste strategy under the Environment Act 1995 and perhaps also the air quality strategy under the same Act, will be subject to SEA. Planning policy guidance notes would also be covered, so we might see their adoption becoming rather more formalised than is the case at present.

SEA would operate in a similar way to project-based assessment. There would be a requirement to prepare an ES (termed an 'environmental report') setting out information on the assessment of the effects of implementing the plan or programme. This would include information on, amongst other things:

(a)   existing environmental problems relevant to the plan or programme;
(b)   the environmental characteristics of the area affected;
(c)   environmental obligations imposed to meet international, European, and national objectives and how the plan or programme meets those objectives;
(d)   the likely significant environmental effects which would be brought about by implementing the plan or programme, including consideration of things like cumulative and synergistic effects, and both temporary and long-term effects;
(e)   any envisaged mitigating measures (which must be as full as possible); and
(f)   a non-technical summary.

A key feature of the new proposals is the attention to the consideration of alternatives. Information about the plan or programme, or the area affected, would always have to consider as well any 'reasonable alternatives' such as alternative types of development or alternative locations for it. There is a watered down version of a requirement to describe the 'zero-option' (the do nothing alternative), and the authority would also have to provide both a statement of how the assessment was conducted and the reasons for not adopting alternatives considered. These clearly go well beyond the provisions relating to alternatives under project-based EIA.

Once the information was provided in an environmental report, there would be consultation with statutory consultees (including relevant environmental NGOs) and with the public in a similar way to EIA. Unlike EIA, however, public authorities would have to consult the public on the scope and level of detail of information to be included in the report, effectively providing for mandatory scoping and giving the public two stages in the plan-making process to express their views. A further notable difference is that environmental information would have to be taken into consideration *during* the plan-making process, rather than simply before adoption; the public must be given an 'early and effective opportunity within appropriate time frames' to comment, although precisely what this means is left up to the Member States. Also, there must be measures for monitoring the implementation of the plan or programme. Both of these go some way towards making SEA a more iterative process than EIA. However, the fact that the same body prepares the environmental report and the assessment may give rise to allegations of bias.

SEA goes some of the way towards integrating environmental considerations into wider decision-making. But also relevant are provisions like Article 6 of the EC Treaty which provides for integration at policy level in the EC (see p. 125). Experience elsewhere, such as with EC structural funds and trans-European networks, indicates some of the difficulties of effective integration.

THIRTEEN
Integrated pollution control

Unlike other chapters in Part II of this book which are concerned with the general control of particular polluting substances such as emissions to water or air, or the deposit of waste on land (regardless of the identity of the polluter), this chapter is concerned with the control of the specific processes which produce such emissions. Although there is a clear overlap between the two in the sense that industrial processes can be controlled under the different legislative regimes which are covered elsewhere (e.g. under the Water Resources Act 1991 or the waste provisions of the EPA 1990), this chapter deals with the specific regulation of all of the emissions from certain prescribed industrial processes under a system known as Integrated Pollution Control (IPC) and the introduction of a wider system of control dealing with emissions and other environmental impacts (e.g. noise and energy efficiency) under the Pollution Prevention and Control Act 1999 (PPCA 1999) and associated regulations.

What distinguishes these controls from other pollution control regimes is the relative narrowness of the scope of control in the sense that a small number of processes are covered; and the relative breadth of the controls imposed in the sense that authorisations which are issued cover emissions to all three environmental media (IPC) and other environmental impacts (PPCA 1999). The introduction of IPC in the EPA 1990 was phased in over a period of six years. Although there were significant teething problems in the transitional period (particularly with a shift from an emissions standards approach to a vaguer process standard approach to setting conditions), the IPC system has now been implemented fully, bringing with it new approaches to such things as public participation (triggered by a controversy over the secrecy surrounding the burning of substitute liquid fuels (SLF)), the assessment of environmental impacts, the selection of the Best Practicable Environmental Option (BPEO) for a particular process and the development of basic techniques of cost benefit analysis and proportionality in relation to upgrading standards for different industrial sectors.

These new developments give the UK somewhat of an advantage when it comes to the implementation of the corresponding European initiative dealing with the controls over industrial processes, the Integrated Pollution Prevention and Control Directive (96/91). This Directive should have been transposed and implemented into national legislation by the end of October 1999. Although this original deadline was missed, the PPCA 1999 provides a statutory framework which enables more detailed regulations to be introduced (which should take place nearly a year late in September 2000). The impact of the Directive will be phased in over a period (for existing installations) and although the scope of the controls under the Directive will be significantly wider than existing IPC controls, the full effect of the new legislation will be reduced as a result of the introduction of a system of IPC in the EPA 1990.

The history of controls over industrial processes

Traditionally, the role of environmental law was targeted towards the protection of public health. Although the secondary purpose of such controls was that the environment was protected from harm, this was not the main purpose of the legislation. In the 1830s, standards of sanitation in the major cities created a great deal of concern amongst those enlightened individuals who took an interest in the poorer classes. Consequently, between the years 1840 and 1875, attempts were made to deal with the problem by the setting up of special local boards of commissioners which were the predecessors of today's local authorities. These boards were made responsible for the enforcement of minimal sanitation standards.

At approximately the same time, industry started to utilise new materials and new industrial sectors were formed, such as alkali works, which produced highly noxious and polluting chemicals as a by-product of their processes. Even in this respect, the problem was not viewed in purely environmental terms and the main thrust of the controls was based on technological answers to what were perceived as scientific problems. Thus the Alkali Inspectorate was created in 1863 to fulfil a technical and advisory role in the combating of pollution. However, the legislation was neither properly enforced nor did it address all the difficulties emissions into the atmosphere could cause. Consequently, although noxious fumes were controlled, there was no prohibition on the emission of smoke into the atmosphere, which brought about problems of lower-level pollution with the production of smog. Thus, although the law sought to deal with one problem another problem arose elsewhere.

As new environmental issues emerged, legislation was introduced which often resulted in separate bodies being responsible for enforcement in respect of overlapping emissions. For example, in relation to air pollution the Alkali Inspectorate dealt with noxious fumes under the Alkali etc. Works Regulation Act 1906, but local authorities were responsible for the control of smoke under the Clean Air Acts 1956 and 1968. Other bodies were created to deal with a variety of subject matters such as the control of health and safety within factories, the control of nuclear installations and the control of mines and quarries. The control of emissions to the atmosphere was pieced together by a haphazard jigsaw of administrative controls enforced by a number of different bodies. Although the aims of these statutory bodies were different, the reactive approach often meant that the mechanisms used to control individual areas of concern overlapped. This resulted in over-complicated and ineffective enforcement.

The 'modern' era

The Robens Committee was set up in the early 1970s to report on health and safety at work and to answer specifically some of the criticisms that had been levelled at the many different authorities administering different sectors. In 1972, the Committee recommended that a new unified body should be set up to deal with all aspects of health, safety and welfare at work. Traditionally, there had been some confusion as to the role of the Alkali Inspectorate and whether or not its aim was to protect the environment or to safeguard the health of workers. The Robens Committee recommended that a new Health and Safety Executive (HSE) should be established to include the Alkali Inspectorate. This was duly formed in 1974, in the first real attempt to unify a number of different inspectorates under one organisational umbrella.

Alongside the creation of the HSE, different measures were being taken to introduce controls over waste disposal and water pollution. In relation to waste, the Control of Pollution Act 1974 created new bodies which were known as waste disposal authorities and had responsibility for the disposal of waste to land. These functions were primarily the responsibility of county authorities. Clearly, this protection was not part of the factory-based approach but, unfortunately, in practice there was little or no coordination between the HSE and those controlling waste disposal, notwithstanding that there is a connection between the production of waste in factories regulated by the HSE and the disposal of waste on sites controlled by waste disposal authorities.

Although attempts were made by the Department of the Environment to rationalise environmental control, the plethora of enforcement agencies, including such bodies as the HSE, local authorities, the water authorities, and later the successor to the Alkali Inspectorate (the Industrial Air Pollution Inspectorate) and the waste disposal authorities, created a complicated web of fragmented control. There was no unified concept of environmental protection; a theoretical and unrealistic sectoral approach had fundamental flaws which constantly served to undermine the authority of the law.

In addition to the jungle of administrative bodies, environmental control was also hampered by the vast number of powers and procedures available to each individual enforcement agency. Where powers to control pollution were available to a number of bodies, overlapping controls often meant that a particular incident or process could be regulated by as many as four different authorities. For example, a factory which was subject to control under the Alkali etc. Works Regulation Act 1906, which produced dark smoke and discharged trade effluent into the nearby river could be controlled by the Alkali Inspectorate, the local environmental health department, and the water authority. This often created difficulties, particularly as a particular problem could be approached by each different enforcement body using different enforcement powers. In many cases there were elements of 'too many cooks spoiling the broth'.

The consequences of the fragmented approach

Overall, as Britain entered the 1980s, there was a fragmented, individualised, sectoral approach which did not reflect the growing trend within Europe for an integrated approach to the environment with specific quality objectives. As the move to make a fundamental change from the 'British approach' gathered pace, the consequences of the traditional basis of pollution control became clear.

(a) Failure to view the environment as a whole
One of the main concerns of those who criticised the sectoral approach to pollution control in Britain was that there was a failure to deal with the environment as a whole. Each individual medium was seen as a separate area of control and no consideration was given to the possible consequences of imposing control on one sector in relation to others. For instance, where strict controls were placed upon the levels of effluent discharge into water, a simple alteration to the production process may shift the disposal of the effluent to another sector, such as by incineration (air) or landfill. The environment as a concept is a series of interdependent sectors. When individual bodies controlled separate sectors there was often a reluctance to deal with a problem on a unified basis. Administratively, the idea of two separate bodies with overlapping responsibilities created tremendous logistical difficulties, misunderstandings arose, inter-departmental communication had its own problems, which led to inefficient control.

(b) The discretionary decision-making process
The different regulatory bodies possessed wide discretionary powers with which to enforce their statutory duties. Too much discretion led to uncertainty. Certain bodies took a more rigorous view of enforcement whereas others were content to pursue a conciliatory approach. When a number of statutory bodies controlled the same process, the use of these different criteria led to an imbalance in the protection of the environment as a whole. Where an enforcement body showed a tendency to pursue rigorous levels of enforcement, emissions in that sector were kept at an artificially low level. However, this was often counterbalanced by an increase of emission levels to another medium in relation to which the alternative enforcement bodies exercised their discretion leniently.

(c) The development of a co-operational approach to enforcement
The lack of definitive standards in many areas saw the development of the co-operative approach by many enforcement agencies. It has been argued in favour of such an approach that compliance with standards has resulted

rather than producing a wholesale enforcement holiday. However, other consequences have also been identified (see Chapter 9).

(d)   Overlapping controls

One of the consequences of failing to deal with the environment as a whole was that each individual enforcement agency had a prescribed area of responsibility. Where, however, there were overlaps in that responsibility, an uncoordinated approach brought about ineffective enforcement of the regulations in question. Where complex administrative mechanisms are required to cope with a simple single incident there is a chance that the proper mechanism is not utilised. The nature of the bureaucratic system of control was such that where administrative controls overlapped, any failure of communication between the enforcement agencies rendered proper enforcement more difficult.

(e)   Lack of public accountability

Lastly, where there were so many enforcement agencies, there was often a problem with a lack of public accountability. The trained professional could have difficulty in ascertaining which body was responsible for a particular activity. The person in the street had very little chance of knowing to whom to turn. Normally, the local environmental health officer was the first person to receive complaints, not necessarily because the local authority was the proper controlling body for a particular process, but because the public identified the environmental health department of a local authority as being the 'right place' to which to complain. Other more obscure agencies were not fully recognised by members of the public. Where there was such uncertainty then the accountability of these bodies was also obscured. For an administrative and bureaucratic system to work effectively, the public needed to recognise who controls what and how they did so.

Beyond the 'modern' era — the shift towards unification of regulatory bodies and controls

In 1976, the Royal Commission on Environmental Pollution recognised some of these defects in its Fifth Report on air pollution (Cmnd 6731, 1976). The Commission recognised that substantive unification of pollution control legislation had to be preceded by the creation of an administrative body which could implement and enforce the unified powers effectively. Thus the Commission recommended, first, that there should be a single unified body to ensure that any regulatory system imposed could be enforced effectively and the full range of environmental emissions of the more polluting processes controlled. Secondly, in order to assess the full environmental effect of a process rather than assessing its impact in terms of different media, it recommended that there should be a move away from the emissions based concepts such as the use of the best practicable means standard (BPM) to the wider notion of 'best practicable environmental option' (BPEO). This test allowed for the setting of emission standards relating to specific prescribed processes and substances whilst maintaining a scientific and technological approach to pollution abatement with incidental powers to improve process standards. In 1988, the RCEP in its Twelfth Report adopted a broader definition, suggesting that the assessment of BPEO was:

> . . . the outcome of a systematic consultative and decision-making procedure which emphasises the protection of the environment across land, air and water. The BPEO procedure establishes, for a given set of objectives, the option that provides the most benefit or least damage to the environment as a whole, at acceptable cost, in the long as well as short term.

Although the RCEP's recommendations were ignored by central government for political reasons, the 1980s saw a gradual shift towards the unification of powers brought about not only as a result of the need to implement the concept of BPEO but also because of the need to move away from the British approach of flexible standard setting towards European-style emission standards defined with reference to 'permissible maximum concentrations of substances' and 'quality objectives'.

In addition different Member States within the EC were starting to develop their own distinct methodologies of pollution control. In particular, in West Germany (as it then was) environmental control evolved around the somewhat different mechanism of the *Vorsorgeprinzip*. This was a stated principle which was to be adhered to when considering the environmental impact of a process and which operated on two bases: first, that the environment should be able to restore itself notwithstanding the effect of industrial activity; and secondly that environmental controls on emissions standards should be set as high as they could, taking into account available technology. These two principles were countered by the general principle of proportionality, which takes into account the balance between the environmental improvement achieved and the cost needed to attain that improvement.

This three-pronged approach was adopted into European legislation in the Directive on Atmospheric Emissions from Industrial Plant (84/360). This required that all appropriate measures against air pollution be taken, including the application of the best available technology which did not entail excessive cost. This concept of the 'best available technology not entailing excessive cost' was viewed by some as being an extension of the BPM, but the method of its utilisation within British legislation, when coupled with the need to meet specific environmental quality objectives, ensured that there was to be a fundamental restructuring of pollution control within Britain.

Her Majesty's Inspectorate of Pollution and the Environment Agency

The move towards a unified regulatory agency was partially secured with the introduction of Her Majesty's Inspectorate of Pollution (HMIP) in 1987 although the division of responsibility for particular areas of pollution control continued beyond the creation of the National Rivers Authority in 1989. It was only with the creation of the Environment Agency in 1996 that true integration of many of the pollution control functions took place.

IPC and IPPC

With the creation of HMIP in 1987, the way was open for the introduction of a system of pollution control which took account of the requirements of assessing impacts upon the environment as a whole. Many of the aspects of the new system of integrated pollution control (IPC) contained some similarities to the pre-existing environmental legislation. There were, however a number of new concepts which were introduced to enable Britain to fulfil its obligations under European law and also to take a proactive approach to environmental protection.

The introduction of IPC in Part I of the EPA 1990 established two systems of control with one dealing with emissions to all media and the other, containing the same principal mechanisms of control, dealing with atmospheric emissions alone (thereby replacing antiquated provisions on air pollution under the Health and Safety at Work Act 1974 and the Alkali etc. Works Regulations Act 1906). At the same time as the IPC provisions were being implemented in Britain, the European Commission was putting forward its proposals on 'integrated permitting' for industrial processes. This rapidly developed into a directive on integrated pollution control which met considerable resistance from some Member States who objected to the concept of a single permit for all environmental releases. Subsequently the proposal metamorphosed into the Directive on Integrated Pollution Prevention and Control which placed an emphasis on the preventive nature of the control mechanism rather than the integration of the permitting system.

In many ways, the Directive echoed the existing IPC system in the UK although there was a shift from control over environmental emissions to wider environmental impacts and from isolated industrial processes to a wider definition of activities and installations (both of which reflected a recognition that the general effects of industrial activity stretch much wider than a mere consideration of what comes out of the end of pipes). Ironically, the UK was in the forefront of the argument in favour of bringing forward the requirements of this Directive for existing operations, primarily as a result of its experience with the system of IPC and the desire to ensure that the affected industrial sectors in other Member States did not gain any competitive advantage during the implementation period. Although the final implementation of the IPPC Directive will require some substantive changes to UK pollution control, the general scheme of the IPC system has meant that procedural and administrative upheaval will be kept to a minimum. Having said that, the practical implementation of the IPPC Directive is to be phased in over a period leading up to 2007 for installations which were in existence at the end of October 1999. This means that there will be a degree of overlap between the IPC controls and the new controls under the IPPC scheme (brought into force under the PPCA 1999 but referred to as IPPC for the rest of this chapter) during this nine-year transitional period.

At the time of writing the final draft regulations which implement the system had been published but not brought into force. Thus, references to 'the Regulations' in this chapter are references to the draft Pollution Prevention and Control (England and Wales) Regulations 2000 and the system is described as found in these final draft regulations. Where possible, specific reference has been made to regulation numbers (with a warning that there is a slight chance that these may change in the final version). In addition, there is some comparative analysis of the new and old systems. Finally, as the IPC regime is still relevant in the short and medium term, there is some consideration of the key aspects of IPC under Part I of the EPA 1990.

The main features of the control over industrial processes

These are as follows:

(a)   The system of IPC applies to certain categories of industrial processes which have been prescribed for control by the Secretary of State. IPC controls all emissions (to air, water and land) from the more polluting industrial processes (known as Part A processes). There is a separate but related system of control (known as Air Pollution Control) which covers atmospheric emissions from the same categories of industrial processes covered by IPC but from less polluting processes (known as Part B processes).

(b)   This dual system of control is to be replaced by a single system of control under the Pollution Prevention and Control Act 1999 (which in turn implements the Integrated Pollution Prevention and Control Directive 96/61). This control applies to activities carried out at installations (as opposed to processes) but is broadly similar to IPC. The IPPC system will be phased in over an eight-year period for all activities which were in existence (or finalised) in November 1999. New installations should have been controlled from 31 October 1999 (raising questions about the effect of late transposition of the Directive).

(c)   The IPC system is administered centrally by the Environment Agency as are the majority of the most polluting installations under IPPC (these are known as Part A(1) installations). The less polluting installations are controlled under IPPC by local authorities (either for all environmental impacts, known as Part A(2) installations or just atmospheric emissions, known as Part B installations).

(d)   Both IPC and IPPC utilise process standards to control emissions and environmental impacts. These process standards are aimed at ensuring that emissions or environmental impacts are minimised particularly by using the best available techniques (BAT) to prevent pollution. Guidance on what constitutes BAT is found in guidance notes. The use of BAT is balanced with the costs of doing so.

(e)   IPPC controls apply to a wide range of environmental impacts over and above environmental emissions. These include energy efficiency, waste minimisation, noise production, accident prevention and clean up after an installation has been closed.

(f)   Applications for authorisations (IPC) and permits (IPPC) are granted conditionally with conditions relating to the achievement of BAT. Applications can be refused on the ground of technical incompetence or likelihood of failure to comply with any condition.

(g)   Under IPPC there are controls over the cessation of prescribed activities, with an operator being required to satisfy the regulator that there is no pollution risk and that the site of the installation is not contaminated from the carrying out of the activity prior to the surrender of any permit being accepted by the regulatory authority.

(h)   Enforcement under both systems is discretionary but underpinned by a duty to supervise permitted installations. The enforcement powers include the power to vary or revoke an authorisation/permit, or to enforce for breach or anticipated breach of condition.

(i)   There are powers for the regulatory agency to prevent or remedy pollution at the permit authorisation holder's expense.

(j)   There are a range of criminal offences including operating a pre-scribed process or activity without a permit, breaching the condition of a permit authorisation, or failing to comply with an enforcement notice.

IPPC and EC law

As with many other areas of environmental law, the PPCA 1999 and associated legislation needs to be seen primarily in the context of the IPPC Directive (96/61). The Directive requires Member States to prevent or, where that cannot be done, reduce pollution and environmental impacts from a range of installations set out in Annex 1 to the Directive. This is to be achieved through an integrated permitting process which will require each installation to hold a permit from a Member State's competent authority.

The permits are to be based on the application of the principle that the best available techniques are to be employed. These techniques must affect all of the site's environmental impacts including emissions to all three environment-al media and also energy use and efficiency, consumption of raw materials, noise and vibration and thermal effects. It is also clear that the permitting process is not simply concerned with the operation of the installation but also with what happens after the closure of the plant particularly as regards site remediation. Permits are to be based on local conditions, environmental quality standards and should address trans-boundary conditions.

The IPPC legislation applies to installations carrying out activities which are listed in Annex 1. Such installations will need to comply with the Directive if they commence operations after 30 October 1999. The Directive allows for an exception for certain developments which were 'in the pipeline' on this date (i.e. consent had been given but not implemented) and are brought into operation by 30 October 2000. This exception means that the delay in implementing the legislation is not a significant as other examples of late transposition (in particular the Environment Assessment Directive). Other installations which were 'existing' at the time of the directive being brought into effect will not have to brought into IPPC regulation until 30 October 2007. In the UK, given the experience of introducing IPC and local authority air pollution control (LAAPC) under EPA 1990 Part I, the government has decided that there should be a phased application to the various installations covered over the eight-year grace period. In addition, in the transitional period between 2000 and 2007 existing installations which undergo substantial changes will also have to seek an IPPC permit.

Although the Directive sets down minimum standards in many areas, it leaves Member States free to extend the scope of activities covered (the UK Government has included Part B processes under the new legislation which would not otherwise be covered under the Directive); to superimpose national policies and strategies for the prevention of pollution; and to select from different permitting procedures.

Transposing and implementing the IPPC Directive

The IPPC Directive is one of the first pieces of EC environmental legislation which is to be transposed and implemented in a devolved United Kingdom. Although there was only one consultation exercise for the new legislation in England and Wales, the final decision on the arrangements under the new legislation and particularly the power to make regulations, rests theoretically with the Welsh National Assembly rather than the Secretary of State (and this will have a knock-on effect in respect of any guidance or directions issued by the English Secretary of State). Scotland has separate legislation (which mirrors that in England and Wales). The position in Northern Ireland is unclear (although it is anticipated that transposition and implementation will be late). For the sake of simplicity, the English law will be described here.

As mentioned above, the transposing legislation is found in the Pollution Prevention and Control Act 1999. The provisions of this Act are, however, wide even for environmental legislation and they provide a very basic framework which gives little idea of the details of the system of control. Sections 1 and 2 of the 1999 Act give the Secretary of State the power to make regulations with the purpose of meeting the requirements of the IPPC Directive and for other measures to prevent and control pollution. When the Bill was first introduced, the power to make regulations was criticised as it granted an almost unfettered discretion to make a wide range of environmental legislation without any significant Parliamentary scrutiny. Consequently, certain safeguards were introduced to ensure that the Act was not unlimited in its scope and that adequate opportunity was given for Parliamentary scrutiny of certain aspects of new Regulations made under the powers in the Act. Section 2 of the Act limits the scope of the Secretary of State's power in that any regulations made under the Act must meet the general purpose under s. 1 (i.e. implementing the IPPC Directive and other pollution prevention measures) and the specific purposes set out in Schedule 1 to the Act. These purposes include the creation of offences; public registers; rights of appeal; rights of enforcement; and descriptions of regulated installations and activities. In addition, s. 2 and sch. 1 enable some of the powers which were found in the waste management licensing provisions under Part II of the EPA 1990 (dealing with waste regulation) to be implemented in relation to waste management activities regulated under IPPC. These include such things as technical competence requirements for applicants ('fit and proper person'), and the procedure for the surrender of permits when an installation closes.

Procedural safeguards have also been built into the Act. The initial regulations are subject to the affirmative Parliamentary procedure for passing secondary legislation which requires regulations to be debated in both Houses of Parliament. Any amendments to these regulations which create a new offence, increase criminal penalties, or seek to amend or repeal any of the provisions of the Act must also comply with the affirmative procedure. There is also a requirement to consult interested parties prior to making any new regulations.

IPC and IPPC — the similarities

There are a number of similarities between the old system of IPC and the new system under IPPC (notwithstanding the introduction of completely new legislation). These include:

(a)   Both systems take an integrated approach to the protection of all environmental media. The underlying objectives of the two systems are broadly similar, being to prevent and where that is not practicable to reduce environmental emissions and their impact on the environment as a whole.

(b)   IPPC permit conditions are to be worked out on a site-by-site basis taking into account the individual characteristics of the environmental impact and the costs and benefits of the adoption of particular techniques.

(c)   Although the IPPC Directive adopts a process standard known as BAT (best available techniques), when combined with the EC principle of 'proportionality' (i.e. costs and economic feasibility must be taken into account), it is very similar to the pre-existing process standard under IPC which is known as BATNEEC (best available techniques not entailing excessive cost).

(d)   Most of the processes controlled under IPC are also controlled under IPPC. This has meant that those processes which were already controlled will have to adapt to the new legislation.

(e)   There is provision for public access to information and the establishment of a Polluting Emissions Register which may be similar to the EA's Pollutant Inventory (see p. 234).

(f)   Many procedural aspects of the two systems are broadly similar including consultation and application procedures, fees and charging schemes, the range of offences and other enforcement options and the system of appeals.

(g)   The permits under IPPC are to be reviewed on an on-going basis to ensure that the BAT standard is adapted to changing circumstances. Under IPC this took place every four years at a minimum.

IPC and IPPC — the differences

Although the broad similarities in the two systems indicate that the changes brought about by the implementation of the IPPC Directive might not be significant, there are a number of substantial differences between the old and the new. These include:

(a)   The range of activities controlled under IPPC is larger than under IPC. It is estimated that in total some 7000 installations will fall within IPPC at the end of the transitional period. This compares with approximately 2000 under IPC. Moreover, IPPC is directed at activities connected to the whole 'installation' not at a particular process as happened with IPC. This means that there has been a move away from the focus on process components which dominated the IPC system (e.g. in relation to charging). However, the definition of installation contained in the Directive provides limitations which are not easily resolved. This will mean that not all site activities on an IPPC installation will be subject to its permitting requirements (see further below).

(b)   The change in the number of installations subject to IPPC is coupled with a change in the nature of the installations controlled. It has been estimated that of the 2000 pre-existing IPC processes about 1800 fall within IPPC. In addition, some 200 processes are within IPC but outside IPPC (e.g. one area where the Directive is of more limited effect than IPC is over the control of mobile plant). There are significant groups of new installations brought within integrated control for the first time including landfill sites, the food and drink industry and livestock units. Even in cases where the same industry groups are included, IPPC demonstrates some distinctive features such as using different threshold limits for certain groups and excluding research and development from the scope of control.

(c)   The identity of the regulator has changed. Under IPC the EA had sole responsibility for controlling emissions to all environmental media from processes which were prescribed for central control. Local authorities were given a residual role in respect of atmospheric emissions from less polluting processes under APC. In the IPPC system, the regulation continues to be divided between the EA and local authorities but the local authorities have been given greater responsibilities. The EA controls activities from installations which give rise to significant emissions to all environmental media (these are known as Part A(1) activities). Local authorities control activities which give rise to less significant emissions to all environmental media (these are known as Part A(2) activities). In addition local authorities control activities which are not listed within the IPPC Directive in respect of atmospheric emissions only (these are known as Part B activities).

(d)   Probably the most important distinctive feature of IPPC is the holistic nature of its regulation. Whilst IPC sought to regulate emissions to all three media, IPPC looks at a wider range of matters including the assessment and regulation of environmental impacts across a wide spectrum. The Directive refers to energy efficiency, raw material usage, noise, vibration, and heat outputs as well as polluting emissions.

(e)   IPPC sets out different arrangements for dealing with changes to existing installations. The Directive does not set out any time period within which installation permits should be reviewed by the competent authority. Under IPC, there was a statutory duty to review authorisation conditions at least every four years. Under IPPC there is no prescribed period, with the government preferring that different periods apply to different industry sectors. The exact nature of the review period will be found in the sector specific guidance notes.

(f)   In the IPC system there is an exemption for processes where the emissions from that process would be 'trivial' in terms of the environmental impact. Under the Directive there are objective threshold levels for exemptions and therefore no subjective criteria. This lack of exemptions under IPPC can arguably be justified on the basis that the wide nature of the environmental impacts covered would mean that very few, if any installations could be said to have a trivial environmental impact.

Transitional arrangements

As the system of IPPC is being phased in over an eight-year period, there are provisions dealing with the transition from IPC to IPPC. New installations (i.e. those commencing operations after the implementating regulations are brought into force and 'pipeline' installations which were planned before 31 October 1999) fall within the terms of the IPPC Directive and any implementing regulations. In addition, existing installations carrying out activities which undergo a 'substantial change' will also trigger the IPPC controls. Substantial change is defined in Art. 2(10) of the Directive as meaning a change in the operation which may have significant negative effects on human beings or the environment. The significance of this is that under the Directive (which appears to have been accepted by the Government) positive substantial changes would not have to undergo a full application (as they would be dealt with as variations to existing authorisations/permits).

Thus, for existing installations and installations which are coming within integrated control for the first time, there is a timetable for the transitional arrangements set out in sch. 3 to the regulations. Generally the proposed timetable for Part A(1) activities follows the order of production of the process guidance notes which are to be agreed at EC level (known as the BREF documents). In circumstances where installations are regulated under IPC and the conditions of the relevant IPC authorisation are to be reviewed within the IPPC implementation date, such a review will be delayed pending the implementation of the IPPC controls. Part A(2) activities will follow approximately one year after the respective Part A(1) activity. Part B processes will be phased in at some stage after 2000 (the precise details were uncertain at the time of writing). Crucially, Part A installations will be required to submit a fresh application for consent which will cover the new aspects of IPPC permitting. Part B installations will not need to do anything as their application will be treated as being deemed and granted (with any new conditions) automatically.

IPPC objectives

The key to the operation of the system of IPPC is the overriding statutory objectives which are designed to underpin the granting of permits. The general approach of the IPPC legislation is to prevent, reduce and if possible eliminate pollution and environmental impact as a whole. The definition of pollution is more extensive than it was under IPC (see s. 1(3), EPA 1990). Under IPPC it is defined as including emissions as a result of human activity which may be harmful to human health or the quality of the environment, cause offence to any human senses, result in damage to material property, or impair or interfere with amenities and other legitimate uses of the environment; and 'pollutant' means any substance, vibration, heat or noise released as a result of such emission which may have such an effect (reg. 2).

This widened definition reflects the move away from the IPC-based controls over emissions (with a traditional definition of pollution), to the IPPC approach which concentrates on environmental impacts from diffuse sources.

IPPC — the activities and installations controlled

As mentioned above, the scope of activities controlled under IPPC is broadly similar to that under IPC. The list of controlled activities is found in sch. 1 to the Regulations and is divided into six chapters of industrial activity including the energy industry; the chemicals industry; the production and processing of metals; the minerals industry; waste management; and a generic category referred to as 'other activities'. Each chapter is sub-divided into more specific definitions of particular groups of activities in that industrial sector. These groups are further subdivided into categories for the purposes of allocating to a regulatory agency, Part A(1) to the control of the Environment Agency, and Part A(2) and B activities to the relevant local authority.

The most significant changes in the types of activities controlled are as a result of the 'extra' activities which are regulated for the first time. These fall into several broad groups.

(a)   Waste management installations (including landfill sites) which were previously controlled under the waste management licensing system under Part II, EPA 1990. Their inclusion means that the IPPC system has had to incorporate aspects of the waste management licensing regime (e.g. the 'fit and proper person' test).

(b)   Those activities which were controlled under differing regimes (e.g. local authority air pollution control, discharge consents and/or trade effluent consents) which come within the classes of activities prescribed for IPPC under the directive (e.g. food and drink manufacturing).

(c)   Those activities which were not specifically controlled under any regime or alternatively were not comprehensively controlled (e.g. intensive agricultural units).

(a)   Meaning of 'installation'

The shift away from a system of control based upon process components to one based upon installations gives rise to a number of practical implementation problems. Although the Directive covers installations rather than processes this does not mean that all activities within an installation will be controlled under IPPC. 'Installation' is defined as any stationary technical unit (thus excluding mobile plant) where a prescribed activity is carried out and any other directly associated activities carried out on the same site which have a technical connection with the prescribed activities and which could have an effect on pollution (reg. 2). Thus, the crucial test appears to be whether or not the activity in question is directly associated with, or has a technical connection with, or could have an effect on emissions and pollution from the installation. The example given by the Government in a consultation paper suggested that in the case of a manufacturing unit, the fuel storage facilities and abatement equipment could form part of an installation whereas the production line itself would not. Given that the control under the directive includes such things as noise and raw material consumption, it is difficult to see how the production line would *not* have an environmental impact under the terms of the Directive.

In addition to general problems of interpretation, there are a number of areas of difficulty with interpreting the definitions in Annex 1 to the Directive, particularly in respect of thresholds which trigger the control over the activity. Some of these technical uncertainties are likely to be resolved by the production of the BAT reference documents which are to be produced under the 'information exchange' programme.

(b) Exemptions
Under IPC the legislation exempted certain processes from control, for example where the emissions from the process were deemed to be trivial in terms of their environmental impact. In practice these exemptions have not had a tremendous practical effect but the Directive makes it clear that all installations listed in Annex I must be subject to the requirement to seek a permit. Thus, there are no exemptions under the IPPC legislation. The Government has, however, indicated that installations which are deemed to have a trivial environmental impact should be subject to a streamlined permitting procedure using uniform simplified conditions. Guidance on the definition of 'trivial' will be published by the Environment Agency.

(c) Control over substances
IPPC controls the emissions of particular substances which are listed in sch. 5 to the Regulations. The lists are divided into two to cover substances which might be released into the atmosphere and others which might be released to water. Where the activity is likely to cause an emission of one of the listed substances in significant quantities, the permit must include conditions imposing emission limit values (or environmental quality standards for that substance if these are lower) for that substance.

Overlapping controls

Although the introduction of IPC and later IPPC has seen a simplification of the administration and control of many environmental impacts from industrial processes, there is still a degree of overlap between different systems of pollution control.

(a) Waste management
Although some aspects of waste management control came within IPC (e.g. where these were an integral part of the overall process), the final deposit of

waste on land was excluded (see s. 28(1), EPA 1990). One of the innovations of IPPC is the introduction of integrated controls over waste disposal sites. Some 900 existing landfill sites come under IPPC (under the transitional arrangements). The remainder of the sites (below the capacity thresholds, set under the Directive, of 710 tonnes of waste in any day or with a total capacity of 25,000 tonnes) will continue to be controlled under the waste management licensing regime under Part II of the EPA 1990. This arrangement should ensure that there is no overlap between the two systems.

IPPC requirements for landfill sites will be phased in for 2003 after the legislation implementing the Landfill Directive is in force (scheduled in 2001 (see p. 472)). The technical requirements of the Landfill Directive will effectively constitute the requirements for BAT for landfill sites with the IPPC legislation covering the procedure for applications, enforcement, appeals and the content of permits and public registers.

There are other aspects of waste management which will be covered under IPPC. Waste disposal (other than landfill sites) and recovery processes are covered in a separate category in the draft regulations. In certain cases where an A(2) installation (i.e. IPPC controlled by local authorities) operates a waste management facility which does not come within IPPC, this activity will form part of the whole installation and come within the IPPC permit. In cases where a Part B installation operates a non-IPPC waste management activity, there will be a division of responsibility between EA (waste regulator) and local authority (regulator of atmosphere emissions).

(b)   Water pollution

The key overlap in respect of water pollution can be found in the case of Part A(2) installations which are controlled by local authorities. Traditionally, discharge consents have been regulated by specialised public bodies (see further p. 574) and local authorities have not developed any expertise in dealing with water quality issues and the imposition of conditions. Dealing with this aspect of permits was considered to be a major challenge for local authorities. The Environment Agency, with the greatest expertise in this area, has been given an overriding supervisory role in the setting of conditions for discharges to water for all Part A(2) installations. In the case of a Part A(2) installation, the Environment Agency has the power to give notice to the relevant local authority specifying the minimum conditions controlling discharges to water. There is a discretion to impose more onerous conditions but there would have to be some specific justification based around site specific circumstances. Under s. 88 of the Water Resources Act 1991, discharges made in accordance with an IPPC permit are not an offence under s. 85 of that Act (i.e. causing or permitting the pollution of controlled waters).

(c)   Discharge of trade effluent into sewers

The discharge of trade effluent into sewers can be controlled under IPPC permits. Indirect discharges to water (i.e. via sewers/treatment plant) are taken into account when setting permit conditions. The effect of any pre-treatment prior to discharge into water will be taken into account when determining emissions limit values for particular pollutants provided that there would not be any increase in levels of pollution as a result of the treatment. There continues to be an overlap of controls, however, as all discharges to sewers require consent from the sewerage undertaker under s. 118, Water industry Act 1991. Such a consent may set limits on the volume, composition and temperature of the discharge in addition to setting out the charges for the consent.

(d)   Statutory nuisances and noise
As an IPPC permit is designed to address all environmental impacts from an installation, a permit should include controls over impacts which could give rise to statutory nuisances. Thus, in cases where there is an IPPC permit covering an installation, the relevant local authority has no right to serve an abatement notice in relation to anything which would otherwise be a statutory nuisance (including noise nuisance) where there are powers to take enforcement action for breach under IPPC legislation (i.e. the PPCA 1999 and the associated regulations). In circumstances where there is no power to take enforcement action under IPPC legislation (e.g. because the nuisance does not arise from the installation or regulated activities, such as in the case of burglar alarms), the power to take action against the nuisance is still available. In addition, the right of a private individual to bring a complaint under s. 82, EPA 1990 is still unaffected by IPPC legislation (although compliance with permit conditions may create a presumption that such a nuisance does not exist).

(e)   Contaminated land
In theory, there is no overlap between the IPPC legislation and the controls over the clean up of historically contaminated land under Part IIA of the EPA 1990. Where contamination arises as a result of activities permitted under IPPC legislation, the power to clean up arises after site closure. On the other hand, contamination which is in existence prior to the application for an IPPC permit should be dealt with under controls to be found in concurrent legislation (e.g. s. 27, EPA 1990 for contamination arising out of breaches of IPC authorisations) or under the provisions dealing with historic contamination under Part IIA. In practice, however, the information on site contamination which is a necessary part of the application for an IPPC permit will give local authorities and the Environment Agency (as regulators under Part IIA) the opportunity of identifying those sites which might be historically contaminated and therefore be potentially designated sites under the contaminated land regime. The dilemma for operators is that they will have to balance a desire to portray the site in its 'warts and all' state prior to commencement of IPPC activities in order to establish a 'dirty' comparator when it comes to site closure, against the inevitable investigations and enforcement under other legislation (including Part IIA) where the site condition report discloses heavy contamination. One important technical distinction between the use of clean up powers under Part IIA and the post-closure IPPC requirements is that the standard of clean up under IPPC

legislation is much higher than under the contaminated land regime. Under IPPC, the land must be cleaned up to a standard based upon the site conditions before the permitted activity was commenced (i.e. before the date of issue of the permit). Under Part IIA the clean up must be to a 'suitable for use' standard (see p. 527).

(f)   Town and country planning and environment assessment

Unlike some of the other pollution control regimes, there is no legislative reference to any connection between the planning system and IPPC. There is no obligation to obtain a planning permission for any development associated with a new or altered installation prior to obtaining a permit under the IPPC legislation (the reverse is also true). However, as a wide range of environmental impacts are material considerations in applications for permits, there is a practical link between environmental assessment under the planning regime and under IPPC legislation. Many of the installations which require a permit to operate will also be subject to the need for environmental assessment under the relevant legislation (see p. 352). In these cases, much of the information included within an environmental statement would form the basis of the information submitted with an IPPC application. The IPPC Directive and the EIA Directive allow for information produced for the purposes of one directive to be recycled for the purposes of the other. In practice therefore it would be appropriate to submit an environmental statement with both applications (although the IPPC application would need to concentrate on additional technical matters such as emission limit values and BAT).

Another important practical overlap is in the decision-making process. When dealing with a planning application, local authorities are advised to consider only the land-use implications of the development. This leads to inevitable questions about the nature of 'land-use' implications. The courts have examined the nature of the overlap between planning and pollution control in relation to the IPC system (which for the purposes of the discussion is the same as the IPPC system) in *Gateshead Metropolitan Borough Council* v *Secretary of State for the Environment* [1995] Env LR 37. In that case the Secretary of State granted planning permission for a clinical waste incinerator in the North-east. The inspector appointed to hear the appeal recommended that permission be refused. One of the issues which was taken into account by the inspector was the public fear that pollution from the site would be unacceptable. The Secretary of State concluded that the issue could be satisfactorily addressed as part of the IPC application and granted planning permission. That decision was challenged by the local planning authority on the basis that the two systems were so closely inter-linked that it was unreasonable to grant planning permission without knowing if emissions could be adequately controlled under the IPC system. In the High Court, Sullivan J decided that although the two statutory regimes overlapped, the extent of the overlap would vary on each occasion. It was envisaged that there would be a range of cases, from those where environmental considerations could be dealt with adequately under the IPC system to those where environmental considerations could not incorporated satisfactorily into an IPC authorisation. The correct legal test was whether or not it was reasonable in the *Wednesbury* sense to arrive at the decision reached by the decision-maker.

On appeal, the Court of Appeal affirmed this decision with only a slight variation of judgment. The issue of whether there was an unacceptable risk was, in the Court's view, a matter for the pollution control authority and the fact that the public had expressed concern about the issue was not conclusive. The Court went on to say, however, that the fact that planning permission had been granted should not have been viewed as a restriction on the pollution control authority's discretion to refuse the IPC application if it thought it fit to do so. Thus, it would appear as if the courts have affirmed the view that there is no definite dividing line between planning and pollution control and that each decision-maker is entitled to arrive at different conclusions if it exercises its discretion reasonably. Although this decision would apply to the overlap between IPPC and the planning system, the dividing line will be much more blurred as the consideration of environmental impacts in each system will be largely similar. Therefore it would be unusual (but seemingly not unlawful) if one regulatory body arrived at a different conclusion from another even with the same information supporting the application (or in the case of the Part A(2) installations, the same regulatory body arriving at two different conclusions).

(g) IPC and IPPC
Perhaps the most significant practical overlap between IPPC and other statutory controls will be during the transitional phase when the old IPC processes continue to be controlled under Part I of the EPA 1990. In a theoretical sense, at least, there is no overlap between the two systems. When the application for IPPC permit is ultimately determined (on appeal if necessary), the IPC authorisation for existing processes will cease to apply (see sch. 3 PPCA 1999). There are, however, many practical overlaps between the two systems. For example, there is unlikely to be a significant shift in the process standards which are used during the initial transitional period. Where guidance on standards (which will be found in BAT reference — BREFs documents) are unavailable at the time when a sector is scheduled to come within IPPC (and given the difficult problems of agreeing a European process standard it is not particularly controversial to predict that not all of the BREF documents should be expected to arrive on time), the existing IPC process guidance notes will be adapted for use to guide decisions on granting IPPC permits. In addition there will be a degree in continuity in the approach to decision-making and enforcement under IPPC. One of the advantages of having implemented an integrated system of pollution control is that many of the teething problems which are associated with introducing an integrated permitting system (e.g. setting conditions, assessing environmental impacts, upgrading existing processes to new standards, cost benefit analysis) have been addressed under the system of IPC. The IPC system will continue to operate during the transitional period and an outline of the provisions is included at the end of this chapter.

IPPC — the permitting system

The controls under IPPC are based around a permitting system (as opposed to an authorisation under IPC). There is nothing significant in the change of name other than the addition of another confusing term to add to licences, permissions, consents etc.

An application for an IPPC permit is generally to be determined on a site-by-site basis rather than by reference to prescriptive principles or rules; the exception is where generally binding rules are adopted (see below). The application procedure is set out in the Regulations (see regs 7, 10 and sch. 4). An application must contain a wide variety of information including: information on the condition of the site (and any associated pollution risks) on which the installation is situated (which is used as a baseline study for comparative purposes when the installation is closed); the raw materials and energy used in the carrying out of the activity; waste minimisation and prevention measures; the foreseeable emissions and environmental effects of the activity; information on the technology and other techniques used for reducing emissions and other environmental impacts; and arrangements for monitoring impacts. In addition, the application must be accompanied by a non-technical summary (in an echo of the requirements under the EIA legislation). Each application must be accompanied by the payment of the appropriate fee.

(a) Public participation and other consultation procedures

There are extensive provisions for public participation in the application procedure alongside other appointed statutory consultees (see sch. 4 to the Regulations). There is an obligation on every applicant to advertise all applications for authorisation and all variations involving a substantial change. The advertisement must be placed in a local newspaper circulating in the area in which the activity is to be carried out and in the case of Part A activities it must be advertised in the *London Gazette*. The advertisement must contain details of the name and address of the applicant and the installation where the activity is to be carried out; a brief description of the activities; reference to the availability of information about the application on public registers; and an invitation to make representations within 28 days of the date of the advertisement.

Other statutory consultees are given the right to make representations. The list of consultees reflects the varied nature of the impacts caused by an activity in terms not only of the environment but also the workplace. The bodies entitled to be consulted include: the Health and Safety Executive; the health authority in whose area the installation will be situated; the relevant Nature Conservancy Council where a potential emission might affect an SSSI; and the water services company or any other sewerage undertaker, in relation to release to a sewer. In addition there is to be close liaison between local authorities and the EA on all Part A applications (see further below). Where an operation at an installation involves a waste management activity the relevant planning authority must be consulted. There is also provision for trans-boundary consultation. Where the Secretary of State is 'aware' that an activity is likely to have significant negative effects on another member state, he is under a duty to notify that other member state of the application so that 'consultation' may take place within a framework of bilateral relations.

All of these consultees are entitled to notification within 14 days of receipt of an application for a permit or variation. They are then given 28 days in which to make representations (although in practice this period can be extended). These representations are to be taken into account as a material consideration in addition to any further information which has been obtained under any environmental assessment which has been carried out (e.g. where planning permission was required for the commencement of the activity).

In normal circumstances, the time period for determining an application for a permit is four months from the date of receipt or any longer period which has been agreed between the applicant and the regulatory body. The exceptions to this rule are where the application has been 'called in' by the Secretary of State and where the application has been notified to another member state and bilateral consultation is taking place.

(b)   Call-in procedure

As with an application for planning permission, the Secretary of State has the ability to 'call in' an application for a permit, thus ousting the jurisdiction of the regulatory agency (sch. 4, para. 14). This power can be exercised at the discretion of the Secretary of State. Given the breadth of this discretion, it will probably only be exercised for particularly sensitive applications, applications of local or national importance, or applications which arouse a great deal of public interest.

When an application is called in, the Secretary of State has no power to grant the authorisation, but instead must direct the enforcing authority as to whether to grant the application and, if so, as to the conditions which are to be attached. The manner by which the Secretary of State decides such an issue may be by public local inquiry or by means of informal hearings.

(c)   Commercial confidentiality and national security

In normal circumstances, the public is allowed free access to information regarding an application for a permit and associated matters. There are, however, exceptions to this on the ground of commercial confidentiality and in relation to issues affecting national security (see regs 30–31 of the Regulations). Where an applicant believes that any information contained within an application should be restricted, then an application may be made to exclude such information from the public registers. This application is included along with the information relating to the permit, and the regulatory agency has to determine whether or not such information is commercially confidential.

In the case of information affecting national security, the only criterion is that the Secretary of State has to be of the opinion that the inclusion in the register of that information would be contrary to the interests of national security. On commercial confidentiality grounds the regulatory agency has 14 days in which to determine whether the information is not commercially confidential, if it is undetermined within that period it is deemed to be treated as such. Where the enforcing authority determines that the information is not commercially confidential, it must not enter such information on the register for 21 days so as to allow an applicant time to appeal against the decision to the Secretary of State. Pending any appeal the information is also excluded from the register.

(d)   The determination of the application

When considering how to determine an application for an IPPC period the authority can take one of two approaches. As with IPC, applications can be determined on a case-by-case basis with consideration of individual circumstances. Under the IPPC Directive, however, there is the possibility of determining applications in accordance with general binding rules. The government has suggested that some permits may have all of their conditions set by general binding rules (GBRs) rather than being individually tailored. Although this option will not be used widely, it has been suggested in various consultation documents that some of the simpler installations such as some of the agricultural sector. The idea behind GBRs is that they could be used to set all or just some permit conditions. Rather strangely the government has suggested that there would be the possibility of opting out from the applications of GBRs, creating general binding rules which are not always generally binding! The Directive itself allows for the passing of daughter directives setting emissions limits for particular installations — these may have a similar effect to GBRs.

Once the regulatory agency has received all representations, it is entitled to grant the permit subject to any necessary conditions, or to refuse it. There is a duty to refuse the permit where the enforcement agency considers that the applicant will not operate the installation concerned so as to comply with the conditions which would be included in the permit (see reg. 10(3)). Although there was a corresponding provision under Part I of the EPA 1990 (see s. 6(4), EPA 1990), there has been a move away from the old definition, which concentrated on the operator's ability to comply with conditions, towards a simpler, wider test. It is likely that the new definition will incorporate elements of fitness to carry out the activity which could include consideration of past compliance (see further in relation to s. 6(4), *R* v *Secretary of State for the Environment, ex parte West Wiltshire District Council* [1996] Env LR 312). In the case of waste management activities which come under IPPC applications will be refused where the applicant is not a fit and proper person to carry out the activity (see reg. 4 and p. 498) or where there is no planning permission in force and such a permission is required. In addition, where the regulatory agency requests further information from the applicant and no information is supplied within the specified time period, the agency is entitled to notify the applicant that the application is deemed to have been withdrawn.

In considering whether or not to grant a permit, there a number of general principles which must be taken into account. In the case of all activities (Parts A and B), installations should be operated in such a way that all appropriate preventive measures are taken against pollution, in particular through the application of best available techniques (BAT) and that no significant pollution is caused. In relation to Part A activities (which cover the activities prescribed under the directive) there is an additional requirement to operate an installation so as to avoid the production of waste; to recover any waste which is produced; where recovery is impossible to dispose of waste to avoid or reduce environmental impacts; to use energy efficiently; and to prevent accidents (see regs 11–13).

These general principles have to be taken into account in determining every application for a permit and in setting permit conditions. In addition, the regulations set out various methods of setting emission limit values for individual pollutants or groups of pollutants. These should be applied at the point where the emission leaves the installation and be based upon the BAT process standard taking into account the technical requirements of the installation, its geographical location and the local environmental conditions, thus clarifying the point that the BAT standard is not necessarily prescriptive but will be determined on a case-by-case basis. However, the BAT standard can be overridden where a specific environmental quality standard would require stricter emission limits than would be applied under the BAT standard. Other specific conditions which should be imposed cover such areas as: minimising long distance and transboundary pollution; protection of soil and groundwater; waste management; abnormal operating conditions; monitoring of compliance with conditions; and pre-commencement and post closure procedures.

BAT and BATNEEC

All of the activities which are controlled under the IPPC Directive (Part A activities) are subject to the requirement of BAT. BAT is to be applied on a case-by-case basis (unless generally binding rules apply to any group of Part A activities). The concept of BAT is somewhat different from the concept of BATNEEC which was used in determining IPC applications. The distinctions, which may at first glance seem insignificant, could take on a greater importance in practice. Under IPC, BATNEEC included not only the technical means and the technology of pollution abatement, but also the number, qualifications, training and supervision of persons employed in the process, in addition to the design, construction, lay-out and maintenance of the buildings in which the process was carried on. BAT under IPPC includes both the technology used and the way in which the installation is designed, built, maintained and decommissioned. The Regulations list matters which should be taken into account which will be supplemented by the production of BREF notes (see regs 12–14).

(a) 'Best available techniques'
The phrase 'best available techniques' is further broken down in the regulations. 'Best' is defined in relation to the effectiveness of the techniques in achieving a high level of protection of the environment as a whole (under BATNEEC it was related to the effectiveness of the techniques in minimising, preventing or rendering harmless noxious emissions). 'Best' is not an absolute term and there may be a number of different techniques which would fall

within this definition. 'Available' techniques are those which have been developed on a scale which allows implementation by the relevant industrial sector under economically and technically viable conditions, taking into consideration the costs and advantages, whether or not the techniques are used or produced inside the UK as long as they are accessible to the operator (this can be contrasted with the definition under BATNEEC which referred to techniques being able to be procured by the operator even if not in general use). This should exclude experimental techniques or techniques which have only been tested under conditions which are peculiar to other countries. 'Techniques' includes both the technology used and the way in which the installation is designed, built, maintained and decommissioned.

The statutory terms are vague which allows the regulatory agencies some discretion in determining applications on a case-by-case basis. There is, however, some supplementary guidance to be found in process guidance notes and the BREF documents. The IPPC Directive (art. 16(2)) requires the European Commission to establish an exchange of information between Member States and the industries which are controlled under IPPC in order to establish best available techniques, associated monitoring and developments in these areas. There is now an IPPC Information Exchange Forum (IPPCIEF) on which all Member States are represented. Trade associations and NGOs also attend the meetings. The Commission must publish the results of the information exchange every three years.

The main purpose of the IPPCIEF will be to comment on draft BAT reference documents which will influence the way in which Member States implement the practical aspects of the directive. The reference documents will describe levels of environmental performance (emission levels, raw materials and energy consumption) which can be achieved through the use of BAT. These BAT reference documents (BREFs) will have to be taken into account when determining BAT either for a sector or for an installation. However, individual circumstances will be taken into account and the BAT reference document will not set down uniform emission limits. Where the BAT reference document is widely accepted across all of the Member States, it may form the basis for sectoral daughter directives to the main IPPC Directive.

(b) BAT and costs

In general the cost of employing BAT under IPPC is still a relevant consideration as the costs and benefits of all BAT standards are to be assessed under the proportionality principle under EC law. Under IPC and LAAPC the costs of implementing BAT were balanced with the benefits. More specifically the BATNEEC test was applied taking into account two broad criteria: the economic and environmental costs and benefits of particular techniques of pollution control; and the affordability of such techniques in the sector of industry concerned. Although there have been no concrete decisions on the application of costs benefit analysis to the BAT test, the Government has expressed a desire to review the second of these two criteria (i.e. sectoral affordability). The main argument against the use of this criterion is that its presence may result in the subsidising of inefficient industrial sectors in the sense that certain sectors should not be permitted to avoid making environmental improvements merely because the industry sector as a whole is not sufficiently profitable. In the Government's view sectoral affordability may be retained under IPPC but it is suggesting its removal so that decisions are based purely on an assessment of costs and benefits. It is far from clear that the sector affordability criterion has had any major impact in practice.

IPPC and wider environmental impacts

Under IPC wider environmental impacts were considered in the context of operators having to demonstrate that the BATNEEC represented the best practicable environmental option (BPEO) in minimising the release of substances to the environment. Although IPPC does not have any corresponding requirement to undertake an assessment of the BPEO for an activity, an operator has to consider all of the environmental impacts of an activity. This represents perhaps the biggest change from the pre-existing controls. In determining the BAT for a particular activity these impacts must be considered but balanced against the likely costs and benefits of using BAT and the precautionary and preventive principles. Special consideration must be given to a list of matters found in the regulations. These considerations are not exclusive but include: the use of waste minimisation technology; the use of less hazardous substances; comparable processes which have been tried with success on an industrial scale; changes in the understanding of environmental risks and abatement technology; and the nature, effects and volume of the emissions from the activity. The more significant changes include the following:

(a)   There is a requirement in the Directive that after an installation has closed it should then be returned to a satisfactory state and pollution risks arising as a result of the permitted activities should be avoided. Every Part A application must include an installation site condition report which should set out the pre-commencement site conditions. If the report includes information on pre-existing contamination this could form the trigger for remedial action under other statutory controls over clean up of contaminated land (e.g. Part IIA, EPA 1990; s. 161A, Water Resources Act 1991). In addition the report will establish a base line survey of site conditions which can be used for the purposes of comparison after the installation has closed in order to identify the pollution risks from contamination caused by the permitted activities.

(b)   The regulation of raw material usage and energy efficiency is a novelty. The government has suggested that operators will be required to take up all energy efficiency measures which are cost effective on normal commercial criteria. For existing installations, it is expected that energy efficiency measures will only become a major issue when existing plant and equipment is replaced at the end of its operating life. The regulation of energy efficiency is likely to be implemented across a range of regulatory techniques. These might include incentives such as an installation being allowed to make greater emissions if it was energy efficient to use energy from combustion on site. The Government foresees the use of negotiated agreements between the regulator and installation on efficiency as a way forward. The first such agreement was concluded between the Chemical Industries Association and the government late last year (see further p. 211).

(c)   The regulation of noise and vibration raises problems over expertise in the regulator. In relation to Part A(1) processes, it is certainly true that HMIP and more recently the Environment Agency have focused their expertise on emissions control rather than wider environmental impacts such as noise pollution. Local authorities criticised what they saw as a transfer of controls over noise from A(1) activities to the Environment Agency. There are proposed three safeguards: First, in setting noise conditions in an IPPC permit, the Agency must have regard to the recommendations of the local authority unless it 'has good reason not to'. Secondly, the removal of the right to serve an abatement notice under the statutory nuisance provisions of Part III of the EPA 1990 only applies to elements of the installation which are covered by the permit. Sources of unregulated noise (e.g. barking dogs or burglar alarms) which do not form part of the installation can still be controlled under the statutory nuisance provisions. Thirdly, the right of a private individual to take action against a statutory nuisance under s. 82, EPA 1990 would continue (see further on overlapping controls above).

(d)   The Directive requires IPPC to address accident prevention. In the UK in many cases the same information may be used in IPPC as will be required for the installation under the Directive on the Control of Major Accident Hazards (96/82/EC).

(e)   As the range of relevant impacts which must be considered in any application for permit is wide, an important part of the application for a permit will be an EIA. As mentioned above, IPC required a more limited form of impact assessment to fulfil the statutory requirements of best practicable environmental option (under s. 7, EPA 1990). Clearly given the scope of regulation under IPPC this will need to be a much broader assessment. The government has suggested that a full EIA will not be needed for all IPPC applications — this will depend presumably on site complexity. However where planning consent is needed for an installation and an EIA is needed as part of the application for planning permission, it is envisaged that it would be worthwhile running the two consenting procedures together. It seems sensible and would overcome the current problems raised by having separate consent systems which may come to different or incompatible conclusions.

Statutory guidance notes

In addition to the limited definition of the considerations contained within the regulations, a regulatory body, when determining an application for permit must have regard to any other guidance note applicable to the class of activities. The guidance notes are supposed to provide a coherent context in which decisions can be made in relation to permit conditions. The government's proposals for statutory IPPC guidance notes will replace the IPC process guidance notes. The statutory guidance notes will be based upon the European BAT Reference documents which will be produced during the transitional period. This gap in the production of guidance will mean that there will be certain new and substantially changed installations which will need an IPPC permit before the relevant sectoral guidance becomes available. During this interim period, the government proposes to rely upon existing IPC and LAAPC process guidance notes which will be supplemented by generic guidance prepared by the Environment Agency covering the wider environmental impacts such as energy efficiency, site remediation and noise. In addition interim guidance notes will be produced for those activities which are coming under integrated control for the first time (e.g. food and drink and intensive agricultural units).

IPPC notes will be non-prescriptive, providing indicative standards for both new and existing installations with clear timetables for upgrading in the case of existing plant. These guidance notes will be much more specific than under the IPC guidance. Arguably this will limit the discretion of inspectors who have been criticised at times for inconsistency in approach when granting authorisations under IPC. Each application will, however, fall to be considered individually, and the government has also accepted that variations from the guidance note standard may be acceptable in certain circumstances. It has been suggested that where the indicative standards and timetables found in the guidance notes are not followed, the regulator should be required to provide a public justification for this. Furthermore, the regulator should provide general data on the extent to which the indicative guidance notes have been applied. It is not clear how these indicative standards will interact with the EC-wide BAT reference documents.

Transfer of permits

A permit is personal to an applicant/operator. It is, however, possible to transfer a permit from one operator to another (see reg. 18). Therefore if a business has been sold, it is possible to transfer an existing permit to the new owner/operator. The Regulations provide that the operator and the proposed transferee have to make a joint application to the regulator to effect the transfer of the permit. There are provisions for partial transfer in cases where part of the installation will remain within the control of the original operator. The only grounds for refusal to transfer are that the regulator considers that the proposed transferee would not comply with the conditions of the transferred permit or, in the case of waste management installations, that the proposed transferee would not be a 'fit and proper person'. There is a two-month time limit for determination of a transfer. If no determination has been made or no extension of the time period agreed between the parties, the permit is deemed to have been transferred. Otherwise, the transfer is effected on a date which is agreed between the parties.

Surrender of permits

As IPPC regulates the cleanup of pollution which has been caused by permitted activities, there is a need to regulate the cessation of activities by the operator so that an assessment of the condition of the site can be made and remedial works undertaken. Indeed, the risks associated with surrender and other decommissioning of the installation must be taken into account when determining whether the installation meets the requirement of BAT at the design stage. An operator has to submit an application to surrender a Part A permit (see reg. 19). An application to surrender can be made for all of the activities covered under the permit or just parts of the operation of the installation (known as a partial surrender). The application must be accompanied by certain information including the name and address of the operator; a plan identifying the part of the site which is the subject of the surrender; a site report describing the condition of the site which identifies any changes in condition of the site; and a description of the steps taken to avoid any pollution risk or to return the site to a satisfactory state.

It is presumed that the operator is responsible for any material difference between the condition of the site as contained in the original base line report which was submitted with the application and the conditions contained in any report submitted with an application for surrender. This presumption would appear to be irrefutable as the regulator must be satisfied that there is no pollution risk and that no further steps need to be taken to return the site to a satisfactory state, irrespective of the cause of that pollution risk, before accepting the surrender of the permit. Naturally this emphasises the importance of ensuring that the original site report submitted with the application must be as comprehensive as possible, so that pre-commencement liabilities which are attributable to other causes/parties do not appear in the pre-surrender report, as they will not be distinguishable from the contamination caused by the operation of the installation.

The regulator must issue a notice of determination on the application for surrender within three months (or longer if agreed between the parties and where the regulator has requested further information from the applicant which has not been supplied). If no determination is made within that period the application is deemed to have been refused if the operator notifies the regulator of this in writing.

Enforcement powers

There are a wide range of enforcement options to deal with operational breaches of permits. Generally, these follow the pattern of IPC enforcement powers with additional powers imported from the waste management licensing regime under Part II of the EPA 1990 and including the power to serve enforcement notices, to suspend permitted activities, to revoke a permit and to vary the conditions of a permit (see generally regs 23–25). This flexibility will ensure that the regulator has enforcement discretion when dealing with regulatory breaches. Under IPC this was evidenced by the fact that, although prosecution levels were low with approximately 14 cases being brought a year, there was widespread use of enforcement notices and other administrative sanctions. It is likely that this pattern will continue as IPPC is implemented.

The regulators have an overriding duty to supervise the operation of permitted installations (reg. 23). The regulator must take any steps needed for the purpose of ensuring that the conditions of the permit are complied with. The mandatory nature of this duty means that where breaches of permit are occurring or likely to occur, the regulator cannot ignore it. It does *not* mean that the regulator is required to take formal enforcement action against that breach. The duty simply means that necessary steps must be taken to ensure compliance with conditions.

(a)   Variation notices

The ability to vary a permit is not strictly an enforcement power when compared with, for example, enforcement, suspension or revocation notices as there is no explicit sanction for non-compliance (other than general powers for breach of condition). The effect of a variation may, however, be such that an operator would view it as having no practical distinction from an enforcement notice. The distinctive character of a variation notice relates more to a proactive approach of minimising environmental impacts than punishing for breaches of existing conditions.

The regulator is under a duty to review periodically the conditions of permits but is also given a discretion to review at any time (reg. 17). Under IPC, there was a maximum of four years between every review. This period may be altered and will vary for different sectors. The precise period for review will, to some extent, be driven by the triennial information exchange report and the BAT reference documents.

Under IPPC, operators must notify the regulator of all changes to the installation which might have environmental consequences. The regulator must then update the permit as appropriate. In addition, the regulator can vary a permit where different conditions are required from those which are already in the permit either as a result of the periodic review, on application from the operator or where the Environment Agency specifies new conditions in relation to emission limit values for discharges to water under the arrangements for Part A(2) activities (see below). In addition conditions can be varied at any time to incorporate changes in BAT for that particular activity.

An application for variation must be in writing and include the name, address, and telephone number of the operator and the address of the installation. The application must also include a description of the proposed change to the activity with corresponding effects on environmental impacts and any additional information which the operator wishes the regulator to take into account. There is provision for the regulator to request further information from the operator.

(b)   Revocation notices

The regulator has the power to revoke a permit either in part or in whole at any time by serving a revocation notice on the operator (reg. 21). The power to revoke a permit is general in nature and is not restricted. The only legislative guidance on the exercise of the power is that it may be used where it appears to the regulator that the operator is no longer a 'fit and proper person' to carry out a waste management activity.

Although the power to serve a revocation notice would appear to be Draconian, it is subject to the right of appeal and subsequently from challenge by way of judicial review. (The need to resolve any dispute by way of administrative review prior to any judicial review can be seen in *R* v *Environment Agency, ex parte Petrus Oils* [1999] Env LR 732.) Any appeal against a revocation notice suspends the operation of the notice. A revocation notice can be withdrawn at any time before it takes effect.

Under IPC the revocation procedure was used in circumstances where an operator had consistently failed to comply with a programme of improvement for an existing process notwithstanding a number of time extensions, and to prevent an operator from reopening in circumstances where the original closure was a result of failure to achieve upgrading standards.

(c) Enforcement notices

Where the regulator is of the opinion that the operator of an installation has contravened, is contravening, or is likely to contravene any condition of the permit, the regulator has a discretionary power to serve an enforcement notice (reg. 24). The discretionary nature of the power reflects the fact that there are other enforcement options available to the regulator. An enforcement notice must contain the following details: the matters which constitute the contravention; the steps required to remedy the situation; and the period within which those steps must be taken.

(d) Suspension notices

If the regulator is of the opinion that the operation of an installation involves an imminent risk of serious pollution, the regulator is under a duty to serve a suspension notice (reg. 25). The only exception to this mandatory duty is where the regulator intends to take action itself in relation to the risk. This duty to serve a suspension notice is independent of any breach of a permit. In this context, the suspension notice is a descendant of the prohibition notice under IPC. When clarifying the distinction between prohibition notices and enforcement notices, Lord Reay suggested that prohibition notices were more appropriate where events which were external to the process brought about a situation where serious pollution could result from a reaction with a prescribed process which was lawfully being carried out. Although this explanation does not strictly apply to the interpretation of the provisions on suspension notices, it is likely that these powers will be used in similar circumstances. The effect of a suspension notice is dramatic. Any permit ceases to have effect either partially or totally (as stated in the notice).

Offences and remedies

The regulations provide a long list of offences in relation to the IPPC system (reg. 32). It is a criminal offence to:

(a)   operate an installation prescribed for control without a permit;
(b)   contravene the conditions of permit;
(c)   fail to give notice of transfer of permit;
(d)   fail to comply with an enforcement or prohibition notice; or
(e)   intentionally make a false entry in any record required to be kept as a
condition of permit.

All offences are triable either way, with the more serious offences having a
maximum fine level in the magistrates' court of £20,000. In the Crown Court
all offences are subject to a maximum term of imprisonment of two years
and/or an unlimited fine (reg. 32(2).

In any trial the onus of proof falls upon the operator to show that there was
no better available technique which could be employed for that particular
installation.

It is open to any court in sentencing an offender for failure to comply with
an enforcement or suspension notice to order that the effects of the offence
be remedied. This allows for cleanup and compensation costs to come
directly out of the offender's pocket. In many instances, these costs will far
outstrip any reasonable fine that could be imposed. Perhaps even more
importantly, where an installation has been operated without any permit or
has not been in compliance with a condition of a permit, the regulatory
agency can arrange for reasonable steps to be taken towards remedying any
harm caused as a consequence and recover the costs of taking such steps from
any person committing the offence. Before doing so, however, the regulatory
agency must obtain the Secretary of State's approval in writing. Thus, even
where a court is not willing to impose the high financial burden of cleanup
costs on an offender, it will be open to the agency to remedy such harm.
There are further remedies available to the regulatory agency in the High
Court. Where there has been a failure to comply with an enforcement or a
suspension notice. This allows the regulatory agency to seek injunctions
where the enforcement of the criminal law is not securing adequate compliance. It must, however, exhaust other remedies before seeking an injunction
(see *Tameside MBC* v *Smith Bros (Hyde) Ltd* [1996] Env LR 312).

Appeals

The regulations provide a right of appeal against:

(a)   revocation, variation, enforcement and suspension notices;
(b)   the refusal to grant or vary a permit;
(c)   the imposition of unreasonable conditions upon a permit.

Furthermore, there is a right of appeal where the regulatory agency has
notified an operator that information contained within a permit, or application for permit, is not commercially confidential (reg. 27).

Generally, the time limit for appeals is similar to that in the planning
system, being six months from the date of refusal, or deemed refusal to grant

a permit. Where there is an appeal against an enforcement, suspension or variation notice, the time limit is two months from the date of the notice. Where the regulatory agency is seeking to revoke a permit, the appeal must be made before the date on which the notice takes effect. Finally, where there is an appeal concerning commercial confidentiality, it must be submitted within 21 days from the date of refusal.

A revocation notice will not take effect pending the hearing of an appeal. In all other cases (i.e. enforcement, suspension or variation) there is no suspension of the notice pending an appeal. Thus an operator cannot gain an economic advantage where there is a rush order by appealing against a notice so as to stop the enforcement process, continuing to pollute until the order is completed, and then stopping the process before the appeal is heard. An appeal must be made in writing to the Secretary of State. The appeal has to be accompanied by any relevant information including any application, permit, correspondence or decision and a statement as to how the appellant wishes the appeal to be determined.

An appeal can be heard in one of two ways: either by written representations or by a hearing. If either party to the appeal requests that it be heard by hearing, the Secretary of State must hold a hearing although there is a discretion as to whether the hearing is held in public. The Secretary of State also has a power to direct that a hearing be held.

The relevance of IPC

The provisions of Part I of the EPA 1990 dealing with IPC will gradually become less important as the PCCA 1999 and associated regulations are brought into force. There are some aspects of the old system which were repealed immediately on the bringing into force of the IPPC legislation (e.g. the application procedure for new IPC processes), although it is anticipated that there will be many practical procedural similarities between the two systems. Moreover, there will be a continuation of many IPC provisions which will apply to those existing processes which are being brought within IPPC during the transitional period. Thus there will be a continuing need to understand the operation of the IPC process for existing processes whilst the IPPC provisions will apply to new installations (or existing ones which undergo a substantial change). As the relevance of IPC will remain but diminish during the transitional period for IPPC, the substantive details of IPC will be kept to an outline only.

Integrated pollution control

The primary legislation dealing with IPC can be found in Part I of the EPA 1990, although the details of the system follow the characteristic of other British pollution control systems in that the primary legislation provides a mere framework which is fleshed out in secondary regulations and tertiary rules (including guidance notes and other informal documents). This complex structure of rules provides sufficient flexibility to amend both regulations and guidance quickly to incorporate new industrial processes, preventive technologies and environmental quality standards. Indeed, the legislation has been amended on a number of occasions since the implementation of the EPA 1990.

Thus, the EPA 1990 is supplemented by the Environmental Protection (Prescribed Processes and Substances) Regulations 1991 (SI 1991/472 as amended), the Environmental Protection (Applications, Appeals and Registers) Regulations 1991 (SI 1991/507) and the Environmental Protection (Authorisation of Processes) (Determination Periods) Order 1991 (SI 1991/513). Furthermore, there is a series of formal process guidance notes and other informal guidance which is issued by the Environment Agency.

(a)   Organisation and administration of IPC
IPC is administered centrally by the EA (SEPA in Scotland). The Secretary of State for the Environment, Transport and the Regions also has a central role in the IPC system which includes: prescribing the industrial processes and the polluting substances which are subject to control; setting standards for such things as emission limits, environmental quality objectives for individual media and monitoring and measurement requirements; having powers to make plans to establish overall emission limits for particular substances for the UK as a whole (e.g. the UK Programme and National Plan for Reducing Emissions of SO_2 and NO_x which sets annual targets for the stated emissions from power stations, refineries and other heavy industries); the power to issue directions to the regulatory agencies which could cover such things as the exercise of enforcement powers, the inclusion of specific conditions within authorisations, the transfer of responsibility for individual processes between different agencies and the removal of information from the public register; the power to determine appeals either personally or by an appointed inspector.

(b)   The requirement for authorisation
The IPC system applies to any process carried out in Britain which has been prescribed as being subject to such control by the Secretary of State. However, prescribed processes which are new or substantially changed (see above) after 31 October 1999 will fall within the IPPC system. The list of processes which fall within IPC can be found in the Environmental Protection (Prescribed Processes and Substances) Regulations 1991 (SI 1991/472 as amended). The descriptions of processes are divided into Part A processes which comprise the more polluting processes and come within IPC, and Part B processes which are controlled by local authorities under Air Pollution Control (APC). There are approximately 2,000 processes which are subject to control under IPC with a further 12,500 processes falling within APC.

Operating a prescribed process without an authorisation is a criminal offence (s. 6, EPA 1990). Unlike the Town and Country Planning Act 1990 (which provides a procedure for assessing whether or not a particular activity or building falls within the definition of development), however, there is no formal mechanism for determining whether or not a process falls within one of the detailed descriptions in the regulations. Some of these difficulties of interpretation are dealt with in the process specific guidance notes issued by the EA and in more general guidance documents issued by the Secretary of State. In theory, however, there is no discretion as to whether or not the description of the prescribed process can be extended to cover particular processes; a restriction which has led to a number of redefinitions of the classes of prescribed processes by way of amendments to the prescribed processes and substances regulations.

(c) Prescribed processes
Essentially, the list of prescribed processes extended the previous list of processes regulated under the Health and Safety at Work Act 1974 by including processes which give rise to the emissions of Red List substances (see p. 614) into sewers or controlled waters. Schedule 1 to the regulations contains a list of prescribed processes which is sub-divided into six main industry groupings: the fuel and power industry; the chemical industry; the minerals industry; the metal industry; the waste disposal industry; and a group of miscellaneous industries. Within these six different groups, the descriptions of processes are further split into Part A and Part B processes with each individual group having a series of subsections. For example, the fuel and power industry is subdivided into: gasification processes; carbonisation processes, combustion processes and petroleum processes. All in all, approximately 105 processes covering some 2,000 installations come within the IPC system.

(d) Meaning of process
Unlike IPPC which controls installations, IPC regulates industrial processes, which are defined in relation to individual operators and locations on the basis of individual components. Thus, under IPC an installation could be made up of a number of processes within the same site. There are, however, a number of rules which simplify the operation of the system. For example, where there are Part A and Part B processes within one site which fall within the same industrial group, they will all be controlled by the Environment Agency under one authorisation.

(e) Exceptions
There are exceptions to the general rule that all prescribed processes are to be controlled under IPC. The list of exemptions from the system can be found in the reg. 4 of the Environmental Protection (Prescribed Processes and Substances) Regulations 1991 and covers specific processes (e.g. working museums and domestic processes incidental to the use of a private dwelling) and general criteria (e.g. where emissions from the process would be trivial to the extent that they would not cause environmental harm).

IPC — process authorisation

The general scheme of applying for and the determination of IPC authorisations, mirrors that in the IPPC system. Most of the significant distinctions between the two systems have already been noted. In outline, IPC authorisations have to take into account and achieve a number of statutory objectives set out in s. 7 of the EPA 1990, as follows:

(a)   ensuring that, in carrying on a prescribed process, the best available techniques not entailing excessive cost (BATNEEC) will be used:

(i)   for preventing the release of substances prescribed for any environmental medium into that medium or, where that is not practicable by such means, for reducing the release of such substances to a minimum and for rendering harmless any such substances which are so released; and
(ii)   for rendering harmless any other substances which might cause harm if released into any environmental medium;

(b)   compliance with any directions by the Secretary of State given for the implementation of any obligations of the United Kingdom under EC Treaties or international law relating to environmental protection;
(c)   compliance with any limits or requirements and achievement of any quality standards or quality objectives prescribed by the Secretary of State under any of the relevant enactments;
(d)   compliance with any requirements applicable to the grant of authorisations specified by or under a statutory plan made by the Secretary of State under s. 3(5) of the EPA 1990.

Section 7(1) provides for three different types of conditions which may be included in an authorisation:

(a)   conditions to meet the statutory objectives as laid down in s. 7(2);
(b)   conditions imposed by the Secretary of State under s. 7(3);
(c)   any other appropriate conditions.

There is also a general implied condition that a process will be carried on using BATNEEC. Additionally, s. 7(7) specifically provides, in relation to IPC processes involving the release of substances into more than one environmental medium, that BATNEEC will be used for minimising the pollution which may be caused to the environment taken as a whole by the releases, having regard to the best practicable environmental option (BPEO) available in respect of the substances which may be released.

Enforcement powers, offences and appeals

The range of enforcement powers available under IPC will continue to operate during the transitional period. The powers closely follow those under IPPC described above. Thus they include variation notices (see ss. 10 and 11, EPA 1990), revocation notices (s. 12, EPA 1990), enforcement notices (s. 13, EPA 1990) and prohibition notices (s. 14, EPA 1990), which are markedly similar to suspension notices. There are also similar provisions in relation to offences (s. 23, EPA 1990) and appeals (s. 15, EPA 1990).

FOURTEEN
Air pollution and air quality

The range of problems affecting the atmosphere stretches across the full range of human activities, from highly toxic fumes emitted from a complicated industrial process to such seemingly mundane activities as lighting a fire, driving a car or using spray-on deodorant. The history of atmospheric pollution dates back to early times. The prohibitions on certain activities producing smoke are probably the first instances of environment pollution legislation in Great Britain.

Because such a wide range of activities affects the atmosphere, the range of environmental issues is also wide. On the one hand, there have always been difficulties with polluting activities affecting the locality in which they were situated. International difficulties have arisen with the creation of acid rain. In recent years we have seen a realisation amongst the international community that individual nations' actions can combine to create truly global difficulties. The destruction of the ozone layer and the issue of global warning have brought home the truly awesome consequences of the combined effect of certain industrial activities.

History and development of early controls over air pollution

The pollution of the local atmosphere from emissions has traditionally been easy to identify. Such problems date back to the early uses of coal in domestic fires. The production of fumes and particulates from fires caused pulmonary infections and related lung diseases. Notwithstanding this effect, coal continued to be used. In 1661, John Evelyn published his famous work on air pollution in city areas, *Fumi Fugium,* which not only outlined the problems that atmospheric pollution from smoke caused, but also, more importantly, tried to suggest methods by which the problems could be resolved.

With the advent of more complicated processes in the late eighteenth century, the problems of atmospheric pollution grew more severe. The industrial revolution increased the use of coal to drive new machinery and, more importantly, produced very acidic emissions as a consequence of the 'alkali works'. These works used the Leblanc process to produce soda, but the by-product of the chemical process used meant that hydrochloric gas was emitted into the atmosphere which, when mixed with water, created a new phenomenon — acid rain.

The consequences of these new processes were that areas of the country were rendered desolate by this very highly acidic moist air, burning trees, shrubs and hedges. One of the centres for the alkali industry, St Helens in Lancashire, was reported as not having a single tree with any foliage on it. Even amongst the people working in such factories, concern was expressed. This concern led to the setting-up of a Royal Commission to look into the problem of alkali pollution, which subsequently made the recommendations which led to the first Alkali Act, passed in 1863. Under this Act, a new Alkali Inspector was appointed who regulated such alkali processes. Although the Act did not attempt to deal with smoke, it did introduce new stricter controls over the production of acidic emissions. It made the first attempts at restricting the composition of emissions with the introduction of primitive emission standard requirements. Under the Act, there was a requirement that 95 per cent of all noxious emissions should be arrested within the plant, so that only 5 per cent of the previously emitted fumes were allowed into the atmosphere.

Even though there were strict emission standards on the volume of noxious gases produced, there were also the first signs of a proactive approach from the newly created Alkali Inspectorate in that they would encourage manufacturers to reduce the emissions to less than 5 per cent in order to protect the environment.

The initial effect of the legislation was a dramatic reduction in the production of acidic emissions from almost 14,000 tonnes to about 45 tonnes. This improvement, however, was only temporary. Within a short time the inadequacy of the legislation was brought home. The imposition of individualised emission standards could not take into account the cumulative effect of a large concentration of such operations. As the Act had only set a reduction for acidic emissions in terms of a percentage for each plant, the overall concentration of such emissions rose as the number of factories increased.

The introduction of the Alkali Act of 1874 attempted to redress the balance by introducing the concept of best practicable means (BPM). The application of BPM was used to widen the scope of the previous emission limits to include all noxious or offensive gases. In essence, the application of BPM relied upon these presumptive limits. The limits saw the introduction of the first proper emission standards in British legislation by specifying actual amounts of certain substances per cubic metre of emitted gas. If these emission limits were being met, then it was presumed that any legislation was being complied with and that the best practicable means were being used. The use of the concept of best practicable means ensured that there was to be a conciliatory and co-operational approach as the Alkali Inspectorate sought a method of enforcement which would not place 'an undue burden on manufacturing industry'.

(a) Controls over smoke

Neither of these Acts, nor the consolidation Act of 1906, dealt specifically with the control of smoke from either industrial or commercial premises. Attempts were made to control the emission of smoke through such Acts as the Public Health Act 1875, the Public Health (Smoke Abatement) Act 1926 and the Public Health Act 1936, but these dealt generally with smoke nuisances. These powers could not rid industrial cities of the problems of smoke pollution. The physical evidence of this pollution could be seen on blackened buildings, and by the frequency of smog, which was prevalent from Victorian times. Such smog was caused by fog forming in winter months and combining with smoke particles to produce a compound of gases which could cut visibility to very low levels. Of more concern, however, was the effect that these smogs had upon the dispersion of pollution. With a heavy concentration of smog hanging over a city the air was very still and convection was low. With the onset of these calm conditions, the dispersal of emissions was much more difficult. Such a lethal cocktail was bound to produce tragic effects, but these were fairly minimal until December 1952 when a smog descended upon London which did not clear for five days. Nothing unusual was noticed until prize cattle at the Smithfield Show started to suffer from respiratory problems. The smog got everywhere, even inside the Sadler's Wells Theatre, which resulted in the stoppage of a performance because of the difficulty of seeing the stage. When the smog had lifted it was estimated that nearly 4,000 people had lost their lives as a consequence of the smoke and other emissions.

The government immediately responded by setting up the Beaver Committee to report on the difficulties surrounding smoke pollution. The recommendation of the Committee was to introduce legislation to eliminate particulate emissions such as smoke, dust and grit so that such conditions would not arise again. With the introduction of the Clean Air Act 1956, later supplemented by the Clean Air Act 1968, controls were introduced for the first time to restrict the production of smoke, grit and dust from all commercial and industrial activities not covered by the Alkali Acts but also, more importantly, domestic fires as well. The Acts introduced such concepts as smoke control areas and the complete prohibition on 'dark smoke' from chimneys.

(b) Acid rain

During the 1970s, the problems of the emission of smoke, dirt, dust and grit lessened and coupled with the new approach to industrial processes a gradual improvement took place in the quality of the atmosphere in the UK. There was a move away from the use of coal as fuel to smokeless substances such as coke and gas. Additionally, the gap left behind with the introduction of clean air zones was met by an increase in the use of electricity for power and heat. The main generator of electricity in Britain, the Central Electricity Generating Board, changed its practices in a direct reaction to the difficulties encountered with local pollution by replacing the short chimneys traditionally used in power stations with larger and taller stacks. The basis of this change was to disperse pollution at a higher level in the hope that any substances would be diluted over greater distances. The consequence would be a reduction in the concentrations of pollutants in the nearby locality. Unfortunately, this reduction in the levels of local pollution only shifted the problems to a different location. Whilst the pollution of the atmosphere declined nationally, the concern internationally rose. The change of policy from short to tall stacks for chimneys saw the creation of the first environmental problem which could properly be identified across national boundaries — the problem of acid rain.

The combination of sulphur dioxide and other acids from power stations and traffic combined with the atmosphere to produce not only acid rain, but also acid deposits in the atmosphere made of ammonium sulphate particles.

The effects of the production of such substances into the atmosphere has increased the acidity of rainfall in some areas to over 40 times the natural level. This has had a terrible effect upon areas of not only England, Scotland and Wales but also other countries within Europe where the prevailing winds have carried such emissions. The Scandinavian countries in particular have received a large percentage of the 'export' of Britain's production of sulphur dioxide and acid rain. The specific effects of certain pollutants can range from speckled areas on leaves brought about by acidic deposits through to complete death. These problems require a co-operative approach to be taken between nations. There has been a long running dispute between Britain and the Scandinavian countries as to the cause of the acidic deposits on their countries. The EC has made some steps towards introducing a desulphurisation programme, but it remains to be seen whether or not this is to be successful.

(c) Global warming and ozone depletion

The Department of the Environment's White Paper, *This Common Inheritance*, published in September 1990, brought the international problem of global warming to the top of the environmental agenda.

> Global warming is one of the biggest environmental challenges now facing the world. It calls for action by all the world's nations, as no single nation can solve the problem on its own.

The greenhouse effect, as it has come to be known, has arisen because the production of various 'greenhouse' gases have increased in the past century with progressive industrialisation. In the lower atmosphere the production of emissions from power stations, car exhausts and industrial plants have increased by almost 100 per cent. These emissions absorb radiated heat and create a higher ambient temperature level which has led to speculation that there could be shrinking global icecaps and rising water levels.

Additionally, the amount of ozone in the upper atmosphere screens the earth from harmful UV-B radiation. This screen has deteriorated and there have been studies showing a 'hole' above Antarctica. This depletion of ozone has been linked to the use of chlorofluorocarbons (CFCs). The creation of greenhouse gases and the depletion of the ozone layer are worldwide problems which require international co-operation to solve. The use of international law as a mechanism for environmental protection is relatively unproven and there are some limitations to its usefulness. However, the nature of the problems facing the world in terms of these two issues have led to significant steps being taken to prevent any further harm.

The main features of the regulation of air pollution

One of the main difficulties with any comprehensive system of regulating air pollution is that the range of polluters and the sources of pollutant are varied and diverse. This means that there is no single regulatory mechanism which will have more than a contributory effect. Having said this, there are certain regulatory and policy mechanisms which provide a basic framework.

(a)   There is provision made for a National Air Quality Strategy which should ensure that air quality standards for certain pollutants are set centrally and provide overall targets which must not be exceeded. These targets are to be achieved through a variety of mechanisms but principally under pollution control legislation through the setting of emission limits.

(b)   Generally, local authorities have control over the management of air quality through the identification of Air Quality Management Areas. In addition they regulate the less polluting industrial processes (under air pollution control and integrated pollution prevention and control), whereas the Environment Agency regulates air emissions from the more polluting processes (under IPC and IPPC). There are a number of scientific bodies which advise government on the setting of standards for particular pollutants.

(c)   There are controls over emissions from industrial processes which are a mixture of process-based controls (e.g. using the best available techniques) for a range of polluting emissions. Conditions are set to achieve the statutory quality standards.

(d)   There are separate controls over the production of smoke, grit, dust and fumes from industrial and domestic premises (only where such emissions are otherwise uncontrolled under the statutory provisions mentioned in (b)). The controls operate by way of blanket prohibition of emissions with classified exemptions. There are simple emission limits set down in legislation (e.g. based around colour and density).

(e)   There is a strong emphasis on product standards to reduce emissions from, in particular, vehicles. There are various economic instruments which are used to reflect the different environmental costs of using such things as unleaded fuel.

(f)   The common law of nuisance acts as a balancing factor where emissions unreasonably interfere with the enjoyment of private rights or property. These controls continue to apply even where emissions are made in compliance with a statutory authorisation. On the other hand the ability to take action under the statutory nuisance provisions is normally ousted when there are other statutory controls which apply.

Air pollution policy

The control of air pollution has, as noted above, been the classic example of the use of reactive legal controls to regulate specific problems as they arise.

Policy approaches had hitherto been sparse and incoherent. Although the legal controls had been modernised and broadened, it was only in the 1990s that a coherent strategy was developed to deal with the problems of atmospheric pollution. When the then Conservative Government published its policy on sustainable development in January 1994, urban air quality was identified as a priority area for improvement. In March 1994 the DoE issued a consultation paper on air quality which bluntly described previous policy initiatives on air pollution as 'the fortuitous sum of a large number of unrelated regulatory decisions and individual choices'. It was not until the beginning of 1995 that the first steps were taken towards a coherent air quality management system and the Environment Act 1995 has a variety of framework provisions which are described below.

A number of factors led to this acceleration of policy-making. First, there was increasing evidence linking health problems with poor air quality, with the increase of the incidence of asthma and other diseases connected with a variety of atmospheric pollutants. There were a number of occasions (particularly in the summer months) when pollution levels rose to dangerous levels in cities.

Secondly, the quality of provision of information on air quality was improved with an increase in the number of background monitoring stations. Although air quality standards (AQS) were introduced for a number of pollutants any assessment of measuring improvement depended to a large extent upon the availability of long-term data. Most of England's major cities now have stations to monitor base data in order to assess compliance with standards for the main polluting emissions. It is anticipated that this will increase as the move towards established AQS grows (for more on monitoring see p. 421). Thirdly, the link between air pollution and transport, in particular motor transport, had become much more pronounced. The RCEP's Eighteenth Report concentrated on the environmental effects of vehicle emissions. In addition there had been a range of measures designed to tackle pollution from motor vehicles (see p. 430). Finally, as in other areas of environmental policy, the EC has made moves towards streamlining policy on atmospheric pollution. This culminated in a new framework directive on air quality assessment and management with proposals to set AQS for 12 significant pollutants (see p. 417).

Economic instruments and air pollution

Economic instruments have been used significantly in relation to air pollution primarily in relation to a range of measures which have been used in order to reduce the amount and impact of vehicle emissions. Thus duties on fuel have been increased over a long period of time with the intention of reflecting the environmental cost of vehicle use and promoting the benefits of fuel efficiency. In order to indicate the varying levels of environmental impact from different fuels, there are fuel duty differentials to encourage, for example, the use of ultra low diesel fuel over normal diesel.

Perhaps the most controversial economic instrument, however, is the so-called climate change levy, or tax on energy usage which will be introduced as a means of assisting with meeting the UK's climate change treaty commitments on, in particular, carbon dioxide reduction. It is scheduled for introduction in April 2001. In conjunction with the tax, the government would like to see the introduction of industry sector voluntary agreements and informal and formal emissions trading schemes (the statutory mechanism for formal schemes is found in sch. 1, para. 1, Pollution Prevention and Control Act 1999).

International law and air pollution

The influence of international law on the regulation of air pollution has been significant. Perhaps in recognition of the fact that many of the problems caused by air pollution can have impacts across a large geographical area (and in certain circumstances cause truly global effects), there have been a number of areas where international law has helped to shape policies and rules on both a continental and domestic level. In addition, the level of co-operation on such issues is sometimes higher than in other areas as there is a general acceptance that there is a mutual responsibility amongst the nation states of the world.

(a)   Transboundary pollution

As the description of the development of the controls over air pollution demonstrates, addressing local problems can often lead to a translocation of the impacts of pollutants over large distances. The Geneva Convention on Long-Range Transboundary Air Pollution, agreed under the UN Economic Commission for Europe (UNECE) in 1979, was the first real attempt to set up a formal framework of controls over air pollution between nations. The Convention has a limited application amongst those countries for whom acid rain has been a recurring problem, namely Europe, the USA and Canada. The Convention only provides a general framework within which detailed protocols set down emission limits for specific pollutants. The most important protocols include: the 1994 Oslo Protocol on the reduction of sulphur dioxide (which replaced a similar protocol agreed in 1985); the 1988 Sofia Protocol on freezing NO_x emissions at 1987 levels; and the 1991 Geneva Protocol on the reduction of volatile organic compounds.

(b)   The protection of the ozone layer

The protection of the ozone layer has had a wider impact than acid rain in that the issue affects more countries. Accordingly, the 1985 Vienna Convention on the Protection of the Ozone Layer and subsequently the 1987 Montreal Protocol set up controls which aim to reduce and ultimately phase out of use the main ozone depleting substances. The Protocol has been amended on a number of occasions in the light of experience and new information. One of the interesting aspects of the Protocol is that it has the effect of binding non-signatories in the sense that signatories cannot trade either the substances themselves or goods which contain those substances to any country (although the banning of certain substances has triggered an illegal market in any remaining stock).

(c) Climate change

The Earth Summit in 1992 was seen as a watershed in the fight against climate change. The conference saw the presentation of the UN Framework Convention on Change Convention which set down a framework for the reduction of so-called greenhouse gas emissions. The Treaty was ratified by 50 countries (including the EC and the UK) and came into force in March 1994. The details of the legally binding reduction targets were left until the end of 1997 when, after much discussion, the Kyoto Protocol was agreed. The Kyoto Protocol sets various reduction targets for different countries in relation to six gases: carbon dioxide, NO_x, hydrofluorocarbons (HFCs), perfluorocarbons (PFCs), methane and sulphur hexafluoride (SF_6). The cuts average out at a 5.2 per cent reduction of 1990 levels of these gases at some time between 2008 and 2012.

The Protocol was the subject of tough negotiations primarily as a result of the political difficulties faced by the US in setting significant reduction targets. This resulted in an number of novel mechanisms which can be used by countries in order to assist in meeting the targets. These include the following.

(i)   Emissions trading systems   This would enable countries with a significant 'surplus' of emissions reduction as a result of exceeding targets, either to sell that surplus to countries which have a 'deficit' (i.e. are having difficulties in meeting their own target) or 'stockpile' it as a safeguard against meeting future reduction targets.

(ii)   The clean development mechanism   As the developing nations are not subjected to any reduction targets, there was some concern expressed that there was little incentive for them to adopt measures which would contribute to the overall achievement of the aims of the Climate Change Convention. Thus, under the Protocol, the countries which are subject to the reduction targets can gain credit for assisting the developing countries in the creation of project activities which result in certified emission reductions. Where a Protocol country assists a developing country with the construction of a power station which will reduce overall emission levels, the reduction achieved can be offset against the Protocol country's own target (as long as the emission reductions achieved are 'additional' to those that would have occurred anyway).

(iii)   Carbon sinks   The creation of carbon sinks — land uses such as afforestation which reduce the amount of certain greenhouse gases — can be taken into account in certain circumstances. The calculation of the actual extent of the reduction is a matter of some controversy as the amount of the reduction in heavily forested countries could be significant in the overall total reduction (e.g. it is estimated that Russia could claim over 25 per cent reduction of its overall target from the use of managed forests).

European law and air pollution

The protection of the atmosphere was not seen as a priority by the EC until the mid 1980s. Indeed, relatively few proposals based purely on environmental protection (as opposed to market harmonisation) were published before 1984. The reasons for this were twofold. First, a lack of political will and, secondly, a genuine desire to move forward in other areas. As a result of the effects of acid rain, however, the German government pressed for swift action in 1983 and the main framework Directive on emissions from industrial plant (84/360) was introduced nearly 10 years after the framework directives for waste and water pollution. Since that time, though, the concern about trans-boundary pollution and wider issues such as global warming and ozone depletion has led to a wide range of directives being introduced.

The Commission's approach to the protection of the atmosphere has been wide-ranging in its scope. Various mechanisms have been used including the following:

(a)   Environmental quality standards

A Framework Directive on Air Quality was formally agreed in 1996 (96/62). In time, the Directive will help to establish new air quality standards and objectives and in relation to specific substances replace a number of directives discussed below. It is intended that the framework Directive will apply three types of quality objective: a limit value, a guide value and an alert threshold (which mirrors the approach taken under the national air quality strategy which is discussed below). The Directive identifies 12 pollutants for which limits will be set in subsequent daughter directives. The first daughter Directive (99/30) was formally adopted in July 1999 setting binding limits for sulphur dioxide, nitrogen dioxide, small particles known as PM_{10} and lead. Further draft 'daughter' directives have been issued for ozone, carbon monoxide and benzene. The final series of daughter directives will cover polyaromatic hydrocarbons (PAHs), cadmium, arsenic, nickel and mercury.

(b)   Emission limits

The Framework Directive (84/360) is fleshed out by daughter directives which set specific emission limits for pollutants from a variety of operations. These include limits on sulphur dioxide, NO_x, and dust from incinerators (94/67 for hazardous waste, and 89/369 for municipal waste) and large combustion plants (88/609). The provisions of these directives have been implemented through the controls over emissions found in Part I of the EPA 1990 and in future under the Pollution Prevention and Control Act 1999.

In 1997, the European Commission published a proposed acidification strategy which was designed to reduce the emission of sulphur dioxide, oxides of nitrogen and ammonia beyond preexisting commitments. The strategy will be implemented through a variety of mechanisms, including a proposal to amend the Large Combustion Plant Directive to lower emissions in the light of technological improvements over the last ten years. The primary implementing mechanism is a proposal for a directive to set national emissions ceilings for each member state for sulphur dioxide, nitrogen dioxide, ammonia and volatile organic compounds.

(c) Product standards
Product standards have been used extensively in the regulation of air pollution. One of the main reasons for this is that, before the amendments to the EC Treaty which permitted environmental protection measures, the introduction of such standards was seen to be justifiable in terms of market harmonisation where environmental justifications were not accepted by every member state. Relevant directives include: sulphur content of certain liquid fuels (99/32); emissions from vehicles (88/76, 89/458, 91/441 and 98/69); and content of fuels (98/70).

(d) Prohibitions
The phasing out and prohibition of CFCs under Regulations 3322/88 and 594/91 is one of the few examples of that mechanism.

(e) Market mechanisms
Proposals for an EC carbon/energy tax have been progressing through various stages for some time. Compulsory taxation on carbon-based fuel has been accepted by the majority of Member States, with Britain being the main dissenter.

(f) EC action on a worldwide basis
The EC has encouraged a number of worldwide initiatives by negotiating in its own right on issues which require global action. Thus, the EC is a signatory to the Vienna Convention on Ozone Layer Protection. This in turn led to the implementation of Regulations 3322/88 and 594/91 on CFCs. Other examples include the Climate Change Convention and the Kyoto Protocol which will be implemented across the EC through a process which allocates reduction targets or, in some cases, permitted increases which are calculated with reference to regional policies rather than environmental considerations.

Overlapping controls

There are few overlapping controls in relation to air pollution and other aspects of pollution control. There is, however, some degree of overlap within the provisions dealing with air pollution alone.

(a) Statutory nuisances and the Clean Air Act 1993
Smoke, dust and other emissions from a chimney (industrial or domestic) are excluded from the definition of a statutory nuisance found in the EPA 1990 (s. 79(7)). In addition, under s. 79(10) of the EPA 1990, statutory nuisance actions cannot be taken in respect of emissions which could be the subject of enforcement action under Part I of the EPA 1990. In both cases, the rationale behind these provisions is that there are co-existing provisions which should be used to deal with the problems arising from the emissions (namely, the Clean Air Act 1993 and the air pollution control provisions of the EPA 1990). The provisions of the Clean Air Act 1993 do not apply to processes

which are prescribed for control under Part I of the EPA 1990 (s. 41, Clean Air Act 1993).

(b) IPC, APC and IPPC

There is a good deal of overlap between the controls under Part I of the EPA 1990 (i.e. air pollution control and integrated pollution control). These are explained in more detail on p. 385. As the provisions dealing with IPPC are brought into force for existing installations these overlaps will be transferred (see p. 392).

(c) Town and country planning

In relation to development control, air quality issues have increased in significance throughout the 1990s. Central government planning guidance on retail development (PPG6) and transport (PPG13) has emphasised the importance of taking into account the environmental impact of transport emissions on air quality when local planning authorities are making decisions on such things as out-of-town shopping centres. Other factors which need to be taken into account in development proposals include restricted parking for commuters, facilities for cyclists and pedestrians and a clear provision for integrated public transport.

In relation to strategic development planning, central guidance found in LAQM 94(97), *Air Quality and Land Use Planning* suggests that land use development planning and strategic air quality planning should have a symbiotic relationship in that neither should be drawn up without regard for the other.

Managing air quality

The Environment Act 1995, Part IV was the first real attempt to introduce a system of air quality management and the legislative initiatives were two-fold. First, the introduction of a national air quality strategy which would set down standards and objectives along with the measures which were required to achieve those objectives. The first strategy was produced in 1997 and proposals for review were published in 1999. These standards and objectives provide the foundation for air quality policy and set the context within which detailed legislation must be implemented and enforced. For example, the Environment Agency is to have regard to the Strategy when exercising its pollution control functions (s. 81, Environment Act 1995).

The strategy does not, however, have statutory force and imposes no direct obligations upon any regulatory body. Thus, the Environment Act 1995 provides a power to prescribe standards and/or objectives by way of regulation (ss. 87 and 91 of the 1995 Act). These regulations in turn impose obligations upon local authorities thereby ensuring national compliance through local implementation. The 1995 Act provides for the creation of a system of local air quality management which obliges local authorities to undertake an assessment of air quality in their areas and to take action where statutory objectives are not being met. These statutory objectives have been incorporated into the Air Quality (England) Regulations 2000 (SI 2000/928) which set down the targets for air quality in each local area for the period between the end of 2003 to the end of 2008. The regulations set down air quality objectives for seven pollutants including sulphur dioxide, nitrogen dioxide, benzene and carbon monoxide. The standards are set in relation to the effect of the pollutant upon human health, although the effect upon the wider environment is also a material consideration.

Where any of the statutory objectives are not likely to be met during the specified period, the relevant local authority must designate the area as an Air Quality Management Area (AQMA) and prepare an action plan indicating how the objectives are intended to be met. There is a range of powers available to local authorities which can be used to implement any action plan including the following.

(a)   The use of smoke control powers under the Clean Air Act 1993
The control of smoke from industrial and domestic premises is an important part of the national air quality strategy. Local authorities have the power to declare a smoke control area (which prohibits the emission of smoke from chimneys and the use of unauthorised fuels) in order to secure objectives contained in an action plan. In practice, however, most of the areas of the country where smoke has been a problem have already been designated as smoke control areas (see further p. 429).

(b)   The use of traffic management and planning powers
The ability of local authorities to tackle local hotspots of poor air quality which result mainly from vehicles has been enhanced with the introduction of Local Transport Plans (LTPs) (which were first discussed in the Integrated Transport White Paper, Cm 3950, 1998). An LTP is designed to tackle the adverse effects of traffic including any deterioration of air quality. Each local authority has a power to produce a LTP which should set out policies for promoting public transport and charging for road users and parking. Although the production of LTPs is only an administrative power, the government is committed to introducing legislation which will put them on a statutory basis. In addition to the strategic management of traffic through LTPs, there are statutory powers available to control traffic under a number of different statutes. The Road Traffic Reduction Act 1997 places a duty upon local authorities to review the levels of traffic on local roads and to produce targets for reducing numbers. This will be supplemented nationally by the traffic reduction targets produced under the Road Traffic Reduction (National Targets) Act 1999. Under the Road Traffic Regulation Act 1984, local authorities have wide powers to regulate traffic under Traffic Regulation Orders (TROs) which can be used to restrict traffic in certain areas (e.g. pedestrianised areas of city centres) or even single roads. TROs can be made in order to achieve air quality objectives (s. 1(g) of the Road Traffic Regulation Act 1984). Further measures to reduce traffic and contribute to air quality improvements can be made by using traffic calming under the Highways (Traffic Calming) Regulations 1999 (SI 1999/1026) which allow local authorities to create narrow 'gateways' into urban centres.

(c)   The use of pollution control measures

This covers measure such as Local Authority Air Pollution Control (LAAPC), Integrated Pollution Control (IPC), and Pollution Prevention and Control (PPC) provisions (see below). Other measures include proposed controls over the emissions of VOCs from the storage and distribution of petrol.

(d)   The control of land uses under by way of planning controls

The link between land use planning and air pollution has been recognised explicitly in Planning Policy Guidance Notes 6 and 13 (see above). The impact of a development upon air quality in an AQMA would be a material consideration which would be taken into account when considering whether to grant planning permission. In addition the designation of an AQMA would have to be taken into account when drawing up development plan policies in regional and local development plans. The procedure for declaring an AQMA is similar to that of the designation of a smoke control area involving prior consultation with a variety of bodies and interested parties.

Advisory bodies with responsibility for air pollution

There are a number of bodies carrying out an advisory function within the area of air pollution. Three of particular importance are:

(a)   The Expert Panel on Air Quality Standards (EPAQS), set up by the DoE which makes recommendations in respect of AQS. Although the government seeks advice from a variety of bodies, this group, made up of both medical and air pollution experts, is seen to have the greatest influence when setting new AQS. It has made recommendations for AQS for ozone, benzene, 1,3-butadiene and carbon monoxide, with other pollutants to follow over a period of time.

(b)   The Quality of Urban Air Review Group (QUARG) reviews the state of urban air quality and makes recommendations in relation to monitoring stations/networks, types of pollutants monitored, information made available to the public and areas for further research.

(c)   The National Environmental Technology Centre (NETCEN) is responsible for a variety of functions relating to the measurement of air pollution. It coordinates the UK Smoke and Sulphur Dioxide Monitoring Network, prepares an annual National Atmospheric Emissions Inventory giving estimates of atmospheric pollution from all sources and provides training for local authorities in relation to the monitoring of local air pollution (see below).

Monitoring of air pollution

The effectiveness of the national air quality strategy can only be assessed with a comprehensive system for measuring pollutants in the atmosphere. Monitoring of smoke, sulphur dioxide, grit and dust has, in fact, taken place since the early twentieth century. This is unsurprising given the major impact that these pollutants have had upon health and the environment and the relatively unsophisticated methods of measurement. In 1961, the establishment of the national survey of air pollution led to a coordinated network of monitoring sites situated throughout the country. These sites concentrated on the accumulation of data on smoke and sulphur dioxide. The network was, however, unwieldy (with approximately 1,200 sites) and unreliable. Over time this network has been replaced and upgraded and the monitoring programme is now organized into ten different networks made up of automatic and sampler-based monitoring systems.

These monitoring systems are supplemented by emissions inventories on a national and local level. The national atmospheric emissions inventory includes information and emissions estimates for a range of pollutants. The inventory is broken down into information on industry sectors and provides data on trends from 1970 to 1997. Local emissions inventories are in operation in certain urban areas where specific air quality problems have been known to occur. These include West Yorkshire, West Midlands, Greater Manchester, London and Glasgow. The information found in the inventories assists with the identification of problems and cost effective solutions.

There are specific and separate requirements for the monitoring and dissemination of information on ozone levels. The Ozone Monitoring and Information Regulations 1994 (SI 1994/440) implemented the EC Directive on Air Pollution by Ozone (92/72). The Regulations require the establishment of a monitoring network, the dissemination of information, and a system whereby the public are warned when excessive levels of ozone are in the atmosphere. These warnings should be communicated as soon as possible and on a sufficiently wide scale to enable the public to take precautionary measures. The warnings should contain details of the area affected, the length of time that levels are likely to be excessive and precautionary measures which should be taken.

The introduction and expansion of the systems for monitoring and disseminating information on air pollution has been widely welcomed but the quality and accuracy of past monitoring has been criticised strongly. The main criticisms have centred around the selection and quantity of sites. The effectiveness of any monitoring network is primarily dependent upon the location of the monitoring equipment. It has been argued that the monitoring sites are not generally located in areas of high exposure and therefore give a false impression of levels of pollution. Also, although coverage of monitoring sites is spreading there are still large gaps, particularly in some areas of heavy industry and traffic. More specifically, the EC has criticised the UK for failing to provide an adequate number of sites to monitor nitrogen dioxide levels. The introduction of a national air quality strategy based around specific standards and objectives means that the base data provided by the monitoring system has to be credible and sufficiently broad to indicate true levels of improvement.

Air pollution control consents and permits

The main regulatory tools for controlling polluting atmospheric emissions fall within three systems: first, local air pollution control and, secondly, integrated pollution control under Part I of the Environmental Protection Act 1990 and, thirdly, the system which will supersede these two, the permitting system under the Pollution Prevention and Control Act 1999. The details of these systems are dealt with in Chapter 13. In general, the systems operate as follows:

(a)   The controls do not apply generally to all emissions. The systems are limited to emissions released from specifically prescribed industrial processes.

(b)   The systems operate by way of process standard. That is to say that although emission limits are set for atmospheric pollutants in each individual consent, the main thrust of the regulatory scheme is that processes must utilise the best available techniques to prevent the release of harmful pollutants into the atmosphere. There is an element of cost benefit analysis in determining the best available techniques in that excessively expensive techniques are excluded.

(c)   There is a split in administrative responsibility between the local authorities which control the less polluting processes and the Environment Agency which has responsibility for the processes which give rise to more significant pollution. This administrative split is also reflected in the scope of control. The Environment Agency controls processes in relation to all environmental releases (under IPC), or impacts (under IPPC), whilst the local authorities control atmospheric releases in relation to all processes which are prescribed for local control (under APC or IPPC). In addition, in relation to certain installations which are prescribed for local control under IPPC, local authorities control all environmental impacts.

(d)   The conditions attached to an authorisation or permit will be designed to help achieve the overall air quality objectives set in the national air quality strategy or indeed any specific objectives set out in an AQMA. In setting conditions, the regulatory agencies must ensure that there are no breaches of European or national environmental quality standards.

(e)   Unlike water pollution, there is no direct liability for the emission of polluting substances to the atmosphere (other than those matters controlled under the Clean Air Act 1993, see below). The controls are mainly continuing in the sense that to operate a prescribed process without the necessary authorisation, or in breach of the conditions of any authorisation, would be a criminal offence.

The control of smoke, fumes, dust and grit under the Clean Air Act 1993

As we have seen, the control of smoke, dust and dirt from industrial and domestic fires was largely ineffective in dealing with the problems associated with such emissions in the early part of the twentieth century. Although the Public Health (Smoke Abatement) Act 1926 attempted to control certain categories of industrial smoke, domestic smoke was prohibited only if it amounted to a 'nuisance'. The Clean Air Act 1956, later amended and supplemented by the Clean Air Act 1968, provided a comprehensive control mechanism for the protection of the environment from smoke, dust and fumes. These Acts were consolidated in the Clean Air Act 1993.

This Act constitutes a separate and distinct area of control. Essentially, it controls smoke, dust and grit from all fires and furnaces.

(a) Control of smoke from chimneys

Section 1 of the 1993 Act prohibits the emission of 'dark smoke' from the chimney of any building. Any occupier who breaches s. 1 will be guilty of a criminal offence. The section applies to all types of buildings, from domestic houses to industrial premises and crematoria. The mechanism of control specifically applies to chimneys from buildings. Although the definition of the word 'building' covers such structures as a greenhouse, it would have to be a part of a recognised structure (*Clifford* v *Holt* [1899] 1 Ch 698).

The prohibition applies only to 'dark smoke'; other types of emissions are covered either elsewhere in the Act or under different statutes. In attempting to determine whether smoke is 'dark', enforcement officers are forced to make a visual assessment of the shade of the smoke emission by comparing the darkness of the smoke with a uniform chart known as a Ringelmann chart. The chart contains five shades of grey by cross hatching black lines on a white background from clear (number 0) to black (number 4). The chart is rectangular in shape, measuring some 581 mm × 127 mm. The chart is used in accordance with certain guidelines laid down in British Standard 2742. It is held up by the operator and compared to the smoke from a distance of at least 15 metres and then comparisons are made between the colour of the smoke and the colour on the chart. If the colour of the smoke is as dark as, or darker than, shade 2 on the Ringelmann Scale it then qualifies as dark smoke (s. 3(1)). Where, however, an operator is experienced, s. 3(2) allows for an assessment to be made independent of the Ringelmann chart, often by the use of a smaller, more portable smoke chart (129 mm × 69 mm). Some officers rely purely on their experience to assess whether or not the smoke is darker than shade 2.

The prohibition also only covers smoke emitted from chimneys. The definition of a chimney can be found in s. 64 and is wide enough to cover all structures or openings through which smoke is emitted. Thus, smoke from outdoor fires or, for instance, burning straw or stubble is not covered by s. 1.

(b) Strict liability

As in other environmental legislation, liability is strict, therefore prima facie *any* dark smoke emitted from a chimney would give rise to liability under s. 1. The Act imposes liabililty on an occupier of a building from which smoke is emitted, irrespective of responsibility.

(c) Exemptions and defences

Section 1(3) provides for certain exemptions to be made by the Secretary of State. These exemptions are restricted by the duration of emissions. The Dark Smoke (Permitted Periods) Regulations 1958 (SI 1958/498) allows three main exemptions for smoke from chimneys. First, there are time-limits imposed of anything between 10 and 40 minutes during any period of eight hours for emission of dark smoke depending on both the number of furnaces used and whether or not soot is blowing. Secondly, there is a limit of four minutes of continuous emissions of dark smoke where the cause is not owed to burning soot. Lastly, there is a limit of two minutes in each period of 30 minutes where smoke is black (that is, smoke as dark as, or darker than, shade 4 on the Ringelmann chart).

Furthermore, s. 1(4) lays down three statutory defences. These defences are not absolute and require certain qualifying steps to be taken to ensure that the defences apply. The section provides that it is a defence to a charge under s. 1(1) that the emission was:

(i)   solely due to the lighting of a furnace, and that all practicable steps were taken to minimise or prevent emissions;

(ii)   solely due to the failure of a furnace, and that the contravention of s. 1(1) could not reasonably have been foreseen or provided against and prevented by action taken after the failure;

(iii)   solely due to the unavoidable use of the least unsuitable fuel available when suitable fuel was unavailable, and that practicable steps were taken to minimise or prevent emissions;

(iv)   any combination of (i), (ii) and (iii).

(d)   Enforcement and offences

Local authorities can take action against dark smoke emitted from outside the area which they control if it affects their area (s. 55(2)). An important prerequisite of bringing a prosecution is that the enforcement authority are under a duty to notify occupiers of the existence of the offence 'as soon as may be'. This notification will normally be given orally by the relevant enforcement officer. If such oral notification is given, it must be confirmed in writing within four days of the date on which the officer became aware of the offence. In any event, written notice of the offence must be given within that time. If notification is not given, it is a defence to charges under ss. 1, 2 or 20 of the Act (s. 51(3)). The offence is only triable in the magistrates' court. There are different maximum levels of fine for emissions from private dwellings (level 3 on the standard scale) and for any other case (level 5 on the standard scale) (s. 1(5)).

(e)   Emissions of dark smoke from industrial plants

Section 2 of the Act prohibits the emissions of dark smoke from industrial trade premises other than from a chimney of a building (which is covered under s. 1). 'Premises' include the grounds of factories and open areas such as demolition sites (*Sheffield County Council* v *ADH Demolition Ltd* (1983) 82 LGR 177). Section 2(2)(b) gives the Secretary of State power to pass regulations giving an exemption to the burning of prescribed matter which emits dark smoke in the open. The Clean Air (Emission of Dark Smoke) (Exemption) Regulations 1969 (SI 1969/1263) exempt certain material such as timber, explosives, tar, and waste from animal or poultry carcases. Section 2(6) provides that industrial or trade premises include premises not used for

Air pollution and air quality

industrial or trade purposes but on which substances or matter are burnt in connection with such processes. Thus, open areas without any connection to industrial activities would fall within control under this section.

Section 2(3) refers to the burden of proof required when attempting to show the causation of dark smoke. On trade or business premises, where circumstances are such that the burning of material would be likely to give rise to an emission of dark smoke, such an emission can be taken as proved unless the occupier or person accused of the offence can show that no dark smoke actually was emitted. When fires have been extinguished but dark smoke has already been emitted there has often been difficulty in proving the source of the dark smoke. This section allows environmental health officers to act against smoke pollution even though there is no smoke emanating from the premises. The prohibition under s. 2 applies not only to occupiers but also to any person who causes or permits the emission of dark smoke from industrial or trade premises.

There is a statutory defence under s. 2(4) that the emission of dark smoke was 'inadvertent'. This would suggest that although the offence has an absolute liability, some degree of blameworthiness is necessary for an action to be successful. If the emission was inadvertent, it is also necessary to show that all practicable steps have been taken to prevent or minimise the emission of dark smoke. Practicability is defined in s. 64 as meaning reasonably practicable having regard to local conditions and circumstances, to the financial implications and to the current state of technical knowledge. An offence under s. 2 is triable only in a magistrates' court, the maximum fine being set at level 5 on the standard scale (s. 2(5)).

(f) The control of grit, dust and fumes
The Act does not only cover smoke. Emissions from furnaces can also contain particulate matter and the Act extends to cover such particulate matter, ranging from the largest (being grit as defined in the Clean Air (Emission of Grit and Dust from Furnaces) Regulations 1971 (SI 1971/162)), through dust and small solid particles between 1 and 75 μm in diameter (as defined in BS3405), to fumes (which are defined as any airborne solid matter smaller than dust) (s. 64). There are proactive measures for preventing smoke, dust, grit and fumes being emitted from furnaces. Section 4 provides that furnaces over a certain energy value (excluding domestic boilers) should, as far as practicable, be smokeless when using a fuel for which it was designed. This control is implemented by s. 4(1), under which anyone wishing to install a furnace has to notify the local authority before doing so. Where the local authority is notified and authorisation has been given, then the furnace is deemed to comply with the provision. This, however, does not exempt the furnace from being subject to the prohibition on dark smoke under s. 1. Where a furnace is operated without such an approval then the person who installed the furnace will be guilty of an offence (s. 4(4)).

This proactive approach is further strengthened by the requirement for grit and dust arrestment plant to be fitted to furnaces. This power is extended by ss. 6 and 7, which control all furnaces partly installed or for which there is an agreement to install after 1 October 1969. Again, details of the type of arrestment plant must be given to the local authority. Prior to 1 October 1969, the only furnaces covered were those in buildings burning pulverised fuel or solid waste or fuel at a rate of 1 tonne or more an hour. After that date, the Clean Air Act 1968 extended the powers to include furnaces in which solid, liquid or gaseous matter is burnt as well as reducing the rate of the use of solid matter to a minimum 100 pounds per hour. The statutory requirements are fleshed out by the Clean Air (Emission of Grit and Dust from Furnaces) Regulations 1971 (SI 1971/162), which contain information as to the quantities of grit and dust which may be emitted by reference to either the heat put out by the furnace or the heat taken in by the furnace.

(g)   Exemptions

There are exemptions to the requirement to supply details of plant to the local authority under s. 6; s. 7 gives two main areas of exemption. First, the Secretary of State can exempt certain furnaces by way of the Clean Air (Arrestment Plant) (Exemption) Regulations 1969 (SI 1969/1262), which exclude mobile or transportable furnaces, and certain other furnaces. Secondly, the local authority has a power to exempt a specific furnace if it is satisfied that the emissions from the furnace will not be prejudicial to health or a nuisance. Application for this exemption has to be made by the person installing the furnace. The local authority has eight weeks in which to give a written decision and if no decision is forthcoming in that period then exemption is deemed to have been granted. Where there is a refusal of an application, there is a right of appeal within 28 days from the date of the decision.

(h)   Monitoring provisions

To enable the local authority to enforce its responsibilities effectively, s. 10 allows the Secretary of State to make regulations which allow the local authority to monitor the emission of grit and dust from furnaces. This provision does not apply to fumes unless they are controlled specifically under other legislation.

The provisions regulating the measurement of grit and dust are contained in the Clean Air (Measurement of Grit and Dust) Regulations 1971 (SI 1971/616) and the Clean Air (Units of Measurement) Regulations 1992 (SI 1992/35). Under these regulations, the local authority has to give occupiers of premises not less than six weeks' notice in writing requiring them to make adaptations to any chimney serving a furnace to allow for plant and machinery to be installed to monitor the dust and grit from the furnace. Thereafter the local authority must give at least 28 days' notice in writing requiring a test to be carried out in accordance with the procedure specified in an otherwise obscure book, *The Measurement of Solids in Flue Gases* by P. G. W. Hawksley, S. Badzioch and J. H. Blackett. Then, after giving at least 48 hours' notice in writing of the date and time of the tests, the occupier must send to the local authority within 14 days the report of the results of the test, including the date, the number of furnaces and the results in terms of pounds of grit and dust emitted per hour.

These provisions apply only to a number of specific types of furnace including those that burn pulverised fuel or any other solid matter at a rate of 45 kilograms or more per hour.

(i)   The control of height of chimneys

As one of the main mechanisms for the control of environmental pollution into the atmosphere was to increase the height of chimneys to disperse the pollutant over a wider area, there is specific legislation to control the height of chimneys. The argument used by many scientists has been that the higher the chimney the higher the emission point, and thus the more diluted any emissions will be when they eventually come back down to the ground.

Under ss. 14 and 15, an application for chimney height approval is required to enable the local authority to assess the height required, taking into account the geographical features and the constitution of the emissions, so as to avoid localised pollution. If approval is not obtained, it will only be an offence if the chimney is used once it has been constructed. The application form is prescribed by the Clean Air (Height of Chimneys) (Prescribed Form) Regulations 1969 (SI 1969/412). An application must be made in the following circumstances:

(i)   where a new chimney is erected;

(ii)   where the combustion space of a furnace serving an existing chimney is enlarged by adding a new furnace to an existing number of furnaces all serving the same chimney;

(iii)   where a furnace is removed, or replaced, but only where a furnace burns pulverised fuel, or burns solid matter at a rate of 100 pounds or more per hour, or burns more than 1.25 million BTU per hour of any liquid or gas.

In addition to these controls, planning permission must also be applied for.

When deciding whether or not to grant chimney height approval, the local authority must be satisfied that the chimney height will be sufficient to prevent, so far as is practicable, the smoke, grit, dust, gases or fumes emitted from the chimney from being prejudicial to health or a nuisance when taking into account (s. 15(2)):

(i)   the purpose of the chimney;
(ii)   the position and descriptions of buildings near it;
(iii)   the levels of the neighbouring ground;
(iv)   any other matters requiring consideration in the circumstances.

If the local authority decides to grant approval, it can grant it with or without conditions, but these must relate only to the rate and quality of emissions from the chimney (s. 15(3)). If the local authority turns down an application, it has to notify the applicant of its decision in writing with its reasons and an indication as to what it thinks the lowest acceptable height would be. The applicant may appeal to the Secretary of State within 28 days of notification of the decision (s. 15(6)).

As in other areas of control in the Clean Air Act, the Secretary of State has the power to exempt certain boilers or plants from this control for chimney height approval. These exemptions can be found in the Clean Air (Heights of Chimneys) (Exemption) Regulations 1969 (SI 1969/411). The regulations specifically relate to the need for approval to construct a chimney under s. 10 and include mostly temporary or mobile boilers or plant.

The guidelines on assessing chimney heights are contained in the *Third Memorandum on Chimney Heights*, published by HMSO. This provides specific mathematical calculations which take into account background levels of pollution. Where pollution levels are higher there is a requirement that a chimney should be higher as well. The memorandum indicates that the chimney height required should vary according to the type of area concerned among other factors. It identifies the following types of areas:

(i)   an undeveloped area where development is unlikely;
(ii)   a partially developed area with scattered houses;
(iii)   a built-up residential area;
(iv)   an urban area of mixed industrial and residential development;
(v)   a large city or an urban area of mixed heavy industrial and dense residential development.

By assessing the level of pollution in the atmosphere in these generalised ways, it is hoped to achieve an idea of the required height for a particular chimney. In a large city or urban area it will be a requirement that chimneys should be at their highest.

(j)   Miscellaneous controls

Aside from chimneys serving a furnace, s. 16 applies similar restrictions on chimneys serving a non-combustion process. There is a much simpler procedure for obtaining approval by submitting building regulation plans. The local authority is entitled to reject the plans if the chimney is not adequate to prevent emissions from becoming prejudicial to health or a nuisance. There is a right of appeal against refusal.

The Building Regulations 1991 (SI 1991/2768) apply not only to non-combustible furnace chimneys but also to those controlled by s. 15. Building regulation approval is therefore required for all chimneys.

(k)   Smoke control areas

In order to improve conditions over wide areas and to control non-dark smoke, s. 18 allows local authorities to designate areas which will be smoke control areas. As there are difficulties in defining areas in relation to land, two or more authorities are entitled to join together and declare that a larger area than their own area is to be a smoke control area (s. 61(3)). Most smoke control areas were designated soon after the introduction of the Clean Air Act 1956. Although the process has slowed down since that time, the number of smoke control orders continues to rise. By 1990, nearly 10 million premises were subject to control, and the success of the orders was a major factor in the achievement of compliance with EC Directive 80/779.

The effect of designating a smoke control area is to make it an offence for occupiers of premises to allow any smoke emissions from a chimney.

The Act exempts both authorised fuel and certain fireplaces from control. The Smoke Control Areas (Authorised Fuels) Regulations 1991 (SI 1991/ 1282), consolidate 17 different regulations made since 1956. These regulations include all the types of material which can be burnt without emitting smoke. Fireplaces are exempted under various Smoke Control (Exempted Fireplaces) Orders. Therefore, either authorised fuel can be used *per se* or unauthorised fuel can be used on exempted fireplaces, and the use of either could amount to a defence to a prosecution under s. 20. The burden of proof for showing that such exemptions apply falls upon the occupier.

The local authority is entitled under s. 18(2) to exempt specified buildings, classes of building or fireplaces from the smoke control area. It may make different provision for different parts of the area or limit their operation to specified classes of buildings in the area, such as factories rather than houses.

The process for making an order designating a smoke control area is contained in sch. 1. There is a requirement for general publicity, which enables the public to make objections. This publicity is effected by placing advertisements in the *London Gazette* in addition to notices being posted around the area. If there are any objections to the order they must be taken into account as material considerations in deciding whether or not to ratify the order. Where an order is made, its operation is delayed for a minimum of six months whilst the authority brings the effect of the order to the notice of the people within the area.

Department of the Environment Circular 11/81 suggests that there should be sufficient supplies of authorised fuel in the area and the operation of the order should be implemented at some time between 1 July and 1 November to ensure that there are adequate provisions of fuel stocks.

The control of emissions from motor vehicles

The effect of transport on the environment is varied. In addition to the obvious effects from emissions, noise, land-take for roads and other projects and the use of raw materials (petrol, diesel, in addition to manufacturing materials). Emissions from vehicles are, however, probably the most significant issue which needs to be regulated and controlled.

The problems of pollution from motor vehicles was acknowledged as significant in the RCEP's First Report (Cmnd 4585, 1971) where the Royal Commission warned of the dangers of ignoring the environmental implications of traffic growth. With growth forecasts for road traffic of over 140% between 1988 and 2025 the original warnings have taken on a repetitive nature. In particular, the RCEP's Eighteenth Report on Transport and the Environment (Cm 2674, 1994) set out eight key objectives which were intended to make transport policy more sustainable. In relation to atmospheric pollution this included targets for air quality and the reduction of carbon dioxide emissions.

The law in relation to the control of emissions from motor vehicles is under constant review and too detailed to be covered, other than in principle, in a book of this type. Most controls target product standards in relation to vehicle-type approval, specified emission limits from vehicles, the content of fuel and maintenance tests. Most limits have their origin within EC legislation (see below).

When a new motor vehicle is produced it must comply with all relevant standards, including EC emission limits. The Motor Vehicles (Type Approval) (Great Britain) Regulations (SI 1994/981) sets out type-approval procedures which are applied to specimen examples of vehicles prior to general sale.

The Road Vehicle (Construction and Use) Regulations, are a series of regulations which set out requirements in reaction to a variety of construction details, including catalytic convertors, the use of unleaded petrol, and emission levels for vehicles in use. In particular, the annual MOT tests (and, more recently, roadside checks) have standards for smoke and carbon monoxide which must not be exceeded.

European policy on motor vehicles

The EC has combined policy with legislative initiatives on transport generally, and motor vehicles specifically, for some time (the earliest Directive on emissions from engines dates back to 1970). European transport policy is to be found in a Green Paper on the Impact of Transport on the Environment, adopted in 1992 (a policy which is due to be updated within the near future). UK policy mirrors the approach contained in this document with its integrated approach to transport policy ('sustainable mobility') with an increasing overlap between transport policy and other areas, such as planning and economic policy.

Vehicle emissions have been controlled under a number of increasingly complex amendments to the original controlling Directive 70/220. Generally, directives have set product standards by fixing emission limits for carbon monoxide, hydrocarbons, nitrogen dioxide and particulates. Various amendments have culminated in Directive 99/102 which sets out limits for cars and light vans which came into force in 1999. Emissions from larger vans and heavy duty vehicles are controlled under separate directives.

In addition to the fixed emission limits, there have been a number of directives controlling the roadworthiness of vehicles to ensure that the original product standards are being maintained. Directives 99/52 set out procedures for checking the roadworthiness of private cars. These Directives are implemented in UK legislation through the Construction and Use Regulations and the Type Approval Regulations (see above).

FIFTEEN
Statutory nuisance

The law of statutory nuisance represents a bridge between the private law of nuisance and the more characteristic statutory mechanisms. Like the various torts considered in Chapter 10, however, statutory nuisance really provides indirect protection for the environment, having developed as a public health mechanism. Nevertheless, there are many ways in which statutory nuisance can be used to combat environmental concerns such as air pollution or the deposit of sewage on beaches, and it is often used to deal with complaints about unacceptable noise levels. The main aim of the statutory nuisance provisions is to provide a quick and easy remedy to abate nuisances with which private law is too slow or too expensive to deal.

History and development of controls

Statutory nuisance law goes back a long way, dating back to public health statutes from 1848, 1855, 1860 and 1875. What underpinned these Acts was a desire to control matters which, although nuisances in the private law sense, were thought to affect sanitation levels and thus public health. It is worth mentioning, however, that before the discovery that diseases like cholera were spread contagiously (mainly through the water supply), the early Victorians laid the blame on foul air, or 'miasms'. Accordingly, this focused attention on things like drainage and the removal of all kinds of refuse (often into the nearest watercourse).

The Victorian legislation was consolidated in the Public Health Act 1936, and updated again, and further consolidated, in Part III of the Environmental Protection Act (EPA) 1990 (to which all references in this chapter relate unless otherwise indicated). This lineage means that even very old authorities may still be relevant, and in some cases even determinative (see, e.g. the meaning of 'premises'). It also means, however, that the boundaries of statutory nuisance tend to be fairly well-settled; this can make it difficult for statutory nuisance to evolve from its public health background into a more genuinely environmental protection mechanisms befitting its place within the EPA 1990.

The control of statutory nuisances

District councils, London borough councils and unitary authorities are under a duty periodically to inspect their areas for statutory nuisances. In addition, if an individual within an area complains of a statutory nuisance emanating from within that area then a district council is obliged to investigate a more responsive duty (s. 79). The EPA 1990 implies that the level of the local authorities general inspection duty is only to take such steps as are reasonably practicable. Although the duty imposed is only that inspection be periodic, it is clear that if there is strong evidence to suggest that a statutory nuisance exists within an area, and a local authority refuses to inspect, then it is possible that the remedy of judicial review will lie to any aggrieved applicant. It is important, therefore, for any individual wishing to complain to a local authority to ensure that proper evidence is gathered (e.g. dates, times and length of the nuisance if it has already occurred, or strong evidence to show that the statutory nuisance is about to occur). There are default powers under sch. 3, para. 4 which allow the Secretary of State to take action if local authorities are not carrying out their duty.

The general control of statutory nuisance is contained in s. 80. This provides that where a local authority is satisfied that a statutory nuisance exists, or is likely to occur or recur, it is under a mandatory duty to serve an abatement notice on the person responsible for the nuisance or, if that person cannot be found, the owner or occupier of the premises on which the statutory nuisance is present.

The nature of this duty was considered in *R v Carrick District Council, ex parte Shelley* [1996] Env LR 273. The applicants were two residents of a Cornish village. They complained to the council about discharges of sewage from two outlets some of which ended up on the village beach. Each outfall was subject to a discharge consent under the Water Resources Act 1991. The applicants asked the council to exercise its powers to deal with statutory nuisances. Instead of taking action the council resolved to do nothing (having taken into account the fact that the discharges of sewage were being considered by the Secretary of State in an appeal made by the relevant water company, South West Water). The applicants challenged this refusal by way of judicial review. It was held that the council was under a duty to investigate its area for the existence of statutory nuisances. Once it was found that a statutory nuisance existed, the council was under a duty to serve an abatement notice. Thus the council could not simply resolve to do nothing in the light of a determination that the statutory nuisance existed. A decision has to be made on the state of affairs which are before the council at any given time and it was not possible to wait for any anticipated improvements before coming to a view on the existence of a statutory nuisance.

In some situations, serving an abatement notice might be thought too blunt an instrument to resolve a situation which may have many underlying causes and involve other public bodies exercising their functions. In *R v Falmouth and Truro Port Health Authority, ex parte South West Water Ltd* [2000] NPC 36, for example, the statutory nuisance was sewage effluent being discharged by

South West Water, the sewerage undertaker for the area. The undertaker was acting under a discharge consent, and was also subject to a range of statutory duties concerning the environment and the adequate provision of sewerage services in its area. The wider problem was not one that could be resolved simply by turning the effluent pumps off and might have been thought a situation better resolved by co-operation rather than criminal enforcement. Nevertheless, the Court of Appeal refused to find that the enforcing authority needed to consult on possible abatement action. This might have been desirable as a matter of policy, but the Court of Appeal overruled the decision of the lower court that this might be required as a matter of legal fairness, a further decision emphasising the extent of the duties that local authorities have to abate statutory nuisances.

The categories of statutory nuisance

There are a number of categories of statutory nuisance contained in s. 79. These are supplemented by other statutes which declare specific categories to be a statutory nuisance and thus controlled under the provisions of the Act (s. 79(1)(h)). Much of the language used in s. 79 is somewhat antiquated and difficult to reconcile with modern technology. The categories of statutory nuisance are listed in the headings below. The Act lays down certain activities or states of affairs which will amount to a statutory nuisance if 'prejudicial to health or a nuisance'.

'Prejudicial to health or a nuisance'

The main criterion for the existence of a statutory nuisance is that anything complained of must be either 'prejudicial to health or a nuisance'. These are not to be read conjunctively.

'Prejudicial to health' is defined under s. 79(7) as meaning injurious, or likely to cause injury, to health. In *Coventry City Council* v *Cartwright* [1975] 1 WLR 845, the Council owned a vacant site within a residential area on which it allowed people to dump all sorts of materials. These included not only normal household refuse, but also building and construction materials. Occasionally, the Council would move household materials. A nearby resident complained of a statutory nuisance under the Public Health Act 1936. The Divisional Court held that, where the accumulation complained of was inert rather than putrescible, there was no likelihood of disease or that vermin would be attracted which could spread disease. Although there was a chance that physical injury could be caused to people who walked on the site, that did not amount to being prejudicial to health in the context of public health legislation. This approach has recently been confirmed in *R* v *Bristol City Council, ex parte Everett* [1999] Env LR 587, where steep stairs were held not to be prejudicial to the health of a tenant with a back injury.

In defining the word 'nuisance', it is generally accepted that the word contained within the EPA 1990 has the same definition as that under the common law. In *National Coal Board* v *Thorne* [1976] 1 WLR 543, the nuisance complained of amounted to defective guttering and windows within premises. The complainant argued that the physical condition of the building amounted to a nuisance under the Public Health Act. Watkins J said that a 'nuisance coming within the meaning of the Public Health Act 1936 must be either a public or private nuisance as understood by common law'. Thus, when deciding on the point of whether or not a statutory nuisance could arise when it was the inhabitants of premises who were suffering, such a state of affairs could not amount to nuisance because it was not an interference with the use or enjoyment of neighbouring property. Recent cases, however, indicate a relaxation of this requirement, so that there may be a nuisance where there is no emanation from one property affecting others (see *Network Housing Association Ltd* v *Westminster City Council* [1995] 93 LGR 280 and especially *Carr* v *London Borough of Hackney* [1995] Env LR 372).

Some cases suggest that the nuisance must involve some kind of personal discomfort, rather than any interference to property or its enjoyment as private nuisance requires. In *Wivenhoe Port Ltd* v *Colchester Borough Council* [1985] JPL 175 it was said that dust falling only on a garden would not be a statutory nuisance. In the *ex parte Shelley* case, discussed above, it was argued that the transfer of the statutory nuisance provisions from the Public Health Acts to the EPA 1990 meant that 'nuisance' should be given a wider meaning. The judge did not have to decide the issue, but it may well have to be decided in the future (see e.g. below, concerning sewers as premises).

It is now clear that whether something is prejudicial to health must be judged objectively. So in *Cunningham* v *Birmingham City Council* [1998] Env LR 1 the claims that a property was hazardous to an autistic child failed, since the property was not a statutory nuisance for an 'ordinary' child. As with the common law of nuisance, however, if the state of affairs would be prejudicial to the health of an ordinary person, it is no defence to say that the person affected is more than usually sensitive, e.g. someone with asthma suffering from dampness and mould (see also *Southwark Borough Council* v *Simpson* [1999] Env LR 553).

(a) Any premises in such a state as to be prejudicial to health or a nuisance

Section 79(1)(a) provides that where premises are kept in a state which is prejudicial to health or a nuisance then this will amount to a statutory nuisance. 'Premises' includes land and any vessel not powered by steam-reciprocating machinery. The physical extent of the premises must be viewed in context. In *Stevenage Borough Council* v *Wilson* [1993] Env LR 214, premises extended to the garden of a house where an abatement notice had included only the word 'dwelling'. The provision covers the physical state of premises rather than any use to which those premises are put. Therefore, where noise or dust etc. is emitted from those premises from a use, this is not covered. The aim is to prevent situations where there are physical elements which are either prejudicial to health or a nuisance.

The courts have always been reluctant to characterise sewers as 'premises'. This appears to have been for the policy reasons of not extending the scope of statutory nuisance provisions to public infrastructure works, or because by their nature sewers may have caused nuisances in the interest of preventing the spread of disease (the objective of the Public Health Acts). This approach has been continued in a recent case concerning a public sewer (*East Riding of Yorkshire Council* v *Yorkshire Water Services Ltd*, 23 March 2000, unreported). The case is notable because arguments that the law on statutory nuisance was now contained in an environmental statute were dismissed, and old authority relied upon.

Land, or water, in its 'natural' state is unlikely to amount to 'premises', so any nuisance caused simply by a natural build-up of, e.g. stagnant water is unlikely to be a statutory nuisance where the category of nuisance must involve premises (although it might well be a nuisance under other heads; see s. 79(1)(e) and (h) below).

Until recently the position was that exposure to traffic noise due to a lack of proper sound insulation of council-owned flats might be remedied by a statutory nuisance action (*Southwark London Borough Council* v *Ince* (1989) 21 HLR 504). But in *London Borough of Haringey* v *Jowett* [1999] NPC 52 it was held that the changes made under the Noise and Statutory Nuisance Act 1993 (see s. 79(1)(ga), below) not only extended statutory nuisances to include noise from vehicles in the street but at the same time completely excluded traffic noise from being a statutory nuisance. This is a rather surprising outcome, and appears to be heavily influenced by policy factors, especially cost implications for local authorities and the fact that the premises were otherwise of an acceptable standard. It also means that noise from railways can still be a statutory nuisance, a distinction that is irrelevant as far as human health or loss of amenity is concerned.

(b)   Smoke emitted from premises so as to be prejudicial to health or a nuisance
Section 79(1)(b) replaced the Clean Air Act 1956, s. 16, which previously made separate provision for the control of smoke from premises. There are exemptions contained within s. 79(3) so that:

(i)   smoke emitted from a chimney of a private dwelling within a smoke control area;
(ii)   dark smoke emitted from a chimney of a building, or a chimney serving the furnace of a boiler or industrial plant attached to a building, or for the time being installed on any land;
(iii)   smoke emitted from a railway locomotive steam engine;
(iv)   dark smoke emitted, otherwise than as mentioned above, from industrial or trade premises

will not be statutory nuisances.

(c)   Fumes or gases emitted from premises so as to be prejudicial to health or a nuisance
Section 79(1)(c) and (4) controls fumes or gases emitted from private dwellings. Fumes are defined as 'any airborne solid matter smaller than dust, gases including vapour and moisture precipitating from vapour' (s. 79(7)).

(d)   Any dust, steam, smell or other effluvia arising on industrial, trade or business premises and being prejudicial to health or a nuisance
The meanings of dust, steam and smell are fairly well established. However, the term 'effluvia' was defined in *Malton Board of Health* v *Malton Manure Co.* (1879) 4 ExD 302. This case involved the production of manure by the defendant company which produced vapours. It could not be conclusively demonstrated that these vapours were prejudicial to healthy people in the locality, although the Board of Health did demonstrate that it had the effect of making people who were ill more ill. The court held that this effect could amount to effluvia which were prejudicial to health. It is suggested that the meaning of effluvia covers the outflow of harmful or unpleasant substances.

(e)   Any accumulation or deposit which is prejudicial to health or a nuisance
To come within s. 79(1)(e), the accumulation or deposit has to be capable of causing disease rather than injury (see *Coventry City Council* v *Cartwright* [1975] 1 WLR 845, above). The wide range of accumulations or deposits covered by this section have included sheep dung (*Draper* v *Sperring* (1869) 10 CB 113) and cinders which emitted offensive smells (*Bishop Auckland Local Board* v *Bishop Auckland Iron and Steel Co.* (1882) 10 QBD 138). This section can also include discharges of sewage on beaches (see *R* v *Carrick District Council, ex parte Shelley* [1996] Env LR 273). The deposit does not need to be caused by human action, and the natural accumulation of a substance such as seaweed can amount to a statutory nuisance, so long as it causes illness (*Margate Pier* v *Town Council of Margate* (1869) 33 JP 437). What will be important in these cases is determining by whose 'default or sufferance' there has been the accumulation; will this be the landowner if a public body had a responsibility to prevent, say, the seaweed coming ashore and causing a nuisance?

(f)   Any animal kept in such a place or manner as to be prejudicial to health or a nuisance
The keeping of a large number of animals on premises can give rise to a number of different enforcement actions. First, the keeping of a large number of animals may amount to sufficient intensification of a use to give rise to a change of use, which could result in enforcement action under the Town and Country Planning Act 1990 (see *Wallington* v *Secretary of State for Wales* (1990) 62 P & CR 150). Secondly, there may be common law actions which could be brought for nuisance. Thirdly, there could be action taken by the local authority under by-laws passed under the Public Health Act 1936, s. 81(2), and finally, there could be action taken under the statutory nuisance provisions of s. 79(1)(f).

(g)   Noise emitted from premises so as to be prejudicial to health or a nuisance
Section 79(1)(g) replaced that part of Part III of the Control of Pollution Act 1974 dealing with noise from premises. Noise here includes vibration (general

problem issues in relation to quantifying noise nuisance are discussed below). Noise from model aircraft is included; otherwise aircraft noise is excluded (s. 79(6)). The difference between sub-section (g) and s. 79(1)(a) is that the focus is on the premises where the noise comes from rather than the premises affected by noise. It has been held (in the Crown Court) that if noise levels fall within advisory standards (e.g. BS 8233) then, despite well-founded complaints, the action was not well founded (*London Borough of Lewisham* v *Fenner* (1995) 248 ENDS Report 44). There seems to be no principled reason, however, why this should be taken as a general rule.

(h)   Noise that is prejudicial to health or a nuisance and is emitted from or caused by a vehicle, machinery or equipment in a street
Section 79(1)(ga) was added by the Noise and Statutory Nuisance Act 1993 to deal with certain kinds of street noise. It does not apply to noise made by traffic (see *London Borough of Haringey* v *Jowett* [1999] NPC 52, discussed above), the armed forces or political or other demonstrations. Because it is not concerned with 'premises', slightly different procedures apply to things like identifying the person responsible, and the service of abatement notices.

(i)   Smoke, fumes or gases emitted from any vehicle, machinery or equipment on a street so as to be prejudicial to health or a nuisance
This provision, which does not apply to any vehicle, machinery or equipment being used for fire brigade purposes, only applies in London boroughs (see s. 79(1)(gb), and the London Local Authorities Act 1996, s. 24). However, a significant exclusion is that it does not apply to smoke, fumes or gases emitted from vehicle exhaust systems (s. 6B), which are regulated under specific statutory provisions (see p. 431).

(j)   Any other matter declared by any enactment to be a statutory nuisance
This provision (s. 79(1)(h)) is to include any statutory nuisance provided for under future statutes. It also includes nuisances from mines, shafts and quarries under the Mines and Quarries Act 1954, s. 151, and various nuisances from the condition of ditches, ponds etc and certain watercourses (see further p. 605).

What is required to satisfy the local authority?

In practice, it is the responsibility of the local environmental health officer to decide whether or not a statutory nuisance is occurring or is likely to occur. As has been stated, the test is whether or not a statutory nuisance is prejudicial to health or a nuisance. An environmental health officer will visit the premises and make an objective decision as to whether or not the state of the premises or anything on those premises amounts to a nuisance. When reverting to the common law for the definition of nuisance, it is up to the environmental health officer to balance the many different factors used when deciding on whether or not a common law nuisance exists. The most important of these factors are:

(a)   the nature and the location of the nuisance;
(b)   the time and duration of the nuisance; and
(c)   the utility of the activity concerned.

Balancing all these factors together is the only way in which an environmental health officer can make an adjudication between respective neighbours' rights, because it is quite clear that a statutory nuisance will only apply to affected neighbours' properties. If the complaint is about prejudice to health, then the environmental health officer will need to have suitable training in the relation between the conditions of premises and ill health, although this does not mean that a medical qualification is needed (*Southwark Borough Council v Simpson* [1999] Env LR 553).

Section 80(1) provides that for a local authority to act, the statutory nuisance must exist or be likely to occur or recur. Although statutory nuisance law has a criminal enforcement mechanism, the local authority must be satisfied only on the balance of probabilities. In the case of anticipated nuisances, however, there must be evidence that the forthcoming activity is likely to give rise to a statutory nuisance, which may be a high hurdle to overcome. However, where these problems can be overcome, such as in the case of a party where there is more than a suggestion that powerful audio equipment will be used, this may well be the only method of prohibiting certain types of nuisances in advance. Where a local authority has delegated enforcement powers to individual officers then those officers are able to carry out the enforcement procedures on behalf of the local authority.

Who is the 'person responsible'?

The enforcement of a statutory nuisance is normally against the 'person responsible', which is defined in s. 79(7) as being 'the person to whose act, default or sufferance the nuisance is attributable'. This is a particularly wide definition and can include a local authority (see *Rossall* v *London Borough of Southwark*, unreported), or a landlord who has allowed a tenant to carry on offensive activities, and can include those who fail to abate nuisances which arise naturally (*Margate Pier* v *Town Council of Margate* (1869) 33 JP 437). It can also include a tenant who has denied access to a landlord who wished to carry out works to abate a nuisance (see *Carr* v *London Borough of Hackney* [1995] Env LR 372). However, the courts will look to see whether there has been some failure to meet acceptable standards, e.g. sound insulation standards at the time of construction (see *Salford City Council* v *McNally* [1976] AC 379; *London Borough of Haringey* v *Jowett* [1999] NPC 52). This is motivated by policy concerns, especially about resources, which would be irrelevant in a common law nuisance claim.

If there are any difficulties in locating the 'person responsible' for the existence of a statutory nuisance, s. 80(2)(c) states that the definition of the person responsible can be extended to include the owner or occupier of the premises in question.

The abatement notice

Once the local authority, through its environmental health officers, is satisfied that a statutory nuisance exists, it is under a duty to serve an abatement notice which must require any or all of the following:

(a)   the abatement of the nuisance or the prohibiting or restricting of its occurrence or recurrence;
(b)   the execution of works or other steps necessary to comply with the notice.

There has been some uncertainty about precisely what this provision means. It has always been clear that there are some kinds of statutory nuisances where the local authority can, in the abatement notice, simply require the cessation of the nuisance. For example, an abatement notice can simply state that the nuisance is 'dogs barking', and leave it to the recipient of the notice to choose the most desirable manner of abatement (*Budd v Colchester Borough Council* [1999] Env LR 739). In noise nuisance cases, e.g. it might be noted that the abatement notice does not need to specify maximum noise levels (see *East Northamptonshire District Council v Fossett* [1994] Env LR 388) and even if it does, this does not necessarily amount to specifying 'steps' which need to be taken (*Sevenoaks District Council v Brands Hatch Leisure Group Ltd*, 8 May 2000, unreported). On the other hand, it is clear that if works *are* specified in the abatement notice, the requirement must be clear and precise as the recipient needs to know what must be done to comply. This is because criminal sanctions apply if the notice is breached (see *Sterling Homes v Birmingham County Council* [1996] Env LR 121). A letter accompanying an abatement notice can, if it specifies works, mean that an otherwise silent abatement notice can be construed as requiring works (*Camden London Borough Council v London Underground Ltd* [2000] Env LR 369).

However, certain cases suggested that there could be situations where the notice would *have to* stipulate the works required. Thus in *Kirklees Metropolitan Council v Field & Others* [1998] Env LR 337, a case about a rock-face and wall which were in imminent danger of collapsing on to a row of cottages, the Court of Appeal held that by not specifying the necessary works the abatement notice was invalid. In contrast to cases like *Budd*, where the nuisance could be abated by some activity being stopped, in *Kirklees* it was obvious that major works of a positive nature were necessary, and the Court held that these should have been specified. The same approach was originally taken in *R v Falmouth and Truro Port Health Authority, ex parte South West Water Ltd* [2000] NPC 36 (see above), where the High Court held that the abatement notice had to say what the sewerage undertaker should do to abate the nuisance because the problem could not be abated simply by turning off the effluent pumps. In the Court of Appeal, however, the *Kirklees* case was overruled and it was held that local authorities could not as a rule be obliged to specify works where work was needed. Instead, as where works did not need to be undertaken, the recipient of the notice should be free to choose their own course of action, so long as in doing so they would comply with the abatement notice.

The Court of Appeal did indicate, however, that there might be extreme cases where this general principle might not be appropriate. The recipient will, of course, always be best placed to choose the method of abatement on grounds of cost and convenience. However, it is at least arguable that where works require considerable technical expertise, then it might be a relevant factor whether the recipient can reasonably be expected to have knowledge of this, or know where to obtain it. In cases like *Kirklees*, therefore, knowledge of what was needed to abate the nuisance might be seen as beyond the reach of the residents of the cottages, and therefore something on which they should properly be advised by the local authority. Thus, it might still be appropriate to distinguish between cases according to the relative degree of awareness and technical expertise as between the local authority and the recipient.

Finally, there is no requirement that the notice be corroborated by evidence of a particular occupier who has suffered unreasonable interference with the enjoyment of property (see *Cooke* v *Adatia* (1988) 153 JP 129). The notice should specify the time within which compliance is required.

Where an individual has been served with an abatement notice, the contravention of that notice, without reasonable excuse, makes that person guilty of a criminal offence under s. 80(4). The criminal nature of statutory nuisance is an obvious contrast with the civil law of private nuisance. It means that the criminal standard of proof applies at the enforcement stage, and also that compensation payments under criminal law may be payable, although they are rarely ordered (but see *Botross* v *London Borough of Hammersmith and Fulham* [1995] Env LR 217; *Davenport* v *Walsall Metropolitan Borough Council* [1997] Env LR 24). Once a notice is served it takes effect in perpetuity even in the case of a notice served under the old Control of Pollution Act powers (see *Aitken* v *South Hams District Council* [1994] 2 All ER 400).

'Reasonable excuse'

Part III of the EPA 1990 is somewhat unusual in that having a 'reasonable excuse' for carrying out the activity which results in the contravention is not a *defence* to an offence committed under s. 80(4) but rather a component part of the offence itself. If there is a reasonable excuse, the offence is simply not made out (for a contrast, see the offence of polluting controlled waters under the Water Resources Act 1991, s. 85). The importance of this is that if the defendant puts forward an excuse, the burden is on the local authority to show, on the criminal standard, that it is not reasonable (see *Polychronakis* v *Richards and Jerrom Ltd* [1998] Env LR 346).

The test laid down for this would seem to be an objective one, i.e. 'would a reasonable person think that the excuse given was consistent with a reasonable standard of conduct?'. The defence is not available where an abatement notice has been contravened deliberately and intentionally in circumstances wholly under the control of the defendant. Thus, a defendant

could not argue that because there had been a three-year gap between the
service of an abatement notice and its breach and no one had complained
about the breach as it was of minimum inconvenience, there was a 'reasonable excuse' (*Wellingborough Borough Council* v *Gordon* [1993] Env LR 218).
It is not sufficient to say that there would be a defence to a private law action
in nuisance. Indeed, in *A. Lambert Flat Management Ltd* v *Lomas* [1981] 1
WLR 898, it was said that COPA 1974, s. 58(4) was designed to provide a
defence to a criminal charge where an individual had some reasonable excuse,
such as some special difficulty in relation to compliance with the abatement
notice. It was not an opportunity to challenge the notice; that should only
properly be done on an appeal (see, in relation to the EPA 1990, *AMEC
Building Ltd* v *London Borough of Camden* [1997] Env LR 330).

Defences

The EPA 1990 does contain some defences where there is an offence under
s. 80(4).

(a) Best practicable means
Where an abatement notice is served on trade or business premises and the
nuisance complained of is caused in the course of the trade or business, it is
a defence under certain heads of s. 79(1), to show that the best practicable
means have been used to prevent or counteract the nuisance (s. 80(7)). This
does not apply to fumes or gases emitted from premises (s. 79(1)(c)), or the
provision under s. 79(1)(h) relating to nuisances in other statutes. Although
there is not any complete definition contained within the EPA 1990, certain
elements are required to be taken into account under s. 79(9). These include
local conditions and circumstances, the current state of technical knowledge,
the financial implications, and the design, installation, maintenance, manner
and periods of operation of plant and machinery.

The defence has to be established on a balance of probabilities, and the
burden of proof lies on the defendant to show that it had taken reasonable
steps to prevent or counteract the nuisance. Thus, where a defendant had
submitted a planning application for noise reducing bunding to counteract a
noise nuisance, but failed to answer the local planning authority's request for
further information, it failed to discharge the burden of proof that it was using
best practicable means to prevent or counteract the nuisance (*Chapman* v
Gosberton Farm Produce Co. Ltd [1993] Env LR 191).

The extent of the defence, and thus a limitation of statutory nuisance, is
illustrated in *Manley* v *New Forest District Council* (29 July 1999, unreported)
where an abatement notice was served against a dog breeding establishment
following complaints about noise. The best practicable means were already
being used at the premises to restrict noise levels, but the Crown Court
thought that moving the establishment to a non-residential area could be
included within best practicable means. The High Court disagreed, in effect
holding that statutory nuisance law is intended to regulate existing trade or
business premises, and not to engage in industrial relocation.

(b)   Special defences

There are specific defences available in relation to noise and nuisances on construction sites and in areas where there are registered noise levels under the noise abatement zone procedure (see EPA 1990, s. 80(9) and COPA, ss. 60, 61 and 65–67, discussed further at p. 457).

The right of appeal against an abatement notice

Where an individual is served with an abatement notice there is a right of appeal against the notice to a magistrates' court. One advantage of the appeal system over a defence to a prosecution under contravention proceedings is that it allows for a far greater range of appeal grounds and therefore provides a greater scope for disputing the nuisance. An appeal normally lies within 21 days of the service of the notice. The grounds of appeal are set down in regulations made under EPA 1990. The Statutory Nuisance (Appeals) Regulations 1995 (SI 1995/2644) set out the grounds of appeal against an abatement notice, which include:

(a)   that the abatement notice is not justified in the terms of s. 80;

(b)   that there has been a substantive or procedural error in the service of the notice;

(c)   that the authority has unreasonably refused to accept compliance with alternative requirements, or that its requirements are unreasonable or unnecessary;

(d)   that the period for compliance is unreasonable;

(e)   that the best practicable means were used to counteract the effect of a nuisance from trade or business premises.

Furthermore, the regulations allow for the suspension of an abatement notice pending the court's decision, unless the local authority overrides the suspension in the abatement notice with a statement to the effect that the notice is to have effect regardless, and that:

(a)   the nuisance is prejudicial to health;

(b)   suspension would render the notice of no practical effect (e.g. where nuisances are to cease before the action can be heard in court); or

(c)   any expenditure incurred before an appeal would be disproportionate to the public benefit.

Individual actions by any person

It is often the case that local authorities' environmental health departments are overworked and understaffed and have neither the resources nor sometimes the inclination to deal with disputes regarding statutory nuisances. Section 82 allows a complaint to be made to a local magistrates' court by any person who is aggrieved by the existence of a statutory nuisance. This procedure allows for any person within an area to bring a more affordable and expeditious proceeding than a private law action. Ironically, complaints are most frequently made against local authorities about the poor state of their housing.

One particular limitation upon this procedure is that the nuisance must be in existence and therefore cannot be used to anticipate problems. Therefore, a person has no right of action under this section to stop a nuisance which is likely to occur in the future (e.g. loud parties). If the person can satisfy the magistrates that there is an existing nuisance, or that there is likely to be a recurring nuisance, they are under a duty to issue an abatement notice requiring the defendant to abate the nuisance within a specified time, and to execute any works necessary for that purpose and/or prohibiting a recurrence of the nuisance, and requiring the defendant, within a specified time, to carry out any works necessary to prevent the recurrence. The magistrates may fine a defendant up to £5,000 for non-compliance (s. 82(2)). There is a notice procedure, which differs slightly from that which governs local authority actions, in that s. 80(6) provides that where an individual is bringing an action they must give not less than three days' notice in relation to a noise nuisance and, in relation to other statutory nuisances, 21 days' notice, before the bringing of proceedings under s. 80(2).

Section 82(12) provides that if a complaint is brought while the statutory nuisance exists then the person complaining is entitled to the costs of any expenses properly incurred, even if the nuisance is abated by the time of any hearing. In *R v Dudley Magistrates Court, ex parte Hollis* [1998] Env LR 354 the court interpreted this strictly in favour of the complainants, an important decision which could mean that complaints under s. 82 will be taken more readily.

Sentencing powers for contravention of an abatement notice

Section 80(5) and (6) provide for penalties for a person who is guilty of an offence of contravening an abatement notice. The matter is triable only in the magistrates' court and, if found guilty, a private offender is liable to a maximum fine of £5,000. If the offence continues after the conviction they are liable to a further fine not exceeding £500 for each day on which the offence continues. The previous levels of fine included under the Public Health Act and Control of Pollution Act indicated that for major industrial uses there were no real disincentives to carry out works to improve premises. Indeed, it was often cost effective to pay fines at a low level in order to ensure that a particular activity could be carried on rather than abated. Section 80(6) closes this particular loophole by imposing a maximum fine of £20,000 on industrial, trade or business offenders. In addition to these sanctions, the magistrates have a 'discretion to award compensation' up to a maximum of £5,000.

The use of injunctions and proceedings in the High Court

In many cases the provisions of s. 80 would not provide an adequate remedy in terms of either gravity or speed. Under s. 81(5), a local authority may take action in the High Court for the purpose of securing the abatement, prohibition or restriction of any statutory nuisance where it is of the opinion that proceedings for an offence of contravening an abatement notice would not provide a sufficient remedy. The usual method for doing this would be by seeking an injunction in the High Court. In *Hammersmith London Borough Council* v *Magnum Automated Forecourts Ltd* [1978] 1 WLR 50, the Court of Appeal decided that this was an additional power to that contained under the statutory noise nuisance provisions contained within COPA 1974 (and now contained in the EPA 1990, s. 79(1)(g)). Thus, the right to take proceedings in the High Court could be used after an abatement notice had been served, but before the prosecution for contravention had been heard, in order to expedite the cessation of the nuisance.

The scope for injunctions has widened considerably with the decision in *Lloyds Bank* v *Guardian Assurance* (1987) 35 BLR 34, which stated that the jurisdiction of the High Court was not affected by any proceedings under the statutory nuisance provisions of COPA 1974. The real effect of this decision has been to suggest that it will not be open to any individual to apply for an injunction under the common law which is in stricter terms than any abatement notice which has already been served under COPA 1974 or the EPA 1990. However, it is open to the local authority to tighten up on a weak abatement notice by applying for an injunction in the High Court under s. 81(5). In such proceedings it will be a defence to prove that noise was authorised by a construction site consent under COPA 1974, s. 61.

Injunctions are a discretionary remedy and will not be granted lightly. The activity complained of must be of sufficient gravity and/or duration to justify stopping it (*Goldsmith* v *Tunbridge Wells Improvement Commission* (1866) LR 1 Ch App 349).

The powers available to local authorities may flow from primary statute (e.g. EPA 1990) or from s. 222 of the Local Government Act 1972. This general power is available only in circumstances where the local authority has expressly considered that the powers available under the specific provisions would afford an inadequate remedy (see *Vale of White Horse District Council* v *Allen & Partners* [1997] Env LR 212).

SIXTEEN
Noise

The most frequent use of the law relating to statutory nuisance contained in Part III of the EPA 1990, and discussed in the previous chapter, is to control noise. However, as in other areas of environmental law, noise is controlled by a variety of standards, not just the flexible standards of nuisance law. This chapter considers these other mechanisms, which include a range of product and process controls, as well as controls on noise in particular areas or from particular activities. As with statutory nuisance, it is worth noting that the legal controls discussed here are often found in controls relating to public health, and in some cases from the realm of public order legislation. In this sense they are not tailored environmental controls, but may indirectly regulate ambient noise levels more generally.

Noise and its perception

Noise is now regarded as a serious object of concern. Complaints about noise nuisance to local authorities in England and Wales have risen dramatically over recent years, from just over 55,370 in 1980 to 232,437 in 1995/6. By far the largest numeric and percentage increases have been in relation to domestic noise. The Chartered Institute of Environmental Health has described this rise as 'apparently inexorable', although figures for 1996/7 (242,181 complaints) suggest a levelling off in the number of complaints overall. However, these figures reflect the fact that they are made to environmental health officers and so, although they do include complaints about things like road traffic and aircraft noise, it is highly likely that these will be under-represented relative to the extent to which they create a problem.

As an object of regulation, 'noise pollution' poses some particular problems, the most important being as follows:

(a) Other than in severe cases, the effects of noise are experienced subjectively. The sound of music coming from a neighbouring property may be enjoyed or it may be suffered.

(b)   What is important about noise levels is the level where the sound is heard, not where it is produced. (Indeed, 'noise' without a hearer is just vibration.) In this sense most noise standards are ambient standards, although some emissions standards regulate the sound made by objects like aircraft and lawnmowers.

(c)   Related to this, noise will be experienced differently according to changing lifestyles. For example, as the 'rush hour' lengthens, the burden of noise pollution is increased, even though the area may not change in character and sound insulation levels remain the same. Noise which is normal for the daytime may cause disturbance to those who work at home or at nights. The '24 hour society' undoubtedly creates noise problems.

(d)   It is not simply the level of noise that may cause annoyance. Low whines and repetitive sounds may irritate as much as ill-tempered car horns.

All these features are captured by the non-statutory definition of noise as 'sound which is undesired by the recipient' (*Final Report of the Parliamentary Committee on the Problem of Noise*, Cmnd 2056, 1963, the 'Wilson Committee'). It is this inherently subjective nature that means that any statistics about noise pollution must be handled cautiously. For example, in 1995/6 just less than 30 per cent of complaints were confirmed as nuisances. Bearing in mind the subjective nature of nuisance, it is still revealing that there appears to be a steady decline over recent years in the percentage of confirmed nuisances as a fraction of the total number of complaints, the proportion of unsubstantiated complaints rising significantly in 1996/7 to over 80 per cent. As the Chartered Institute of Environmental Health comments: 'Whether this indicates that nuisance is no longer the appropriate standard to use or that the public has unrealistic expectations of the noise climate is unclear' (Annual Report 1997, p. 4)

Particularly telling is the relative rise in the number of complaints about domestic noise nuisance. In 1983/4 these were roughly equal to the number of complaints about industrial and commercial noise. By 1995/6, noise from domestic sources accounted for more than the number of complaints from all other recognised categories of noise combined. This has led some, e.g. Fitzpatrick, to argue that 'It would appear that it is less noise in itself that is the problem, but much more that it is coming from next door, or at least that it is more legitimate to complain about it' (see bibliography). The same care must be taken with statistics about the number of noise-related deaths, of which around 20 have been reported in recent years. There is a tendency to report a noise disturbance as the cause of such incidents, rather than as one aspect of much more bitter and tragic neighbour disputes.

Policy approaches

A feature of noise pollution is that it is transient rather than persistent: noise does not accumulate in the environment the way that toxic chemicals do. This has consequences both for the setting and the enforcement of noise controls. Beyond simple tolerance, noise levels can be controlled at two main points:

(a)   where it is produced, through preventive standards. These centre around standards for the decibel levels of manufactured goods; and

(b)   *en route* to the hearer, by some form of barrier. This can be a physical barrier such as sound insulation, or a roadside embankment to muffle traffic noise. Or it may be a spatial barrier such as the separation of the source of the noise from those likely to be affected. This is the realm of planning controls, and planning guidance seeks to separate noise generating and noise sensitive developments.

The after-effects of noise pollution cannot be measured in quite the same way that the consequences of a water pollution incident can be. This also has an impact on the use of strategic mechanisms since, regardless of the subjective experience of noise, it is still much more difficult to categorise any particular area as 'noisy' than, e.g. to categorise a river as of 'poor quality' or land as 'contaminated'. Nevertheless, the general policy approach has been the use of environmental quality standards through nuisance-based controls. In relation to enforcement, this means measuring noise at the time and at the point at which it is experienced, or producing other evidence which attests to the nature of the noise. It also means that, in appropriate situations, emissions standards on machinery or products may be used. These reduce enforcement costs, but the tendency has been to use them selectively.

The development of statutory controls

Statutory controls over noise emissions have been relatively late in coming. Noise nuisances were dealt with in some local Acts and in by-laws, but problems tended to be left to individually initiated action. Private law remedies were generally relied on, although in the case of aircraft noise these were *removed* quite early on under the Air Navigation Act 1920. The Noise Abatement Act 1960 was the first general Act on noise control, although this only added certain noise nuisances to the range of statutory nuisances controllable under public health law (and now regulated under Part III of the EPA 1990, see Chapter 15). Following the report of the Scott Committee on *Neighbourhood Noise* in 1971, further controls on noise were introduced in Part III of the Control of Pollution Act 1974, which introduced provisions on street noise, noise from construction sites and noise abatement zone provisions.

There has never been consolidated legislation on noise, no doubt partly because noise controls are often one aspect of wider legislative provisions. This is certainly the case with a number of public order controls under general criminal justice and other 'behaviour control' legislation. But it also applies to quite a wide range of noise provisions in, e.g. the Civil Aviation Act 1978 and the Road Traffic Act 1988 (and to worker safety legislation and entertainment controls, which are outside the scope of this chapter). The impact of EC law has largely been in regulating the free movement of an odd assortment of goods under directives that contain what are in effect noise emission standards. The net result is an incomplete, incoherent and unprincipled body of law, an 'ugly mosaic of separate legal controls' (McManus and

Burns, 'The Impact of EC Law on Noise Law in the United Kingdom', in Holder (ed.) *The Impact of EC Environmental Law in the United Kingdom* (Wiley, 1997, p. 185)) which makes classification difficult. However, there are moves to integrate the control of noise emissions with other pollutants, such as under the EIA and IPPC Directives.

International law and noise

Because of its subjective and localised nature, the impact of international law on noise pollution has been comparatively slight. What is of most importance, however, is the way in which international regimes effect hard legal standards. This is the case with the 1944 Chicago Convention on International Civil Aviation, which established the International Civil Aviation Organisation. Annex 16 of the Convention effectively lays down standards for aircraft noise, which are translated into EC directives that oblige Member States to comply with these standards, and the revisions to them that are made every few years. A 'softer' example is provided by the World Health Organisation's standards for noise. Although these cannot be enforced directly, they play an important role in practice when, for example, common law or statutory nuisance actions are being brought. However, the mere fact that noise exceeds WHO levels may not in itself be sufficient to found a claim of nuisance, if the noise is judged reasonable in all the circumstances (*Murdoch* v *Glacier Metal Co. Ltd* [1998] Env LR 732).

The EC and noise

At EC level, although the available data on noise exposure is relatively poor, it has been estimated that around 20 per cent of the EC's population (around 80 million people) suffer from noise levels considered to be unacceptable. An additional 170 million citizens live in so-called 'grey areas' where noise levels cause serious annoyance during the daytime.

Existing environmental noise control legislation generally stems from the Second Environmental Action Programme (1977–81) and can be divided into four categories of product-focused provisions relating to construction plant; aircraft; household appliances; and permissible sound levels and exhaust systems for motor vehicles. These provisions are essentially concerned with the free movement of goods, with technical harmonisation of standards being the basic approach. However, even as regards product standards, regulation of noise is far from comprehensive, being described as no more than a 'regulatory patchwork' (Rehbinder and Stewart, *Environmental Protection Policy*, de Gruyter, 1985, p. 203). Standards are generally highly specific, giving rise to the possibility of challenges to the non-enforcement of directives, although in the case of noise emissions from household appliances, Directive 86/594 is an information-providing mechanism under which noise levels are labelled and other information about noise levels of products made available.

A good example of how noise directives operate can be seen in relation to directives that regulate sound levels from motor vehicles under Directive

70/157, as amended. Member states may not refuse to grant EC or national type-approval to vehicles or exhaust systems, or restrict their free movement, if the requirements of the directive are met. But in *R v London Boroughs Transport Committee, ex parte Freight Transport Association Ltd* [1991] 1 WLR 828, the House of Lords held that a distinction was to be made between controlling the free circulation of vehicles manufactured in accordance with the directive, and legitimate traffic control measures, and allowed the latter (see also *R v London Borough of Greenwich* (1996) 255 ENDS Report 49).

An illustration of how EC noise law (in this case, Directive 80/51 on noise from subsonic aircraft) works alongside rules on free movement of goods is Case C-389/96 *Aher-Waggon GmbH v Germany* [1998] ECRI-4473. The standards in the directive are formulated as minimum requirements, and the Court held that a Member State could provide for stricter measures on the grounds of public health or environmental protection so long as these did not constitute an unjustified barrier to trade. A German national measure which prohibited the registration, after the coming into force of the Directive, of aircraft falling below this stricter standard, was not therefore disproportionate, even if aircraft in the national fleet of a similar specification could retain their registration. The national policy of seeking to reduce aircraft noise over time justified the provision.

At EC level the wider environmental impact of noise pollution has generally avoided regulation, and neighbourhood noise has generally been seen as a local problem for which EC action would be inappropriate. But there is now a Green Paper on a *Future Noise Policy* (COM(96)540) which builds on a number of basic targets set out in the Fifth Environmental Action Programme for reducing exposure to noise by 2000. The Green Paper emphasises product-based and information provisions, but in some areas, such as rail noise, emission limit values are considered. Specific changes to controls over noise emissions from construction plant and outdoor equipment are recommended. It seems clear that any move to a more environmentally-based noise policy will both mark a significant departure from a concern with the free movement of goods and services, and raise serious scrutiny in the light of subsidiarity.

Domestic controls over noise

In addition to controls under statutory nuisance and under the common law of nuisance, there is a range of other national controls on noise. The approach taken here is to look first at the remaining provisions, other than those contained in the EPA 1990, that are most central to regulating neighbourhood noise, before considering controls on noise from specific sources; preventive and strategic controls; and overlapping controls.

Further controls on neighbourhood noise

There are a range of statutory provisions which govern neighbourhood noise. While some of these provisions relate to 'neighbour-type' disputes, there is an increasing tendency to regulate noise more generally.

(a)   Night noise

The stated purpose behind the Noise Act 1996 is to make it easier to take action against night noise disturbances. To this end, a new criminal offence has been created. The offence is committed if, after a warning, a person is responsible for the emission of noise from a dwelling between 11pm and 7am and the noise level (in the complainant's dwelling) is above prescribed levels. The test for whether a person is responsible is the same as that used in statutory nuisance. The prescribed levels are set out in Circular 8/97, and provide that the noise level must be at least 35 decibels, if the underlying noise level is 25 decibels or less. Alternatively, if the background noise level is above 25 decibels, then the noise being emitted must be at least 10 decibels above that. To give an indication of how loud this is, the sound of an ordinary bedroom at night is around 25 decibels, and the sound of a library about 40 decibels. An increase of 10 decibels is approximately a doubling of loudness. The offence attracts a fine of up to £1000, a £100 on-the-spot fixed penalty notice and the summary seizure by the local authority of the sound equipment. There is a defence of proving there is a reasonable excuse for the noise.

There are three key features about the Noise Act 1996. First, it differs from nuisance law in that the determination of whether there is a nuisance is judged according to more or less objective standards. While the locality of the area is taken into account by reference to underlying noise levels, the way in which this is done is much less flexible. Many of the factors taken into account in nuisance law — such as duration and the nature of the activity causing the nuisance — are effectively ignored. Secondly, there is a clear break between an essentially civil (or civil-cum-criminal) law approach and the full use of criminal law sanctions. Third, the 1996 Act only applies in areas where the local authority has adopted its provisions, and the local authority has an absolute discretion whether to do so. In this respect the Act is reminiscent of many of the early planning and environmental statutory provisions. It is revealing that by June 1999, only nine local authorities had adopted the powers. A central reason appears to be that the 1996 Act really covers little that could not be regulated under ordinary statutory nuisance law. It is also more draining on local authority budgets, since the duty to investigate complaints must be complied with immediately the complaint is made: authorities cannot wait until the following day when environmental health staff are paid on ordinary rates. There must also be a question mark as to whether environmental health officers are generally enthusiastic about the use of inflexible standards in this area.

(b)   Housing Act 1996

Part V of the Housing Act 1996 makes it easier for both social and private landlords to evict tenants causing 'nuisance and annoyance' to neighbours. This extends to nuisance arising from a tenant's behaviour anywhere in the locality. As with the Noise Act 1996, a key approach is to amend the relevant procedural requirements. The Housing Act 1996 therefore makes it easier to possess noise-making equipment, and provides for the use of 'professional' local authority witnesses, so that those affected do not need to give evidence.

(c)   Anti-social behaviour orders

The Crime and Disorder Act 1998 came into force on 1 April 1999. Section 1 provides for antisocial behaviour orders to combat threatening and disruptive antisocial behaviour which causes, or is likely to cause, harassment, alarm and distress. The orders are ostensibly designed to curb disorder on estates and in communities, rather than to be used in disputes between neighbours. Although they can be used even where one person is affected, strongly worded Home Office guidance counsels against their use in pure neighbour disputes. They may well be sought, however, where there is serious street noise disturbance, since this is not regulated by statutory nuisance provisions. The orders can be sought by a local authority in consultation with a chief police officer, or vice versa, and are made by the magistrates' courts. To this extent they are civil powers, and civil standards of proof apply when they are being sought, but breach of an order is a criminal offence punishable by up to five years' imprisonment or an unlimited fine. Antisocial behaviour orders have been roundly condemned for the inroads they make on civil liberties, and for their rather pernicious blend of civil and criminal provisions.

Noise from specific sources

There is a patchy collection of provisions that regulate noise from specific sources. These tend to control things like noise from outdoor sources such as construction sites and transport, or be reactions to public order concerns such as raves. There is no common approach taken. Controls include 'stop' and notice provisions, licensing, product and specification standards. It might be noted that noise generally from industrial premises is not regulated as a specific object of control.

(a)   Construction noise

There are powers given to local authorities under COPA 1974 for the control of noise from construction sites. Sections 59A, 60 and 61 allow councils to serve notices imposing requirements about the way that work is carried out. These may include quite prescriptive conditions about the type of plant and machinery used, but conditions about the time the noise is emitted and its level are more usually imposed. It is a criminal offence to contravene such a notice without reasonable excuse, but it is a defence that the work was carried out under a consent issued under s. 61. Such consents may be applied for in advance of construction work being carried out, which avoids changes to the work being needed because a notice is served after the work has begun. It is a criminal offence to carry out works or knowingly permit works to be carried out which contravene a consent. Such consents are, however, rarely sought, the fear being that stricter standards will be imposed in advance compared with those which might be imposed under notice once the work has begun (see *Report of the Noise Review Working Party*, 1990), an example of the law's reluctance to disturb activities on environmental grounds once wealth generation has begun.

(b) Transport noise

Transport noise, especially from road traffic and from aircraft, has the capacity to cause noise levels which seriously damage quality of life and which are therefore incompatible with sustainable development (see *Transport and the Environment*, Royal Commission on Environmental Pollution, Eighteenth Report, Cm 2674, 1994, paras. 4.4 to 4.17). Because of their mobile nature, specification and emission standards are often used, while other source-based approaches used include things like speed restrictions and curbs on night flights, although a small number of 'barrier' or 'separation' controls are also used. In practice, planning controls are probably as important a mechanism as any in regulating traffic noise, since these are crucial in determining exposure to noise. As a matter of planning policy, however, it appears that there is an emphasis on locating noise-sensitive developments away from noisy areas or activities (planning controls are discussed in more detail on p. 458). As a general point it is probably better to label emission controls on vehicles as regulations about vehicle noise rather than traffic noise, since they have no direct bearing on overall noise levels and can be rendered ineffective through increases in traffic levels.

(i)   Road traffic noise
Road traffic noise comes mainly from engine noise and from the impact of tyres on the road surface. Noises from these sources are mainly tackled by a mixture of legislatively prescribed design standards and emission limits. EC law has been important here, although not always to tighten standards. The impact of Directive 70/157 in the UK was to tighten noise limits slightly for cars, but relax standards for buses and lorries (on this directive see also p. 132). Since then, however, EC directives have imposed more stringent standards over time (see Directives 77/212, 81/334, 84/372, 84/424, 92/97), leading to a near halving of 'noise values' for cars from 82 dB(A) in 1970 to 74 dB(A) in 1992 (dB(A) being a decibel measure of loudness). This is not to say, however, that there has been a concomitant reduction in actual noise emissions from such vehicles, which are estimated to have fallen by only 1 to 2dB(A) because of factors including the slow replacement of older vehicles, significant growth in traffic and questions over whether the test procedures reflect actual driving conditions.

Standards and measurement rules are now contained in the Road Vehicles (Construction and Use) Regulations 1986 (SI 1986/1078), as numerously amended, made under the Road Traffic Act 1988, s. 41. These lay down minimum standards, with particular emphasis on the maintenance of an effective silencer. The 1986 Regulations also make it an offence to drive causing unnecessarily high noise levels, or to leave an engine running unnecessarily when stationary (reg. 98). The Motor Vehicles (Type Approval) (Great Britain) Regulations 1984 (SI 1984/81), made under s. 54 of the 1988 Act, and the Motor Vehicles (EC Type Approval) Regulations 1998 (SI 1998/2051) lay down national-based and EC-based standards in relation to noise respectively. Similar provisions apply to lorries and motor cycles.

Where increased noise levels are caused by the construction or alteration of a highway, highway authorities must carry our noise insulation works to combat the effect of traffic noise on certain properties. Alternatively, they may provide grants for noise insulation to be fitted, a flexible means of implementing a specification standard rather than the use of economic tools (see the Land Compensation Act 1973, s. 20, and the Noise Insulation Regulations 1975, SI 1975/1763, as amended by SI 1988/2000). There are also powers under the Highways Act 1980 for highways authorities to undertake works to mitigate the adverse effects of constructing or improving highways, e.g. noise bunding (Highways Act 1980, s. 282). A similar scheme applies in relation to noise from railways and tramways (see the Noise Insulation (Railways and Other Guided Transport Systems) Regulations 1996, SI 1996/428).

The composition of the road surface also leads to significant differences in noise levels; for example, porous asphalt surfaces are quieter than conventional concrete surfaces by anything from 4 to 8 dB, although they also have environmental disadvantages such as greater use of quarried aggregates. However, there are so far no statutory controls governing road surfaces, and the composition of public road surfaces is determined only by Department of the Environment, Transport and the Regions practice in the case of trunk roads, and otherwise by local authorities. The impact of traffic noise can also be reduced by things like urban bypasses, although not all bypasses reduce traffic movements to the extent intended, as the controversial Newbury bypass illustrates. In any event, such policies have other environmental consequences.

The continuing 'Cinderella' status of noise is emphasised by the low profile of noise issues in the government White Paper, *A New Deal for Transport* (Cm 3950, 1998). Indeed, 'noise' as such is not mentioned so much as the need for preserving the 'tranquillity' of the countryside, at least as far as designated 'quiet roads' are concerned. This suggests both an anti-urban policy focus, as well as an 'enclave' approach to noise control rather than a desire to reduce noise levels generally.

(ii)   Aircraft and airport noise
The main control on aircraft noise is under emissions standards which have been set under the framework of the 1944 Chicago Convention, in particular Annex 16. These standards have been tightened over the years, and (in so far as they relate to subsonic planes) are included in EC Directives 80/51, 83/206 and 89/629, implemented by the Air Navigation (Noise Certification) Order 1990 (SI 1990/1514, as amended by SI 1999/1452). This Order prohibits any plane to which it applies from taking off or landing in the UK unless it has a noise certificate issued by the Civil Aviation Authority, or by the competent authority of countries deemed to operate equivalent standards, or issued in pursuance of the 1944 Chicago Convention. The process of acquiring a noise certificate is essentially a licensing procedure, and conditions may be set regulating things like maximum take off and landing weights. Certificates can be varied, suspended or revoked.

The basic policy approach has been first to prevent the addition of noisier aircraft to national registers, before eventually phasing them out altogether. In the case of subsonic jets, this second stage is effected by Directive 92/14, although there are exemptions for aircraft less than 25 years old which still meet basic standards, which can operate until 1 April 2002. Directive 92/14 has recently been amended by Directive 98/20 on the limitation of the operation of so-called 'Chapter 2' aircraft, although there are certain exceptions (until 2002) for planes of developing countries. Implementing measures are consolidated in the Aeroplane Noise Regulations 1999 (SI 1999/1452). However, increases in the average size of aircraft over the years, and in the number of flights, have reduced the impact of improvements from the significant tightening of standards (a phenomenon also experienced in relation to lorry movements). For example, although general noise levels are down at Heathrow and Gatwick, they have increased at Stansted, and night noise levels at Gatwick are deteriorating (see *Night Restrictions at Heathrow, Gatwick and Stansted: Second Stage Consultation*, DETR, 1998). This is a vivid illustration of the inadequacy of relying only on emission control standards.

The general legal approach to airport and aerodrome noise is to give the Secretary of State a power to designate certain airports in order to subject them to specific controls on the frequency or time of aircraft movements (s. 78, Civil Aviation Act 1982). So far, Heathrow, Gatwick, Stansted and Manchester have been designated, although it is in fact the aircraft operators who must comply with the restrictions and, on the direction of the Secretary of State, withhold facilities from defaulting operators. This section has been used to fix the total allowable number of night flights, although not without legal controversy (see *R* v *Secretary of State for Transport, ex parte Richmond upon Thames London Borough* [1994] 1 WLR 74; *(No. 2)* [1995] 7 ELM 52; *(No. 3)* [1995] 7 ELM 127; *(No. 4)* [1996] 8 ELM 77). An interesting feature of these provisions is that they give power to central government, rather than the courts, and only on the initiative of the Secretary of State, not those affected (see Leeson, *Environmental Law*, Longman, 1995, p. 335). Under s. 79 of the 1982 Act, schemes may be established which require designated aerodromes to make grants towards the cost of insulating certain buildings in the vicinity which require protection from noise. Statutory noise insulation grants schemes have been made for Heathrow and Gatwick, and non-statutory schemes for three other airports.

There are also environmental and noise considerations when air transport licences are granted, although not to the extent that there is a clash with British airlines competing effectively or with public demand (ss. 4 and 68(1) and (3), Civil Aviation Act 1982)

Finally, it should be noted that civil liability for trespass, or for damage caused by nuisance, from the flight of an aircraft over property is generally excluded, so long as the conduct of the flight is reasonable (s. 76, Civil Aviation Act 1982). There is a similar exclusion for nuisance from noise on the land, i.e. from the airport itself, where this is caused at an aerodrome complying with an Air Navigation Order (s. 77). The legality of these exclusions was challenged in *Powell and Rayner* v *United Kingdom* (1990) 12 EHRR 355, where it was claimed that s. 76(1) violated Articles 6, 8 and 13 of the European Convention on Human Rights since there could not be a fair hearing of possible nuisance claims, and the noise interfered with the claimants' home and private lives contrary to the Convention. The claim was rejected on the grounds that a private law claim could still be brought if the flight was outside the terms of the statutory exemption, and because a proper balance was deemed to have been struck between the residents' rights and wider community interests. This may be true in the case of Heathrow, the airport complained about in *Powell and Rayner*, but it may not be in relation to the majority of airports in Britain which are used for private flying. (The Noise Review Working Group Report of 1990 recommended the abolition of immunity for all but commercial flights. See also *Review of Aircraft Noise Legislation*, 1993.)

(iii)   Noise from boats
It is briefly worth mentioning s. 13(2) of the Countryside Act 1968 which allows a local authority to make by-laws, amongst other things, to prevent excessive noise nuisances in National Parks. Such by-laws may, e.g. regulate noise from boats or vessels by requiring the use of silencers or otherwise regulating noise or vibration levels. By-laws imposing a 10 mph speed limit on Lake Windermere, effectively ending high-speed power-boating and water-skiing there, have recently been confirmed by central government and will come into force in 2005.

(c)   Music from raves
The Criminal Justice and Public Order Act 1994 contains some rather Draconian measures ostensibly designed to combat noise from raves. A rave is defined as a gathering of 100 or more people on land in the open air that includes the playing of amplified music. In an attempt to make sure that all rave music was caught by the 1994 Act, 'music' is famously defined as including 'sounds wholly or predominantly characterised by the emission of a succession of repetitive beats'. If the music is likely to cause serious distress to local residents the police can take steps to secure its cessation (s. 63). This includes certain powers to prevent people reasonably suspected of travelling to raves from 'proceeding in the direction of the gathering' (s. 65). In seeking to stop raves, these powers clearly go well beyond what could be expected of public nuisance law, which could apply (*R v Shorrock* [1993] 3 All ER 917).

(d)   Noise controls on other specific sources
There are a number of other disparate provisions which regulate noise from specific sources. Some of these have origins in EC directives, such as harmonisation measures on noise levels from construction plant and equipment (79/113), compressors (84/533), tower cranes (84/534), welding generators (84/535), power generators (84/536), powered hand-held concrete-breakers and picks (84/537), lawnmowers (84/538) and various kinds of excavators (86/662), all of which have since been amended (see the Construction Plant and Equipment (Harmonisation of Noise Emission Standards) Regulations 1985, SI 1985/1127, as amended). There is a proposal to replace these directives with a single text, which would also cover some other sources of noise, although the coverage remains extremely limited (COM(98)46).

At national level, regulations can be made to control noise from plant or machinery under s. 68 of COPA 1974, but the policy preference has been to use codes of practice to minimise noise, which have been issued (under s. 71) in relation to various sources such as ice cream van chimes (SI 1981/1828) and model aircraft (SI 1981/1830). Although breach of a code of practice is not itself a criminal offence, codes may be taken into account in legal proceedings, for example in determining whether best practicable means have been employed.

Noise from loudspeakers and audible intruder alarms are regulated separately. It is generally an offence to use a loudspeaker in the street between 9pm and 8am, although exceptions are made for things like the emergency services and mobile grocers (COPA 1974, s. 62). The Noise and Statutory Nuisance Act 1993 tempered this approach by introducing the right to obtain a consent from the local authority, although only where the local authority has adopted the powers in its area (s. 8 and sch. 2). A similar power to adopt noise control powers under the 1993 Act applies to audible intruder alarms (s. 9 and sch. 3). This gives local authorities the power to require alarms to comply with prescribed standards, coupled with obligations to notify the police and the local authority. There are also powers for local authorities to turn off alarms, if need be by getting the consent of a justice of the peace and entering by force.

General preventive and strategic controls

In addition to regulating specific sources of noise, there are a number of more general preventive mechanisms which might be used, of which in practice the town and country planning system is perhaps the most important.

(a) Noise abatement zones

Under the Control of Pollution Act 1974 a local authority may designate all or part of its area as a noise abatement zone. Designation of a zone is at the local authority's discretion (s. 63), although authorities must inspect their areas with the need for designating zones in mind (s. 57). When a noise abatement zone is in operation the local authority records the levels of noise from specified premises (see the Control of Noise (Measurement and Registers) Regulations 1976, SI 1976/37). These are usually trade and business premises, but places such as concert halls could also be covered. Recorded noise levels are then entered in a noise level register, which is open to public inspection. Once noise levels have been registered they can only be exceeded with the local authority's consent, in effect setting a ceiling on noise levels. There is, however, a right for affected premises to request the local authority's consent to exceed a recorded noise level. Consents can be made subject to conditions, and must also be recorded on the register. It is an offence to breach register levels or consent conditions (s. 65(5)). After conviction, the magistrates may make an order requiring works to be done, if the breach is likely to continue or recur. There is a power for the local authority to undertake such works itself and recover expenses from the person convicted (s. 69).

Noise abatement zones are therefore intended to control noise from premises in the long term by preventing an increase in noise levels, but under s. 66, noise reductions can be sought if they would secure public benefit and are practicable at reasonable cost. However, a further qualification to this is that for trade and business premises there is still a best practicable means defence to any charge of breaching a noise reduction notice.

Where zones have been designated, relatively small areas such as industrial estates tend to be designated, while some zones govern single noisy industrial premises. However, the noise reduction provisions are generously worded to business, and the main use of zones is to avoid increases in noise levels. Of course, their restriction to premises makes them of little use in combating noise from mobile sources such as traffic, and thus general increases in noise levels. This, coupled with high enforcement costs and the statutory nuisance powers, may explain why, in practice, only about 60 zones have been designated in England and Wales (McManus and Burns, above, at p. 185).

(b)   Other preventive approaches

There is a range of other provisions that aim to control noise arising from states of affairs. Specification standards are used in the case of building design. Under the Building Regulations 1991 (SI 1991/2768) buildings must be constructed to prevent undue noise. The 1991 Regulations only apply to houses in buildings (such as flats) or to semi-detached or terraced properties: detached properties are not covered.

(c)   Planning controls

Planning controls will often be the principal, or only, means of regulating noise. This is certainly the case with things like wind turbines, which have no legal standards attached to their noise output. It is also true of general traffic noise from new road developments, where conditions can be imposed relating to things like earth banking, tree screening and proximity from housing. However, the planning system is of little use in regulating an increase in noise due to traffic growth, since this is not 'development'. (No matter how much the noise and traffic intensifies, the land is still a road: there cannot be a material change of use.) This illustrates the extent to which law is rather better at controlling new activities than regulating existing ones, especially incremental changes to existing uses.

Guidance on 'Planning and Noise' is given in PPG 24. This counsels the use of development plans and the development control system in separating new noise-sensitive developments from major sources of noise. Planning conditions are often used to minimise the impact of noise, e.g. by putting restrictions on the time when noisy activities may take place. A local planning authority can impose a planning condition which is more onerous than restrictions required under an abatement notice served under the statutory nuisance powers of the EPA 1990 (*R* v *Kennet District Council, ex parte Somerfield Property Co. Ltd* [1999] JPL 361). There is no legal requirement for planning officers and environmental health officers to reach the same decision about what level of noise is acceptable, although this might be thought desirable.

Although attempts by the Royal Commission on Environmental Pollution in its Eighteenth Report on *Transport and the Environment* (Cm 2674, 1994) to have general targets for acceptable day and night noise accepted by government were rejected, PPG 24 goes some way towards introducing these through planning policy. The levels recommended by the RCEP are at the lower end of the noise exposure category which advises that development falling within it should normally be refused planning permission on noise grounds, unless noise reduction measures are taken.

Other environmental controls

With notable exceptions like those relating to aircraft noise, actions under private or public nuisance can still be taken despite the specific statutory provisions discussed above, although if a privately initiated remedy is sought it is more likely that statutory nuisance law will be used if this is possible. A modern example of an attempt to use public nuisance law to combat traffic noise is *Gillingham Borough Council* v *Medway (Chatham) Dock Co. Ltd* [1993] QB 343 (see p. 284).

As discussed in Chapter 13, noise emissions are not within the remit of integrated pollution control under Part 1 of the EPA 1990, but are a relevant factor in determining the wider concept of BPEO under the IPPC Directive (96/61). Environmental statements for developments requiring assessment under the Directive on Environmental Impact Assessment (85/337, as amended) must include estimates of noise emissions. The need for an environmental statement to cover secondary and indirect impact means that noise from increased or altered traffic flows must also be considered.

SEVENTEEN
Waste management

The production of waste is a natural consequence of life in an industrialised society. In the past, both the volume and the types of waste produced were easily dealt with in small, country rubbish dumps. This, of course, was in the days before plastic packaging, aluminium cans and other composite materials which make up a large amount of domestic waste in Britain. Furthermore, the amount of domestic waste disposed of in Britain represents only a small fraction of the total amount of waste produced. Other types of waste include liquid industrial effluent, agricultural waste, waste from mines and quarries, sewage sludge, waste from power stations, solid industrial waste and hazardous waste.

Methods of waste disposal

Most of the waste disposed of in Britain is deposited in large holes in the ground, such as old quarries. The difficulties of burying waste are numerous. Substances may break down after a number of years to produce contaminating liquids or hazardous gases, which may then escape from the site. Britain has already experienced the dangers of waste disposal sites. In 1986, methane produced from a landfill site at Loscoe in Derbyshire exploded, causing injury. Other examples could be given from around the world of housing estates that have been abandoned because of contamination of the land on which they were built, severely polluted water supplies, deaths caused by indiscriminate dumping of waste, and areas that are wholly unusable owing to long-term pollution problems caused by dumping (see further, Chapter 18 on contaminated land).

Landfill is not the only option for the disposal of waste. Large quantities of waste are discharged to sewers or to natural waters, both matters which are dealt with elsewhere in this book. A small percentage of waste is incinerated and, until 1998, a small percentage was also dumped at sea.

Each of these methods of disposal creates its own pollution problems and controversies. As suggested above, landfill sites may give rise to problems of methane emissions and of water pollution as a result of leachate. They also give rise to effects that will be only too obvious to those who live nearby, such as smells, noise, air-borne dust and rubbish, and increased traffic generation. As a result, landfill sites are amongst the uses of land that are most vigorously opposed by local communities. A further factor is that there is a marked tendency for landfill sites to be proposed on 'waste land', which is often precisely that land which is of greatest importance in nature conservation and amenity terms. However, at the beginning of the 21st century the most important point is simply that many existing sites are reaching their full capacity and that the supply of suitable new locations for landfill sites is very limited indeed. In some areas the problem is acute, leading to the need to transport waste long distances. A particular problem for Britain is that, unlike many other European countries, it has traditionally followed a policy of co-disposal on landfill sites, meaning that different sorts of waste are mixed together. The amount of waste going to landfill is set to fall dramatically over the next 15 years when the targets for reduction imposed by the Landfill Directive take effect. Assuming that the targets are not met through natural waste minimisation initiatives, there will have to be a huge increase in alternative disposal routes, principally in incineration capacity.

In relation to incineration, there are obvious problems of air pollution, especially concerning the release of such things as dioxins as a result of incomplete combustion. It is becoming clear that the application of EC standards on air pollution to British incinerators led to a reduction in their number and that replacement facilities are being opposed and delayed through the town and country planning system and latterly the authorisation process under EPA 1990, Part I. However, in May 1993, the Royal Commission on Environmental Pollution in its Seventeenth Report, *Incineration of Waste* (Cm 2181, 1993), recommended that waste incineration should play a key role in the future development of waste disposal, though critics have pointed to the weakness of the Royal Commission's arguments on waste minimisation.

These problems illustrate the need to establish a clear framework of policy to provide for the proper disposal of waste, particularly toxic and hazardous waste. However, more importantly, they establish the need to develop policies relating to the reduction of waste and its recycling or re-use.

Scope of this chapter

The focal point of this chapter is the definition of waste. Attempts to refine this definition in statutes and case law illustrate many of the difficult questions surrounding the regulation of the management of waste. This central issue is followed by discussion and explanation of the waste management licensing system. Other areas covered include the contribution of EC law and the regulation of international trade in the import and export of hazardous waste. Finally, there is some discussion of waste management policy and in particular the role that it has to play in minimising the production of waste and encouraging recycling.

The challenge of regulating waste management

Some areas of pollution control target emissions and/or environmental quality (e.g. air and water). The management of waste provides some different if not unique challenges (although it is arguably indirectly associated with certain aspects of environmental quality, in particular soil and groundwater in the case of landfill, and air in the case of incineration).

First, the definition of waste is not clear. Most of the problems associated with defining waste adequately stem from the fact it is not necessarily synonymous with actual pollution or harm. The threat to the environment may arise as a result of the risk of pollution or harm in circumstances where the waste is mishandled or abandoned. Therefore there is a need to regulate the whole waste cycle from the production of the waste through the handling, storing, transportation and treatment of waste up to and including the final disposal, independently of whether there is any actual pollution or harm caused. Consequently, there are many 'grey areas' which can lead to uncertainty and confusion. These include such things as whether something which can be reused but which is discarded should be classified as waste (e.g. electrical equipment which is placed into a dustbin but which functions perfectly); whether something which is not wanted by one person (and is therefore 'got rid of') but is valued by another (which is evidenced by the fact that they will 'buy' it) can be waste; or finally, whether a residue or a by-product from an industrial process which can be used as a replacement for a raw material should be classified as waste.

Secondly, there is the problem of trying to blend different types of legal measures to encourage waste minimisation and reuse. There is an inevitable requirement to replace those things which have been discarded and consequently there are issues of resource depletion which can only be tackled through the minimisation, reuse and recovery of waste. Traditional forms of regulation are useful when addressing the control of environmental risks (e.g. from the disposal of waste) but in doing so they can often fail to address this issue. In this sense legislative controls over the management of waste have proved to be inadequate as positive mechanisms for environmental improvement. Traditionally, the 'command and control' mechanisms have focused on the regulation of activities after the production of the waste. For example, a system which licenses the treatment or disposal of waste is not necessarily efficient when it comes to promoting the reduction of the production of waste or encouraging recycling and recovery.

Finally, and linked closely to the last point, there is the difficult challenge of sustainable waste management. Ultimately, the main indicator of sustainability would be a continuous reduction in the volume of waste arisings. Up until recently, there have been few legal measures introduced to meet this goal. A lack of sufficient information on waste arisings, the use of 'predict and provide' methods which base future growth in waste facilities on extrapolated historic figures and a lack of coordinated waste policies on a national basis have contributed to the failure to address sustainability issues. As with so many other areas, the picture is being changed as a result of European legislation which sets binding targets for the recycling, recovery and reduction of waste (e.g. through the Packaging Waste Directive and the Landfill Directive.

History

The modern era of legislative controls over waste can be traced back to the series of Public Health Acts which date back to the late nineteenth century. These provisions were not primarily environmental in nature, being based around the concept of statutory nuisance which depended largely upon either harm to human health or the common law test of nuisance. In addition the controls were not used to prevent harm but were used to clean up existing problems. Indeed up until the introduction of modern planning legislation there was little in the way of preventive controls. As the final disposal of waste involves land use considerations it fell naturally into the planning system. This continues to the present day with the existence of some form of planning permission (or latterly an established use certificate) being a prerequisite for the consideration of an application for a waste management licence. The very strengths of the system of land use planning are also its weaknesses in that planning considerations are not adequate to deal with all of the technical problems of waste disposal or management. In particular the planning system is not suited to controlling post operational activities on a waste management site (i.e. dealing with long term aftercare of a landfill site).

In a typically British approach to environmental legislation, two governmental reports on waste disposal set out long-term objectives in developing a new system of regulation for waste disposal. Before these could be considered in any detail, however, a public outcry over the dumping of toxic wastes on a playground in the West Midlands brought a kneejerk legislative reaction with the introduction of the Deposit of Poisonous Wastes Act 1972. This Act was a classic example of the reactive nature of environmental legislation in Britain, since it approached the deposit of waste from a narrow viewpoint and sought mainly to combat the type of incident that had occurred. It remains the case, however, that the 1972 Act was one of the first controls over the deposit of hazardous waste in the world.

The 1972 Act was soon supplemented in respect of controls over non-hazardous wastes in Part I of the Control of Pollution Act (COPA)1974. This Act introduced a more comprehensive system in which a waste disposal licence was required before 'controlled waste' could be finally disposed of either in a landfill site or by incineration. Although the system was not without its flaws it provided a framework which was adopted by other countries, and in particular for the first major European legislation on waste, the Framework Directive (75/442).

The defects of the Control of Pollution Act 1974

Following the implementation of COPA 1974, it became increasingly clear that there were still problems dealing with the management of waste (as compared with its final disposal) and that the scope of the Act was too narrow. Some of the defects should have been obvious at the time the Act was passed whereas others only became clear as time passed. In 1989, the failure of the Act and those responsible for implementing its provisions was heavily criticised by the House of Commons Environment Committee in its Second Report, *Toxic Waste* (1988–89 Session). The following defects in the implementation of COPA were identified:

(a)   There was a failure to produce any strategic plans for the disposal of waste. Although local waste disposal authorities were responsible for producing waste disposal plans which dealt with future waste strategies, only 23 out of a possible 79 were produced in the first 15 years of operation of COPA 1974.

(b)   There was a lack of a national policy on how the provisions should have been applied in practice. Although the then government committed itself to producing at least 13 waste management papers in the 1980s, this target was missed and many papers were not produced on time. This led to inconsistency in the setting and enforcement of conditions across the country.

(c)   The emphasis on waste disposal rather than management led to difficulties of enforcement. Whilst COPA 1974 controlled the deposit of waste, problems arose with the storage, treatment and transportation of waste. For example, where waste had been fly-tipped, it was only possible to prosecute the person who had actually caused or knowingly permitted the deposit of the waste, leaving others further up the chain of waste management free from control notwithstanding the fact that these others may have had a significant degree of responsibility for what had happened. Other enforcement difficulties included the low level of penalties on conviction and the absence of an offence of failing to comply with a licence condition. This latter problem was compounded by the decision in *Leigh Land Reclamation Ltd* v *Walsall Metropolitan Borough Council* (1991) 155 JP 547 where it was held that as long as the deposit of waste was in accordance with the licence conditions, it was irrelevant if other conditions relating to the site were not being complied with. In the absence of a 'breach of condition offence', the case had the effect of ensuring that many operational and administrative licence conditions were practically unenforceable.

(d)   There were some severe defects in the licensing system which meant that proper control over standards was difficult. For example, there were limited grounds to refuse a grant of a waste disposal licence or to refuse a transfer, or to vary or revoke a licence. The discretion in the decision-making process fell largely within the planning regime. In the case of some operators, planning permission had been granted many years in the past often before environmental considerations were given any significant weight. In addition the technical requirements of holding a waste disposal licence were not necessarily relevant matters which could be taken into account at the stage of determining whether or not to grant planning permission. Finally, regulatory authorities were unable to attach aftercare and restoration conditions to waste disposal licences although certain aspects could be dealt with by way of planning condition. The overall effect of this lack of control was that it was possible for technically incompetent or unsuitable people to be granted a waste disposal licence.

(e)   Licence holders had the right to surrender a disposal licence at any time, in which case any conditions attached to it would automatically cease to have any effect. In practice, this meant that an operator could abandon a site and relinquish any future responsibility for supervision of it. Thus an operator who was financially or technically incompetent to deal with problems that had arisen on site could avoid them simply by giving notice to the regulatory authorities. Although the COPA 1974 controls ceased on surrender it should also be noted that any obligations under a planning permission or the common law continued to bind the operator.

(f)   There was a significant overlap in regulatory and operational responsibilities. The regulatory authorities created by COPA 1974, were also the main operators of waste disposal sites. The inherent conflict between these two roles led to an undermining of public confidence in the ability of the regulator to control its own activities.

The shift from waste disposal to management — the Environmental Protection Act 1990

Many of these defects were addressed with the introduction of Part II of the Environmental Protection Act (EPA) 1990 which established a new system of waste management. The shift away from 'disposal' to management was significant as it illustrated that increased control was to be exercised over the whole of the waste cycle 'from cradle to grave'. In particular, the EPA 1990 created greater controls over waste producers and carriers and restructured the administration of waste regulation. Unfortunately, the implementation of Part II EPA 1990 was beset with problems and has still not been fully implemented at the time of writing (in particular there is an issue in relation to the classification of wastes such as agricultural wastes). No timetable for its introduction was originally written into the Act or promised in the debate on the Bill. To some extent this uncertainty was understandable given the nature of some of the challenges facing those who would be drafting the details of the secondary legislation which would flesh out the base concepts within the primary legislation. Extensive consultation (both formal and informal) took place in relation to various aspects of the new provisions and this process has yet to be completed. Some of the provisions gave rise to great controversy within the waste disposal industry and continue to present problems for the regulators (e.g. exemptions from the licensing system and the spreading of wastes on land). As a result there were persistent delays, a situation which was exacerbated by the indecision over the creation of the Environment Agency. In the end, the implementation of the provisions (and accompanying secondary legislation) has been piecemeal. Although some of the provisions were brought into force on 1 April 1992 (e.g. the duty of care) the main bulk of Part II was brought into operation on 1 May 1994.

The main statutory provisions in Part II EPA 1990 are fleshed out in numerous other documents. In addition to the Waste Management Licensing

Regulations 1994 (SI 1994/1056) which form the main body of supplement-ary legislation, there is a charging scheme dealing with licence fees, technical guidance in the form of waste management papers and policy guidance in Department of the Environment Circular 11/94 on Waste Management Licensing and the Framework Directive on Waste. The main statutory provisions are supplemented by the provisions of the Control of Pollution (Amendment) Act 1989, which was brought into force in 1992. This Act introduced a system of registration for carriers of waste, with strong penalties for operating an unregistered vehicle. Additional controls over litter can be found in Part IV of the EPA 1990.

There is further legislation and guidance on the management of special waste in the form of the Special Waste Regulations 1996 (SI 1996/972) as amended and technical guidance on the meaning of special waste. The effect of all this is that the law has become even more complex and difficult to interpret.

The main features of waste management regulation

These are as follows:

(a)   There is a national waste strategy for England and Wales which sets out the policy framework and goals for waste regulation. This is formulated by the Secretary of State with full public consultation. The strategy sets out targets for waste management including reduction, recycling and recovery. The strategy is not legally binding but influences national and local decision-making on waste facilities and licensing.

(b)   The concept of 'waste' is broadly defined by reference to whether something has been 'discarded'. This covers the disposal, recycling and recovery of materials although there is a difficult distinction which must be drawn between the use of raw materials in industrial processes (e.g. use of something as a fuel) and the recovery of waste. Within this broad definition there are classes of waste (e.g. household, industrial and commercial) which are relevant, for example, when considering waste licensing or targets for reduction.

(c)   Certain wastes known as 'special wastes' are subject to extra controls. Categories of special wastes can be found in detailed lists or the term is defined by reference to general hazardous properties.

(d)   The management of waste (which includes keeping, treating or disposing) requires a licence from the Environment Agency. Certain activities are exempt from the need for a licence subject to specified limits (e.g. time and quantity limits for the storage of particular wastes).

(e)   There is a general 'duty of care' which applies to all those who are involved in the waste chain from production to final disposal. Breach of the duty is a criminal offence. Compliance with the duty requires reasonable steps to be taken to ensure that waste is handled safely by an authorised person and that an offence is not committed. There is a Code of Practice which gives some guidance on the types of steps which would be considered to be reasonable.

(f)   A waste management licence can only be granted where there is a planning permission in force (if planning permission is required); the applicant is a 'fit and proper' person in terms of their technical competence, financial security and absence of criminal conviction; there has been an adequate investigation of whether the activities will lead to the pollution of groundwater; and there will be no pollution of the environment or harm to human health.

(g)   There is limited consultation on an application and no requirement for public participation (which should have taken place at the planning stage).

(h)   Licence conditions can relate to any activities which the licence authorises and can cover matters after the authorised activities have ceased (e.g. monitoring and other aftercare matters) or off-site controls (e.g. leachate management).

(i)   The EA has a duty to supervise licensed activities and can exercise wide powers including the variation, suspension or revocation of existing licences.

(j)   There are controls over the transportation of waste with the registration of waste carriers within domestic legislation. There are also strict controls over import and export of wastes between the UK and other countries.

International law and waste management

Generally, waste regulation has been concerned with controlling the management of waste within the domestic context. As waste regulation became tighter in some countries (mainly the US and Europe) the costs of disposal rose and it became common practice to export hazardous wastes to developing countries where it could be disposed of at a lower cost (as a result of lower standards). As a result, there was increasing pressure for the introduction of controls over the transportation of waste between countries. Consequently, there are rules which govern the import and export of wastes between countries. Originally, these rules were concentrated solely on the control over the transportation of hazardous wastes and although there has been a broadening of the categories of waste within EC law, international law is still primarily focused upon hazardous waste.

The United Nations Convention on the Control of Transboundary Movements of Hazardous Wastes and their Disposal (known as the Basel Convention) was first proposed in 1989 but only entered into force in 1992. The Basel Convention establishes a system whereby the exporter of waste must obtain the consent of the regulatory authorities in the importing country prior to shipping that waste. That consent must include a written confirmation that the importer of the waste will deal with the waste in an environmentally sound manner. Where the consignment of waste cannot take place (e.g. where it would not be handled in an environmentally sound manner), the exporter of the waste is bound to take back the waste within 90 days. Failure to comply with the Basel Convention is a criminal offence.

The Basel Convention is supplemented by the 1989 Lomé IV Convention which prohibits the direct or indirect export of hazardous wastes from the EC to a number of African, Caribbean and Pacific states and the 1991 Bamako Convention which bans the direct or indirect import of waste into African states.

(a) Implementation of the Basel Convention

The EC Regulation on the Supervision and Control of Shipments of Waste within, into and out of the European Community (259/93) gives effect to the Basel Convention throughout the EC (this replaced an earlier Directive (84/631) on transfrontier shipment of hazardous waste). The Regulation subjects the transfer of waste between countries to a system of 'prior informed consent' of the regulatory agencies in the two respective countries. Under Council Decision 93/98/EEC, Member States were required to ratify the Basel Convention. The UK subsequently ratified in 1994 and implemented the requirements of the Basel Convention under the Transfrontier Shipment of Waste Regulations 1994 and the UK Management Plan for the Imports and Exports of Waste. This management plan sets out the policy behind the regulations. It is advisory and non-binding (although it gains its force through the regulations).

The type of notification which must be given differs depending upon the nature of the waste which is shipped, whether the waste is destined for recovery or disposal and finally whether the waste is transferred between two Member States or out of the EC. Waste which is being transported for disposal is relatively straightforward and must comply with the requirements of the Basel Convention (see above). In the UK the Management Plan for the Imports and Exports of Waste bans all exports of waste for disposal and bans most imports for disposal other than in exceptional cases where wider environmental considerations apply.

Waste transported for recovery is controlled under a more complicated system. The EC Regulation adopts a classification for all wastes (mainly taken from an OECD Council Decision) which divides wastes into three lists: Green; Amber; and Red. The categories are exclusive in the sense that any waste not on the list is treated as Red list waste and there is no provision for mixtures of wastes even where they are on the same list. In *R v Environment Agency, ex parte Dockgrange Ltd* [1997] Env LR 575, the High Court held that a policy which treated mixtures of different Green list wastes as unassigned (and therefore treated as Red list waste with the consequent tightening of procedures) was unlawful and that the correct approach was to identify such a shipment as a mixture of assigned wastes which were to be found on the Green list. It was, however, pointed out that the situation might be different were there to be a mixture of Amber or Red list wastes as the combination of such wastes might give rise to separate environmental risks which needed to be notified separately.

The Green list can be found in Annex II to the EC Regulation. Shipments of such waste need to be accompanied by basic information such as a description of the waste, quantity shipped, the name and address of the person to whom the waste is consigned and a description of the recovery operation involved. The only other requirement is that the waste should be shipped to a facility licensed in accordance with the Waste Framework Directive.

Amber list wastes can be found in Annex III to the Regulation. Shipments of Amber waste must be subject to the pre-notification procedures found in the Basel Convention. The notification must contain details of the type, source and quantity of the waste (Art. 6). In addition, Amber list wastes can be shipped under a general notification procedure whereby certain types of shipments going to a particular facility do not have to obtain approval on each occasion (Art. 9).

Red list wastes (and any waste which has not been assigned to one of the lists) are subject to the greatest level of control. The regulatory authority in the exporting country must give notification to the importing regulatory authority prior to export and there is no provision for a general approval as with Amber wastes.

European waste management law and policy

The implementation of COPA 1974 was carried out in parallel with the development of European legislation. In common with other areas of environmental protection there is a directive which sets out a framework of objectives and general provisions (known as the Framework Directive) which is further supplemented by more specific directives in relation to general or precise categories of waste (e.g. in the former case hazardous waste and in the latter such things as sewage sludge, waste oils, packaging waste and waste polychlorinated biphenyls (PCBs)). In addition there are two directives on the management of waste by means of incineration for both municipal waste and hazardous waste. These two directives are, however, slightly different in the sense that they are mostly implemented under the Integrated Pollution Control regime rather than the waste management licensing system. Finally, there has been the recent adoption of a Directive on the disposal of waste in landfills (i.e. within the ground), a Directive which will have a tremendous impact upon domestic law and practice which is considered in more detail below.

In keeping with the general aims of EC environmental policy set out in Art. 174(2) of the EC Treaty, the EC has adopted as a specific aim the prevention of waste at source through proper design of products and processes. This is linked with such initiatives as the development of clean technology, eco-labelling and the discipline of life cycle analysis. A second aim is to recycle or to reuse waste which is produced, with particular emphasis to be placed on the use of waste as a source of energy, for example through combined heat and power schemes linked to waste incinerators. An obvious example of the EC's role in this area is its development of a directive on the recycling of packaging waste (although this was, in fact, based upon existing legislation in other Member States). A third aim is that waste should be disposed of in its country of origin, thus leading to restrictions on the transfrontier shipment of waste which reflect the content of international treaties on the issue.

The European Commission has set out these general policy objectives in its Fifth Action Programme which broadly reflects the legislative objectives in the Framework Directive by adopting a waste hierarchy of, in order of priority: prevention of the production of waste; recycling and reuse; and finally safe disposal by combustion as fuel, incineration and landfill. The Fifth Action Programme is supplemented by a Community Waste Strategy which places a great deal of emphasis on the concept of producer responsibility for waste, that is to say that the producer of the thing which becomes waste has a responsibility to ensure that when the thing becomes waste it is recovered or recycled.

The Framework Directive on waste

The 1975 Framework Directive was largely replaced in 1991 by a new Directive 91/156. These amendments were scheduled to be implemented in Member States by April 1993 and were transposed into UK national law by the Waste Management Licensing Regulations 1994 (SI 1994/1056) over a year late. The Framework Directive is of fundamental importance within the domestic context as it has been directly transposed (sometimes referred to as 'copied out') and contains a number of vital provisions. First it provides a definition of waste which has been incorporated into the domestic legislation under the definition of 'directive waste'. Secondly, it sets out a number of objectives which should provide a framework for all other policies on waste. These objectives represent a waste hierarchy when considering options for waste management. These are:

(a)   to prevent or reduce the production of waste;
(b)   to recover waste by means of recycling, reuse or reclamation, or any other process including the use of waste as an energy source (Art. 3(1)).

Thirdly, it requires Member States to take all necessary measures to ensure that waste is recovered or disposed of without endangering human health or the environment (Art. 4).

What then is the status of these objectives? They have been transposed into UK law in Schedule 4 to the Waste Management Licensing Regulations 1994. Although the ECJ has held that these objectives do not have 'direct effect' (see *Comitato di Coordianmento per la Difesa della Cava and others* v *Regione Lombardia and others* [1994] Env LR 281), the UK domestic courts have considered the status of the objectives in *R* v *Bolton MBC, ex parte Kirkman* [1998] Env LR 719 and *R* v *Environment Agency, ex parte Gibson and another* [1999] Env LR 73. Although these decisions were concerned with the status of the duty where there were overlapping controls (i.e. planning permission and integrated pollution control respectively), they still give a general view on the status of the objectives.

In respect of the waste hierarchy in Art. 3, the Court of Appeal in *Kirkman* took the view that the Framework Directive could only express an objective rather than a requirement. Thus where an application for an incinerator was being considered, an authority was not obliged to consider the availability of other facilities which would deal with waste in a manner which was higher up the hierarchy.

In respect of Art. 4, however, the Court of Appeal in *Kirkman* held that although the obligations were not directly effective, the consequence of transposing the Framework Directive into domestic legislation was such that there was now a separate self-standing duty upon regulatory authorities to ensure that the objectives set out in Schedule 4 to the Waste Management Licensing Regulations were achieved. The decisions in both cases do not, however, go on to consider how this duty should be carried out. In both cases the courts seem to link the duty to the discretionary consideration of the material factors (i.e. the decision-maker must consider whether waste is disposed of or recovered without endangering human health or harming the environment). If this were to be the accepted position it would appear that the duty resembles a material planning consideration. Thus, under this view, the duty does no more than ensure that the decision-maker takes all of the relevant factors into account. It does not greatly matter how much attention is paid to the fulfilment of the duty as that falls entirely within the decision-maker's discretion (a view which was subsequently adopted by Richards J. in *R* v *Leicester County Council, Hepworth Building Products Limited and Onyx (UK) Ltd, ex parte Blackfordby and Boothcorpe Action Group Ltd,* 15 March 2000, unreported). An alternative view would be that the duty is mandatory rather than discretionary in nature and that the purpose of the duty (i.e. to ensure that waste is disposed of without endangering human health or harming the environment) means that pollution must be prevented and the decision-maker's discretion is limited to achieving that consideration.

In addition to these overriding objectives, the Framework Directive sets out a number of other provisions including:

(a)   a goal of self-sufficiency of waste disposal capacity within the EC with the establishment of a network of disposal installations to deal with waste produced (Art. 5);

(b)   the need for waste management plans to be drawn up by national authorities (Art. 6, represented in the UK by the National Waste Strategies, waste local plans and waste recycling plans);

(c)   the imposition of a duty to ensure that waste is only handled by authorised operators (Art. 8, transposed by the duty of care provisions under EPA 1990, s. 34);

(d)   the licensing of waste disposal and waste recovery operations (Arts. 9, 10 transposed under EPA 1990, ss. 35–42); and

(e)   the keeping of records of the nature of waste, its transport and its treatment (Art. 14, transposed under the consignment note system under the duty of care).

Whilst the Framework Directive sets out objectives and controls over waste generally, it also provides for the adoption of further directives dealing with the management of certain categories of waste. The Hazardous Waste

Directive (91/689, amending 78/319) makes provision for the management of certain wastes which are specifically regulated because of their hazardous or toxic properties. The annexes to the Directive set out the properties which bring wastes within the definition of 'hazardous'. A list has been drawn up under the directive (see Decision 94/904), which catalogues the wastes which fall within the definition of 'hazardous'. There are additional provisions in the Directive dealing with licensing, exemptions and the keeping of records in relation to hazardous waste. Most of these provisions have been transposed and are implemented under the Special Waste Regulations 1996 (SI 1996/972).

The Landfill Directive

The most significant waste directive to be agreed in recent years is the Landfill Directive (99/31). As with other European legislation, its significance can be assessed against the background of disagreement between Member States which postponed the adoption of the directive for approximately nine years (with an early version abandoned as a result of the controversy). The Directive is intended to harmonise landfill standards across the Member States with particular emphasis on standards of design, operation and aftercare for landfill sites. The main impact upon the UK will be in the changes to current policies and practice as opposed to legislative change although some new implementing legislation will be required.

The Directive came into force on 16 July 1999 and the deadline for transposition into UK law is 16 July 2001. Much of the implementation of the directive will be brought about with the adoption of the National Waste Strategy (particularly in respect of waste reduction targets).

The main part of the Directive sets out targets for the reduction of the amount of biodegradable municipal waste (i.e. household or similar waste which is capable of decomposition) put into landfills and thereby reduce the amount of methane produced. Thus Art. 5 of the directive requires the amount of biodegradable municipal waste which is disposed of in landfills to be reduced in three stages: by 25 per cent, 50 per cent, and 65 per cent of the 1995 levels by 2006, 2009 and 2016 respectively (these targets were relaxed as a result of lobbying from the UK and other Member States). Even these deadlines can be extended where, as in the case of the UK, more than 80 per cent of biodegradable municipal waste was disposed of in landfills in 1995 (which would make the deadlines 2010, 2013 and 2020 respectively).

The targets are set for the UK as a whole and there will be an apportionment between the devolved countries although the method of transposition will be uniform in order to ensure that the targets are met. At the time of writing, the exact method of attaining the Directive's targets has yet to be decided although it is likely that there will be a statutory instrument (possibly made under the powers of transposition under the Pollution Prevention and Control Act 1999) limiting the amount of municipal waste being sent to landfill. In practical terms, the targets will be met by amending existing waste management licences at landfills either to ban or limit the disposal of municipal waste.

Although the new targets are the most significant parts of the Directive, there are other aspects which will require amendments to existing policies and legislation. The Directive imposes:

(a)   a ban on the current practice of co-disposing of hazardous, non-hazardous and inert wastes in the same landfill and on certain hazardous waste, liquid wastes and tyres;

(b)   a requirement that all waste must be pre-treated before disposal (which includes sorting and compaction of wastes);

(c)   a requirement that an operator makes adequate financial provision for maintenance and aftercare (reflecting to some extent the approach taken in the UK with the requirement that an operator be a 'fit and proper person');

(d)   a requirement for controls over gas and leachate produced at landfill sites. In particular, all landfill gases must be either used to produce energy or flared off; only a minority of current sites do this.

Many of these changes will be brought about through amendments to existing waste management licences or through the introduction of new standards for IPPC permits for sites which fall within this system.

Other directives on waste

In addition to the general controls under the Waste Framework Directive (91/156) and the Hazardous Waste Directive (91/689), there are a series of subject specific directives dealing with different categories of waste. These include:

(a)   A Directive on Packaging and Packaging Waste (94/62). This directive aims to prevent the production of packaging waste and to encourage its recycling, reuse and recovery. Under the Directive, Member States are required to set up systems to enable the achievement of these objectives and to meet targets of between 50 and 65 per cent of all packaging waste to be recovered and 25–45 per cent of all packaging waste to be recycled by June 2001. In the UK, this Directive is transposed and implemented under the producer responsibility legislation made under ss. 93–5 of the Environment Act 1995 (see below).

(b)   Directives on Waste Oils (75/439), Batteries and Accumulators (91/157), Titanium Dioxide (78/176) and PCBs and polychlorinated triphenyls (PCTs). Although the Directives deal with these materials specifically, the transposition of the Directives' requirements is generally through the normal waste management licensing system (although there are slight variations for batteries and PCBs).

(c)   Lastly there are Directives on the incineration of waste. Directives 89/369 and 89/429 respectively cover new and old municipal incinerators. Both are 'daughter directives' of the Directive on Air Pollution from Industrial Plant (84/360). They lay down EC standards based on the best available technology and have caused the shutdown of many domestic incinerators which could not attain the necessary standards. There is a Directive on Hazardous Waste Incineration (94/67) which amongst other things lays down strict emission limits based on best available techniques. These Directives are implemented in the UK through Part I of the Environmental Protection Act 1990 (under IPC and APC) and the permitting system under the Pollution Prevention and Control Act 1999.

Domestic waste management policy

For many years the development of waste policy mirrored that of the law in that the primary aim was to address the environmental risks involved in the disposal of waste. The first steps towards a wider policy base were made with the introduction of the Framework Directive which required Member States not only to control the disposal of waste but to encourage the prevention, recycling and reuse of waste. The Conservative Government took up this approach in *This Common Inheritance* (Cm 1200, 1990) by placing a firm emphasis on policies which would tackle the production of waste at source if at all possible. In addition the concept of the waste hierarchy was adopted, namely that the preferred policy options for the management of waste would be ranked with waste minimisation followed by recycling then recovery and finally disposal.

Although these principles provided a good foundation upon which to build waste policy, the growth of detailed policies was largely unstructured with the effect that the overall objectives were often difficult to discern. In addition, the implementation of waste disposal plans and waste local plans dealing with strategic waste management and planning respectively had been patchy, leading to inconsistent local guidance. In the light of the amendments to the Framework Directive (by Directive 91/156) it became clear that there was a need to introduce some coherence into both national and local waste policies. The Framework Directive sets out a number of objectives which provide the basis for all other waste policies. These objectives have been directly transposed into UK law in the Waste Management Licensing Regulations 1994, sch. 4.

In addition to these explicit legal objectives the development of waste policy has entered a new phase with the introduction of a formal waste strategy. Scotland will have a separate strategy and Northern Ireland has a draft strategy issued in June 1998. Section 44A of the EPA 1990 gives the Secretary of State powers to prepare a statement containing policies in relation to the recovery and disposal of waste. It is intended that this national strategy will replace waste disposal plans which were drawn up by the old Waste Regulation Authorities under EPA 1990, s. 50 in addition to meeting the Framework Directive's requirements in relation to waste management plans under Art. 7.

The process of producing the National Waste Strategy has been far from easy. The House of Commons Environment Select Committee in its Sixth Report in 1998 criticised the 'inertia' which characterised the development of a sustainable waste policy. Indeed the failure to produce an adequate national waste management plan resulted in the European Commission issuing a 'reasoned opinion' against the UK for failure to comply with the terms of the Framework Directive. Although the Commission had been notified of 160 waste plans which had been prepared by local bodies, these did not provide a national coverage and only eight were considered to meet the requirements for such plans which were laid down in the directive.

One of the major obstacles to the production of a national strategy was the collation of data on waste arisings. On the basis that it is difficult to set targets for waste management without knowing the nature and extent of waste arisings, the compilation of credible information is a prerequisite for the production of a meaningful waste strategy. The information is not yet complete although reasonable estimates of the amount of municipal waste (i.e. the household and other waste which is collected by local authorities) have been collected in relation to the year 1997/8. Commercial and industrial waste arisings are still only preliminary estimates. Even these two main groups only form a relatively small part of the overall picture. It is estimated that of the 400 million tonnes of waste produced each year only 130 million tonnes come from the sources listed above with the remainder coming from construction and demolition wastes, sewage sludge, agricultural wastes, mining wastes and dredged spoils. It is interesting to note that most of these categories either fall outside the current definition of waste or are exempt from waste management licensing controls.

With progress being made on the collation of the data on waste arisings the production of a coherent waste strategy has developed over a relatively short period. The final version of the strategy, *Waste Strategy 2000 for England and Wales* (Cm 4693, 2000), was published in May 2000. This strategy constitutes the waste management plan for the purposes of the Waste Framework Directive. It also represents the necessary management plans for the purposes of the Hazardous Waste Directive, Packaging Waste Directive and the Landfill Directive. The Strategy sets out targets over a 20-year period with reviews every five years.

The Strategy sets out specific targets for the reduction of waste. These targets are:

(a)   By 2005 to reduce the amount of industrial and commercial waste going to landfill to 85 per cent of 1998 levels.

(b)   By 2005 to recover 40 per cent of municipal waste with a separate target of recycling 25 per cent of all household waste.

(c)   By 2010 to recover 45 per cent of municipal waste with a separate target of recycling 30 per cent of all household waste.

Figures suggest that less than 10 per cent of household waste is currently recycled which would mean that there is a difficult task ahead if we are to more than double the amount of household waste recycling within the necessary time period, let alone reduce other types of waste by 85 per cent. What is interesting about these targets is that the main regulatory controls are not designed to assist with the implementation of these policy goals. The provisions in Part II of the EPA 1990 are designed to minimise the risk of harm to the environment or human health. The legal instruments which are designed to assist in meeting these policy goals are much more diverse in character. The Government has placed a lot of emphasis upon the use of economic instruments and charging mechanisms. The landfill tax and the producer responsibility initiative (see further below) are seen as the two main instruments to provide the incentive to reduce waste production and increase recycling. The other main legal instrument which should trigger a move towards these targets will be the implementation of the requirements of the Landfill Directive (also see below).

The cumulative impact of the Strategy and the legal instruments associated with it is clear, particularly when coupled with the developments in relation to discharges to sewers and controls over incineration. Waste minimisation is to be encouraged because the costs of disposal, by whatever route, are likely to increase significantly as the national strategy is implemented. Indeed, the Waste Strategy makes it clear that voluntary initiatives and self-regulation (e.g. best practice programmes for industry sectors) play a vital role in the achievement of the policy targets. In addition there has been discussion of the greater use of economic instruments in waste management with both trade-able permits and the setting of quotas for each waste authority being options to be utilised in the meeting of the new targets.

Economic instruments and waste management

The use of economic instruments is more common in relation to waste management than in other areas of pollution control perhaps as it is one of the best ways of reflecting the true environmental cost of managing and disposing of waste and can help to provide an incentive to minimise production. The two main instruments (other than the recovery of adminis-tration costs through charging schemes) are provisions which encourage producer responsibility for waste (and in particular packaging waste) and a tax on wastes which are disposed of in landfill sites.

The landfill tax

The landfill tax was introduced under the Finance Act 1996. There are various secondary regulations and guidance notes which flesh out the main statutory provisions including the Landfill Tax Regulations 1996, the Landfill Tax (Qualifying Materials) Order 1996 and the Landfill Tax (Contaminated Land) Order 1996. The provisions came into force in October 1996 and have the effect that the vast majority of waste disposed of in landfill sites is subject to a tax at the point of disposal. There are three classes of material, the main class which is subject to the highest rate of tax (currently £10 a tonne which will rise to £15 over time), a second group of specific 'inactive' materials which is subject to a lower rate of tax (currently £2 a tonne) and a third class of waste which is exempt from the tax. The tax is paid by the operators of the landfill sites to the Customs and Excise on a quarterly basis although it is envisaged that this cost will be passed on to the disposers of the waste (and then theoretically to the producers of the waste). Although the main purpose of the tax was to ensure that environmental costs of waste disposal were acknowledged, it is also a source of revenue for central government. Some of the income raised by the tax is used to reduce employers' National Insurance contributions.

At the time the tax was introduced, there was some criticism of the failure to use the revenue for environmental purposes. The Landfill Tax Credit Scheme (LTCS) was introduced to address these concerns. Under the scheme, landfill operators which are subject to the tax can claim a credit against any payment of tax for any contribution which is made to an approved environmental body to pay for a project which is approved under the Landfill Tax Regulations. These cover a wide range of environmental projects including: the reclamation and restoration of contaminated land (where it does not benefit the original polluter); education and training in sustainable waste management; the creation of public amenity space or a wildlife habitat; and maintaining historic buildings and churches within the vicinity of a landfill site. The reclaimed credit must not be greater than 20 per cent of the total landfill tax payable and there is a ceiling of 90 per cent credit on each contribution made (i.e. the landfill tax payer must pay at least 10 per cent of the contribution from their own income).

The tax has been in operation for some time and a number of studies and surveys have been undertaken to see if the tax is effective (see HC Environment Select Committee, *The Operation of the Landfill Tax*, 1999; HM Customs and Excise, *Review of Landfill Tax*, 1998; and Coopers and Lybrand, *Landfill Tax — Is it Working?*, 1997). The evidence suggests that the tax is not high enough to make a significant impact upon the amount of waste arising and that there appear to be more approved projects which are funded under the LTCS which are connected to local amenity (and therefore good for public relations) rather than based upon long-term research and development towards sustainable waste management and waste minimisation. In addition there is some evidence that tax avoidance schemes have exploited loopholes in the waste management legislation (such as using inert waste for landscaping purposes — which is exempt from the waste management licensing system) and that fly-tipping of waste has increased. Although these concerns reflect more than mere teething troubles with a new regulatory scheme, the landfill tax is becoming an accepted regulatory tool which is to be used in conjunction with other mechanisms to assist in reducing waste arisings and encouraging reuse, recycling and recovery.

Recycling

Although there are administrative and legislative provisions dealing with the promotion of waste recycling, the current emphasis is on voluntary and economic instruments rather than compulsory regulation. As a result, British legislation does not include many formal duties to recycle (with the notable exceptions of the packaging waste obligations and the forthcoming waste reduction targets which will be set under the Landfill Directive). This also explains the government's opposition to the introduction of such targets and the difficulties which have been experienced in achieving the targets or in setting up regulatory systems to implement the European legislation.

The authority with the most important role in relation to recycling is the waste collection authority, since it collects most domestic and commercial waste and is able to separate recyclable wastes at an early stage. The authority may require separate receptacles to be used for household wastes that are to be recycled and those which are not (EPA 1990, s. 46(2)). It may buy or acquire waste with a view to recycling it (s. 55) and, if it makes arrangements for recycling waste, it does not have to deliver the waste to the waste disposal authority, as it would otherwise have to do under s. 48. It is also under a duty to draw up a waste recycling plan for its area, which involves publicising the arrangements it intends to make to facilitate recycling (s. 49).

Perhaps most significant in the light of government policy on economic instruments is that the waste collection authority is entitled to a recycling credit from the waste disposal authority under s. 52 where it recycles waste. The idea behind this provision is that it acts as an incentive to recycle waste by getting the waste disposal authority to pay the waste collection authority the amount of money it saves by not having to dispose of the waste. The amount payable is based on the net saving the waste disposal authority makes as a result of the recycling activities. At present the rate is fixed at half the average cost saving to the waste disposal authority, but the Government has announced that this is to rise to the full amount. The waste disposal authority *may* also make such a payment to anyone else who recycles waste and thus removes it from the waste stream (s. 52(3)).

Producer responsibility

Section 93 of the Environment Act 1995 provides for the introduction of regulations to impose obligations on the producers of materials or products to recycle, recover or re-use those products or materials. The first set of regulations imposing such an obligation introduced an obligation to recover and recycle certain percentages of packaging waste. These regulations came into force at the beginning of March 1997. Under the EC Directive on Packaging and Packaging Waste (94/62/EC), the UK has been set targets for recycling and recovering packaging waste, under which 50 per cent of waste packaging must be reutilised through recycling and other recovery methods by 2001.

The legislation which translates the EC Directive into UK law is the Producer Responsibility Obligations (Packaging Waste) Regulations 1997 (SI 1997/648 (as amended)). A key feature of the Regulations is the shared approach which spreads the responsibility for meeting the recovery and recycling targets right along the packaging chain from production through to retail.

Not all businesses are forced to comply with the regulations. The criteria for businesses falling under the Regulations are that they must:

(a)   be involved in one or more of the following activities:

(i)   manufacturing raw material used for packaging (e.g. making the cardboard for boxes),
(ii)   converting raw materials into packaging (e.g. turning the cardboard into a box),
(iii)   packing or filling packaging (e.g. putting goods into the box),
(iv)   selling packaging to the end user (selling the boxed goods to the final user);

(b)   produce, handle or supply more than 50 tonnes of packaging materials or packaging each year, including imported, but not exported, packaging;
(c)   have a turnover of more than £5 million (although from 2000, businesses with a turnover of over £2 million will fall under the regulations).

(a)   The definition of packaging
The definition of packaging includes products made from any materials which are used or are intended to contain and protect goods, or to aid their handling, delivery or presentation. Examples include boxes, plastic shrink-wrap, pallets, jars, and bottles. 'Recycling' is defined as including the reprocessing of packaging waste so that it can be used again either for its original or another purpose. 'Recovery' covers a number of processes whereby benefit is derived from using the waste packaging (this means that recycling is also a recovery process). The main process which can be defined as recovery is incineration where waste is turned into energy.

(b)   The obligations
There are three obligations which apply to companies which fall within the above categories. First they must register with the Environment Agency and supply data on packaging handled, recovered and recycled. There is an annual registration fee. An obligated company must register before April for each calendar year. The supplied data relates to the previous calendar year. This data is then used as the basis for the second obligation which is that obligated companies must recover and recycle certain percentages of the packaging handled in the previous year (i.e. based upon the data submitted by the obligated company).

Finally, obligated companies must complete a certificate of compliance which states that the company has met its obligation in the preceding year and send that certificate to the Environment Agency. Companies should be subject to monitoring from the Agency to verify the data supplied and compliance with the recovery and recycling obligation.

(c)   Meeting the obligations
An obligated company can choose to meet its obligations individually or join a 'compliance scheme' which takes on the legal responsibility for complying with the regulations on behalf of its members. Where companies join a

compliance scheme, they fall outside the operation of the regulations (although in practice the compliance scheme passes on the requirements under the terms of membership). In these cases the compliance scheme is subject to the regulations with the consequent need to comply with the obligations on an aggregate basis on behalf of its members.

(d)   The obligation to recover and recycle
The extent of the obligation to recover and recycle depends upon the nature of the activity carried out by the obligated company. As the obligation is shared out amongst the packaging chain, the manufacturers of packaging have a 6 per cent share, convertors a 9 per cent share, packer/fillers a 37 per cent share and sellers a 48 per cent share (these figures differ slightly from the original percentage shares which were thought to be unfair to convertors). Thus in order to calculate the obligation, an obligated company must take the amount of packaging waste which it is responsible for in the UK market and multiply it by the activity percentage. Finally, this figure must be multiplied once again by the overall national targets for packaging waste recycling and recovery.

(e)   Producer responsibility for packaging waste in practice
Given that the targets laid down in the directive were significantly higher than rates of recovery and recycling which were achieved in 1997, it was thought appropriate to stagger the domestic targets in the years running up to the adoption of the full directive targets in 2001. In addition, after the regulations were brought into force there was some concern about the setting of targets which would only just secure the directive targets as a minimum (with consequential problems of non-implementation were the targets to be missed). Therefore, the national targets have been increased for the final two years of the interim period (i.e. 1999 and 2000) in order to ensure that there is sufficient provision of recovery and recycling facilities in place in 2001 and to provide a little 'slack' which should mean a small shortfall will not necessarily be critical. Thus, the regulations were amended in 1999 with 43 per cent of packaging waste to be recovered in 1999 and 45 per cent in 2000, rising to 52 per cent in 2001. The recycling obligation was 10 per cent in 1999, 13 per cent in 2000 and 16 per cent in 2001.

Notwithstanding the tinkering with these targets, the forecasts of packaging recovery and recycling in 2001 suggest that the UK will not comply with the requirements of the directive with a possible shortfall of some 10 per cent of the target (see further DETR, *Increasing the Recovery and Recycling of Packaging Waste: A Forward Look for Planning Purposes*). Moreover, the Commission is in the process of revising the Directive which would undoubtedly lead to increases in the targets (possibly to 65 per cent recovery and 45 per cent recycling by 2006) but also switching the emphasis from general waste to household waste. Whatever happens, the UK will have to adopt radical measures to ensure continuing compliance.

There are a number of producer responsibility offences under the regulations. It is an offence to: fail to register; fail to take 'reasonable steps' to recycle or recover the required amount of packaging waste; and to supply misleading data. These offences are subject to a maximum fine of £5,000 on summary conviction or an unlimited fine on conviction on indictment.

The producer responsibility obligation for packaging waste is probably just the first in a series of regulations which will be introduced under s. 93 of the Environment Act 1995. It is likely that similar regulations will be introduced to encourage the recycling and recovery of other products and materials including newspapers, electrical goods and batteries. What is most interesting about the scheme of the regulations is the way that a variety of different mechanisms are used to secure the overall objective. The system operates in practice by compelling obligated businesses to purchase evidence of compliance from reprocessors who recover and recycle packaging materials in the form of packaging recovery notes (PRNs). Thus the regulations mix the use of the market in these PRNs (which will fluctuate in price under the normal principles of supply and demand) with the prospect of criminal sanctions for non-compliance to encourage businesses to consider the amount of packaging which they use.

Waste disposal and town and country planning

The disposal of waste on land presents some difficult questions of a land use nature, indeed the Town and Country Planning Acts were the primary control over waste before COPA 1974 was enacted. The development of land for waste management purposes is controlled under an additional and complementary layer of regulations which has remained largely unchanged through the introduction of waste management licensing legislation. The deposit of waste in land is deemed to be development which requires planning permission (see below). Furthermore, the use of land for waste management purposes other than disposal may require planning permission if it amounts to a material change of use. In most cases, the storage of waste on land will be incidental to the main use (e.g. in the case of an unrelated industrial use) although there may be cases such as the change of fuel in a cement kiln from conventional fuels to waste derived fuels where the boundary is not clearly distinguishable.

(a) The administration of waste planning

The main responsibility for waste planning falls to waste planning authorities (normally at a county, metropolitan or unitary level). Waste planning does, however, need to be taken into account at a regional level as so many issues need to be addressed on a regional basis. Thus Regional Planning Bodies (RPBs) are under an obligation to incorporate planning policies for regional waste management capacity when revising Regional Planning Guidance (RPG). The RPBs are advised on these issues by Regional Technical Advisory Bodies which provide data and assistance with technical issues when determining strategies which will be incorporated into RPG.

(b)   Development plans

There is specific provision for development plans for waste which set out policies against which planning applications for waste management facilities must be considered. Generally, in most non-metropolitan areas these policies can be found in a combination of the structure plan and the waste local plan or minerals and waste local plan. In other areas, the policies will be found within the unitary development plan. For many years, county planning authorities incorporated waste disposal policies into county structure plans. Some counties prepared subject local plans, but coverage was sparse. The Planning and Compensation Act 1991 amended the development plan provisions of the Town and Country Planning Act 1990 and amongst other things imposed a duty upon county planning authorities and some unitary authorities to prepare a waste local plan or a minerals and waste local plan (s. 38, TCPA 1990, as amended). Other unitary authorities may include waste policies in the district wide local plan when authorised to do so by the Secretary of State (see also s. 14(5)(d), Local Government Act 1992). National Park authorities are required to include waste policies in their park wide local plan or prepare a separate waste local plan (s. 38(3), TCPA 1990). Finally in metropolitan areas, unitary development plans must include waste policies in Part II of the Plan.

The content and form of waste development plans are set out in the Town and Country (Development Plan) (England) Regulations 1999 (SI 1999/ 3280) which also set out the procedures for making and altering such plans (see further p. 304). When drawing up waste development plans, the waste planning authority is obliged to consult the Environment Agency and to take into account the content of any waste disposal plan made under s. 50, EPA 1990 and in time the National Waste Strategy.

(c)   Development control

Section 55(3)(b) of the Town and Country Planning Act 1990 provides that the deposit of refuse or waste materials on land involves the material change in the use of that land if the area of the deposit is extended or the height of the deposit is extended above the original ground level. In addition, depending upon the facts of the case, tipping can amount to an engineering operation (if it involves technical supervision for instance), or even fall within the catch-all definition of an 'other operation'.

A planning application for the use of land, or the carrying out of operations in or on land, for the deposit of refuse or waste materials and/or the erection of any building, plant or machinery designed to be used wholly or mainly for the purposes of treating, storing, processing or disposing of refuse or waste materials is a county matter (see Town and Country Planning Act 1990, sch. 1). The application is made direct to the county planning authority, which is then under a duty to notify the district authority within 14 days as part of the consultation procedure (art. 12 of the GDPO).

(d)   Planning conditions and obligations

The difficulties with using planning conditions to control environmentally sensitive developments have been covered elsewhere (see p. 328). Planning permissions for waste disposal operations require special consideration. The main criterion for conditions on a planning permission for waste disposal is that they be for a planning purpose. Examples of matters which would normally be dealt with by way of conditions on the planning permission include:

(a) phasing of operations;
(b) the extent of tipping;
(c) access to and from the site;
(d) the *general* nature of the waste;
(e) restoration plans, including site contours, minimum depth of top soil etc.;
(f) aftercare for a short-term period.

To avoid duplicating environmental controls there are certain areas which should not normally be covered as they are more properly dealt with under the waste management regime. These include:

(a) the duration of activity;
(b) supervision of activities (including site offices and other administrative responsibilities);
(c) the specific types of waste to be covered;
(d) keeping of records;
(e) associated works.

Although it is advisable to separate the two areas of control, it is not unlawful to impose conditions which overlap.

Other overlapping controls

(a) Integrated pollution control and air pollution control (overlap with EPA 1990, Part I)

Regulation 16 of the Waste Management Licensing Regulations 1994 covers the overlap between control under Parts I and II of the EPA 1990. In relation to integrated pollution control, reg. 16(1)(a) provides that the recovery or disposal of waste under an IPC authorisation, where the activity is or forms part of a process, is exempt from the licensing. What is not clear is the extent to which an activity is 'part of the process'. The problem is particularly acute in respect of incineration and other combustion processes which use waste fuels. In particular, where waste is stored or treated on the site of an incinerator it is unclear as to whether a waste management licence is required.

In addition, despite the fact that it is meant to provide an integrated system of control, no condition can be attached to an authorisation which regulates the final disposal of directive waste in or on land (s. 28(1)).

In relation to other processes, most incinerators (except for very small ones), a number of waste recovery operations, and some other processes in which waste is burned as a fuel are subject to control under the local authority air pollution control provisions of Part I of the EPA 1990 (see Part B of section 5.1 (incineration) of the Prescribed Processes etc. Regulations 1991 (SI 1991/472). In these restricted circumstances, where an authorisation is required under Part I of the EPA 1990, this will exempt the premises from the need for a waste management licence. In practice, however, many operators will have operations ancillary to the main process (e.g. waste storage or delivery) and will seek a waste management licence to cover these aspects.

(b)   Integrated pollution prevention and control
There is an overlap in European law between the Framework Directive on Waste (75/442) and the Integrated Pollution Prevention and Control Directive (96/61) in that certain waste management installations are covered by both directives (detailed coverage of this overlaps on p. 389). In the UK, control over such installations has traditionally fallen within the waste management licensing system. The implementation of the Integrated Pollution Prevention and Control (IPPC) Directive under the Pollution Prevention and Control Act 1999 and associated regulations will see aspects of waste management (and in particular waste disposal) taken out of the licensing regime and put into the integrated permitting system. The draft regulations make it clear that all waste management installations which are subject to the requirements of the IPPC Directive will also be subject to the requirements of the Waste Framework Directive. The regulations also import two of the pre-existing mechanisms of regulating waste sites into the IPPC system. Thus, operators of IPPC waste management installations have to pass the 'fit and proper persons' test before being granted a permit and the requirements under the IPPC Directive for post operative restoration and monitoring are implemented by means of the transfer of the surrender provisions under Part II of the EPA 1990 (see p. 401).

There is an overlap between the requirements of the IPPC Directive and the Landfill Directive. The technical requirements of the Landfill Directive will be incorporated into the permitting system via the BAT standard when the Landfill Directive is implemented in domestic legislation. Thus, existing waste management installations will only be brought within the permitting system when the Landfill Directive has been implemented within the UK (probably after 2003). New waste management installations (which are prescribed for control) which wish to operate after 31 October 1999 must apply for a permit and use the best available techniques for reducing environmental impacts (see further p. 388).

There is, however, no explicit overlap between the two regimes. Under the permitting system, waste management installations are excluded from the waste management licensing system and the waste management licensing regime excludes installations which are subject to the permitting system.

(c)   Contaminated land
The deposit or discharge of waste (whether knowingly or otherwise) is a significant cause of contamination and there is a good deal of interaction between the waste management licensing regime and the provisions dealing with the clean up of contaminated land. First, where contamination arises as

a result of the illegal deposit of controlled waste, the right to serve a remediation notice under Part IIA is removed (s. 78YB(3), EPA 1990). This is because there is an equivalent power to remove such waste under s. 59, EPA 1990 (see p. 548). This would cover a situation where there was an active deposit of waste (i.e. in the case of an unlicensed landfill) rather than passive leakage of waste (e.g. seeping from an underground tank). Secondly, where there is an extant waste management licence in force in relation to a site which is contaminated, the land cannot be identified as contaminated land as there are enforcement powers under the licence to deal with any clean up (s. 78YB(2), EPA 1990). Finally, where clean up operations are required under a remediation notice, such operations may require a waste management licence as a disposal or recovery operation.

(d) Water pollution

The treatment of liquid effluent prior to discharge into sewer or into controlled waters is arguably the treatment of waste and there has been some confusion about the extent to which effluent treatment plant fell under the waste management licensing regime. Under the Framework Directive, the physico-chemical or biological treatment of 'waste' is defined as a disposal operation which would be subject to the requirement for licensing. However the Department of the Environment determined in 1996 that such treatment was excepted from the waste licensing system as it was 'waste in liquid form' which was controlled under other legislation, namely the Urban Waste Water Treatment Directive (91/271) and the corresponding domestic legislation, the Urban Waste Water Treatment (England and Wales) Regulations 1994 (SI 1994/2841) and/or the Water Resources Act 1991.

The landfilling of waste can provide a threat to groundwater quality. In order to implement the Groundwater Directive (80/68), there are provisions which set out requirements in respect of groundwater protection which must be met when determining any waste management licence application. Under the Waste Management Licensing Regulations 1994, reg. 15, a waste management licence can only be granted where there are adequate measures for preventing groundwater pollution by substances listed in List I and II in the Directive (see further p. 498). As a result of these controls, activities which are carried out under a waste management licence are exempt from the requirements of the Groundwater Regulations 1998 (see p. 587). There is, however, a gap between the two legislative regimes as the groundwater protection measures under the waste management licensing system only apply to waste disposal. This means that there are other activities which are covered under a waste management licence (e.g. recycling) which may give rise to a risk of groundwater pollution but which are not required to implement the measures found in the Groundwater Directive.

Waste authorities

The administration of waste management is divided into three. Under s. 30 of the EPA 1990, as amended by the Environment Act 1995, the

Environment Agency is the main regulatory agency taking over responsibility from the waste regulation authorities in April 1996. Circular 15/95 gives guidance on the transfer of property rights and liabilities from the WRAs to the Agency. The Agency has responsibility for the main regulatory functions in relation to waste management including the administration, supervision and enforcement of licensed activities (ss. 35–42). In addition the Agency is responsible for the system of licensing waste carriers, the special waste provisions, and the operation and enforcement of the duty of care. The waste collection authorities (WCAs) are the relevant district councils or London borough councils. They have the responsibility for arranging the collection of household waste (and on request the collection of commercial or industrial waste) (s. 45), drawing up plans for recycling household and commercial waste (s. 49) and making arrangements for the provision of waste bins for household and commercial waste (ss. 46–7).

The waste disposal authorities (WDAs) are the county councils in English non-metropolitan areas or the unitary authorities in such areas. In some metropolitan areas special arrangements apply (e.g. Greater London and Greater Manchester), but generally the metropolitan district council or London borough council will be the waste disposal authority. The WDA was responsible for the formation of the privatised waste disposal companies (s. 32), and continues to be responsible for arranging for the disposal of waste collected by the WCA (s. 51), arranging for the provision of waste transfer stations and civic amenity sites (s. 51) and waste recycling (s. 55).

What is waste? — general considerations

Before examining the details of waste management licensing regulation, there are a number of preliminary issues. First, as the statutory regime only applies to the management of waste, there is the general definition of waste. Secondly, there is the categorisation of the type of waste management operation which is used to manage the waste (either recovery or disposal). Finally, there is the issue of whether the waste is exempted from the statutory regime.

The concept of waste has proved to be particularly difficult to define with any certainty. There are a number of reasons for this. First, there is no inherent physical characteristic which can be used to define waste. Unlike other areas of pollution control the idea of waste is not necessarily associated with pollution (although all pollution is associated with waste). The link between waste and environmental harm is that unless waste is managed properly (and therefore regulated accordingly) there is a *potential* for pollution. Secondly, there is the subjective nature of the view which one can take when considering whether the material is waste. In particular, one person's waste can be another person's raw material. This can be closely linked to the third reason, that there is an implicit connection between the concept of waste and a lack of value or worth of an object (i.e. something can only be waste if it is not wanted). There are, however, some categories of objects which have been discarded by the original holder, but which have a value because they can be used either for their original or another purpose (there may be some sort of treatment required prior to reuse). Fourthly, the adoption of the waste management hierarchy simply adds to the problem. Where there is an emphasis placed upon the reuse and recycling of material there is no sense in over regulation by drawing up a very wide definition of waste as this would discourage environmentally beneficial activities which would reduce the amount of raw materials required and consequently the waste produced. On the other hand, many recycling and reclamation processes have the capability of causing harm if left unregulated. In drawing up any definition, the rule maker must seek to strike a balance between these two competing considerations.

For many years the definition of waste included substances or articles which were scrap or which were required to be disposed of because they were broken, worn out, contaminated or otherwise spoilt (s. 30, COPA 1974 and s. 75, EPA 1990). Under the 1991 amendments to the Framework Directive, however, a common definition of waste was agreed to apply to all Member States. This differed from the previous definition and required amendments to UK legislation. Other amendments have been necessary to ensure full implementation of the Directive. All of the amendments have been incorporated within the Waste Management Licensing Regulations 1994 with subsequent amendments to the EPA 1990. Although the definition of waste and waste management activities is very complex, there are two broad principles which apply. First, the only waste which is regulated under the EPA 1990 is known as 'Directive waste' to reflect the description of waste as found in the Directive. Secondly, the activities which are subject to the licensing requirements under Part II of the EPA 1990 are known as Directive disposal and Directive recovery. These two phrases replace the old single phrase of 'treating, keeping or disposing of waste' which was found in the original version of s. 33 of the EPA 1990.

What is waste — Directive waste

The concept of 'Directive waste' as found in art. 1 of the Framework Directive is implemented through a repeal of s. 75(2), EPA 1990 which provided for the previous statutory definition of waste. There has been a delay with the formal repeal of this definition which has been caused by the lack of progress over bringing certain wastes (e.g. agricultural wastes) within the new general definition. Notwithstanding this delay, Directive waste has been incorporated into domestic legislation through the licensing system in the Waste Management Licensing Regulations 1994.

Therefore, the definition of Directive waste can be found in regs. 1(3), 24(8) of, and sch. 4, para. 9 to the Waste Management Licensing Regulations 1994. These provisions also amend the definition of controlled waste so as to exclude any waste which does not fall within the definition of Directive waste from the definition of controlled waste (and therefore it falls outside the scheme of control of Part II of the EPA 1990).

The general definition of Directive waste is to be found in art. 1(a) of the Framework Directive (and in the Waste Management Licensing Regulations 1994) which provides the following definition:

any substance or object in the categories set out in Annex I [to the Framework Directive] which the holder discards or intends or is required to discard.

The starting point for the definition of waste is therefore the list of 'categories' which can be found in Annex I of the directive (Part II of sch. 4 to the regulations). There are sixteen categories (Q1–Q16) covering a range of descriptions of production residues and contaminated or adulterated materials. Whilst these descriptions are helpful in determining whether something is waste, on closer examination it becomes clear that the description of various categories of waste is illustrative rather than determinative. The first thing to note is that the list sets out substances or objects which are waste *only* when they are discarded. Thus, a substance or object in one of the categories in the list will not necessarily be waste unless it can be demonstrated that it falls within the general definition in art. 1(a). Secondly, there is a totally inclusive category, Q16, which covers all 'materials, substances or products' which are not contained in any of the other categories. This would cover everything which could conceivably exist. The inclusion of this general category suggests that there is a specific purpose in setting out other more detailed categories (otherwise the all-inclusive category would render the others superfluous).

It is clear from the descriptions of the categories that they cover substances or objects which may be presumed to be discarded (or will be discarded in the near future). At best this could set up a rebuttable presumption which could be contradicted by specific evidence of an absence to discard. In addition to these general categories of waste, there is an extensive list of wastes (known as the European Waste Catalogue) prepared by the European Commission (see Decision 94/3). In common with the Annex I list, this is merely illustrative (as its main purpose is to ensure uniformity in the classification of wastes across Member States) and is not conclusive in determining whether any of the listed substances is actually waste.

The practical effect of the general category of waste means that there is a two-stage test which applies to the question of whether a substance, material or product is directive waste. First, is it a substance, material or product and does it therefore come within any of the categories set out in the specific definitions in sch. 4? If the answer is yes (and for practical purposes it will almost certainly be the case), the second question is, has the substance, material or product been discarded by its holder or is there an intention or requirement to discard it?

It is the second of these two questions which gives the key to the definition of directive waste. As we shall see, the case law on the definition of waste suggests that material is not waste merely because it fall within a class set out in sch. 4, but that the critical question is whether it has been discarded and on that issue, one of the important factors is whether the substance has been consigned to a waste recovery or disposal operation. This interrelationship between the concept of 'discarding', 'waste recovery operation' and 'waste disposal operation' lies at the heart of the problem of providing a general definition of waste.

In *Mayer Parry Recycling Limited* v *Environment Agency* [1999] Env LR 489, the High Court followed the ECJ's ruling in two important cases on the definition of waste. In these cases, the ECJ held that the meaning of the word 'discards' within the definition of directive waste has a special meaning which covers both the consignment of waste for disposal (i.e. getting rid of something) and the consignment of waste to a recovery operation (see *Euro Tombesi* [1998] Env LR 59 and *Inter-Environnement Wallonie* v *Regione Wallone* [1998] Env LR 625). This approach has the advantage that there is no need to discuss the possible meanings of the word 'discards' (which is tortuously deconstructed in policy guidance found in Circular 11/94) but it has the disadvantage that the emphasis shifts to the definitions of disposal and recovery operations (i.e. has the substance, material or object been consigned to a disposal or recovery operation — if so, it is waste).

(a)   Disposal operations and recovery operations
The definition of 'disposal operations' is relatively straightforward. Annex IIA of the Framework Directive (sch. 4, Part III of the Waste Management Licensing Regulations 1994) lists a series of operations which are standard ways of finally disposing of waste (including varieties of incineration and landfill). By definition consigning a substance to one of these operations will be deemed to be 'discarding' that substance as the operation is final. One point which should be made, however, is that the list is not exhaustive and there are other types of disposal which are not included (particularly in relation to such things as deliberate discharges of pollutants into the atmosphere) where they are controlled under separate legislation.

The definition of 'recovery operations' is, however, more complicated. The starting point is the list of operations which are found in Annex IIB of the Directive and Part IV of the Waste Management Licensing Regulations. On closer consideration, the list includes operations which take place within the 'normal industrial cycle' (i.e. the recovery process is part and parcel of a bigger industrial process). For example, category R9 ('Use principally as a fuel') and R8 ('Reuse of oil') can take place without the specific recovery of waste (e.g. the use of primary fuels such as coal). The dividing line between the use of raw materials in a normal industrial cycle and the consignment of waste to a recovery operation can, in certain cases, be very fine indeed. Indeed, in *Tombesi* and *Inter-Wallonie*, the Advocate-General made it clear that the issue of where to draw the dividing line would be a matter for Member States to determine on a case by case basis. In the UK this has been done both in policy guidance in Circular 11/94 by means of the definition of a specialised recovery operation, and through the courts as a result of the *Mayer Parry* case.

(b)   Specialised recovery operations
The first way of differentiating between recovery operations and industrial processes has been the adoption of a separate concept of the 'specialised recovery operation'. There is no specific legislative definition of this phrase but it is described in Circular 11/94 as being intended to cover operations

which either reuse substances or objects which are waste because they have fallen out of normal use, or recycle them in a way which eliminates or diminishes sufficiently the threat posed by their original production as waste and produces a raw material which can be used in the same way as raw material of a non-waste compound. In cases where substances are consigned to a specialised recovery operation they will always be waste. Although this approach has been viewed favourably by the ECJ and the High Court, it is still not a legal test. Given the lack of judicial criticism, however, and the difficult nature of the issue, it would seem that this can form the basis of a practical test.

(c)   The *Mayer Parry* case

The *Mayer Parry* decision concerned, amongst other things, the sorting of scrap metals and whether or not this involved a recovery operation. The High Court followed the decisions in *Tombesi* and *Inter-Wallonie* but added a gloss of matters which could be taken into account when determining whether an operation was a normal industrial process or a recovery operation. In doing so, the High Court considered a range of factors which contributed an overall picture of whether an operation was a recovery operation.

First, the nature of the business was an important factor. If the business was involved with an operation which was listed in the Directive as a recovery operation (e.g. the recovery or recycling of metals), it was fair to presume that the operations carried out by the company would constitute recovery operations, in the absence of evidence to the contrary. The fact that some of the operations had no environmental consequences (e.g. the physical sorting or grading of metals) was irrelevant unless the sorting was carried out for economic reasons only. On the facts of the case, the sorting of reusable metals was found to be 'economic sorting' whereas the division of reusable metals from that which was to be disposed of was a recovery operation.

Secondly, the High Court considered that it was appropriate to take into account an 'equivalent replacement' test, namely, 'did the operation meet normal health and safety requirements applicable to non-waste products or processes?' or put another way, 'would there be any greater risk of environmental harm from the use of the material in the operation than would have been the case were a non-waste material to have been used?'. If the answer was yes then it would presumed that it was not an equivalent replacement and the operation would be deemed to be a waste recovery operation. Finally, there was a level where an operation would be so small as to be insignificant although there was no indication of what that level would be.

One other aspect of the case which is notable is that the High Court reaffirmed the previous case law in finding that waste can cease to be waste where it is recovered (see *Kent County Council* v *Queenborough Rolling Mill Co. Ltd* (1990) 89 LGR 306, below). The waste is 'recovered' when it is a substance of sufficient beneficial use to eliminate or sufficiently diminish the threat posed by the original production of the waste. In addition, the waste can be altered by a change of intention on behalf of the recipient of the waste. For example, someone who receives a broken, discarded product can mend it so that it ceases to be waste.

What is controlled waste?

Most of the provisions of the EPA 1990 apply to 'controlled waste'. The primary definition of controlled waste is set out in EPA 1990, s. 75(4) as meaning household, industrial or commercial waste or any such waste. In *Thanet District Council* v *Kent County Council* [1993] Env LR 391 the Divisional Court held that the phrase 'any such waste' is limited to waste coming within any of the named categories and would not cover seaweed deposited on agricultural land. The definition of controlled waste has been amended by the Waste Management Licensing Regulations 1994. Regulation 24(8) amends the Controlled Waste Regulations 1992 (SI 1992/588) by providing that waste which is not directive waste must not be treated as household, industrial or commercial waste. Thus, the practical effect is that the previous categories of household, industrial or commercial waste have been amended to the single class of directive waste.

Case law on the general definition of waste

In addition to the cases already referred to, the courts have examined the definition of waste on a number of previous occasions. Although these decisions are based upon the definition under previous legislation they assist in helping with the interpretation of directive waste as the principles can, in some cases, be extended to cover the new definition. In *Long* v *Brook* [1980] Crim LR 109 the Crown Court decided that, upon its true construction, COPA 1974 defined 'waste' from the point of view of the person discarding the material. This was followed in *Kent County Council* v *Queenborough Rolling Mill Co. Ltd* (1990) 89 LGR 306, where the defendant company was charged with depositing waste on land without a disposal licence contrary to COPA 1974 (s. 3). The material concerned consisted of ballast, china, china clay and broken pottery from a disused site which was being cleared by a demolition company. It was used to fill an area subject to subsidence. The magistrates decided that such material was not waste as it was inert and was being used for the purposes of infill. On appeal to the Divisional Court the council argued that the material was waste by its very nature. The defendant company argued that the material was not waste because it was put to a useful purpose and therefore was not unwanted. The Divisional Court held that, although the material was put to a useful purpose, that was not a relevant factor in deciding whether the material was waste. The important factor was the nature of the material when it was discarded. If it was waste it would always remain waste until it was adequately reconstituted or recycled. This would still be the case with the redefintion of waste under the Waste Management Licensing Regulations 1994.

In *Cheshire County Council* v *Armstrong's Transport (Wigan) Ltd* [1995] Env LR 62 the defendant company was responsible for processing building site rubble before returning the crushed material to its original site to assist in rebuilding works. The defendant was prosecuted as it did not seek a waste disposal licence under COPA 1974. The magistrates found that the material was not waste as it was a product. The defendant was able to demonstrate that there was no intention to discard on behalf of the last holder of the material as they were under a contractual obligation to return the material to the site once it had been processed. The Divisional Court held that this obligation meant that the rubble was not waste as the original holder had not wished to dispose of it.

In *Meston Technical Services Ltd* v *Warwickshire County Council* [1995] Env LR 380 the defendants operated a waste recycling business from a site in an industrial park. They traded in the receipt of liquid controlled waste which was received from various companies and was reprocessed into substances which would either be sold on for industrial or commercial use or otherwise disposed of by way of landfill or incineration. The defendants were prosecuted for breach of licence conditions under COPA 1974. On appeal the defendants argued that the drums of material were not 'waste' within the meaning of COPA 1974 and that the licence did not apply to the storage of the drums. It was argued that the drums (and the material within it) were not waste because they were wanted by the defendants and were valuable to them. Secondly, it was argued that the defendants could only be guilty of an offence where they themselves regarded the relevant material as waste. If they did not regard it as waste but intended to sell it on if they could, it was not waste and no offence was committed. The Divisional Court held that the value of the material or the views of the defendants were irrelevant when considering the definition of the material as waste, and it was not appropriate to examine the aims and purposes of the holder of the waste when considering what was waste under the Environmental Protection Act 1990. The introduction of the wider definition of directive waste does nothing to change the fundamental principles behind these decisions. Indeed, in *Tombesi*, the ECJ held that directive waste extended to all objects and substances discarded by their owners, even if they had a commercial value and were collected on a commercial basis for recycling, reclamation or re-use.

The national decisions are in line with a decision of the ECJ in Cases C-206 & 207/88 *Vessoso* [1990] ECR I-1461. In these cases, two Italians had been charged with collecting, transporting and storing waste without authorisation, contrary to Italian Presidential Decree. It was argued on their behalf that the material was recyclable raw material and not waste. In its judgment, the Court stated that the definition of waste contained in the original Framework Directive on Waste (75/442) was concerned with the potential health and pollution hazard that the materials could bring, and concluded by finding that although recycling was to be encouraged, material could be waste notwithstanding its potential for future use. This has now been clarified with the expansion of the definition of waste in the updated Framework Directive (91/156) and the amendments to the UK legislation.

Exceptions — what is not waste

There are various categories of waste which fall outside the waste management licensing system altogether. These should be distinguished from exemptions which are categories of waste which are exempt from statutory control because they fall within set limits laid down in legislation (this distinction mirrors the difference between those things which are not 'development' under the Town and Country Planning Act 1990 and development which is granted automatic planning permission).

Regulation 1(3) of the 1994 Regulations excludes anything excluded from the scope of the Directive from the definition of directive waste (and thus controlled waste). The justification for these exceptions is that they are already covered under existing legislation. There are, however, a few anomalies. Six main categories of waste are excepted.

(a) Gaseous effluent emitted into the atmosphere: controlled under Part I of the EPA 1990 and the Clean Air Act 1993. Emissions from waste management are, however, covered under the directive (e.g. from incineration).

(b) Radioactive waste: controlled under the Radioactive Substances Act 1993.

(c) Waste resulting from prospecting, extraction, treatment, and storage of mineral resources and the working of quarries: controlled under the Mines and Quarries (Tips) Act 1969. This also accords with s. 75(7) of EPA 1990 which excludes all waste from mines and quarries from the definition of controlled waste. The issue of non-mineral waste from mines and quarries is, however, far from clear-cut. Although the EPA 1990 would exclude this waste from the definition of controlled waste the DoE has said that this would fall within the definition of directive waste.

(d) Animal carcasses and the following agricultural waste, namely faecal matter and other natural, non-dangerous substances used in farming: controlled under the Animal By-Products Order 1992 (SI 1992/3303); there is, however, a similar problem to the position in respect of minerals wastes. Agricultural waste is excluded from the definition of controlled waste under s. 75(7) of EPA 1990, yet the DETR takes the view that it should fall within the definition of directive waste where it falls outside the above exemption.

(e) Waste waters, with the exception of waste in liquid form: broadly controlled under the Water Resources Act 1991 and Water Industry Act 1991. After much debate the treatment of effluent in treatment plants is not considered to require a waste management licence (see above, p. 485).

(f) Decommissioned explosives: controlled under the Explosives Act 1875, the Control of Explosives Regulations 1991 (SI 1991/1531), various regulations under the Health and Safety at Work etc Act 1974 and the Road Traffic (Carriage of Explosives) Regulations 1989 (SI 1989/615).

There is a residual degree of control over non-directive waste. Any person who deposits or who knowingly causes or knowingly permits the deposit of any non-controlled waste commits an offence if the waste has the characteristics of special waste and is not deposited in accordance with a licence or permission of some description (EPA 1990, s. 63(2)). This rather convoluted subsection appears designed to cover such things as the irresponsible disposal of toxic materials. The maximum penalty is the same as under s. 33. In addition, the Secretary of State may make regulations under s. 63(1) applying specified parts of the EPA 1990 to exempt wastes (specifically agricultural and mine wastes), although no such regulations have ever been made.

The meaning of 'deposit'

The definition of 'deposit' is central to the operation of the EPA 1990 and the courts have adopted a relatively wide definition. Initially in *Leigh Land Reclamation Ltd* v *Walsall Metropolitan Borough Council* (1991) 155 JP 547 it was held that waste was deposited at a landfill site only when there was no realistic prospect of further examination or inspection and it had reached its final resting place. This decision caused enormous practical problems for waste regulation authorities as it became difficult to prove that waste had definitely reached its final resting place when defendants argued it was going to be moved on a future occasion. The decision in *Leigh* was overturned by the Divisional Court in *R* v *Metropolitan Stipendiary Magistrate, ex parte London Waste Regulation Authority* [1993] All ER 113, where it was held that 'deposit' applies to temporary deposits as well as to permanent ones, which seems to reflect both common sense and the wider scope of the EPA 1990 in dealing with waste *management* rather than *disposal*. This definition was widened once again in *Thames Waste Management Ltd* v *Surrey County Council* [1997] Env LR 148. In that case, the defendant, TWML, was convicted of unlawfully depositing controlled waste on land other than in accordance with the conditions in a waste disposal licence. A condition of the licence required any deposit of waste to be covered over in the prescribed manner on the day that waste was deposited. TWML argued that the failure to cover the waste was not an unlawful deposit because the failure to cover took place after the initial deposit. The court held that 'deposit' could cover continuing activities where the context of the waste management licence would suggest that it was appropriate to do so. On the facts of the case it was reasonable to assume that the deposit continued until such time as it was covered. Thus there has been a significant movement away from a relatively narrow notion where 'deposit' was viewed only in terms of permanence to a view where deposit may take a significant period whilst other activities are carried out.

The waste management licensing system

The statutory framework dealing with the licensing of waste management activities can be largely found in Part II of the Environmental Protection Act 1990. The main features of the regulatory framework include:

(a)   Waste management functions, which are split between regulatory and operational functions. The Environment Agency has regulatory control over waste management whilst operational functions are split between the waste collection authorities, waste disposal authorities, and the private sector waste disposal companies.

(b)   A criminal duty of care, which applies to all those who deal with waste and which ensures that waste is properly handled throughout from production through to final disposal.

(c)   An all-embracing criminal offence of treating, keeping or disposing of waste in a manner likely to cause pollution of the environment or harm to human health. This operates independently of the licensing system and effectively imposes minimum standards for the handling of all wastes.

(d)   A comprehensive system of waste management licensing dealing with all aspects of waste management. In particular, there are expanded powers to refuse licences on the ground that the applicant is not a 'fit and proper person', sophisticated powers of enforcement and increased maximum penalties in the event of breach.

(e)   The licensing of directive disposal operations and directive recovery operations. These phrases have assumed greater significance following the decisions in *Inter-Environment Wallonie, Tombesi* and *Mayer Parry* which linked the definition of waste and the concept of 'discarding' to the consignment of a substance either to a disposal or recovery operation (see above). The list of directive disposal operations can be found in Part III of sch. 4 to the Waste Management Licensing Regulations 1994. It includes landfill, incineration on land and at sea, permanent storage of waste, the treatment of waste prior to final disposal and the injection of waste into the earth. The list of directive recovery operations can be found in Part I of sch. 4. It includes the reclamation or recycling of a variety of substances (e.g. solvents, organic substances, acids and metals) and the use of wastes obtained from recycling or reclamation. These categories do not, however, give a complete picture as some recovery operations are indistinguishable from normal industrial activities (see the discussion of 'recovery and disposal operations', above).

(a)   Exemptions
A lengthy list of exemptions from the need for a waste management licence is set out in reg. 17 and sch. 3. It is not possible in a book of this nature to go through the whole list, or to provide exact details of those things that are mentioned, but the main types of activity that are covered are as follows:

(a)   activities that are carried on in accordance with the provisions of consents or authorisations granted under other legislation (e.g. a discharge consent granted under the Water Resources Act 1991, or a licence to dump at sea granted under the Food and Environment Protection Act 1985);

(b)   the storage of directive waste at the place at which it is produced pending its treatment or disposal elsewhere (this will cover such things as storing waste in a skip — there is no time limit as long as the producer can show that it is genuinely going to be collected);

(c)   the storage of special waste at the place at which it is produced pending its treatment or disposal elsewhere, as long as certain conditions on quantity and security are met;

(d)   various activities relating to the recovery or reuse of waste, such as sorting waste at the place at which it is produced, baling it, shredding it and compacting it;

(e)   storage or deposit of demolition or construction wastes for the purposes of construction work being undertaken on the land;

(f) deposit of certain organic matter for the purposes of fertilising or conditioning land;

(g) in order to encourage recycling, a great variety of recycling activities are exempted, although often subject to detailed restrictions on quantity (for example, the collection of paper and cardboard, aluminium and steel cans, plastics, glass and textiles for recycling, or the cleaning and washing of packaging or containers so that they can be reused).

In most of these categories the exemption will not apply if the waste is special waste.

The requirement for a waste management licence (and the exemptions from the need for a licence) must be read in conjunction with the offence of unlawful waste management set out in s. 33. The general offence in s. 33(1)(c) of keeping, treating or disposing of directive waste in a manner likely to cause pollution of the environment or harm to human health will remain applicable in all the above exemptions apart from those in category (a). By contrast household waste from a private dwelling which is treated, kept or disposed of within the curtilage of the dwelling by, or with the permission of, the occupier, is entirely exempt from s. 33 (s. 33(2)).

(b) Registration

A requirement of the 1994 Regulations, made necessary by the provisions of Article II of the Framework Directive, is that certain activities must be registered with the EA even though exempted from the waste management licensing system. The registration system is based around an offence in support of the requirement to register. Under reg. 18(1) it is an offence to carry on an exempt activity involving the recovery or disposal of waste without being registered with the appropriate registration authority. The requirement to register covers 'establishments or undertakings'; it does not include private individuals. Registration is effected simply by notifying the EA of the relevant activities, where they are carried on, and the exemption which is being relied on (reg. 18(3)). The EA is required to keep a register of exemptions containing the particulars of the registration (reg. 18(4)). The tone of government advice in Circular 11/94 is that the requirement to register is more administrative in nature than any great step forward in environmental protection. Indeed, the advice in the circular would suggest that prosecution for the failure to register an exempt activity would only be a last resort. Where serious environmental harm had arisen from exempt activities it would be preferable to rely upon prosecution powers under s. 33(1)(c), if possible (see p. 511).

(c) Applications for a licence

If a waste management licence is required, an application must be made in writing to the EA. There is a standard application form available from the EA. It is an offence to make a statement in an application for a licence (or in an application for modification, transfer or surrender) knowing it to be false in a material particular, or reckless as to such an event (s. 44). The maximum penalty on conviction in the magistrates' court is a £5,000 fine, but in the Crown Court the maximum penalty is an unlimited fine and/or two years in prison. Where an application form does not provide the requisite information, the Environment Agency is entitled to refuse to proceed with an application and it will not be deemed to have been refused when the statutory period for determination (four months) runs out.

Where the licence relates to the keeping, treating, or disposal of waste in or on land the licence is called a 'site licence', and the application is made to the EA where the site is situated. An application for a licence for mobile plant is made to the EA where the applicant has its principal place of business, thus allowing for a number of pieces of plant to be covered by one licence. Section 35(2) states that only the occupier of the land or the operator of a mobile plant can apply for a licence. There is no definition of an occupier in the Act, but it must be assumed that it relates to the ability to control the waste operation and the use of the land.

The EA must consult with a number of other public bodies if it proposes to issue a licence, and must consider any representations that those bodies make within 21 days. The Health and Safety Executive is a statutory consultee in all cases. In any case where the site is notified as a site of special scientific interest (SSSI), the relevant NCC is also a statutory consultee, reflecting the fact that a number of SSSIs have been lost to waste disposal over the years — though current planning guidance makes it less likely that planning permission will be granted for waste disposal on a SSSI in the future.

The EA must also take into account any central government guidance (s. 35(8)). This will be provided in the form of waste management papers and it is intended that they should produce a situation where a more uniform approach is adopted across the country than has been the case in the past. The most significant paper is Waste Management Paper No. 4, *Licensing of Waste Facilities*, which seeks to provide comprehensive guidance on the criteria for granting a licence, such as the definition of a 'fit and proper person' and on conditions. WMP4 contains a policy that licences should be reviewed annually and fully reconsidered at least every five years. It will also be appropriate to consider the guidance to be found in Circular 11/94.

One feature that is missing is any element of public participation, since the application does not have to be advertised. This situation arises because it is perceived that the grant of a waste management licence is a technical question: the wider question of the appropriateness of the site will have been considered when planning permission was sought.

(d)   The powers of the EA
The EA has a discretion to grant or refuse a licence, but this is subject to a number of restrictions. (Similar restrictions apply to the EA's discretion on questions relating to the transfer, modification, suspension or revocation of a licence, though the wording of the relevant sections is usually more restrictive — see below.)

First, an application *must* be refused if planning permission is required for the use of the land and there is no such permission (s. 36(2)). For these purposes, a lawful development certificate granted under the Town and Country Planning Act 1990, s. 191, is treated as a planning permission. An established use certificate granted under earlier legislation will also normally suffice.

Secondly, the EA *may* refuse a licence if it is satisfied that such a step is necessary to prevent pollution of the environment or harm to human health. This gives a fairly wide discretion to the EA, since s. 29 defines pollution of the environment to mean pollution due to the release or escape of substances capable of causing harm to any living organism from the land in or on which waste is kept, treated or deposited. Where there is no planning permission in force (i.e. because it was not required — this would cover a site open since before 1948), the EA may refuse a licence if that is necessary to prevent serious detriment to the amenities of the locality (s. 36(3)).

Further guidance on this point is provided by the Waste Management Licensing Regulations 1994. In order to ensure compliance with the Groundwater Directive (80/68), the EA is required only to grant applications if technical precautions, enforceable through conditions, can be taken to prevent the discharge of List I substances and to prevent groundwater pollution by List II substances. The EA is also required to review existing licences that may lead to discharges of List I or List II substances and to use its modification and revocation powers accordingly. The risk of groundwater pollution is an important consideration in the grant of any licence. There is a strong set of policies for the protection of groundwater, which were formulated by the NRA (see NRA, *Policy and Practice for the Protection of Groundwater*, 1992). There are some doubts over the ability of measures taken to prevent contamination of groundwater from landfill sites. On most sites the preventive measures will involve some form of impermeable membrane to prevent the egress of leachate. Research has shown that over time even the sturdiest membrane can degrade and the groundwater be threatened. The technical decision on the adequacy of any preventive measures is, however, a question of policy and the decision-maker is entitled to rely upon one technical view even if there are competing views (see *R v Vale of Glamorgan Borough Council, ex parte James* [1996] Env LR 102, where a WRA was held to be entitled to rely on the view of the NRA even though another view was put forward).

Thirdly, a licence *may* be refused if the applicant is not a fit and proper person. The meaning of this phrase is set out in general terms in s. 74 and in more specific terms in the Waste Management Licensing Regulations. The final form of the regulations and the guidance on their use was the subject of great controversy and debate between the government and the waste disposal industry in 1992 and 1993, leading to a position where the standards are not as strict as was once envisaged.

Section 74(3) states that an applicant is not a fit and proper person if:

(a)   the applicant or any other relevant person has committed a relevant offence; or

(b)   the mangement of the site will not be in the hands of a technically competent person; or

(c) the applicant cannot make financial provision adequate to discharge the obligations arising under the licence.

Section 74(7) explains that a relevant person has committed a relevant offence in this context if:

(a) any employee of the applicant has been convicted of a relevant offence;

(b) a company of which the applicant was a director, manager, secretary or similar officer has been convicted of a relevant offence; or

(c) where the applicant is a company, any current director, manager, secretary or similar officer of the company has been convicted of a relevant offence, or was an officer of another company when that company was convicted of a relevant offence. The question of who constitutes a manager will be construed narrowly to mean someone who is part of the 'controlling mind' of the company (see *R* v *Boal* [1992] QB 591 and *Woodhouse* v *Walsall Metropolitan Borough Council* [1994] Env LR 30).

For the purpose of these provisions, a list of relevant offences is contained in the Waste Management Licensing Regulations 1994, reg. 3. Since the list is wide (but by no means exhaustive of environmental offences), the EA can choose to ignore a conviction if it wishes to do so (s. 74(4)). Waste Management Paper No. 4, Chapter 3, contains guidance on these provisions. It suggests that four factors should be taken into account in exercising the discretion to ignore a conviction. These are: the type of applicant (i.e. individual, partnership or corporate body); whether it is the applicant or another relevant person who has been convicted of the relevant offence; the nature and gravity of the relevant offence(s); and the number of relevant offences which have been committed.

As far as technical competence is concerned reg. 4 applies to the person responsible for the proper management of the site. The regulation provides that a person is technically competent in relation to the prescribed facilities set out in reg. 4 only if they are the holder of the relevant certificate of technical competence awarded by the Waste Management Industry Training Board (WAMITAB).

There are various transitional arrangements for those managers who have experience within the waste industry prior to the implementation of Part II of the EPA 1990 (known as 'existing managers'). A person will qualify as an existing manager if they registered with WAMITAB before 10 August 1994 and in the 12 months prior to that date were a manager of a relevant type of facility. An operator of a site previously controlled under COPA 1974 is also assumed to be a 'fit and proper' person. Full implementation of the technical competence rules will only take place in early 2001.

The position with regard to financial provision is much less clear cut. WMP4 suggests that the main way of providing such financial provision is through insurance via a third party or, if that is not possible, through self-insurance. The paper also identifies four stages in relation to landfill where financial provision may be relevant: site acquisition and preparation; site operation; site restoration and landscaping, or aftercare for a new use; and post-closure control and monitoring. Specific financial provision may be included in a licence in order to meet specified obligations under the licence. The assessment of the financial provision of an applicant is not to be specifically detailed. It is only to be considered in general terms in relation to the obligations under the licence. WMP4 suggests that the main thing that the EA will want to see when assessing financial capability will be a business plan showing the various stages of the life of the landfill. Unfortunately, as history has shown, the provision of a sound business plan does not necessarily guarantee the long-term success of the operation. It is this long-term position which remains to be assessed.

If the EA decides that the applicant is a fit and proper person, it is under a duty to grant a licence (s. 36(3)). This suggests that if the impediment can be avoided by the imposition of appropriate conditions, the licence should be granted with those conditions attached.

(e) Conditions
The EA is given a wide discretion to attach 'appropriate' conditions to a licence (s. 35(3)). Applying ordinary public law principles, conditions must relate to the purposes of Part II of the EPA 1990. In *Attorney-General's Reference (No. 2 of 1988)* [1990] 1 QB 77, the Court of Appeal decided that a condition requiring the site to be operated so as to avoid creating a nuisance was not permissible under COPA 1974, since it did not relate to the purposes of that Act. Even though the purposes of the EPA 1990 are wider than those of COPA 1974 (in that they relate to the protection of the environment as a whole, rather than the protection of water resources), it is still unclear whether such a condition would be acceptable under s. 35(3), since it is still arguable that such matters are more appropriately dealt with under the statutory nuisance provisions in Part III of the EPA 1990.

Unlike many pieces of environmental legislation, the EPA 1990 does not provide a list of the types of conditions that are appropriate. This function however, is carried out by WMP4. This provides a checklist of matters that should be covered, and stresses that they should relate to the operation and management of the site, so as not to duplicate the conditions attached to the planning permission. The paper also states that conditions should be enforceable, unambiguous, necessary and comprehensive, and that operators should know exactly what they have to do to comply with them. It appears from decisions of the Secretary of State on appeal that conditions should not impose an unreasonable burden on the operator of a site (see Bates, *UK Waste Law* (Sweet & Maxwell, 1997)). This seems to water down somewhat the environmental protection aim of the legislation, though it is clearly in line with government policies on restricting unnecessary regulation and on balancing environmental factors with economic ones.

The range of conditions imposed under the EPA 1990 can be wider than under COPA 1974 in a number of ways. Section 35(3) states that conditions may be imposed which must be complied with before activities begin or after they have ceased. For example, conditions requiring insurance cover to be effected before the site is opened, or the monitoring of a site for methane emissions or for leachate after disposal has finished, are legitimate. Under COPA 1974, such aftercare conditions can be imposed only at the planning permission stage. Section 35(4) provides that conditions may require the applicant to carry out works that need the consent of another person (this also applies to cases where there is a modification or suspension of an existing licence). There are detailed procedures and arrangements for compensating owners and occupiers which are set out in the Waste Management Licences (Consultation and Compensation) Regulations 1999 (SI 1999/481). Where these powers are exercised, the person whose consent is required must grant any rights in relation to the land that will enable the licence holder to comply with the conditions. For example, this subsection could be used to override landlord and tenant law by allowing a tenant to carry out works that would normally require the landlord's consent.

Regulations may be made prescribing conditions which are or are not to be included (s. 35(6)). In addition, the Secretary of State is given wide powers to direct that specified conditions are, or are not, included in a licence (s. 35). For example, the Waste Management Licensing Regulations stipulate that no conditions designed solely to secure health and safety at work can be imposed (reg. 12), and that, in order to comply with Directive 75/439 on Waste Oils, certain conditions relating to waste oils must be included (reg. 14).

(f)   Transfer of a licence

A waste management licence may be transferred by the EA under s. 40 if the holder and the proposed transferee make a joint application to the EA. Unless the EA considers that the proposed transferee is not a fit and proper person, it must make the transfer. An application for a transfer has to be made in writing. It must be determined within two months (or any longer period if agreed between the parties). In the absence of any agreement the application is claimed to have been refused.

(g)   Surrender of a licence

Under s. 39, a site licence cannot be surrendered at will, though a mobile plant licence can. A surrender of a site licence can take place only if the licence holder applies to the EA and it accepts the surrender. Before that happens, the EA must inspect the land and determine whether it is likely or unlikely that the condition of the land will cause pollution of the environment or harm to human health. In making that determination, it must take into account only matters that relate to the keeping, treatment or disposal of waste on the site, and not extraneous factors.

If the EA considers that the condition of the land is likely to cause such pollution or harm, it *must* refuse the application (s. 39(6)). But if it is satisfied that the condition of the land is unlikely to cause pollution or harm, it *must* accept the surrender. Where a surrender is accepted, the EA will issue a certificate of completion, and any obligations under the licence (such as to monitor for methane emissions) then come to an end. Since s. 39 requires the EA to issue a certificate where pollution or harm is unlikely, it is possible that an operator will be able to surrender a licence even though it has not fully complied with the licence conditions. However, any conditions attached to the planning permission for the site will still apply after surrender: these could cover such things as a requirement to restore the land to its previous use or to landscape it appropriately.

This procedure is of great importance, since until the implementation of the EPA 1990 holders of waste disposal licences could surrender them at will, and thus relinquish any continuing responsibilities for the site. This is no longer possible under the EPA 1990. One side effect of this change was that, in anticipation of the introduction of stricter standards and more rigorous enforcement powers under the EPA 1990, many holders of waste disposal licences under COPA 1974 surrendered them prior to the implementation of the new system, resulting in a significant shake-out of the waste disposal industry.

Detailed guidance for applying for a surrender has been set out in WMP 4 and WMP 26A which must, as a result of s. 35(8), be taken into account by the EA. Applications for the surrender of a licence must include: information on the licence holder; site location; number of the site licence; and a description of all the different activities (whether licensed or not) which were carried out on the site, the location of those activities, the period over which they were carried out and an estimate of the quantity of waste dealt with at the site. Where the site has involved the disposal of waste to landfill, further detailed information is required relating to such matters as hydrogeology, production of gas and leachate and the quality of groundwater.

Once all the formalities have been complied with, the certificate can be issued and the licence ceases to have effect. Experience has shown that only a small number of applications are rejected on an annual basis although the acceptance of surrendered licences is also relatively low at approximately 50 to 60 per cent of all applications (which leaves the rest undetermined, presumably whilst technical checks are made).

Enforcement powers

It is one of the features of most modern systems of pollution control that the regulatory agencies have strong enforcement powers. These are not limited to bringing prosecutions for breaches of the law, but extend to powers to vary and to revoke licences without compensation. These administrative remedies often represent a greater threat to operators than prosecution because of the potential financial consequences. The EA has some of the widest and most varied sets of powers in this respect, including powers to modify a licence, to revoke it in whole or in part, to suspend the operation of licensed activities, and to order the carrying out of specified works. In order to ensure that these powers are used, s. 42 imposes supervisory duties on the EA. In a number of cases the legislation places the EA under a duty to take enforcement action.

(a) Supervision of a licence
Section 42 puts the EA under a duty to supervise waste management licences. It must take the steps that are needed to ensure that pollution of the

environment, harm to human health or serious detriment to the amenities of the locality do not occur. It must also take steps to ensure that licence conditions are complied with.

Where there is an emergency, specific powers are given by s. 42(3). The EA may carry out necessary works on land or in relation to plant or equipment, and may recover any expenditure from the licence holder.

(b) Modification of a licence

Powers to modify a licence are of particular importance where circumstances have changed since the initial grant of the licence. The EA may, at its discretion, modify the conditions of a licence where it considers this is desirable and is unlikely to require unreasonable expense on the part of the licence holder (s. 37(1)(a)). But if it considers that in order to ensure that the authorised activities do not cause pollution of the environment or harm to human health, or become seriously detrimental to the amenities of the locality, it is necessary to modify the conditions, it *must* do so to the extent necessary (s. 37(2)). Alternatively, in such circumstances it may decide to revoke the licence under s. 38(1). The consultation requirements apply to an EA proposal to modify a licence in virtually the same way that they apply to an application under s. 36, except that, in an emergency, a reference to a consultee may be postponed. There is a separate right for the licence holder to apply for a modification (s. 37(1)(b)). In each situation any modification made under s. 37 must be by notice and must specify when it takes effect (s. 37(4)).

(c) Suspension of a licence

The powers to suspend and to revoke a licence are of great use where licensed activities are giving rise to problems, for example where the site is being inadequately managed or is causing pollution. The grounds for their use are, in general terms, similar to those relating to the refusal of an initial licence application, though they are in fact slightly less wide. They provide an opportunity to police the licence on a continuing basis and may be used in addition to other enforcement mechanisms, such as prosecution or ordering a clean-up.

The EA may suspend a licence by serving a notice on the licence holder. Such a notice must specify when the suspension is to take effect and when it is to cease. This may be on the occurrence either of a specified date or a specified event. A suspension cannot be of the whole of a licence, but can only relate to those parts of the licence that authorise the carrying on of activities. For example, the EA may suspend a licence in so far as it allows certain types of waste to be deposited, whilst retaining in force any conditions that relate to measures the licence holder must take to protect against pollution. Whilst a part of a licence is suspended it does not authorise the licence holder to carry on the activities specified.

The power to suspend is provided for in two separate sections: one where there has been a failure to comply with the licence (s. 42(6)), and another which applies more generally (s. 38(6)).

(a)   Under s. 38(6), if the EA considers that the site is no longer in the hands of a technically competent person, it may suspend those parts of the licence that authorise the carrying on of activities. The same power applies if the EA considers that serious pollution of the environment or serious harm to human health has been caused, or is about to be caused, or that the continuation of the activities will cause serious pollution of the environment or serious harm to human health.

(b)   The alternative power is that if, in exercising its supervisory powers under s. 42, it appears to the EA that a condition is not being complied with, it may by notice require the licence holder to comply within a specified time. If the licence holder does not do so, the EA may suspend the licence (s. 42(6)). In this situation, the availability of the suspension power acts as an incentive to the proper implementation of conditions.

One limitation on these powers is that, if the Secretary of State determines on appeal that the EA acted unreasonably in suspending a licence, the licence holder can claim compensation for consequential loss from the EA (s. 43(7)). This potential financial liability may act as a brake on the use of suspension notices by the EA.

Whilst a licence is suspended, the EA may require the licence holder to take such measures to deal with or avert pollution or harm as it thinks fit (s. 38(9)). Significantly, this may include matters which fall outside the scope of the original licence conditions. It is an offence to fail to comply with such a requirement (s. 38(10)). The maximum penalty is, on conviction in the magistrates' court, a fine of £5,000 or, on conviction in the Crown Court, two years' imprisonment and/or an unlimited fine. If the waste is special waste, a magistrates' court may imprison for up to six months, and the maximum term of imprisonment on conviction in the Crown Court is five years (this is the highest custodial sentence which can be imposed in relation to pure pollution control offences).

(d)   Revocation of a licence

The EA may revoke a licence by serving a notice on the licence holder, specifying when the revocation is to take effect. A revocation may be of the whole of a licence or of part of it — this includes revocation of those parts of the licence that authorise the carrying on of activities, whilst retaining other parts. For example, the EA may revoke a licence in so far as it allows special waste to be deposited, leaving the rest of the licence in force. Revocation of the whole of the licence is likely to be inappropriate in many cases, since it means that any conditions attached to the licence cease to have effect (s. 35(11)). As these may include conditions requiring the licence holder to carry out works of pollution control, or conditions relating to the restoration and aftercare of a site, revocation would effectively remove most of the licence holder's responsibilities. It was once possible that the EA could avoid this difficulty by exercising its powers under s. 61 (a section which has now been repealed), but that section only allowed costs to be recovered from the owner of the site, who may not be the same person as the former licence holder, particularly if the pollution occurs some years later. A licence can be revoked in a number of circumstances.

(i)   Under s. 38(1), if the EA considers that the holder of a licence has ceased to be a fit and proper person by reason of being convicted of a relevant offence, it may revoke the licence, wholly or in part. The same power applies if the EA considers that the continuation of the activities authorised by the licence would cause pollution of the environment or harm to human health, or would be seriously detrimental to the amenities of the locality, except that, in such a case, it must also consider that the pollution, harm or detriment cannot be avoided by modifying the conditions of the licence.

(ii)   Under s. 38(2), if the EA considers that the site is no longer in the hands of a technically competent person, it may revoke those parts of the licence that authorise the carrying out of activities, but not the rest of it.

(iii)   The same power of partial revocation applies if the licence holder fails to pay an annual subsistence charge (s. 41(7)).

(iv)   As with the power to suspend a licence, if the licence holder fails to comply with a notice served under s. 42 requiring compliance with a condition, the EA may revoke the licence, either wholly or in part (s. 42(6)).

Fees and charges

As part of the shift towards transferring funding of the regulation of pollution from the public to polluters, the Environment Act 1995, s. 41, provides for an annual fees and charges scheme (see the Waste Management Licensing (Fees and Charges) Scheme). The scheme is a cost-recovery scheme, meaning that the levels are supposed to be fixed by the Secretary of State so as to cover, in general terms, the cost to the EA of processing an application and supervising a licence.

In order to achieve this objective and to ensure that different operations pay a reasonably fair charge relative to each other, a fairly complex scheme has been implemented. The types of licensable activity are divided into four main classes, although these are then subdivided to take account of such things as whether the waste is being reused, reclaimed or recycled. These classes are: the treatment of controlled waste; the keeping of controlled waste; the disposal of controlled waste; and situations where a site has closed and a certificate of completion is being sought. Having established these general classes, the type of waste which is concerned (for example, whether it is inert waste, household waste, industrial waste or special waste), and the amount of waste that the site is licensed to receive annually, are taken into account so that the precise category into which the activity falls can be ascertained. The various fees and charges are then worked out by reference to that category.

There are separate fees for initial applications for a licence, and for applications for transfer, modification and surrender respectively. An annual subsistence charge is also payable, which will normally run into thousands of pounds, depending on the type of facility. The EA has a power to revoke a licence in part if the annual charge is not paid (s. 41(6)).

Public registers

The EA is under a duty to maintain a public register of a wide range of information relating to the waste management licensing system (s. 64, supplemented by the Waste Management Licensing Regulations 1994).

In outline, the registers must contain details of the following: all current or recently current licences and applications, together with any relevant supporting documentation, representations and directions; modification, suspension and revocation notices; matters relating to an application to surrender a licence; reports and monitoring information produced or obtained by the EA in discharging its functions; remedial action taken by the EA; consignment notes and records made for the purposes of the special waste provisions; convictions of licence holders under Part II of the Act; and appeals. A licence is no longer recent 12 months after it ceases to be in force, and an application no longer recent 12 months after its rejection, meaning that the registers are of limited use for historical purposes.

There are powers for the Secretary of State to exclude information from the registers on the ground that its inclusion would be contrary to the interests of national security (s. 65), and for the EA to exclude information on commercial confidentiality grounds (s. 66), though there is an appeal to the Secretary of State if the EA refuses to do so. In relation to exclusions dealt with under s. 66, the register will contain an entry indicating the existence of the information.

These fairly comprehensive registers will provide much useful information to environmental groups. But they will also be of great help to those who need to comply with the duty of care, since a search of the register may answer many relevant questions about waste carriers and waste disposal sites.

The powers of the Secretary of State

Apart from the wide-ranging powers to make regulations under the Act and to issue policy guidance, the Secretary of State is provided with very wide powers to give directions to the EA. For example, where an application is made, the Secretary of State may give a binding direction to the EA in relation to the terms and conditions that must, or must not, be included in the licence (s. 35(7)). This power is the equivalent of the call-in powers that exist in other areas of the law. There are similar powers to give binding directions relating to modification (s. 37(3)) and to suspension and revocation (ss. 38(7) and 42(8)) — in these cases the Secretary of State can effectively force the EA to take action.

Appeals

There are wide-ranging rights of appeal to the Secretary of State contained in s. 43. An appeal can be made where:

(a)   an application for a licence is rejected (or is not determined within four months);
(b)   a licence is subject to conditions;

(c)   the conditions are modified;

(d)   an application for a modification of conditions is rejected (or is not determined within two months);

(e)   a licence is suspended;

(f)   a licence is revoked;

(g)   an application to surrender a licence is rejected (or is not determined within three months);

(h)   an application for a transfer of a licence is rejected (or is not determined within two months).

One exception is where the Secretary of State made the original decision under the various powers of direction. In such a case, an action for judicial review would be the only available option.

There are no specified grounds of appeal. The procedures relating to appeals will be set out in regulations. The Waste Management Licensing Regulations 1994 state that an appeal must be brought within six months of the relevant decision (or deemed decision in cases where the appeal is against a non-determination within the required timescale). As is normal in environmental matters the appellant and the EA have a choice as to whether the appeal is in the form of a hearing or by written representations. Unusually, if a hearing is held, s. 43(2)(c) states that it is open to the person who hears the appeal to hold it in private, in whole or in part. The appeal will commonly be referred to an inspector or other person, who will normally make the decision on behalf of the Secretary of State.

Modifications and revocations normally have no effect while an appeal is pending or being heard (s. 43(4)). However, the EA may reverse this rule by stating in its notice that this is necessary for the purpose of preventing or minimising pollution of the environment or harm to human health (s. 43(6)). Suspension notices are not affected by an appeal (s. 43(5)). One limitation on the exercise of the power under s. 43(6) is that a licence holder may ask the Secretary of State to determine whether the EA acted unreasonably in activating s. 43(6), or in suspending a licence. If the decision goes in favour of the licence holder, it can claim compensation for consequential loss from the EA (s. 43(7)). This may limit the use of suspension notices and of s. 43(6).

Offences

With the introduction of the concepts of directive waste and directive disposal and recovery operations, the original offences under the EPA 1990, s. 33 have now been reinterpreted. Unless one of the exemptions or exemptions apply, a combination of s. 33(1) of EPA 1990 and the Waste Management Licensing Regulations 1994, reg. 1(3) and sch. 4, makes it a criminal offence to do the following:

(a)   deposit directive waste in or on land unless it is in accordance with a waste management licence. This applies to any deposit, whether temporary or permanent, and is not restricted to directive disposal and recovery operations;

(b) treat, keep or dispose of directive waste unless it is under and in accordance with a waste management licence — this offence can be committed either in or on land, or by means of mobile plant. As pointed out above this offence now extends only to directive disposal and recovery operations;

(c) knowingly cause or knowingly permit either of the above.

These offences are considerably wider than those under COPA 1974 because they are not limited to deposits but extend to keeping, treating or disposing of controlled waste. However, many acts of storage and treatment will in fact be exempted, as the Waste Management Licensing Regulations 1994 show. It is clear that offences in categories (a) and (b) above are ones of strict liability, but it should be noted that (c) interposes 'knowingly' in front of both 'cause' and 'permit'.

There was some uncertainty over the exact number of offences which could be committed under s. 33. Is the treating, keeping or disposing of directive waste a single offence committed in the alternative or are there three separate offences? The practical difficulty which arises as a result of this uncertainty is that if the latter position is correct, any indictment alleging all three in one charge would be duplicitous (as the situation is in relation to causing or knowingly permitting pollution of controlled waters, see p. 589). In *R v Leighton and Town and Country Refuse Collections Ltd* [1997] Env LR 411 the court considered the specific question of whether there are a number of alternative ways of committing the same offence. The court found that although each relevant paragraph of s. 33(1) created a separate offence, each of those offences could be committed in any of the ways specified within the paragraph. For example, it was possible to bring a charge of disposing or treating or keeping of controlled waste in a manner likely to cause pollution of the environment or harm to human health contrary to s. 33(1)(c) of the EPA 1990. This eases the evidential burden on the prosecution when framing an indictment.

The courts have interpreted the phrase 'knowingly' very strictly. In *Shanks and McEwan (Teesside) Ltd v Environment Agency* [1997] Env LR 305 the defendant was charged with knowingly permitting the deposit of controlled waste in contravention of a licence condition. It was argued that although the defendant knew of the deposit of the waste it did not know it was in breach of condition. The court followed the previous decision in *Ashcroft v Cambro Waste Products Ltd* [1981] 1 WLR 1349 in taking a very strict view of the phrase. The prosecution need only prove knowledge of the deposit of the waste material. It is not necessary to demonstrate knowledge of the breach of the licence condition which gives rise to the offence. Thus, once the prosecution demonstrate that waste had been knowingly permitted to be deposited, the burden then falls on the defence to establish that the deposit was made in accordance with the conditions of the licence.

It is also possible to infer knowledge. In *Kent County Council v Beaney* [1993] Env LR 225 it was held that knowing permission may be inferred from the facts of a case where the deposit of waste was obvious from surrounding events. This concept of constructive knowledge was developed further in the *Shanks and McEwan (Teesside)* decision (see above). In that case, Mance J took the view that it was sufficient that the defendant company (including its senior management) knowingly operated and held out its site for the reception and deposit of controlled waste. Once this was established it was not necessary to demonstrate that there was any knowledge of the specific breach of the licence condition. This approach broadens the offence considerably and in effect places the operators of landfill sites under a strict liability for breaches of waste management licence conditions.

As far as the concept of causation is concerned, this has been discussed on a number of occasions in relation to the similar offences under the Water Resources Act 1991 (see p. 589). However, analogies with these cases should be made with care, since they do not consider the situation where 'knowingly' is inserted in front of 'cause'. This appears to suggest that someone who orders another to deposit waste will be guilty under this section only if it is shown that they knew the deposit was to take place unlawfully. One subsection that may help here is s. 33(5), which states that where controlled waste is deposited from a motor vehicle, the person who controls the vehicle, or who is in a position to control its use, will be treated as knowingly causing the deposit. There is a separate strict liability offence of contravening any condition of a waste management licence (s. 33(6)). This removes the loophole revealed by *Leigh Land Reclamation Ltd* v *Walsall Metropolitan Borough Council* (1991) 155 JP 547 (see p. 464).

The maximum penalty for these offences is, on conviction in the magistrates' court, six months' imprisonment and/or a fine of £20,000 or, on conviction in the Crown Court, two years' imprisonment and/or an unlimited fine. If the waste is special waste, the maximum term of imprisonment on conviction in the Crown Court is five years. An injunction may also be sought in appropriate cases.

Any director, manager, secretary or other similar officer of a corporate body can be prosecuted personally if the offence is committed with their consent or connivance, or is attributable to their neglect (s. 157). As stated earlier, a 'manager' only covers someone who is part of the 'controlling mind' of the company (see *R v Boal* [1992] QB 591, a case on very similar wording in the Fire Precautions Act 1971). This liability is additional to the individual liability of the person who carried out, or knowingly caused or knowingly permitted the deposit. Waste management is one area of environmental law where sentences of imprisonment have actually been imposed, though they have been reserved for serious offences and where an offender offends repeatedly.

The decision in *Boal* has been applied in relation to waste management offences under COPA 1974. In *Woodhouse* v *Walsall Metropolitan Borough Council* [1994] Env LR 30, the general manager of a waste disposal site (along with his employers) was convicted of a waste offence under the Act. Following the decision in *Boal* the crucial issue in determining personal (as opposed to corporate) liability was whether the defendant was 'in a position of real authority' having both 'the power and responsibility to decide corporate policy and strategy'. This is something more than mere authority itself (such as the power to 'hire and fire'). The important test was whether a defendant was in a position to control and guide the corporate body in terms of policy and strategy. This is, of course, a question of fact and degree in every case. For a possible view of the other side of the coin (i.e. corporate vicarious liability for the actions of its employees in relation to the Water Resources Act 1991) see *National Rivers Authority* v *Alfred McAlpine Homes East Ltd* [1994] 4 All ER 286 and p. 252. In *Shanks and McEwan (Teesside) Ltd* v *Environment Agency* [1997] Env LR 305 there was some discussion of the nature of such vicarious liability and although the views were not central to the specific point which was decided, it was thought that where an employee had knowledge of a deposit of waste there would, following the *Alfred McAlpine* case, be a 'powerful' argument in favour of fixing the employer with vicarious knowledge of that deposit.

Defences

There is a defence under s. 33(7)(a) where the defendant took all reasonable precautions and exercised all due diligence to avoid the commission of the offence. This is a familiar defence that is included in many pieces of regulatory legislation. Essentially, it involves the defendant showing either that it took the appropriate steps on the facts of the case, or that it set up an adequate system. In many ways, the requirements are similar to those laid down by the duty of care. For example, the defence is of great use for receivers of waste (i.e. carriers and waste disposal site operators), who may inadvertently deal with it in an illegal fashion if they are misled by the consignor. However, it does impose quite a high standard on them to take steps to ensure that the consignment contains what it is meant to contain. It is arguable that this defence introduces an element of self-policing into the waste disposal chain. For example, in *Durham County Council* v *Peter Connors Industrial Services Ltd* [1993] Env LR 197, a system of operation which relied upon the person disposing of waste regularly collecting a skip which had been filled with waste by another without checking on the contents of the skip every time, was not sufficient to come within an analogous defence under s. 3(4) of COPA 1974. In that case, the court said that the collector of waste had to take care to inform itself on each occasion that it collected the waste as to the nature of the contents of the skip. The defence required a specific enquiry to be made of any person who knew what the waste was and whether or not the future deposit of that waste would involve a breach of the Act.

There are further defences in s. 33(7)(b) and (c) relating respectively to employees who act under instructions from their employer and in ignorance of the offence, and to acts carried out in an emergency in order to avoid danger to the public (although not danger to the environment). The onus of proof establishing whether or not an emergency exists rests with the defendant upon the balance of probabilities. In *Waste Incineration Services Ltd* v *Dudley Metropolitan Borough Council* [1993] Env LR 29 the court viewed the phrase 'emergency' (as used in a condition of a waste disposal licence) objectively and without reference to how the licence holder perceived a given set of facts.

Dangerous disposal of waste

There is a very important further offence created by s. 33(1)(c). It is an offence to treat, keep or dispose of controlled waste in a manner likely to cause pollution of the environment or harm to human health. The importance of this paragraph is that it applies irrespective of the need for a waste management licence. In other words, activities which are exempted from the need for a licence are still governed by what is in effect a general requirement to act safely. The paragraph could also be said to supplement the licensing system by acting as a form of residual condition attached to a licence, since in theory it applies even where a licence is being complied with. The offence is drafted remarkably widely, as pollution of the environment is defined in s. 29 by reference to harm to *any* living organism. Harm in this context means any harm to the health of living organisms or interference with the ecological systems of which they form a part.

The paragraph is mainly targeted at providing a straightforward offence that can be used in relation to fly-tipping and other forms of irresponsible waste disposal. However, it also covers such things as storage of wastes on the production site — the harm to human health could be a harm to employees. The maximum penalty for breach of s. 33(1)(c) is the same as for offences relating to a waste management licence. The section does not, however, apply to activities which are under regulations made under s. 33(3). This has only been done in the cases of activities which are adequately controlled under regimes other than waste management.

Clean-up powers

Section 59 gives the EA and waste collection authorities powers to require the removal of controlled waste. They apply whenever controlled waste has been deposited on land in contravention of s. 33(1), i.e. the deposit was not in accordance with a waste management licence or it breached s. 33(1)(c).

The initial responsibility falls on the occupier of the land. The EA may serve a notice on the occupier requiring the waste to be removed, or steps to be taken to mitigate the consequences of the deposit. The notice must specify a period within which this action should be taken, though it cannot be less than 21 days. There is a right to appeal to the magistrates' court during the 21-day period. Such an appeal must be allowed if the court is satisfied that the appellant neither deposited nor knowingly caused or knowingly permitted the deposit, or if there is a material defect in the notice (s. 59(3)). An appeal suspends the operation of the notice until it is determined (s. 59(4)). It is a summary offence, with a maximum fine of £5,000 to fail to comply with a notice served under s. 59 (s. 59(5)). This offence is a continuing one and a further fine of up to £1,000 can be imposed for every day on which the failure to comply continues after conviction. Ultimately, the EA has default powers to carry out the steps specified in the notice itself and to recover any expenses reasonably incurred from the person on whom it was served (s. 59(6)).

Where the occupier did not make or knowingly permit the unlawful deposit, or there is no occupier, the EA may remove the waste or take mitigating steps immediately. This course of action is also available if these steps were immediately necessary to remove or prevent pollution or harm to human health (s. 59(7)). The EA may then recover its costs from any person who deposited the waste, or knowingly caused or knowingly permitted its deposit, unless that person can show that the cost was incurred unnecessarily (s. 59(8)). Ultimate responsibility for unlawfully deposited waste therefore falls on the person who deposited it rather than on the occupier. However, it may not be possible to trace the person responsible, or they may have no money to pay the EA's costs, in which case the position is in practice that the EA has a choice whether to leave the waste where it is or pick up the bill itself. Nevertheless, this is an important power which can be used in addition to a prosecution under s. 33, since it tackles directly the problem that faces the EA.

The EA's powers under the Water Resources Act 1991, s. 161, should also be considered in this context, since they may be used to deal with deposits of waste that threaten controlled waters (see p. 599).

Duty of care

The most significant new control introduced by the EPA 1990 was the criminal duty of care imposed by s. 34, which came into force on 1 April 1992. All those who deal with controlled waste are required to take reasonable and appropriate steps in relation to it, otherwise they commit a criminal offence. This entails such things as storing and packaging waste properly, describing clearly what it consists of, dealing only with an authorised carrier, providing the carrier with an accurate transfer note relating to the waste, and taking steps to ensure that it is ultimately disposed of correctly. What is reasonable will depend on the exact circumstances and on the identity and resources of the person concerned. Additional, more specific, requirements apply to special waste (see p. 518).

The introduction of the duty of care was prompted primarily by the publication of the Eleventh Report of the Royal Commission on Environmental Pollution, *Managing Waste: The Duty of Care*, in 1985 (Cmnd 9675). This concluded:

The first task is for society to identify where the responsibility lies for ensuring that wastes are properly handled and disposed of. In our judgment, this must rest with the individual or organisation who produces the wastes. The producer incurs a duty of care which is owed to society, and we would like to see this duty reflected in public attitudes and enshrined in legislation and codes of practice.

The Royal Commission went on to stress the need to pass the responsibility for waste from person to person down the disposal chain, thereby suggesting that, rather than the producer retaining total responsibility for the waste, the duty of care would operate by ensuring that everyone in the chain checks the competence of those with whom they deal with regard to handling the waste safely and without harm to the environment. The main purpose behind the duty of care is thus clear. It is to encourage anyone who holds waste to deal with it in a responsible fashion, so that a 'cradle to grave' approach is applied to its management and disposal. It is no longer the case that producers and others necessarily lose responsibility for waste when they cease to have possession of it.

(a)   What does the duty entail?

Section 34 provides that the duty of care applies to any person who produces, imports, carries, keeps, treats or disposes of controlled waste, or who, as a broker, has control of it. The only exception is that occupiers of domestic premises are not subject to the duty with regard to household waste produced on the property (s. 34(2)). The duty applies only to controlled waste.

The section itself states that any person to whom the duty applies should take reasonable steps to do the following (each of which is discussed below):

(i)   prevent any other person contravening s. 33 (i.e. the law relating to the unauthorised deposit, keeping, treatment or disposal of controlled waste);

(ii)   prevent the escape of waste;

(iii)   ensure that the waste is transferred only to an authorised person;

(iv)   ensure that an adequate written description of the waste is given to anyone to whom the waste is transferred.

The bare duty in s. 34 is supplemented by the Environmental Protection (Duty of Care) Regulations 1991 (SI 1991/2839), which lay down some additional documentation requirements. Contravention of these regulations automatically results in the commission of a criminal offence. There is also a *Code of Practice on the Duty of Care*, made by the Secretary of State. This is a statutory code, made under s. 34(7). Contravention of its provisions is not of itself a criminal offence, but it could be said that contravention gives rise to a presumption that the duty has been breached, since s. 34(10) states that it should be taken into account in deciding whether the duty has been complied with and in fixing any penalty. (The Code may also be used as evidence in civil cases and in prosecutions under s. 33.) The combined effect of s. 34, the regulations and the Code of Practice is to lay down a mixture of general and specific requirements.

It is a criminal offence to breach the duty of care. The maximum penalty is, on conviction in the magistrates' court, a £5,000 fine or, on conviction in the Crown Court, an unlimited fine.

The steps required to be taken under s. 34 (see above) comprise the following:

(i)   The prevention of breaches of s. 33   This part of the duty of care is concerned with ensuring that a holder of waste (i.e. the person who has control of it at any time) takes responsibility for checking that the waste is dealt with properly by others further down the waste disposal chain. For example, it entails that the transferor of waste should know where the waste is going before parting with it, which in turn involves checking that the site where the waste is to be taken is licensed to take it and that the carrier is actually taking it there. The Code of Practice requires that a transferor of waste must be prepared to stop a transfer of waste if not satisfied that it is being dealt with properly. The standard is objective in the sense that holders of waste ought to act on signs that something is amiss. For example, a transferor of waste who suspects that a carrier is not tipping the waste where it says it is (for instance, because of the short periods of time between journeys), or who is quoted an unrealistically low price for the disposal of waste, ought to check what is actually happening. However, the standard is also related to the resources and knowledge of the individual, with the result that large firms may be expected to carry out more rigorous investigations than small ones.

(ii)   Prevention of the escape of waste   This requirement is mainly related to the correct packaging and labelling of waste. For instance, if waste spills from inadequate drums whilst they are on the back of a lorry, the transferor of the drums may be in breach as well as the lorry driver. Other examples relate to the nature of the packaging; for example, fire resistant packaging should be used for inflammable wastes. This limb also imposes a duty to ensure that waste is properly stored — using an open skip which allows waste to be blown off by the wind may amount to a breach.

(iii)   Transfer to an authorised person   There are various stages to the disposal of waste and who constitutes an authorised person will vary from stage to stage. If waste is entrusted to a carrier, the duty of care clearly establishes that it should only be given to a carrier who is registered under the Control of Pollution (Amendment) Act 1989 (see below), or who is exempted from registration under that Act. Accordingly, the Code of Practice states that a transferor should check the carrier's certificate of registration, or its grounds for exemption. It even states that a photocopy of the registration certificate is not adequate for this purpose, only an original copy issued by the EA. If waste is being delivered to a waste disposal site or an incinerator, an authorised person is one who holds a waste management or waste disposal licence or is exempt from the need for one.

(iv)   Description of the waste   The purpose behind this requirement is fairly clear. It is to enable everyone who deals with the waste to know what it consists of. In that way, it should not be treated incorrectly through ignorance. The detail required in a description will depend on the nature of the waste. For example, if it is hazardous the exact nature of the hazard should be identified, whereas in many other cases a general description will suffice. Consideration of the purpose of the requirement should enable decisions to be taken on what is an adequate description. For example, omitting to mention that a skip includes a small amount of dangerous

chemicals may lead to the contents being deposited at a site that is not equipped to take it, or to an undesirable mixing of incompatible wastes. Alternatively, a false description could have catastrophic results in the event of a road accident if it meant that the emergency services dealt with it inappropriately.

The requirement of an adequate description is supplemented by the 1991 Regulations (SI 1991/2839). These require that when controlled waste is transferred there must be a transfer note, though this does not actually have to travel with the waste. The transfer note must identify the waste and state its quantity, the kind of container it is in, the time and place of transfer, and the name, address and other relevant details of the transferor and transferee. The regulations also require that the transferor and transferee sign the transfer note and that the transfer note and the written description are kept for at least two years from the date of transfer. The EA has powers to demand production of the transfer note or written description within this period. The written description and the transfer note may be combined in one document as long as each requirement is fully met. A standard form of transfer note is set out in the Code of Practice. Because of the width of the concept of a transfer, these requirements cover a range of circumstances where the recipient may not at first glance seem like a typical 'waste disposal firm' — for example, a landlord of an industrial estate, office block or large shopping centre could require a transfer note if the waste was collected centrally, unless the transfer was construed as being 'within the same premises'. It is permissible for multiple consignments of waste up to one year to be covered by one transfer note, as long as the description of the waste, the identity of the parties and all other details remain the same for each consignment.

(b)   Enforcement of the duty of care

It should be noted that the duty of care is broken irrespective of whether harm is caused. It is the failure to take reasonable steps that is the criminal offence, not any damage that results from it. This creates a position where offences will be committed frequently. The control mechanism is whether any breach comes to the attention of the EA and whether it considers any enforcement action is justified. In this context, central government guidance suggests that the EA is meant to be reactive in its approach to policing the duty of care and is not expected to go out of its way to look for breaches. Instead, it should treat enforcement work as part of its existing duty to supervise the waste management licensing system. Certainly no extra resources have been given to the EA in order to enable it to monitor the duty of care provisions.

It should also be remembered that everyone in the waste chain is subject to the duty of care. The system should therefore have an element of self-policing. For example, a producer of waste would be well advised not to transfer it to someone they suspect of being a 'cowboy', because if the waste is fly-tipped that could lead the EA to prosecute the producer for breach of the duty of care (and also give rise to possible criminal actions for knowingly permitting the deposit, and to potential liability in civil law, or under the clean-up powers). Equally, a waste carrier should not accept improperly labelled or packaged waste, and should make periodic checks on the waste it receives, since it will have responsibility under the duty of care if there is something wrong.

In summary, the preceding discussion suggests that the main function of the duty of care is to encourage responsible behaviour and the development of appropriate management systems for the storage, transfer and monitoring of waste, rather than to punish wrongdoing. Because of the documentation procedures, it also makes waste consignments easier to trace. Some of the reported prosecutions for breaches of the duty illustrate these points. For example, in one case a demolition contractor was fined £800 for failing to ensure that a skip contained only materials described in the transfer note — the infringement came about because employees had not been given sufficient instruction that only certain materials could be put in the skip. When it comes to sentencing for the offence, however, many of the breaches, such as failing to make out a transfer note, are seen by the courts as technical in nature, and thus only small fines are imposed. This seems to underplay the importance of this type of management-based control.

Carriage of waste

Intimately connected with the duty of care is the requirement that all carriers of waste are registered with the EA. The requirements in this respect arise out of the Control of Pollution (Amendment) Act 1989. This was a private member's bill (although it did ultimately have government support) which sought to deal with the growing problem of fly-tipping by providing some powers over carriers. The Act is supplemented by the Controlled Waste (Registration of Carriers and Seizure of Vehicles) Regulations 1991 (SI 1991/1624) as amended by SI 1998/605. It came into force on 1 April 1992.

It is an offence under the 1989 Act, s. 1(1), to carry controlled waste without being registered with the EA. The offence is a summary one only, with a maximum fine of £5,000. The defences are very similar to those available for offences under the EPA 1990, s. 33 (see p. 507). It should be remembered that it is normally a separate offence under the duty of care to deal with an unregistered carrier.

Certain bodies such as local authorities, charities and voluntary groups are specifically exempt from the requirement to register by virtue of reg. 2, which also states that a producer may carry its own wastes without having to seek registration, as long as the waste is not demolition or construction waste. In addition, s. 1(1) refers only to carrying waste in the course of a business or with a view to profit, meaning that such things as carrying waste to a local authority waste site on behalf of a neighbour are not covered.

An application for registration must be made to the regional office of the EA where the carrier has its principal place of business (reg. 4). There is only one substantive ground for refusal of registration, which is that the applicant is not a desirable carrier. This fulfils a similar function to the 'fit and proper person' requirement in the waste management licensing system. It has two elements: (i) that the carrier, or someone closely connected with the carrier's business, has been convicted of one of the relevant offences listed in sch. 1 to the regulations; and (ii) that the EA considers it undesirable for the carrier to be authorised to carry controlled waste (reg. 5). There is a power to revoke a registration on these grounds (reg. 10). However, the impact of these provisions is limited somewhat by the Rehabilitation of Offenders Act 1974, which effectively will allow most convictions to become spent after five years. In addition, there is a right to appeal to the Secretary of State against refusal or revocation and, in accordance with the advice in Circular 11/91, a refusal to register was overturned even though the applicant had been convicted of seven waste offences in the past (see (1993) 217 ENDS Report 13). Unless revoked, a registration lasts for three years, when it must be renewed, though the carrier may surrender a registration at any time. A fee is payable for an application or a renewal (reg. 4(9)). The EA must keep a public register, to be open for inspection free of charge, of firms that are registered in their area (reg. 3).

Enforcement of the Act is mainly in the hands of the EA. Appointed officers (and also police officers) are given powers to stop and search vehicles, as long as they have reasonable grounds for believing that controlled waste is being carried by an unregistered carrier (s. 5(1)). They may also require the carrier to produce its certificate of registration. It is a summary offence intentionally to obstruct an officer exercising these powers, with a maximum penalty of £5,000. Environment Agency officers also have the powers provided under the EPA 1990, s. 71, and the Environment Act 1995, ss. 108 and 109 (see below).

In addition, there are separate powers relating to the seizure of vehicles used for unlawful activities (s. 6). If the EA is unable to obtain through its general powers information about the ownership of a vehicle it has reason to believe has been involved in unlawful disposal operations, it may apply for a warrant from a magistrate to seize the vehicle. Once the vehicle has been seized, the EA may take specified publicity measures and, if no one claims it, dispose of it (reg. 23). If the EA does discover who owns the vehicle it can bring a prosecution under the 1989 Act and/or under the EPA 1990, ss. 33 and 34, though in those circumstances it has no power to seize the vehicle.

Waste brokers

There is a growing business in arranging for the disposal or movement of other people's wastes. These people may not require a waste management licence because they never actually handle the waste themselves. The Waste Management Licensing Regulations 1994 now control such brokers/dealers in waste. Regulation 20 makes it an offence for any establishment or undertaking to arrange, as a dealer or broker, for the disposal or recovery of directive waste on behalf of another person unless they are registered with the EA. Exemptions apply to those with a waste management licence, or other statutory consents (e.g. a discharge consent), charitable or voluntary registered waste carriers, and bodies with statutory responsibilities for waste management (e.g. waste collection and disposal authorities).

Schedule 5 to the regulations sets out the procedure for registration. Perhaps the most important consideration in determining whether an establishment/undertaking is to be registered is the number of 'relevant offences' committed by the applicant or connected persons. Generally the considerations are the same as the test for 'fit and proper persons' in relation to applications for a waste management licence. A fee is payable on application for registration and the entry in the register is available to the general public. The entry in the register lasts for a maximum of three years unless it is renewed.

General powers of the EA

Section 7 of the EPA supplements the general powers available to the EA under the Environment Act 1995, ss. 108 and 109. These powers can be exercised in relation to any of their functions, not just in relation to waste management licensing. There are wide powers to require information by written notice (s. 71). It is a criminal offence to fail to provide, without reasonable excuse, the information required, or knowingly to provide false information. Case law suggests that this power to serve written requisitions provides an almost unfettered discretion to gather information as a refusal to answer on the grounds of self-incrimination is not a 'reasonable excuse' (although any information gathered cannot be used against the supplier — see *R* v *Hertfordshire CC ex parte Green Environmental Industries Ltd* [2000] 1 All ER 773; [2000] 2 WLR 373). The maximum penalty is a fine of £5,000 on summary conviction, or an unlimited fine and/or two years in prison on conviction on indictment. When serving such a notice, the EA must have admissible evidence upon which they can base an argument as to their reasons for needing the information in order to fulfil their statutory functions. It is not possible to use these powers as a 'fishing expedition' where no other evidence is available, as there must be cogent evidence available which can form the foundation of any further requests (*JB and M Motor Haulage Ltd* v *London Waste Regulation Authority* [1993] Env LR 243).

Environment Agency officers have wide powers which are set out in s. 108 of the Environment Act 1995. These include rights of entry, rights to carry out investigations on premises, and rights to take and remove samples, including the power to take samples which will be used as evidence and taken into account by the Secretary of State on appeal (*Polymeric Treatments Ltd* v *Walsall Metropolitan Borough Council* [1993] Env LR 427). The inspector may also require any person to answer questions and provide information relevant to the investigation.

A further power in s. 109 allows inspectors who are carrying out investigations to seize and render harmless any article or substance (not just waste) which appears to be a cause of imminent danger of serious pollution or serious harm to human health.

Special waste

As stated earlier, there are additional controls over hazardous waste, which is referred to in the UK context as 'special waste'. Such waste is primarily controlled under the Special Waste Regulations 1996 (SI 1996/972) which came into effect on 1 September 1996. The regulations were primarily introduced in order to transpose the Hazardous Waste Directive (91/689) into UK law. Detailed guidance on the regulations has been produced by the DETR in the form of a Technical Guidance Note (see *Special Wastes: A Technical Guidance Note on their Definition and Classification*, 1999).

The Regulations are intended to meet a number of objectives including:

(a)   the introduction of criteria for determining whether or not waste is special;

(b)   a requirement to pre-notify movements to the Environment Agency by consignment note;

(c)   the provision of better descriptions of waste and their associated hazards by means of a revised design for the consignment note;

(d)   the simplification of arrangements for repetitive movements and collection rounds;

(e)   a ban on mixing by carriers and consignees of categories of special wastes, and of special with non-special wastes, unless for safe disposal;

(f)   a requirement to carry out periodic inspections by regulators of special waste producers; and

(g)   the introduction of fees for many consignments of special wastes.

The regulations broaden the scope of waste to be treated as special and effectively broaden the scope of control over sites receiving a variety of wastes. Many sites were restricted to receiving waste which was not considered special under the previous legislation and this required amendments to extant licences.

Regulation 2 defines special waste as any controlled waste which:

(a)   is listed with a six-digit code in part I of sch. 2 to the Regulations (the Hazardous Waste List, taken from the Council Decision 94/904 mentioned above) and displays any of the properties given in part II of sch. 2 (which reproduces Annex III to the Hazardous Waste Directive); or

(b)   does not appear in the list set out in part I of sch. 2, but displays any of a restricted range of those properties specified in part II of the schedule (namely: highly flammable, irritant, harmful, toxic (including very toxic), carcinogenic or corrosive); or

(c)   is a waste prescription-only medicine.

Fourteen hazard criteria are listed in part II of sch. 2 and, with the exception of 'infectious' and 'formation of hazardous products after disposal', they match the classifications contained in the Chemicals (Hazard Information and Packaging for Supply) Regulations 1994 (SI 1994/3247).

The 1996 Regulations also apply to radioactive waste, which is not controlled waste by virtue of s. 78 of the Environmental Protection Act 1990, that would come within the definition of special waste but for the fact that it is radioactive. Thus, for example, radioactive waste which is also corrosive will still not be controlled waste, but it will be special waste.

Regulation 2 provides for two exceptions: first, household waste is not special waste unless it consists of clinical waste, asbestos or any mineral or synthetic oil or grease; and secondly, controlled waste that would be special waste because it has any of the restricted range of properties specified in part II of sch. 2 (listed in paragraph (b) above) is not special waste if any of the properties are below the threshold given in part III of sch. 2. For example, a waste in which the total concentration of substances classified as toxic is less than 3 per cent will not be classed as special waste.

Although explosives are specifically named in part I of sch. 2, and 'explosive' is one of the hazardous properties in part II of the schedule, explosives are already controlled under the Explosives Act 1875 and are not subject to the regulations.

(a) Pre-notification procedure

A key feature of the new system remains the requirement, in most cases, to pre-notify the Environment Agency of any consignments of special waste. (While the regulations simply state that pre-notification should be made to the Agency, the guidance states that, in practice, this will mean the local or area office for the place to which the waste is being consigned.) The exceptions are lead acid motor vehicle batteries, off-specification products being returned to manufacturers or suppliers, consignments within the same group of companies where the waste is being removed for the purpose of storage, and certain landed ships' waste.

The main points of the new system are:

(a)   Parties are referred to as the 'consignor' and 'consignee'.

(b)   The content of the consignment note is prescribed in sch. 1 to the regulations and, under reg. 23, this obviates the need for a duty of care transfer note as required by the EPA 1990, s. 34. The EA produces consignment notes and supplies them on request. However, users are still able to produce their own or purchase them from commercial suppliers.

(c)   Between three days' and one month's notice is required, although fax and email is acceptable on condition that paper copies are forwarded before the waste is consigned.

(d)   The consignment note is to be sent to the local Agency office for the area to which the waste is being consigned. This office will, within two weeks, send a photocopy of the note to the consignor's local Agency office.

(e)   A single pre-notification is allowed for carriers' rounds and repetitive consignments. The latter will be valid for up to 12 months.

(f)   Each consignment note must contain a unique identifying number issued by the EA. In the case of repetitive consignments, each consignment must contain its own unique number and also refer to the original number issued by the EA. Consignment notes produced by the EA are pre-coded; others have to obtain codes direct from the EA. Bulk purchases of codes are allowed.

(g)   Consignment code numbers should be obtained from the local EA offfice for the place to which the waste is being taken.

(h)   A fee of £15 (£10 for loads consisting entirely of lead acid motor vehicle batteries) is payable for each consignment. This fee also applies to each consignment in a series of repetitive transfers.

(b)   Record keeping

In addition to maintaining registers of consignment notes, anyone who deposits special waste in or on any land is also required to record the location of each deposit. Such records are to be cross-referenced to the register of consignment notes except in cases where the waste was disposed of via a pipeline or at the premises where the waste was produced, where no consignment notes will have been produced.

The records may consist of either a site plan marked with a grid or a site plan with overlays showing the deposits in relation to the contours of the site. The records must be maintained and kept for the lifetime of the site and forwarded to the EA when the site's waste management licence is surrendered or revoked.

The Regulations introduce restrictions on mixing different categories of special waste or mixing special with non-special waste. The restrictions apply to collectors and carriers or to those who recover or dispose of special waste. However, they do not apply if the mixing is authorised by a waste management licence or an IPC authorisation (and this will be extended to cover IPPC permits). Nor do they apply to an activity exempt from waste management licensing.

The regulations also place a duty on the EA to inspect producers of special waste periodically. This is a requirement of the Hazardous Waste Directive and is achieved by amending the Waste Management Licensing Regulations 1994, sch. 4, para. 13(1). This paragraph already requires 'appropriate periodic inspections' by the Agency on other waste operations. The periodicity of inspections is not stipulated, but is left to the discretion of the EA, giving due consideration to advice contained in DoE Circular 11/94 (waste management licensing guidance).

(c)   Offences

The regulations create the offences of failing to comply with the regulations, knowingly or recklessly making statements which are false or misleading, or intentionally making a false entry in records. The penalties for each offence are a fine of up to £5,000 on summary conviction (i.e. in a magistrates' court) or an unlimited fine and/or up to two years in prison on conviction on indictment (i.e. in the Crown Court).

Civil liability for unlawful disposal of waste

Civil liability is provided for in s. 73(6), which is significantly wider than the equivalent provision in COPA 1974, s. 88). This subsection applies where any damage is caused by a deposit of controlled waste in contravention of ss. 33(1) or 63(2) (i.e. the deposit was not in accordance with a waste management licence, or it breached s. 33(1)(c), or it breached the provision on unlawful disposal of non-controlled waste). Any person who deposited the waste is liable to pay damages for any personal injury or property damage that was caused, except where it was due wholly to the fault of the person who suffered it, or they voluntarily accepted the risk of the damage. Liability also attaches to any person who knowingly caused or knowingly permitted such waste to be deposited, with the result that anyone who orders an unlawful deposit, or who stands by in the knowledge that it is happening, will also be liable. Since liability is linked to the commission of an offence under ss. 33 or 63(2), it is strict and fault need not be shown, though the defences available under those sections will also apply.

Section 73(6) provides an alternative to the common law causes of action which are explained in Chapter 10. The leading case on waste sites is the Canadian case of *Gertsen* v *Municipality of Toronto* (1973) 41 DLR (3d) 646, where an occupier of land successfully claimed damages for personal injury. His injuries were the result of an explosion caused by the spark from his car engine when he started it up in his garage, which had filled with high levels of methane escaping from the disused landfill site on which it was built. The action was successful under the rule in *Rylands* v *Fletcher*, nuisance and negligence, although it must be doubted whether, on the current state of the law, all these causes of action would have succeeded in an English court. Section 73(6) will avoid some of the difficulties associated with the common law actions where there has been an unlawful deposit.

EIGHTEEN
Contaminated land

This chapter deals with the rules and policy which control the clean up of land which has become 'contaminated'. The debate about the regulation of contaminated land is relatively recent, reflecting the fact that, in contrast to other areas of pollution control, the problems of soil contamination are comparatively well concealed and the legal issues (particularly in respect of liability for historic contamination) arguably more complex and controversial. The main area which will be covered is the clean up of 'historic' contamination which is controlled under a specific statutory scheme found in Part IIA of the Environmental Protection Act 1990 (as inserted by the Environment Act 1995 and referred to as 'Part IIA' for the remainder of this chapter) and a package of other 'rules' found in regulations and statutory guidance (all statutory references in this chapter are to Part IIA or the regulations as appropriate). The rules are made up of an extremely complicated mixture of law, policy, and technical guidance. It is not possible to deal with every aspect of these provisions in a book of this sort. Therefore, the emphasis is placed upon an analysis of the key aspects such as the definition of contaminated land and the vexed question of who pays for the clean up works (i.e. the allocation of liability). Other parts of the statutory framework are covered in outline only.

As contamination can also be caused by continuing activities which are controlled under extant licences/permissions or otherwise under general pollution control provisions, there is brief coverage of the ways in which the various statutory schemes overlap.

In the 1970s, during the period of the modernisation of pollution control regulation, the issue of soil pollution was only addressed indirectly, i.e. through the introduction of tighter controls to prevent new contamination arising (e.g. under the waste disposal provisions of COPA 1974). In addition, although there have been a number of 'incidents' which were connected to land contamination, such as the explosion caused by the escape of landfill gas at Loscoe in Derbyshire in 1986, there was no perceived need to introduce reactive legislation to respond to a public outcry or specific set of circumstances which demanded a quick regulatory response. Thus although there were individual attempts to regulate new sources of contamination, it was not until 1990 that any serious attempt to introduce a comprehensive system of controls over historically contaminated land in the UK. Since that time there have been a number of unsuccessful steps towards the full implementation of the system but the final 'package' of rules (including regulations and technical guidance) was finally introduced in England in April 2000. In Scotland the package of guidance and regulations came into force in July. Wales and Northern Ireland are expected to implement the detailed provisions towards the end of 2000 at the earliest.

What is 'contaminated land'?

Although the phrase 'contaminated land' has become somewhat of a term of art, it is far from being clear and precise. The presence of 'contamination' in land does not necessarily lead to harm, whether actual or potential, to the environment or human health. The existence of contamination needs, therefore, to be put into some form of context against which the need to intervene and require clean up can be assessed. Relevant factors include the nature of the polluting substance; the presence and identity of a 'target' which is being affected by the contamination (e.g. humans, nature conservation or property interests); and the costs and benefits of carrying out clean up works. It is in this sense that the definition of 'contamination' reflects some of the problems with the definition of 'pollution' (see further p. 25) in that scientific, economic and political factors need to be considered in deciding whether any regulatory control is required. In deciding to take action against contamination, the policy maker and the rule maker must identify the point at which contamination poses an unacceptable risk.

The vague nature of the definition of contamination is reflected in the fact that there are no definite figures for the amount of contaminated land within the UK. Estimates have varied depending upon whether the numbers are based upon location or area and perhaps more crucially the definition of 'contaminated land' which is adopted. Environment Select Committee Reports have suggested anything from 5,000 to 100,000 'sites' and 27,000 to 100,000 hectares in terms of land area. Indeed, one of the primary purposes behind the introduction of Part IIA was to assist the ordered identification of contaminated land and one of the first aspects of the implementation of the statutory provisions will be the preparation of strategies to carry out this identification duty.

Sources of contamination

Although there may be doubts about the extent of the problem, it is clear that there are areas of land which pose unacceptable risks to human health and the environment as a result of the presence of historic contamination. The sources of contamination can be traced as far back as Roman times (from lead and copper mining) although the Industrial Revolution and subsequent activities provide the major cause of contemporary problems.

There have been a number of attempts to identify categories of activity which has the potential to contaminate (the most formal of which was the implementation of the ill-fated register of potentially contaminative uses). The House of Commons Environment Select Committee identified 19 categories of use which were thought to represent the vast majority of the sources of contamination. These included waste disposal sites; chemical works; leather tanning works; sewage works; docks and railway land; and heavy engineering works.

The main difficulty with this type of categorisation (and one which was closely linked to many of the objections to the proposed register) is that the existence of one of these categories of use cannot be linked conclusively with the presence of contamination nor is the reverse true (i.e. contamination cannot be conclusively linked to a particular type of use). Clearly, uses of land which involve toxic or potentially polluting substances can cause contamination either directly and intentionally (e.g. on site waste disposal) or indirectly and accidentally (e.g. spillages, leakages or from airborne emissions). There may be situations, however, where contamination arises on land which has not been subject to one of the categorised uses. For example, agricultural activities, which are not listed, can be a major source of contamination (see e.g. nitrate pollution from the use of fertilisers in *Savage* v *Fairclough* [2000] Env LR 183). In addition, contamination can be found on land which has not been subject to any use where the contamination has migrated from another location through groundwater or the air.

The threats posed by contaminated land

The potential consequences of contamination are as many and varied as the sources. They include:

(a)   Explosion and fire caused by the accumulation of combustible gases (as occurred at Loscoe, Derbyshire). These problems are often associated with the waste disposal and the degradation of putrescible matter in tips producing flammable methane gas.

(b)   Toxic effects on human health brought on by the presence of noxious substances. These are caused by direct contact with or indirect intake of a contaminant through such things as inhalation of contaminants (see the effects of asbestos contamination in *Hancock and Margereson* v *JW Roberts Ltd* [1996] Env LR 304) or eating vegetables grown in contaminated soil. Relevant effects includes disease, illness and birth defects.

(c)   Toxic effects on the environment including water pollution caused by the movement of contaminants from soil to water (see e.g. the spillages of solvent which caused groundwater pollution in *Cambridge Water Co.* v *Eastern Counties Leather* [1993] Env LR 161). Another example is the harm caused to habitats through phytotoxic chemicals which can inhibit plant growth.

(d)   Toxic effects upon property including crops and livestock which are affected by soil contamination.

(e)   Corrosive effects on property such as contaminants which attack the foundations of a building or underground pipes etc.

These consequences reflect the general categories of harm which are controlled under Part IIA.

The difficulties of regulating contaminated land

In recent years our understanding of the potential consequences of contamination has improved dramatically. Accompanying that understanding has
been a general consensus that there has to be some way of addressing the
problem of historically contaminated land in a systematic and considered
manner. The description of the development of policy and legal framework
discussed below demonstrates, however, that the path to a solution has been
long and tortuous involving two different legislative schemes and a series of
consultation exercises. This reflects the controversial and complex nature of
the problems which need to be addressed when attempting to regulate the
clean up of historically contaminated land. Some of the difficult factors which
need to be considered include the following.

(a)   The nature of contamination
The physical nature of contamination can present complex challenges for a
policy maker or a rule maker. Contamination is not necessarily identifiable
on the basis of discrete geographical boundaries. It may have migrated over
long distances to contaminate areas other than the place where the contamination originated. It may have moved from land into controlled waters (either
within the ground or other surface waters). Even where contamination may
be identified in relation to a single site it may be caused by different
contaminants which pose different risks which require different solutions.
Certain substances could be harmless when they enter the ground in isolation
but present a serious hazard when combined with other contaminants or after
degradation over time.

(b)   Stigma/blight
The formal classification of land as 'contaminated' may have detrimental
consequences in terms of the effective and productive use of resources. These
consequences include the effects of blight and stigma which would cover loss
in the value of the land and an inability to sell. These phrases can often be
interchanged when used in the context of contamination. They are used here,
however, to represent two different facets of the same issue. Where there are
areas of land which have been subject to potentially contaminative uses, the
risk of contamination is often associated with all of the land in that area
regardless of whether it is actually contaminated. This presumption of
contamination can have a blighting effect which can sterilise land which
would otherwise be brought into effective use.

There is a slightly different problem with land which has been identified as
being contaminated but has been subjected to clean up works. In such cases
the land may continue to be stigmatised with the label of 'contaminated' with
the consequence that it too may be sterilised in terms of a productive future
use. A good example of this type of stigma can be found in *Blue Circle* v

Ministry of Defence [1999] Env LR 22 where a site which was in the process of being sold was contaminated with radioactive soil. Although the site was subsequently cleaned up, the sale fell through as a result of the stigma of contamination.

(c) Standard setting

One of the key problems in regulating the clean up of historically contaminated land is the setting of standards in relation to the level of contamination which will trigger regulatory action and the level of clean up which is required. As mentioned above, the assessment of unacceptable levels of contamination always requires some form of risk assessment which takes into account a range of factors. Such risk assessments do not lend themselves to rigid rules. In addition, once it has been established that the risks arising from the contamination are unacceptable, there is the problem of deciding on the question of what clean up works will be required.

The two clean up levels which are most commonly adopted refer to the use to which the land is put and the level of clean up which is required to put the land to such a use without any of the risks associated with the original contamination. The 'multifunctional' approach requires land to be cleaned up to a level so that it is fit for any possible use. On the other hand, the 'suitable for use' standard only requires that any clean up works enable the land to be used for its current use (although this can include a future use which has received planning permission). Of course, in addition to these two general approaches to standard setting there is the problem of setting the specific levels of contaminants which apply in particular cases.

The adoption of either of these two general approaches has its advantages and disadvantages. For example, the 'suitable for use' approach can ensure that action is only taken where there are current risks but this may mean that significant amounts of contaminants are left after clean up works have taken place. Under the 'multifunctional' approach unnecessary work may be required which can have significant financial consequences without any environmental benefits (indeed Holland, which is the country most associated with 'multifunctionality', abandoned this approach as annual clean up costs rocketed).

(d) The allocation and apportionment of retrospective liability

In any system which deals with the clean up of historic contamination there will be a need to introduce retrospective liability. By its very nature, historic contamination is the consequence of actions which occurred in the past, sometimes many years distant. In many circumstances, the activities which caused the contamination will have been lawful. Therefore, in addition to retrospective effect, an efficient regulatory scheme of liability to cover such lawful past actions must impose strict (i.e. without fault) liability. The introduction of such retrospective strict liability could be, in many circumstances, inherently unfair and unduly punitive. In the case of contaminated land, however, this unfairness is arguably balanced by the need to address the long-term consequences of contamination and the implications for sustainable development should land be left to present environmental problems for many years into the future.

There are also great practical difficulties when attempting to allocate or apportion liability for historic contamination. The factual background can be particularly complex with many different occupiers and operators who may have used numerous substances which have combined to contaminate the land. The physical nature of the contamination referred to above may mean that it has moved from its original location complicating any effort to trace the original responsible parties. Those parties may have ceased to exist (e.g. through death in the case of individuals or dissolution in the case of companies), changed identity in some way (through corporate restructuring) or simply be unable to pay for the works which are required. There are also difficulties in knowing where to draw the line in defining the concept of who is 'responsible' for the contamination. A very wide definition might include anyone with a connection to the site (including banks who lend money to pay for the site or landlords who leased it to polluting occupiers). A very narrow definition might restrict the definition to the last person with knowledge of the contamination. Any definition is almost certain to result in 'hard cases' which might lead to unfairness or ineffectiveness.

History

The first formal moves towards a system to deal with historically contaminated land can be traced back to 1989 when the House of Commons Environment Committee reported on the subject and recommended the abolition of the 'buyer beware' rule in relation to the sale and purchase of land so that the seller was under an obligation to inform the buyer of any defects associated with the land (including contamination). The governmental response was a consultation paper, *Let the Buyer be Better Informed,* which proposed a register of land which had been used for certain categories of potentially contaminative uses. The statutory framework for this new register was to be found in s. 143 of the Environmental Protection Act 1990. The response to the consultation exercise was negative and resulted in a further round of consultation. This second exercise proposed a much more restricted range of potentially contaminative uses.

Many objections were raised at both stages of the consultation process. Perhaps the most fundamental objection was that the register would not record actual contamination. The reliance on recording the previous or existing use of the land would not provide sufficient certainty of the presence of contamination. Indeed, there would have been a significant number of sites which were heavily contaminated which would not have appeared on the register at all. Thus the key issue was not the identification of *potentially* contaminated land but the detection of *actual* contamination. Of equal importance was the fact that there was nothing in the proposals which sought to introduce positive instruments to assist in the clean up of identified contamination nor address the crucial questions of who should pay the costs of remediation.

In the light of these criticisms it was announced in March 1993 that the government was withdrawing its proposals to set up the register of contaminative uses. At the same time it was announced that there would be a wide-ranging review of the clean-up of contaminated land including such issues as treatment, allocation of liabilities and cost recovery. The consultation paper *Paying for Our Past* was issued in March 1994. The aim of the paper was to set out a number of 'preliminary conclusions' on a series of seven issues dealing with: government policy objectives; the statutory framework; the relationship with the common law; the extension of strict liability; the identity of the person liable for clean-up; providing the markets with information; and the role of public sector bodies.

In November 1994 the government announced the outcome of the consultation exercise. The result was a policy document, *The Framework for Contaminated Land*, which set out the broad future strategy for dealing with contaminated land (which is discussed below). These policy aims were implemented in part with the introduction of the Environment Act 1995 which set out the statutory framework as inserted into the EPA 1990 as a new Part IIA. Like many other areas of environmental law the framework of the legislation only gives a small part of the legislative picture. Most of the detail is fleshed out in secondary legislation and more commonly in the guise of government guidance.

European policy on contaminated land

In comparison to other areas of environmental protection, there have been few significant European initiatives in relation to contaminated land. Perhaps the main reason for this is the extreme political sensitivity involved in trying to reach a consensus on measures which would introduce retrospective liability for soil contamination. There are, however, pieces of European legislation which are relevant. For example the Groundwater Directive (80/68) is designed to prevent the entry of certain contaminants into groundwater (see p. 587) and breaches of the Drinking Water Directive's quality parameters are used as a trigger for defining more harmful categories of contaminated land in domestic legislation. Other initiatives such as the recent White Paper on liability for environmental damage are specifically designed to exclude historic damage (although there are some arguments about the position of latent damage such as that caused by contamination; see p. 287).

Domestic contaminated land policy

The development of the policies which underpin the legal framework dealing with the clean up of historically contaminated land needs to be viewed in the wider context of the extensive impacts which such contamination has upon sustainable development. In addition to the direct threats to the environment and human health caused by harmful contamination, there are significant consequences in terms of resource depletion. This arises out of the inability to re-use previously developed land and the supplementary increase in pressure to develop green field sites. This has to be balanced against the high cost of cleaning up contamination with its knock-on economic effects on an individual, local, regional and even national scale.

As a result of the response to *Paying for Our Past* referred to above, the government adopted a broad strategy for dealing with historically contaminated land. The principal elements of this strategy are:

(a) to seek to bring damaged land back into beneficial use;

(b) the adoption of the 'suitable for use' approach when dealing with the issue of clean-up. Thus, remedial action will only be required where the contamination poses unacceptable actual or potential risks to health or the environment. This is to be balanced against the appropriateness and cost effectiveness of the measures taking into account the actual or intended use of the site. Therefore the measures required to clean up a site which was to be used for housing would be more stringent than if it were to be used for car-parking;

(c) to prioritise action to deal with the most urgent and real problems whilst balancing the economic constraints within the economy as a whole and on private businesses and landowners; and

(d) To clarify the law on the clean up of contaminated sites thus enabling a proper market to be created for those who own sites which are or have been contaminated.

The key component of this strategy is the adoption of the 'suitable for use' standard for clean up. This approach means that sites are assessed on a case-by-case basis taking into account the site specific risks. In addition, the 'suitable for use' standard is assessed against the current use or during the determination of any permission which is required for a future use (e.g. the land is cleaned up prior to the commencement of development to a standard which is suitable for the future use). Finally, the requirements for clean up are limited to the minimum necessary to prevent unacceptable risks to either the current use or officially permitted future use (e.g. with the benefit of planning permission), thus ensuring that the action is proportionate and does not have to address possible unknown future risks.

Although the 'suitable for use' approach is used in most situations, there is an exception where contamination has been caused as a result of activities which are covered by an extant statutory authorisation or licence. Where the relevant statutory provisions provide for a power to order clean up, the requisite standard is to a reinstatement level (i.e. to remove the contamination completely).

As with other areas of environmental regulation, the imposition of an administrative statutory framework is used in conjunction with other policy initiatives. In particular, there a number of programmes which are designed to meet the objective of recycling previously developed land including targets of 60 per cent of new housing to be built on 'brownfield' sites and 100 per cent of all contaminated land to be brought into beneficial use by 2030 (the latter being proposed by the Urban Task Force). The main thrust of these policies is to try to deal with the barriers to the redevelopment of contaminated land. Thus there are financial incentives in the form of grants and subsidies administered by bodies such as English Partnerships and the regional development agencies; research and development programmes to ensure that the risks associated with contaminated land can be evaluated objectively; and not least the imposition of a legal structure which clarifies the position in respect of potential liabilities for contamination. On this last point, it is arguable whether the implementation of the complex package of rules associated with Part IIA clarifies matters in the short term but certainty and confidence should result after an initial period of uncertainty.

The main features of the controls over historically contaminated land

These are as follows:

(a)   The local authority has the primary role in inspecting land within its area and identifying land which is deemed to be 'contaminated' for the purposes of Part IIA.

(b)   The definition of 'contaminated land' is narrow for the purposes of Part IIA and only covers situations where the contamination gives rise to significant harm, significant risk of significant harm or pollution of controlled waters.

(c)   Once 'contaminated land' has been identified, responsibility is divided, with the Environment Agency taking control over sites where the risks from the contamination are perceived to be higher (known as 'special sites') and all other sites remaining within the control of the local authorities.

(d)   In the absence of an emergency, the appropriate enforcing authority is under a duty to ascertain the person or persons who is/are responsible for cleaning up the land.

(e)   In cases where there is an emergency, the enforcing authority can carry out the clean up works and seek to recover the costs of doing so from the person or persons who would otherwise have had to carry out the works.

(f)   In cases where there is no emergency, the enforcing authority must identify all persons who might be affected by any requirement to carry out clean up works. This includes owners, occupiers and those responsible for the contamination.

(g)   The enforcing authority must come up with a scheme for the clean up of the land. Any scheme must take into account the costs and benefits of carrying out the works.

(h)   After the scheme has been drawn up, the enforcing authority must consult the potentially affected parties. Where voluntary works are agreed, no further action can be taken by the enforcing authority.

(i)   Responsibility for clean up works rests primarily with the original polluters (although this relatively simple phrase conceals a number of complex issues) and in cases where the original polluter cannot be found, responsibility is transferred to the owners or occupiers of the land. After identifying the person or persons who should pay for the clean up, the enforcing authorities must exclude less blameworthy persons in accordance with various tests set down in statutory guidance (known as 'exclusion tests'). After these exclusion tests have been applied, the costs of carrying out the clean up works must be apportioned between the remaining responsible persons.

(j) The enforcing authority is under a *duty* to serve the remediation notice if it is able to do so. It cannot serve a remediation notice in certain circumstances (e.g. if any person would suffer 'hardship' if the costs of carrying out the works would be recovered from them or where the responsible person agrees to carry out clean up works voluntarily). If the enforcing authority cannot serve a remediation notice, there is a *power* to carry out the works and to seek to recover all or any part of the costs of doing so.

(k) There are rights of appeal against the service of a remediation notice. Appeals are made to the magistrates' court or the Secretary of State (in relation to special sites only). A notice is suspended until the appeal is finally determined or withdrawn.

(l) It is an offence to fail to comply with the requirements of a remediation notice without reasonable excuse.

(m) Each enforcing authority is required to maintain a system of public registers which should contain details of remediation notices and areas of contaminated land for which that authority is responsible.

The statutory package of rules

The statutory framework in Part IIA sets out the structure of the system to deal with contaminated land. There is supplementary secondary legislation in the form of the Contaminated Land (England) Regulations 2000 (SI 2000/227) with corresponding regulations in the devolved countries (the references to regulations in the rest of this chapter refer to the English regulations). These regulations deal with certain aspects of the contaminated land regime including: the definition of 'special sites'; the detailed arrangements for remediation notices including content, service and appeals; and public registers.

In practice, however, the most important elements of the new system are to be found in tertiary rules which can be found in statutory guidance documents and in Circular 2/2000, *Contaminated Land: Implementation of Part IIA of the Environmental Protection Act 1990.* There is a significant difference in the status of these two sets of guidance. The Circular sets out the context for the operation of the rest of the legislation and provides a general description of how the system operates. The statutory guidance, on the other hand, is capable of binding the enforcing authorities. In particular, enforcing authorities have to 'act in accordance with' certain aspects of the guidance (this covers the definition and identification of contaminated land and the allocation and apportionment of liability), whilst they must 'have regard to' the remainder (this covers the remediation requirements and the recovery of the costs of remediation).

The fact that there are two 'levels' of guidance suggests that there is some legal significance in the distinction. The 'have regard to' guidance is akin to the 'material consideration' in a planning decision. Thus it is one factor in the decision-making process but it must be weighed against other matters. Decisions which do not follow such guidance will be lawful so long as they are accord with the general administrative decision-making (e.g. *Wednesbury* reasonableness, fairness, lack of bias etc.).

The guidance which enforcing authorities are to 'act in accordance with' is somewhat more problematic. Arguably, this guidance gives very little discretion to the enforcing authorities when making decisions and there would not appear to be anything which would justify a departure from such guidance (other than areas where the meaning of the guidance was debatable).

Administrative and regulatory responsibilities

The primary responsibility for regulating the clean up of historically contaminated land rests with local authorities and in particular the borough and district councils or the unitary authorities. In this context, the Environment Agency plays an important role providing technical guidance (e.g. for priority contaminants and in relation to site specific matters). In addition, the EA plays an active role in regulating the clean up of the most contaminated sites after notification by the local authorities (see below). Finally, the EA is under an obligation to prepare a report on the state of contaminated land with assistance from the local authorities (s. 78U, EPA 1990).

The definition of contaminated land

The definition of contaminated land is central to the operation of Part IIA. Section 78A(2), EPA 1990 provides that for the purposes of Part IIA (and those purposes alone) contaminated land is:

> any land which appears to the local authority in whose area it is situated to be in such a condition, by reason of substances in, on or under land, that—
>
> (a)   significant harm is being caused or there is a significant possibility of such harm being caused; or
> (b)   pollution of controlled waters is being or is likely to be, caused.

Section 78(4) defines harm as meaning:

> harm to the health of living organisms or other interference with the ecological systems of which they form part and, in the case of man, includes harm to his property.

The two categories of contaminated land are defined to reflect the policy of only requiring clean up when the contamination is causing unacceptable risks to the environment or human health. Although this definition provides the trigger for the operation of Part IIA, the statutory phrases are deliberately vague. It should therefore be noted that the statutory definition is meaningless without the backing of the statutory guidance. The importance of the guidance definition is emphasised by the fact that the enforcing authorities are to 'act in accordance with' the guidance on the definition of contaminated land. The definition can be broken down into smaller sub-definitions.

(a)   The existence of a pollutant linkage

The guidance fleshes out the statutory definition of 'significant harm and significant possibility' by introducing the concept of the 'pollutant linkage'. A pollutant linkage is formed when there is a linkage between a contaminant (a pollutant) and a receptor or target (e.g. humans or property) by means of a pathway. If any one aspect is missing, no linkage is formed. For example where there is contamination but it is self contained in the ground with no route into the wider environment, there is no pathway and the linkage cannot be formed. Where such a linkage is present, it must be 'significant' (forming what is known as a 'significant pollutant linkage' (SPL)) for the land to come within the definition of 'contaminated land'. Significance is assessed in relation to the types of targets which are being harmed by the contamination; the degree or nature of that harm; and the possibility of the harm being caused.

(b)   The types of receptor/target

The guidance narrowly defines the types of receptors or targets which can form part of the SPL. These are: human beings; nature conservation sites (which includes all of the sites which are protected under nature conservation laws); buildings; and other property (which covers crops and animals which are subject to property rights such as livestock). Anything which is a target which falls outside these categories (e.g. wild animals, nature conservation sites which are not protected under nature conservation laws or personal property such as cars) does not fall within Part IIA.

(c)   The nature of the harm

The guidance provides that in assessing the significance of the harm the local authority needs to consider whether the harm caused to the specified receptors falls within specified categories in relation to each of those receptors. For example in relation to humans this includes serious injury, birth defects and impairment of reproductive functions. In relation to nature conservation sites it includes any harm which results in an irreversible or substantial adverse change to the functioning of the ecosystems which form a substantial part of the site. In relation to property it includes substantial loss in crop value or substantial damage to buildings.

(d)   The possibility of significant harm being caused

In the absence of actual significant harm, the local authority must assess whether there is a significant possibility of significant harm being caused. The guidance explains that this should be based on an assessment of the risks involved with the contamination and in particular the 'magnitude or consequences' of the different types of significant harm being caused. This is a complicated exercise which should take account of the nature and degree of the harm (e.g. an explosion of methane gas or toxic effects on the growth of crops); the susceptibility of the receptors (e.g. a nearby school or a building with concrete foundations); and the timescale within which the harm might occur (imminent or over a period of 50 to 100 years). Putting all the factors together it might be found that the possibility of a methane gas explosion on a site next to a school which could occur imminently would have more significance than a site which was leaching corrosive chemical which might destroy the foundations of a building over a 100-year period. When considering the statistical assessment of the possibility of significant harm, the guidance provides that in all cases other than harm to human health this is assessed on the balance of probabilities (i.e. is it more likely than not to cause significant harm). In cases of harm to human health the relevant standard is that the risk must be medically 'unacceptable'.

(e) Pollution of controlled waters
The second limb of the statutory definition of contaminated land covers situations where poisonous, noxious or polluting matter is entering or is likely to enter controlled waters from the land in question (s. 78A(9), EPA 1990). The statutory guidance provides that the likelihood of the entry of the contaminant is to be assessed on the balance of probabilities. It should be noted that this definition excludes substances which have entered controlled waters at some time in the past and the entry has now ceased and is unlikely to recur (e.g. contamination which is caused by past leaks from underground storage tanks which are currently empty).

Unlike the other limb of 'contaminated land', the statutory definition is not fleshed out in guidance. The definition in s. 78A(9) mirrors the provision in the pollution control provisions of the Water Resources Act 1991 (see p. xxx). Case law on that definition suggests that very small quantities of contaminant could be considered to be 'polluting'. This would mean that there is no risk assessment involved when determining whether Part IIA applies to water pollution. At present, the government has merely pointed out that clean up works for small amounts of contamination may be unreasonable when subjected to a cost benefit analysis.

Although the local authorities have a seemingly straightforward task in relation to water pollution, it is quite clear from the guidance that local authorities are being given a very complicated set of tasks to implement when determining whether land is 'contaminated' within the terms of Part IIA and the accompanying statutory guidance. In particular, the guidance is certainly not prescriptive in terms when discussing the various factors which should be taken into account when carrying out the risk assessment in determining 'significance'.

The identification of contaminated land

Under s. 78B(1), EPA 1990, local authorities are under a duty to inspect their areas from time to time for the purposes of identifying:

(a)   contaminated land;
(b)   special sites.

In undertaking this duty local authorities must 'act in accordance' with the
statutory guidance. When identifying contaminated land, a local authority is
entitled to take into account the cumulative impact of two or more separate
sites when assessing whether there is 'significant harm' or 'pollution of
controlled waters'. This will be important where the 'cocktail' effect of a
number of contaminated sites causes significant harm whereas any individual
site will not give rise to any notable pollution (s. 78X(2)).

(a)   Contaminated land

In seeking to identify contaminated land, local authorities may rely upon
information from a number of sources including the owners or occupiers in
question (who may have carried out a voluntary investigation of their own
land). Where pollution of controlled waters is being caused or the contamination is harming a nature conservation site, the local authority must consult
the EA and English Nature respectively and have regard to any comments
which they make before making the determination as to whether the land
should be designated as 'contaminated land'. In cases where this information
is not sufficient to enable the local authority to identify the land as contaminated, it can carry out an inspection of the land where there is a
'reasonable possibility' that there is a pollutant linkage on the land. For the
purposes of the identification duty, local authorities have the same powers of
inspection and entry as the EA has under s. 108 (see p. 170).

(b)   Special sites

When contaminated land has been identified, local authorities must consider
whether the site falls within one of the categories of special sites as defined
under the regulations. Special sites are regulated directly by the EA. The
general criteria for special sites are the seriousness of the harm or water
pollution which would be (or is being) caused and whether the EA is more
likely to have the expertise to act on those particular sites. More specifically
the categories include: land on which an IPC process is carried on; Ministry
of Defence land; nuclear sites; land on which waste acid tars are present; and
in respect of the pollution of controlled waters, contamination which is
causing breaches of drinking water quality standards (regs. 2 and 3).

For special sites to be designated, the local authority must first formally
identify the land as contaminated for the purposes of Part IIA. In practice,
however, the Environment Agency has a role to play in the identification of
special sites either in conjunction with the local authority (by carrying out any
investigation on behalf of the authority) or on its own account.

Where the authority considers that the land should be designated as a
special site it is under a duty to notify the EA (after seeking its advice), the
owner/occupier, and any person who might be responsible for paying the
costs of remediation (s. 78C(1)–(3)). The EA has inspection and entry
powers in relation to special sites (s. 78Q). The EA also has the power to

terminate the designation of a special site where it appears to the EA that it is no longer suitable for designation (see s. 78Q(4), although the land will continue to remain 'contaminated land' as identified by the local authority).

Notification and consultation

Once land has been identified as being contaminated, the local authority is under a duty to notify this fact to all owners, occupiers, people who appear to the local authority to be liable to pay the clean up costs and the Environment Agency (s. 78B(3)). In practice, many of those people will already be aware of the potential designation as a result of supplying information as part of the identification process. The notification to the EA enables it to consider whether the site should be designated as a special site and whether there is any need for site specific guidance on the level or nature of the clean up work.

After notification, there follows a period of consultation with the notified parties (s. 78(1)). This duty does not apply in cases of where it appears to the authority that there is an imminent danger of serious harm or pollution of controlled waters (s. 78G(4) and s. 78H(4)). There is a minimum period of three months for consultation (before the service of a remediation notice) and the government has expressed the desire that this period be used at best to achieve agreement between the enforcing authorities and the persons who are carrying out the remediation and at worst to narrow the areas of disagreement. Indeed, the emphasis on the voluntary nature of this process is formalised with the preclusion of any further formal action (i.e. the service of a remediation notice) where a person has undertaken to carry out voluntary remediation works. Where such agreement is reached, the person must describe the works in a Remediation Statement which is published on the public register (s. 78H(7)).

The second main purpose of the consultation period is to discuss the works which are necessary and in particular whether they should be phased or whether a single action could deal with a number of SPLs (e.g. digging out contaminated soil and disposing of it might deal with a number of different contaminants which have been caused by different people). Alternatively, the enforcing authority may consider that remediation would not be reasonable bearing in mind the costs and the benefits (e.g. where there were very low levels of water pollution). In such circumstances, the enforcing authority must publish a remediation declaration explaining that no remediation is required notwithstanding the formal identification of the land as con-taminated under Part IIA (s. 78H(6)).

The duty to serve a remediation notice

Once land has been identified as contaminated and consultation has taken place between the enforcing authority and the relevant persons, the authority must serve a remediation notice (s. 78E). Although this duty is similar to the duty to serve an abatement notice under the statutory nuisance regime (see

p. 433 and the discussion there of *R* v *Carrick DC, ex parte Shelley* [1996] Env LR 273), there are limits to the mandatory nature of the duty. Unlike statutory nuisances, the enforcing authority is specifically precluded from serving a remediation notice in certain circumstances. These include:

(a) where there are other statutory powers which can be used to enforce a clean up of the land (see overlapping controls below). The justification for the primacy of these other statutory provisions is that the introduction of Part IIA was not intended to add to the pre-existing regulatory burden: the policy aim was merely to clarify the law on contamination rather then introduce new liabilities;

(b) where any requirement to carry out remediation would be unreasonable (s. 78H(5)(a)). For example because the costs outweighed the benefits or where the statutory guidance suggests that particular works would be unreasonable. In such cases a remediation declaration is required (s. 78H(6));

(c) where the appropriate person has agreed to undertake voluntary remediation (s. 78H(5)(b));

(d) where one of the persons who would be served with a remediation notice would suffer 'hardship' if they were required to pay for their share of any of the costs of remediation (s. 78N(3)(e)). 'Hardship' is undefined in Part IIA and the guidance suggests that it should be determined on a case-by-case basis and having regard to the statutory guidance on the issue (see chapter E). In such cases, the enforcing authority is precluded from serving the notice on *any* of the parties who would have been served with the notice (where there is more than one party responsible, see s. 78H(5)(d));

(e) where the enforcing authority is itself the appropriate person (e.g. as a result of owning a contaminated site or by being the original polluter, see s. 78H(5)(c));

(f) where it is considered that there is imminent danger of serious harm or pollution (s. 78N(3)(a));

(g) where there is pollution of controlled waters and the only appropriate persons who can be found are owners/occupiers (s. 78J);

(h) where, after reasonable inquiry, no appropriate person can be found (s. 78N(3)(f)).

If the enforcing authority is precluded from serving a remediation notice, it has a *power* to carry out the works itself and to seek to recover the costs of doing so (if that is possible) from the appropriate persons. The importance of these exceptions cannot be underestimated as they are wide (particularly in the case of hardship) and shift the regulatory focus from mandatory duties to discretionary powers.

The remediation notice is to be served on the 'appropriate person' and is required to set out what must be done and the time period for carrying out the specified steps (s. 78E(1)). In specifying the steps required under a remediation notice the authority is under a duty to have regard to the statutory guidance and to balance the costs of carrying out the work with the seriousness of the harm/pollution caused (s. 78E(4)). The statutory guidance makes it clear that environmental benefits should be considered in addition to any financial benefits.

The 'appropriate person'

The issue of the identity of the 'appropriate person' on whom the remediation notice is served is, together with the definition of contaminated land, one of the central elements of Part IIA. The question of 'who pays?' in a liability regime which imposes costs on a retrospective basis for something as complicated as historic contamination was always going to require the resolution of difficult issues. In accordance with the 'polluter pays' principle the appropriate person is defined as the person, or any of the persons, who caused or knowingly permitted the substances, or any of the substances, which have been the cause of the contamination to be in or under the land (s. 78F(2)). On some interpretations of this section, however, it could be argued that the 'polluter pays' principle is given a wide meaning which would cover a person who brought potentially polluting substances onto land regardless of whether the substances polluted whilst under their control. In addition to contamination on the site where it was originally present, the appropriate person can also be responsible for contamination which has escaped onto other land (s. 78K). Within the statutory guidance those appropriate persons who have caused or knowingly permitted the presence of the substances are known as 'Class A persons'.

The phrase 'caused or knowingly permitted' is familiar in the context of environmental offences (particularly in relation to water pollution), however, great care must be taken in extrapolating the principles in those cases and applying them in the contaminated land context.

(a) 'Caused'
Whether a person has 'caused' the presence of contamination should be viewed as a question of fact in each case. Following the existing case law, liability is strict (i.e. fault, negligence or knowledge are not required). There might be arguments which could be put forward to justify a distinction between the strictness of the liability for causing environmental criminal offences (where the strictness is mitigated by varying the punishment to reflect the blameworthiness of the defendant) and causing historic contamination (where the financial 'penalty' is fixed and potentially much more significant than any fine). The counter to these arguments would be that the statutory regime has other mechanisms for promoting fairness (e.g. the exclusion tests and the 'hardship' exemption) and that the policy aims behind the legislation would be defeated should 'innocent' parties be allowed to escape liability on the basis of their lack of fault. In particular, the government rejected a suggestion that there should be a 'state of the art' defence (i.e. liability would not attach to a person who could demonstrate that they had adopted 'state of the art' practices at the time the original contamination arose.

The government has suggested that, in line with the water pollution cases on the issue, causation would be established where the person concerned was involved in some active operation to which the presence of the contaminating substance was attributable although a failure to act could amount to causation in certain circumstances (for a more detailed analysis of these cases see p. 589). In practice, in most cases where contamination is found on a site, there would be a rebuttable presumption (i.e. assumed unless the contrary could be proved) that the operator/occupier of the site at the time of the contamination had caused the presence of the pollutant. The presumption would be particularly strong where it could be demonstrated that the operator/occupier had generated or used the substances in question.

Causation could be direct (e.g. the person was responsible for placing pollutants in the ground) or indirect (e.g. through leaks from equipment). In addition, more than one person could be said to have 'caused' the presence of the contaminant (e.g. a contractor dumping the operator's waste contaminants on the operator's site — both parties would be appropriate persons).

(b) 'Knowingly permitted'
The definition of 'knowingly permitted' raises more complex issues than under the 'caused' limb. When the Environment Act 1995 was passing through Parliament, a ministerial statement suggested that the government's view of the phrase was that it required both knowledge that the substances were in, on or under the land and the existence of a power to prevent that presence. This does not deal with all of the issues with the phrase. Other matters which are subject to argument include the following.

(i) The extent of the required knowledge
There is an important distinction between knowing that a substance is present in, on or under land and knowing that it has the potential to be present in such a way as to render the land as contaminated for the purposes of Part IIA. For example, land could be transferred through a number of ownerships with each owner knowing that a substance had been stored on the land some time in the past (e.g. in underground storage tanks). On the former interpretation, the date on which the substances left the storage tank and entered into the land would be irrelevant, the determining factor would be the presence of the substance, regardless of whether it was safely contained in the storage tank. On the latter interpretation only knowledge of the escape of the substance into the land and the knowledge of the requisite standard of harm would give rise to a potential liability (with the date of escape being the trigger date).

(ii) The standard of the knowledge
This point is connected to the extent of the knowledge in the sense that the word 'knowingly' could be narrowly construed to mean actual knowledge of the presence of the substance. Alternatively, and the view which would accord most readily with other areas of environmental regulation (e.g. water pollution, see *Schulmans Incorporated Limited* v *NRA* [1993] Env LR D1 and waste

management, see *Kent CC* v *Beaney* [1993] Env LR 225), knowledge can be implied from the factual circumstances. This would include constructive knowledge (i.e. a reasonable person would have known given the circumstances) and wilful blindness (i.e. shutting one's mind to the obvious). Thus, buying a site where an operator had carried on an operation using hazardous substances might be sufficient to raise the presumption of knowledge in the absence of actual information.

(iii) *'Permitting'*
Although there is case law on the definition of 'permitting' in relation to regulatory matters, most of it relates to one-off incidents (e.g. permitting the entry of polluting matter into controlled waters). Permission in this context is generally a positive act in the sense that involves some form of explicit or implied consent for the thing to be done. The *presence* of substances, on the other hand, is a continuing state of affairs where permission may be assumed from a failure to address the presence of the pollutant. As in the example above, this could arise from ownership of land and knowledge of the presence of substances, regardless of a positive permission.

Aggregating these three issues (i.e. (i) to (iii)), it would be possible to argue that owning land for even a short period with the knowledge that substances are stored on the land (which could be constructive i.e. there are storage tanks on or in the land) may be sufficient for the owner to become a 'knowing permitter' even in the absence of the escape of the pollutant. On this interpretation, the only way to avoid this classification would be to ensure that the substance was no longer present on the land (i.e. in this case to empty the storage tanks).

(c)   Owners and occupiers
Where the owner or the occupier of the land is not a Class A person, they can only be the appropriate person where no Class A person can be 'found' after reasonable inquiry (s. 78F(4)). In these circumstances, owners and occupiers are known as Class B persons for the purposes of the statutory guidance. 'Found' in this context would not include people who had died or companies which had ceased to exist. There are situations where owners/occupiers could fall within both Class A and Class B where they are responsible for the presence of some but not all of the substances on the land (as a Class A person) and the parties who are responsible for the residual contamination cannot be found (as a Class B person). One final important point to note is that Class B persons cannot be served with a remediation notice in respect of works relating to pollution of controlled waters or in respect of contamination which has escaped from other land onto their land other than remediation in respect of land or water which they own or occupy (ss. 78J and 78K(3), (4) respectively).
'Owner' is defined in s. 78A as being the person entitled to receive a market rent (as opposed to a token or peppercorn rent) for the property. It specifically excludes mortgagees not in possession which means that lenders can receive remediation notices where they are mortgagees in possession.

Insolvency practitioners are also protected from personal liability unless the contamination is attributable to their own negligence (s. 78X(3)). 'Occupier' is not defined.

(d)   Practical issues
Although these provisions in respect of responsibility for contamination provide a complicated hierarchy of liability, the practical difficulties of establishing responsibility must not be overlooked. Unfortunately contamination does not necessarily carry clear identification of responsibility. In particular in areas where there has been a long history of industrial activity, distinguishing between different polluters will present evidential hurdles which will have to be overcome before a remediation notice can be served. The rules provide a framework for the allocation of liability but the evidential problems of linking individuals or companies with particular pollutant linkages will undoubtedly provide the enforcing authorities with an extremely difficult task. The standard of proof in relation to these issues is the balance of probabilities.

Allocation of liability

The identification of the potential appropriate persons is an integral part of the notification of the identification of contaminated land under Part IIA. This is, however, only one stage of the process of allocating liability for the clean up of historically contaminated land. The other significant stages in the process include the following.

(a)   Forming liability groups
First, the enforcing authority must identify the numbers of SPLs on the land (i.e. the number of different pollutants which are giving rise to significant harm etc. via a pollutant linkage). This could be a single pollutant (with one SPL) or a number of different pollutants (with corresponding numbers of SPLs). The enforcing authorities must then identify each Class A person who is linked to each SPL (i.e. those parties who caused or knowingly permitted the presence of the contaminant). This group is referred to as the Class A liability group in relation to each SPL. Alternatively, in the absence of Class A persons in relation to any SPL, the owners/occupiers of the land form what is known as the Class B liability group in relation to that SPL. Thus, areas of contaminated land might have different substances which form different SPLs where either some or all of the persons who caused or knowingly permitted the presence of the substance can be found (forming Class A liability groups) or in cases where none of the Class A persons can be found, the owners and occupiers of the land on which the SPL is found form the Class B liability group.

(b)   Applying the exclusion tests
Where a liability group has two or more members, the enforcing authority is obliged to apply a series of 'exclusion tests'. These tests exclude appropriate

persons from liability. The tests are applied in a specific order and seek to exclude what might be perceived to be categories of appropriate persons who might appear to be less blameworthy. Thus where there are large liability groups the tests seek to differentiate between different causers and permitters. The rationale behind the exclusion tests would seem to be to mitigate any unfairness inherent in a system based upon strict and retrospective liability. The main flaw in this rationale is that the tests might, in certain circumstances, operate to increase the unfairness where liability groups are small.

There are six main tests for excluding Class A liability group members which can be grouped under three headings. The first test (Test 1 — 'Excluded activities') excludes all those persons who have Class A liability solely by reason of carrying out certain specified activities including: providing financial assistance, such as lending money; underwriting insurance; being a landlord where the tenant has caused the pollution; and providing technical, legal or scientific advice. The second group of tests excludes parties who have transferred the responsibility for the contamination either by reducing the price of the land in question to reflect the condition of the land (Test 2 — 'Payments made for remediation') or by selling the land with information on the condition of the land such that it is reasonable to expect that the purchaser of the land should pay for the clean up of the land (Test 3 — 'Sold with information'). The last group of tests excludes parties who are less blameworthy as a result of a change in circumstances from the date when the substance was originally in, on or under the land. These include: harmful changes to the original substance brought about by the unforeseeable introduction of later substances (Test 4 — 'Changes to substances'); new activities which have caused the substances to escape from the original land (Test 5 — 'Escaped substances'); and the introduction of new developments which cause the creation of a SPL (Test 6 — 'Introduction of pathways or receptors').

Class B exclusion is much simpler excluding occupiers and tenants paying a market rent. These parties are excluded on the basis that they have no interest in the long-term value of the land and therefore will not benefit from any increase in the value should it be cleaned up.

There are a number of general rules which apply to all of the tests. First, the rules cannot exclude parties if the result would be to exclude all of the liability group. Secondly, exclusion is only referable to the specified liability group and not across all liability groups (i.e. an appropriate person may be excluded from one group but not necessarily from another). Thirdly, the tests must be applied in numerical order. Fourthly, where members of liability groups have reached a private agreement on the basis upon which liability should be allocated between them, and a copy of the agreement has been provided to the enforcing authority, the authority must allocate and apportion any liability on the basis of that agreement, in relation to the parties to the agreement alone. For example a buyer of land might agree to pay for any future liabilities which would be allocated to the seller of the land in return for a slightly reduced price. Any liabilities allocated to other appropriate persons would not fall within this agreement. A private agreement can be disregarded if it would have the effect of transferring liabilities to a person who would suffer hardship (on the basis that in these circumstances, the enforcing authority would be precluded from serving a remediation notice and private agreements could be drafted as a liability avoidance mechanism). Fifthly, the financial circumstances of the parties are disregarded when carrying out the exclusion tests (avoiding the problems of the so called 'deep pockets' discrimination where the enforcing authority targets only those who can afford to pay). Finally, where two or more of the persons within the liability group are part of the same group of companies, they are treated as a single person.

Apportionment of liability

Once the exclusion tests have been carried out and the liability groups finalised, the enforcing authority must determine how much of the costs of carrying out the remedial works should be apportioned to each appropriate person. In general terms, the starting point is that liability should be apportioned on the basis of relative responsibility of each of the group members for creating or continuing the risk caused by the SPL. This might be related to the extent of time of occupation of the land or the use of a substance. In the absence of reasonable information upon which to base such an assessment of responsibility, the enforcing authority should apportion the costs equally between the group members.

Remediation notices

Once the enforcing authority has allocated and apportioned liability it must serve the remediation notice. Section 78E(1) and reg. 4 make provision for the details which must be included in the notice. Although there are certain prescribed pieces of information which must be included, the government is hoping to avoid some of the legalistic issues which have been raised in relation to abatement notices (see p. 440). The contents of the notice are likely to be much more detailed and complicated than an equivalent statutory notice but the government's stated aim for the notice is to give the recipients a clear picture of the nature of the work; who is required to carry it out; where there is more than one appropriate person, what proportion of the costs of the work must be borne by each of them; by when the work must be carried out; the identity of the other appropriate persons; the reasons for serving the notice; the rights of appeal and any other information which can help to clarify any uncertainty. In order to promote consistency of approach, the DETR and the EA are proposing the use of standardised 'model' notices (which raises interesting questions of accountability and delegation of responsibility).

Appeals

Any person who is the recipient of a remediation notice has the right of appeal within 21 days of the service of the notice (s. 78L(1)). Where the notice was served by a local authority the appeal is made to the magistrates' court; in relation to special sites, the right of appeal is to the Secretary of State. Regulation 7 sets out the 19 main grounds of appeal. In summary these cover such things as: whether the land is 'contaminated land' for the purposes of Part IIA; whether the appellant is an appropriate person; whether the appellant should have been excluded form the relevant liability group; whether the enforcing authority was precluded from serving a remediation notice; whether the requirements of the notice were reasonable; and whether the enforcing authority has acted in accordance with the statutory guidance.

An appeal suspends the operation of the notice until the determination or withdrawal of the appeal (reg. 15). The distinction between the appeal procedure in relation to special sites and other contaminated land is significant in a number of ways. First, the Secretary of State may hold a public inquiry (reg. 11(1)(b)) where third parties are able to make representations. Secondly, the Secretary of State may delegate the decision to the Planning Inspectorate (indeed it is anticipated that most appeals will be determined in this way). Inspectors appointed may be technically qualified and may be assisted by assessors with experience in contaminated land issues. On the other hand, 'contaminated land' appeals are to be allocated to stipendiary magistrates who are not necessarily equipped to deal with the complicated technical issues involved. Finally, 'just and reasonable' costs are normally awarded against the unsuccessful party in the magistrates' court, whereas costs in relation to special site appeals will not be awarded in written representation appeals and in other cases (i.e. hearings and inquiries) except where there has been unreasonable behaviour on behalf of one of the parties which has led to unnecessary expense. Whilst this division of responsibility is understandable (with the division reflecting procedures for statutory nuisance appeals and pollution control appeals respectively), there would not appear to be any coherent justification for this.

Compliance with a remediation notice

After 21 days from the date of service of the notice, there are two possible outcomes. First the notice is complied with. In such circumstances, it may be necessary to serve an additional remediation notice if it becomes clear as a result of complying with the original notice that further or different works are required. Alternatively, the works may be sufficient to address the risks brought about by the SPL. Although there is no formal procedure for declassifying the land as 'contaminated', the enforcing authority must enter the details of the remediation carried out on the public register (see below) and it may confirm that no further enforcement action is anticipated.

Non-compliance with a remediation notice

The second possible outcome after the service of a remediation notice is that it is either not complied with or partially complied with. It is an offence to fail to comply with a remediation notice without reasonable excuse (s. 78M). There are, however, relatively minor penalties which undermines the deterrence factor. The offence can only be tried in the magistrates' court. Where the contaminated land is currently industrial, trade or business premises the maximum penalty is a fine of £20,000 with a further daily fine of up to £2,000 for every day before the enforcing authority has carried out any remediation (s. 78M(4)). In cases of other contaminated land the maximum fine is £5,000 with a maximum daily fine of £500 (10 per cent of Level 5) (s. 78M(3)).

The relevant authority has the power to carry out remediation works where the recipient of the remediation has failed to comply either with or without the appropriate person's agreement (s. 78N). The Agency has the power to recover all or part of its reasonable costs (s. 78P). In recovering costs regard must be had to any hardship which the cost-recovery might impose. In England and Wales the relevant authority also has the power to serve a charging notice on the owner which will constitute a charge on the premises which consist of or include the contaminated land in question. The costs of any charge may be paid by instalments over a maximum thirty-year period. A person served with the charging notice has a right of appeal which must be made to the county court within 21 days of the receipt of the notice (s. 78P(8)).

Registers

Each enforcing authority is required to keep a public register of information in relation to Part IIA (s. 78R). Schedule 3 to the regulations sets out the details of the information which is to be kept on the register. These include: particulars of remediation statements, declarations and notices; appeals; convictions; notices in relation to special sites; and information about remediation work notified to the authority although there is no official guarantee of compliance with remediation notices (s. 78R(3)).

Overlapping controls — The distinguishing features of Part IIA

The main focus of the Part IIA provisions is to deal with historic contamination which would not be cleaned up under other provisions. In this context, the new provisions should be seen as a last resort as in most (but not all) situations, if there is an alternative statutory mechanism for enforcing clean up, this will oust the Part IIA provisions. Thus, when considering how contamination must be dealt with, there is a range of alternative statutory mechanisms for preventing harm to either the environment or health arising from regulated operations or processes. There are some significant differences between the historic provisions and these continuing controls. These include the following.

(a) Risk assessment
Part IIA operates within narrow margins. The definition of 'contamination' is drawn fairly tightly and requires a sophisticated analysis of the risks associated with contamination before clean up works can be demanded. Other statutory regimes operate on a much wider definition of 'pollution'/ 'harm' or are based on breaches of extant statutory consents. Enforcing

authorities are therefore much more likely to use such mechanisms as they tend to be simpler, easier and quicker to use.

(b) Allocation and apportionment of liability
Under Part IIA, the enforcing authorities are required to go through compli-cated tests for the allocation and apportionment of liability. These tests mean that, amongst other things, enforcing authorities have to: give effect to private agreements made between people who are responsible for the clean up; estimate the respective proportions of contamination caused by responsible persons; and assess whether the costs of carrying out such works as are deemed necessary would cause 'hardship'. In contrast most other statutory clean up schemes are straightforward with joint and several liability (i.e. one party is responsible for all of the cost of clean up regardless of whether there are other parties who are also responsible).

(c) Mandatory duties and discretionary powers
Once land has been identified as contaminated and there are parties who would be liable, there is no discretion over the question of whether to enforce the clean up. The enforcing authority is under a duty to serve a remediation notice. The counterpoint to this is that the Part IIA provisions preclude the service of a remediation notice in certain circumstances. This suggests that there is an 'all or nothing' aspect to the operation of the system (i.e. the enforcing authority *must* serve a notice or it *is not able* to serve a notice).

Although a comparable duty exists in relation to statutory nuisances (see *R* v *Carrick DC, ex parte Shelley* [1996] Env LR 276), clean up provisions in relation to other areas of pollution control are discretionary in nature. This gives the enforcing authority a good deal more flexibility in dealing with clean up works.

(d) Differing clean up standards
The issue of clean up standards is closely linked to the question of risk assessment. With historic contamination the 'suitable for use' standard is adopted for clean up as this reflects the existing risks to the environment or human health (see further below). This may mean that the required works only need to address the risks associated with the contamination in relation to the *current* use of the land (e.g. more significant works may be required where the land is residential in use as compared with land which is industrial use). Under other pollution control provisions the emphasis is placed upon the remedying of harm caused irrespective of the use of the land. This approach is based upon a requirement to reinstate the environment to the state that it was in prior to the pollution.

Overlapping controls

(a) Integrated pollution control (IPC) and integrated pollution prevention and control (IPPC)
There are two aspects to the overlap between the contaminated land regime and the integrated authorisation or permitting systems under IPC and rules,

and the replacement regime under IPPC. First, contamination which is caused as a result of the operation of a process or an installation which is prescribed for control under either system falls outside the Part IIA rules on historic contamination. There are powers to remedy harm caused by a breach of an IPC authorisation or an IPPC permit (s. 27, EPA 1990). Where the harm is caused by contamination, the enforcing authority under the contaminated land regime is precluded from serving a remediation notice to remedy the harm (although there is nothing to prevent the site being designated as 'contaminated land' for the purposes of Part IIA; see s. 78YB(1), EPA 1990).

The second aspect of the overlap is brought about by the implementation of the assessment and mitigation of a wide range of environmental impacts under the Pollution Prevention and Control Act 1999. Where an installation is prescribed for control under the permitting regime, there is a requirement to carry out an investigation into the site conditions in order to provide a benchmark which can be used to assess the contamination which is caused by the future operations of the installation. This in turn is used to guide clean up requirements when the installation is closed. Although this procedure is adopted primarily for the purposes of the 1999 Act regime, the results of the initial survey can yield evidence which can be used by an enforcing authority in any assessment of the land for the purposes of Part IIA.

(b)   Waste management licensing

Where contamination arises on a site which is covered by a waste management licence and the cause of the contamination is attributable to either a breach of the conditions of the licence or an activity which is authorised by the licence in accordance with its terms and conditions and the licence is still in force, the enforcing authority is precluded from serving a remediation notice (s. 78YB(2), EPA 1990). This is also true in any circumstances where the contamination is caused by an illegal deposit of controlled waste (s. 78YB(3), EPA 1990). The justification for these exceptions is that there are alternative powers to deal with the contamination. In the former case, there are powers to enforce against breaches of extant waste management licences under Part II of the EPA 1990 (see p. 502). In the latter case, the Environment Agency has powers to remove the waste and remedy any harm caused (s. 59, EPA 1990). This is likely to apply only to wastes which were discarded after May 1994 when the current waste management licensing regime came into force. It is worth pointing out that the s. 59 power (like s. 161, Water Resources Act 1991, the equivalent power in relation to water pollution) does not involve any of the complex questions of allocation and apportionment of liability associated with Part IIA.

(c)   Water pollution

As the definition of contaminated land applies to the pollution of controlled waters (see above), there is a significant overlap between the works notice provisions of the Water Resources Act 1991 (s. 161–161D) and Part IIA. The works notice provisions apply when there is or is likely to be pollution of controlled waters. In such circumstances, a notice can be served upon the person who 'caused or knowingly permitted' the presence (or likely presence) of the substance, requiring them to take action to prevent the pollution. This means that the powers to serve a remediation notice and works notice are concurrent and as a result of the differences between the two regimes (not the least of which is the relatively straightforward allocation and apportionment of liability under the works notice provisions as compared with the complexities of the contaminated land regime) the implications of the selection of the appropriate mechanism are substantial.

The Environment Agency has published guidance on the use of works notices in situations where there is an overlap in the two powers. These guidelines suggest that there should be close cooperation between local authorities and the Environment Agency when identifying sites which might be designated as contaminated land for the purposes of Part IIA. This cooperation is designed to ensure that each body understands the position of the other when it comes to the statutory powers which are being considered. Where land is formally identified as 'contaminated' then Part IIA powers should be used in preference to the works notice provisions. The main justification for this is that there is a *requirement* to serve a remediation notice whilst the power to serve a works notice is merely *discretionary* (see *Environment Agency Policy and Guidance on the Use of Anti-Pollution Works Notices* published by the Environment Agency). Thus it would seem that a works notice will only be served in cases where the Part IIA regime does not apply (e.g. where the substances are no longer in, on or under the land as they have migrated into the controlled waters completely) or where, in consultation between the Agency and the relevant local authority, the Agency serves a notice prior to any formal designation of the site from which the pollutant emanates.

(d) Statutory nuisances
The original purpose behind the introduction of Part IIA was to clarify the existing statutory nuisance provisions which were available (it was suggested) to help local authorities deal with contaminated land. Accordingly, although there is a great deal in common between the two regimes, there has been a concerted attempt to separate and distinguish the operation of Part IIA from the normal statutory nuisance provisions.

Where land is in a 'contaminated state' it is excluded from the definition of a statutory nuisance (see sch. 2, para. 89, Environment Act 1995). 'Contaminated state' is defined more widely than the definition of 'contaminated land' found in Part IIA as it includes circumstances where there is mere harm or a possibility of such harm being caused and therefore excludes any element of 'significance' which is found in the Part IIA definition. The consequence of this wide definition is that there is a gap between the two regimes which will mean that land which is giving rise to harm which is not 'significant' under the terms of Part IIA cannot be cleaned up by way of an abatement notice under the statutory nuisance provisions of the EPA 1990.

The justification given by the government for this gap is that the package of rules associated with Part IIA provides the 'right level' of protection for the environment and human health and that it would be 'inappropriate' to allow local authorities to use an abatement notice in circumstances where a remediation notice could not be used. This gap emphasises once again that the narrow nature of the statutory definition and the complex issues which are at the heart of that definition are crucial when considering the practical impact of the Part IIA regime.

(e) Amenity notices

Local planning authorities have the power to require steps to be taken to remedy the condition of land which adversely affects the amenity of their area by serving an appropriate notice on the owner or occupier of the land (Town and Country Planning Act 1990, s. 215). These notices are designed to cover situations where the harm is not severe enough to amount to a statutory nuisance (e.g. weeds or overgrown, unkempt land) and therefore there is little chance of an overlap in controls in relation to contaminated land.

(f) Town and Country Planning

It is quite clear from the guidance documents on the practical implementation of Part IIA, that the great weight is given to the clean up of contaminated land as part of the development process. Thus, although the clean up powers available under Part IIA are separate and distinct from the planning process the two systems operate in parallel. Contamination would amount to a material consideration when determining planning applications. In particular, local planning authorities should consider the risks associated with any contamination in the context of the existing use (as with Part IIA) *and* any future use which is proposed in any planning application. The primary control mechanism in the planning system which will ensure that contamination is adequately addressed is through the imposition and enforcement of planning conditions. For example these might require an investigation and clean up of the site prior to the commencement of development or they might specify limitations on the nature of the use of land where contamination would give rise to significant risks. Policy guidance on the issue of contamination is provided in PPG23 and Circular 1/95 but it should be remembered that 'contaminated land' within this policy guidance has a much broader meaning than that adopted in relation to Part IIA.

In addition to development control matters, the planning system has a role in dealing with historically contaminated land through development planning. Policies in development plans might deal with the regeneration of contaminated land generally or more specifically in relation to Part IIA.

Civil liability and contamination

In addition to the statutory powers which can be used to clean up historic contamination, there are potential civil liabilities for damage caused by contamination. These liabilities depend upon actual loss rather than anticipated loss, although it is possible to bring a mandatory injunction to prevent any damage arising (see p. 275).

Statutory civil liability is imposed where any damage is caused by a deposit of controlled waste in contravention of waste management provisions (s. 73, EPA 1990, see further, p. 521). Common law liabilities for contamination may arise under the rule in *Rylands* v *Fletcher* and nuisance (see further p. 257). In both cases, the main bar to claims for damages in relation to historic contamination is the requirement of foreseeability of the type of damage (see the discussion of *Cambridge Water Co.* v *Eastern Counties Leather* at p. 261 or *Savage* v *Fairclough* [2000] Env LR 183). There are other more fundamental problems with the common law as a mechanism to deal with historically contaminated land including problems of proof, flexibility of standards and remedies which do not necessarily prevent environmental harm (see p. 277). In summary, the courts have consistently rejected the idea of developing the common law as a means of dealing with historic contamination (see p. 20).

NINETEEN
Water pollution and water quality

This chapter is about the quality of the water environment. It concentrates on the control of pollution of inland and coastal waters and does not seek to cover in any detail wider issues about water resource management such as land drainage or flood defence. While the quality of the public water supply is discussed briefly, the regulation of the abstraction of water from the natural environment is not discussed in any detail, despite the acknowledged importance of water quantity for water quality. Discharges to sewers, which have as much in common with waste disposal as with water pollution and which have their own, more basic, regulatory system operated by sewerage undertakers, are dealt with in Chapter 20.

Because of the central importance of the system for 'licensing' water pollution (the discharge consent system), both legally and in policy terms, we consider it in detail before looking at the water pollution offences it guards against, and the general water pollution offence which applies when pollution is caused by other matters. This is followed by discussion of various mechanisms and various overlapping controls to prevent harm occurring, such as integrated pollution control or common law principles. These are preceded by looking at the history of the water sector and controls on water quality and a short summary of the present legal controls and current policy, and an assessment of the contribution of international and (especially) EC law in this area. There is also a short excursion looking at the supply and financing of clean water, which illustrates the importance of economic regulation to water quality.

Water pollutants and their sources

Pollutants of water come in many forms, including:

(a) deoxygenating materials, for example, sewage and other organic wastes, such as silage, farm wastes and wastes from a number of heavily polluting industrial processes (e.g. food processing and the production of smokeless fuel, textiles, paper and dairy products);

(b)   nutrient enrichment by such things as fertilisers, which may give rise to eutrophication, causing an accelerated growth of plants and algae and leading to a decline in water quality;

(c)   solids, which may impede flows, or block out light for growth;

(d)   toxic materials: some materials, such as heavy metals, pesticides or nitrate, are toxic to humans, animals, plants, or all three, often depending on the level of the dose received;

(e)   materials which cause an impact on amenity, such as car tyres or shopping trolleys, or old boots in canals;

(f)   disease-carrying agents, such as bacteria;

(g)   heat, which may affect biological conditions and also deoxygenates water.

The effect of any potential pollutant will vary according to the size, temperature, rate of flow and oxygen content of the receiving waters, as well as the local geology and the presence of other pollutants and any resulting synergistic effects. The use made of a stream is also of enormous importance in deciding whether it can be said to be polluted, and this factor has a large impact on the attitude of the regulatory bodies towards the setting of standards and their enforcement. It is not sufficient to look only at pollution of surface waters, since 30 per cent of the public water supply is taken from ground waters. As a result the control of water pollution encompasses the control of liquid discharges to land.

The sources of pollution are also varied. For example:

(a)   There are around 75,000 discharges where there is a consent for discharge to waters. Many of these involve toxic materials or organic pollutants.

(b)   Most consents (around 62,000) relate to sewage works, where the organic content of the discharge makes it highly polluting. Regulating sewage pollution has been a central concern in the history of water pollution.

(c)   Agricultural pollution is problematic, giving rise both to a significant number of pollution incidents annually, as well as the more diffuse entry of pollutants from pesticide and fertiliser run-off. Groundwater contamination from pollutants like sheep dips is also a major problem for regulation.

(d)   Spills of oils and fuels are now the most common source of water pollution incident (see *Water Pollution Incidents in England and Wales — 1998*, EA, 1999).

(e)   Accidents are frequent causes of pollution, particularly from the storage and transport of hazardous chemicals.

(f)   Leachate from waste sites, including disused ones, and discharges from mines are often highly contaminated.

Natural events can also influence water quality: heavy rainfall may lead to greater pollution from farm run-off, while drought will tend to concentrate pollutants. Also, the more the environment is already under some form of 'stress', the more severe pollution incidents will tend to be.

The state of the water environment

The general state of water quality is measured by the Environment Agency (EA) using the General Quality Assessment (GQA) scheme. This has two separate elements, covering chemical and biological quality. Taking 1990 as a baseline, the GQA shows a marked improvement overall in chemical quality until 1995, followed by a slight downturn by 1997 (see *The Quality of Rivers and Canals in England and Wales*, EA, 1995 and the Environment Agency's *State of the Environment* website). The general improvement is largely attributed to better treatment of effluent by sewerage undertakers, following significant investment by the water industry following privatisation in 1989. The reasons for the recent downturn are not yet clear, but may relate partly to dry weather and partly to water abstraction, emphasising the importance of proper regulation over water quantity if water quality is to be improved.

By also including biological assessment (based on small water fauna), however, the GQA provides a better picture of the overall effect of all pollutants on the river ecosystem, although the grading of waters in this way is rather imprecise and biological quality depends on factors other than the quality of discharges. Figures from 1990 and 1995, adjusted to take improvements in monitoring into account, indicate a net improvement in biological water quality of around 25 per cent, with improvements recorded in all regions of the EA. Further GQAs based on nutrient and aesthetic quality will be used from 2001.

Taken together, the GQA and the EA's recording of water pollution incidents show some significant results in combating pollution from point sources, although differences in quality between areas and regions still persist and the quality of some stretches of river can still decline between surveys. What is undeniable, however, is that water quality is far removed from the nineteenth century when a letter could be written with river water (see Royal Commission on Rivers Pollution, Third Report, *Pollution Arising from the Woollen Manufacture*, 1871, Vol. 1, p. 12) and the lower reaches of the River Thames were little more than an open sewer.

The regulatory challenges

As the title of the chapter suggests, the central regulatory and environmental issue here is not simply preventing or controlling unwanted substances from entering the natural water environment. Indeed, the traditional British approach to water quality regulation has been to defend the view that it makes no sense to start by asking 'what dangerous substances should we prevent from entering water?' since many substances can have a damaging impact on water quality in sufficient quantities. For example, there has been a successful water pollution prosecution following a spill of carbonated apple juice, and milk has a polluting effect around 300 times that of sewage. This illustrates that, in part, water quality regulation is about controlling the discharge of substances which are not inherently toxic or harmful, but which may have negative impacts depending on how much is discharged and where such substances are discharged.

The counterpart of this is that there is usually 'water pollution' only where waters are rendered unfit for some desirable use such as drinking water supply or supporting fish life. The law therefore tends to aim to ensure a particular quality of water for various purposes, rather than just preventing or minimising the entry of 'pollutants' (although some standards are clearly set to eliminate certain substances being present in certain waters, even where there is little evidence of actual harm being likely: the pesticides standards in the Directive on Drinking Water are fairly clear examples of this). This also allows for natural differences in the composition of water, and things like the rate and amount of flow, to be taken into account. In legal terms, this is reflected in a preference for standards based on the character of the receiving environment rather than the adoption of emission standards reducing certain harmful substances from the water environment. (This preferred approach has, with one or two notable exceptions, basically been followed in EC water directives.) It is also reflected in the particular approach taken to regulating individual discharges, which is that official permission is not strictly needed before substances are discharged. Rather, the purpose of a discharge consent, issued by the EA, is to act as a defence to any charge of polluting water.

This peculiar legal nature of discharge consents has some important implications, most notably that in the setting of consents, the adoption of process-based standards such as best available techniques to minimise pollution has not generally been required. (There was a defence for companies under the Rivers Pollution Prevention Act 1876 to use 'best practicable means'.) In the context of quality standards, such an approach could lead to over-regulation and inefficiencies, although another way of looking at this is to emphasise that, as a result, discharge consents do not necessarily encourage a progressive tightening up of standards. On the other hand, however, strict water quality objectives have never been favoured. Instead, consents have tended to be set (and enforced) on an individualised basis, having general regard to the quality of the river and its catchment, and to particular things like the location of abstraction points for public supply.

Many of the more obvious sources of pollution are being brought under control. This is focusing attention on the release of substances into the environment which have an uncertain impact, such as whether nitrate pollution leads to eutrophication (or whether phosphate is the principal cause as the government contends), or the impact of hormone disrupting substances (so-called 'gender-bender' chemicals) which appear to feminise male fish like roach, leading to concerns over their impact on humans. But perhaps the most important regulatory problem is the increasing contribution of diffuse sources, such as agricultural run-off and pollution from urban development and vehicle emissions, to reductions in water quality. Such non-point sources of water pollution cannot really be controlled by consents, and instead need an imaginative mix of policy and legal mechanisms.

A final issue is that, as with certain air pollution limits, once it is decided that a certain overall level of pollution is to be tolerated, it must be decided how 'rights' to pollute as between those who want to use the natural resource in question are divided up, and on what basis. This is something determined in the day-to-day setting and revision of consents, but it illustrates the more profound issues the consent regime raises than simply protecting individual dischargers from criminal liability. The consent system, as well as other mechanisms to prevent or reduce water pollution, must be transparent, participatory and accountable if it is to operate with any legitimacy.

History of the water sector and controls on water quality

Over the years, the law on water pollution has tended to be the most developed of the systems of pollution control. It has also had the greatest degree of coherence, both in terms of the institutional arrangements and in terms of substance law. These institutional arrangements have changed markedly over time, and must be appreciated alongside changes to the structure of the water sector.

(a) The water sector
The water industry has traditionally been thought of as including a wide range of rather different matters: water collection, treatment and supply; the provision of sewers, sewage works and sewage disposal; water pollution control; the regulation of bodies providing water services; fisheries; navigation; flood defence and land drainage; recreational activities; and conservation responsibilities. From this list it is clear that in reality this is a set of activities, connected in the sense that they all relate to the water cycle, but separate in their objectives. Not all of these matters are relevant to the themes of this book; pollution control is only one function of the water industry, but its place in relation to these other activities needs to be understood.

The industry has historically been dominated by water supply and sewage disposal. Up to the Second World War these tasks were largely carried out by municipal authorities. However, activities such as fishing and pollution control increasingly came to be organised on a river basin basis through a number of specialist, river-related institutions, such as catchment boards (for land drainage), fisheries boards and internal drainage boards, although a significant responsibility for pollution control still rested with the local authorities through their public health functions.

These trends led to an attempt to create a more logical system. The River Boards Act 1948 established 32 river boards, organised on a catchment area basis, which took over a number of regulatory functions. In 1963 the Water Resources Act converted these boards into 27 river authorities, which had a range of regulatory functions, including pollution control and responsibility for the new system of licensing abstractions of water. Water supply and sewage disposal remained in general a local authority function, although the number of water supply undertakings was steadily reduced over the years.

The Water Act 1973 established a fully integrated system of river and water management. Ten regional water authorities became responsible for all water related functions within river basin areas. These included the management of water provision, water treatment and water supply, sewerage, sewage works and sewage disposal, land drainage and flood defence, pollution control, inland fisheries, recreational uses of water and ecological and amenity matters. The idea was to set up a completely planned and integrated service as opposed to the fragmented system then in existence (prior to 1973, there were 27 river authorities, 157 water supply undertakings and no less than 1,393 sewage authorities). The only real exception was the retention of 29 private water companies responsible for water supply in defined areas.

However, this system came to be seen as ineffective. For a start, the industry was clearly massively underfunded, with the result that capital and other works were postponed and the quality of service declined. In consequence, the problem of water quality was never really addressed and this contributed to a general decline in standards. A particular cause of these declining standards was the inadequacy of many sewage works operated by the regional water authorities themselves, which came to be seen as acting the part of both poacher and gamekeeper in relation to water pollution. This conflict of interest led to specific changes in the Water Act 1989.

(b) Water privatisation
The Water Act 1989 carried out a fundamental restructuring of the water industry. The main impetus was undoubtedly the government's policy of privatisation. One stated aim of this was to increase accountability, though exactly whether this means the industry should be accountable to the public, the government, or to shareholders is unclear. A further aim was to remove the previous cash limits on public spending that had restricted the regional water authorities, thus opening the way for improvements in the quality of water services, but at a cost to the consumer of those services, who now pays for them.

Originally it was intended to privatise the whole industry en bloc, but the inadequacy of the proposed regulatory mechanisms, particularly those for pollution control (see, e.g. p. 147), led to the privatisation of the operational end of the industry only (i.e. water supply, sewerage services and certain recreational services) in the form of 10 water services companies. These double as water undertakers and sewerage undertakers in areas corresponding with the old regional water authority ones. The 29 water companies (now 15 through mergers and takeovers) were retained as statutory water companies, having responsibility for water supply only.

The position of Director General of Water Services, who is in charge of the Office of Water Services (OFWAT), was created to exercise regulatory functions in relation to water supply and sewerage provision. The National Rivers Authority (NRA) was created as a wide-ranging and independent regulatory agency with responsibility for tackling water pollution amongst other things. Unlike the old regional water authorities, it had no operational responsibilities in relation to sewage works to conflict with its environmental protection role. These arrangements were consolidated in the Water Resources Act 1991 and the Water Industry Act 1991. However, from 1 April 1996 the NRA was subsumed within the Environment Agency (see p. 162).

(c) Legal controls on water quality
The modern system of control really begins with the Rivers (Prevention of Pollution) Act 1951, a rather rudimentary control system in which consent

from the river board was required for industrial or sewage discharges into most inland waters. Prior to that, there had been the Rivers Pollution Prevention Act 1876, which imposed an absolute prohibition on pollution but proved almost totally unworkable. The Clean Rivers (Estuaries and Tidal Waters) Act 1960 extended the controls to tidal and estuarial waters and the Rivers (Prevention of Pollution) Act 1961 ensured that a large number of discharges that had hitherto been exempted were controlled, including those commenced prior to 1951. The Water Resources Act 1963 extended the system to discharges to certain underground waters. However, the system remained essentially secret and with little public accountability. Control over sewage effluents was also compromised because of the local authorities' control of the river authorities.

The next major step forward was in the Control of Pollution Act 1974, which again extended the geographical coverage of the controls so that most discharges to inland, underground, tidal or coastal waters out to the 'three-mile limit' were covered. More importantly, COPA 1974 introduced some advanced provisions on public participation in decisions, established public registers of information and allowed for private prosecutions, which had previously been excluded. In addition a more sophisticated set of preventive and remedial measures was introduced.

However COPA 1974 did not come into force immediately. Like much environmental legislation its implementation relied on commencement orders, and the main measures were not brought into force until the mid-1980s: a delay mainly due to the government's worries over the economic cost of the new controls, particularly in relation to underperforming sewage works operated by the regional water authorities. Even when COPA 1974 was brought into force, the transitional provisions meant that the full impact was not felt immediately, and indeed certain of the provisions were never implemented.

As explained above, the Water Act 1989 created the NRA. It also continued the process of refining and improving the law. The system of consents set out in COPA 1974 remained roughly the same, though with a few amendments. Important changes included the introduction of sections providing for statutory water quality objectives for the first time, the introduction of a system of charging for trade and sewage discharges, and the improvement of the available preventive and remedial powers. Water pollution law was then consolidated in the Water Resources Act 1991.

The EPA 1990 did not alter the main structure of water pollution law, but, under the Act, Her Majesty's Inspectorate of Pollution took the lead role in relation to processes subject to integrated pollution control, thus robbing the NRA of total control over discharges to inland and coastal waters. The bringing together of the NRA and HMIP in the Environment Agency means that the institutional control of water pollution is once more unified (although the Drinking Water Inspectorate remains outside the EA, and there are some areas of uncertainty about the role of local authorities in relation to discharges to water under the integrated permitting system in the Pollution Prevention and Control Act 1999).

Throughout this history the emphasis has been on flexible standards, with most consents being set on an individualised basis by reference to the effect of a discharge on the receiving waters. Particular emphasis has been placed on biochemical oxygen demand (BOD) and the level of suspended solids, rather than on such things as metals and toxic substances, especially in relation to sewage discharges. In a sense, the method of setting consents could almost be described as a 'rule of thumb' method. This approach is, however, changing in response to EC directives and as a result of creating a more uniform system of control nationwide, begun under the NRA.

(d) Water quality policy style and techniques

Until 1989, it was difficult to identify a coherent national water quality policy. The Department of the Environment had overall responsibility for all water matters, but most policy decisions were left to the regional water authorities, with the DoE appearing more preoccupied with financial matters than with water quality. The one national body in this area, the National Water Council, was abolished in 1983 as superfluous. Of course, there were often unspoken aims, such as that of getting treatable wastes into the sewerage system if possible, and cleaning up waters for economic reasons, since the public water supply was increasingly taken from them. In addition, EC standards effectively laid down a set of priorities, leading to such things as a policy to minimise the discharge of dangerous substances and if possible to cut them out entirely — effectively a precautionary policy.

The establishment of the NRA meant that the opportunity could be taken to establish a truly national policy on water quality — or at least one applicable to England and Wales. At a general level, this was achieved through the NRA's Corporate Plans, which set out a number of aims on water quality, such as the assessment of the present quality of waters, the establishment of classification systems so that comparisons could be made, the review of existing policy in relation to the granting of consents and compliance with them, increased attention to prevention of harm in such areas as farm pollution and pollution from abandoned mines, and a more rigorous enforcement policy involving greater use of prosecution. The general approach adopted by the NRA (and continued by the EA) was that river catchments should be managed on an integrated basis. This process is a good example of aspects of environmental policy being set by a body other than central government. However, the government also has an important role to play here. *River Quality: The Government's Proposals* (DoE, 1992) set out a general strategy for water quality which arguably is still being followed. This makes it quite clear that the cost-effectiveness of environmental improvements — and the question of who should pay for them — was a major factor in government policy, hence the slow progress that is being made on such things as statutory water quality objectives.

More specifically, the NRA was involved in trying to establish uniformity and consistency on such things as sampling, setting of consents and public participation, where in the past there had tended to be different attitudes in different regions. In the Kinnersley Report (*Discharge Consent and Compliance*

Policy: A Blueprint for the Future, NRA, 1990), the NRA suggested some mechanisms for unifying the totally different procedures and levels of consents that it inherited from the 10 regional water authorities. It established a national strategy for reviewing all existing consents on a catchment area basis, and this included bringing sewage works consents into line with industrial consents. However, it remains the case that consents are mainly set on an individualised basis, with the main determinant being the effect on the receiving waters.

Scotland, Wales and Northern Ireland

It should be noted that in Scotland a slightly different system applies, since the water industry has not been privatised there. Previously, regional councils were responsible for the provision of the water supply and for sewerage and sewage disposal. Apart from the three island councils, which were all-purpose authorities, water pollution was the responsibility of the seven river purification boards. These were independent catchment area bodies with their own budgets financed out of precepts on the regional councils, and with one third of their members appointed by each of the following, namely, regional councils, district councils and the Secretary of State. The Water Act 1989 did not make any institutional changes, but in sch. 23 it did amend the Control of Pollution Act 1974, which still remains in force in Scotland. Unfortunately, this has meant that there are slightly different wordings for some sections on each side of the border. Whilst water pollution law is thus very similar in Scotland, it cannot always be guaranteed that it is exactly the same.

This position was altered by the Local Government etc (Scotland) Act 1994, which restructured local government in Scotland by introducing unitary authorities for the mainland, although the three existing island councils were retained. It also established three publicly owned combined water and sewerage authorities to take over from the regional councils. The Environment Act 1995 established the Scottish Environment Protection Agency (SEPA), which replaced the river purification boards and Her Majesty's Industrial Pollution Inspectorate (HMIPI) and thus brings together all water pollution functions in one body (although SEPA does not have functions in relation to fisheries and, therefore, fisheries-related water pollution offences). Following the Scotland Act 1998, water pollution is a matter for the Scottish Parliament, although importantly the negotiation of EC directives remains with the UK government.

Under the Government of Wales Act 1998, responsibility for water pollution is a matter for the National Assembly for Wales although the Assembly cannot amend primary legislation such as the Water Resources Act 1991. As with Scotland there is also the significant limitation that matters concerning EC water law and policy remain the responsibility of central government. General references to 'the Secretary of State' or 'the Minister' should be read as including the Welsh Assembly where appropriate.

Water quality matters in Northern Ireland are the responsibility of the Environment and Heritage Service of the Department of the Environment

(Northern Ireland). The water legislation has recently been overhauled by the Water (Northern Ireland) Order 1999 (SI 1999/662) (NI.6) which brought the controls on discharge consents more into line with practice elsewhere in the UK and gave more powers to the DoE (NI) to make pollution prevention regulations. However, the Order will not come into force before the end of 2000 and the full effect of the Order will not be apparent for several years.

Summary of present legal controls

The present legal controls in England and Wales are as follows:

(a)   The body with general responsibility for water quality in England and Wales is the Environment Agency (EA), acting under the Water Resources Act 1991. There is no overall statutory national strategy comparable to those found in the air quality and waste management sectors. Although the EA has an *Environmental Strategy for the Millennium and Beyond* (EA, 1997) which is fleshed out by a *Functional Action Plan* concerning Water Quality (EA, 1998), these are not documents which required public participation and consultation before adoption.

(b)   The addition of any substance to an inland or coastal water is not generally prejudged as being a harmful act; it is only harmful if it interferes with some desirable use for the water.

(c)   This is reflected in a preference for an approach based on environmental quality standards rather than controlling harmful substances entering water (indeed, the idea of a substance added to water being 'harmful' only makes sense when judged against some consequent restriction on a use for water).

(d)   However, this policy approach does not mean that precedence is given to binding objectives for water quality. At national level, such objectives tend to be non-binding, although the impact of EC directives has changed this in relation to certain waters such as bathing waters. Otherwise, quality objectives act to guide the EA in setting discharge consents.

(e)   EC law is increasingly the most important force in determining new water quality standards, and in driving up the costs of compliance (and thus of water supply and sewerage services). The introduction of more precise standards has also contributed enormously to raising public debate about water quality, and increased the scope for legal challenges to poor water quality.

(f)   It is an offence to 'cause or knowingly permit' water pollution, but acting in accordance with a discharge consent acts as a defence. Understanding what it means in particular to 'cause' water pollution is important in relation to questions of liability, since the judicial interpretation of what amounts to 'polluting matter' is very wide, extending to substances *capable* of causing harm to humans or the water environment and not just those which cause *actual* harm.

(g)   In limited situations, certain activities are specifically stated under the Water Resources Act 1991 to amount to water pollution offences. An example of this is disposing of dangerous substances in a way that might lead to groundwater pollution.

(h)   Given the basic nature of water pollution regulation, this breadth is perhaps surprising, although it is generally tempered by selective enforcement. But it does mean that dischargers such as sewage undertakers and industrial operators, who contribute most to water pollution loading by the discharges for which their consents gives them a defence, must protect themselves against a wide range of possible liabilities through their consents. This means that the setting of such consents is centrally important to water quality regulation.

(i)   Pollution from, e.g. agricultural run-off is not consented, because there are no specific discharge points that can be monitored. Pollution loading from, e.g. pesticide and fertiliser usage must therefore be controlled using other methods. The need for more integrated solutions is particularly relevant to discharges from very diffuse sources, such as acidification from vehicle exhausts, because of the indirect effects involved.

(j)   The methods most commonly used to control such non-point (or diffuse) discharges are specification standards, such as apply to the storage of farm slurry, or area-based controls over sites designated because of, e.g. high nitrate levels in drinking water. A programmatic approach to reduction may also be taken, such as under the EC Directive on Nitrates.

(k)   Financial controls are increasingly used. The charges levied by the EA for discharge consents go some way towards making the polluter pay, while subsidies are sometimes (controversially) used to encourage farmers in certain areas to reduce their nitrate loading. The future is likely to see, e.g. full cost recovery charges introduced for all discharges, with the more remote possibility of tradable discharge consents and specialist taxes for, e.g. pesticides.

(l)   International law has tended to affect national standard-setting only indirectly, for example through World Health Organisation standards influencing EC standards. In recent years, the international treaty regime concerning the North Sea has become more influential. At this stage, this has tended to be by setting general targets and principles, although these have been sufficient to change the political climate over things like radioactive discharges.

International law and water quality

Not surprisingly, international law has mostly been concerned with marine waters rather than water quality at national level, although it is the nature of the water cycle that there is no clear divide between the two. Compared with EC law, its impact has been less dramatic, although there are instances where EC standards and policy originate in hard and soft international law (see p. 90). The International Conferences for the Protection of the North Sea, for example, have been of considerable importance, especially in relation to development of the precautionary principle and, in line with this, banning the disposal of sewage sludge at sea, a measure now contained in the Urban Waste Water Treatment Directive (91/271). The impact of this on national disposal practices, such as greater spreading of sludge on land, as well as similar bans on the dumping and incineration of industrial waste, and coastal dumping of colliery spoil and power station ash, illustrates the way in which measures to protect the marine environment may have direct consequences at national level, to say nothing of the significant costs involved.

This impact of international law on national practices is also seen with the various international provisions aimed at preventing marine pollution from ships, notably the 1973/78 'MARPOL' Convention, which regulates deliberate, operational discharges of oil and, through Protocols, certain other substances (e.g. noxious liquid substances and sewage) from vessels. These provisions must be enforced both by flag states and against foreign vessels by port states, and apply to the territorial sea as well as (in some situations) the exclusive economic zone. The Convention also regulates design, construction and maintenance standards for oil tankers, although it originally contained rather generous provisions for existing vessels which, because of the life span of tankers, limited its effectiveness. This was addressed in amendments to the Convention adopted in 1992, which both strengthened the inspection procedures for older vessels and added a requirement to retrofit double hulls or an equivalent to tankers of 25 years of age and older.

The MARPOL Convention regime therefore takes a preventive approach to marine oil pollution. This is in contrast to other international agreements in this area. These include the 1969 Intervention Convention, which allows for intervention on the high seas in the case of accidental oil spills from vessels in distress (introduced following the *Torrey Canyon* incident in 1967). They also include measures regulating liability and compensation for oil pollution damage under the 1992 Conventions on Civil Liability for Oil Pollution Damage and Establishment of an International Fund for Compensation for Oil Pollution Damage. Crucially, however, the definition of 'pollution damage' under the 1992 Convention only includes the reasonable costs of reinstating impairment to the environment. Since natural recovery is often the quickest way for the environment to be restored, this may have the effect of limiting liability to minor aspects of environmental damage, and would not penalise damage leading to irreparable environmental harm. The extensive claims submitted to the International Fund following the *Sea Empress* disaster in 1996 show how these provisions can have direct national implications: some of the £60m damages claimed were for clean-up costs incurred by bodies such as the EA, costs which might otherwise have been recovered under the Water Resources Act 1991 (see p. 599).

By contrast with what are quite tightly defined obligations in relation to oil and other noxious substances, there are more general provisions in the 1982 UN Convention on the Law of the Sea on preventing, reducing and controlling pollution of the marine environment from land based sources (art. 207) and similar obligations for pollution from things like oil rigs and sea bed mining (art. 208). There are also rules about pollution from dumping (art. 210), though as with many provisions of UNCLOS in this area, states are encouraged to seek regional solutions and the 1992 Paris Convention dealing with the North Sea and North East Atlantic area (the 'OSPAR' Convention) is important, at least in relation to the development of policy. Specifically, following the *Brent Spar* affair, the parties to OSPAR agreed in 1998 to a ban on the disposal of redundant steel oil and gas platforms at sea, which will have knock-on consequences for waste disposal on land (although concrete platforms can still be dumped). The parties also agreed to reduce to 'close to zero' by 2020 concentrations of artificial radioactive substances. The UK approach to meeting this objective can be seen by the way that the Government approved the approach of the Environment Agency to reducing controversial technetium-99 discharges from Sellafield. While the authorised discharge limit was reduced by slightly more than one-half, a range of further conditions were attached to the licence, requiring BNFL to explore a range of additional abatement technologies. This decision is broadly in line with taking a preventive and precautionary approach as the OSPAR Convention demands. The UK dropping its reservation to provisions banning the dumping of radioactive waste at sea will also affect disposal options. Taken together, these developments seem to mark a continuing move away from a 'dilute and disperse' approach, although it is also interesting that, in the case of oil rig decommissioning, the use of individual BPEO assessments has also now been rejected in favour of a more prescriptive policy approach. This suggests a subtle shift towards an emission standards approach based on the political unacceptability of some high profile 'discharges' to the water environment.

The EC and water quality

The EC has had an enormous impact on water pollution law and policy over the years. The First Action Programme on the Environment in 1973 picked out water pollution as a priority matter, and there has been a steady stream of directives since. These have tackled such diverse topics as the reduction of pollution from dangerous substances, the improvement of the quality of bathing waters, nitrates in water and the progressive introduction of adequate sewage treatment systems. However, it remains the case that EC law only covers water pollution in a selective manner — not all pollutants in all waters are yet covered. The proposed Water Framework Directive (see p. 570) may address this deficiency.

EC water directives tend to follow two basic models as regards standard setting (see Somsen, 'EC Water Directives' [1990] Water Law 93):

(a)   those which adopt emission standards, which are mainly used for reducing dangerous substances; and

(b)   those which impose quality objectives on waters that are mainly set according to the use that is to be made of those waters.

There are also isolated cases where directives take different approaches to control, focusing on particular kinds of pollutants. Directive 73/404 on Detergents sets a product standard by prohibiting the marketing of detergents with average biodegradability of less than 90 per cent. Directive 78/176 on Titanium Dioxide sets standards in relation to a specific industry. The 1991

Directives on Urban Waste Water Treatment (91/271) and on Nitrates from Agricultural Sources (91/676) illustrate a more modern trend to regulate particular polluting activities, and for this reason are considered separately (see p. 568). For a full discussion of all the EC directives relating to water and their implementation, see Haigh, *Manual of Environmental Policy: The EC and Britain*, Longman, loose leaf.

(a) Emission standard approaches

One of the first water directives, and arguably the most important, is 76/464 on Dangerous Substances in Water. This is a framework directive passed with the aim of reducing or eliminating certain dangerous substances from water. It covers essentially the same waters as those controlled by the EA and has led to very tight controls over certain dangerous substances in discharge consents.

The Directive lays down two lists of substances:

(a) List I (the 'black list'); and
(b) List II (the 'grey list').

In relation to black list substances, the Directive seeks the elimination of pollution. Any discharge of a black list substance must be subject to some form of authorisation granted by a competent national authority. Such an authorisation must conform to very strict requirements. It must *either* set an emission standard which does not exceed the appropriate EC limit value, or the emission standard must be set so that the EC environmental quality standard for the receiving waters is kept to at all times. Only Britain has adopted the second approach (see below), the competent authority being the EA, which operates the discharge consent systems so as to ensure that the EC environmental quality standards are met at all times.

However, implementation of this part of the Directive is proceeding slowly. The Directive itself identifies potential black list substances in general terms only — they are those which are highly toxic, persistent, carcinogenic or liable to bio-accumulate. Although in 1982 the EC Commission published a specific list of 129 potential black list substances (made up mainly of pesticides, organic solvents, and a small number of heavy metals), implementation of the Directive ultimately depends on the adoption of subsidiary 'daughter directives' which set the EC standards for individual substances. Only a few such daughter directives have been agreed, covering the following substances: cadmium (83/513); mercury (82/176 and 84/156); hexachlorocyclohexane (84/491); carbon tetrachloride, pentachlorophenol and DDT (86/280); chloroform, hexachlorobenzene, hexachlorobutadiene and the pesticides aldrin, dieldrin, endrin and isodrin (88/347); and 1, 2-dichloroethane, trichloroethylene, tetrachloroethylene and trichlorobenzene (90/415). Where a daughter directive has not been agreed for a potential black list substance, the substance is treated as on the grey list (see below). The list of 129 (amended slightly in the intervening years) therefore acts as a priority list for future daughter directives.

For grey list substances, the Directive again lays down a fairly general list. This includes a range of metals (such as zinc, copper, tin, nickel and chromium), biocides, cyanides, fluorides, ammonia and nitrites. The objective is that pollution by these substances should be reduced. Accordingly, if any such substance has a deleterious effect on the aquatic environment, the Directive requires Member States to develop a national environmental quality standard and to ensure that it is met in the receiving waters. These standards are set at a national, rather than at an EC, level. The member state must also introduce a reduction programme for grey list substances and must control discharges by setting standards in discharge consents which enable the environmental quality standards to be achieved.

It was Directive 76/464 which first demonstrated the differences between Britain and the rest of the EC over standard setting. Britain's system of a decentralised setting of non-uniform consents by reference to the quality of the receiving waters was seen to be directly contradictory to the desire of other Member States for uniform, centrally set emission standards for dangerous substances. After much argument, this led to the agreement of the alternative approaches for 'black list' substances in the Directive explained above. The same conflict has also led to delays in the process of agreeing daughter directives, since unanimity is required on the setting of the limit values and environmental quality objectives.

Directive 76/464 has had an enormous impact on British pollution control. Having claimed that it set its consents by reference to quality objectives for the receiving waters, the British government was forced to introduce such a system on a formal basis, and water quality objectives were introduced for the first time in the late 1970s, at first by administrative action. This was insufficient for compliance with EC law and sections relating to *statutory* water quality objectives were first introduced in the Water Act 1989.

The Directive also led to specific changes in relation to controls over dangerous substances. For example, whilst many existing discharges were given deemed consent when COPA 1974 was finally brought into force, those involving dangerous substances were subject to specified emission standards. In general, significant discharges of 'black list' and 'grey list' substances are subject to integrated pollution control. The rules providing for control by the EA of prescribed substances discharged to sewers are also a result of this directive.

A similar story attaches to Directive 80/68 on Groundwater, except in this case List I substances are to be prevented from entering ground waters, whilst discharges of List II substances should be limited, in both cases by a consent system. Revisions to the Directive will be covered in the proposed new Framework Directive (see p. 570).

One problem with the emission standards approach is that it does not work well for pollution from non-point (i.e. diffuse) sources, nor where there are multiple polluters in one catchment area (although it may have to deal with what are effectively diffuse discharges; see Case C-231/97 *van Rooij* [1999] ECR I-6355). Directive 86/280 attempts to tackle this issue by requiring all *sources* of 'black list' substances to be monitored.

(b)   Quality objective approaches

For the quality approach there are a number of stages:

(a)   water with particular uses must first be identified (this is usually left to the discretion of the Member States but must be done on objective grounds);

(b)   the EC must establish a number of parameters: these are normally expressed either as Imperative (I) values, which must be kept to, or Guide (G) values, which Member States must try to achieve;

(c)   environmental quality objectives must be set for the waters, having regard to the parameters;

(d)   a competent national authority must be established for monitoring purposes and uniform sampling techniques are set by EC directives (e.g. 79/ 869 on Sampling Surface Water for Drinking);

(e)   procedures are established for updating the I and G values in the light of new knowledge.

Directives which have adopted this approach include those on Surface Water for Drinking 75/440, Shellfish Waters 79/923, Water Standards for Freshwater Fish 78/659, Bathing Waters 76/160 and Drinking Water 80/778.

The Directive on Surface Water for Drinking lays down three classes of waters (A1, A2 and A3), and 46 relevant parameters that waters must comply with to fall within any class (see p. 572 below).

The two Directives on Freshwater Fish and Shellfish lay down standards for waters designated by Member States. The power to designate these waters was delegated to the regional water authorities (now the EA) — another example of a decentralised implementation of policy. The Member State must decide if certain prior conditions exist; if they do, then designations must follow (see Case C-225/96 *Commission* v *Italy* [1998] Env LR 370).

The Directive on Bathing Waters lays down 19 parameters (mainly bacteri-ological) with which all 'traditional' bathing waters must comply, within specified percentile compliance rates. It covers fresh and marine waters although the Directive is very vague as to precisely which waters are covered. The British response was unenthusiastic: identification of the relevant waters was left to the regional water authorities and only 27 were initially identified — fewer than, for example, land-locked Luxembourg. (In addition, no inland bathing waters were identified until nine sites were selected in 1998 — a bemusing approach). No doubt the reason was the fear of the cost of cleaning up discharges of sewage effluent. In consequence of a reasoned opinion on non-implementation from the EC Commission, and intense EC and public pressure, the number of designated beaches in England and Wales is now 473. Nevertheless, Britain was taken to the European Court of Justice over non-implementation of the Directive and in July 1993 was found to be in breach in relation to standards on Blackpool and Southport beaches (see Case C-56/90 *Commission* v *United Kingdom* [1993] ECR I-4109). In 1998 90.4 per cent of designated beaches complied with the standards. The domestic courts have also had occasion to doubt the effectiveness of the implementation of the Directive. In *R* v *National Rivers Authority, ex parte Moreton* [1996] Env LR 234 Harrison J observed that the government had apparently failed to implement the mandatory standard on entero-viruses from the Directive (although the government had argued that there was no scientific basis for maintaining the mandatory level). There have been signs that, following pressure from the Council, the Commission may propose revisions to the Directive that would allow greater differentiation in standards between fresh and coastal waters, and warmer southern and colder northern waters, an example of moves towards greater flexibility and subsidiarity (see p. 132).

The Directive on Drinking Water is probably the best known of the water quality directives. It lays down 62 parameters relating to the quality of all water provided for human consumption or for the purposes of food manufacturing, except for natural mineral waters (as to which, see Directive 80/777). It led directly to the setting in Britain of the first statutory standards of wholesomeness for drinking water, in the Water Supply (Water Quality) Regulations 1989 (SI 1989/1147).

Apart from the delay in complying with the Directive until well after the formal date set for compliance, argument has centred over the provisions for derogating from the Directive, because of problems in some areas in complying with the standards on lead, nitrate and certain pesticides. For example, the government sought to grant derogations for nitrate levels by reference to art. 9 of the Directive, which refers to geological conditions. This was argued by the Commission to be an inaccurate interpretation of art. 9, since nitrate levels result from self-induced effects on the soil. The UK government was held by the European Court of Justice to be in breach of the Directive in relation to nitrate levels in a number of supply areas (see Case C-337/89 *Commission* v *United Kingdom* [1992] ECR I-6103). This case also decided that the duty to comply with the standards laid down in the Directive is absolute, rather than simply to take all practicable steps to comply (for further litigation on this issue see further p. 148). Significant revisions to the Directive have recently been made by Directive 98/83 and take effect from December 2000. These give Member States greater flexibility to derogate from standards where there is no danger to health and the supply of water cannot otherwise be maintained.

(c) Directives regulating particular polluting activities
There are two directives from 1991 which regulate particular polluting activities. The Directive on Waste Water Treatment (91/271) is potentially the most significant directive in terms of compliance costs. It lays down minimum standards for the treatment of urban waste waters (i.e. domestic sewage and industrial waste waters). These treatment standards, and the time-scales within which they must be met, vary according to the population of the area concerned, but the basic idea is that some form of biological treatment ('secondary treatment') should be usual for domestic wastes. For example, a secondary or equivalent system of sewage treatment is required by the end of 2000 for a town with a population equivalent of more than 15,000. Stricter

standards are required in sensitive areas and lower standards are permitted in less-sensitive areas. The Directive also required all Member States to cease dumping sewage sludge at sea by the end of 1998. The Directive therefore grafts an emissions standard approach on to a quality standards framework, and is fairly unusual in that water quality is not protected because of any immediate use value.

The Directive has had a particular impact on Britain, the only member state which carried out sewage sludge dumping and which traditionally employed a 'dilute and disperse' policy of discharging virtually untreated sewage into the sea via outfalls. The Directive was implemented by the Urban Waste Water Treatment (England and Wales) Regulations 1994 (SI 1994/2841). These regulations largely adopt the wording of the directive, except that instead of 'less sensitive areas' the regulations refer to 'high natural dispersion areas'. In 1994, 33 sensitive areas and 58 high natural dispersion areas were initially identified. One area of controversy, however, was the classification of a number of estuarial waters as coastal for the purposes of the regulations, thus allowing lower levels of treatment to be applied. In *R v Secretary of State for the Environment, ex parte Kingston upon Hull City Council* [1996] Env LR 248 the Secretary of State drew the boundaries of the estuary for the Humber and Severn rivers at the Humber and Severn road bridges, thus ensuring lower (and therefore cheaper) levels of treatment for treatment works alongside the rivers. His decision was successfully challenged on the grounds that costs should not have been taken into account, and that the correct way of drawing the boundaries was to carry out a genuine and rational assessment of what actually constituted the estuary. (Subsequently, the estuaries were redefined as a line between the two furthest points of land on each side of the river.) In 1998, a further 47 sensitive areas were designated. As important have been increases to funding under which the amount of sewage outfalls receiving secondary treatment is now well above the 2 per cent level it stood at before the Directive.

The Directive on Nitrate Pollution from Agriculture (91/676) also regulates a particular polluting activity. It required Member States to designate 'nitrate vulnerable zones' by December 1993. These are defined in the Directive as being where inland waters intended for drinking or groundwaters are likely to contain more than 50 mg/l nitrate if protective action is not taken; or where any inland or coastal waters are liable to suffer from eutrophication if protective action is not taken. Within these designated 'nitrate vulnerable zones', detailed regulatory requirements are laid down. The Directive therefore takes a largely quality objective approach, but like Directive 91/271 is distinct in regulating water quality through the control of a particularly polluting activity. For more detail on the Directive and its implementation see p. 603.

Summary of the impact of EC law

The EC has thus had a great impact on British water pollution practice. Whilst there have been many arguments about technical matters, such as the levels laid down for nitrate in drinking water and the need for a Bathing Waters Directive at all, most of the standards required have been introduced in one way or another, although normally belatedly. A formal system of water quality classifications and objectives, statutory regulations on drinking water quality, the introduction of specific standards for dangerous substances, and a dramatic shift in relation to the discharge of sewage effluent to the sea can all be attributed to EC initiatives. The general approach to pollution control has also been altered significantly.

Perhaps the greatest impact, however, has been the great publicity that has been engendered by having specific standards set at EC level against which government action can be measured. This has certainly contributed to the intensity of the debate over nitrate. EC requirements also had an impact on the proposals for the privatisation of the water industry. It became clear that the EC would not accept a private pollution regulator as a 'competent authority' for the purposes of directives, and this was one reason for the creation of the NRA (and also a separate Drinking Water Inspectorate). Finally, when combined with this greater specificity, the public health nature of most water directives may help direct legal challenges to non-implementation (although whether individual rights must be infringed for there to be a remedy is arguable; see p. 140).

The future of EC water pollution policy

EC water pollution policy is on the brink of fundamental change. In 1997, the European Commission issued its long-awaited proposal for a Water Framework Directive (COM(97)49, as amended). The Commission's proposal lays the last major building block in a comprehensive overhaul of the EC's water policy. There is a general recognition that the bulk of the Community's water legislation (which dates back to the 1970s and early 1980s) is a little outdated in the approach to pollution control.

The proposal would result in the abandonment of the proposal for a Directive on the Ecological Quality of Water (COM(93)680 final) and the repeal of the Groundwater Directive (80/68), the Surface Water Directive (75/440), the Fish Water Directive (78/659) and the Shellfish Water Directive (79/923). Following the demise of plans for a 'mini-IPPC' directive covering less polluting sectors, the Dangerous Substances Directive (76/464) would also be incorporated.

Unlike previous water legislation, the framework Directive would cover surface water and groundwater together, as well as estuaries and coastal waters. Its purpose is threefold: to prevent further deterioration in, and to protect and enhance, the status of aquatic ecosystems; to promote sustainable water consumption based on the long-term protection of available water resources; and to contribute to the provision of a supply of water in the qualities and quantities needed for its sustainable use.

It is intended to meet these objectives by using the following mechanisms:

(a)   creating an overall framework within which Community, national and regional authorities can develop integrated and coherent water policies;

(b)   providing a 'safety net' for identifying water issues that are not adequately addressed at present, requiring remedial action to be taken at the appropriate level;

(c)   establishing a sound basis for collecting and analysing a large amount of information on the state of the aquatic environment and the pressures upon it; and

(d)   requiring transparency through the publication and dissemination of information and through public consultation.

The Directive's overriding requirement is that Member States ensure that 'good' status is achieved in all waters by the end of 2010. The intention is to achieve this by river basin management, monitoring and planning. For groundwater, good status is measured in terms of both quantity and chemical purity (i.e. abstractions and alterations to the natural rate of recharge are sustainable in the long term without leading to loss of ecological quality); for surface waters ecological quality is an additional criterion (i.e. in addition to ensuring that concentrations of certain, 'black list', substances do not exceed relevant environmental quality standards and other Community legislation setting such standards, 'good ecological status' means that a body of water which is demonstrated to be significantly influenced by human activity, nevertheless has a rich, balanced and sustainable ecosystem). Although the definition of good status is rudimentary, in many cases it will require Member States to improve on the present situation.

One of the framework Directive's innovations is that rivers and lakes will need to be managed by river basin — the natural geographical unit — instead of according to administrative or political boundaries. With each river basin the directive will make provision for the preparation of a strategic plan, a 'river basin management plan', which will need to be updated every six years. This plan will have to include an analysis of the river basin's characteristics, a review of the impact of human activity on the status of waters in the basin, and an economic analysis of water use in the district. The purpose of the plan will be to establish a programme of measures to ensure that all waters in the river basin achieve the objective of good water status.

The Directive avoids some of the problems of adopting a singular approach to environmental standards. Indeed it recognises the strengths of arguments in favour of both approaches which were put forward at the time of the 1976 directive (see p. 190). It takes a 'combined approach' requiring Member States to set down in their programmes of measures both limit values to control emissions from individual point sources and environmental quality standards to limit the cumulative impact of such emissions.

The emission limit values will be set in line with the IPPC Directive — on the basis of best available techniques — for installations covered by that Directive. The standards laid down by the daughter directives under the 1976 framework directive will be incorporated into the new Directive. Member States will be required to set environmental quality standards for each significant body of water that is used for the abstraction of drinking water or that may be in future. The quality standards must be designed to ensure that, under the expected water treatment regime, the abstracted water will meet the requirements of the Drinking Water Directive.

The draft Framework Directive is also the first piece of EC water legislation to address the issue of water quantity, which is important in part because of the links between water quantity and water quality (see p. 553). One consequence of this is that 'full cost recovery' pricing for water use is envisaged. This would include costs of water use in terms of environmental damage as well as adverse effects on the interests of future generations caused by over-abstraction.

There is no doubting that the proposals would require a fundamental change in existing law — both European and domestic. There are, however, many potential hurdles to be cleared before the Directive, which is presently going through the 'conciliation procedure' between the European Parliament and Council, is adopted. For example, it remains to be seen how some of the key concepts behind the proposals will actually work in practice. In particular, the idea of 'full cost recovery pricing' begs a number of questions about the methodology of calculating the cost of 'environmental harm'. The proposals suggest that it will be left to individual Member States to implement the full cost recovery obligation. If some form of pricing can be agreed which is generally applicable, it may provide a firm basis for valuing the environment as a commodity in other areas. The cost of implementing the proposals is likely to give rise to the most fundamental political objections from Member States. The administrative and regulatory changes which would be required by the proposals would be bound to increase costs dramatically. At present, these extra costs have not been estimated.

Water supply and water industry finance

Strictly speaking, the provision of a clean water supply is a consumer protection rather than an environmental protection measure. However, there is an intimate relationship between water supply and pollution control. The public water supply is abstracted from inland and ground waters, so pollution of those waters will lead to a reduction in the available source and to an increase in the cost of treatment of the water that is abstracted. To this end, it is an offence to pollute any 'waterworks' likely to be used for human consumption, which covers pollution of springs, wells, boreholes and service reservoirs (Water Industry Act 1991, s. 72). In addition, Directive 75/440 on Surface Water for Drinking has imposed controls on the quality of inland waters. This Directive seeks to ensure that surface waters which are abstracted for drinking are fit for that purpose and divides waters into three categories — A1, A2 and A3. Classification in these categories depends on the waters meeting the limits set out in the Directive. Any water of below A3 quality should not be abstracted for drinking except in exceptional circumstances. These requirements are implemented in British law by the Surface Waters (Abstraction for Drinking Water) (Classification) Regulations 1996 (SI 1996/3001) and by the Water Supply (Water Quality) Regulations 1989 (SI 1989/1147) (and see also SI 1989/1148).

There is also a more indirect link which is tied up with the highly charged political question of who should pay for the cost of environmental protection, and which requires some understanding of how the water industry as a whole is regulated and paid for. As pointed out earlier in the chapter, the water industry was massively underfunded when it was in public control prior to 1989, with the result that sewage works were major sources of pollution, and the quality of the public water supply was questionable. Since 1989, the public water supply and sewerage services have been provided by the privatised water undertakers under the regulatory oversight of the Director General of Water Services (OFWAT) and the Secretary of State. Water bills have risen considerably above inflation and, compared with the position prior to 1989, the way in which consumers pay for water and sewerage services is more explicit, since the full amount is paid in charges rather than a proportion being hidden in general taxation. However, the water companies' overall charges for water and sewerage services are regulated by the Director General under the Water Industry Act 1991. This is achieved by reference to a formula, known as RPI + K, under which the weighted average charge is allowed to increase by the retail price index plus a company-specific factor set by the Director General (known as the K factor). The Director General has to take water companies' costs, including the cost of 'environmental' improvements such as upgrading of sewage works and improvements in drinking water quality, into account when setting the K factor. Once the K factor is set, the water companies have to operate within it. This means that the trade-offs between environmental improvements by the water companies (for example, improved performance from sewage works, improved water quality from the public water supply and reduced losses from leakage), improvements in levels of service, efficiency savings and increased company profits and directors' pay, are very clear.

The K factors, which were originally set by the Secretary of State in 1989, were redetermined by the Director General in July 1994. In the run-up to that redetermination, there was a very public debate about the cost of environmental improvements. This debate focused in particular on the cost of complying with EC directives such as Directive 91/271 on Urban Waste Water Treatment, which requires the upgrading of a large number of sewage works, although the whole issue was complicated by wildly differing views on the actual costs involved. Some, including the Director General to some extent, argued that the economic cost of the environmental standards set out in the directives was too high a price for consumers to pay, whilst others argued that basic environmental standards must be paid for, and that water companies rather than consumers should pay by making efficiency savings and reducing excessive profits and directors' pay. The latest round of price determinations was finalised in November 1999. Key issues were the extent to which the water companies should finance desirable but non-mandatory environmental improvements, especially where river SSSIs and bathing waters are affected (on SSSIs see p. 628). The determinations require a considerable amount of such non-essential expenditure at the same time as bills are reduced mainly through a large reduction in 2000–01. As the price review demonstrates, there is a real sense in which decisions of the economic regulator are critical in determining both policy choices and legal obligations.

As far as the quality of the public water supply is concerned, under the Water Industry Act 1991, s. 67, domestic water must be 'wholesome', a term which was defined in legislation for the first time in the Water Supply (Water Quality) Regulations 1989. These regulations lay down a large number of specific criteria with which water must comply if supplied for domestic or food production purposes. These limits are set to comply with Directive 80/778 on Drinking Water (and the regulations are currently being revised to transpose Directive 98/83 by the end of 2000). The regulations require that information on water quality must be made available to the public. In addition, it is an offence under the Water Industry Act 1991, s. 70 to supply water that is 'unfit for human consumption', although prosecution for this offence may only be brought by the Secretary of State or the Director of Public Prosecutions. In practice, the Secretary of State has delegated enforcement powers to the Drinking Water Inspectorate (DWI), based within the DETR. In the last couple of years, the DWI has taken a number of successful prosecutions against water suppliers, mostly under s. 70 for supplying discoloured water. A failed prosecution following a cryptosporidium outbreak because of evidential problems (see [1997] Water Law 161), however, has meant the introduction of stringent monitoring and prevention provisions at supply works under amendments to the regulations (see SI 1999/1524), which in practice amount to the use of a process standard. The general enforcement approach, however, remains cooperative (see p. 241). There is the possibility of an action at common law for breach of statutory duty or negligence (see *Read* v *Croydon Corporation* [1938] 4 All ER 631, where a ratepayer successfully sued in negligence for water supplied to his household which caused his daughter to contract typhoid). Widespread incidents, such as at Camelford in 1988, may give rise to an action in public nuisance (*R* v *South West Water Authority* [1991] LMELR 65).

Standard setting, water quality and consents for the discharge of trade or sewage effluent

As noted previously, most pollution loading comes from discharges where there is a consent in order to avoid liability for a water pollution offence. It is therefore important to think of the consent system and of how consents are set within the context of the principal water pollution offences. Although water quality objectives are discussed at the end of this section, this does not mean they are a final consideration for the EA when determining a consent application. Rather, because of the emphasis on environmental quality standards, they are likely to be central. But even where there are mandatory EC quality standards to be achieved, there will usually be some flexibility in the system when individual consents are set.

A consent is required from the EA for:

(a)   any discharge of trade or sewage effluent into 'controlled waters';

(b)   any discharge of trade or sewage effluent through a pipe from land into the sea outside the limits of 'controlled waters';
(c)   any discharge where a prohibition is in force.

It is an offence under the Water Resources Act 1991, s. 85 to 'cause or knowingly permit' such a discharge, although there is a defence if it is carried out in accordance with a consent. This means it is also an offence to breach any conditions attached to a consent, a point made explicit by s. 85(6). There is no need to show that the discharge has polluted the receiving waters because the offence consists of discharging otherwise than in accordance with the consent.

'Trade effluent' is defined in s. 221 and includes any effluent from trade premises (these include agricultural, fish farming and research establishments), other than domestic sewage or surface water. 'Sewage effluent', also defined in s. 221, includes any effluent, other than surface water, from a sewerage works. The discharge must be of effluent, so it seems that if trade materials, such as fuel oil, escape they are covered by the general pollution offence (see p. 587). But there is some doubt here since effluent is defined in s. 221 to mean 'any liquid' and is not specifically limited to wastes.

A further problem relates to the interpretation of the word 'discharge'. This word is not defined in the Act. It is capable of carrying either an active meaning (i.e. that the release of materials has to be part of a deliberate trade or sewage process) or a passive meaning (as in the discharge of blood from a wound). It is suggested that it carries an active meaning, because otherwise potential dischargers would be in the impossible position of having to apply for a consent for something that was not meant to happen. The effect of this reasoning is that accidental and non-routine emissions of trade or sewage effluent do not require a consent and are covered by the general water pollution offence (see p. 587).

On the other hand, the ECJ has now held that 'discharge' for the purposes of the Dangerous Substances in Water Directive (76/464) can include discharges of listed substances (PAHs) found in wood preservative with which wooden posts used for shoring up riverbanks had been treated (Case C-232/97 *Nederhoff* [1999] ECR I-6385) and discharges of polluted steam precipitating into watercourses (*van Rooij*, p. 566 above). This is clearly a more expansive understanding of what 'discharge' means, and while it clearly applies to discharges regulated under this Directive, it remains to be seen whether the EA will insist on consents for similar discharges regulated solely as a matter of national law (and, if it does, how).

The prohibition is a new device first introduced by the Water Act 1989. It is designed to cover those cases where the type of discharge is not necessarily harmful and thus the blanket requirement of a consent is not justified. By prohibiting discharges on a selective basis, control can be exercised over just those situations where it is required (see s. 86, Water Resources Act 1991).

There are three situations where a prohibition may apply:

(a)   Where the EA by notice prohibits a discharge of trade or sewage effluent from a building or fixed plant to any land or land-locked waters outside the definition of controlled waters. This includes such situations as soakaways from trade premises and some agricultural activities.

(b) Where it prohibits a discharge of matter other than trade or sewage effluent from a drain or sewer. Trade and sewage effluent are automatically covered by the need for a consent, so the intention here is to restrict such things as discharges of dangerous substances from a storm drain.

(c) In addition, any such discharges involving substances prescribed by regulations *automatically* invoke the prohibition.

In relation to the first two categories, the prohibition can only come into force three months after notice to the discharger, unless the EA is satisfied that there is an emergency.

Controlled waters

The discharge consent system, and the water pollution offences, apply to 'controlled waters'. 'Controlled waters' are defined in s. 104 and include virtually all inland and coastal waters. Controlled waters are made up of four sub-categories:

(a) relevant territorial waters (i.e. the sea within a line three miles out from the baselines from which the territorial sea is measured, despite the extension of the territorial limit to 12 miles in the Territorial Sea Act 1987);

(b) coastal waters (i.e. the sea within those baselines up to the line of the highest tide, and tidal waters up to the fresh water limit as defined by the Secretary of State on maps produced for that purpose);

(c) inland waters (i.e. rivers, streams, underground streams, canals, lakes and reservoirs, including those that are temporarily dry); and

(d) groundwaters (i.e. any waters contained in underground strata or in wells or boreholes).

In addition, the courts have held that a river bed can form part of 'controlled waters' (see *National Rivers Authority* v *Biffa Waste* [1996] Env LR 227), as can a man-made ditch, if it drains into controlled waters (*Environment Agency* v *Brock plc* [1998] Env LR 607).

The only waters that are excluded are land-locked waters that do not drain into other controlled waters. However, the Secretary of State has power to include or exclude specific waters by order. This has been done in the Controlled Waters (Lakes and Ponds) Order 1989 (SI 1989/1149), which includes any reservoirs, apart from those intended for public water supply, which would otherwise be excluded. Water supply mains and pipes, and sewers and drains (where separate controls on discharges apply), are also excluded from the definition of controlled waters.

The consent system

The system for acquiring a consent is set out in the Water Resources Act 1991, sch. 10, and the Control of Pollution (Applications, Appeals and

Registers) Regulations 1996 (SI 1996/2971), and it involves a higher degree of public involvement than many other licensing-type systems.

Consents which have already been granted under COPA 1974 or earlier legislation are simply translated into valid consents for the purposes of the 1991 Act. However, they may be varied or revoked in the future under the terms of sch. 10 (see below).

A consent is required for each discharge, so if a factory has three discharge pipes it needs a consent for each one. The applicant applies to the EA, which has a discretion as to the details required. Normally the applicant will have to state the place, nature, quantity, rate of flow, composition and temperature of the proposed discharge. It is an offence under s. 206 to give incorrect information.

The applicant must publicise the application in a local newspaper and in the *London Gazette* and notify any relevant local authorities and water undertakers. However, this publicity may be dispensed with if the EA considers that the discharge will have 'no appreciable effect' on the receiving waters. Great use was made of this dispensation by the regional water authorities in the past, so that an estimated 90 per cent of all applications were exempted from publicity in this way. Guidance on this vague and subjective discretion is given in DoE Circular 17/84, which suggests a complex set of tests to be considered, the main one being that a change is not to be considered appreciable if there is less than a 10 per cent increase on all relevant parameters, unless some significant environmental amenity is affected. This is a good example of the use of administrative methods to define a legal requirement. It is objectionable that the operation of such an important publicity procedure rests on a rather restrictive interpretation given in a departmental circular.

Where the application contains information which would affect matters of national security the EA can exempt the application from the requirement to advertise (s. 191A and reg. 4).

The EA must take into account written representations made within six weeks of the notice appearing in the *London Gazette*. It has the power to grant consent, either unconditionally or subject to conditions, or to refuse consent.

A fee for making an application for a new or revised consent was introduced from 1 October 1990. The intention is that the EA should recover the overall costs incurred in processing applications. A standard charge is payable for each new or revised consent. There is a reduced charge for certain minor discharges of sewage effluent or cooling waters and for those surface water discharges which require consent (see *Scheme of Charges in Respect of Applications and Consents for Discharges to Controlled Waters*).

(a) Conditions

The EA may attach 'such conditions as it may think fit' and sch. 10, para. 2(5) includes a non-exhaustive list. This includes such things as the quality, quantity, nature, composition and temperature of the discharge, the siting and design of the outlet, the provision of meters for measuring these matters, the taking and recording of samples by the discharger, and the provision of information to the EA. Frequently the most significant conditions will relate to biochemical oxygen demand, levels of toxic or dangerous materials, and suspended solids, although the EA is presently considering the introduction of a more sophisticated test based on the toxicity of the discharge to aquatic life. For industrial discharges it is normal to attach absolute numerical limits for the various parameters covered in the consent, with the result that any excess amounts to a breach of the consent.

Conditions requiring a specified treatment process are legal, but are not generally imposed, since in the past it has been government policy to require compliance with environmental standards whilst giving a discharger a choice of methods to achieve the standard. For some discharges, however, the effect of the Urban Waste Water Treatment Directive (91/271) may be that specific treatment methods are required (e.g. biological treatment), although generally the Directive requires quality standards to be met. It is permissible for conditions to be staggered so that they get progressively stricter. A consent is personal to the operator but can be transferred under provisions contained in sch. 10, para. 11.

There is a procedure for granting a retrospective consent in para. 5. This involves the payment of the relevant fee and the same publicity requirements as for any other application. However, the paragraph is not fully retrospective since it affords no immunity for offences committed before the consent was granted. It enables the EA to formalise the legal position in relation to a discharge and also to attach conditions to an existing discharge.

A significant problem under COPA 1974 was the position of new pollutants. This phrase covers substances which the discharger introduces into the discharge after the consent has been obtained, or new substances unknown at the time the consent was set, or substances which were only later traceable or later considered to be polluting. Such substances would not be mentioned in the consent, and it appeared that discharging them may not have been in breach of the consent, since there was a breach only if the conditions were not met. It seems that this possible loophole has been avoided by the Water Resources Act 1991, which requires that the discharge must be 'under and in accordance with' the consent in order for the defence in s. 88 to apply. Following a number of discharge consent appeals brought by sewerage undertakers, however, the Minister has decided that the EA's policy of including a general condition excluding the discharge of any substance not specified in the consent should be qualified so that it usually applies only where it is 'reasonably practicable' for the undertaker to do so (see below).

(b) Sewage discharge consents

Sewage discharges have always caused regulatory problems, both because of their potent polluting power and because of the previous conflict of interest between regulator and regulated when the water authorities were responsible for operating treatment works and policing discharges from such works (see p. 557). However, the same conflict also existed when the local authorities ran the sewage works, since they also provided members for the river authorities and thus exercised an influence on their decisions.

Under the Water Resources Act 1991, there is no conflict of interest. Sewerage undertakers are treated similarly to other dischargers in requiring a consent from the EA. One slight difference relates to the offences under s. 85. Because sewerage undertakers treat wastes discharged by other people, and thus have limited control over what is actually put into the sewers, they have a special defence under s. 87(2). This operates if the contravention of their discharge consent was due to an unconsented discharge made into the sewer by another person which they could not reasonably have prevented (see *National Rivers Authority* v *Yorkshire Water Services Ltd* [1995] 1 AC 444, discussed below at p. 589).

A more significant difference is that sewage works have in the past had their consents set on different terms from other dischargers. Before privatisation, the relative lack of control over the quality of sewage effluent or its containment was comparatively unimportant, since the poacher/gamekeeper relationship meant that there was considerable scope for selective enforcement. With privatisation pending, however, consents were relaxed so that instead of containing absolute numerical limits, with the result that any breach of the limit amounted to a criminal offence, consents were set by reference to 'look-up' tables intended to ensure a 95 per cent compliance rate over a rolling 12-month period. Only in exceptional cases, where a generous maximum (or 'upper tier') limit was exceeded would there be liability for a one-off sewage pollution incident.

These relaxations, which have been described as 'a sort of environmental betrayal' (Kinnersley, *Coming Clean*, Penguin, 1994, p. 149) in order to reduce the undertakers' potential liabilities and make privatisation more attractive, were not however the first time sewage discharge consents had been relaxed. In the late 1970s, the National Water Council commenced a review of consents that led to some relaxations, although the review was never completed and the results never published. Consents were also relaxed in the 1980s in anticipation of the implementation of COPA 1974 and the consequent availability of a right to bring private prosecutions.

Under first the NRA and now the EA, these 'percentile' consents are being replaced by absolute limits when consents come up for review. This has led to a significant rise in the number of prosecutions brought against sewerage undertakers, since only a single sample is now needed rather than a series of samples from a 12-month period. It has also had a knock-on effect on trade effluent consents granted by the sewerage undertakers under the Water Industry Act 1991 (see Chapter 20). But the Secretary of State has decided that some leeway must still be given to take account of events beyond the control of the sewerage undertakers, and revised consents give some protection to sewerage undertakers where they can show that they have operated the works reasonably practicably so as to minimise polluting effects, for example, where there is an overflow of the sewage system during heavy rainfall (the key clauses are reproduced in Payne, *Kinnersley — Discharge Consent Conditions* [1998] Water Law 13).

A final issue is the impact of the Urban Waste Water Treatment Directive (91/271), discussed above. This imposes various restrictions on sewage discharges, although the general tenor of the Directive is purposive rather than standard-setting, that is it seeks to achieve specific goals depending on the area and population concerned rather than mandating that compliance with specific parameters or treatment methods should be met by all sewage works. Unfortunately a practice appears to have emerged whereby many new and revised consents require, in general terms, compliance with the Directive as a consent condition. Taken on its own, such a condition is probably meaningless, and likely to be void for uncertainty.

(c) Revocation and variation

Under sch. 10, para. 7, the EA has a discretion to review consents from time to time. A variation or a revocation can be made simply by notifying the discharger. Alternatively the Secretary of State may direct that a variation take place (sch. 10, para. 9). No compensation is payable except in one case considered below. There is no provision for public participation in relation to a variation or revocation. This power to make variations or revocations is a wide one which reflects the need to cater for new circumstances, such as a new polluter in the catchment area, or a newly perceived pollution threat, or a change in EC or international obligations. It also reasserts the position that no one has a right to pollute.

However, there are limits on when a variation or revocation can be made. A period will be stipulated in the original consent. This cannot be less than four years and a variation or revocation cannot take place within that period (measured from the setting of the original consent or the last variation), except with the permission of the discharger. In practice, only 4 per cent of consents are varied or revoked annually after the four year period has expired. Exceptionally, the Secretary of State may direct a modification within the period in order to give effect to an EC or international obligation, or to protect public health, or flora and fauna dependent on an aquatic environment. There is no right to vary early solely because the discharger has been in breach of the consent, or in order to cater for a new pollutant: both are situations where such a right would be desirable. The EA will have to pay compensation to the discharger if a direction is made on the public health or protection of flora and fauna ground within the period.

Transitional provisions

In any regulatory system, when a new Act comes into force the transitional provisions are of importance. For the Water Act 1989, because most discharges were already covered by the provisions of COPA 1974, the transition was fairly straightforward. Existing consents were simply translated into Water Act consents and later into consents under the Water Resources Act 1991. This hides a continuation of a transitional provision from COPA 1974. Some discharges which did not require a consent before that Act were deemed to have been granted consent for the current level of discharge under COPA 1974, s. 40(4), as long as an application was made. These applications are slowly being decided by the EA but the process is not yet complete. Such discharges include many pre-1974 discharges to estuaries, which are effectively permitted to continue with their previous discharge uncontrolled.

Annual charges for discharge consents

The EA is empowered to make annual charges for discharge consents under the general charging provisions of ss. 41 and 42 of the Environment Act 1995, although any scheme requires the approval of the Secretary of State and the consent of the Treasury (see p. 171).

The basic philosophy underpinning the charging scheme is that of cost-recovery charging, i.e. that the EA should recover from dischargers the actual cost of its activities connected with discharges. This includes the sampling of discharges, inspection of discharges, discharge-related impact monitoring, work on the review of consents, laboratory services and direct administration connected to these matters. Expenditure on general water quality monitoring, general administration and pollution incidents is not recovered by these charges, but will come from the general budget of the EA.

Further principles are that the charges are uniform throughout the country and are not to vary locally; that they relate to what is consented to rather than to the actual discharge; and that they are set according to a formula which has three separate elements — the volume of the discharge, its content, and the nature of the receiving waters. For each of these three elements broad bands have been devised, each being accorded a weighted value (i.e. a number of units). For volume, there are eight broad bands, with larger volume discharges having a higher value than lower ones. There are exceptions for emergency discharges, intermittent discharges and rainwater drains. For content, there are seven bands, reflecting the relative complexity and cost of monitoring the discharge. For receiving waters, there are four bands, with estuarine waters having a higher weighting than inland watercourses, which in turn are weighted more highly than discharges to coastal waters or to groundwaters.

Each discharge thus has three separate values, which are multiplied together to give a final figure in terms of a number of units. This final figure is then multiplied by a national financial factor, so that all dischargers know in advance what their charge is going to be. This financial factor is varied annually. It can be expected that most dischargers will face a significant annual bill for their discharges.

Although limited by the Environment Act 1995 to charging only for the recovery of administrative costs, the charging system does give partial effect to the 'polluter pays' principle. The possibility of going further and introducing charges reflecting the full environmental costs of discharges has been on the political agenda since this was mentioned in the White Paper, *This Common Inheritance* (Cm 1200, 1990) and was taken further in the Sixteenth Report of the Royal Commission on Environmental Pollution on *Freshwater Quality* (Cm 1966, 1992). The Labour Government has consulted on this as part of a wider look at using economic instruments to control water pollution (*Economic Instruments for Water Pollution*, DETR, 1997), but it is unlikely that there will be change before the next general election.

The role of the Secretary of State

The Secretary of State has a general, and very wide, power under s. 40 of the Environment Act 1995 to issue directions of a general or specific nature to the EA in relation to pollution control, amongst other matters. The supplementary powers of the Secretary of State to require information from the EA in s. 202 should also be noted. The reason for the width of this power is the fact that large policy-making powers have effectively been delegated to the EA, making some mechanism for central control desirable. The use of directions to achieve this should be compared with the use of Circular guidance in other areas of environmental law, since they fulfil similar purposes. Directions are often used in relation to EC directives, supplementing implementing regulations (see also p. 159).

At any stage the Secretary of State may call in an application for decision (sch. 10, para. 5). This is an unfettered discretion and ousts the jurisdiction of the EA to consider the consent. It is rarely exercised.

The EA must apply to the Secretary of State if it wishes to make any discharges. Similar procedures apply as for ordinary consent applications (SI 1996/2971, sch. 2). Given the limited operational activities of the EA, few such applications will be necessary.

Appeals

The applicant or discharger has a right to appeal to the Secretary of State against a refusal of consent, the attachment of unreasonable conditions, any adverse variation or revocation of a consent, or the setting of the period in which a consent cannot be varied (s. 91). An application is deemed to have been refused if no decision is given within four months.

An appeal is a general rehearing of the matter in issue and the Secretary of State has the same powers as the EA originally had. As with planning appeals, in practice appeals are heard by the Planning Inspectorate, although the Secretary of State retains the final decision in more important cases. Compared with the system of planning appeals, which accords enormous opportunities for argument on policy, this appeal right is far less commonly used. This may be because there is little perceived difference in policy between the Secretary of State and the EA. However, because of the length of time it takes for appeals to be decided, an understanding of the principles to be applied on appeal is only building up slowly. although the recent decisions on sewerage undertakers' liability for unseen pollutants (see p. 579) are a good indication of thinking.

The procedures for called in applications and for appeals are set out in the Control of Pollution (Applications, Appeals and Registers) Regulations 1996 (SI 1996/2971). These regulations retain the procedures for other applications with modified wording, and also provide for the rights of objectors. One significant change is that the discretion not to publicise where there is no appreciable effect on the receiving waters does not apply.

How are consents set?

The EA, or the Secretary of State on appeal, has a wide discretion in setting the consent and it will be set by reference to a variety of factors. Although sch. 10 is silent as to the factors which must be taken into account, applying ordinary public law principles the EA must have regard to all material considerations. In addition, certain requirements appear from other sections of the Act, especially s. 84, and from EC law.

As stated before, it is important to grasp the individualised and flexible nature of these consents, although uniformity and consistency is now being sought by the EA. Relevant matters include:

(a)   The water quality objectives and standards set for the receiving waters under s. 83 (see below). This emphasises that one of the crucial elements in fixing a consent is the effect on the receiving waters. This in turn depends on the use that is intended for those receiving waters.

(b)   Any other effects on the receiving waters, such as on a fishery or downstream user. In particular, regard will be had to whether the waters are used for abstraction for water supply or irrigation.

(c)   Any relevant EC standards for the discharge concerned or for the quality of the receiving waters.

(d)   Any 'cocktail' effect of the discharge. The EA will consider not only the immediate effect of the discharge but also any impact the discharge will have in combination with the current contents of the waters and any potential future discharges.

(e)   The desirability of minimising discharges of hazardous substances as far as possible in accordance with Directive 76/464.

(f)   The EA's environmental duties laid out in the Environment Act 1995, s. 6 (see p. 167).

(g)   The specific duty in relation to sites of special scientific interest set out in s. 8 of the 1995 Act (see p. 168).

(h)   Any relevant objections and representations made and the results of any consultation carried out.

(i)   Certain informal standard tests for particular types of discharge. For example, 'normal' standards for sewage works were suggested by the Eighth Report of the Royal Commission on Sewage Disposal in 1912 and these were applied for many years. The EA is now seeking to establish some uniformity of standards across the country for all types of discharge.

(j)   Any other material considerations.

There would be scope for having general binding rules applying across an industrial sector but so far there appears to be little enthusiasm for these. In other Member States, their use has been criticised by the regulators for making it harder to establish and maintain a co-operative relationship with dischargers (see [1998] Water Law 195).

Water quality objectives

Although the British approach to the control of water pollution has tended over the years to concentrate on the environmental impact of pollutants, the development of *statutory* water quality objectives owes a great deal to the EC. In the 1970s, in debates on EC directives such as 76/464 on Dangerous Substances in Water, the British government argued that its system of water pollution control was different from the systems operated by other EC Member States in that it was based on individualised consent standards set by reference to local environmental quality objectives, rather than on uniform emission standards or limit values which did not take the environmental effects fully into account. At the time, however, there were no formally set quality objectives, so in order to show that this was indeed how the system worked, the government was forced to introduce more explicit objectives.

(a)   Classification schemes
In 1978, the National Water Council developed a water quality classification (see *River Water Quality: The Next Stage*, National Water Council, 1978). This had five basic classes of river waters (there was a similar but separate classification for estuaries):

1A   High quality waters suitable for all abstraction purposes with only modest treatment. Capable of supporting game or other high class fisheries. High amenity value.
1B   Good quality waters usable for substantially the same purposes as 1A though not as high quality.
2   Fair quality waters viable as coarse fisheries and capable of use for drinking water provided advanced treatment is given. Moderate amenity value.
3   Poor waters polluted to the extent that fish are absent or only sporadically present. Suitable only for low grade industrial abstractions.
4   Bad quality waters which are grossly polluted and likely to cause a nuisance.

This classification was adopted by the regional water authorities in setting informal river quality objectives over the next few years. It was also used for the five-yearly national survey of water quality. However, as an administrative method of implementing EC directives, it was clearly insufficient to satisfy EC law (see p. 136) so it became inevitable that a statutory system would be adopted.
The Water Act 1989 introduced statutory water quality classifications and objectives for the first time. The provisions are now reproduced in the Water Resources Act 1991, ss. 82–84. When fully operational (which will not be for many years), statutory water quality objectives will make the system more open and will be an important element in the general process of establishing a rationally planned, transparent and properly accountable system of water resources management.
The essential features are that, over the next few years, classification regulations should (in theory) be made which set the standards that waters must reach in order to come within a certain classification. This will be done

under s. 82. The Secretary of State will then establish (under s. 83) a water quality *objective* for each stretch of controlled waters. This will set specified classifications as an objective, and will accordingly incorporate the relevant water quality *standards*. These will then act as explicit policy goals for the EA, which will be under a legal duty under s. 84 to exercise its functions, including the granting of discharge consents, so as to achieve and maintain the statutory water quality objective at all times, at least as far as it is practicable to do so. There are thus three different processes involved, although these are intertwined.

The first process is the setting of classification systems for waters under s. 82. In order to comply with certain EC directives, the following regulations have been made:

(a)   The Surface Waters (Abstraction for Drinking Water) (Classification) Regulations 1996 (SI 1996/3001) (and see also SI 1989/1148) (see p. 572).

(b)   The Bathing Waters (Classification) Regulations 1991 (SI 1991/ 1157), which establish a classification that reflects the mandatory standards laid down in the Bathing Waters Directive.

(c)   The Surface Waters (Dangerous Substances) (Classification) Regulations 1989, 1992, 1997 and 1998 (SIs 1989/2286, 1992/337, 1997/2560 and 1998/389) which set classifications in accordance with the Dangerous Substances in Water Directive and its daughter directives.

(d)   The Surface Waters (Fishlife) (Classification) Regulations 1997 (SI 1997/1331) and the Surface Waters (Shellfish) (Classification) Regulations 1997 (SI 1997/1332), which set classifications for the Freshwater Fish Waters and the Shellfish Waters Directives respectively.

To comply with EC law, these classifications have also been issued as initial water quality objectives under s. 83 (see below). This has been done by the Secretary of State under the power to make directions (see p. 582). In doing so the publicity and consultation requirements set out in s. 83(4) are now always dispensed with.

The Surface Waters (River Ecosystem) (Classification) Regulations 1994 (SI 1994/1057) is the only classification that has been made for purely national reasons, which may explain why there is no obligation imposed under the regulations requiring their use as water quality objectives for particular waters under s. 83. The regulations lay down five classifications, RE1–RE5, defined in accordance with seven parameters. Although there are no specific biological parameters there is a link here with the biological GQA (see p. 554), but the regulations do not seem to have been used as the basis for any water quality objective yet imposed.

(b)   Classifying individual waters
The second process is that water quality objectives for individual stretches of controlled waters may be set by the Secretary of State (s. 83). The choice of an objective by the Secretary of State would mean that the appropriate standards laid down for that objective in the classification regulations would apply to the stretch of water. In addition, appropriate EC standards laid down for that objective in the classification regulations would apply to the stretch

of water. In addition, appropriate EC standards laid down in directives would be incorporated where relevant (for example, if the waters were bathing waters designated under Directive 76/160).

The procedures for setting a statutory water quality objective involve at least three months publicity of the proposed objective 'in such manner as the Secretary of State considers appropriate for bringing it to the attention of persons likely to be affected by it' (i.e. these provisions are less specific than many other publicity provisions in relation to pollution control). The EA must also be notified. All representations and objections must be considered, and the Secretary of State may modify the proposals in the light of these representations. A public local inquiry may be held under s. 213. Because of the mandatory nature of EC quality standards, as noted above the publicity and consultation obligations are now always overridden, effectively integrating the classification and designation stages, at least for objectives based on EC law.

(c) The effects of classification

The third process is that, as stated above, under s. 84 the EA and Secretary of State are placed under a duty to exercise their powers under the Act so as to achieve statutory water quality objectives at all times, so far as it is practicable to do so. This duty already applies to the objectives set in the Surface Waters (Dangerous Substances) (Classification) Regulations, but will only apply to other objectives when they are formally established. It does not follow that the EA is in breach of s. 84 simply by failing to achieve the appropriate standards. But it does mean that its powers in relation to the setting and variation of consents, remedial and enforcement action, and preventive controls should be exercised to achieve the standards if practicable, since a judicial review action could conceivably be brought to ensure the enforcement of the duty. Under the EPA 1990, s. 7(2)(c), a similar duty is placed on the EA to try to achieve statutory water quality objectives when considering authorisations for integrated pollution control, and a similar duty is likely to feature in the regulations implementing the PPCA 1999. In both situations, equity issues arise. It is not clear whether, in order to meet water quality objectives, the EA should refuse all new consents or authorisations, or gradually try to tighten all existing consents over time (and if so, whether it should tighten all consents equally).

(d) Criticisms of the system of quality objectives

One of the criticisms of the sections on statutory water quality objectives when they were first passed was that no timetable was set for the introduction of the system. It is now clear that full implementation will take many years. There is still some work to be done on the development of precise classification criteria. After that, the process of setting individual objectives will, in the Conservative government's words, extend 'over a number of years', starting with a very limited number of selected river catchments. Even then, the current proposals relate only to rivers — statutory water quality objectives for estuaries, coastal waters, groundwaters, canals and lakes are clearly many years off. The existing informal river quality objectives will remain in force until superseded by the statutory objectives. There is little doubt that there is little enthusiasm for the costs involved in setting statutory water quality objectives, despite the great benefits they would produce in terms of a rational and transparent system of pollution control.

Groundwater pollution

Different provisions apply to certain activities that may lead to black or grey list substances contaminating groundwater (see p. 566). The Groundwater Regulations 1998 (SI 1998/2746) require the discharge consent system to be used to prevent the entry of black list substances, and pollution from grey lists substances. But the regulations also use consent-type provisions to regulate indirect discharges such as might arise from the disposal and tipping of listed substances, at least where these are not regulated by waste management provisions (reg. 18, and see reg. 15 of the Waste Management Licensing Regulations 1994, discussed at p. 498). They also provide for a 'notice' provision similar to prohibition notices in relation to activities on or in the ground (such as underground storage tanks), although only where pollution might arise (reg. 19). The EA has discretion whether to serve such a notice, and must take account of any Code of Practice issued. There are very limited publicity requirements for these authorisations and notices. A significant difference is that the Groundwater Regulations 1998 also create a specific offence of discharging listed substances where there is a *risk* of *indirect* groundwater pollution, by amending the wording of s. 85, Water Resources Act 1991 specifically to cover this situation. What is unique about this is not that the risk of pollution is covered (see p. 598 below) but that what amounts to a pollution offence is defined in the Water Resources Act 1991 and that no actual entry or discharge into water is required.

Water pollution offences

Turning from the consent system, it is important to remember that a key purpose of this system is to guard against criminal liability for polluting controlled waters. The water pollution offences described below are therefore important in that they provide the context for the consent system (it should be stressed again that the discharge consent system does not require dischargers to be 'licensed' or to meet general process-based standards, as is the case e.g. with industrial operators under the IPC or IPPC systems, although in practice the difference is not that great). However, the water pollution offences are also the key means of imposing criminal liability on those who discharge without a consent, e.g. where substances are illicitly dumped into a river or there is a pollution spill after an incident. The offences below are in addition to the offence of breaching any condition of a discharge consent, which of course only applies to consent holders (s. 85(6)).

(a) General pollution offence
There is a general offence under s. 85(1) of causing or knowingly permitting any poisonous, noxious or polluting matter or any solid waste to enter controlled waters. As is common within the flexible definitions of British

pollution control, the words 'poisonous, noxious or polluting' are not defined. However, the wording is very wide and in *R v Dovermoss Ltd* [1995] Env LR 258, the Court of Appeal decided that 'polluting' requires simply that a likelihood or *capability* of causing harm to animals, plants or those who use the water could be demonstrated. Actual harm is not necessary.

This general offence complements the more specific offence of discharging trade or sewage effluent without consent (s. 85(3)). Obviously it covers any entry of polluting matter which is not trade or sewage effluent. But, unlike COPA 1974, where the general and the specific offences were made exclusive of each other by s. 31(2)(e), under later Acts this exclusivity has been removed, so an illegal discharge of trade or sewage effluent also amounts to an offence under the general offence if it causes pollution.

The general offence also covers accidental and non-routine escapes of trade or sewage effluent because, whilst the specific offence requires a 'discharge', the general offence only requires an entry. In addition, non-point discharges, such as agricultural run-off, are potentially covered by the general offence.

There is a further offence in s. 85(5) of substantially aggravating pollution by impeding the proper flow of inland, non-tidal waters.

(b) Penalties

For all s. 85 offences the potential penalties are the same. On summary conviction there is a maximum fine of £20,000 (this was raised by the EPA 1990, s. 145(1) from the previous maximum of £2,000), and/or three months in prison. On conviction on indictment, there can be an unlimited fine and/ or a two-year jail sentence. The normal six-month period for a summary prosecution to be brought is extended to 12 months by the Water Resources Act 1991, s. 101, as it is for all offences in Part III of the Act.

(c) Defences

A number of defences to these water pollution offences are set out in s. 88. A discharge or entry made in accordance with the following is a defence:

(a)   a consent from the EA, or the equivalent consent granted or deemed to have been granted under COPA 1974 or earlier legislation;

(b)   an authorisation in relation to integrated pollution control granted under Part I of the EPA 1990, or an IPPC permit under the PPCA 1999;

(c)   a waste management licence or a waste disposal licence (except where the offence is of discharging trade or sewage effluent or where a prohibition is in force);

(d)   a licence permitting dumping at sea granted by the Ministry of Agriculture, Fisheries and Food under the Food and Environment Protection Act 1985;

(e)   an Act of Parliament;

(f)   any statutory order (such as a drought order).

Section 89 provides a further defence if the entry or discharge was made in an emergency in order to avoid danger to life or health: in such a case the discharger must inform the EA as soon as reasonably practicable and take reasonable steps to minimise any pollution. It must be assumed that only a danger to human life or health would suffice. In addition, s. 89 excludes from the operation of s. 85 sewage effluent from vessels (which is covered under by-laws) and solid refuse from mines where the EA has given consent for its deposit. There is also a block exemption order relating to certain discharges which had never required a consent until COPA 1974 came into force. This granted transitional exemption for these discharges, but it is being progressively withdrawn and few discharges are now covered. It might be noted that the defence in s. 89(3) for permitting water pollution from abandoned mines was withdrawn on 31 December 1999 (see the Environment Act 1995, s. 60). The Environment Act 1995 also defined the concept of abandonment for the first time and imposes a duty on mine operators to give the Environment Agency at least six months notice of a proposed abandonment.

There are some complex provisions in s. 87 relating to responsibility for discharges from sewage works. In addition to the impact of the wide interpretation given to the concept of 'causing' on sewerage undertakers (see below), s. 87(1) deems sewerage undertakers to have caused a discharge of sewage effluent if they were bound to receive into the sewer or works matter included in the discharge. In other words, they are responsible for all discharges from sewers or works unless the pollution is caused by an illegal (i.e. unconsented) discharge into the sewer. However, s. 87(2) provides a defence where a contravention of s. 85 is attributable to an unconsented discharge into the sewerage system by a third party which the sewerage undertaker could not reasonably have been expected to prevent. In *National Rivers Authority* v *Yorkshire Water Services Ltd* [1995] 1 AC 444, the House of Lords decided that, notwithstanding the precise wording of s. 87(2), the defence applies to all the offences in s. 85. It should be noted that the defence covers the situation where the sewerage undertaker could not reasonably have prevented the discharge *into* the sewer, rather than *from* the sewer, but that the original discharger into the sewer can be prosecuted under s. 85 for causing pollution of controlled waters as well as under the Water Industry Act 1991, s. 118, for the illegal discharge to the sewer (see Chapter 20).

Under COPA 1974, there was a defence to the general offence if it was committed by a farmer acting in accordance with good agricultural practice. This was defined in a Code of Guidance issued by the Ministry of Agriculture, Fisheries and Food. The defence has been repealed. In its place is non-binding guidance (*The Water Code Revised 1998*, issued under SI 1998/3084). Contravention does not amount to a criminal offence and compliance does not afford a legal defence to any criminal charge. However, conformity with the Code will affect any decision whether to prosecute and the level of any fine imposed. Conformity may also influence any decision about whether the actions of a farmer are judged reasonable for the purposes of a nuisance action (see *Savage* v *Fairclough* [2000] Env LR 183).

(d) The meaning of 'cause or knowingly permit'
The offences under s. 85 require that the defendant 'cause or knowingly permit' the relevant discharge or entry. It is clear that there are two separate

offences, 'causing' and 'knowingly permitting', and that the former lays down an offence of strict liability because it is not conditioned by any requirement of knowledge.

Until recently, the leading case in this area was *Alphacell Ltd v Woodward* [1972] AC 824, where the House of Lords provided reasonably clear guidance as to what 'causing' required. In *Alphacell*, settling tanks at a paper factory overflowed into a river. The biochemical oxygen demand (BOD) of the discharge was well above the level permitted in the consent. Although the magistrates did not find that the firm had been negligent (a strange decision since pumps which should have stopped the flow were blocked by brambles and ferns), the House of Lords held that there was no need to prove negligence or fault. Alphacell were guilty of the general offence of causing pollution simply by carrying on the activity that gave rise to the pollution. As long as their activity was itself intentional all that needed to be shown was a causal link between it and the discharge. The directness of the entry was also irrelevant: in this case the entry was via a channel into a river.

This test was reiterated in many cases. For example, in *F.J.H. Wrothwell Ltd v Yorkshire Water Authority* [1984] Crim LR 43, a company director who had poured herbicide into what he thought was a drain leading to the public sewer, but which in fact led to a nearby stream, was guilty of causing pollution, despite the unintended result of his action. In *National Rivers Authority v Yorkshire Water Services Ltd* [1995] 1 AC 444, an industrial solvent had been discharged illegally into the sewers by an unidentified industrial firm. The solvent had travelled through the sewers and, as a result of the design of the sewage works, into controlled waters, in a virtually undiluted condition. The House of Lords, reaffirming *Alphacell*, stated that there was ample evidence on which to find that the sewerage undertaker had caused the discharge from the sewage works (although in fact the conviction was quashed because the undertaker could take advantage of the special defence in s. 87(2)).

Two further cases illustrate the scope of liability. In *CPC (UK) Ltd v National Rivers Authority* [1995] Env LR 131, a factory operator was held to have caused polluting matter to enter controlled waters when a pipe carrying cleaning fluid fractured, allowing the fluid to flow into a river via a storm drain. The conviction was upheld even though the cause of the fracture was defective work carried out by subcontractors for the previous owner, a defect which a rigorous environmental audit of the premises before it was bought by the current owners had failed to detect. The current owners caused the pollution because they were operating it at the time of the polluting incident: this was enough to satisfy the test laid down by Lord Wilberforce in *Alphacell* that causing 'must involve some active operation or chain of operations involving as a result the pollution of the stream'. And in *Attorney-General's Reference (No. 1 of 1994)* [1995] 1 WLR 599, a sewerage undertaker was held to have caused a water pollution incident by running a sewerage system in an unmaintained state. Although it was argued that this was an omission, the court reformulated the issue by pointing out that the active operation was running a sewage disposal system in an unmaintained state. The court also added that it was possible for more than one person to be liable for causing one pollution incident — the offence simply required that the defendant caused the discharge or entry, not that it was the sole, or even the principal, cause. (Thus in the *CPC* case, an action could also have been brought against the subcontractors, or in the *Yorkshire Water Services* case also against the original discharger into the sewer, had they been identified.)

There was a line of cases, however, where the courts held that the defendant had been passive rather than active, and therefore not liable for causing pollution. These began with *Price* v *Cromack* [1975] 1 WLR 988, where a farmer had a contract permitting an animal firm to discharge waste into lagoons on his land. One lagoon wall failed and the resulting escape severely polluted a river. The farmer was acquitted of causing pollution on the ground that he had only permitted the accumulation and had not caused the pollution. *Price* v *Cromack* was followed in *Wychavon District Council* v *National Rivers Authority* [1993] 1 WLR 125 and *National Rivers Authority* v *Welsh Development Agency* [1993] Env LR 407. In the *Wychavon* case, raw sewage escaped from a sewer under the control of the Council acting as agent of the water company in maintaining and repairing the sewerage system. The immediate cause was a blockage in the sewer. The Divisional Court held that the Council was not guilty of the causing offence since it had merely remained inactive. In the *Welsh Development Agency* case, the court decided that the landlord of an industrial estate did not cause a discharge of trade effluent from the estate's surface water drains when the effluent originated from one of the units on the estate. These two cases both purported to follow *Alphacell*, but appeared to ignore that in *Alphacell* it was the underlying operation, not the immediate cause of the pollution, that must be active. (In *Alphacell*, the active operation was identified as a complex one that involved the carrying on of a paper factory with an effluent treatment plant situated next to a river and which had an overflow channel that led directly to a river: it was inevitable that if something went wrong, polluting matter would enter the river.)

In the recent decision of the House of Lords in *Empress Car Company (Abertillery) Ltd* v *National Rivers Authority* [1998] Env LR 396, however, this suspect line of cases was strongly disapproved of as being too restrictive, and an attempt was made to restore the meaning of 'active operation' laid down in *Alphacell*. In *Empress Car*, an oil tank had a protective bund, but to make it easier to use the oil, the tank was connected via a pipe to a smaller drum outside the bund. The outlet from the tank had an unlocked tap, which was vandalised. The drum overfilled, leading to pollution of a river via a storm drain. Following *Alphacell*, Lord Hoffmann held that the defendant must have 'done something', but this something need not be the immediate act which led to the pollution. Maintaining a diesel tank was 'doing something': so was maintaining lagoons or operating sewerage systems.

(e)   Third parties, natural forces and other intervening 'causes'

Despite the apparent strictness of *Alphacell*, there was a line of cases where the courts imposed limits to the wide interpretation of the concept of causing pollution where a third party or other intervening act was thought to interrupt the chain of causation. In *Impress (Worcester) Ltd* v *Rees* [1971] 2 All ER 357, fuel oil from a tank was released into the River Severn. The defendant successfully pleaded that this was the act of a trespasser. In *National Rivers Authority* v *Wright Engineering Co. Ltd* [1994] 4 All ER 281, vandals had interfered with an oil storage tank, which then leaked into controlled waters. Once again, the company was held not to have caused the polluting entry, although it was accepted that the forseeability of the vandalism would be a relevant factor in deciding who caused the pollution incident. In *Alphacell*, however, the presence of leaves and other debris that blocked the overflow channel were to be expected in autumn. Similarly, in *Southern Water Authority* v *Pegrum* (1989) 153 JP 581, the heavy rain which filled up slurry lagoons so that they overflowed and polluted a river was not so out of the ordinary as to break the chain of causation.

In *Empress Car*, Lord Hoffmann reaffirmed what had really already been laid down in *Alphacell* concerning causation, namely that once it was established that something had been done to cause pollution, the only question that needs to be asked is whether the defendant caused the pollution. But he then stated a general test as to when the chain of causation will be broken. He did so by trying to avoid questions of whether the specific intervention was foreseeable (as the court did in *Wright Engineering*), replacing this with a more objective approach.

> The true common sense distinction is, in my view, between acts and events which, although necessarily foreseeable in the particular case, are in the generality a normal and familiar fact of life, and acts or events which are abnormal and extraordinary.

In his view, vandalism is foreseeable, whereas a terrorist attack is not. This approach may make it easier for magistrates to determine whether or not the defendant caused the pollution, but does not wholly remove scope for argument. For example, terrorist attacks may be extraordinary, but they are planned against by water and sewerage companies. On the other hand, incidents of vandalism may be rare in some rural settings. Ultimately, though, the new test does leave some room for arguments that, in individual cases, an event is extraordinary. In *Environment Agency* v *Brock plc* [1998] Env LR 607, a case involving pollution following a fracture to a pipe with a latent defect, however, the Divisional Court seemed to imply that any such defect would always be an 'ordinary fact of life', suggesting that this was a matter of law rather than fact.

(f) 'Knowingly permitting'
The offence of 'knowingly permitting' has given rise to fewer cases and is clearly more limited than the 'causing' offence because of the knowledge requirement. However, it may be of use in situations where a person is passive even after knowing of the polluting incident. For example, in *Price* v *Cromack* the judge suggested the farmer could well have been charged with knowingly permitting the pollution; and in the *Wychavon* case it is fairly clear that the

local authority could have been charged with knowingly permitting the pollution once it had been drawn to its attention (on the facts it had delayed for some time before taking steps to remedy the situation). One issue of great importance to the 'knowingly permitting' offence is the level of knowledge required. In *Schulmans Incorporated Ltd v National Rivers Authority* [1993] Env LR D1 the judge held that constructive knowledge was sufficient, although he did not go on to elaborate the point (see Wilkinson, 'Causing and knowingly permitting pollution offences: a review' [1993] Water Law 25, for a discussion of the possible implications of this case).

(g)   Liability of companies and consent holders
Two final cases are of importance for the s. 85 offences. In *Taylor Woodrow Property Management Ltd v National Rivers Authority* (1994) 158 JP 1101, a property company held a discharge consent relating to an outfall from an industrial estate. Even though it did not itself actually make any discharge, it was held liable under s. 85(6) for contravening the conditions of the consent. It thus appears that the holder of a consent is always capable of being prosecuted for breach of positive conditions attached to the consent. It can also be noted that this is a very neat way of avoiding any argument concerning whether the defendant has carried out an active operation, but only where there is a consent.

Company directors and other senior managers can be guilty of a water pollution offence in addition to any charge brought against the company, if there is consent or connivance on that person's part, or some form of neglect (s. 217(1)) although this has never been used. And in *National Rivers Authority v Alfred McAlpine Homes East Ltd* [1994] 4 All ER 286, the company was held to be vicariously liable for acts of its employees, irrespective of whether those employees exercised 'the controlling mind' of the company. This appears to be a straightforward application of the principle of vicarious liability, but it does illustrate the need for companies to establish proper environmental management systems.

(h)   Summary of judicial attitudes to the general water pollution offences
It is quite clear, from comments in the cases referred to above, that the judges have been prepared to adopt a fairly purposive view of the legislation in order to further the aim of environmental protection. One result has been that the s. 85 offences have been given a very wide interpretation. This has had a number of implications. First, a wide range of accidental occurrences are offences. Secondly, any excess over the requirements of a numerical consent amounts to a criminal offence, no matter how small it is. Thirdly, firms are given a clear incentive to adopt an appropriate environmental management system so that accidents and breaches of consent do not occur. Fourthly, when a prosecution is brought there is a very high success rate (it is currently around 95 per cent). However, the EA has a discretion whether to prosecute and has adopted a policy which means that a prosecution will not be brought in every possible case (see Chapter 9 and p. 596 below).

The courts also have a discretion in sentencing, which may mitigate perceived injustices: in the *CPC* case, the defendants were eventually given an absolute discharge. This discretion on prosecuting and on sentencing, however, means that it would be dangerous for the courts to import the interpretation of 'causing' given in *Empress Car* into other provisions such as those in relation to contaminated land (see p. 539) or water pollution clean up powers (see p. 599), where there is less discretion to mitigate the strictness of liability.

(i)   Other water pollution offences

There are a number of other offences which may be committed in relation to water pollution. A few of the main ones are considered here: to these should be added offences concerning the dumping of waste, which often involve the pollution of water, and many by-laws of a local or specific nature.

Under the Water Resources Act 1991, s. 90(1), it is an offence to remove any part of the bed of inland waters so as to cause it to be carried away in suspension. Section 90(2) provides for an offence of causing or permitting vegetation to be cut or uprooted so as to fall into inland waters, and then failing to take reasonable steps to remove it. In both cases the EA may grant its consent subject to any conditions it considers appropriate. The offences are summary only, with a maximum fine of £2,500.

Under the Water Resources Act 1991, sch. 25, the EA has powers to make by-laws in relation to the washing or cleaning of anything in controlled waters, or in relation to sanitary appliances on vessels. The maximum fine for an offence under these by-laws is £2,500.

Under the Salmon and Freshwater Fisheries Act 1975, s. 4(1), it is an offence to cause or knowingly permit any liquid or solid matter to flow or be put into waters containing fish so as to cause those waters to be poisonous or injurious to fish, their food or their spawning grounds. This offence is more limited than the Water Resoures Act 1991, s. 85; it requires proof of the presence of fish and injury to them. A prosecution cannot be brought except by the EA or anyone who has obtained a certificate from the Minister of Agriculture, Fisheries and Food (or, in Wales, the National Assembly) that they have a material interest in the waters affected. The maximum fine on summary conviction is also less than for s. 85 (£5,000 rather than £20,000) although the penalties for conviction on indictment are the same. The Water Consolidation (Consequential Provisions) Act 1991, sch. 1 provides that a consent under the 1991 Act is a defence to the offence under the 1975 Act.

Under EPA 1990, s. 140, the Secretary of State is given powers to make regulations to prohibit the importation, use, supply or storage of any substance or article for the purpose of preventing it causing pollution of the environment, or harm to the health of humans, animals or plants. This very wide power includes the power to order the disposal or treatment of restricted articles. It replaces the similar power under COPA 1974, s. 100. That section was used to make regulations banning the supply of lead weights for use by anglers (see Control of Pollution (Anglers' Lead Weights) Regulations 1986 (SI 1986/1992)), prohibiting the supply and use of PCBs (see Control of

Pollution (Supply and Use of Injurious Substances) Regulations 1986 (SI 1986/902)), and prohibiting the supply of tri-organotin compound paints (see Control of Pollution (Anti-Fouling Paints and Treatments) Regulations 1987 (SI 1987/783)). Interestingly, the regulations on anglers' lead weights have been amended as a result of the EC single internal market. The original regulations had banned the import of lead weights as well as their supply. The Control of Pollution (Anglers' Lead Weights) (Amendment) Regulations 1993 (SI 1993/49) amended this so that only their supply is banned, since the government considered, despite the clear implications of the *Danish Bottles* case (see p. 135), that the import ban could no longer be justified.

Sampling and enforcement powers

Environment Agency officers have wide rights of entry to property under s. 108 of the Environment Act 1995. These include a right to take samples of water or effluent or to install monitoring equipment. But changes made under s. 111, albeit against significant pressure from industrial interests, mean that a sample is admissible in evidence even though it is not a 'legal', or tripartite, sample (i.e. one that was taken in a specified way and divided into three parts, one being sent for analysis, one given to the occupier and one retained for future comparison). The requirement of a 'legal' sample led to a number of cases where the status of the results of things like continuous monitoring were questioned, although these are now of historic interest. In any event, the need to take tripartite samples never seemed to apply to samples taken other than by or on behalf of the NRA, so a privately taken sample was always admissible even if its scientific accuracy would probably be challenged. It is worth noting that a private sample taken by trespassing on the discharger's land, although admissible, may be excluded as improperly obtained evidence at the discretion of the court, although such a course of action is unlikely (see the Police and Criminal Evidence Act 1984, s. 78).

In practice, some form of monitoring requirement, typically self-monitoring, is now included in most discharge consents, and s. 111 states simply that information provided or obtained as a result of a licence condition is admissible, including where it is provided by means of an apparatus (i.e. some form of measuring device). There is a rebuttable presumption that such an apparatus is accurate. The new position therefore makes it clear that the results of self-monitoring (where there is no tripartite division) can be used for enforcement purposes, at least where required under a consent. It should also reduce the number of offenders who escape prosecution on evidential technicalities. In practice, most consents which require self-monitoring will also make it a condition to pass on information gathered, so that failure to do will also be an offence.

There is also a potential problem relating to the admissibility of the public registers, since it is fairly clearly hearsay evidence. It appears that samples taken by the EA are admissible under the Criminal Justice Act 1988, s. 24. This section also seems to avoid any problem relating to self-incrimination where the discharger's own voluntarily taken data are used, as that data will count as a confession (see the Police and Criminal Evidence Act 1984, ss. 76 and 82). Although it is arguable that the decision in *Saunders* v *United Kingdom* (1997) 23 EHRR 313 changes this, the decision in *R* v *Hertfordshire County Council, ex parte Green Environmental Industries Ltd* [2000] 1 All ER 773 indicates that information placed on the registers can be relied on, because it is not sought as part of a specific criminal investigation.

Enforcement policy

A central issue relating to water pollution, and indeed of this whole book, is whether the rules are actually enforced by the regulators (see generally Chapter 9). The NRA established a national prosecution policy and it became clear that the traditional recipe of a conciliatory approach to enforcement with very low prosecution rates was rapidly reformulated.

For example, from 1980 to 1987 the regional water authorities collectively prosecuted between 91 and 254 cases of water pollution each year (Birch, *Poison in the System*, Greenpeace, 1988). By comparison, the NRA brought 592 prosecutions for incidents occurring in 1990, although this figure was especially high because of drought conditions in many areas that year which led to a higher number of incidents. In addition in a further 206 cases a formal caution was issued, this course of action being used where the polluter admits the offence yet a prosecution is considered unnecessary.

This increase in prosecution activity was linked to the NRA's internal practices. It divided pollution incidents into three categories according to their severity — major, significant and minor. Major incidents involved one or more of the following:

(a) a potential or actual persistent effect on water quality or aquatic life;
(b) the closure of a potable water, industrial or agricultural abstraction point;
(c) an extensive fish kill;
(d) excessive breaches of consents conditions;
(e) a major effect on amenity values; or
(f) extensive remedial measures being necessary.

It then applied its internal prosecution policy. Although this was never formally published it involved prosecuting for major incidents where there was sufficient evidence to do so, and left it to the discretion of individual officers where a significant incident occurred (see Jewell, 'Agricultural water pollution issues and NRA enforcement policy' [1991] LMELR 110).

Prosecution policy is now governed by the EA's revised *Enforcement and Prosecution Policy* (discussed on p. 253). Essentially, this takes the same approach to major pollution incidents, although these are renamed Category 1 incidents and include significant adverse effects to sites of conservation importance, and there is a presumption that cautions will be used for significant (Category 2) incidents. Statistics on water pollution incidents and enforcement are given in annual reports by the NRA and now the EA. The latest report (*Water Pollution Incidents in England and Wales — 1998*, EA, 1999) records 17,863 substantiated pollution incidents in 1998 and states that by the end of 1998, 92 prosecutions had been brought with a further 95 cases still to come to court. This is a drop — in incidents and prosecutions — compared with the mid-1990s. However, the proportion of incidents leading to prosecution remains relatively constant, at just over 1 per cent, although a greater proportion of major incidents are now being prosecuted.

One difficulty with the annual published statistics is that they do not include breaches of discharge consents, and it remains the case that most prosecutions are for accidental or other unusual incidents rather than for consistent breaches of consent. This has led to complaints from environmental groups that the NRA (and now the EA) has not taken action against persistent polluters with significant rigour. In this regard, the scope to bring a private prosecution under the Water Resources Act 1991 is important. While little used, its availability remains a threat to dischargers, particularly in the light of the information on the public registers, and it may also be used by environmental groups as a means of registering their disquiet over official inaction over certain discharges. This was the case, for example, when Greenpeace successfully prosecuted Albright & Wilson in 1991, and the threat of a private prosecution following the *Sea Empress* spill may have galvanised the EA into prosecuting (see p. 238).

Owing to the strict liability nature of the offences most prosecutions are successful, although the success rate dropped from 97 per cent in 1993 to 93 per cent in 1997. Also, the level of fines imposed by magistrates is rising. Before the EPA 1990 raised the maximum fine on summary conviction to £20,000 it was £2,000. However, even this was rarely imposed and the average fine in the late 1980s was estimated to be around £250. This has clearly increased since then, most probably as a result of greater publicity of the costs of environmental pollution. The maximum fine was imposed for the first time in 1998, and a fine of over £1000 would be expected in most cases. Another emerging trend is an increased willingness by the EA to bring prosecutions in the Crown Court, where fines may be higher. This has resulted in several large fines, most notably the £4m fine imposed following the *Sea Empress* incident (*Environment Agency* v *Milford Haven Port Authority and Andrews* [1999] 1 Lloyd's Rep 673), a fine which the judge remarked would have been significantly higher had the defendant been a private business. (The fine was later reduced to £750,000 by the Court of Appeal; see further p. 247.) In contrast to waste management offences, scant use has been made of custodial sentences: so far, only one two-month sentence has been imposed for a water pollution offence following an agricultural oil pollution incident (see [1998] Water Law 66).

Access to information

For the first time, the Control of Pollution Act 1974 provided for public registers of a range of environmental information relating to water pollution, although these provisions were not implemented until 1985. Prior to that the system tended to be operated with a fair degree of secrecy about consents and samples taken. The relevant provisions are repeated in the Water Resources Act 1991 with some amendments.

Under s. 190, a public register must be kept by the EA of all applications for consent, consents actually granted, any conditions attached to a consent, and notices of water quality objectives made under s. 83. Prescribed details of authorisations granted for the purposes of integrated pollution control must also be recorded on the water registers. In addition, the results of any samples of the receiving waters or of effluent, and any information produced by analysis of them, must be registered. This requirement is worded more widely than under COPA 1974, and samples taken by *any* person must be registered; this includes samples taken by a discharger as a condition of consent.

Registers must be open for inspection by any member of the public free of charge at all reasonable times, with reasonable facilities for taking copies afforded on payment of a reasonable fee. The Control of Pollution (Applications, Appeals and Registers) Regulations 1996 (SI 1996/2971) specify the detailed shape of the registers. Details of any sample must be entered on the register within two months of the date of the sample.

The public register provides an invaluable database for groups and individuals wishing to monitor water quality. It can be used to mount a private prosecution (as in *Wales* v *Thames Water Authority* (1987) 1(3) *Environmental Law* 3, where the water authority was successfully prosecuted for pollution from a sewage works in reliance on the information which it had itself recorded on the register), or to provide evidence for a civil claim, but its use in providing general information on the state of the water environment is rather limited (see further p. 229). The admissibility of the registers as evidence seems quite clear now that they are kept by the EA (see p. 596).

In addition, s. 204 prohibits the EA or any officer from disclosing information obtained under the Act. Any person who does disclose such information without the permission of the person or company which provided it is guilty of an offence and liable, on summary conviction, to a fine not exceeding £5,000, and on conviction on indictment, to imprisonment for up to two years or an unlimited fine, or both. Of course, this restriction does not apply to matters required to be entered on the register. Nor does it apply to such things as the disclosure of information for criminal proceedings, or in pursuance of an EC obligation, and a range of other matters listed in s. 204. Nor does it apply where a company has ceased trading.

Preventative and remedial powers

In common with other areas of pollution control, the regulatory system which controls water pollution has a range of powers in relation to the prevention of harm. The exercise of these powers is undoubtedly aided by the presence of water quality objectives against which action may be judged. These powers can be used both for consented discharges (where 'enforcement notices' are used) and for activities which are unconsented but where water pollution may need to be prevented (where the EA can either recover the costs of preventing or remedying harm or serve a notice on the responsible person to do so).

(a) Works notices

Under s. 161, the EA has widely drafted powers to prevent pollution incidents where there is a threat of water pollution, to clean up after them and to carry out remedial or restorative works. For example, s. 161 covers such things as diverting a potential pollutant spilt in an accident in order to prevent it from entering a watercourse, cleaning up the effects of a spillage, and restocking a river with fish. Following an amendment made by the Environment Act 1995, s. 60, it also covers investigations into pollution incidents.

The EA can recover the costs incurred in these works, operations or investigations from anyone who has caused or knowingly permitted the pollutant to be present in controlled waters, or who has caused or knowingly permitted the pollutant to be a threat to controlled waters. There is a degree of overlap between these powers and the power to clean up contaminated sites. The Environment Agency has issued guidance on the manner in which each of these powers should be exercised (see further p. 549). There are two exceptions: expenses cannot normally be recovered in relation to waters from an abandoned mine, although this exemption lapsed on 31 December 1999; and these powers cannot be exercised so as to impede or prevent the making of a discharge in pursuance of a consent. In this second case the EA is limited to a consideration of whether the consent should be varied, although there is no power to override the period of immunity against variation merely on the grounds that a discharger has committed a breach or an act of pollution.

Section 161 is mainly used for accidental acts of pollution, although it can be used where there has been a breach of the conditions of a consent (although it is much more likely that the EA would choose to issue an enforcement notice: see below). It is particularly useful because the potential cost may act as a greater deterrent than the threat of prosecution. The costs of a clean-up operation are likely in many cases to be higher than the potential fine. For example, in *National Rivers Authority* v *Shell (UK)* [1990] Water Law 40, Shell was fined £1m for a major leak of oil into the River Mersey, but it has been reported as having paid over £6m in clean-up costs. In *Bruton* v *Clarke* [1994] Water Law 145, a county court case concerning damage to a fishery, the approach to valuing a claim under s. 161 is shown, with the judge limiting the NRA to costs necessarily incurred as a result of the pollution incident and not allowing costs incurred in *improving* the fishery. The case also illustrated that there does not have to be a successful prosecution for s. 161 to be successful. Following criticism by the National Audit Office in 1994 about the low level of cost-recovery, the NRA introduced guidelines in 1995 to standardise and improve cost-recovery. Although the amount obtained in 1998 increased to £1.3m, the number of incidents where there was a recovery of costs fell significantly from the previous year, and costs are recovered following only 18 per cent of incidents, still a low figure considering the EA's stated policy approach that polluters should pay for the consequences of their actions.

The main problem with s. 161 is that it requires the EA to undertake works or operations before recovering the costs, thus adding to uncertainty over the prospect of cost-recovery which can, in turn, mean that the power to carry out works is often not exercised. There are, however, two provisions added by the Environment Act 1995 which allow the EA to require specific works to be undertaken so as to avoid or mitigate a pollution incident. First, where there has been or is likely to be a breach of a discharge consent condition, the EA may serve an *enforcement notice* under s. 90B, Water Resources Act 1991. This must identify the breach (or likely breach), the steps required to remedy the breach and the time within which these must be carried out. Failure to comply with an enforcement notice is an offence and there are the normal rights of appeal (see above). Enforcement notices give the EA another option other than prosecution when faced with a pollution incident. They are also useful in preventing pollution from non-accidental sources and requiring improvements in situations where there is an 'accident waiting to happen'. Secondly, under s. 161A–D, the EA can serve a *works notice* on the appropriate responsible person requiring them to prevent or clean up pollution, unless it is necessary to carry out works 'forthwith' or the polluter cannot be found. Failure to comply with a works notice is an offence (procedural issues are dealt with in the Anti-Pollution Works Regulations 1999, SI 1999/1006). Where there is an overlap with the contaminated land regime, Part IIA of the EPA 1990 should be used, since this is a mandatory provision. This also has the benefit that the contaminated land provisions ought to remediate harm caused to other parts of the environment.

(b)   Other preventive and precautionary tools
There are also other mechanisms which can be used against activities which cannot be consented because they do not generally 'discharge' (e.g. slurry tanks) and which do not necessarily give rise to an immediate risk of harm. In this sense, some of the measures described below might be said to be precautionary rather than merely preventive controls, in the sense that they include measures which, e.g. seek to create what in effect are 'buffer zones' between water pollutants like oil or (in some areas) chemical stores, and controlled waters.

(i)   Precautions against pollution
Under s. 92, the Secretary of State is empowered to make regulations concerning precautions to be taken in relation to any poisonous, noxious or polluting matter to prevent it from entering controlled waters. Such regulations may prevent anyone having custody or control of poisonous, noxious or polluting matter unless the steps required in the regulations or specified by the EA are carried out. These regulations may create additional criminal offences and administrative remedies in relation to breaches, although these may not have penalties higher than for the pollution offences under s. 85.

The Control of Pollution (Silage, Slurry and Agricultural Fuel Oil) Regulations 1991 (SI 1991/324, as amended by SI 1997/547) are, as yet, the only regulations made under s. 92. They introduce precautionary controls over the design and operation of some potentially very polluting activities by imposing specific controls over silage making operations, slurry stores and agricultural fuel oil stores. All new or substantially altered facilities are covered by the new standards (many of which are performance standards rather than strict design requirements), though it is possible for the EA to bring existing activities under control if it is satisfied there is a significant risk of pollution to controlled waters. These regulations have the potential to complement the planning system in preventing pollution problems arising. However, control is exercisable over operational details in a more specific way than is possible through the planning system, oversight and monitoring will be carried out by a more specialist body, and the controls relate to agricultural matters not normally covered by planning powers. A second set of regulations relating to industrial fuel oil stores has been contemplated since 1996. These might usefully tackle the fact that although there has been a steady decrease in oil pollution incidents over this period, oil spills are now the most common source of pollution incident. The Government has recently proposed draft Regulations on this topic, although it is notable that they would not extend to underground tanks (covered by the Groundwater Regulations 1998). However, no new rules on chemical storage have been proposed.

(ii)   Water protection zones
Under s. 93, the Secretary of State may designate water protection zones by order. Such an order may effectively establish a system of local law within the zone with regard to water pollution. Orders under this section may either prohibit or restrict specified activities within the designated zone with a view to preventing or controlling the entry of poisonous, noxious or polluting matter into controlled waters, or provide for a system whereby the EA determine prohibited or restricted activities. It is not possible to require the carrying out of positive works. An order may also include provisions relating to procedures for obtaining consent for such restricted activities from the EA, with criminal sanctions being available for breaches.

The procedure for the making of an order is set out in sch. 11. This requires that the EA must apply for an order by submitting a draft to the Secretary of State. Fairly precise publicity requirements are laid down, including a duty to notify any local authority and water undertaker within the designated area. The Secretary of State may modify the order and has a power (not a duty) to hold a public inquiry before making it. In England, the Secretary of State must consult with the Minister of Agriculture, Fisheries and Food.

Similar provisions were included in COPA 1974 but never used. The first water protection zone was eventually designated in 1999, covering most of the River Dee catchment (Water Protection Zone (River Dee Catchment) Designation Order 1999, SI 1999/915). The order effectively provides for a specialist consent regime within the zone to regulate the storage and use of certain controlled substances by industrial and other processes, although construction sites, retail premises, farms and sites covered by integrated pollution control are excluded. Consents are determined following a risk assessment, and BATNEEC principles apply where there is an appreciable risk of pollution (see the Water Protection Zone (River Dee Catchment) (Procedural and Other Provisions) Regulations 1999, SI 1999/916). It is thought that there will be such a risk in relation to about 100 of the 300 to 500 sites affected. Undertaking activities without a consent or in breach of its conditions is an offence, although by contrast with the strictness of the main water pollution offences there is a 'due diligence' defence, and also rather generous defences of showing genuine lack of knowledge that the activity was being carried on or an excessive amount of substances being kept or used. There are also transitional provisions which effectively deem consent to be given to any ongoing activity. This consent cannot be varied within two years, unless there are changes in circumstances. While generous in places to industry, these provisions should contribute to protecting the catchment from accidental and diffuse discharges such as fertiliser run-off at least cost overall. They also make explicit provision for precautionary consent conditions to apply.

One limitation, in s. 93(3), is that a water protection zone should not concern itself with nitrate from agricultural sources. This is because protection against nitrate is provided for in s. 94: a section which was hurriedly written into the legislation during its passage in response to public worries about nitrate in groundwaters used for water supply and the action against the UK government in the European Court of Justice for non-compliance with EC Directive 80/778 on Drinking Water (see p. 148). From a legal point of view it is difficult to see why the nitrate problem could not have been tackled through the designation of water protection zones, and it is hard to avoid the conclusion that specific nitrate sensitive area provisions are something of a political gesture.

(iii)   Nitrate sensitive areas
The powers in relation to nitrate are set out in s. 94, which provides that an area may be designated a nitrate sensitive area by order with a view to preventing or controlling the entry of nitrate into controlled waters as a result of agriculture. In this case the designation is made by the Secretary of State and the Minister of Agriculture, Fisheries and Food acting jointly if the area is in England, and by the National Assembly for Wales if it is in Wales. An order can only be made if requested by the EA, which must identify controlled waters likely to be affected and the agricultural land likely to result in the entry of nitrate into waters. It must also appear to the EA that its other powers are inadequate to control nitrate pollution before applying for an order. The consent of the Treasury is required before an order is made.

There are two types of order that may be made, respectively imposing voluntary and mandatory controls. Voluntary controls are available where *any* nitrate sensitive area has been designated: the Minister of Agriculture, Fisheries and Food may enter into a management agreement with any owner of an interest in agricultural land, with compensation payable. Such an agreement will bind those deriving title from the original party.

A mandatory order is similar to an order designating a water protection zone. However, there are significant differences. In nitrate sensitive areas the order may require positive obligations, such as the construction of containment walls around agricultural stores, as well as prohibitions and restrictions on activities. If consent is required, it is obtained from the Minister responsible for the designation, not the EA. In addition, the order may provide for compensation to be paid to anyone affected by the obligations. No guidelines on the criteria for awarding compensation are set out in the Act.

The procedure for making a mandatory order is set out in sch. 12. This requires that the EA must apply for an order by submitting a draft to the relevant Minister. Once again, precise publicity requirements are laid down, including a duty to notify any local authority and water undertaker within the designated area, and to notify any owner or occupier appearing to the relevant Minister to be likely to be affected by the compensation provisions. The relevant Minister may modify an order and has a power (not a duty) to hold a public inquiry before making an order.

The Conservative Government made public its intention to use only the voluntary methods initially, in keeping with its stated preference for such methods. It designated 10 pilot areas in the Nitrate Sensitive Areas (Designation) Order 1990 (SI 1990/1013), which provided for two types of scheme, a 'basic scheme' and a 'premium scheme', with more significant restrictions on agricultural operations (and higher payments) available in the latter than in the former. The take-up rate was, in general, good (about 87 per cent of the agricultural land in the 10 areas), but the premium scheme was little used, so the payment rates were increased in an amendment order (SI 1993/3198).

Subsequently a new scheme was introduced in the Nitrate Sensitive Areas Regulations 1994 (SI 1994/1729) and a further 22 areas designated. These regulations are formally made under the European Communities Act 1972, s. 2(2), to comply with the EC Agri-Environment Regulation 2078/92, and thus technically concern the de-intensification of agriculture rather than pollution control. They provide for various schemes under which farmers are required to give undertakings as to their farming operations for a period of five years in return for payments of specified amounts per hectare per year. It is significant that the payment rates have been revised during the five years. In line with reforms to the Common Agriculture Policy, the regulations have been modified so that new applicants must show that participation in the scheme will be of 'unquestionable environmental benefit' (SI 1998/2138). However, because all nitrate sensitive areas are in NVZs (see below), the scheme has been closed to new applicants since 1998 (highlighting its essentially discretionary nature).

(iv)   Nitrate vulnerable zones

Although the Nitrate Sensitive Areas Regulations 1994 (as amended) represent a fairly sophisticated response to nitrate pollution in designated areas, they are insufficient to comply with Directive 91/676 on Nitrates, which has more programmatic objectives (see p. 569). As a result, the Protection of Water against Agricultural and Nitrate Pollution (England and Wales) Regulations 1996 (SI 1996/888) were introduced. The regulations designate Nitrate Vulnerable Zones (NVZs) in specific areas where there are excessive levels of nitrate pollution from agricultural sources. Following consultation,

68 NVZs were designated on the basis that nitrate levels were either above Drinking Water Directive levels (for surface water) or in the case of groundwater in excess of 50mg/l. The EA is under a duty to monitor nitrate levels so that designations can be continuously assessed and revised (see below). The Secretary of State must then draw up action plans for each NVZ which are designed to reduce and prevent water pollution from nitrates and agricultural sources (see Action Programmes for Nitrate Vulnerable Zones (England and Wales) Regulations 1998, SI 1998/1202).

Two crucial differences between nitrate sensitive areas and NVZs are that the latter are always mandatory, and there is no prospect of compensation payments for farmers in NVZs. This helps explain the concerns raised by many farmers to the designations, which culminated in a legal challenge in Case C-293/97 *R* v *Secretary of State for the Environment and Minister of Agriculture, Fisheries and Food, ex parte Standley* [1999] Env LR 801. The main ground of challenge was that the government, when drawing up the NVZs, had failed to consider whether the excessive nitrate levels were caused by non-agricultural sources. It was argued, on behalf of the farmers, that this failure discriminated against agricultural users in the NVZ as the cost of reducing the nitrate concentrations to an acceptable level was to be borne wholly by the farmers when there were other users which may have been responsible for the nitrate pollution. The case was referred to the European Court of Justice, which upheld the approach of the Government in identifying waters where agricultural sources made a 'sufficient contribution' to excessive nitrate levels, in line with a purposive interpretation of the Directive. Indeed, the Court hinted that something rather less than a significant contribution might have been enough, showing the amount of freedom that Member States have. This flexibility is also seen in the Court's rejection of an argument that the UK violated the 'polluter pays' principle (see now Article 174(2), EC Treaty), since the Directive had sufficient room to ensure that action programmes targeted the contribution of farmers proportionate to those of other polluters. (The Directive says little about how such other sources are to be regulated, although other sources like sewage treatment works will probably be subject to duties to reduce nitrate pollution under measures like the Urban Waste Water Treatment Directive, under which sensitive areas have been designated because of risks from nitrate (see [1997] Water Law 61).) One danger with flexibility here, though, is that it might be used to implement the Directive minimally. There are concerns that the area covered by NVZs in the UK is too small: by contrast, the whole of the Netherlands, Denmark and Germany have been designated and, partly in response to Commission action, the designation of zones in the UK is currently under review.

Overlapping controls

(a) Land use planning controls
Local planning authorities have the ability to make important decisions relating to water pollution through the town and country planning system.

However, it is clearly recommended in central government guidance, such as Circular 11/95 on planning conditions and Planning Policy Guidance Note 23, *Planning and Pollution Control* (PPG 23), that planning powers should be used mainly for locational and siting decisions and that matters about the regulation of pollution should be left to the specialist regulators to control through the specialist consent systems.

It is clear that potential water pollution arising from a proposed development is a material consideration in any planning decision, and the EA is a statutory consultee under the General Development Procedure Order in relation to many applications for planning permission. This is of great importance in relation to groundwaters, since the NRA published a set of very strong policy statements on the protection of groundwater (*Policy and Practice for the Protection of Groundwater*, NRA, 1992). In addition, planning permission may be refused because of inadequate sewerage in the area. Of course, the EA will also have an important role to play in the making of development plans. The generous exemptions for agricultural activities and buildings may be of significance in the context of increasing evidence of water pollution by agriculture.

It is notable that specific regulations governing certain abstractions of water which may have environmentally harmful effects are being drafted for which the Environment Agency would be the competent authority (these should have been made by 14 March 1999, under the revised EIA Directive). However, there is nothing comparable as regards water quality, with the result that in relation to environmental impact assessment and water quality matters, the EA is only ever a consultee in the assessment process.

(b) Integrated pollution control

There are separate controls for those processes prescribed for Part I of the Environmental Protection Act 1990 (i.e. those processes subject to integrated pollution control) and processes for which an IPPC permit is required. Acting in accordance with an IPC authorisation or IPPC permit will be a defence to the water pollution offences under s. 85 of the Water Resources Act 1991 (see generally Chapter 13).

(c) Radioactive discharges

Under the Control of Pollution (Radioactive Waste) Regulations 1989 (SI 1989/1158), the radioactivity of a discharge is to be ignored for the purposes of the Water Resources Act 1991. In other words, the non-radioactive elements of a discharge or entry are dealt with under the Water Resources Act 1991 and the radioactive elements under the Radioactive Substances Act 1993 by the EA.

(d) Statutory nuisances

In addition to the statutory nuisances listed in Part III of the EPA 1990 (see p. 435), two further statutory nuisances are provided for in the Public Health Act 1936, s. 259. Section 259(1)(a) provides that any pool, pond, ditch, gutter or watercourse which is in a state that is prejudicial to health or a nuisance is a statutory nuisance. This will cover small ponds and ditches which are not within the consent system, as well as controlled waters although not estuarial or coastal waters (*R* v *Falmouth and Truro Port Health Authority, ex parte South West Water Ltd* [2000] NPC 36). Section 259(1)(b) covers any watercourse which is silted up or choked so as to obstruct the proper flow of water and thus causing a nuisance or which is prejudicial to health. This is limited to watercourses which are not normally navigated. The normal procedures for statutory nuisance apply to these situations, thus creating an alternative course of action for a local authority or individual wishing to clean up a grossly polluted watercourse.

Water pollution and private law controls

Private law controls still play a significant role in the control of water pollution. Indeed, for various technical reasons they are probably of greater use for water pollution than for other forms of pollution and may be used to produce, directly or indirectly, environmental improvements although they have at best a limited strategic role.

One right which has already been mentioned is the right of private prosecution for breaches of the criminal law. This has been available for many water pollution offences since 1985 as a result of the removal by COPA 1974 of the restrictions on it. More significant, however, are the various civil law claims that may be brought. For example, the Anglers' Conservation Association is estimated to have been involved in over 1,000 cases involving water pollution since the Second World War. The two main remedies available are damages to compensate an owner of the river bed, the river banks, or a fishery for any losses caused, and an injunction to restrain future breaches of the law.

It is important to note that acting within the terms of a discharge consent does not act as a defence to a civil action, since the private law system operates separately from the public regulatory mechanisms. This is made explicit in the Water Resources Act 1991, s. 100(b), but it can also be implied from the important decision in *Wheeler* v *J.J. Saunders Ltd* [1996] Ch 19, which decided that a planning permission cannot license what is otherwise a nuisance (see further p. 284).

There are a number of reasons why water pollution cases have proved easier to bring than e.g. air pollution cases:

(a) Causation is easier to show because of the defined channels in which water normally flows.

(b) Many rural landowners have the money to bring an action: indeed, pollution to fisheries will often justify an action in commercial terms.

(c) There are a number of campaigning and amenity bodies concerned with water problems, far more than are concerned with air (or noise) pollution.

(d) The acquisition of evidence is more straightforward, particularly since the advent of the public registers, which may provide evidence relating to the quality of the receiving waters before and after an incident and also relating to discharges. Nevertheless there are areas of scientific uncertainty, such as whether nitrate loading leads to entrophication.

(a) Riparian rights

The usefulness of the civil law in this area stems mainly from the nature of riparian rights. Owners of land adjoining a watercourse (including estuaries), termed riparian owners, normally own the river bed, but not the water itself. However, as a natural incident of the soil itself, they have the right to receive the water in its natural state, subject only to reasonable usage by an upstream owner for ordinary purposes (*Chasemore* v *Richards* (1859) 7 HL Cas 349). Owners of other property rights such as fisheries have the same right.

The most authoritative statement of this principle was given by Lord Macnaghten in *John Young & Co.* v *Bankier Distillery Co.* [1893] AC 691. He stated, at p. 698:

> A riparian proprietor is entitled to have the water of the stream, on the bank of which his property lies, flow down as it has been accustomed to flow down to his property, subject to the ordinary use of the flowing water by upper proprietors, and to such further use, if any, on their part in connection with their property as may be reasonable in the circumstances. Every riparian owner is thus entitled to the water of his stream, in its natural flow, without sensible diminution or increase, and without sensible alteration in its character or quality.

This means that any interference with the natural quantity or quality of the water is an actionable nuisance. The strictness of this test was shown in *John Young & Co.* v *Bankier Distillery Co.* An upstream mineowner discharged water into a stream from a mine. This altered the chemistry of the water from soft to hard and thus altered the quality of the downstream distillery's whisky. The water had not been made impure, but the distillery obtained an injunction because the nature of the water had been changed. The case illustrates the relative nature of the definition of water pollution and indeed emphasises that the common law does not lay down any absolute standards in relation to water quality. It is worth noting, however, that this test only applies where the upstream usage is not ordinary; a good example of the balancing process the law of nuisance tries to carry out.

Some of the technical difficulties relating to the law of nuisance, such as the causation question and the locality doctrine, have been neatly answered in the water pollution cases. It appears from the reasoning in *Young & Co.* v *Bankier Distillery Co.* (above) that an invasion of the natural right to water is treated as equivalent to damage to land, thus circumventing the locality doctrine. It is also clear that actual harm need not be shown, merely a 'sensible alteration', a position that is supported by *Nicholls* v *Ely Beet Sugar Factory Ltd* [1936] Ch 343, where the claim of interference with riparian rights was held to be analogous to trespass. It follows that an action can be brought against any upstream polluter, even if only one of many and responsible for only a part of the whole pollution. All that needs to be shown is that the polluter is contributing to the pollution (*Crossley and Sons Ltd* v *Lightowler* (1867) LR 2 Ch App 478).

(b) Pollution of groundwater

Liability may also arise in nuisance for polluting percolating groundwaters, as long as causation can be shown. This was first established in *Ballard* v *Tomlinson* (1885) 29 ChD 115, where a brewery successfully sued for the contamination of its well caused by a neighbour who used his own well for the disposal of sewage. However, the extent of this liability was clarified in *Cambridge Water Co.* v *Eastern Counties Leather plc* [1994] 2 AC 264, a case discussed in detail on p. 261. As explained there, the House of Lords took the opportunity to move the law of nuisance and the law under the rule in *Rylands* v *Fletcher* towards negligence, by requiring the defendant to show that the type of damage that occurred was foreseeable. *Ballard* v *Tomlinson*, where forseeability did not arise, was distinguished. This decision satisfied those whose primary concern was with avoiding the prospect of retrospective civil liability, but disappointed those commentators who argued for the primacy of strict liability in the civil law of water pollution as a reflection of the polluter pays principle.

The decision also casts great doubt on whether there is anything particularly strict about liability for groundwater pollution law any more, at least as far as liability for past activities is concerned. However, it does not necessarily restrict the recovery of damages, or the imposition of an injunction, in cases where polluting activities currently cause damage to groundwaters or, indeed, where the cause of the pollution was recent. It must be pointed out that liability in nuisance is personal in the sense that, even if the original polluter is liable for pollution damage, it does not follow that a subsequent purchaser of the site would also be liable. But, purchasers of potentially contaminated land must bear in mind the possible implications of cases such as *Goldman* v *Hargrave* [1967] 1 AC 645, which establish that there is liability for 'adopting' a nuisance in certain circumstances. A final point worth making is that, unlike riparian rights, there is no right to any particular *quantity* of groundwater, which reduces the potency of private law to protect groundwaters and seems to make something of a nonsense of private law here in terms of its coherence.

(c) Other claims

Other common law claims may also be available. In *Jones* v *Llanrwst Urban District Council* [1911] 1 Ch 393, the owner of a river bed claimed successfully in trespass for deposits of solid wastes. In restricted cases, a claim in negligence might also be upheld (see further p. 268).

In the context of water pollution, the High Court has struck out a claim under breach of statutory duty following damage to shellfish beds which the claimant alleged were attributed to unlawful acts of a sewerage undertaker, holding that such claims had to be pursued in public law (*Bowden* v *South West Water Services Ltd* [1998] Env LR 445). In a follow up to this case (reported at [1999] Env LR 438), however, the Court of Appeal allowed the claimant to pursue a claim based on liability against the state (a '*Francovich*' claim; see p. 141 above) because of the extent to which the Directive on Shellfish Waters (79/923) might be said to confer rights on individual shellfishermen. However, similar claims under the Urban Waste Treatment Waters Directive (91/271) and the Bathing Waters Directive (76/160) were rejected because the claimant could not say that he derived individual rights under them. This decision gives a good indication of the extent to which the need to prove an individual right to take a state liability claim may, in practice, mean showing that an individual economic interest might be infringed, rather than appealing to any wider environmental interests, limiting such claims to quite narrow classes of claimants.

Lastly, it is often stated that a prescriptive right to acquire an easement to pollute can be acquired. Whilst this remains true as a matter of principle, such an occurrence will be rare because it is not possible to acquire a prescriptive right where the act relied upon to gain the right is illegal. In most water pollution cases the polluting activity will be illegal.

(d) Remedies
Damages will be recoverable for any loss to the person whose rights have been infringed. This will include such things as any clean-up costs, the cost of restocking the water with fish, any loss of profits from subscriptions for such things as fishing rights and, in some circumstances, loss of amenity (see *Bruton* v *Clarke* [1994] Water Law 145).

Injunctions are also available for water pollution, though they will normally be suspended to allow the defendants time to correct matters. For example, in *Pride of Derby and Derbyshire Angling Association Ltd* v *British Celanese Ltd* [1953] Ch 149, injunctions and damages were obtained against British Celanese Ltd (for industrial effluent), Derby Corporation (for untreated sewage), and the British Electricity Authority (for thermal pollution from a power station).

TWENTY

Disposal of waste to sewers

In this book disposals of waste to the sewerage system are dealt with in a self-contained chapter because they are a separate form of waste disposal with their own particular and unique regulatory regime. The treatment of wastes at sewage works is an integral part of general policies on waste disposal and protection of the natural environment. The alternative to such disposal (waste minimisation apart) is often some form of direct discharge to the environment, so sewage treatment offers an important weapon in the search for the best practicable environmental option (BPEO).

There are other links with environmental protection that justify detailed consideration of sewage disposal. Sewage treatment is only an intermediate step in the ultimate disposal of waste and the operators of sewers and sewage works must dispose of their own wastes. This will often (though not always) be after a treatment process and will involve a combination of liquid discharges into watercourses or the sea, the dumping of sludge on land and incineration. Indeed, sewage works have been responsible for the low quality of many of our inland and coastal waters (see *The Quality of Rivers, Canals and Estuaries in England and Wales,* NRA, 1991). The Government announced a commitment to phase out the dumping of sewage sludge at sea by 1998 at the Third International Conference for the Protection of the North Sea in March 1990 (an obligation later contained in the Urban Waste Water Treatment Directive (91/271): see p. 568).

Sewerage and sewage treatment have always been closely related with the water industry and most books have tended to treat discharges to sewers as a part of the law on water pollution. This can be explained on the grounds that discharges to sewers are liquid and that most sewage works themselves discharge into watercourses, but it also relates to the historical institutional connections. Sewerage, public water supply and the prevention of water pollution have often been carried out by the same bodies, most notably between 1974 and 1989 when the 10 regional water authorities in England and Wales carried out all functions in relation to water and sewage on an integrated basis. This included regulating discharges both to the sewers and to surface waters.

Since 1 September 1989 there has been a reversion to a system of split responsibilities for liquid effluent. Private sewerage undertakers own and operate the sewerage network and the sewage works, as well as regulating discharges to sewers, whilst the EA (originally the NRA) regulates discharges to the natural environment and has responsibility for combating surface water pollution.

Trade effluent discharges

The sewerage undertaker plays its most important environmental protection role in the regulation of trade effluent discharges, although since 1989 certain dangerous discharges have been regulated by HMIP and now the EA (see below). Measured in terms of pollutant load, a far greater quantity of industrial effluent is discharged into the sewers than directly into surface waters or by any other disposal route.

The regulatory regime relating to discharges to sewers is an old and somewhat rudimentary one, though there have been periodic developments designed to bring it more up-to-date. It involves a rather basic system of individualised consents set by the operators of the sewers, involving little input from other bodies or from the public at any of the various stages of policy-making, standard-setting, consent-setting or enforcement. The legislation is contained in the Water Industry Act 1991, to which all section numbers refer.

It is a criminal offence to discharge any trade effluent from trade premises into sewers unless a trade effluent consent is obtained from the sewerage undertaker (s. 118). 'Trade effluent' and 'trade premises' are defined widely in s. 141 to include all liquid discharges from industry, shops, research establishments, launderettes and agriculture, except for domestic sewage. It is also an offence to breach the terms of a consent. This is a unique system of control in that it is the only example in this country of a private body exercising regulatory functions with regard to environmental protection.

Applying for a trade effluent consent

The discharger applies for a trade effluent consent by serving a trade effluent notice on the sewerage undertaker at least two months prior to the commencement of the discharge. This notice is effectively an application and must state the nature and composition of the proposed effluent, the maximum daily volume and the maximum rate of discharge in order to enable the sewerage undertaker to establish its likely effect.

The sewerage undertaker then has a discretion whether to grant or refuse consent, though if the sewerage system can cope with the discharge, it is normal for consent to be granted subject to conditions. The scope of these conditions is laid down in s. 121. They may include such matters as the place of discharge, the nature, temperature and composition of the discharge (including requirements as to the elimination or maximum concentration of any specified constituent), the rate and timing of discharges, and ancillary matters such as the fixing of meters to register the volume of the discharge, the monitoring of the nature and volume of the discharge and the keeping of records. Most importantly, conditions on the payment of effluent charges will also be included. Conditions must be imposed to meet the requirements of sch. 4 to the Urban Waste Water Treatment (England and Wales) Regulations 1994 (SI 1994/2841), although it appears in practice that there is little discretion in doing so (see p. 579).

It is not usual to attach conditions which require the fitting of specified treatment plant. The normal practice has been to specify the effluent standards that must be met and to leave it to the discharger to determine how to meet those standards, albeit often with advice from the sewerage undertaker. One reason for this has been a widespread belief that most effluent is better and more efficiently treated at the sewage works than at each factory, but it also reflects the policy of preserving some element of choice for producers. An impact of the Urban Waste Water Treatment Directive, however, is that the increased cost of treating effluent to the higher standards required is being reflected in much higher trade effluent charges; as a result, many more firms are likely to do more pre-treatment work at their sites to lower their costs.

How are consents set?

Since discharges to sewers are distinct from other discharges in being to an artificial environment, the matters that are taken into account in setting a consent differ from other consents and licences. In particular, environmental protection is only one factor.

The objectives of trade effluent control are set out clearly in a booklet produced by the Water Authorities Association in September 1986 entitled *Trade Effluent Discharged to the Sewer*. They are that the system of control seeks:

(a)   to protect the sewerage system and the personnel who work in it;
(b)   to protect the sewage works and their efficient operation (for example, most sewage works operate by a biological process and care has to be taken not to neutralise that process);
(c)   to protect the environment generally from the residues of the sewage treatment process or from direct discharges from parts of the system such as storm drains; and
(d)   to ensure that dischargers pay a reasonable charge for the cost of the treatment.

In addition, the booklet stresses that it is important for correct information on discharges to be kept, so that dischargers can know how to improve their trade effluent control and sewerage undertakers can plan for future sewerage provision and operate the treatment process efficiently.

With these factors in mind, the consent will in general be set by reference to the receiving capabilities of the sewer and sewage works. If the works are already overburdened, the consent may be refused or subject to tight limits, whereas if there is spare capacity at the works, the limits will be much more generous. Certain pollutants, such as heavy metals or persistent chemicals, may be unsuitable for sewage treatment and may be banned from the discharge. The discharger may then have to pre-treat the effluent to remove these constituents, or find an alternative method of disposal. Other relevant matters are taken into account, such as the sewerage undertaker's own potential liability for discharges from the works under the Water Resources Act 1991 and the requirements of EC law.

The sewerage undertaker has a power to vary a consent unilaterally by giving two months' notice to the discharger (s. 124). This enables it to take steps to meet the terms of the consent for the sewage works set by the EA. Since 1989, variation has been a common occurrence, as sewerage undertakers have renegotiated consents inherited from the regional water authorities and established a more uniform system for their areas and also as, formerly, the NRA and now the EA tightened consents relating to discharges from sewage works. It should be noted, however, that there is no power for the sewerage undertaker to revoke a consent.

Variation of a consent is, however, possible only after two years have elapsed from the grant of the consent or the last variation. Exceptionally, a variation may be made within this period if it is necessary to provide proper protection for people likely to be affected by the discharge. In this situation, compensation will be payable to the discharger unless the variation was necessary as a result of a change of circumstances unforeseeable at the time of the grant of the consent or its last variation (s. 125). A variation can be made on environmental grounds to comply with the Urban Waste Water Treatment Regulations 1994 (SI 1994/2841, reg. 7(6)). In this case, no compensation is payable.

The discharger has a right of appeal to the Director General of Water Services (i.e. to OFWAT) against a refusal or variation of consent or the imposition of conditions, except that there is no appeal against trade effluent charges (ss. 122, 126). An appeal against a deemed refusal may also be brought if no decision is given on the trade effluent notice within two months. (It used to be the case that such a failure to determine an application led to an automatic consent, but that rule was removed by the Water Act 1989.) As with planning appeals, an appeal is effectively a rehearing and the Director General may make any decision that the sewerage undertaker could have made. There is a further right of appeal to the High Court on a matter of law. The right of appeal being to the economic regulator emphasises the essentially commercial nature of the arrangement.

An alternative to seeking a consent is for the discharger and the sewerage undertaker to reach an agreement for the reception or disposal of trade effluent under s. 129. Such an agreement may provide for the discharger to pay for works necessary to treat the wastes, such as an extension to a sewage works.

Trade effluent charges

Trade effluent charges are levied for discharges to sewers and a charges scheme may be made under the Water Industry Act 1991, s. 143. (Under

their terms of appointment, sewerage undertakers must always have such a
scheme in force.) All the sewerage undertakers currently use a similar formula
based on the so-called 'Mogden Formula', in which charges are calculated
according to the volume and strength of the effluent, as measured by the
chemical oxygen demand (COD) and the solids content. Dischargers are
therefore advised to consider whether their processes can be changed so as to
minimise wastes, and thus costs. No extra charges are currently levied by the
sewerage undertakers in relation to metals or other hazardous items: undesirable levels of these are controlled by the consent limits rather than by
charging mechanisms. However, levels of charges are rising fast as a consequence of the fact that sewerage undertakers are themselves liable for charges
for their own discharges from sewage works. The charging system thus
operates in tandem with the consent system to reduce discharges. To a
limited extent it encourages the reduction of pollution, although it does not
make dischargers fully responsible for the environmental costs of their
discharges. It remains to be seen whether a system of incentive charging will
be introduced in this area: that would require legislation.

Public participation

Public rights in relation to the trade effluent system are very limited. There
is no right for a member of the public to be informed of an application for a
trade effluent consent and no right to participate in the decision whether to
grant one, or in any appeal. Under the Water Industry Act 1991, s. 196, all
consents, variations, agreements and directions by the sewerage undertaker
or the Director General, and all decisions by the Secretary of State (effectively
the EA in this context) must be placed on a public register.

However, this is a limited right, since there is no public right to information
on any samples taken. Indeed, it is a criminal offence under s. 206 for an
employee of the sewerage undertaker to disclose information furnished under
the Act. There is also no right of private prosecution for breach of a consent,
except by a 'person aggrieved' or with the consent of the Attorney-General.
Uncertainty over the application of the Environmental Information Regulations 1992 (SI 1992/3240) to sewerage undertakers, and to sewers, has posed
problems for conferring wider rights (see p. 225).

'Red List' substances

In order to ensure compliance with EC directives, such as 76/464 on
Dangerous Substances in Water, an additional control has been introduced
for specified dangerous substances. The Secretary of State is empowered to
prescribe certain substances or processes for which the EA is effectively made
the consenting body. Currently 24 such substances are listed in sch. 1 to the
Trade Effluents (Prescribed Processes and Substances) Regulations 1989 (SI
1989/1156, as amended by SI 1990/1629), and five processes involving
asbestos or chloroform are listed in sch. 2. The 24 prescribed substances
consist of the 'Red List' (a dangerous substance list similar to the EC 'black

list' — see p. 565 — but with origins in the OSPAR treaty regime), plus carbon tetrachloride.

All discharges where any of these substances is present in more than background concentration, or where a prescribed process is carried on (often known collectively as 'special category effluent'), must be referred to the EA, which may then issue a direction (against which there is no appeal) to the sewerage undertaker on whether to grant a consent and on any conditions it might impose. Before deciding an application, the EA must provide the sewerage undertaker and the applicant with an opportunity to make representations. The same procedures apply where more than 30 kg per year of trichloroethylene or perchloroethylene is discharged (Trade Effluent (Prescribed Processes and Substances) Regulations (SI 1992/339)).

Existing discharges covered by the regulations are also reviewable by the EA. As with ordinary trade effluent discharges, a review may not normally be made within two years of the previous review. However, review is possible within two years if there has been a contravention of a consent or agreement, to give effect to an international or EC obligation, or to protect public health or aquatic flora and fauna. Compensation is payable in some of these circumstances, unless the review resulted from a change of circumstances unforeseeable at the time of the setting of the consent or the previous review.

Any process discharging significant amounts of 'Red List' substances will normally be a prescribed process for the purposes of integrated pollution control under Part I of the EPA 1990 and therefore require an authorisation from the EA. This is in addition to the trade effluent consent that will also be required. In relation to further processes regulated under the IPPC Directive (96/61) and the Pollution Prevention and Control Act 1999, it remains to be seen whether these will be treated as releases into 'the environment'. It is also unclear how the Directive duty to avoid waste production is tempered by the power to take any effluent treatment into account if there is an indirect discharge to water (see Chapter 13).

Enforcement

The penalty for the offence of discharging into a sewer without consent, or in breach of a condition, is, on summary conviction, a fine not exceeding £5,000, and on conviction on indictment, an unlimited fine (ss. 118, 121). It is possible for the same unlawful event to lead both to this offence, and to a water pollution offence under the Water Resources Act 1991. But only the actual occupier of the premises can be found guilty of the former.

There are no 'enforcement notice'— type provisions here. Enforcement of the legislation is by the sewerage undertaker so this would mean one company dictating operational matters to another company. In the past this has led to a conciliatory approach to enforcement, since officials have seen themselves as problem-solvers rather than as police officers. One of the main surveys of enforcement attitudes (Richardson, Ogus and Burrows, *Policing Pollution*, Clarendon, 1983) was a survey of trade effluent control officers.

Discharges from sewage works

Under the Water Resources Act 1991, sewerage undertakers have consents set for their own discharges into controlled waters and may be prosecuted by the EA or any individual if they breach them. They are responsible for all discharges from their sewers or works, subject only to a defence that the breach was caused by an illegal discharge to the sewer that they could not reasonably have been expected to prevent (Water Resources Act 1991, s. 87(2) and *National Rivers Authority* v *Yorkshire Water Services Ltd* [1995] 1 AC 444). This means that sewerage undertakers are ultimately responsible if they are unable to treat adequately discharges they have permitted. They thus have an incentive to restrict discharges to those which are treatable.

Domestic sewage discharges

Some discharges are prohibited entirely by the Water Industry Act 1991, s. 111 (although a trade effluent consent is a defence). These are discharges of anything liable to damage the sewer, or to stop its flow, or to prejudice the sewage works treatment; any chemicals, or any liquids over 110°F, which will be dangerous or a nuisance; and any petroleum spirit, including motor oils. For example, drainage of used car oils is an offence under this section. The maximum penalties are, on summary conviction, a fine of up to £5,000, and, on conviction on indictment, an unlimited fine and/or up to two years imprisonment.

Otherwise, there is no restriction on discharges of domestic sewage. There is a right of connection to the public sewer conferred on owners and occupiers by the Water Industry Act 1991, s. 106, with very limited powers of refusal. These do not include the potential overloading of the system: as Upjohn J stated in *Smeaton* v *Ilford Corporation* [1954] Ch 450, 'they [i.e. the sewerage undertakers] are bound to permit occupiers of premises to make connections to the sewer and to discharge their sewage therein'. Indeed, the duty has been held to require connections notwithstanding that the sewer is already over-loaded, with obvious consequences (*Tayside Regional Council* v *Secretary of State for Scotland* [1996] SLT 473, concerning near identical provisions to s. 106 in the Sewerage (Scotland) Act 1968, s. 12). The counterpart of this duty is the restriction on criminal liability for water pollution caused by sewage which the undertaker must accept (see above, and p. 589). Powers to requisition new sewers for domestic purposes are set out in the Water Industry Act 1991, s. 98.

However, it is permissible for the local planning authority to refuse planning permission on the ground that the local sewage works are overburdened or inadequate, since that is a material consideration. Alternatively, it could seek some planning gain in relation to the provision of sewers by the use of conditions or planning obligations under the Town and Country Planning Act 1990 (see Chapter 11 for the limitations on this course of action).

TWENTY-ONE
The conservation of nature

This chapter looks at the laws that aim specifically to protect plants, animals and habitats. This has become a popular subject in recent years, for a variety of reasons. These include increasing interest in all things connected with nature and conservation, and alarm at the appalling rate of decline in and loss of the natural environment. But also relevant is a keener scientific and cultural (and even economic) appreciation of the importance of conserving biological diversity (or biodiversity), that is, diversity within and between species and of ecosystems, or quite simply, the diversity of life on earth. But it is also a controversial policy area. The Wildlife and Countryside Act 1981, the major piece of legislation in this area, still holds the record for the number of amendments tabled to a Parliamentary Bill. However, it is arguable that the debate may be shifting slightly away from *whether* resources and environmental space should be found for species and habitats, to *how* this can be achieved without undue restrictions on private property rights.

At the outset, a distinction must be made between nature conservation and matters of amenity and landscape, which are dealt with in Chapter 22. Traditionally, it has been possible to distinguish between those laws that are justified as a matter of straight wildlife protection and those which relate to management of the environment for more aesthetic or cultural reasons. But doing so is becoming less easy: there is an increasing integration of conservation and landscape matters both at an institutional level (the Countryside Council for Wales and Scottish Natural Heritage combine conservation and landscape functions) and at policy level (such as the use of 'Character Areas' like the Surrey Heaths, or chalk downland, where conservation, landscape and recreational objectives are pursued collectively). And often the substantive law tries to protect both the natural and cultural heritage, as the Hedgerows Regulations 1997 (discussed on p. 678) demonstrate. It must also be borne in mind that the effective conservation of biodiversity depends as much on the responses to the other environmental threats covered in this book, such as pollution and development, as on the specific methods of protection mentioned in this chapter, which would probably be useless if applied in isolation.

A final point is that this chapter proceeds through discussion of what are considered to be the key nature conservation provisions at national and EC level, before ending with a brief analysis of international treaty law. This ordering is to help explain the development of both the law and policy in this area. The coverage of international conservation law is of course not comprehensive, but is intended to illustrate how this level of law operates and its impact closer to the ground at national and EC level.

The history and development of controls

A brief history of nature conservation will help to explain the current structure of the law. Until the nineteenth century, the need to protect wildlife was normally perceived solely in human terms, such as the desirability of preserving game and quarry species and protected areas in which to hunt them. There is little doubt that an incidental benefit of this human-centred approach was the protection of other animals and plants and the preservation of whole areas (for example the New Forest) in a fairly natural state, but there were few laws designed specifically to protect wildlife.

(a)   Early controls

From Victorian times, the tendency was to enact legislation outlawing unwelcome activities in response to particular problems as they were identified. The rationale for this intervention was as much based on concern about cruelty as on any positive desire to conserve nature for its own sake. Some good examples are the Sea Birds Protection Acts of 1869, 1872 and 1880, passed to combat the slaughter of birds at places such as Flamborough Head, and various pieces of legislation intended to restrict the international trade in feathers for clothing and hats. However, there was no grand design underlying these restrictions. The weight of conservation fell on voluntary organisations — indeed Britain had the world's first developed conservation movement — and no official bodies were established to monitor or enforce the legislation that did exist. This unplanned approach persisted; the Protection of Birds Act 1954, which established protection for birds that was far stronger than that for other animals and plants, was a Private Member's Bill brought forward on behalf of the Royal Society for the Protection of Birds.

These voluntary organisations gradually developed a strategy which became, and remains, the typical approach to nature conservation. This is the designation of selected areas or sites that are specially protected. The first modern uses of this technique related to the protection of common lands for recreational purposes, but it was soon used for the development of nature reserves, even though at this time they were seen as a somewhat peripheral interest of the nature conservation movement. For example, the National Trust acquired parts of Wicken Fen in 1899, the Norfolk Naturalists Trust was founded to buy Cley Marshes in 1926 and the Royal Society for the Protection of Birds bought its first nature reserve (on Romney Marsh) in 1929. However, in the absence of any legislative protection for such sites, their safety lay in the exercise of ordinary property rights. After all, the property owner's freedom to exclude others and to use the land for any purposes is one mechanism for controlling land use in limited areas. The limitations of this approach are well illustrated by the RSPB's first reserve, which had to be abandoned when drainage activities on neighbouring land destroyed its natural interest.

(b)   The post-war period

After 1945, the site designation approach was adopted as a matter of national policy. The beginning of the modern age of nature conservation can be traced to that time in the publication of two influential reports, *Conservation of Nature in England and Wales* from the Wildlife Conservation Special Committee (the Huxley Committee, Cmd 7122) and *Nature Reserves in Scotland* from the Scottish Wild Life Conservation Committee (the Ritchie Committee, Cmd 7184), many (though not all) of whose recommendations were accepted and acted upon.

A specialist national nature conservation body — the Nature Conservancy — was established and one of its main roles was to create a series of protected sites across the nation, rather than the somewhat random series produced by private acquisition. The two main habitat protection measures, the national nature reserve (NNR) and the site of special scientific interest (SSSI), both date from this period. The scientific basis of nature conservation was emphasised and it was linked firmly to education and research on the natural environment. Nature conservation was also split from amenity, recreation and landscape matters, which were given their own separate institutions and laws, and it is worth reflecting that the powers for nature conservation at that time were both stronger and met with far less opposition than those for recreation in the countryside. However, nature conservation law was intimately bound up with two key Acts from this period dealing with the promotion of agriculture (the Agriculture Act 1947) and with development control (the Town and Country Planning Act 1947, which excluded agricultural land use from the meaning of 'development'). Together, they reflected the view that the main threat to nature was from urban sprawl, rather than from changing agricultural practices, and set the scene for the decades ahead.

(c)   Current policy

Many of the features of this structure remain, but the climate in which they operate has changed radically, with the result that many of the similarities the current system has with that structure are illusory. There have been devastating changes in both the urban and rural environments and these have altered the role of site designation dramatically from an educational to a safeguarding one. One result has been the expansion of the NNR and SSSI system way beyond that envisaged, or indeed considered necessary, by the Huxley and Ritchie Committees, in order to ensure that at least a basic pool of key sites is protected.

Another result is that general environmental awareness has now shifted the focus of policy away from the designation and protection of certain key sites towards the protection of the wider countryside. It is now accepted that there is little future in having isolated and ever-decreasing areas of protected wildlife in an otherwise barren countryside, and so nature conservation is increasingly seen as a factor to weigh in the balance when considering all rural policies. This adds to the political dimension which nature conservation has rapidly acquired. It also leads nature conservation law into a potential head-on collision with traditional views of property and personal rights.

In addition, the enjoyment of nature has emerged as a major leisure pursuit, blurring the distinction in the public mind and in policy between nature conservation as a scientifically justified discipline and as a recreation. There has been an undreamt-of increase in voluntary activity in relation to the countryside, resulting in large numbers of reserves and sites protected by voluntary bodies and non-statutory designations.

(d) The impact of EC and international law
There has been a significant increase in international activity on nature conservation. This has been through treaties such as the Ramsar Convention on Wetlands of International Importance (1971) and the Washington Convention on International Trade in Endangered Species (1973, usually known as CITES), which have put considerable pressure on the government to carry out internationally agreed policies. Conventions like the Bonn Convention on the Conservation of Migratory Species of Wild Animals and, especially, the Berne Convention on the Conservation of European Wildlife and Natural Habitats, both from 1979, have influenced the development of EC directives on wild birds and habitats conservation. The Wild Birds Directive (79/409) required changes in British law and led to the Wildlife and Countryside Act 1981, effectively the first major government-sponsored measure on nature conservation. The Convention on Biological Diversity (1992) and the EC Habitats Directive (92/43) have both addressed site protection as well as requiring wider and more programmatic obligations.

Types of legal protection

From this brief historical survey it can be seen that the protections offered by the law can be divided into four rough categories:

(a) Protecting individual animals and plants
This is still done on a somewhat ad hoc basis, though a degree of coherence is provided by the Wildlife and Countryside Act 1981. Nature conservation is not the only aim being pursued: there is still a large element of protection against cruelty, and there are important exceptions relating to game and quarry species.

(b) Habitat protection through the designation of key sites
This has been a favoured technique, and a bewildering array of legislative designations has built up, the special rules and protections differing for each one. There is quite a degree of overlap here and many designations are cumulative. In *Nature Conservation in Great Britain* (1984), the Nature

Conservancy Council set out its policy that 10 per cent of the country be covered by one designation or another, so that a bedrock of essential sites may be protected.

(c)   Conservation in the wider countryside
The realisation that the protection of isolated sites is insufficient, both in scientific terms and in terms of the expectations of people who are interested in nature, has led to the search for general policies conducive to nature conservation, especially as part of agriculture and forestry policy. Grants and incentives are often used to meet these policy objectives. This is all part of the general trend towards integrating environnfental considerations into all aspects of policy.

(d)   Incidental protection
It remains clear that nature conservation interests are often served by taking advantage of legal powers which were not designed with nature conservation in mind. The best example is the purchase of private nature reserves by voluntary bodies, thus taking advantage of ordinary property rights, but another good example is the nature conservation value of the large tracts of land used for Ministry of Defence training grounds.

The nature conservation agencies

In 1949, on the basis of recommendations contained in the Huxley and Ritchie Reports, the Nature Conservancy was established by Royal Charter. This was a scientifically-orientated national body with responsibility throughout Great Britain for nature conservation matters ranging from education and research to the designation and management of national nature reserves. Under the Nature Conservancy Council Act 1973, this body became the Nature Conservancy Council (NCC), an autonomous body independent of government departments, but whose Council members were appointed by the Secretaries of State. However, the new NCC was split from its active research ecology arm (this is now the Institute of Terrestrial Ecology), a separation which resulted in a greater concentration on its remaining roles of advice and site protection. When coupled with the increasingly political flavour of nature conservation in the 1970s and 1980s, this turned the NCC into what could almost be described as a pressure group within government.

Under the EPA 1990, from 1 April 1991 the NCC (and hence responsibilty for nature conservation) was split into three national bodies; an NCC for England (called English Nature); a Countryside Council for Wales, combining the functions of the NCC and the (then) Countryside Commission in the principality (i.e. combining nature conservation with amenity and recreational matters); and an NCC for Scotland. In the case of Scotland, the position was further changed by the Natural Heritage (Scotland) Act 1991. This Act established a new body called Scottish Natural Heritage, effectively through a merger of the NCC for Scotland with the Countryside Commission for Scotland. In the EPA 1990, the three national bodies — English Nature, the Countryside Council for Wales and Scottish Natural Heritage — inherited most of the responsibilities of the NCC within the appropriate geographical area and thus have very similar powers and duties relating to nature conservation to each other. For ease of explanation, the name 'NCC' is retained throughout this book to refer to the relevant national body in its own area. (In Northern Ireland, nature conservation is a matter for the Environment and Heritage Service of the Department of the Environment.)

Each of the three national bodies is established on a similar basis to the old NCC (see EPA 1990, sch. 6). They receive annual grant in aid from the Treasury and have to submit annual reports and accounts to Parliament. Council members are appointed by the appropriate Secretary of State. They are the government's statutory advisers on nature conservation issues, with specific responsibilities for advising on species and habitat protection, the dissemination of knowledge about nature conservation, the support and conduct of research into nature conservation, and the safeguarding of protected sites (see EPA 1990, s. 132). In particular, they are responsible for the selection and management of NNRs and for the designation and oversight of SSSIs. They are also statutory consultees in relation to a large number of decisions made by other public bodies, including decisions on applications for planning permission and for pollution consents. In one sense, therefore, the three bodies are classic quangos and could be said to be largely unaccountable for many of their decisions: but they could also be said to be accountable to the interests of wildlife and ecology.

The dismantling of the NCC was undoubtedly the most controversial part of the EPA 1990. The Conservative government sought to justify it on the ground of administrative efficiency, but the result has been to add to the adminstrative complexity (and thus to the administrative cost) of nature conservation activities. A further justification was that power was devolved to Scotland and Wales and away from a GB-wide body based in Peterborough. Whilst there was a significant degree of support for such devolution, particularly in Scotland, this explanation scarcely squared with the Conservative Government's general record on devolution of powers. The clear impression left was that the main motivation behind the splitting up of the NCC was the political desirability of reducing the NCC's power in Scotland, where it had been active in opposing such things as the inappropriate afforestation of the unique Flow Country of Caithness and Sutherland.

Critics of the dismantling of the NCC point to the irrationality of dividing responsibility for nature conservation along national borders, when ecological criteria demand that a wider approach is adopted. They also stress that three smaller bodies are inevitably weaker than one large one. In addition, there is a significant possibility that uniformity in the implementation of the law will be lost. This follows inexorably from the wide discretions in the legislation and the fact that in Scotland and Wales in particular there is a greater willingness to accept that economic factors outweigh nature conservation considerations. As the last Chairman of the NCC, Sir William Wilkinson, put it when presenting the NCC's 16th Annual Report, 'As a result of the Government's attitude, nature conservation has been set back three, or possibly up to five, years'. In hindsight, although the progress of these separate bodies has not been without difficulty, their existence has helped pave the way for what looks like an early diversification of approaches, both policy and legal, the impact of which will have to be assessed in the light of experience.

The controversy over the splitting up of the NCC led to the establishment in the EPA 1990 of a further GB-wide body. There was initial opposition to such an idea from the then government, but during the debates on the Bill a separate Joint Nature Conservation Committee emerged. The final form of this body is provided for in sch. 7. It has few executive functions, but carries out important roles in relation to the international responsibilities of the old NCC (e.g. under the Ramsar Convention and other international agreements), matters affecting Great Britain as a whole, and the retention of common standards throughout Great Britain (for example, common criteria for the designation of SSSIs). Since it is really a committee of the three national bodies, the Joint Nature Conservation Committee relies on them for its funding, staffing and other resources. It consists of an independent chair and three other independent people appointed by the Secretary of State, together with two representatives from each of the three national bodies and the chair of the English Countryside Commission. Two non-voting members are appointed by the Department of the Environment for Northern Ireland.

The protection of individual animals and plants

The common law is generally unsympathetic to wild creatures, according them no rights of their own. However, property rights may usefully be exercised in order to protect them. Wild animals are subject to the qualified ownership of the landowner whose land they are on, whilst wild plants are part of the land itself. As a result, wild animals and plants have no common law protection against the landowner. But anyone else who kills or injures a wild animal or picks a wild plant commits the torts of trespass and interference with property. Whilst the normal remedy would be damages for the value of the item taken (and thus is of little practical use), it would be possible to seek an injunction to restrain continued breaches. An owner of a nature reserve could in theory use these property rights to protect against threats to the wildlife on it. In addition, a person who uproots plants may commit the crimes of theft and criminal damage, though there is an exception in the Theft Act 1968, s. 4(3) for picking flowers, fruit, foliage and fungi.

As a consequence of the limitations of the common law, the main protection for wild creatures is statutory. The Wildlife and Countryside Act 1981, Part I, contains the bulk of the law in this area, although the Conservation (Natural Habitats etc.) Regulations 1994 (SI 1994/2716) have made some changes to ensure compliance with the Habitats Directive 92/43. Three more specific conservation Acts are the Conservation of Seals Act 1970, the Protection of Badgers Act 1992 and the Wild Mammals (Protection) Act 1996. There are numerous pieces of legislation relating to hunted species, such as deer, game birds, wildfowl, rabbits and of course fish, though in all these Acts protection of individual animals is incidental. Reference to specialist books is recommended.

The chosen method of control is to establish blanket criminal offences of interfering with specified wildlife, together with a long list of exceptions and defences for acceptable activities, many of which require permission or a licence from an official body. The strongest provisions relate to wild birds (a legacy of the historical influence of the voluntary bodies here, but also a result of the EC Directive on Wild Birds 79/409, which requires certain legislative protections) in the sense that they are reverse listed — i.e. the 1981 Act applies unless they are exempted in the Schedules covering pest and quarry species. Animals and plants are covered only if specifically listed in other Schedules. As with all Schedules to the Act, the Secretary of State has powers to vary them by order to include or exclude species (s. 22), and this power has been exercised fairly frequently to take account of changes in the conservation status of the species concerned. The Joint Nature Conservation Committee has a specific duty to carry out a quinquennial review of schs. 5 and 8, which deal with protected animals and plants respectively, although its advice is not binding on the Secretary of State.

(a) **Wild birds**
It is an offence intentionally to kill, injure or take any wild bird and this is backed up by offences of intentionally taking, damaging or destroying a nest whilst it is in use or being built and intentionally taking or destroying eggs (Wildlife and Countryside Act 1981, s. 1(1)). It is also an offence to be in possession of a wild bird or egg, live or dead (s. 1(2)). There are further offences relating to illegal methods of killing or taking wild birds (s. 5) and the sale or advertising for sale of wild birds (s. 6). For these purposes a bird is presumed to be wild unless proved otherwise.

Birds are divided into two categories. Rarer birds are listed in sch. 1 and are specially protected. This means that the maximum penalty for committing any of these offences is increased from the normal £1,000 to £5,000 (s. 1(4)). In addition, intentionally disturbing a Schedule 1 bird on or near its nest, or disturbing its dependent young, is an offence (s. 1(5)).

Areas may be designated as bird sanctuaries by the Secretary of State, but only with the consent or acquiescence of the owners and occupiers. By-laws may be made for bird sanctuaries which create extra offences, including unauthorised access to the site (s. 3).

There are a number of exceptions and defences to these various offences. Game birds (i.e. pheasant, partridge, grouse and ptarmigan) are excluded from the protection provided by the Act, apart from that relating to illegal methods of killing or taking them (s. 27). Wildfowl listed in sch. 2, Part I may be killed or taken outside the close season (s. 2(1)). (The close season can be varied by the Secretary of State and there is also a power to provide for special protection periods in the event of bad weather in the open season.) Pest species listed in sch. 2, Part II may be killed or taken and their nests or eggs destroyed, but only by the owner or occupier of the land or any other authorised person (s. 2(2)).

Under s. 4, there are defences relating to the killing of injured birds and where the action is an 'incidental result of a lawful operation and could not reasonably have been avoided', or where it is necessary for crop protection, disease prevention or the protection of public health and safety. None of these defences requires permission, though the last three are only available to owners and occupiers and other authorised persons.

Section 16 also includes a long list of further exceptions which apply if a licence has been obtained from the appropriate official authority. It includes such things as the carrying out of research, educational activities, ringing of birds, falconry and keeping bird or egg collections.

(b) Animals

Only the animals listed in sch. 5 are protected by the legislation. This includes all bats, reptiles and amphibians, but only the rarest mammals, fish, butterflies and other forms of life.

For those animals which are protected, there is a range of offences similar to those for wild birds. It is an offence intentionally to kill, injure or take any scheduled wild animal (s. 9(1)), or to have in one's possession any such animal, live or dead, or any part of one (s. 9(2)). Additional offences relate to the sale or advertisement for sale of wild animals (s. 9(5)), illegal methods of killing or taking any wild animal (s. 11(1)), and illegal methods of killing or taking those animals listed in sch. 6 (s. 11(2)). There is also an offence of intentionally damaging, destroying or obstructing any structure or place used for shelter or protection by a sch. 5 animal, or disturbing such an animal whilst it is occupying such a structure (s. 9(4)). This provision is of greatest significance for the protection of bats roosting in such typical places as attics, outbuildings, caves and belfries, since they cannot be disturbed by, for example, rebuilding or timber treatment unless the NCC is notified in advance. For all these offences the maximum penalty is £5,000. In ss. 10 and 16 there are similar provisions relating to defences and licences to those available for wild birds.

In addition, the Conservation (Natural Habitats etc.) Regulations 1994 (SI 1994/2716) create some further offences in relation to the animals defined as 'European protected species', which are listed in sch. 2 to the regulations (this is a short list which includes all native bats, the dormouse, the great crested newt, the otter, the large blue butterfly and a few other species). In order to ensure compliance with the Habitats Directive 92/43, the Government chose to set out the requirements of the Directive in full, rather than seek to amend the existing legislation. The result is that the regulations cover similar ground to the 1981 Act, but with some occasional subtle changes in wording to make the offences wider: for example, it is an offence under reg. 39 deliberately to disturb an animal of a European protected species or deliberately to take or destroy the eggs of such an animal.

There is more general protection for wild mammals which are not covered under the Wildlife and Countryside Act 1981. Under the Wild Mammals (Protection) Act 1996 it is an offence to commit a wide range of cruel acts to any wild mammal with intent to inflict unnecessary suffering, although the

Act is deliberately worded so that normal hunting with dogs cannot be an offence. There are defences if the acts constituted a mercy killing or were otherwise lawful (e.g. trapping or the use of poisons). The maximum fine is £5,000 per animal affected. The operation of the 1996 Act is somewhat restricted by the range of defences and the need to prove the mental element of the offence but it does at least bring a degree of parity in the law relating to domestic animals and that relating to wild mammals.

(c) Badgers

Badgers are given special protection under their own legislation. This has been developed over many years and is now consolidated in the Protection of Badgers Act 1992. The general scheme is similar to that for animals protected under the Wildlife and Countryside Act 1981, sch. 5, but there are some unique features to the provisions. It is an offence to do any of the following: wilfully kill, injure or take a badger, or attempt any of those things (s. 1(1)); possess a dead badger (s. 1(3)); cruelly ill-treat a badger, use badger tongs, or dig for a badger (s. 2); sell or have possession of a live badger (s. 4); mark or attach a marking device to a badger, except under licence (s. 5). In recognition of the evidential problems thrown up in prosecutions for the barbaric activity of badger baiting, in relation to the attempt offences under s. 1(1) and the offence of digging for a badger, the burden of proof is effectively reversed. Once there is reasonable evidence of the offence it is up to the defendant to prove that no offence has been committed. For all these offences there is a defence if a licence is obtained from the appropriate authority (s. 10).

There is a further, very important, offence of interference with a badger sett that shows signs of current use (s. 3). This covers such things as damaging the sett, destroying it, obstructing access to it, causing a dog to enter it, or disturbing a badger that is in occupation. The provisions are unusually strong in that, even where there is a valid planning permission, a separate licence will be required under s. 10 if the carrying out of the permission would involve damage or disturbance to a sett. This has led to a situation where the existence of a badger sett is a very significant factor if development is envisaged. There is a general defence if the action was the incidental result of a lawful operation and could not reasonably have been avoided, and a more specific defence in relation to temporary interference in the course of fox-hunting (s. 8).

The maximum fine for all the offences under the 1992 Act is £5,000 per badger affected, and in relation to most of the offences a prison term of up to six months may also be imposed. If a dog is used in connection with the offence, the court may order its destruction or disposal.

(d) Plants

Section 13 of the Wildlife and Countryside Act 1981 makes it an offence for anyone other than the owner, occupier or other authorised person intentionally to uproot any wild plant. In addition, it is an offence for anyone intentionally to pick, uproot or destroy any of the numerous species of rare wild plants listed in sch. 8. The sale or advertisement for sale of sch. 8 plants is also an offence. Once again, there are similar provisions relating to defences and licences to those available for wild birds.

In addition, the Conservation (Natural Habitats etc.) Regulations 1994 (SI 1994/2716) create some further offences in relation to the small number of European protected species of plants which are listed in sch. 4. As with the offences concerning European protected species of animals, in order to ensure compliance with the Habitats Directive 92/43, the offences are similar to, but slightly wider than, those in the 1981 Act: for example, it is an offence deliberately to collect or cut a wild plant of a European protected species.

(e)   Introducing foreign animals or plants to Great Britain
A further section of the 1981 Act worth mentioning is s. 14, which makes it an offence to introduce into the wild any animal not normally resident in Great Britain or any wild animal or plant listed in sch. 9. This section aims to protect against further repetitions of the ecological havoc wrought by alien introductions such as grey squirrel, coypu and giant hogweed.

Habitat protection

Although there is a rapidly growing number of protective designations for areas of habitat, the main domestic ones remain the interrelated categories of NNR and SSSI. The increasingly important international designations are discussed later in this chapter. Both NNRs and SSSIs were originally introduced in the National Parks and Access to the Countryside Act 1949 on the recommendation of the Huxley and Ritchie Committees. The NNR powers remain essentially those enacted in 1949, but the SSSI provisions have been significantly altered and strengthened by the Wildlife and Countryside Act 1981, Part II. This reflects the changing role of SSSIs in the light of the enormous environmental changes since 1949.

Two preliminary points need to be made about the 1981 Act, the passage of which would justify a book by itself. First, the whole structure of Part II rests on the policy of voluntariness favoured by the Conservative Government. This is the view that compulsory controls should only be used as a last resort, because they will only serve to antagonise landowners, who are seen as having the main responsibility for site protection. Pursuant to this policy, the favoured mechanism of control is the management agreement: the NCC is to seek to enter into agreements with landowners to protect the site, with compensation being paid for losses incurred by owners (see p. 636). In order to achieve this, many of the legal requirements focus on a duty to notify the NCC of threats to sites.

Secondly, Part II was significantly altered during its passage through Parliament. Originally the Conservative Government had intended to confer statutory protection only on the limited number of sites to be accorded nature conservation order status, leaving the majority of SSSIs protected by the narrow existing limitations on development in the planning system. Many saw this as wholly inadequate, particularly when the NCC released statistics showing that between 10 and 15 per cent of SSSIs had suffered significant damage or loss in 1980 alone, the majority of the damage being caused by agriculture rather than urban-type developments. Statutory powers relating to *all* SSSIs were hurriedly introduced. One effect is that the provisions on SSSIs (and the confusingly similar nature conservation orders) are not well drafted and many detailed matters remain particularly unclear, although there have subsequently been drafting amendments in the Wildlife and Countryside (Amendment) Act 1985, the Wildlife and Countryside (Service of Notices) Act 1985 and the EPA 1990.

The difference between NNRs and SSSIs can best be explained by saying that NNRs are actively controlled and managed by the NCC, whereas in SSSIs the occupier of the land retains control subject to a number of restrictions on use decided by the NCC. In one sense, therefore, the NNRs are the top tier of sites which merit extra controls and the expenditure of money on positive management. However, since they are all notified as SSSIs and benefit from the restrictions on them, it is clearer if the protections available to SSSIs are explained first.

Sites of special scientific interest (SSSIs)

It is important to understand the function of SSSIs. In an explanatory paper, *The Selection of Sites of Special Scientific Interest,* it is explained that they are a representative sample of British habitats, with each site seen as 'an integral part of a national series' established with the aim of 'maintaining the present diversity of wild animals and plants in Great Britain'. It is emphasised that selection is on scientific grounds rather than to enhance amenity or provide recreation. For biological sites, the best examples of various habitat types (including natural, semi-natural and man-made landscapes) are chosen, determined on the basis of 'naturalness, diversity, typicalness and size', along with sites catering for rare habitats and species. A geographical spread is ensured by selecting typical sites within sub-regional areas (see, in general, *Guidelines for Selection of Biological SSSIs,* NCC, 1989). Geological SSSIs are treated differently, the intention being to 'conserve those localities essential to the continued conduct of research and education in the earth sciences', again in the context of a national representative series (see *Geological Conservation Review,* NCC).

By the end of March 1999, throughout Great Britain there were 6,455 SSSIs notified under the 1981 Act (4,045 in England, 962 in Wales, and 1,448 in Scotland). Together they covered 2,178,418 hectares, which is over 7 per cent of the land area, though the proportion is far higher in some areas, notably Scotland (11.6 per cent). The size of individual SSSIs ranges from over 10,000 hectares for some upland moorland sites, to less than one hectare. Also included are a number of linear sites, such as rivers.

The NCC is given a wide discretion both to formulate reasonable criteria for notification and to carry out the task of individual selection. The 1981 Act, s. 28(1), states:

Where the Nature Conservancy Council are of the opinion that any area of land is of special interest by reason of any of its flora, fauna, or geological

or physiographical features, it shall be the duty of the Council to notify that
fact —

(a)   to the local planning authority in whose area the land is situated;
(b)   to every owner and occupier of any of that land; and
(c)   to the Secretary of State.

One effect of this definition is that the list is not unchanging. New SSSIs will
be notified as new information about sites is acquired, and as the importance
of safeguarding certain habitats increases. It must also be understood that, in
an age when sites are being damaged and destroyed, one site may become of
greater importance simply because of the loss of another site. The NCC will,
in practice, denotify a site which loses its scientific interest, although it is
unclear whether there is any legislative basis for such a step.

Section 28(1) states that it is the 'duty' of the NCC to notify the people
and bodies listed. This is a very rare example, as far as environmental
legislation is concerned, of a duty rather than a discretionary power being
referred to. It is especially remarkable given the largely unaccountable nature
of the notifying agencies. The nature of the duty was discussed in *R v Nature
Conservancy Council, ex parte London Brick Co. Ltd* [1996] Env LR 1, which
concerned a challenge to the notification of a SSSI relating to old clay pits on
a brickworks in Peterborough. May J discussed the procedures for establishing a SSSI and decided that there are, in fact, two steps involved.

(a)   Under s. 28(1), a *duty* is imposed on the NCC to notify a site which
fulfils the appropriate scientific criteria. This notification has provisional
effect, but a period of three months is provided during which representations
or objections can be made (s. 28(2), as inserted by the Wildlife and
Countryside (Amendment) Act 1985).

(b)   The NCC must consider these representations or objections and then
has a *discretion* under s. 28(4A) whether to confirm the notification (with or
without modifications). If confirmation is not made within nine months of
the date when the notification was served, the notification lapses.

May J then went on to accept that English Nature's policy normally to
confirm a notification unless the site is unavoidably going to be destroyed is
a reasonable policy, and he upheld the confirmation. In the interests of
natural justice, however, confirmation must be on the same basis as notification (*R v Nature Conservancy Council, ex parte Bolton Metropolitan Borough
Council* [1995] Env LR 237).

The implications of the decision in *ex parte London Brick Co. Ltd* are
significant, since it suggests that it would be illegal for the NCC to refuse to
notify on political or tactical grounds (although it could arguably refuse to
confirm a notification), and that it may well be possible for an environmental
group to succeed in an action to compel the NCC to notify a site. Conversely,
it appears that it will be difficult to mount a successful challenge against an
unwelcome notification where the requisite special interest can be shown. It

is notable that, in Scotland, there is an independent review body which advises the Secretary of State when the scientific basis for notification is challenged (s. 12, Natural Heritage (Scotland) Act 1991).

It is up to the NCC to define the boundaries of the SSSI and it appears from *Sweet* v *Secretary of State and Nature Conservancy Council* [1989] JEL 245 (actually a case about s. 29, as to which, see below) that it is permissible for land of lesser intrinsic scientific interest to be notified if it is part of the same environmental unit as land which is of interest. However the position of surrounding buffer lands is less clear and it must be doubted whether they could be notified. One geographical limitation is that SSSIs cannot be notified for waters below the low water mark (thus excluding many estuaries), although inland waters are included within the definition of land in the Act.

In carrying out the notification to owners and occupiers, the NCC must specify the features of the land which are of special interest and must also specify any operations which are likely to damage those features. These have traditionally been called 'potentially damaging operations' and it is clear from the decision in *Sweet* that a very wide interpretation will be given to this phrase. It can include virtually anything that has an impact on the site and 'operations' is not limited to its meaning under the Town and Country Planning Act 1990. In *Sweet*, it was held to include:

cultivation, including ploughing, rotavation, harrowing and reseeding; grazing; mowing or other methods of cutting vegetation; application of manure, fertilisers and lime; burning; the release into the site of any wild feral or domestic animal, reptile, amphibian, bird, fish or invertebrate, or any plant or seed; the storage of materials; the use of materials; the use of vehicles or craft likely to damage or disturb features of interest.

Such things as drainage, building operations and the application of pesticides are clearly covered. One thing which is not covered, however, is doing nothing, and on many sites neglect, as much as wilful damage, will be detrimental to the conservation interest. A good example of this is the species of water beetle threatened in the *London Brick* case following the decision to stop pumping out the pits.

In the Scottish case of *North Uist Fisheries Ltd* v *Secretary of State for Scotland* 1992 SLT 333 (again a case on similar wording in s. 29), the judge suggested that the use of the word 'likely' required any potential damage to be probable rather than a bare possibility. If this interpretation (which was strictly *obiter*) is correct, it would undermine the whole of the legislation on SSSIs. It is submitted that the judge's reasoning should not be followed, since it seems to be based on an entirely incorrect understanding of the context of the legislation.

Duties on owners and occupiers

The process of notification is a lengthy one, since every owner and occupier, which includes over 40,000 people, must be notified in relation to the whole of each site. The NCC has only recently finished the process, started in 1981, of renotifying all the sites which existed at that time. This was important because, until it did so, the protection of the 1981 Act did not apply to those sites.

Once they have been notified, owners and occupiers are placed under a reciprocal duty. They must notify the NCC in writing before carrying out any potentially damaging operation. However, four months after this notification, or earlier if the written consent of the NCC is obtained, the operation can go ahead unimpeded — unless of course it requires and fails to get planning permission, which must still be sought for operations and material changes of use as defined in the Town and Country Planning Act 1990. It is an offence 'without reasonable excuse' to carry out a potentially damaging operation either without notifying the NCC, or within the four-month period, but the maximum penalty is only a £2,500 fine. The restrictive effect of designation as an SSSI is therefore to impose a four-month ban on potentially damaging operations.

Liability for the commission of the offence is strict, but it can only be committed by owners and occupiers of the SSSI. They should know about the designation, either because they have been notified, or because it is a local land charge (s. 28(11)). There are two specific defences available: that the operation was carried out in an emergency, and that planning permission had been granted by the local planning authority. This does not include an automatic permission granted by the General Permitted Development Order (s. 28(8)), but it does mean that a planning permission overrides a SSSI designation.

These provisions illustrate the 'voluntary' mechanism which was favoured by the Conservative Government. The whole purpose of the reciprocal notification requirement and the four-month ban is to give the NCC an opportunity to arrange a management agreement with the owner or occupier.

One question which has often arisen relates to the meaning of the word 'occupier' in this context. This is important because there is no need for the NCC to notify anyone who is less than an occupier. It is also true that such a person cannot commit an offence under s. 28 and cannot be offered a management agreement. In *Southern Water Authority* v *Nature Conservancy Council* [1992] 1 WLR 775, the House of Lords decided that for the purposes of s. 28 someone is an occupier if they have some form of stable relationship with the land. As a result, a water authority which carried out drainage works whilst temporarily on an SSSI did not commit an offence under s. 28, even though it knew that these were potentially damaging operations and that they would cause significant harm (the House of Lords referred to its actions as 'ecological vandalism'). This decision did not specifically answer the important question whether commoners are covered by the definition of an occupier, but it is the practice of the NCC to treat them as such, relying on a clear statement to that effect given by a Government Minister during the debates on the Environmental Protection Bill (see Withrington & Jones, 'The Enforcement of Conservation Legislation' in *Agriculture, Conservation and Land Use*, ed. Howarth and Rodgers, University of Wales Press, 1992). Support for this stance can now be gained from the House of Lords decision in *Pepper* v *Hart* [1993] AC 593 that it is permissible to refer to Parliamentary debates in certain limited circumstances to establish the meaning of a statute, since the statement was given in the context of a refusal to bring forward an amendment to clarify the situation on the grounds that the position was already clear.

Specific nature conservation duties

Specific duties in relation to SSSIs are imposed upon the Environment Agency and the NCCs in the Environment Act 1995, s. 8. Similar duties apply to the water and sewerage undertakers under the Water Industry Act 1991, s. 4. The NCC must notify the EA of SSSIs that may be affected by its activities (including operational and regulatory functions). If the EA is notified, it must consult the NCC over any operation or activity it intends to carry out which it thinks is likely to damage or destroy the SSSI. In addition the EA is obliged to consult the NCC before authorising anything it thinks is likely to damage the SSSI. This covers all the range of the EA's functions, including IPC authorisations, waste management licensing, abstraction licences, discharge consents and land drainage consents. There is a code of practice which suggests that *all* operations should be notified to the NCC, rather than just those that the EA or undertaker *thinks* will damage the SSSI, otherwise detrimental ones may be inadvertently missed (*Code of Practice on Conservation, Access and Recreation*, 2000) (see further p. 168).

These duties are wider than the normal ones imposed on owners and occupiers. They apply to all operations, not just to potentially damaging operations notified by the NCC, and they cover activities in the vicinity of an SSSI which may affect it, such as drainage works, an upstream discharge or even an industrial process with potentially detrimental atmospheric emissions some distance away. However, there is no remedy if the relevant body fails to consult the NCC, and these duties are unenforceable unless the NCC brings a successful action for judicial review. This reflects that the real purpose of these duties is to bring the matter to the attention of the NCC so that it may give advice (it does not normally offer a management agreement to public bodies, considering that their general environmental duties should suffice to make them act in a responsible fashion). Note should therefore be made of the general environmental duties in the Environment Act 1995, ss. 6, 7 and 9 (see p. 167).

Nature conservation orders

Section 29 provides stronger powers for areas subject to a nature conservation order. Even so, they have been sparingly used. About 40 have been made over the years, mainly to protect sites imminently threatened with destruction.

The powers in relation to nature conservation orders are superficially similar to those on SSSIs, but there are significant differences. The order will list potentially damaging operations which must be notified to the NCC before being carried out, and a three-month ban is imposed. The NCC can extend this ban to 12 months by offering a management agreement, or by offering to purchase the interest of the person seeking to carry out the operation. At the end of the 12 months, the operation can go ahead. Once again, the purpose of this ban is to enable the NCC to conclude a management agreement, or terms for the purchase of the site.

It is an offence to carry out a potentially damaging operation without notifying the NCC, or within the period of the ban. The offence carries a maximum fine of £5,000 on summary conviction, or an unlimited fine for a conviction on indictment, and it can be committed by anyone, not just owners and occupiers. Thus, contractors, trespassers or visiting members of the public could be prosecuted under this section, a position justified by the publicity given to a nature conservation order (see below).

Certain ancillary arrangements differ from s. 28. The NCC is authorised to enter land to see if an order ought to be made, or to see if an offence against one has been committed (s. 51), powers which are not available for SSSIs (a significant gap in the legislation). Anyone can prosecute for a s. 29 offence (under s. 28 it is only the NCC and anyone who has the permission of the Director of Public Prosecutions). A convicting court has powers to make a restoration order (s. 31), ordering that the offender carry out specified works for the purpose of restoring the land to its former condition, although in many cases this power will be next to useless because the damage will be irreversible. Compensation is also payable to the owner or occupier for any reduction in the value of an agricultural holding as a result of an order, and for any loss directly attributable to the ban on operations (s. 30).

These wider powers are complemented by a much more complex system for making nature conservation orders. After consulting the NCC, the Secretary of State is empowered to designate areas by order. They must be of special interest and national importance, or required to ensure the survival in Great Britain of a plant or animal, or to comply with an international obligation. Although it is arguable that all SSSIs are of national importance, it is apparent that the Secretary of State has in practice refused to designate some SSSIs under s. 29 on the grounds that the land was not of national importance, even when the NCC has requested it. On the other hand, an order was eventually made in 1997 on land in Sussex being damaged by ploughing, even though some of the land was not of national importance. It is clear from *Sweet* v *Secretary of State and Nature Conservancy Council* [1989] JEL 245 that it is permissible to designate the whole of an environmental unit even though only part of it is of national importance.

Schedule 11 provides for the making of an order. It comes into effect immediately it is made. It must then be notified to owners, occupiers and the local planning authority and must be publicised generally for any objections to be made. Twenty-eight days are allowed for representations to the Secretary of State, who must appoint an inspector or hold a public inquiry if any objections are not withdrawn. The Secretary of State has a discretion to confirm the order, or to amend or revoke it.

Despite their complexity, nature conservation orders provide the NCC with few extra powers not available for all SSSIs. They are basically used to provide more time for the NCC to negotiate a management agreement where the owner or occupier is being awkward. They also serve notice of intent to use whatever powers are available to protect the site. This may include compulsory purchase (see below). For example, in *Sweet* the land was eventually obtained in 1989 as part of a new national nature reserve.

National nature reserves (NNRs)

NNRs owe their existence to the National Parks and Access to the Country-side Act 1949, s. 15, which defines them as areas managed for study or research into flora, fauna or geological or physiographical interest, or for preserving such features which are of special interest. Before declaring an area an NNR, the NCC must consider that it is expedient in the national interest to manage the area as an NNR.

Designation as an NNR is a simple process: the NCC merely declares that an area is one. In order to do this it has to have control of the site so that it can manage it. Control may be achieved either by buying the land, leasing it, or entering into a nature reserve agreement with the owner under the National Parks and Access to the Countryside Act 1949, s. 16. Such an agreement is enforceable against successors in title.

In addition, the Wildlife and Countryside Act 1981, s. 35 permits the NCC to declare an NNR on land which is of national importance and which is being managed by an approved body (meaning a voluntary conservation organisation). Strictly, only sites designated under s. 35 are NNRs; those designated under s. 15 of the 1949 Act are strictly 'nature reserves', but they have always been referred to as national nature reserves, the term used here.

The NCC also has powers to seek a compulsory purchase order if it is unable to conclude a satisfactory management agreement with the owner (1949 Act, s. 17), or if an unremedied breach of an agreement occurs. An order will require the approval of the Secretary of State. These compulsory powers are intended as reserve powers only and are very rarely used. However, they remain the only compulsory powers available to the NCC: if a maverick landowner were to refuse to enter into a management agreement on an SSSI and refused to sell the property, a compulsory purchase order would be the only remaining weapon.

There are no additional statutory restrictions on the use of an NNR other than those imposed on all SSSIs (as a matter of practice all NNRs are designated as SSSIs), since the nature reserve agreement will cover anything extra. However, the NCC may make by-laws for the protection of the reserve (1949 Act, s. 20). They require confirmation by the Secretary of State and the procedures for making them are set out in the 1949 Act, s. 106. These by-laws may include wide restrictions on such things as entry to the reserve, taking, killing or interference with animals, plants or the soil, dropping litter and lighting fires. Shooting of birds can also be restricted in areas surround-ing the reserve. By-laws may not restrict the rights of the owner or occupier, public rights of way (though this does not include rights of navigation — *Evans v Godber* [1974] 1 WLR 1317), or statutory undertakers and some other public bodies carrying out their statutory functions.

There are over 320 NNRs in Great Britain as at March 1998, covering over 200,000 hectares, but it cannot be assumed that they are necessarily the very best sites. Designation of a site as an NNR imposes heavy costs on the NCC, which has accordingly to be selective, and it has tended to follow a policy of opportunism. Given a chronic shortage of money, it will buy or take control of sites that are threatened or available, rather than those which are in safe hands, such as those owned by a voluntary conservation body.

Local nature reserves (LNRs)

Under the National Parks and Access to the Countryside Act 1949, s. 21, local authorities are given the same powers to designate and manage local nature reserves as the NCC has in relation to NNRs. A local nature reserve must have local, as opposed to national, importance and the local authority must consult with the NCC before designation. At March 1999 there were 718 LNRs in Great Britain, covering 43,186 hectares, the vast majority of these in England where a policy of using LNRs to promote conservation education in urban areas has been pioneered.

Marine nature reserves (MNRs)

MNRs are the counterparts to NNRs in tidal and coastal waters and may be designated for any area of land or water from the high tide mark to a line three miles from the baselines established for measuring the territorial sea (see the Territorial Sea Act 1987). They are provided for in the Wildlife and Countryside Act 1981, s. 36, and may be designated on the same grounds of conservation and study as NNRs. They are actively managed by the NCC.

There are a number of differences from NNRs. Some stem from the absence of property rights over most of the potential area of MNRs, others are a consequence of the limited vision of MNRs in the 1981 Act. Designation of an MNR is by the Secretary of State on the application of the NCC. There is a lengthy procedure, similar to that for nature conservation orders, in which the proposed designation and any by-laws are publicised, followed by a period for representations from interested parties, with the possibility of a public inquiry and of a judicial review both being catered for (see Wildlife and Countryside Act 1981, sch. 12). Only two MNRs have ever been designated (around the islands of Lundy and Skomer), although this may reflect the fact that the NCC's priorities lay elsewhere in the 1980s. It is also true that there are a few voluntary marine reserves.

In common with NNRs, the main additional control conferred by MNR status is the power of the NCC to make by-laws. These may be made as part of the original designation, or may be issued separately, but in either case require confirmation by the Secretary of State. The 1981 Act, s. 37, sets out the range of possible by-laws, which is much more limited than the range for NNRs. Restrictions may be introduced on the killing, taking and disturbance of plants and animals and on the deposit of litter. The by-laws may also prohibit or restrict access by people or vessels to the MNR, but this is limited

by the provision in s. 37(3) that by-laws may not restrict any lawful right of
passage by vessels, except for pleasure boats. This is an important limitation,
since most boats will be able to take advantage of the right of passage in tidal
waters, and there are no proprietary limitations on access in such waters.
Also, the maximum fine for breach of a by-law is only £1000. In addition, it
must be noted that MNRs cannot take any real advantage from the protection
relating to SSSIs, since SSSIs cannot be designated below the low water
mark.

Limestone pavements

Limestone pavements are rare landscape features limited to a small number
of areas in North-West Europe. In the light of the devastating damage that
has been done to them, particularly in gathering stone for garden rockeries,
specific powers to protect them were introduced in the Wildlife and Countryside Act 1981, s. 34.

There are two distinct controls. Under s. 34(1), the NCC or the Countryside Agency must notify limestone pavements of special interest to the local
planning authority. Amongst other things this will then be taken into account
in any planning application. Under s. 34(2), the Secretary of State, a county
planning authority or a national park authority may by order prohibit the
removal from, or disturbance of, any limestone on a site notified under
s. 34(1), if they consider it is likely to be affected adversely by such acts. The
making of a limestone pavement order is subject to the same procedures as a
nature conservation order (1981 Act, sch. 11). It is an offence without
reasonable excuse to remove or disturb any limestone on or in an area subject
to an order, although it is a defence to have planning permission to do so.
The penalty is a maximum fine of £5,000 on summary conviction and an
unlimited fine on conviction on indictment. It was originally intended to
protect most areas of substantial pavement, but the cumbersome nature of
designation has meant that only a handful of orders have ever been made,
mainly (as with nature conservation orders) to deal with threats of imminent
damage.

This dual form of protection differs from all other conservation designations. But it must be noted that this is the form that the government originally
proposed in 1981 should apply to SSSIs, with only a few specially protected
areas having extra restrictions and the ordinary SSSIs being protected only
by notification to the local planning authority.

Management agreements

The NCC has a power to enter into management agreements with owners
and occupiers of SSSIs (Countryside Act 1968, s. 15). This was extended by
the EPA 1990, sch. 9 to enable agreements to be made with owners or
occupiers of land adjoining an SSSI, which should be of use, for example, in
wetland areas to control drainage. There is a similar power to make nature
reserve agreements for NNRs (National Parks and Access to the Countryside

Act 1949, s. 16), although these normally provide for the NCC to manage the land itself.

Management agreements underpin the voluntary approach to nature conservation favoured by successive administrations. They are effectively contracts in which owners or occupiers of land agree to manage it in the interests of nature conservation in return for payment from the NCC. They normally provide for positive management of the site as well as for restrictions, but it appears that only restrictive arrangements in the agreement will be binding on successors in title (s. 15(4)).

Prior to the Wildlife and Countryside Act 1981, little use was made of management agreements — only 70 were in force in 1980/81. But since the 1981 Act, numbers have grown, so that in 1990/91 the NCC paid out over £6.85m on 2,032 management agreements on SSSIs (see NCC 16th Annual Report).

The current figures for Great Britain are £9.53m being paid out under 3,505 agreements, a steady increase since 1991. In large part this reflects the fact that the costs of management schemes far exceeded original estimates and eventually became prohibitively expensive for the NCC. In 1981, for example, only £600,000 was allocated. But s. 50 of the 1981 Act laid down standard rates of compensation established in financial guidelines made by Ministers (these are set out in the Appendix to Circular 4/83) which are generous to landowners. This is because they are based on the principle of profits foregone, which includes such things as lost agricultural grants or lost revenues had the land been converted to a more profitable use.

An obvious drawback of such payments is that they compensate people for *not* doing something desirable, in this case positive management, which is both inefficient and poor conservation policy. (A good example of how the guidelines work is *Cameron v Nature Conservancy Council* 1991 SLT (Lands Tribunal) 85.) Increasingly, such compensatory agreements are being replaced by agreements under which positive management is encouraged, notably English Nature's Wildlife Enhancement Scheme. Introduced nationally in 1996, this scheme now accounts for over 44 per cent of all agreements and over 36 per cent of all payments. As well as encouraging positive management, another advantage of the scheme is that standard payments are made for a range of conservation activities. This is an improvement on the compensatory agreements which had to be negotiated individually, using up valuable time and resources. The new scheme may help explain why the average cost of negotiating agreements has halved since 1991. But it is also a good example of how an important shift in regulatory approach can be made without resort either to a change in primary legislation, or even (remarkably) to a change in the guidance, which remains in force.

In Wales, the pilot Tir Cymen scheme also provided for positive management, and this has now been superseded by the Tir Gofal scheme, which also integrates environmentally sensitive area payments. A notable feature of this scheme is that it applies to the 'whole farm', and thus extends beyond land notified as SSSI. Land of outstanding scientific interest may also qualify for tax relief (see *Capital Taxation and Nature Conservation*, English Nature, 1992).

Planning permission

In addition to any controls specific to SSSIs and NNRs, planning permission will be required for operations and material changes of use which fall within the definition of development in the Town and Country Planning Act 1990, s. 55 (see p. 310). Where the application relates to an SSSI or is likely to affect an SSSI, or relates to development within a 2-km 'consultation area' around an SSSI, the Town and Country Planning (General Development Procedure) Order 1995, art. 10, requires the local planning authority to consult with the NCC before making a decision. The objective is the familiar one of informing the NCC in advance of a potential threat to the site, so it may give advice or offer a management agreement. Prior to the 1981 Act, this was the *only* legal protection for SSSIs.

These requirements are very limited in practice. Many activities likely to damage SSSIs, such as those relating to agriculture, forestry and works carried out by statutory undertakers, are not covered by the need for planning permission, either because they are not development or because they are granted exemption (see further Chapter 22). In any case, the local planning authority is not bound by the NCC's advice — it is just one material consideration to be taken into account. The economic and other arguments in favour of the development may well outweigh the need to protect the SSSI. For example, in 1990 Havering DC granted outline planning permission for a large theme park on Rainham Marshes, the largest SSSI in Greater London. The Secretary of State refused to call the application in, even though this would have been the largest ever loss of SSSI land to a development with planning permission (it has not gone ahead, although the planning authority still wishes to develop the site). In another example, Poole BC granted itself planning permission for housing on Canford Heath, an SSSI within the town's boundaries. After an unsuccessful High Court challenge (see *R v Poole Borough Council, ex parte Beebee* [1991] JPL 643), the Secretary of State took the almost unprecedented step of revoking the planning permission under the Town and Country Planning Act 1990, s. 100.

Government policy on planning and nature conservation is now set out in Planning Policy Guidance Note 9, *Nature Conservation* (PPG 9, October 1994). As well as explaining the various statutory and international protections, PPG 9 emphasises that the nature conservation interest of a site, and the importance of the site in national and international terms, is clearly a material consideration when it comes to a decision whether to grant planning permission, although it does refer to the potential use of conditions or planning obligations to avoid damaging impacts. In particular, PPG 9 includes some especially strong policies in relation to international sites, including that environmental assessment will normally be required where such a site (including a proposed site) could be affected (see below for a discussion of internationally important sites).

However, there is a difficulty here concerning the relationship between safeguarding sites through the planning machinery and the formal designation of SSSIs. If a formal policy against granting planning permission on internationally important sites is adopted, which is likely, many people would then argue that the procedures for designation of those sites need to be upgraded so as to include rights of objection, the possibility of a public inquiry and so on, since such a restraint policy would effectively take away any real chance of realising the development value of the land.

If planning permission is granted for development, it acts as a defence to a prosecution for damaging an SSSI (1981 Act, s. 28(8)). This does not just apply to new permissions. It also exempts existing mineral and peat extraction permissions over SSSIs from the 1981 Act. These are on sites which tend not to have been identified as of importance when the permission was originally granted. The NCC's options are limited and all involve the payment of potentially large sums of money: revocation of the planning permission entails a liability to pay compensation, a management agreement would have to compensate for lost profits, and purchase would normally be at the market price.

Loss and damage to SSSIs

Despite the strengthening of the law relating to SSSIs in the 1981 Act, loss of, and damage to, sites continues, though probably at lower rates than previously. The three national conservation agencies now all work to a document, *Common Standards for Monitoring Designated Sites* (JNCC, 1997), which divides incidents into no recovery (either the whole feature or a part of it), long-term and short-term recovery, and unknown. Before 1997, each of the agencies used slightly different criteria — which were also criticised for varying between years — which must be borne in mind when looking at relevant statistics.

The latest figures for 1998/99 indicate that very few sites have been lost completely in recent years. English Nature identified 62 reports of damaging activities at 55 sites in the year, including 8 incidents that resulted in partial or total loss of the sites' notified features, while in Wales there were 22 cases of damage on 21 SSSIs, 3 incidents resulting in partial or total loss of the notified features. Figures from a 1994 study by the National Audit Office reported that 869 SSSIs in England suffered loss and damage between 1987 and 1993, which amounted to over one-fifth of the total number notified, although there was some element of double-counting in those figures. Between 1981 and 1991, however, English Nature denotified 579 SSSIs, around 15 per cent of the total.

The *Common Standards* also apply to monitoring the condition of sites. In English Nature's 1998/99 Report, for example, 56 per cent were found to be favourable; 16 per cent unfavourable but improving; 11 per cent unfavourable and declining; and 17 per cent unfavourable but with no change, figures which show little change from 1997/98. In its 1997/98 Report, English Nature stated that it would only use figures on loss and condition in future reports, effectively removing figures on damage. This suggests a desire to avoid publicising 'incidents' in the same way as, for example, the Environment Agency does in relation to water pollution. This would have avoided calls for 'naming and shaming' those responsible for damage to SSSIs (recommended by the Public Accounts Committee in 1994), and allow for a continuing co-operative relationship between the NCC and landowners, but the latest report suggests that damage to sites will still be recorded.

What the statistics on loss and damage show clearly, however, is that the causes of damage have changed somewhat over the years, a point reinforced by a number of independent analyses (see Rowell, *SSSIs: A Health Check*, Wildlife Link, 1991; WWF-UK, *A Muzzled Watchdog? Is English Nature Protecting Wildlife*, WWF-UK, 1997). While agricultural activities are still the biggest single cause of incidents, only a small proportion of these lead to loss of a site. The major problems in relation to agriculture appear to be those with which the 1981 Act is ill-equipped to deal, such as overgrazing (especially by commoners) and neglect, both of which create difficult issues of management and control. And other activities giving rise to damage are also ones with which the 1981 Act cannot deal because they are effectively exempt from its provisions, such as: activities granted planning permission (e.g. the perpetual extractions for peat extractions on lowland moors); major development promoted by government departments (such as the Channel Tunnel, or the road-building programme); activities by statutory undertakers (the prosecution of Southern Water Authority mentioned above is a good example); recreational activities, which are often not controlled because those who are neither owners nor occupiers cannot commit an offence under s.28; and activities taking place below the low-water mark.

SSSIs: proposals for reform

The cases of loss and damage mentioned above (as well as damage caused by things like water abstraction, drainage and pollution) all point towards the existence of a number of defects in the scheme of the 1981 Act which urgently require to be addressed. But more generally, the protection afforded from activities that *are* covered by the 1981 Act leaves a lot to be desired. As Lord Mustill observed in *Southern Water Authority* v *Nature Conservancy Council* [1992] 1 WLR 775 (at p. 778):

> It needs only a moment to see that this regime is toothless, for it demands no more from the owner or occupier of an SSSI than a little patience . . . In truth the Act does no more in the great majority of cases than give the council a breathing space within which to apply moral pressure, with a view to persuading the owner or occupier to make a voluntary agreement.

Many of these shortcomings were addressed in a consultation paper covering England and Wales: *Sites of Special Scientific Interest: Better Protection and Management* (DETR, 1998) and are now covered in the Countryside and Rights of Way Bill that is presently before Parliament. The key proposals of Government are two-fold. First, a power to refuse consent for a potentially damaging operation. Although there would still be no right to appeal the notification of an SSSI, consents (or their conditions) could be appealed to the Secretary of State in cases of conflict. Secondly, the Bill envisages securing the positive management of sites in the case of neglect. This would be by the NCC making a 'management scheme' and serving this on every owner and occupier, and then enforcing this by serving 'management notices' in cases of non-compliance. If the notice is not complied with, the NCC would have the power to enter the site and carry out the works itself, including restoration works, charging any reasonable costs incurred to the owner or occupier.

These proposals strike at the heart of the voluntary principle, and if enacted would profoundly affect the relationship between the NCC and landowners, which involves the NCC in an often uneasy balance between being a scientific authority, partner in management, and regulator. Almost certainly they would legalise every aspect of SSSI policy, since the negative restrictions of owners and occupiers would give them greater incentive to challenge both the decision to notify and any decision not to consent or to require management. Other important proposals are:

(a)   that all payments under management agreements would only be made to secure appropriate management of the site, to ensure preservation of its nature conservation value;

(b)   that the NCC could enter into management agreements not merely in relation to SSSIs and adjacent sites, but *any* other sites (thus avoiding problems where ecological impacts are being caused by activities well away from the SSSI, e.g. drainage or water abstraction);

(c)   placing on owners of public land a legal duty of care in relation to site management (a more general duty of care is rejected);

(d)   that all SSSIs be declared in legislation to be of national importance, thus removing the distinction between s. 28 and s. 29 of the 1981 Act (a distinction would remain between controls relating to the actions of owners and occupiers, and of third parties). This will probably mean that some sites will, under explicit new powers, be denotified because they are of less than national importance;

(e)   powers to enter SSSIs;

(f)   increased penalties for deliberate damage;

(g)   a duty on statutory undertakers to give notice to the conservation agencies of all proposed operations (except emergency works) within or likely to affect SSSIs, and a power for agencies to refuse consent; and

(h)   enforceable means to require restoration of the conservation interest (currently provided for only under s. 29).

It is not surprising that the proposals were warmly, and in many cases enthusiastically, received by the conservation NGOs. However, some problem areas are not addressed. Most notable is protection of the marine environment, a depressing acknowledgement of the secondary status accorded to marine conservation at national level.

Legislation is also promised in Scotland (see *People and Nature*, 1998), although geographic, cultural and economic differences mean that reform proposals there take a slightly different shape. In particular, it is notable that emphasis is being placed on public involvement in site designation and management, albeit in the context of sites still being designated on scientific grounds. Thus, references to 'the NCC' in relation to reform proposals should be treated with caution.

EC conservation law

The development of EC conservation law has partly been in response to international developments (see p. 620), but it has also responded to particularly 'European' concerns. This is seen in a number of measures relating to things like restricting the import of pelts from animals caught by leghold traps (Regulation 3254/91), and banning certain imports of seal skins (Directive 83/129) and whale products (Regulation 348/81). Arguably it is also seen in the EC response to international regulation of the trade in endangered species, which goes beyond what is required by the CITES Convention (see Regulation 338/97).

However, in terms of the impact on UK law, it is the Wild Birds Directive (79/409) and the Habitats Directive (92/43) that have had the greatest influence and will continue to be of importance in the future. These contain some important provisions on the protection of individual animals and plants (which have been discussed above) but their greatest impact is in relation to habitat conservation. To a greater extent than with sites protected under national law, the best approach to understand the law in this area is to keep a clear distinction between the law relating to the designation of sites, and the laws governing the level of protection of such sites. Usually, the latter are weaker than the former.

EC Wild Birds Directive 79/409

Under the Wild Birds Directive, Member States are required in general terms to take measures, including the creation of protected areas, to maintain a sufficient diversity of habitats for *all* European bird species (Arts. 1, 2 and 3). They are also required to take special conservation measures to conserve the habitats of the rare or vulnerable species listed in Annex I and of all regularly occurring migratory species (Art. 4). These special measures should include the designation of special protection areas (SPAs) for such birds. Once an SPA has been designated, Member States must take appropriate steps to avoid significant pollution or deterioration of the habitat or disturbance of the birds within it (Art. 4(4)).

In Case C-355/90 *Commission* v *Spain* [1993] ECR I-4221, the European Court of Justice held that the Spanish government was in breach of Art. 4 by failing to designate an important wetland area, the Marismas de Santoña (or 'Santoña Marshes'), as an SPA. The case established that a Member State is effectively under a duty to designate an area as a SPA (and thus to protect it) if it fulfils the objective ornithological criteria laid down in the directive.

Subsequent decisions of the European Court of Justice have followed this strict approach to the duty of Member States to designate special protection areas. In Case C-44/95 *R* v *Secretary of State for the Environment, ex parte Royal Society for the Protection of Birds* [1997] QB 206, the RSPB challenged the failure of the Government to designate an area known as 'Lappel Bank' within the Medway Estuary and Marshes as an SPA. The UK government argued that economic considerations were relevant, whilst the RSPB relied on the ECJ decision in the *Santoña Marshes* case to argue that at the designation stage ornithological criteria were the only relevant considerations. The ECJ essentially took the latter view of the Directive, holding that the duty to designate sites was an obligation on Member States that was unaffected by economic considerations. However, the House of Lords had refused interim relief (with the consequent destruction of the habitat by the building of a 22 hectare car park) (see [1997] Env LR 431).

In the more recent case of Case C-3/96 *Commission* v *Netherlands* [1999] Env LR 147 the issue for the ECJ was not the failure to designate a particular site, or part of a site, but rather whether the Netherlands had breached its obligations under the Directive by not designating a *sufficient* number (and total area) of sites. A study in 1989 had suggested that 70 sites (covering 797,920 hectares) should have been designated, but in fact only 23 sites (covering 327,602 hectares) had been designated. The Court held that the Member States' discretion extended only to the application of objective ornithological criteria in identifying the most suitable territories for the conservation of Annex I species. The Netherlands could not argue that other conservation methods were being used.

The meaning of Art. 4(4) of the Directive was considered by the ECJ in Case C-57/89 *Commission* v *Germany* [1991] ECR I-883, a case about an area known as the 'Leybucht Dykes'. It established that reduction in the area of a SPA was only justified on very limited grounds, such as where the works were necessary for reasons of public health or public safety (which was actually the situation in the case itself), and that works could not be permitted for economic or recreational reasons, thus creating a strong presumption against development in such an area. This point was reinforced by the *Santoña Marshes* case, which applied the same test to the deterioration of a site as a result of pollution or other works and also suggested that Art. 4(4) is sufficiently clear to be directly effective. The effect of these rulings, however, was very quickly mitigated by an amendment that was made to Art. 4(4) by the Habitats Directive, which brought the Wild Birds Directive into line with the less restrictive exceptions laid down in Art. 6(4) of the Habitats Directive (see below).

Apart from the requirement to designate special protection areas, the Wild Birds Directive does not specify how its objectives are to be achieved, giving a degree of flexibility to Member States. In Britain, the approach that was adopted was initially to provide protection through the town planning and SSSI systems. All SPAs are, in practice, notified as SSSIs before being designated, but it should be noted that, prior to the passage of the Conservation (Natural Habitats etc.) Regulations 1994 (which are discussed in detail below), designation as an SPA (or as a Ramsar site, where a similar policy was adopted) did not impose any additional domestic requirements on owners or occupiers to those applicable to all SSSIs. There is also a crucial gap in the legislation on SSSIs in that there is no SSSI protection for parts of many SPAs (and also many Ramsar sites) because they are below low-water mark. Estuarine sites in particular are under great pressure; an NCC report has shown that 56 out of 136 estuarine SSSIs suffered damage between 1986 and 1989, many through permanent developments (see *Nature Conservation and Estuaries in Great Britain*, NCC, 1991). The European Court of Justice decisions in the Commission actions against Germany and Spain suggested that the British approach was no longer adequate and the position has now been radically altered by the 1994 Regulations.

The NCC has produced some extensive criteria for qualification as a special protection area (see *Protecting Internationally Important Bird Sites*, NCC, 1990, in which it identified a total of 218 candidate sites and stated that it was considering the merits of a further 43). As at 31 August 1999 there were 201 SPAs in the UK covering 934,574 hectares. Only a very small number of additional such areas are designated annually, and the Government has indicated that the series, at least the land-based and inter-tidal sites, will be largely complete by the end of 2000. In June 1999 selection guidelines were published, somewhat belatedly, by the JNCC. It is also important to note that the government has accepted, as a matter of planning policy, that all sites that meet the criteria for designation as an SPA should be treated as if they had been formally designated. For example, in July 1992 the Secretary of State refused planning permission for a number of major developments in North Kent, giving the need to protect a potential SPA as one of the main reasons (see [1993] Water Law 89). This policy is now enshrined in Planning Policy Guidance Note 9, *Nature Conservation* (PPG 9, October 1994).

EC Habitats Directive 92/43

The full title of this Directive refers to the Conservation of Natural Habitats and of Wild Fauna and Flora. However, whilst it does require some measures of importance to the protection of individual animals and plants to be taken, its main importance relates to habitat protection. Accordingly, it is commonly referred to as the Habitats Directive. It was adopted in May 1992 after many years of argument within the EC and has led to some important changes to British law and policy on habitat protection, which are discussed below.

(a) Site designation
The central feature of the Directive is that it provides for the creation of a coherent ecological network of special areas of conservation, which will make up a system of European sites known as Natura 2000. The network will consist of sites containing the natural habitat types listed in Annex I of the Directive and sites containing the habitats of the species listed in Annex II. It will incorporate the special protection areas classified under the Wild Birds Directive. However, the Directive also includes some more general duties, including a requirement that Member States monitor the conservation status of *all* habitats and species (Art. 11) and a general duty relating to the management of certain important landscape features (Art. 10).

(i)   Selecting SACs

The procedures for producing the list of special areas of conservation (SACs) are complex. By June 1995, Member States were required to send to the Commission a list of proposed sites, drawn up by reference to the criteria laid down in Annex III (Stage 1). By June 1999, 340 sites in the UK had been submitted to the Commission, with the Government indicating that this marked the end of this stage. Since then, however, the Government has been forced to review its selection of sites, following criticism. The Commission was then under a duty to draw up, by June 1998, a draft list of 'sites of Community importance', taking account of the criteria set out in Annex III (Stage 2). Given the delay in receiving submissions from most Member States, this has been delayed. The Commission adopts a final list thereafter in the light of scientific advice from a committee of independent experts. The Commission will produce a separate list of those sites which host one or more of the *priority* habitat types or species which are identified in Annexes I and II (these can be termed 'priority sites'). There are provisions for a bilateral consultation process between the Commission and a member state where the Commission considers that a priority site has been left off a member state's list, with ultimate recourse to the EC Council (Art. 5). In addition, the Commission is under a duty to review the list in the future, whilst Member States and the Commission are required to submit detailed implementation reports. Once the Commission has adopted the list of sites of Community importance, Member States are under a duty to designate any site on the list as a special area of conservation as soon as possible and within six years at the latest (Art. 4(4)).

(ii)   Economic considerations

Compared with the Wild Birds Directive, the provisions of the Habitats Directive appear to elevate the general importance to be attached to economic considerations (Art. 2(3)). It is not yet clear whether this affects the obligations on Member States when submitting candidate SACs, that is, whether they can take into account economic factors alongside the scientific considerations in Annex III. This issue is currently before the European Court of Justice in a reference from the High Court in Case C-371/98 *R v Secretary of State for the Environment, Transport and the Regions, ex parte First Corporate Shipping Limited*. In the Advocate General's Opinion (of 7 March 2000, unpublished), Member States should not take economic considerations into account when submitting candidate sites. However, this is tempered by the fact that, according to later guidance on site selection issued by the Commission in 1996, they must also send to the Commission information about 'impacts and activities in and around the site', defined as 'all human activities and natural processes that may have an influence, either positive and negative, on the conservation and management of the site'. On this reasoning, the conclusion must be that the Commission can take economic impacts into account when finalising the list of SACs. If this is upheld, it would mark a dramatic shift from the judgments of the ECJ in relation to SPAs under the Wild Birds Directive, where it has consistently held that the wording of that

Directive prevents economic consideration being taken into account at this stage. As things stand, however, the case illustrates the huge legal importance that may attach to low-profile EC guidance.

(iii) UK case law on site designation

Designation under the Habitats Directive has, however, been considered on at least three occasions by the UK courts (including the *ex parte Greenpeace* case, referred to below at p. 651). In *R v Secretary of State for Transport, ex parte Berkshire, Buckinghamshire and Oxfordshire Naturalists Trust* [1997] Env LR 80 an application for judicial review of the construction of the Newbury bypass was rejected. It was argued that the decision to proceed with the bypass necessarily frustrated any future decision to submit the site as a candidate SAC due to the presence of terrestrial pulmonate snails which, given the importance of the site for the snail, would have been likely. A significant reason why the site was not a candidate SAC was because the government takes the view that all terrestrial sites must first be SSSIs, an approach to implementation of the Directive which has no basis in law and which, as here, has presented problems for a significant minority of sites. But Sedley J could not find any basis for striking down the Government's approach, partly because of efforts by English Nature and the Highways Agency to translocate the snail population off the site. However, he did reach his decision with regret, noting that 'one can appreciate the force of the view that if the protection of the natural environment keeps coming second we shall end up by destroying our own habitat'.

Most recently in *World Wildlife Fund-UK Ltd and Royal Society for the Protection of Birds v Secretary of State for Scotland and others* [1999] Env LR 632, WWF and RSPB sought judicial review in the Scottish courts of various decisions connected with the exclusion of areas of Cairngorm from a candidate SAC. The area excluded was to be used for a funicular railway to take skiers up the mountain. However, it was held that although choosing sites and drawing boundaries was all part of one exercise, there was room for discretion in the drawing of boundaries so long as the discretion was exercised only on ornithological grounds. But these did not need to be so objective that a court could rule on them. The Scottish Office and its advisers had taken one view, the objectors another. It was not for the judge to say that the official line was wrong. An interesting feature of the case, however, is that the area was excluded from the candidate site in part because it was already developed, begging questions about the extent to which the presence of existing development can justify not designating areas of otherwise important sites.

The practical implication of this case is that decisions on the drawing of boundaries around sites, unless the boundaries are wholly irrational, are unlikely to be interfered with by the courts, which may lessen the impact of any decision about taking economic considerations into account on designation. Reasoning from the *Commission v Netherlands* case on SPAs, the prospect is that the government may, if it chooses, implement a minimalist designations policy involving designating a 'not insufficient' number of sites, and then drawing the boundaries around such sites as tightly as the courts hostility to reviewing such decisions as being irrational allows. Needless to say, such an approach would hardly fall within the spirit of the Directive, although in September 1999 the government agreed, just before a meeting of Member States in the Atlantic bioregion of the EC, to review its selection of SACs.

(b)   Site conservation
The protection provided by the Habitats Directive is as follows:

(a)   for special areas of conservation (once designated), Member States must adopt 'necessary conservation measures' and 'appropriate statutory, administrative or contractual measures' (Art 6(1));

(b)   for sites adopted by the Commission as sites of Community importance, SPAs designated under the Wild Birds Directive and sites subject to the Art. 5 consultation procedure, Member States are required to take appropriate steps to avoid the deterioration of the sites and significant disturbance of the species for which the areas have been designated (Art. 6(2)); and

(c)   for sites adopted by the Commission as sites of Community importance and SPAs designated under the Wild Birds Directive, any plan or project not directly connected with the management of the site which is likely to have a significant effect on it must be subject to an appropriate assessment of the implications; the competent national authorities can then agree to the plan or project only if it will not 'adversely affect the integrity of the site concerned' (Art. 6(3)).

However, if there is no alternative solution, a plan or project may be carried out if there are 'imperative reasons of overriding public interest, including those of a social or economic nature' (Art. 6(4)). In such a case, the member state has to take compensatory measures in order to ensure the overall coherence of Natura 2000 and must inform the Commission of those measures. When compared with the position set out in Case C-57/89 *Commission* v *Germany* [1991] ECR I-883 (the *Leybucht Dykes* case), this exception lessens the protection that is offered. However, for priority sites Art. 6(4) limits the exception to considerations relating to human health or public safety, situations where the impact is beneficial to the environment, and where the Commission has accepted that there are reasons of overriding public interest, in effect retaining the *Leybucht Dykes* position for priority sites. It is of relevance, therefore, that there are no priority bird species, and thus the stronger controls applicable to priority sites cannot apply to SPAs designated under the Wild Birds Directive.

It is notable, however, that in giving its Opinion on proposals to route the A20 motorway through the Peene Valley in Germany, intersecting two SPAs, the Commission was able to find that there were imperative reasons of overriding public interest to warrant a 300km link between two Baltic Sea ports. This was because the project was part of the trans-European road network, the region was in receipt of European social funding, because of the 'special value' that the German government placed upon it, and because of the lack of alternatives. The effect of this Opinion, and a similar draft Opinion relating to plans to route the same road through other SPAs and areas hosting priority natural habitat types under the Habitats Directive, therefore seems to be to reintroduce economic considerations into the derogations procedure. This seems contrary to the clear intention of Art. 6(4).

In Case C-355/90 *Commission* v *Spain* [1993] ECR I-4221 (*Santoña Marshes*), the ECJ suggested that Art. 4(4) of the Wild Birds Directive had direct effect. Since paras (2)–(4) of Art. 6 of the Habitats Directive are in very similar terms, in that they lay down clear requirements, it is arguable that they are also directly effective, with all the implications for enforcement of the law in Member States that this entails.

The 1994 Regulations

Initially, the then British government envisaged that the Habitats Directive could be implemented without new legislation. It intended to adopt the approach that had hitherto been used in relation to the Wild Birds Directive, i.e. judicious use of the SSSI and town planning systems. However, in the light of the *Leybucht Dykes* and *Santoña Marshes* cases it became clear that this would be inadequate in legal terms. As a result, in order to implement the provisions of the Directive, the European Communities Act 1972, s. 2(2) was used to pass the Conservation (Natural Habitats etc.) Regulations 1994 (SI 1994/2716).

However, rather than remodel the law on nature conservation entirely, the Government adopted a minimalist approach. It simply engrafted onto the existing SSSI and town planning mechanisms the additional protections required by the Directive, and then only where absolutely necessary. In essence, the regulations apply additional protections to 'European sites', which are defined as follows:

(a)   a special area of conservation (once designated — the regulations reproduce the procedures and timetable in the directive relating to designation, the Secretary of State being placed under a duty to propose a list of sites on or before 5 June 1995 (reg. 7) and required to designate sites adopted by the Commission as special areas of conservation 'as soon as possible and within six years at most' (reg. 8));

(b)   a site adopted by the Commission as a site of Community importance;

(c)   a special protection area designated under the Wild Birds Directive;

(d)   a site subject to consultation under Art. 5 of the Habitats Directive (although in this case the protection is limited in the same way as under the directive to the obligations under Art. 6(2)); and

(e)   candidate SACs submitted to the Commission, until such time as these sites are either adopted as SACs or fail to make the final list (this provision was added by SI 2000/192, and corrects the failure to classify candidate SACs as European sites in the 1994 Regulations).

The Secretary of State will draw up a public register of European sites (reg. 11) and notify them to the NCC (reg. 12), which will then notify local planning authorities, owners and occupiers and anyone else the Secretary of State may direct (reg. 13).

Under the regulations, the basic protection given to terrestrial European sites is the same as under the Wildlife and Countryside Act 1981, s. 28 for all SSSIs, with the following exceptions:

(a)   the NCC may amend the original notification made under s. 28 of the special interest of the site and of the potentially damaging operations (reg. 18);

(b)   the process through which the NCC grants consent for potentially damaging operations is altered in the light of Art. 6 of the directive so that:

(i)   if it appears to the NCC that a plan or project is likely to have a significant effect on the site, it must carry out an appropriate assessment and may only give consent if the plan or project will not affect the integrity of the site; and

(ii)   if it considers that there is a risk that the operation will be carried out without consent, it must notify the Secretary of State, who has the powers described below to make a special nature conservation order (reg. 20);

(c)   existing consents must be reviewed by the NCC and may be withdrawn or modified without compensation (reg. 21); and

(d)   by-laws may be made for terrestrial European sites (and over surrounding or adjoining sites) as if they were 'national' nature reserves (reg. 28).

In addition, the Secretary of State has a power to make a special nature conservation order over a European site (reg. 22). This is a new type of protection, which, although based on the Wildlife and Countryside Act 1981, s. 29, is potentially far stronger because it produces a situation where the ban on potentially damaging operations is permanent.

Where a special nature conservation order has been made, reg. 24 sets out the procedure to be followed where an owner or occupier applies for consent to carry out a plan or project. If it appears to the NCC that the plan or project is likely to have a significant effect on the site, it must carry out an appropriate assessment and *must* refuse consent, unless it is satisfied that the plan or project will not affect the integrity of the site. The owner or occupier may refer the refusal to the Secretary of State, who is given a power to direct the NCC to grant consent. But this power of direction can be used only if: (i) there is no alternative solution; and (ii) the plan or project must be carried out 'for imperative reasons of overriding public interest' (which is defined as in Art. 6(4) of the Directive and includes the more restrictive test for priority sites). If consent is granted, appropriate compensatory measures must be carried out.

This is the central feature of the whole Regulations, since it provides a form of absolute protection by introducing a mechanism through which a damaging activity may be prevented permanently. However, the success of the whole regulations (at least in terms of whether the Directive is properly implemented in practice) depends on the willingness of the Secretary of State to make a special nature conservation order and then to refuse consent where appropriate. These are matters that may not become clear for some time since, until the Commission adopts the list of sites of Community importance, until recently the only sites that were covered by the Habitats Directive were the special protection areas designated under the Wild Birds Directive although the recent changes to include candidate SACs as 'European sites' may change things here (see p. 648). Nevertheless, it is clear from the whole scheme of protection that the government envisages special nature conservation orders as instruments of last resort to be used only when absolutely necessary and only two such orders have been made by the NCC, the first in February 1998 in relation to drainage works on the Peak Moors special protection area. (Some orders under s. 29 of the 1981 Act have become special nature conservation orders under reg. 27.) Set against that, reg. 3(2) requires the Secretary of State and the nature conservation bodies to exercise their nature conservation functions 'so as to secure compliance' with the Directive. It must also be noted that the regulations repeat many of the opaque words and phrases used in the Directive; in line with standard principles of EC law, these should be interpreted in accordance with the Directive.

European marine sites

As far as European sites which are marine or tidal are concerned, the regulations are far more loosely worded. Every public body having functions relevant to marine conservation is required to exercise its functions so as to secure compliance with the requirements of the Directive (reg. 3(3)). In addition, more specific powers and duties are laid down in regs. 33 to 36. The NCC must advise other relevant authorities (a term which includes local authorities, the Environment Agency, water and sewerage undertakers, internal drainage boards, navigation authorities, harbour authorities and fisheries committees) as to the conservation objectives for the site and any potentially damaging operations. Any relevant authority *may* then establish a management scheme for the site and the NCC *may* make by-laws under the Wildlife and Countryside Act 1981, s. 37 as if the site were a marine nature reserve. The relevant Minister is given a wide power to make directions to the relevant authorities concerning management schemes. Although guidance was published by the Department of the Environment, Transport and the Regions, and the Welsh Office in 1998, it must be doubted whether these vague arrangements, which in the absence of town planning and SSSI controls are the only real powers available below the low-water mark, are adequate to ensure the proper implementation of the directive. Having said that, marine habitats and species are poorly represented in the Directive itself, which has an almost exclusive focus on territorial and coastal habitats. Although the view of the UK Government was that the Directive, which applies to the 'European territory of the Member States', did not extend to the continental shelf, the High Court has now held that it does. In a purposive decision in *R v Secretary of State for Trade and Industry, ex parte Greenpeace (No. 2)* [2000] Env LR 221, a challenge to the awarding of oil exploration licences, the Court took into account that some distant water species are listed in the Directive. Perhaps more importantly, however, the place of the Directive within a matrix of other conservation measures, most of which did extend beyond territorial waters (e.g. the Biodiversity Convention, on which see p. 654), was judged to be an important consideration.

One implication of this case is that the Conservation (Natural Habitats etc.) Regulations 1994 will need to be revised so that they extend to the UK continental shelf and superjacent waters out to 200 nautical miles. Another consequence is that the functions of the NCCs will need to be revised so that they can exercise their functions out to this limit.

European sites and other regulatory systems

The regulations also make important amendments to a number of regulatory systems. Where a plan or project is likely to have a significant effect on a European site, before granting such things as planning permission or a pollution authorisation, the relevant regulatory agency must consult with the NCC and carry out an appropriate assessment of the implications of the plan or project for the site (reg. 48). The agency must agree to the plan or project only if it will not adversely affect the integrity of the site, unless the provisions of regs. 49 and 53 are satisfied (these repeat the exceptions laid down in Art. 6(4) of the Directive). The Secretary of State is also given powers to prohibit the plan or project, either temporarily or permanently. In addition, existing permissions, consents and authorisations must be reviewed as soon as reasonably practicable (reg. 50). If the integrity of the site is adversely affected, the agency should use its normal powers of revocation or modification, paying compensation if that would be the usual position. There are also restrictions on a developer taking advantage of a development order in order to carry out development on a European site (regs. 60 to 64).

An example of how these provisions work is the first such action of its kind under the 1994 Regulations. In November 1998 the Secretary of State confirmed the revocation of a planning permission which would have resulted in the loss of 82 hectares of grazing marsh in the Medway Estuary by the disposal of river dredgings. The planning permission pre-dated the classification in 1993 of the Medway Estuary and Marshes as a special protection area (the same area formed the wider background to the *Lappel Bank* litigation, discussed on p. 642 above). The Minister accepted that there were alternatives to the disposal of the dredged material on the Marshes which would be less damaging to wildlife, and judged that cost factors were irrelevant in reaching this decision.

In relation to applications for planning permission, PPG 9, *Nature Conservation* (October 1994), creates some additional protections as a matter of policy, including that, for development control purposes, potential SPAs and candidate SACs included in the list sent to the EC Commission (although see now SI 2000/192, at p. 648) should be treated in the same way as designated sites, and that environmental assessment will normally be required where a Ramsar site or a candidate or designated European site could be affected.

Summary of protection under EC conservation law

There is little doubt that the 1994 Regulations have increased the protection available to European sites and that PPG 9 reinforces that protection within the planning system. However, it is difficult to say whether they implement the Habitats Directive fully, since the crucial issues relate to whether the powers will be used in practice. As pointed out above, the willingness of the Secretary of State to designate European sites and then to protect them by making special nature conservation orders is central. The then government's approach to the selection of appropriate sites was set out in *A List of Possible Special Areas of Conservation in the UK*, issued in March 1995, which confirmed that there will be few priority sites in the UK.

There are other potential defects with the regulations. They impose a very heavy administrative burden on the NCC and the various regulatory agencies which are required to review consents. This burden may well prove to be too great. It must also be asked whether the extra attention paid to European sites means that, in practice, the resources and goodwill available to protect other sites are being downgraded. Many commentators have already queried why, in the light of the defects identified in the legislation relating to SSSIs, the opportunity was not taken in 1994 to improve the protection given to *all* SSSIs.

International conservation law

In customary international law, nature conservation objectives are problematic because of the principle of national sovereignty over natural resources (see p. 96). For terrestrial species, there are few restrictions on unchallenged exploitation, although the Stockholm Declaration does refer to states' duties to safeguard wildlife, which would extend both to harm done within states and to neighbouring states (Principles 2 and 4). Another important text is the World Charter for Nature (1982), adopted by the UN General Assembly, a strongly worded, soft law document emphasising ecosystem conservation. Customary international law has more to say in relation to shared or common resources, especially living marine resources, but as the *Behring Fur Seals Arbitration* (see p. 95) indicates, this may not be to the advantage of conservation. Rather more encouraging was the statement by the International Court of Justice in the *Fisheries Jurisdiction* cases that states must have 'due regard' to the 'needs of conservation for the benefit of all' (see *United Kingdom* v *Iceland* (Merits) 1974 ICJ Rep. 3).

But in practice, it is clear that for all the enforcement problems, international biodiversity conservation is likely to be best realised using treaty law, and there are a number of international conventions relating to nature conservation whose significance in the context of domestic law should not be underestimated. Arguably, the 1979 Berne Convention on the Conservation of European Wildlife and Natural Habitats, and to a lesser extent the 1979 Bonn Convention on the Conservation of Migratory Species of Wild Animals, can be seen as driving forces behind the Wild Birds and Habitats Directives discussed above. Another key conservation treaty is the 1973 Washington Convention on International Trade in Endangered Species of Wild Flora and Fauna (CITES). The CITES treaty is interesting legally because, although it cannot be a party to it, the EC has nevertheless introduced legislation which, in some respects, imposes even stricter obligations than is required under the treaty. In particular, Council Regulation 338/97 puts tougher demands on countries exporting endangered species or products made from such species than are required under CITES. To the extent that the regulation conflicts with the Control of Endangered Species (Import and Export) Act 1976, the UK's national measures to implement CITES, the regulation prevails.

(a)   The Ramsar Convention
The Ramsar Convention on Wetlands of International Importance Especially as Waterfowl Habitat, 1971, was the first international convention dealing solely with habitat. It came into force in 1975 and currently there are 120 Contracting Parties, of which the UK is one.

The Convention establishes a number of protections, though it can be criticised for being too general and unenforceable. First it imposes on the Contracting Parties a general duty to promote the conservation of wetlands and waterfowl, especially by establishing nature reserves. Secondly it adopts a site designation approach and provides for the compilation of a list of wetlands of international importance. Contracting Parties are under a duty to formulate their planning so as to promote the conservation of wetlands included in the list. Each Contracting Party must designate at least one site within its territory and deletion or reduction in size of a site is allowed only on the grounds of 'urgent national interests'. Guidelines on the definition of international importance have been drawn up, although ultimately it is up to each Contracting Party to decide whether and where it will designate. In addition to these powers, there are provisions under the Convention for the monitoring of wetlands, the establishment of a database, the funding of projects, educational work and publications. It also provides for a Ramsar Bureau, which is based in Switzerland. Notably, the focus of the Convention has shifted over the years to emphasise financial and other support mechanisms for wetlands conservation rather than prohibitive measures.

'Wetland' is interpreted very widely to include 'areas of marsh, fen, peatland or water, whether natural or artificial, permanent or temporary, with water that is static or flowing, fresh, brackish or salt, including areas of marine water the depth of which does not exceed six metres'. Designation may also include adjacent areas of land, such as coasts, riverbanks and islands.

As with the Wild Birds Directive, the Ramsar Convention was initially implemented through the planning and SSSI systems. In practice, this still remains the case, since the sites are not necessarily European sites for the

purposes of the 1994 Regulations. However, it must be pointed out that
Ramsar sites are now given significant protection in practice through PPG 9
and that many of the 139 sites designated in the UK (which cover 713,339
hectares) by August 1999 are also SPAs under the Wild Birds Directive or
candidate SACs. Proposals in the Countryside and Rights of Way Bill (see
p. 640) would make it a formal requirement for the Secretary of State to
notify the NCCs of Ramsar sites.

The Convention has therefore played a key role in protecting one particular
habitat that the UK has in relative abundance. The meetings of the parties to
the Convention every two or three years helps focus attention on the
government's obligations, and often provides the impetus for the designation
of further sites or other conservation measures. In practice, however, domestic considerations may be more influential. Despite featuring on the 'Mon-
treaux record', an 'at risk register' for the Convention, the timing of the
additional protection given to the cross-border Dee catchment through the
designation of the first water protection zone (see p. 601) owed more to the
immanence of Welsh devolution (it being easier to pass regulations through
one legislature rather than two), and in any case is focused on protecting
public water supplies.

(b) The Convention on Biological Diversity
The 1992 Convention on Biological Diversity came into force by the end of
1993, very quickly for a major multilateral treaty. It aims to conserve
biological diversity through a variety of means including species and habitat
conservation. Under art. 6 of the Convention the contracting parties must, in
accordance with their particular conditions and capabilities, develop or adapt
national strategies, plans and programmes for biodiversity conservation, and
integrate the conservation and sustainable use of biological diversity into
relevant sectoral or cross-sectoral plans, programmes and policies.

Under art. 6, the UK Biodiversity Action Plan 1994 was produced, an
important document guiding subsequent policy in this area. This in turn has
led to the development of action plans for 172 species of plants and animals
(a further 200 species are under review) and 24 habitats. The scheme is
intended to increase public awareness and involvement, but also to develop
costed targets for key species. An important tool used is to seek 'champions'
for species, especially from the voluntary and private sectors, as well as
government funding. For example, Water UK, the body representing the
water industry, has invested £1m in otter conservation over three years, the
largest such funding arrangement. Alongside changes contained in the Countryside and Rights of Way Bill, these plans are the most important development in conservation policy since the 1981 Act. There is a prospect that the
Bill might put such plans on a statutory footing (as is already the case with
the Greater London Authority Act 1999, s. 352), which might alleviate some
of the funding problems the NCC is experiencing in their implementation.

Also in accordance with art. 6, the Commission has adopted a Communication on a European Community Biodiversity Strategy (COM(98)42), the
EC having ratified the Convention in 1993. Amongst the policy approaches

envisaged for promoting conservation outside protected areas is the promotion of eco-labelling schemes for products whose production, distribution, use or disposal could affect biodiversity. But the more general integration of biodiversity concerns into relevant sectoral policies such as agriculture, fisheries and regional policies is also envisaged. The Convention also includes measures about in-situ conservation (art. 8), which cover, for example, provisions requiring degraded ecosystems to be rehabilitated and restored through, among other things, plans and management strategies, and impact assessments (art. 14).

Many have judged the Convention weak and misguided. Most of the articles of the Convention require action only 'as far as possible and as appropriate', which weakens their legal status. Also, many aspects of the Convention are premised on the economic utilisation of biodiversity for things like pharmaceutical products. The intention was to create mechanisms, especially in relation to intellectual property rights and technology transfer, under which developing countries in particular would have economic incentives to conserve their natural stock of biodiversity. It is largely because of objections to these provisions that the United States has still not ratified the Convention. Nevertheless, provisions such as art. 6 go beyond a 'protected area' approach to conservation, and at least in the UK appear to have given considerable impetus to the development of wider conservation initiatives. On the other hand, it is debatable whether provisions like art. 10 of the Convention, which require the integration of biodiversity conservation into national decision-making, have provided anything more than a basis for policy arguments along these lines. The tendency has been to isolate conservation from the pressures of the wider economy, without doing anything to lessen the forces creating those pressures. A conservation 'stamp collecting' approach, through a focus on protected sites, still appears to dominate.

TWENTY TWO
Landscape management

This chapter looks at the legal protection and management of various features of the British countryside: its landscape, trees, forests, and hedgerows. There are a number of different things involved here. As regards landscape there is the restriction of urban expansion and urban development in the countryside; the preservation of the particular rural character of an area; and the protection of distinctive landscapes or landscape types. All are strongly affected by social changes, especially population migration from urban to rural areas. But they are also affected by the economic prosperity of rural areas, making the sharp decline in farm incomes in the wake of the BSE crisis particularly relevant here. This has put further pressure on farmers to diversify their businesses, which may significantly alter the character of rural areas. In many cases, farms have been sold, often leading to the creation of larger agricultural units or to 'hobby farms' whose emergence may lead to a loss of the local knowledge needed to maintain local features.

With trees, forests and hedgerows the focus is generally on smaller, sometimes individual, environmental features, the key problem for the law being in grappling with two familiar and related difficulties — controlling destructive, rather than constructive, acts and establishing adequate control over natural things. In both cases, however, protection and management pose some difficult problems, since the shape of most of what is to be protected is the result of hundreds of years of human intervention. There is also the problem, common to environmental law, that loss or damage to individual features is unlikely to be critical ecologically, although individual loss of amenity may be more acutely felt. A good example is the role of trees and woodlands as 'carbon sinks', mitigating global warming: it is difficult to argue that small losses are significant other than in amenity terms. In the wider context of sustainable development, this poses difficult issues of what exactly to preserve and why. Some of the difficulties here can be seen in the statement of the Countryside Commission (now the Countryside Agency, see p. 661 below) that future generations must be passed a national inheritance 'with all its richness intact' (*Protecting our Finest Countryside: Advice to Government*, 1998), a suitably obscure objective.

A further consideration is the role that landscape plays in the construction of identity, and it might tentatively be suggested that issues concerning landscape will play some part in the forging of regional identities in England in the longer term. (It is certainly the main motivation behind a 1998 draft Council of Europe European Landscape Convention.) This might form one part of a more 'bioregional' approach to decision-making, in which nature conservation would also play an important part. As discussed briefly in Chapter 21, nature conservation and landscape issues are increasingly being yoked together, following many decades of relative isolation.

Regulatory mechanisms

Three main methods of control may be discerned:

(a)   One is to rely on the town and country planning legislation to control developments in the countryside in the same way they are controlled in towns.

(b)   A second is to impose special protections in designated areas, or in relation to designated features such as hedgerows. In practice, these added protections often tend to stem from the town and country planning system as well, though there are some that do not.

(c)   A third mechanism is to utilise grants and other incentives to ensure the proper care of the countryside or natural features, again with special schemes available in selected areas. Economic tools are widely used in the promotion of desirable objectives such as tree planting and hedge laying.

A particular feature of both the second and third mechanisms is the reliance on voluntary controls, rather than on compulsion. Since most countryside land is privately owned it is perhaps inevitable that positive action, as much as restrictive controls, will be used.

The international and EC dimension

By comparison with most other topics covered in this book, international and EC law has had relatively little direct impact on national law and policy relating to landscape management. This is undoubtedly because of the often local and subjective nature of this topic, although some conventions have in recent years included landscape features within a general definition of 'the environment', as is the case with the 1991 Espoo Convention on Environmental Impact Assessment in a Transboundary Context and the 1992 Transboundary Watercourses Convention. Attempts to conclude a global convention on forests have so far been unsuccessful, and only a Non-binding Statement of Forest Principles was agreed at the Earth Summit in 1992, although there are emerging signs that a global treaty may now be more acceptable to countries such as Indonesia which strongly resisted such a development at Rio.

The 1972 World Heritage Convention, however, is a notable example of an attempt to use international law to protect national features of global significance. As well as cultural treasures, the treaty aims to protect natural heritage of 'outstanding universal value' for aesthetic or scientific reasons. The treaty is unusual since states are obliged not only to protect sites which are eventually accepted onto a 'World Heritage List', but are also under general obligations to protect any areas worthy of inclusion on such a list. States must keep under review heritage covered by the treaty, and protect it even if it is not accepted on to the list, although it is unlikely that any decision about an area forming part of the world heritage would be reviewable by the courts (for an Australian example see *Queensland* v *Commonwealth* (1989) 167 CLR 232). The added protection of being listed is that sites are eligible for assistance from the World Heritage Fund, run by UNESCO. The list is currently biased in favour of cultural heritage, and the 17 sites for which the UK is responsible are also mostly built heritage, e.g. Canterbury Cathedral. Although there is no planning policy on World Heritage sites, there is a Ministerial statement to the effect that inappropriate development should be avoided at such sites. This may extend to development affecting the wider setting of such sites, which may provide extended landscape protection in a small number of areas (see *Coal Contractors* v *Secretary of State for the Environment* [1995] JPL 421, a case concerning Hadrian's Wall).

At EC level, there is no legislation relating directly to landscape, although the Environmental Impact Assessment Directive (85/337) requires information about the effects of projects on landscape and cultural heritage to be assessed. Rather, the impact of the EC is most closely felt through the Common Agricultural Policy and from EC regulations aimed at integrating agricultural and environmental objectives (see below). Under the Habitats Directive (92/43), Member States must encourage in their land-use planning and development policies the conservation of linear landscape features, such as hedgerows, which play an important part in biodiversity conservation. This obligation marks an important break from a pure protected areas approach to conservation (on which see generally Chapter 21) and emphasises the links between nature conservation and landscape management that are increasingly being made.

Town and country planning

The starting point for the protection of the countryside has always been the development control system. But it has never proved particularly successful because, despite its name, it has always had an urban bias. There have been very few adaptations of the basic structure to cope with countryside matters. Indeed, it is commonly referred to as the 'town planning' system, the countryside aspect being forgotten.

There are a number of reasons for this. A major one is the history of the system, which had a consequent effect on the nature of the legal mechanisms that were adopted. The town and country planning system developed in 1947 was specifically designed to meet predominantly urban problems, such as community layout and design, industrial location, post-war reconstruction, public health and overcrowding, and transportation changes. As far as the rural environment was concerned, the main policy was the protection of the countryside against urban creep and expansion. The legal mechanisms that were adopted were thus mainly negative, such as the need for planning permission, and did not reflect the need for positive management in the countryside.

In addition, there was in 1947 perceived to be little need to control developments in the countryside, since it was generally considered that landowners and farmers had done a good job in shaping the landscape, and in any case agriculture itself required protection after the rural depression of the 1930s and the Atlantic Blockade of the Second World War. Agriculture and forestry, the two main activities likely to have an impact on the landscape, were granted generous exemptions in the legislation which, despite some minor changes, still remain today.

As a result there are distinct limitations on the use of development control in the countryside, and its most important role is in controlling new buildings and structures:

(a)   Many rural activities which have a significant impact on the landscape do not constitute development. For example, afforestation or deforestation, hedgerow or stone wall removal, ploughing, and the cultivation of new crops (such as oil seed rape) are all entirely excluded from the development control system.

(b)   The Town and Country Planning Act 1990, s. 55(2)(e), provides that a change of use to agriculture or forestry is not development. Whilst it is obvious that this covers a change from an urban to a rural use, in landscape terms it is more significant that this paragraph excludes from development control a change from unused land (often of high nature conservation or landscape value) to agriculture or forestry, or from agriculture to forestry, or from forestry to agriculture, or from one type of agriculture or forestry to another. 'Agriculture' is defined very widely in the Town and Country Planning Act 1990, s. 336, to include such diverse things as intensive livestock production, fish farming, horticulture and extensive grazing.

(c)   Further exemptions are set out in the Town and Country Planning (General Permitted Development) Order 1995 (SI 1995/418) (the GPDO) sch. 2, under which blanket automatic planning permissions (permitted development rights) are granted. For example, the GPDO exempts the construction of fences and walls up to 2 metres in height, and temporary uses up to 28 days per year (although not war games, motor sports and clay pigeon shooting within SSSIs).

(d)   The GPDO, sch. 2, parts 6 and 7 provide permitted development rights for a wide range of agricultural and forestry operations, such as new roads, buildings, drainage works and excavations, subject to some generous limitations on size and height (for example, each building may be up to 465 square metres in area and 12 metres in height). There are other, more technical limitations, such as that the erection or alteration of structures for the accommodation of livestock, or for storing slurry or sewage sludge, within 400 metres of non-agricultural dwellings or other buildings is not permitted under the GPDO.

(e) A final limitation on the usefulness of the development control system in the countryside is that this is a political system. Decisions are made by local planning authorities and are likely to reflect the economic needs and policy preferences of local residents, although reference must always be made to Planning Policy Guidance Note 7, *The Countryside and the Rural Economy*, which sets out general government planning policies towards the countryside. Local authorities may also underestimate the importance of a local area in national terms. (In passing it should be noted that these same limitations explain why the network of SSSIs is not protected properly by controls dependent on the town and country planning system (see p. 631).)

Extra protections under planning law

In some circumstances, there are extra protections provided by the town and country planning system in the countryside:

(a) The extent of development permitted under the GPDO is limited in national parks, the Norfolk and Suffolk Broads, areas of outstanding natural beauty, conservation areas and any area specified by the Secretary of State and Minister of Agriculture under the Wildlife and Countryside Act 1981, s. 41(3) (collectively these areas are known as Article 1(5) land). Whilst the limitations are not great, this does mean that stricter controls apply to such things as extensions to houses and other buildings.

(b) A system of prior notification applies to farm or forestry developments otherwise permitted by the GPDO, sch. 2, parts 6 and 7. This means that 28 days' prior notification of the proposed development must be submitted to the local planning authority, which may then impose conditions relating to the siting, design and external appearance of the development in the light of the likely effects on the surroundings. In making this decision, the local planning authority must take into account not only the visual aspects of the development, but also the desirability of preserving ancient monuments and their settings, archaeological sites, the setting of listed buildings and sites of recognised nature conservation value.

Since 1999, prior notification procedures now also apply to mobile phone masts, although only ground-based masts (as opposed to antenna and masts on buildings) require publicity, which explains the current preference for masts on buildings like schools and churches. For ground-based masts, policy guidance 'strongly encourages' additional publicity beyond a notice at the proposed site, e.g. through advertisements in local newspapers (Circular 4/99, *Planning for Telecommunications*). The Telecommunications Code, made under the Telecommunications Act 1984 and separate from planning law, lays down notification procedures for any 'telecommunications apparatus', but then restricts those who can object to landowners on whose land the apparatus is installed or those having 'nearby' land interests.

(c)   As a matter of policy, the local planning authority may impose restrictive conditions on activities requiring permission. For example, specific design criteria are commonly imposed where there is a local style. It may also make non-statutory designations of such things as sites of high landscape value in its development plan.

(d)   An Article 4 direction may be imposed under the GPDO, requiring planning permission to be sought for something that would otherwise be granted automatic permission (see p. 315). For example, this mechanism was used on Halvergate Marsh in the Norfolk grazing marshes in 1984 to prevent agricultural drainage and ploughing damaging the landscape importance of the area, though in confirming the direction, the DoE stressed that the main purpose was to compel the farmer involved to accept a management agreement on the land. Since Article 4 directions entail the payment of compensation by the local planning authority if planning permission is then refused, their use is rare (even though the cost is sometimes grant-aided by central government agencies).

It is important to note that green belts, creatures of planning policy but never planning law, are primarily intended to act as a brake on suburban growth. There is a policy presumption against major development in green belts, unless 'very special circumstances' dictate otherwise (see Planning Policy Guidance Note 2, *Green Belts* (1995)), which around many urban areas entrenches the divide between urban and rural. While green belts are not designated on nature conservation or landscape grounds, they undoubtedly contribute indirectly to these objectives.

The Countryside Agency

In England, landscape matters were for many years the responsibility of the Countryside Commission, originally created in 1949 as the National Parks Commission. In April 1999, a new Countryside Agency was formed by changing the name of the Countryside Commission to the Countryside Agency, and then transferring certain functions of the Rural Development Commission (RDC) to the new Agency (see SI 1999/416). The result is that the functions of the Countryside Agency are still found in ss. 1 and 2 of the Countryside Act 1968, which provide that the Agency has responsibilities for the conservation and enhancement of natural beauty in England and the provision of recreational activities. These amenity functions distinguish it from English Nature. Constitutional matters and funding are governed by sch. 13 to the Wildlife and Countryside Act 1981, which provides that its members are appointed by the Secretary of State and its finance is provided by central government grant aid. The Agency has few operational powers, apart from the designation of national parks and areas of outstanding natural beauty, but it has an important role in providing advice and finance in relation to its objectives. It is important to note that the creation of the Countryside Agency is bound up with the establishment of Regional Development Agencies in England, under the Regional Development Agencies Act 1998, which have inherited rural regeneration functions from the RDC.

Equivalent responsibilities to those of the Countryside Agency are carried out in Scotland by Scottish Natural Heritage and in Wales by the Countryside Council for Wales, although neither body has assumed the rural development remit of the former RDC.

Finally, all the landscape agencies, and all Ministers, government departments and public bodies, must have regard to the desirability of conserving the 'natural beauty and amenity' (in Scotland, the 'natural heritage'; see Countryside (Scotland) Act 1967, s. 66) of the countryside (Countryside Act 1968, s. 11). These are broad-ranging duties, applying to the functions of these bodies under any enactment, but their usefulness is limited by the weakness of their formulation.

Landscape protection and management agreements

Apart from the limited protection accorded to landscapes by planning law, there are a number of designations of land that may be made. However, these depend ultimately either on the town planning system, or on voluntary powers. There are few, if any, compulsory powers to support landscape protection.

In line with this voluntary philosophy, there is a power for any local planning authority to enter into a management agreement with any owner of land for conserving or enhancing its natural beauty or amenity, or for promoting its enjoyment by the public (Wildlife and Countryside Act 1981, s. 39). Such an agreement is grant aided by the Countryside Agency. Unlike the position for agreements made in relation to SSSIs, the financial guidelines laid down in the Wildlife and Countryside Act 1981, s. 50 do not apply to agreements made under s. 39 (see p. 637 for these guidelines).

(a) National parks
National parks in Britain do not equate to the concept of a national park used in most other countries. Instead of being wilderness areas with few, if any, inhabitants, they contain land on which large numbers of people live. They are effectively working environments. The aim of national park designation is to plan and manage the area so as to create a balance between recreation, amenity, wildlife and economic development. Land ownership is unaffected by designation, although various public bodies are given powers to purchase land, and in practice much of some parks is in the ownership of a public body, or of the National Trust.

(i) General objectives and duties
National parks were first provided for in the National Parks and Access to the Countryside Act 1949. This Act still provides the basic structure of the legislation on national parks, although it has been much amended, especially by the Countryside Act 1968 and the Environment Act 1995, Part III. The purposes of national parks were originally stated in the Hobhouse Report (*National Parks in England and Wales*, 1947), and set out in the National Parks and Access to the Countryside Act 1949, s. 5, in terms of two general

objectives: the preservation and enhancement of the natural beauty of the areas; and the promotion of their enjoyment by the public. In recognition of the way that attitudes towards the national parks have changed since 1949, the Environment Act 1995, s. 61 substitutes a new s. 5 which sets out somewhat wider purposes:

(a)   conserving and enhancing the natural beauty, wildlife and cultural heritage of the areas . . .; and

(b)   . . . promoting opportunities for the understanding and enjoyment of the special qualities of those areas by the public.

The impact of the changed purposes is reinforced by a new s. 11A(2) to the 1949 Act, which requires all public bodies and statutory undertakers to have regard to the new purposes when exercising or performing any functions affecting land in a national park. The new s. 11A(2) also gives statutory effect to the so-called 'Sandford principle', which is that where there is a conflict between purposes (a) and (b), then greater weight should be attached to purpose (a). The balance between environmental, amenity and economic factors is also made explicit in a new s. 11A(1), which requires national park authorities to seek to foster the economic and social well-being of local communities within the national park, albeit in the context of pursuing the purposes set out in s. 5.

Responsibility for proposing and designating a national park originally lay with the National Parks Commission, which designated the 10 existing parks in the 1950s. This responsibility has now devolved to the Countryside Agency and the Countryside Council for Wales.

Currently there are 10 national parks, covering 9 per cent of the area of England and Wales and with almost 250,000 permanent residents. The parks are the Peak District, the Lake District, the Yorkshire Dales, the North York Moors, Northumberland, Snowdonia, the Brecon Beacons, the Pembrokeshire Coast, Exmoor and Dartmoor. In addition, the Broads Authority was established by the Norfolk and Suffolk Broads Act 1988. This has a similar constitution and powers to the national parks, with the inclusion of powers over navigation and water space. For the purposes of most legal protections it is treated as a national park. If a new park is proposed, this would require extensive publicity and consultation and would normally also require a public inquiry, after which the designation would need confirmation by the Secretary of State.

In September 1999, the Government announced that it was asking the Countryside Agency to consider designating national parks in the South Downs and the New Forest. Latterly, the Countryside Commission/Agency had taken the view that further designations of national parks in England would devalue the concept, although in 1998 they eventually supported designation of the New Forest (it might be noted that there is already a New Forest Heritage Area in which the same planning principles that govern development in national parks are applied). What is interesting about the recent development is that, despite responsibility for proposing and designating parks resting with the Countryside Agency, what has happened is that central government, whose confirmation and funding is needed, is able to initiate the designation process by political direction.

There is no national park in Scotland, although there are designations with a roughly similar impact, and clear signs that the Scottish Parliament may designate Loch Lomond and the Trossachs as Scotland's first park (followed by the Cairngorms) if the National Parks (Scotland) Bill is enacted.

(ii)   Administrative responsibilities
The national parks are the only areas where a new institutional structure has been created in an attempt to protect the countryside. However, control remains essentially local, since the Countryside Agency and the Countryside Council for Wales have no executive functions. Under s. 63 of the Environment Act 1995, the Secretary of State has power to establish by order a national park authority in the form set out in sch. 7. This has altered the previous arrangements whereby each national park was administered by an authority run by a committee of the relevant county council or a separate, autonomous board. This has had the effect of creating autonomous local authorities for national parks with primary responsibility for planning functions.

The national park authorities were formally established on 1 April 1997. Schedule 7 provides that a national park authority is a body corporate and is subject to most legislative provisions affecting local authorities, including those on access to meetings, audit, competitive tendering and the jurisdiction of the Commissioner for Local Administration (the Ombudsman). Following a late amendment to the 1995 Act, for national parks in England the balance between the various appointees to the authorities was altered, a change that led to accusations from some quarters that national park authorities will be turned into centralised quangos. (In Wales, half the members are appointed by the National Assembly, after consultation with the Countryside Council for Wales, and half appointed by the constituent local authorities.) One half plus one of the members are appointed by the constituent county and district councils, with the remainder appointed by the Secretary of State, after consultation with the Countryside Agency. Of those Secretary of State appointees, half minus one must be members of parish councils in the national park. The total number on the authority and the exact number of appointees from each local authority is set out in the specific order establishing each national park authority. The authority then elects its own chair and deputy chair.

Under the previous legislation each national park had a national park officer and a national park management plan. This position remains the same for the new authorities, which are empowered to adopt the existing management plan, subject to provisions concerning regular review (Environment Act 1995, s. 66). There are new powers to provide funding for the national park authorities. Under the Environment Act 1995, s. 72, the relevant Secretary of State has a wide discretion to make grants to a national park authority, whilst s. 71 empowers the authorities to issue levies to the constituent local authorities and the principle of 75 per cent central funding remains. In addition, it should be noted that grants from the Countryside Agency and the Countryside Council for Wales for works and schemes are normally payable at a higher rate in a national park than they are outside.

(iii) Controls on development

Protection of the parks has always been strongly tied to the town and country planning system. The national park authority is designated the sole local planning authority for its area, taking over all of the planning functions from the national park committee or board. One exception concerns tree preservation orders, where the district council retains concurrent jurisdiction with the national park authority. Strategic planning in national parks centres around the national park development plan that was first required by the Planning and Compensation Act 1991 (as with all plan-making in national parks, this requires consultation with the Countryside Agency or the Countryside Council for Wales). In addition under s. 66 of the Environment Act 1995 the national park authorities had to prepare a national park management plan before April 1999. These replace the national park plans made under the Local Government Act 1972 (though existing plans can be adopted as the management plan). The management plan performs a different strategic function from the purely planning-based development plan, covering wider management policy issues.

As far as the substantive detail of planning law is concerned, apart from the limited restrictions referred to above, the main protection lies in the formulation and application of sensitive policies for the protection of the park through the planning process. But national parks are certainly not inviolable, as the siting of Fylingdales Early Warning Station, Milford Haven Oil Terminal, and numerous quarries in the Peak District illustrate. National park authorities also have positive powers in relation to such things as the purchase of land, the arrangement of public access, the provision of facilities and the appointment of rangers.

Every national park authority is under a duty to prepare a map of 'any area of mountain, moor, heath, woodland, down, cliff or foreshore' within the national park, whose natural beauty it is important to conserve (Wildlife and Countryside Act 1981, s. 43, as amended by the Wildlife and Countryside (Amendment) Act 1985). These maps will provide a reliable picture of the landscape of the parks and how it is changing. They will be used as the basis for policies relating to landscape protection within the parks, in line with guidance issued by the Countryside Commission.

(b) Areas of outstanding natural beauty

Areas of outstanding natural beauty (AONBs) are designated under the National Parks and Access to the Countryside Act 1949, s. 87, solely for their natural beauty, with the objective of protecting and enhancing these features. Even though in landscape terms they are meant to be the equivalent of national parks, by comparison with the parks they are little known and understood. Unlike national parks, there is no duty to consider their designation and many of the powers available within them are optional for the local planning authority. Indeed, Marion Shoard in *The Theft of the Countryside* (Temple Smith, 1980) described them as the 'Cinderellas of the planning system'.

AONBs have a number of similarities with national parks. They tend to be extensive areas: 41 have been designated, covering over 14 per cent of England and Wales. They are designated in the same way as national parks, i.e. the Countryside Agency makes a proposal for designation which requires confirmation by the Secretary of State, normally after extensive consultation (in only one case has there also been a public inquiry). They rely on town planning procedures for their legal protection and the town planning powers are essentially the same as in national parks, including the duty to consult with the Countryside Agency over the making of development plans.

However, there are significant differences too. AONBs do not have a statutory role as far as recreation is concerned, nor are there general duties on all public bodies as there are with national parks. Nor is extra finance specifically provided for AONBs, although the establishment of the Countryside Agency has brought with it some increased funding. But perhaps the major difference from national parks is that the local planning authority generally remains unchanged. To combat some of these inherent weaknesses, the Countryside Commission revised its policy in 1991 with the result that nearly all AONBs have a management plan and at least one AONB officer, similar to national parks officers. Where more than one local authority has responsibility for the area, the policy of encouraging non-statutory Joint Advisory Committees to bring together the different local authorities but also local people and non-governmental organisations has generally been successful (see PPG 7, *The Countryside: Environmental Quality and Economic and Social Development*).

(c) Other landscape protections

A further type of designation is heritage coast. Areas are selected by the Countryside Agency and the local planning authority acting together and are subject to protective policies within the planning process. Forty-four areas covering 1,493 km of coast have been designated although there have been no new designations since 1991. It should also be noted that there is a fairly strong Planning Policy Guidance Note No. 20, entitled *Coastal Planning*, which establishes a number of restraint policies on coastal development. Balanced against this, however, is the general policy of 'managed retreat', meaning that in certain cases coastal land is allowed to erode naturally, because stemming the erosion would not be useful.

There is a power for the Secretary of State and the Minister of Agriculture to make moorland conservation orders by statutory instrument (Wildlife and Countryside Act 1981, s. 42). These orders impose a notification requirement similar to that applied to SSSIs, with the intention that the national park authority may offer a management agreement. It is accordingly a criminal offence to plough or convert any moor or heath subject to an order which has not been agricultural land within the preceding 20 years, unless the national park authority has been notified in advance. This section is distinctly limited. Orders can only be made in a national park and only provide for a temporary ban on operations, and works can go ahead after 12 months even if the national park authority refuses consent for them. It does not appear that any such orders have ever been made.

Landscape protection orders were recommended by the House of Commons Select Committee on the Environment in 1985. Despite support from the Countryside Commission, this proposal produced a very limited response from the government, which envisaged their use only as a stopgap power pending the making of a management agreement, and the proposals have never been acted upon.

Agriculture and landscape

There is insufficient space in this book to trace the history of agricultural grants and their relationship with damage to the countryside, but in the past their availability has often been held responsible for a great number of damaging changes (see, for example, Shoard's *The Theft of The Countryside*). The nature of agricultural grants and, indeed, of the whole shape of agriculture has changed dramatically in recent years, and this is reflected in such things as the so-called EC Agri-Environment Regulation 2078/92, the EC scheme on agricultural set-aside, and the domestic Farm and Conservation Grant Scheme.

There are three protective procedures which have an important impact on the protection of the landscape and deserve greater attention:

(a) Prior notification

Since 1980 there has been a scheme in which farmers in national parks and the Broads should give advance notification to the national park authority of their intention to seek agricultural grants. (A similar scheme applies in relation to SSSIs, requiring prior notification of the relevant NCC.) The scheme is non-statutory and therefore is not backed up by any legal sanctions, but it has had a high success rate in preventing objectionable proposals from being carried out (see *Farm Grant Notifications in National Parks*, Countryside Commission, 1987). The then Countryside Commission recommended that the scheme be extended to cover AONBs.

The scheme works as follows. The farmer should notify the national park authority of an intention to seek agricultural grant. If no objection is received, the work may go ahead. If there is an objection, discussions follow between the two parties, and the Agricultural Development and Advisory Service of the Ministry of Agriculture, Fisheries and Food (ADAS) is able to mediate at this stage. If a satisfactory arrangement cannot be reached informally, one solution is for a management agreement to be concluded under the Wildlife and Countryside Act 1981, s. 39.

If no agreement can be reached, the farmer may seek a decision on the grant from the Minister of Agriculture, who may approve or refuse it. The possibilities for damaging development are thus either:

(a)   that the Minister approves the grant against the opposition of the national park authority; or

(b)   that the farmer goes ahead with the works without grant.

It should be noted that, in making the decision, the Minister is under a duty to seek to achieve a reasonable balance between the interests of agriculture and of conservation of the natural beauty of the countryside (Agriculture Act 1986, s. 17), and this may be given as the reason for a refusal. However, the Minister may give as the reason for the refusal of grant the objection by the national park authority, in which case the authority is under a duty to offer a management agreement, to which the financial guidelines made under the Wildlife and Countryside Act 1981, s. 50 will apply (see the 1981 Act, s. 41(4)), although it does not appear that this procedure has ever been used.

(b)   Environmentally sensitive areas (ESAs)
These designations formally date from EC Regulation 797/85 on Improving the Efficiency of Agricultural Structures, which permitted Member States to give special aid to farmers in environmentally sensitive areas. However, the current powers are modelled on an experimental scheme established earlier in the Broads to solve the problems experienced in Halvergate Marsh as a result of proposals to plough part of the Marsh (see the Broads Grazing Marshes Conservation Scheme 1985 to 1988). Effect was given to the EC Regulation in Britain by the Agriculture Act 1986, s. 18, which allows MAFF to designate an ESA after consultation with the Countryside Agency and English Nature, or with the Countryside Council for Wales, with the aim of conserving landscape and wildlife. Twenty-two ESAs covering 1.1m hectares have been designated in England. There are six ESAs in Wales covering 165,000 hectares, but the scheme is now closed to new applicants (see the discussion of Tir Gofal below).
Within these ESAs standard rates of annual payment are made by MAFF to farmers in return for their agreeing to farm in accordance with specified practices. The order establishing each ESA includes a list of practices (and of grant rates) specially tailored for that ESA, but the exact terms of each agreement are a matter for the management agreement between the farmer and MAFF. One important point about these protections, apart from the fact that they rely wholly on the voluntary agreement of the farmer, is that payment is made by MAFF rather than by the conservation bodies. Another is that, by providing for standard rates of payment for standard practices, the system is administratively far simpler than the one established for SSSIs, where each management agreement has to be negotiated individually (although this has not prevented strong criticism by the Public Accounts Committee about high administrative costs). As a result, the take-up rate for the ESA scheme is far higher, and in England continues to rise steadily.

(c)   Countryside Stewardship/Tir Gofal
The Countryside Stewardship scheme was originally established in 1991 on a pilot basis by the Countryside Commission in England as a means of wider countryside conservation outside of ESAs. In 1996 responsibility was

switched to the Ministry of Agriculture, although unlike ESAs the scheme is not restricted to farm businesses. The revised scheme aims to protect, restore and re-create targeted landscapes, their wildlife habitats and historical features. A slightly extended range of landscape types are now eligible, including chalk and limestone grassland; lowland heath; waterside land; uplands; old meadows and pastures; and field boundaries. As with ESAs the scheme is entirely voluntary on both sides, and applicants enter into agreements, usually for 10 years, to undertake specified conservation works. One criterion used to determine which applications are successful is opportunity for public access. Between 1991 and the end of March 1999, 8,614 agreements had been entered into, covering 143,055 hectares. Figures for 1998 suggest that interest in the scheme remains constant, with a dramatic recent increase in the amount being paid out for work on field margins.

In Wales the pilot Tir Cymen scheme has recently been replaced by Tir Gofal, which incorporates features not merely of ESAs and Countryside Stewardship, but also incorporates nature conservation management agreements. As with Countryside Stewardship the scheme extends to whole farms, and has no explicit statutory basis.

(d) Grant schemes under the Agri-Environment Regulation 2078/92

Four sets of regulations were made in 1994 in order to assist in the implementation of Regulation 2078/92. Each of them enabled the Minister of Agriculture, Fisheries and Food to make payments for certain types of countryside management and each specified rates of payment and precise management requirements. In keeping with the traditional policy approach in this area, occupiers were given a choice whether to join the schemes or not. The Habitat (Water Fringe) Regulations 1994 (SI 1994/1291) apply where an occupier within 20 metres of a designated watercourse or lake agrees not to use arable land or permanent grassland for agricultural purposes for 20 years and undertakes to manage the land to protect or improve a wildlife habitat. The Habitat (Salt-Marsh) Regulations 1994 (SI 1994/1293) apply where the occupier undertakes to manage land with the objective of establishing an area of salt-marsh. These schemes are now closed to new applicants, and have been incorporated into Countryside Stewardship, from 2000. The Habitat (Former Set-Aside Land) Regulations 1994 (SI 1994/1292) applied, until 1997, a similar system in relation to land which had previously been the subject of agricultural set-aside. The fourth set of regulations, the Nitrate Sensitive Areas Regulations 1994 (SI 1994/1729), are discussed in Chapter 19 in the context of nitrate sensitive areas, although their impact is somewhat wider than pollution control. The Agri-Environment Regulation has been replaced, as from 1 January 2000, by Chapter VI of the EC Rural Development Regulation (1257/99).

Finally, under the Environment Act 1995, s. 98, the Minister of Agriculture, Fisheries and Food and the Welsh Assembly are empowered to make grants for any purposes which are conducive to the conservation or enhancement of the natural beauty or amenity of the countryside (including its flora and fauna) or any features of archaeological interest, or the promotion of the enjoyment of the countryside by the public.

Trees, woodland and hedgerows

The rest of this chapter looks at the protection afforded to trees, woodlands and hedgerows. What we see is a development from early, mainly negative, controls such as the use of tree preservation orders (TPOs), which have existed in town and country planning law since 1932, towards a more varied approach, encompassing the use of economic instruments and consumer information. We also see a slight shift in emphasis from pure amenity considerations (which have always been to the fore with TPOs) towards wider environmental considerations. A good example of these are the limited environmental duties to which the Forestry Commission is subject when granting felling licences, although the primary focus of forestry legislation with trees as commercial items means that this general area is covered only briefly. The conservation of some trees can, of course, be safeguarded through protective designations or agreements of the kind discussed in Chapter 21.

In theory, the use of negative restrictions is particularly unsuitable for the proper management of natural resources such as trees that require positive management. Although some lessons have been learnt, the Hedgerows Regulations 1997 are arguably a throwback to 'command and control' measures, a central weakness of which is the inability to address mismanagement or neglect, now the major threat to hedgerow conservation. But there are also environmental consequences from tree or hedge *planting* (see, e.g. the concerns raised in *Kincardine and Deeside District Council* v *Forestry Commissioners* [1993] Env LR 151). For larger projects this is dealt with through environmental impact assessment (see the Environmental Impact Assessment (Forestry) (England and Wales) Regulations 1999, SI 1999/2228). But tree planting on a smaller scale is unlikely to be legally regulated, falling outside the town and country planning system and being unlikely to give rise to any private law remedy, since there is neither a general right to a view (*Hunter* v *Canary Wharf* [1997] 2 WLR 684) nor to light (other than light to buildings).

Trees and planning permission

Although ordinary town planning rules have a limited impact on tree protection, specific protective measures are found in ss. 197 to 214 of the Town and Country Planning Act 1990, which deal with TPOs. All references to section numbers in relation to TPOs refer to this Act.

Planning permission is not required for the planting or cutting down of trees or woodland, because trees, being natural, are not structures or buildings for the purposes of the development control system. Section 55(2)(e) also excludes from the definition of development any change of use of land to forestry or woodland.

However, s. 197 imposes a general duty on local planning authorities to make adequate provision for trees when planning permission is granted. This may involve attaching conditions relating to trees to the permission (e.g. that certain trees should be retained or replaced by others, or that new trees should be planted as part of the landscaping of the site). It also involves considering whether to impose a TPO on any existing trees. A further possibility is to refuse permission on the grounds that existing trees or woodland should be retained. Full advice on trees and the planning system is given in *Tree Preservation Orders: A Guide to the Law and Good Practice* (DETR, 2000).

Tree preservation orders (TPOs)

A TPO is a means by which individual trees, groups of trees or woodlands may be protected against damage. A woodland TPO is arguably the most restrictive, since it includes trees which take root after the order is made. A TPO may be imposed on specified trees 'if it appears to a local planning authority that it is expedient in the interests of amenity' (s. 198). Since the section refers explictly to amenity, it does not seem that a tree could be protected for nature conservation purposes. Most TPOs are made in urban areas, though rural woodland may also be protected. The DETR Guidance suggests that TPOs will not normally be made on trees under good arboricultural or silvicultural management.

(a) TPO offences
Any person who, in contravention of a TPO, '(a) cuts down, uproots or wilfully destroys a tree, or (b) wilfully damages, tops or lops a tree in such a manner as to be likely to destroy it', commits an offence, unless consent has been obtained from the local planning authority (s. 210(1)). On summary conviction the maximum fine is £20,000. On conviction on indictment the level of the fine is unlimited. In determining the amount of any fine, the court must have regard to the financial benefit accruing, or likely to accrue, to the convicted person in consequence of the offence. This is a significant provision, since many offences against TPOs are committed by developers who stand to make a substantial gain on the development value of their land (see, for example, the £50,000 fine imposed on a property company for deliberately felling 25 trees after designation, which is reported at [1991] JPL 101). There is a further offence of contravening the provisions of a TPO (s. 210(4)), for which the maximum fine is £2,500. This will cover such things as ignoring conditions imposed on works permitted by a TPO. If no other enforcement action works, an injunction to stop contravention of a TPO is available (s. 214A), though courts will be reluctant to exercise their discretion to issue an injunction except in clear cases. One notorious persistent offender (a Kent farmer) has, however, been imprisoned for failing to comply with the terms of an injunction.

These offences may be committed by any person, not just the owner or occupier of the property. They are offences of strict liability. Thus, in *Maidstone Borough Council v Mortimer* [1980] 3 All ER 552, a contractor was held to have committed an offence even though the owner of the site had assured him that consent for the works had been given. (It seems that the owner would also commit an offence in such a situation, because the contractor is acting as an agent.) This strict position is justified by the fact that a TPO is a public document (it is a local land charge), so anyone can check the position before carrying out works.

Part of the offence requires that it be committed 'wilfully'. This has been interpreted to mean that it is the act of damaging or destroying the tree that must be wilful (i.e. deliberate), not the contravention of the TPO. *Barnet London Borough Council* v *Eastern Electricity Board* [1973] 1 WLR 430, illustrates that this may include a negligent act. In that case, contractors negligently damaged the roots of six trees subject to a TPO, shortening their life expectancy. The Divisional Court held that this amounted to a wilful destruction. The case also illustrates that the concept of destruction includes something less than immediate death to the tree.

(b) Making a TPO

The local planning authority has responsibility for making TPOs. This normally means the district planning authority, or the national park authority in a national park, though a county planning authority does have jurisdiction over its own land and where it grants planning permission (e.g. on waste disposal or minerals applications). The authority which imposes the TPO is then the relevant local authority for all procedures for consent and for enforcement purposes. The Secretary of State has a reserve power to make a TPO under s. 202, although this is unlikely to be used much.

The procedures for making a TPO are now set out in the Town and Country Planning (Trees) Regulations 1999 (SI 1999/1892), which have effect under the authority of s. 199. The local planning authority produces a draft TPO, which is placed on public deposit, and all owners, occupiers and those with felling rights are notified. At least 28 days are then allowed for objections, which must be considered before the local planning authority itself confirms the TPO (prior to 1980 a TPO required confirmation by the Secretary of State). There is no appeal against the making of a TPO, though there is right to challenge its validity in the High Court under s. 288. In practice, arguments about the desirability of protecting the tree are considered at the stage of seeking consent to fell.

Normally a TPO does not have effect until it is confirmed. But under s. 201 a provisional (or interim) TPO may be made by the local planning authority. This is done simply by stating that s. 201 applies and the TPO will then have immediate effect, though it will lapse if not confirmed within six months. Such a provisional TPO is of obvious use where there is an imminent threat of felling.

Each TPO is separately drafted and accompanied by a map. This position allows for flexibility (for example, conditions specific to that TPO may be attached, or permitted woodland management operations may be established for a coppiced woodland), but it does make the making of a TPO quite a cumbersome process — certainly more cumberstone than those protective designations where all that is required is that standard rules or restrictions apply to the designated land. However, there is a standard form, which is set out in the schedule to the 1999 Regulations, and accordingly most TPOs will be substantially in the form set out in the schedule. The normal position is therefore that TPOs include a list of permitted operations and of prohibited operations, some of which are especially tailored for that site.

One particular difficulty relates to the definition of a tree. In *Kent County Council v Batchelor* (1976) 33 P & CR 185, Lord Denning MR somewhat arbitrarily suggested that a diameter of 7 to 8 inches at least was needed before something could be said to be a tree. However, this was expressly not accepted by Phillips J in *Bullock v Secretary of State for the Environment* (1980) 40 P & CR 246, who thought that anything ordinarily called a tree could be covered by a TPO. In that case he accepted expressly that a coppiced woodland could be covered, a position which seems sensible, since from an ecological point of view a coppice is effectively a single entity and not a collection of unconnected trees. Phillips J's view is to be preferred and is supported by s. 206(4), which states that a TPO will attach to any tree planted as a replacement for one subject to a TPO — such a replacement will often be a sapling or smaller tree. However, although the dividing line is imprecise, it remains clear that some things cannot be the subject of a TPO, such as hedges, bushes and shrubs. It appears to be accepted that a stump of a tree is capable of remaining a tree if it is still alive — a proposition that enables a TPO to continue to apply to trees which have been felled, but not to those which have been uprooted.

A further issue relates to whether local authorities actually have the resources to make TPOs. It appears that a number of local authorities have adopted a policy of not making any further TPOs because of the time and expense involved. The legality of such a policy must be questioned, as it appears to amount to an effective fettering of discretion.

(c)   Defences to TPO offences
There is a number of exceptions to these offences:

(a)   Some works are permitted in the TPO itself. For example, the standard form of TPO exempts works on cultivated fruit trees, and now also any pruning of a fruit tree if this is in accordance with 'good horticultural practice'. Also exempt are the 'cutting down, topping, lopping or uprooting of a tree' where needed to implement a planning permission (no longer 'immediately required', as the 1969 Regulations, which preceded the 1999 Regulations, stipulated). There has, though, been some narrowing in relation to development permitted under the GPDO. This is only exempted if carried out by a statutory undertaker or body like the Environment Agency.

(b)   It is possible to seek consent from the local planning authority (see below).

(c)   It is an exception to cut down, uproot, top or lop trees which are dead, dying or dangerous, or 'so far as may be necessary for the prevention or abatement of a nuisance' (s. 198(6)). The nuisance exception relates to the position where a tree is a civil nuisance. It is potentially a very wide exception, because it is a civil nuisance for a tree to affect a neighbour's foundations or access. *Elliott v Islington London Borough Council* [1991] 1 EGLR 167 illustrates the potential for conflict between public and private rights when dealing with private nuisance. Mr Elliott obtained a mandatory injunction against Islington LBC requiring that a horse chestnut tree, which was in an adjoining park and was damaging his garden wall, be removed. (The tree was not actually subject to a TPO because it was the council's practice not to designate trees on their own land, but this does not affect the point being made.) It is believed that the injunction was in fact never enforced following a later compromise agreed between the parties, but in the Court of Appeal Lord Donaldson MR showed the primacy accorded to private rights over the public interest when he stated, 'It is not generally appropriate to refuse to enforce specific private rights on the basis that that would cause hardship to the public: the court would be legislating to deprive people of their rights'. However, it is not a nuisance to deprive a neighbour of the right to a view or the right to light (see p. 670), so this section would not justify interference with protected trees on these grounds.

(d) There are further exceptions where the Forestry Commission is already effectively controlling forestry activities on the land through a forestry dedication covenant, or a grant or loan made under the Forestry Acts (s. 200).

(d) Consent

It is possible to apply to the local planning authority for consent to carry out any works which are prohibited by a TPO. Any consent which is granted may be subject to conditions, such as the planting of replacement trees. There are no publicity requirements for an application for consent, though Circular 36/78 encourages it and notification of neighbours and the placing of site notices are common. There is an appeal to the Secretary of State against a refusal of consent, and the procedures and powers on an appeal are similar to those for an appeal against refusal of planning permission, although they give effect to recent proposals on streamlining (see p. 335). There are now powers to vary or revoke a TPO (reg. 9), which would fulfil the same purpose.

(e) Replacement trees

The replacement of trees covered by a TPO may be required by the terms of the TPO itself (e.g. in return for permitted works), by a condition attached to a planning permission, by the terms of a consent, or by s. 206.

Section 206 provides that, if a tree is removed or destroyed in contravention of a TPO, or because it was dead, dying or dangerous, a replacement tree of appropriate size and species must be planted at the same place as soon as reasonably possible. The owner may ask the local planning authority for this requirement to be lifted. The TPO attaches to the replacement tree.

Special provisions apply to woodlands. There is no need to replace a dead, dying or dangerous tree, and the obligation is to replace the same number of trees on or near those removed, or as agreed by the local planning authority. Flexibility has been provided in such a case because it will often be impossible to determine exactly how many trees were removed and from where (reg. 8).

(f) Enforcement notices

Since contravening a TPO is itself a criminal offence, there is less need for an enforcement notice requirement than for ordinary breaches of development control. But there is a power for the local planning authority to serve an enforcement notice where a replanting obligation is not complied with. Such a notice must be served within four years of the failure and may require such replanting as is specified by the authority (s. 207). There is a right of appeal against an enforcement notice to the Secretary of State, who may uphold, modify, or quash it (s. 208).

Failure to comply with an enforcement notice is not a criminal offence but the local planning authority may enter the relevant land, carry out the replanting as required, and recover the cost from the owner (s. 209).

Conservation areas

All trees in a designated conservation area are subject to a statutory restriction (effectively a statutory TPO) which prohibits the cutting down, lopping, topping, uprooting, wilful damage or wilful destruction of the tree (s. 211). This is more limited than most individual TPOs. In addition, regulations may be made by the Secretary of State that exempt specified works (s. 212).

There is one crucial difference between these statutory TPOs and ordinary ones: prohibited acts may go ahead six weeks after notification of an intention to do them has been given to the local planning authority. The purpose of this section is to enable the local planning authority to have prior notification of potentially damaging works to trees in conservation areas. (A similar form of control is applied for the protection of SSSIs — see p. 631.) It then has six weeks in which to decide whether to impose a TPO: if it does not the works may go ahead. It is an offence to do any of the prohibited acts without notifying the local planning authority and waiting six weeks, unless consent is given earlier. The penalties for this offence, and the replanting and enforcement provisions, are the same as for ordinary TPOs.

Compensation

No compensation is payable for the imposition of a TPO, but it is payable where loss or damage is caused by a refusal of consent (including revocation or modification) or by a conditional consent (s. 203).

Originally it was thought that this compensation was payable to compensate for the value of cut timber forgone, but this assumption was shown to be unwarranted by *Bell* v *Canterbury City Council* [1989] 1 JEL 90. In this case the Court of Appeal confirmed that the level of compensation payable was for the loss in value of the land. Accordingly, it awarded compensation at £1,000 per acre to a farmer who was prevented from converting a coppiced woodland to beef or sheep farming. Such large amounts of compensation would obviously limit the use of TPOs by local authorities, especially on woodlands which may have potential for agricultural or urban development.

An immediate response was to alter the existing regulations, namely the TPO Regulations 1969. It had always been possible for the local planning authority to certify that refusal was in the interests of good forestry or that the trees were of outstanding or special amenity value: in such a case no compensation would be payable. This certificate was originally available for individual trees, but the 1969 Regulations were amended (in SI 1988/963) to apply the procedure to woodlands. However, a more significant response was to alter the practice of the Forestry Commission in relation to woodland TPOs. In woodland, the volume of timber being cut will normally require a felling licence from the Forestry Commission (see below). Normally, the Commission would refer any application relating to trees subject to a TPO to the local planning authority. However, a change of practice consequent to *Bell* v *Canterbury CC* was that the Commission agreed to refuse a felling licence if TPO consent would be refused. The effect is that the Commission pays compensation, but at the level set out in the Forestry Act 1967, which relates to the value of the timber. The 1999 Regulations give statutory effect to this position by limiting compensation to loss in value of the timber, and then applying this valuation method to trees covered by felling licences. Losses under £500 cannot be recovered.

Proposals for change

The 1999 Regulations give effect to some of the changes suggested as far back as 1990 when the Conservative Government issued a consultation paper entitled *Review of Tree Preservation Policies and Legislation*, and later in a further review of the legislation in 1994. Many of the proposals made there, however, would require primary legislation, including amending s. 201 so that all TPOs have immediate effect and proposals to give local authorities positive powers to demand works on protected trees.

Afforestation

Outside of any requirement for environmental impact assessment, the main tool used to regulate afforestation is incentive payments, of which there are two main schemes. The removal in the 1988 Budget of the notorious tax breaks relating to forestry was, it appears, effected to ensure that no significant afforestation would occur without the official approval which grant aid effectively provides. This duly happened, although a dramatic reduction in new planting followed. The Woodland Grant Scheme, dating from 1990, marks a clear departure from the previous over-riding policy objective of timber production. The scheme has several purposes, which include the pursuit of landscape, conservation and amenity objectives. This multi-purpose approach is restated in *Our Forests: The Way Ahead: Enterprise, Environment, Access* (Cm 2644, 1994). To be eligible for funding, projects must have regard to landscape considerations, and must include a diversity of tree species. Higher sums are paid for broadleaved woods, reflecting in part their greater landscape and conservation importance, and the majority of new planting is now broadleaved. There is also the Farm Woodland Premium Scheme (SI 1992/905) which, as its name suggests, is designed to encourage the creation of new woodlands on farms, the underlying purpose being to take land out of agricultural production. Payments under this scheme reflect agricultural revenues forgone.

Felling licences

By contrast with the minimal legal controls over afforestation, under s. 9(2) of the Forestry Act 1967, a felling licence is required from the Forestry Commission for the felling of trees over 8 cm in diameter (15 cm in coppices) measured 1.3 m from the ground. It is an offence to fell without a licence, which again may be committed by anyone (see *Forestry Commission* v *Frost* (1989) 154 JP 14). This control is based on commercial factors, rather than on amenity factors. However, the Forestry Commission is under a duty to endeavour to achieve a balance between the management of forests and the conservation of landscape and nature (Forestry Act 1967 s. 1(3A), inserted by the Wildlife and Countryside (Amendment) Act 1985 s. 4). A felling licence is not required for fruit trees, trees in gardens, orchards, churchyards or public open space, topping or lopping of trees, operations under a forestry dedication scheme, thinning trees less than 10cm in diameter, or harvesting less than 5 cubic metres of timber per quarter.

To avoid duplication of effort, if a felling licence is required and there is a TPO in force, the following procedure applies. The application goes to the Forestry Commission, which has three choices: it may refer the matter to the local planning authority, in which case the TPO legislation applies; it may refuse the licence, in which case it will pay compensation under the Forestry Act 1967; or it may grant a licence. A felling licence is the equivalent of a TPO consent, but before the Commission grants a licence it must consult with the local planning authority. If the authority objects to a proposed grant of a licence, the matter is referred to the Secretary of State for decision. If a licence is granted there is an obligation to restock the land, unless the Commission waives it (see the Forestry Act 1986).

Consultation on felling and afforestation

There are no formal requirements for the Forestry Commission (or in the case of the Farm Woodland Premium Scheme, the Agriculture Ministry) to consult on applications for felling licences or grant applications. However, it is Forestry Commission policy to consult local authorities and bodies such as the Countryside Agency and English Nature about grant applications, and all applications for new planting are placed on a public register. In both cases there is an appeal, ultimately to the Minister.

Community forests and the National Forest

There is a 'Forests for the Community' programme run as a joint venture between the Countryside Agency and Forestry Commission, together with local authorities. The aim is to promote the creation, regeneration and multi-purpose use of well-wooded landscapes around major towns and cities. Community forests are non-statutory designations, and their establishment is facilitated in part through planning policy guidance under which development plans should play a facilitative role and provide that any development proposals within them respect the woodland setting. Their establishment therefore relies heavily on the exercise of private rights by the Forestry Commission. To date there are 12 Community Forest areas in England, together with the National Forest in the Midlands, the establishment of which is being facilitated in a similar way.

Consumer information and certification schemes

One consequence to emerge from the Forest Principles and from Agenda 21, both agreed at the Rio Earth Summit (see p. 97), has been the emergence of forest management certification and ecolabelling as a preferred policy approach both of producers and of wider civil society (such as environmental NGOs). At national level, we now have the UK Woodland Assurance Scheme, which aims to assure purchasers of wood products in the scheme that the timber has come from sustainably managed sources. The voluntary scheme is notable for being a partnership between the public and private sectors, and environmental organisations, and operates through a combination of auditing of producers by a certification body, and subsequent use of an ecolabel.

Hedgerows

There has been an enormous loss of hedgerows since 1945, mainly as a result of agricultural intensification. However, hedges have never had the same protection as trees, because the definition of a tree means that the TPO legislation does not apply to hedges, though it is capable of applying to trees in hedgerows. Numerous promises were made in relation to hedgerow protection until finally the Environment Act 1995, s. 97, made provision for the protection of special categories of hedgerows. Under this section, the Secretary of State has the power to make regulations prohibiting the removal, damage or destruction of 'important hedgerows'.

The Hedgerows Regulations 1997 (SI 1997/1160) make provision for the protection of important hedgerows in England and Wales. The Regulations generally apply to a wide class of hedgerows (in particular to hedgerows which are 20 metres or more long or which meet another hedgerow at each end and which, in each case, are on or adjacent to land used for certain specified purposes). Domestic hedgerows are excluded.

The protection is basic, to say the least. An owner (or in certain cases a relevant utility operator) must notify the local planning authority before removing any hedgerow, or stretch of hedgerow. The local planning authority has 42 days in which to serve a retention notice, failing which consent is deemed to have been given. Consent can only be refused if the hedgerow is important. The 'unimportant' hedgerows can be removed after that period.

The accompanying Guidance emphasises cooperation with farmers rather than confrontation, thus continuing the tradition of voluntariness found in other areas.

To qualify as an important hedgerow the hedge must be not less than 30 years old and must comply with certain detailed criteria laid down within the regulations relating to such matters as the number and type of species contained in the hedgerow. Thus, the range of hedgerows which can actually be protected is relatively narrow.

Fines can be imposed on defaulters (the courts being directed to take account of any financial benefit accruing from the removal) and the courts can also order replanting.

The Hedgerow Regulations have been criticised for placing too much emphasis on the need for objectively verifiable indicators of importance, and thus restricting their ambit to a small category of hedges (around 20 per cent) of historic importance. For Holder, this is a consequence of seeing the importance of hedgerows as 'little more than the sum of their parts', rather than trying to give weight to matters of cultural and local importance ([1999] MLR 100). This is also evidenced in the absence of public consultation built into the regulations.

A government review of the Hedgerow Regulations in 1998 merely observed that giving greater powers to local authorities to determine local importance would reduce the consistency, and certainty for business, currently provided for. However, the review went on to recommend various reforms which would allow for local distinctiveness to be a factor in assessing 'importance' (e.g. beech hedges in Exmoor), although this still falls some way short of local recognition of local importance. The review also suggested that the presence of priority species in the UK Biodiversity Action Plan could also be an indicator of 'importance', which would go some way towards the regulations making more of a contribution to nature conservation. Nevertheless, loss of natural and cultural features through neglect, which has now overtaken uprooting as the greatest threat to hedgerows, would still not be addressed in law.

In the absence of control under the regulations, other legal remedies may be possible. These include individual enforcement of the provisions of enclosure Acts, such as in *Seymour* v *Flamborough Parish Council, The Times*, 3 January 1997, where Cracknell J ordered the Council to preserve what was an 'undistinguished, badly maintained, straggly and unkempt' hawthorn hedge because it was still bound by the Flamborough Enclosure Act 1765 which required the parish council to maintain the hedge forever, a somewhat ironic note on which to end a book on environmental regulation.

Bibliography

This bibliography is intended as slightly more than just a list of books mentioned in the text. Because we have tried to keep the use of references to a minimum (on the ground that we think that they can distract the reader), we have sought to identify, with brief comments, some of the more important pieces of writing in each area. In addition, with the growth of information and resources on the internet, we have attempted to direct readers to the more relevant and significant web pages.

As the book tries to illustrate, there is a need to be familiar with the policy of environmental protection as well as with the law: indeed, the two are often indistinguishable. One way to achieve this is to read the official publications. At a European level, these are commonly available from the internet on the DG Environment's web page at *www.europa.eu.int/comm/environment/policy_en.htm*. This contains official policy documents (referred to as COM documents) on the full range of environmental policy areas in addition to more general background papers. These policy documents give an accessible and interesting introduction to many new European policy initiatives. For a specific overview of the European environment, beginners could look at The Global Assessment of the 5th Environmental Action Programme (COM 99(543)) at *www.europa.eu.int/comm/environment/newprg/global.htm* which provides a few pointers to future policy directions.

At the national level, most policy documents are available through the DETR's web page (*www.detr.gov.uk*). There is no general policy document covering all areas of environmental policy (like *This Common Inheritance* (Cm 1200, 1990) under the Conservative Government). There is, however, more detailed coverage in relation to certain areas. These include *A Better Quality of Life: Strategy for Sustainable Development* (Cm 4345, 1999), the *Air Quality Strategy* (Cm 4548, 2000) and the *Waste Strategy 2000* (Cm 4693, 2000). Whilst these are good introductions to these particular areas, they do rather beg the question as to why there are no similarly comprehensive policy documents in relation to other important areas of environmental protection (such as the protection of water resources, or noise).

Any report by the Royal Commission on Environmental Pollution, the House of Commons Select Committee on the Environment, or the House of Lords Select Committee on the European Communities is worth reading as a snap shot of the operation of environmental law and policy. Each of these bodies challenge perceived orthodoxies in a formal and authoritative manner.

However, the best way to get an insight into what is happening is to visit the web pages of environmental organisations such as Greenpeace (*www.greenpeace.org.uk*) which tends to concentrate on global issues and Friends of the Earth (*www.foe.org.uk*) which is more local. These provide up to the minute information on the most significant (or media friendly, depending upon your viewpoint) topics of the moment. In recent years, there have been some interesting books attempting to counter what are seen by some as excessive 'green pessimism': two good examples of the genre are North, *Life on a Modern Planet: A Manifesto for Progress* (Manchester University Press, 1995) or Simon, *Ultimate Resource 2* (Princeton University Press, 1998). Markham, *A Brief History of Pollution* (Earthscan, 1994) provides a good contextual introduction to the issue of what much of environmental law is seeking to control.

There is a need for books which attempt to cross the multi-disciplinary divide between law, politics, science and economics. A good reader (for those with an understanding of the legal aspects) on the complexities of this interrelationship can be found in Elworthy and Holder, *Environmental Protection: Text and Materials* (Butterworths, 1997). Other perspectives can be found in Revesz (ed.), *Foundations of Environmental Law and Policy* (OUP, 1997) which gives an American view (although it is still relevant to the UK) and O'Riordan, *Environmental Science for Environmental Management* (Longman Higher Education, 1999) which gives a non legal view of some of the central issues of environmental protection.

For those seeking an overview of environmental *law*, the books can be divided into two main categories: those for environmental practitioners and those that are written for a more general audience. In the former category, the *Encyclopaedia of Environmental Law* (Sweet & Maxwell), *Commercial Environmental Law and Liability* (Sweet & Maxwell) and *Garner's Environmental Law* (Butterworths) are all looseleaf works which provide comprehensive coverage of environmental statutes (although they all tend to suffer in comparison to internet sources when it comes to the speed of delivery of new laws). There are two major textbooks aimed at the practitioner which deal with most of the mainstream areas of environmental law. Burnett-Hall, *Environmental Law* (Sweet & Maxwell, 1995) and Woolley et al (eds), *Environmental Law* (OUP, 2000) are both comprehensive and detailed, although the coverage tends towards straightforward exposition of the legal provisions rather than any analysis of the role of environmental policy. They both suffer from two main defects, the first of which is characteristic of all non-looseleaf works, namely that they become out of date almost on the day they are published. The second problem is that they are both extremely expensive and fall outside the range of most pockets. The first problem is an issue for all books dealing with environmental law and can be addressed by way of Supplement (Burnett-Hall, *Environmental Law*: 1st Supplement, Sweet & Maxwell, 1998) or through the internet (updates for Woolley et al should be available at *www.oup.co.uk*). The second problem is more fundamental but it should not obscure the fact that both are extremely impressive works.

As far as general textbooks are concerned, Hughes, *Environmental Law* (Butterworths, 1996) contains more detail and breadth of coverage in some areas than we provide in this book, whilst clear, concise and accessible accounts of the law are given in Thornton and Beckwith, *Environmental Law* (Sweet & Maxwell, 1997), and the *NSCA Pollution Handbook* (National Society for Clean Air, published annually). Sunkin, Ong and Wight, *Sourcebook on Environmental Law* (Cavendish, 1997) more than meets the difficult challenge of providing a text which has brief commentary, cases, selective statutory provisions and other relevant materials which can support the traditional textbooks.

There are collections of statutes which are a convenient way of aggregating relevant material. These include Duxbury and Morton, *Blackstone's Statutes on Environmental Law*, (Blackstone Press, 2000) and Fry, *Manual of Environmental Protection Law* (OUP, 1997). As stated above, with the internet providing such easy access to new legislation and policy (see below), the usefulness of these collections is reduced, particularly when there are online services such as Butterworths Direct at *www.butterworths.co.uk* or Westlaw at *www.sweetandmaxwell.co.uk* which are updated instantly and provide an accurate picture of the actual law in force (although outside academic institutions, these services charge a high commercial price).

More general collections dealing with different aspects of environmental law and policy include Robinson and Dunkley (eds) *Public Interest Perspectives in Environmental Law* (Wiley Chancery, 1995) which includes good chapters on public interest environmental litigation in the US and access to justice in the EC, as well as on the Australian experience of environmental courts, legal standing in the UK and the whole concept of public interest environmental law. Jewell and Steele (eds), *Law in Environmental Decision Making* (Clarendon Press, 1998) is another eclectic selection which is slightly more complex for the general reader but provides excellent coverage of different approaches to environmental regulation, the overlap between public law and environmental decision making, access to information, private law and environmental risk, and European and international environmental law.

As we mentioned in the main text, there are a number of books covering the environmental laws in Scotland and Northern Ireland (coverage of Wales may take a little longer until it develops distinctive policies and rules). There is a collection of essays in Reid (ed.), *Green's Guide to Environmental Law in Scotland* (W. Green & Son, 1997) with similar coverage in Smith et al, *Pollution Control in Scotland* (T&T Clark, 1998). The position in Northern Ireland is catered for in Turner and Morrow, *Northern Ireland Environmental Issues* (Gill and Macmillan, 1996) and Morrow and Turner, 'The More Things Change, the More They Stay the Same' [1998] JEL 41.

Journals

Of course one of the most important things in environmental law is keeping up to date. There are a number of journals which attempt to do this, though one thing that any environmental law researcher quickly discovers is just how difficult it is to establish what has happened recently and what is going to happen next. This is perhaps a good illustration of the secrecy traditionally surrounding policy making in this country. There are many consultation papers currently being produced by government on proposed changes in the law. These often summarise the current position and the reasons for change. In the last few years, the vast majority of these have been published on the DETR's web page (see *www.detr.gov.uk*).

Since environmental law includes news and policy from a wide range of sources, the best way to keep up is to read the *ENDS Report* (Environmental Data Services Ltd, monthly), a topical monthly digest of a wide range of news on environmental matters, with excellent coverage of legal and policy matters. *Environmental Law and Management* and *Water Law* (both Wiley Chancery, six times a year) attempt to cover all areas of environmental law and matters connected with the water industry respectively through articles and current survey.

The *Journal of Environmental Law* (Oxford University Press, three times a year) includes more lengthy and reflective articles dealing with national, European, international and comparative environmental law. It has recently been joined by the *Environmental Law Review* (Blackstone Press, four times a year) which covers a similar mix of articles and case law analysis with the addition of a comprehensive update on recent developments.

All these journals — and the *Journal of Planning and Environment Law* (Sweet & Maxwell, monthly with an extra edition covering the proceedings of the Oxford Planning Conference) — include summaries and reports of the more important cases, usually with illuminating commentary. The *Environmental Law Reports* (Sweet & Maxwell, six times a year) are the only published source in which to find the full transcripts of many environmental cases.

On-line information

No list of sources would now be complete without mention of sources of information available on the internet. Of these, these are some sites which are likely to be accessed routinely, and which are free; at national level, these include *www.open.gov.uk* (a general gateway to an enormous amount of governmental and non-departmental material, such as Environment Agency reports), while at EC level primary materials can be accessed via the main Europa site (see Chapter 5 below). There is nothing really comparable in international law; perhaps the best is the PACE University site, although this has something of a US and comparative law focus (*www.law.pace.edu/env*).

We also recommend the use of some more general 'gateway' sites, of which the LawLinks site at the University of Kent is unrivalled and links to just about every key source of information on law that a student might need (see *http://library.ukc.ac.uk/library/lawlinks*). We also recommend the site maintained by Delia Venables, another excellent general 'portal' (*www. venables.co.uk*). ENDS Environmental Links are also useful, though users need to register (*www.ends.co.uk/links/index.htm*). On environmental law and policy, the most useful portal is probably the Greenchannel (*www.greenchannel.com*), which has links to a wide range of environmental organisations, and through its 'Environmental Law' window links to various organisations such as the Institute for European Environmental Policy and the UK Environmental Law Association, the latter containing full text responses to some recent consultation papers.

As noted above, there are also several sites where access to information is charged for, although many libraries may have subscriptions which allow all students to access these without incurring further cost. These tend to provide 'value-added' information, such as consolidated versions of statutory material (e.g. Butterworths Direct: *www.butterworths.co.uk*), or the full text of recent cases. They are all searchable in some way, an indispensable aid to research. Of these, Lawtel (*www.lawtel.co.uk*) is an excellent search tool and good for keeping up to date; Casetrack (*www.casetrack.com*) provides full text of cases at no extra charge per case), while Current Legal Information (*http:// 193.118.187.160*) enables access to what's been published in journal articles as well as UK and EC official publications and newspaper cuttings. CCH New Law (*www.cchnewlaw.co.uk*) provides access to case law which is not found elsewhere (e.g. Chancery cases), and is also organised on a more thematic basis, which allows for searching both in the area of environmental law or specific sectors within the field.

Chapters 1, 3, 6 and 7

These chapters attempt to tackle in introductory form a number of more general issues. An excellent starting point for any deeper reading is Gunningham and Grabosky, *Smart Regulation: Designing Environmental Policy* (Clarendon Press, 1998), though McLoughlin and Bellinger, *Environmental Pollution Control: An Introduction to Principles and Practice of Administration* (Graham & Trotman, 1993) is a very readable (if a little dated) account which combines legal and administrative insights. On the specific issue of the various types of standard that are available (and much more on environmental decision making in general) see the RECP's 21st Report, *Setting Environmental Standards* (Cm 4053, 1998). On the 'British approach' to pollution control, see Vogel, *National Styles of Regulation* (Cornell University Press, 1986), which despite its age still provides a thought provoking comparison between British and American approaches.

An interested reader would find many illuminating parallels with other areas of regulation which are described in general texts on regulatory theory, of which the most accessible and relevant include: Baldwin and Cave, *Understanding Regulation* (OUP, Oxford, 1999) which has excellent chapters on standard setting, regulating risks and regulatory enforcement; Baldwin, Scott and Hood (eds), *A Reader on Regulation* (OUP, Oxford, 1999); and Ogus, *Regulation: Legal Form and Economic Theory*, (OUP, Oxford, 1994). The latter provides a nice bridge into other texts which examine the relationship between economics and environmental law. Although there are many such texts, the starting point should be Pearce, Markandya and Barbier, *Blueprint for a Green Economy* (Earthscan, 1989) which has a number of sequels, the latest of which is Pearce and Barbier, *Blueprint for a Sustainable Economy* (Earthscan, 2000). These provide an interesting study in how economic theory has developed over the last ten or so years. Another useful study is O'Riordan, *Eco-Taxation* (Earthscan, 1996).

The Environment Agency and its internal workings have become more transparent with the publication of many internal papers (including the Agenda and minutes of Board meetings) on the internet (*www.environment-agency.gov.uk/aboutus/board/index.htm*). As a counterpoint to this somewhat sanitised information, the House of Commons Select Committee's 6th Report (1999–2000 Session) on the Environment Agency (*www.parliament. uk/commons/selcom/etrahome.htm*) provides a good picture of the strengths and weaknesses of the Agency as an administrative and policing body, whilst Jewell and Steele, 'UK Regulatory Reform and the Pursuit of "Sustainable Development"': The Environment Act 1995' [1996] JEL 283 gives a deeper analysis of the duties and powers of the Agency under the Environment Act 1995.

Any discussion of environmental law and the future must include some reference to the debate over whether there should be a court to deal with environmental cases. This debate dates back some years and the initial discussion can be found in Woolf, 'Are the Judiciary Environmentally Myopic?' [1992] JEL 1; Carnwath, 'Environmental Enforcement: the Need for a Specialist Court' [1992] JPL 799; and McAuslan, 'The Role of Courts and Other Judicial Type Bodies in Environmental Management' [1991] JEL 195. The last article is an excellent starting point for answering the question 'what is environmental law?' whilst simultaneously providing a good backdrop for identifying the progress that has been made in the last 10 years in defining the area as a subject in its own right. The debate about an environmental court has been brought right up to date with the publication of a research report commissioned by the DETR and available at *www.planning.detr. gov.uk/court/index.htm*

Chapter 2

As we mention in the main text, Alder and Wilkinson, *Environmental Law and Ethics* (Macmillan Press, 1999) is an outstanding text which covers all of the issues associated with environmental ethics within the legal and policy context of environmental law. An extremely interesting portrayal of different ways of looking at environmental issues can be found in Ruhl, 'The Case of the Speluncean Polluters — Six Themes of Environmental Law, Policy, and Ethics' (1997) 27 *Environmental Law* 343, which takes a mythical case before a Supreme Court and presents different judicial perspectives in a manner which is immediately accessible without being simplistic — highly recommended for raising the interest of the disinterested and uninterested student!

Two foundational works which have proved to be very influential in the development of environmental ethics are Sagoff, *The Economy of the Earth: Philosophy, Law and the Environment* (Cambridge University Press, 1988);

and Stone, *Should Trees Have Standing? And Other Essays on Law, Morals and the Environment* (Oceana Publications, 1996). As its name suggests, Farber, *Eco-Pragmatism* (University of Chicago Press, 2000) tries to balance some of the more extreme versions of environmentalism with a practical approach which will work in real environmental decision making.

There is a plethora of material dealing with the perception of risk (including environmental risk). For an entertaining and illuminating examination of the topic see Adams, *Risk* (UCL Press, 1994) complete with idiosyncratic diagrams of angels and fish. A more difficult book (but one which is definitive in the area) is Beck, *Risk Society* (Sage, 1992) which suggests that environmental impacts and the associated risks are part of a fundamental shift in society. For a gentler introduction and one which is influential on the political stage see the House of Lords Science and Technology Committee's 3rd Report (Session 1999–2000) on *Science and Society* (at *www.parliament.the-stationery-office.co.uk/pa/ld/ldsctech.htm*).

For further reading on how decisions about conservation and development might be framed, we recommend Macnaghten and Urry, *Contested Natures* (Sage, 1998) and Harrison, Burgess and Clark, 'Capturing Values for Nature' in Holder and McGillivray (eds) *Locality and Identity: Environmental Issues in Law and Society* (Ashgate, 1999) as good counterpoints to the economic approaches referred to above. There is also a specialist journal — *Environmental Values* (quarterly, White Horse Press) — where much of the debate on values and sustainability is conducted.

For those wanting a general introduction to sustainable development, Dobson, *Green Political Thought* (Routledge, 2000) gives a clear overview. Further works by (or edited by) the same author, *Fairness and Futurity: Essays on Environmental Sustainability and Social Justice* (OUP, 2000) and *Justice and the Environment: Conceptions of Environmental Sustainability and Theories of Distributive Justice* (OUP, 1998) can also be recommended for getting up to speed on where the debate has now reached. Still an interesting starting point for thinking through the substantive legal aspects of sustainability is Brown Weiss, 'Our Rights and Obligations to Future Generations for the Environment' (1990) 84 *American Journal of International Law* 198.

On rights issues, an excellent introduction is Miller, *Environmental Rights: Critical Perspectives* (Routledge, 1998), which critically probes the value of thinking about environmental protection (both generally and in particular areas like air quality or nature conservation) through rights. Equally good as a way in, although with much more of an international and comparative perspective, is Boyle and Anderson (eds), *Human Rights Approaches to Environmental Protection* (OUP, 1996), the opening chapter of which neatly locates environmental rights in the context of the evolution of rights more generally.

Chapter 4

Even with the inclusion of a chapter on international environmental law, the value of excellent and comprehensive texts is not diminished. The best remains Birnie and Boyle, *International Law and the Environment* (OUP,

Oxford, 1992) and Sands, *Principles of International Environmental Law* (Manchester University Press, 1995), the latter containing a significant amount of primary material in separate volumes. There is a good general overview of current concerns in the House of Commons Select Committee on Environment, Transport and Regional Affairs, Sixteenth Report, Session 1998–99, HC 307, *Multilateral Environmental Agreements*. An accessible and enriching set of essays, placing international law in its wider context, is Hurrell and Kingsbury (eds), *The International Politics of the Environment* (Clarendon, 1992). Vogler, *The Global Commons: A Regime Analysis* (Wiley, 1995) is a good account of this particular aspect to international law, and contains a very clear summary of the argument surrounding the 'tragedy of the commons' thesis.

On trade and environment issues more generally, Esty, *Greening the GATT* (Institute for International Economics, 1994) is an excellent way in, while Fijalkowski and Cameron (eds), *Trade and the Environment: Bridging the Gap* (Cameron May, 1998) is a good mixture of 'first hand' accounts of experiences of and difficulties in balancing trade concerns and multilateral environmental agreements. Kingsbury, 'The Tuna-Dolphin Controversy: the World Trade Organisation and the Liberal Project to Reconceptualize International Law' (1994) *Yearbook of International Environmental Law* 1 and Schoenbaum, 'International Trade and Protection of the Environment: The Continuing Search for Reconciliation' (1997) 91 *AJIL* 268 are both valuable. For a UK view, see House of Commons Environment Select Committee, Fourth Report, Session 1995–96, HC 149, *World Trade and the Environment*.

On compliance, Cameron, Werksman and Roderick (eds), *Improving Compliance with International Environmental Law* (Earthscan, 1996) combines general discussion and examples (many about climate change), while Werksman (ed.), *Greening International Institutions* (Earthscan, 1996) is of considerable importance to anyone concerned with finding effective and acceptable ways of empowering such bodies in the search for global sustainability. Sand (ed.), *The Effectiveness of International Environmental Agreements: A Survey of Existing Legal Instruments* (Grotius, 1992) contains numerous case studies assessing compliance compiled for Rio. There is detailed discussion of the Kyoto Climate Change Protocol, often illuminating of the treaty negotiation process, in (1998) 7(2) *RECIEL*.

As regards the work of the ICJ, there is a symposium on the *Gabcikovo* case in (1997) *Yearbook of International Environmental Law*, while some thoughts are offered by McGillivray and Mansell in 'The Water of the Danube: The ICJ Bottles It' [1998] *Water Law* 107. Clark and Sann (eds), *The Case Against the Bomb* (Rutgers University School of Law at Camden, 1996) provides a first hand account of the ICJ's 'Nuclear Weapons' Advisory Opinion, and an excellent way in to understanding the working of the ICJ.

For keeping up to date, the *Review of European Community and International Environmental Law (RECIEL)* and *Environmental Policy and Law* are regular and informative, while the *Yearbook of International Environmental Law* contains both sectoral and country reports, recent primary materials and a useful bibliography, as well as lengthy articles. *International Legal Materials* (ILM) provides most of the major treaties and decisions although the internet is central to keeping up to date, and is the easiest source for WTO decisions (see *www.wto.org*).

Chapter 5

For many years, keeping up to date with developments in EC law and policy was a major problem. Although decision-making is still comparatively secretive, the problem has shifted from there being too little information accessible to, in some cases, too much. Much of this can be found on the central website of the EU, *www.europa.eu.int/eur-lex/en/index.html*, which links to legislation, case law and preparatory documents and now also the *Official Journal*, the definitive source for legislative material.

What is important now is finding a way through the maze, and an excellent companion in this is Gillies, *A Guide to EC Environmental Law* (Earthscan, 1999), which sets out clearly the decision-making processes as they effect environmental law, and also gives helpful guidance on how to bring complaints. Beyond this, Haigh, *Manual of Environmental Policy: The EC and Britain* (Longmans, looseleaf), is an expensive work but updated fairly regularly, and analyses the history and scope of most environmental directives, and how they are implemented at national level. Other ways of keeping up to date are obviously through specialist journals, and the *European Environmental Law Review* (monthly, Kluwer) combines news and articles. Also worth looking at is the European Environmental Law Homepage, at *www.asser.nl/EEL/index.htm*, which has a free email alerting service.

Of more general texts, a superb introduction to the subject is Scott, *EC Environmental Law* (Longmans, 1998). Although narrow in coverage, it is especially good on the arguments for and against EC intervention, which are also covered in a challenging essay by Chalmers, 'Inhabitants in the Field of EC Environmental Law', in Craig and de Búrca (eds) *The Evolution of EC Law* (OUP, 1999), a close read of which will pay dividends. More comprehensive coverage is given in Krämer, *EC Environmental Law* (Sweet & Maxwell, 1999), written by a former Head of Application of Community Law in the Environment Directorate-General of the EC Commission.

Also worth looking at is a collection of essays by the same author, *Focus on European Environmental Law*, 2nd ed. (Sweet & Maxwell, 1997). A number of other essay collections on EC environmental law and policy can also be recommended. An excellent introduction to the way in which policy style has evolved in response to EC membership is Lowe and Ward (eds) *British Environmental Policy and Europe* (Routledge, 1998). As well as thematic coverage, there are sectoral chapters which might usefully be read alongside the chapters in Part II of this book. We also recommend Somsen (ed.), *Protecting the European Environment: The Enforcement of EC Environmental Law* (Blackstone Press, 1997); Holder (ed.) *The Implementation of EC Environmental Law in the UK* (Wiley, 1997); and the companion volumes Collier (ed.) *Deregulation in the European Union: Environmental Perspectives* (Routledge, 1998) and Golub (ed.) *New Instruments for Environmental Policy in the*

EU (Routledge, 1998), the titles of which are fairly explanatory. The essays by Scott and by Ladeur in de Búrca and Scott (eds) *Constitutional Change in the EU: From Uniformity to Flexibility?* (Hart, 2000) cover changes in the environmental area within broader developments at EU level.

Chapters 8 and 9

The Royal Commission on Environmental Pollution has long campaigned for free access to environmental information. See in particular *Air Pollution Control: An Integrated Approach* (5th Report, Cmnd 6371, 1975) and *Tackling Pollution: Experience and Prospects* (10th Report, Cmnd 9149, 1984), the latter giving a good introductory account of the arguments for and against disclosure. A general discussion of the issues can be found in Kimber, 'Understanding Access to Environmental Information: the European Experience', in Jewell and Steele (eds) *Law in Environmental Decision Making* (OUP, 1998). A comparative analysis of the implementation of the Directive on Access to Environmental Information can be found in Hallo (ed.) *Access to Environmental Information in Europe: The Implementation and Implications of Directive 90/313/EEC* (Kluwer, 1996). For an empirical study on the effectiveness of access to information see, Rowan-Robinson et al, 'Public Access to Environmental Information: A Means to what End? [1996] JEL 19.

Anyone looking for some wider reading material on the enforcement of environmental law will find a number of good works and there are additional texts which cover regulatory enforcement generally but can be extremely useful when considering the theory of enforcement. In the former category there is Richardson, Ogus and Burrows, *Policing Pollution — A Study of Regulation and Enforcement* (Clarendon Press, 1982); Hawkins, *Environment and Enforcement: Regulation and the Social Definition of Pollution* (Clarendon Press, 1984); and Hutter, *The Reasonable Arm of the Law* (Clarendon Press, 1988) all of which provide an examination of environmental enforcement officers' experience of enforcing the law in the real world. In the latter category, there is Ayres and Braithwaite, *Responsive Regulation* (Oxford, 1992) which, as the main text explains, provided an alternative view of regulatory enforcement (we hesitate to call it the 'third way'). Readers may also find Lowe et al, *Moralizing the Environment* (UCL Press, 1997) an interesting study of the way in which shifts in the perception of the harm caused by agricultural pollution brought about tighter regulation and enforcement.

Other relevant material includes Rowan-Robinson and Ross, 'The enforcement of environmental regulation in Britain' [1994] JPL 200; Mehta and Hawkins, 'IPC and its Impact: Perspectives from Industry' [1998] JEL 61; and de Prez, 'Excuses, Excuses: The Ritual Trivialisation of Environmental Prosecutions' [2000] JEL 65. A very good, and short, study comparing recent experience in the UK and the US is Wilson, *Making Environmental Laws Work* (Hart, 1999), which probes some of the fundamental questions about the use of criminal law to enforce environmental regulation that we raise.

Any study of the enforcement of environmental law must keep abreast of current developments and figures which can be found in the most recent editions of the Environment Agency's *Enforcement and Prosecution Policy* and its Annual Report (both available from *www.environment-agency.gov.uk*). Alternative views can be found in occasional reports commissioned by environmental organisations such as Friends of the Earth (e.g. see the study 'Slippery Customers' published in 1997 which looked at the enforcement of water pollution).

Chapter 10

This chapter looks at private law, especially tort, from a single perspective and therefore does not attempt to cover all aspects of that particular field. Of the many specialised works in this area Jones, *Textbook on Torts*, 6th ed. (Blackstone, 1998) is a good general text, while Hedley, *Tort* (Butterworths, 1998) is a very useful shorter introduction. In very different ways, both Howarth, *Textbook on Tort* (Butterworths, 1995), and Conaghan and Mansell, *The Wrongs of Tort*, 2nd ed. (Pluto, 1998) discuss the economic and doctrinal underpinnings to tort law, the latter containing an excellent critique of the limitations of tort law for environmental protection. Practical and legal issues are discussed in Pugh and Day, *Pollution and Personal Injury: Toxic Torts 2* (Cameron May, 1994).

Leading journal articles on the common law and the environment include McLaren, 'Nuisance Law and the Industrial Revolution — Some Lessons from Social History' (1983) OJLS 155; Brenner, 'Nuisance Law and the Industrial Revolution' (1974) J. Legal Studies 403; Ogus and Richardson, 'Economics and the Environment: A Study of Private Nuisance' [1977] CLJ 284. All deal with the socio-legal aspects of common law controls. The linkages between common law and regulatory controls are explored in Steele, 'Private Law and the Environment: Nuisance in Context' (1995) 15 LS 236 and 'Remedies and Remediation: Foundational Issues in Environmental Liability' [1995] MLR 615, and in Ball, 'Liability for Environmental Harm' [1995] *Contemporary Issues in Law*, vol. 2. Some ideas are floated in McGillivray and Wightman, 'Private Rights, Public Interests and the Environment', in Hayward and O'Neill (eds), *Justice, Property and the Environment* (Ashgate, 1997) and replied to in Campbell 'Of Coase and Corn: A (Sort of) Defence of Private Nuisance' [2000] MLR 197.

Amongst much written about the *Cambridge* Water case can be recommended Shelbourn, 'Historic Pollution — does the Polluter pay?' [1994] JPL 703; Wilkinson, '*Cambridge Water Company* v *Eastern Counties Leather Plc*: Diluting Liability for Continuing Escapes' (1994) 57 MLR 799; Cross, 'Does Only the Careless Polluter Pay?' (1995) 111 LQR 445; and Hilson, 'Cambridge Water Revisited' [1996] *Water Law* 126. On questions of causation and foreseeability elsewhere, see Holder, 'The Sellafield litigation and questions of causation in environmental law' (1994) 47 CLP 287, and Steele and Wikeley, 'Dust on the Streets and Liability for Environmental Concerns' [1997] MLR 265.

Chapter 11

There are some excellent texts on planning law and policy, the value of the latter being that the high policy content of planning law makes them more accessible than normal here. A very readable general introductory text is Cullingworth and Nadin, *Town and Country Planning in Britain*, 11th ed. (Routledge, 1994) while the extent of the changes to planning that have occurred since the 1947 Act are captured in Cullingworth (ed.), *British Planning: 50 Years of Urban and Regional Policy* (Athlone, 1999). Recent policy developments are discussed in Tewdwr-Jones, 'Planning Modernised?' [1998] JPL 519 and in Healey, 'Collaborative planning in a stakeholder society' (1998) 69 TPR 1.

Still the most useful conceptual framework for thinking about planning law is McAuslan, *Ideologies of Planning Law* (Pergamon Press, 1980), especially Chapters 1 and 6. Modern planning law generally is covered in Moore, *A Practical Approach to Planning Law*, 7th ed. (Blackstone Press, 2000), the clearest of the standard textbooks. Although it is very comprehensive, with useful practical insights, it is oriented rather too much towards the exposition of principles through cases and is rather less preoccupied with policy considerations. Amongst other texts, Telling and Duxbury, *Planning Law and Procedure* 11th ed. (Butterworths, 1999) is readable, but slightly limited in coverage. For completeness, the *Encyclopaedia of Planning Law* (Sweet & Maxwell, looseleaf) includes all the relevant statutory and non-statutory material and is updated monthly, with insightful annotations and analysis. Other useful sources for keeping up to date are the *Journal of Planning and Environment Law* (JPL), which contains information on policy documents, Ministerial decisions and ever-illuminating case law analysis, and publications like *Planning* and the *Estates Gazette*. More discursive pieces on policy are contained in the *Town Planning Review* (TPR) and the *Journal of Environmental Planning and Management*. Familiarisation with the key Planning Policy Guidance Notes and Circulars is usually imperative: the more recent of these are on the internet, at *www.planning.detr.gov.uk*. Looking at copies of development plans is also recommended, on which see Purdue, 'It's not all over until the fat lady sings: challenges in the High Court to the validity of development plans' [1998] JPL 837, and Davoudi, Hull and Healey, 'Environmental concerns and economic imperatives in strategic plan making' (1996) 67 TPR 421 .

In relation to planning and environmental protection more generally, some stimulating thoughts are offered by Fairlie, *Low Impact Development* (Jon Carpenter, 1996), coupled with *Defining Rural Sustainability* (available via *www.enviroweb.org/tlio*), and in Owens, ' "Giants in the path": Planning, sustainability and environmental values' (1997) 68 TPR 293. On planning obligations see Whatmore and Boucher, 'Bargaining with nature: the discourse and practice of "environmental planning gain" ' (1993) 18 *Transactions of the Institute of British Geographers* 166; Healey, Purdue and Ennis, *Negotiating development, rationales and practice for development obligations and planning gain* (Spon, 1995); and Cornford, 'The Control of Planning Gain' [1998] JPL 731. Various angles on planning and environmental risk regulation are discussed in Grove-White, 'Land use law and the environment' [1991] *Journal of Law and Society* 32; Stanley, 'Public concern: the decision-makers' dilemma' [1998] JPL 919; and Tromans, 'Environmental Risk and the Planning System' [1996] JEL 354.

Chapter 12

A good place to begin understanding both the policy and legal issues in EIA (and SEA) is Sheate, *Environmental Impact Assessment: Law and Policy — Making an Impact II* (Cameron May, 1996). Other good introductory accounts of EIA are Glasson, Therivel and Chadwick, *Introduction to Environmental Impact Assessment* (UCL Press, 1994) and Wood, *Environmental Impact Assessment: A Comparative Review* (Longman, 1995). Weston (ed.), *Planning and Environmental Impact Assessment in Practice* (Longman, 1997) contains a number of useful case studies from planning practitioners: the essay by Street on 'EIA and pollution control' is particularly illuminating of the way in which EIA can reach beyond large, single projects to encompass more cumulative and even cross-border concerns. The journal, *Impact Assessment and Project Appraisal* (formerly *Project Appraisal*) can also be recommended, although much of the good, policy-based research tends to be published together with the general planning literature. Of this, Wood and Jones, 'The Effect of Environmental Assessment on UK Local Planning Authorities' 34(8) *Urban Studies* 1237, and Jones, Wood and Dipper, 'Environmental Assessment in the UK Planning Process: A Review of Practice' 69(3) TPR 315 have been the basis for much of the research data in this chapter. Therivel et al, *Strategic Environmental Assessment* (Earthscan, 1992) covers this topic, while Hamblin, 'Environmental Integration Through Strategic Environmental Assessment: Prospects in Europe' (1999) 9 *European Environment* 1 is a good summary of recent developments.

More legalistic issues are covered in Alder, 'Environmental Impact Assessment — The Inadequacies of English Law' [1993] JEL 203, an excellent and accessible account of some of the early case law and implementation problems; Kunzlik, 'Environmental Impact Assessment: The British Cases' [1995] *European Environmental Law Review* 336; Boch, 'The Enforcement of the Environmental Assessment Directive in the National Courts: A Breach in the "Dyke"' [1997] JEL 129; and Stallworthy, 'Planning Law as a Tool of Environmental Protection: The UK's Slow Embrace of Environmental Assessment' [1998] JEL 363. Bryant (ed.), *Twyford Down: Roads, Campaigning and Environmental Law* (E & FN Spon, 1996), written by those directly involved, is an entertaining, illuminating and ultimately depressing account of the unsuccessful attempt to save Twyford Down, and illustrates very clearly the gap between the aspirations for EIA and actual events. Useful web sites include: *www.europa.eu.int/comm/dg11/eia/home.htm* and *www.art.man.ac. uk/eia/eiac.htm*, and *www-penelope.et.ic.ac.uk*

Chapters 13 and 14

There is a single text which covers all of the material in these two chapters (and more). Hughes, Parpworth and Upson, *Air Pollution Law and Regulation* (Jordans, 1998) is a straightforward exposition of the statutory materials in the area and covers international, European and domestic sources of law. For a less legal and more policy based approach, the *National Air Quality Strategy for England, Scotland, Wales and Northern Ireland* (Cm 4548, 2000) covers all of the issues in a reader friendly fashion.

There is relatively little serious analysis of the new system of IPPC other than Backes and Betlem (eds), *Integrated Pollution Prevention and Control: The EEC Directive from a Comparative Legal and Economic Perspective* (Kluwer, 1999) which puts the Directive into a comparative context by examining the position in three Member States (Germany, the UK and the Netherlands). An earlier view of the Directive can be found in Emmott and Haigh, 'Integrated Pollution Prevention and Control: UK and EC Approaches and Possible Next Steps' [1996] JEL 301.

In the period before the legislation 'beds down', readers are advised to download the five Consultation Papers on the subject which are available in the archive section of the DETR's web page. These give a good explanation of the issues and problems involved in implementing the Directive.

In contrast there is a great deal more material on IPC. This deals with empirical studies of the effect of the regime upon industry (see Mehta and Hawkins, 'IPC and its Impact: Perspectives from Industry' [1998] JEL 61); the problems of practical implementation of the regulations (see Allot, *Integrated Pollution Control — The First Three Years* (ENDS, 1994)); and the significance of the introduction of the IPC system in terms of its impact upon environmental standard setting (see Purdue, 'Integrated Pollution Control and the Environmental Protection Act 1990: A Coming of Age for Environmental Law?' [1991] 54 MLR 534).

The historical context for the introduction of the BPEO standard can be found in various Royal Commission on Environmental Pollution Reports: see the 5th Report (Cmnd 6371, 1976); the 10th Report (Cmnd 9149, 1984) and the 12th Report, *Best Practicable Environmental Option* (Cm 310, 1988).

Chapters 15 and 16

In relation to statutory nuisance law, until recently Tromans' annotations to Part III of the EPA 1990 in *The Environment Acts 1990–1995* (Sweet & Maxwell, 1996) were a clear and comprehensive account of the law, but the flood of cases decided by the High Court and Court of Appeal in the last couple of years alters this. Some of the recent cases are covered in Malcolm, 'Statutory Nuisance: enforcement issues and the meaning of "prejudice to health"' (1999) 1 Env L Rev 210, while there is a good discussion of the wider role of statutory nuisance in Moran, 'Statutory Nuisance and Environmental Protection' (1994) *Environmental Policy and Practice* 129. Waite, 'Neighbourhood Noise in the UK' [1994] *Environmental Law and Management* 130, links statutory nuisance and noise.

On noise, a good way to get a feel for the area, and trends over time, is to look at the annual surveys produced by the Chartered Institute of Environmental Health. The technical aspects of noise generation and monitoring are dealt with in Adams and McManus, *Noise and Noise Law: A Practical Approach* (Wiley Chancery, 1994), which is also an excellent short introduction to the law and policy. A more comprehensive survey of the law, if now a little dated, is Penn, *Noise Control: The Law and its Enforcement* (Shaw & Sons, 1995). Future developments are discussed in McManus, 'The EC Green Paper on future noise policy and its impact on the United Kingdom' (1999) *European Public Law* 125. Fitzpatrick, 'A Quiet Life: Right or Duty', in Pardo (ed.), *The Morals of Legitimacy* (Berghahn Books, 2000) is an insightful critique of the creeping use of law to regulate domestic arrangements like neighbour noise disputes.

Chapters 17 and 18

The starting point for any research on waste is the *Waste Strategy for England and Wales 2000* (Cm 4693, 2000) which was published just as this book went to press. This sets the framework for waste management for the foreseeable future and is bound to be the subject of much debate in the waste management community. To see how far we have come, readers could usefully look at the RCEP's 11th Report, *Managing Waste: The Duty of Care* (Cm 9675, 1985). This Report not only deals with the historical context of waste management law and practice but also provides a damning indictment of past practices.

There are two main text books dealing with waste management. Bates, *UK Waste Law* (Sweet & Maxwell, 1997) covers the main areas in detail but does not contain much critical analysis of the provisions. Lawrence, *Waste Regulation Law*, (Butterworths, 2000) has the advantage of being bang up to date and it evaluates the statutory provisions and case law in depth. For a practical and comparative view of the operation of waste management regulation see Lange, 'National Environmental Regulation? A Case Study of Waste Management in England and Germany' [1999] 11 JEL 59.

The problem of defining waste has been the subject of a number of articles and case commentaries. These include: Wilkinson, 'Time to discard the concept of waste' (1999) 1 Env L Rev 172; Purdue, 'Defining Waste' [1990] JEL 250; Smith, 'The Challenges of Environmentally Sound and Efficient Regulation of Waste' [1993] JEL 91; Fluck, 'The Term "Waste" in EU Law' [1994] European Environmental Law Review 79; Cheyne and Purdue, 'Fitting Definition to Purpose: The Search for a Satisfactory Definition of Waste' [1995] JEL 149; Purdue and van Rossem, 'The Distinction Between Using Secondary Raw Materials and the Recovery of Waste: The Directive Definition of Waste' [1998] JEL 116; Van Calster, 'The EC Definition of Waste: The Euro Tombesi Bypass and the Basel Relief Routes' (1997) European Business Law Review 137. All are worth considering as they each cast some distinctive light on this very difficult area.

The starting point for any understanding of the contaminated land regime is the DETR's Circular 2/2000 which provides as clear a picture as possible (given the complexity of the provisions) of the way in which the new law should work in practice. On wider issues related to contaminated land, there is one work which stands head and shoulders above the rest. Tromans and Turrell-Clarke, *Contaminated Land* (Sweet & Maxwell, 1994), together with its first supplement (Sweet & Maxwell, 1998) provides a comprehensive coverage of the pre-Part IIA law including precedents and practical matters such as commercial and property considerations. A second supplement covering the post-implementation position is eagerly awaited.

For a stimulating examination of the problems of trying to regulate the clean-up of contaminated land whilst taking note of market effects (the stumbling block for the ill-fated Contaminative Uses Register) see Steele, 'Remedies and Remediation: Issues in Environmental Liability' (1995) 58 MLR 615.

Chapters 19 and 20

Good starting points for understanding water quality regulation, and the recent development of policy, are Kinnersley, *Coming Clean: The Politics of Water and the Environment* (Penguin, 1994), a refreshingly polemical account and, more academically and historically, Maloney and Richardson, *Managing Policy Change in Britain: The Politics of Water* (Edinburgh University Press, 1995).

The best comprehensive and up-to-date survey of the law relating to water quality, including discharges to sewers, is Bates, *Water and Drainage Law* (Sweet & Maxwell, looseleaf). A more discursive, if now somewhat historical, account is Howarth, *Water Pollution Law* (Shaw and Sons, 1988, supplement 1990), although see also Howarth and McGillivray, *Water Pollution and Water Quality Law* (Shaw & Sons, forthcoming). Elworthy, *Farming for Drinking Water* (Avebury, 1994) is good on agricultural issues, especially nitrate, while Elworthy, 'Finding the Causes of Events or Preventing a "State of Affairs"?: Designation of Nitrate Vulnerable Zones' [1998] JEL 92 is an excellent analysis of the problems of regulating pollution from diffuse sources and of what making the water polluter pays means.

Current water quality policy is best approached through the Environment Agency's *Functional Action Plan* in this area (EA, 1998). EC policy issues are well covered by the House of Lords Select Committee on the European Communities, Eighth Report, Session 1997–8, *Community Water Policy* (1997) and, focusing on implementation, by Stallworthy, 'Water Quality: the Capacity of the European Community to Deliver' [1998] Water Law 127. Some of the policy issues in the negotiation of the 'second generation' of EC water directives are discussed in Jordan, 'European Community Water Policy Standards: Locked in or Watered Down?' (1999) 37(1) JCMS 13, while the views of the Director General of OFWAT on balancing environmental and economic interests are nicely outlined in Byatt, 'The Impact of EC Water Directives on Water Customers in England and Wales' (1996) 3(4) JEPP 665. On future directions, see Howarth, 'Accommodation Without Resolution: Emmission Controls and Environmental Quality Objectives in the Proposed EC Water Framework Directive' (1999) 1 Env L Rev 6.

Recommended writings on water quality law at national level are Wilkinson, 'The Re-determination of the K Factors' [1994] Water Law 153 (still a good discussion of the relationship between prices and environmental protection); Macrory, 'The Privatisation and Regulation of the Water Industry' [1990] MLR 78; Howarth, 'Poisonous, Noxious or Polluting' [1993] MLR 171; Ball, 'Cambridge Water: What Does It Decide?' [1994] Water Law 61 (and see also other works on this case in Chapter 10); Howarth, 'Self-Monitoring, Self-Policing, Self-Incrimination and Pollution Law' [1997] MLR 200; Ryan, 'Unforeseeable but not Unusual: The Validity of the *Empress* Test' [1998] JEL 345; and Stanley, 'The *Empress* Decision and Causing Water Pollution' [1999] Water Law 37, the titles of which are fairly self-explanatory.

Chapters 21 and 22

Reid, *Nature Conservation Law* (W. Green, 1994) provides a clear and full summary of nature conservation law (both north and south of the border). However, it is out of date in the sense that the Conservation (Natural Habitats &c) Regulations 1994 are not covered. Some thoughts on these and on nature conservation generally can be found in Ball, 'Reforming the Law of Habitat Protection' in a very useful set of essays, *Nature Conservation and Countryside Law*, ed. Rodgers (University of Wales Press, 1996). A stimulating analysis of the issues surrounding the Wild Birds Directive and the *Lappel Bank* saga can be found in Harte, 'Nature Conservation: The Framework for Designating Special Protection Areas for Birds' [1995] JEL 267, and the follow-up article, Harte, 'Nature Conservation: The Rule of Law in European Community Environmental Protection' [1997] JEL 168. Nollkaemper, 'Habitat Protection in European Community Law: Evolving Conceptions of a Balance of Interests' [1997] JEL 271 discusses the Commission's opinions on the exercise of its powers under the Habitats Directive to sanction damaging development.

There is a wealth of information on the state of our natural heritage and on nature conservation policy. The starting point for any reading on the shape of modern nature conservation must be the Huxley Report, *Conservation of Nature in England and Wales* (Cmd 7122, 1947), which sets out all the arguments as to why nature conservation is important. There are many good books on the history of nature conservation (and also landscape protection). A stimulating introduction to the science of nature conservation is Moore, *Bird of Time: The Science and Politics of Nature Conservation* (Cambridge University Press, 1987), written by a former Chief Scientist at the NCC who had a special involvement in the drawing up of the current SSSI criteria. Adams, *Nature's Place: Conservation Sites and Countryside Change* (Allen and Unwin, 1986), provides another readable summary of conservation history.

Shoard, *The Theft of the Countryside* (Temple Smith, 1980), is a book which caused enormous controversy when it first appeared in the run-up to the Wildlife and Countryside Act 1981, and it provides a polemical view of what was (and arguably still is) happening in the countryside. Harvey, *The Killing of the Countryside* (Jonathan Cape, 1997) examines wider issues of countryside destruction and attacks the Common Agricultural Policy as one of the primary causes of excessive farming and loss of biodiversity. A more optimistic version of conservation (and landscape amenity) in the wider countryside is Green, *Countryside Conservation* (E&FN, Spon, 1996). The annual reports of the national conservation agencies, especially English Nature, are a valuable source of information about current practice and recent trends.

There is no up to date text on international conservation law. The Biodiversity Convention is very clearly explained, article by article, in Glowka, Burhenne-Guilmin and Synge, *A Guide to the Convention on Biological Diversity* (IUCN, 1994). Davis (ed.), *The Ramsar Convention Manual: A Guide to the Convention on Wetlands of International Importance Especially as Waterfowl Habitat* (Ramsar Convention Bureau, 1994) provides similar coverage of the Ramsar Convention. The key website is *www.biodiv.org/rioconv/websites.html*

In relation to landscape management, there is stimulating general and historical coverage of national developments in Rackham, *The History of the Countryside* (J.M. Dent, 1986) and Thomas, *Man and the Natural World* (Penguin, 1984). Some of the legal issues are discussed in Garner and Jones, *Countryside Law*, 3rd ed. (Shaw & Sons, 1997) while general information about landscape and countryside issues can be found in Countryside Commission, *Protecting our Finest Countryside: Advice to Government*, 1998, and *State of the Countryside 1999*, available on the website of the Countryside Agency (*www.countryside.gov.uk/*).

Rackham, *Trees and Woodlands in the British Landscape* (Routledge, 1996) is the key text on this topic, while Holder, 'Law and Landscape: The Legal Construction and Protection of Hedgerows' [1999] MLR 100 provides coverage of the Hedgerows Regulations 1997. As far as tree protection is concerned, many books of planning law include a brief chapter on this topic.

Index

Index

Index